AC 1 .G7 v.46

Great books of the Western
  World

DATE DUE
**SUBJECT TO RECALL
AFTER 2 WEEKS**

SEP 2 3 2004

NORTH DAKOTA STATE UNIVERSITY
LIBRARIES

WITHDRAWN
NDSU

WITHDRAWN
NDSU

GREAT BOOKS
OF THE WESTERN WORLD

ROBERT MAYNARD HUTCHINS, *EDITOR IN CHIEF*

46.

HEGEL

MORTIMER J. ADLER, *Associate Editor*

Members of the Advisory Board: STRINGFELLOW BARR, SCOTT BUCHANAN, JOHN ERSKINE,
CLARENCE H. FAUST, ALEXANDER MEIKLEJOHN, JOSEPH J. SCHWAB, MARK VAN DOREN.
Editorial Consultants: A. F. B. CLARK, F. L. LUCAS, WALTER MURDOCH.
WALLACE BROCKWAY, *Executive Editor*

The Philosophy of Right

The Philosophy of History

BY GEORG WILHELM FRIEDRICH HEGEL

William Benton, *Publisher*

ENCYCLOPÆDIA BRITANNICA, INC.

CHICAGO · LONDON · TORONTO

The Philosophy of Right, translated by T. M. Knox,
is reprinted by arrangement with OXFORD UNIVERSITY PRESS

THE UNIVERSITY OF CHICAGO

The Great Books
is published with the editorial advice of the faculties
of The University of Chicago

COPYRIGHT IN THE UNITED STATES OF AMERICA, 1952,
BY ENCYCLOPÆDIA BRITANNICA, INC.

COPYRIGHT 1952. COPYRIGHT UNDER INTERNATIONAL COPYRIGHT UNION BY
ENCYCLOPÆDIA BRITANNICA, INC. ALL RIGHTS RESERVED UNDER PAN AMERICAN
COPYRIGHT CONVENTIONS BY ENCYCLOPÆDIA BRITANNICA. INC.

AC
1
.G7
v. A6

BIOGRAPHICAL NOTE
GEORG WILHELM FRIEDRICH HEGEL, 1770–1831

HEGEL was born at Stuttgart, August 27, 1770, the oldest child of a minor state official. His achievement at the local grammar school and *gymnasium* was not remarkable. A journal from that time contains evidence of interest in history, Greek and Latin literature, and theology, and he then began his lifelong habit of making copious extracts from his reading which he annotated and arranged alphabetically. At the age of eighteen he entered the University of Tübingen as a student of theology. But he showed little aptitude for theology; his sermons were a failure, and he found more congenial reading in the classics. The certificate which he received in 1793 commended his excellent talents but declared that his industry and knowledge were mediocre, his speaking poor, and that he was particularly deficient in philosophy. He seems to have profited most from the companionship of his friends, notably Hölderlin and Schelling, with whom he read Kant and Plato.

On leaving Tübingen, Hegel became a tutor in a private family, as had Kant and Fichte before him. He held such a position first at Bern (1793-1796) and then at Frankfurt (1797-1800). From the years when he was a tutor there remains a large number of manuscripts, in various stages of completion and of varying importance, but all indicative of a great deal of study. During his residence in Switzerland he wrote a life of Jesus, a critique of positive religion, and several studies in the history of religion. Later his attention turned to questions of economics and government, and he left writings on the reform of the Prussian land laws, a commentary on James Steuart's *Political Economy,* and other studies of similar character which have since been published. In 1800 he produced a sketch which is generally regarded as the first systematic statement of his philosophy.

In 1799 his father died, and a small inheritance offered Hegel a brief period of independence. He wrote to Schelling, who was already on the way to fame, asking him to suggest a suitable town for a brief period of studious withdrawal, specifying, among other requirements, "a good beer." Expressing his joy at the recent successes of his friend in the academic world, he confessed that he too had ambitions: "The ideal of my youth has necessarily taken a reflective form and been transformed into a system. Now I am asking myself, while still busy with this task, how can I return to influencing the life of mankind?" Schelling's answer must have been enthusiastic, for Hegel abandoned his plans for a quiet vacation and joined him at Jena almost immediately. Here he became a *Privatdocent* at the university, after he had presented as his qualifying dissertation a treatise *On the Orbits of the Planets.* In the winter of 1801 his lectures, delivered in the late afternoon and attended by eleven students, dealt with logic and metaphysics; succeeding series in later years, somewhat better attended, were devoted to a "system of speculative philosophy," the history of philosophy, pure mathematics, and other topics. Before Schelling's departure from Jena, in 1803, he and Hegel collaborated in the publication of the *Journal of Critical Philosophy.*

Although Hegel appeared at first as a follower of Schelling, his own views rapidly became distinct and he set about preparing a systematic exposition. In the preface to his first important work, *The Phenomenology of Spirit,* he went to some length to make a kind of disavowal of Schelling's position. It was while he was engaged in the details of publication of this work that his academic career was brought abruptly to a close by the Napoleonic campaign culminating in the battle of Jena in the autumn of 1806. In a letter written to a friend on the day before the battle, after expressing anxiety regarding the fate of his manuscripts then on the way to the printer, he spoke of seeing Napoleon: "I saw the Emperor—that world-soul—ride through the town to reconnoitre. It is indeed a strange feeling to see such a person, who here, from a single point, sitting on his horse, reaches over and masters the world!"

The Phenomenology of Spirit appeared in 1807 despite the war, but Hegel himself was at loose ends. For a time (1807-1808) he edited the *Bamberger Zeitung,* but finding journalism distasteful, he accepted a position as headmaster of the *Aegidien-gymnasium* at Nuremberg, where he remained until 1816. In 1811 he married. Two volumes of his *Science of Logic* were published in 1812, and a third in 1816, and he was offered professorships at Erlangen, Heidelberg, and Berlin. He accepted the invitation to Heidelberg, but after the publication of his *Encyclopedia of the Philosophical Sciences* in 1817, the offer of Berlin was renewed and accepted, and he occupied the chair vacant since the death of Fichte.

The thirteen years of Hegel's professorship at the University of Berlin (1818-1831) brought him to the summit of his career and made him the recognized leader of philosophic thought in Germany. With every year his personal prestige and following increased, until his name was linked with that of Goethe by his more enthusiastic disciples. In 1821 he published *The Philosophy of Right,* the last of the large works published in his lifetime. His lectures on aesthetics, the philosophy of religion, the philosophy of history, and the history of philosophy were constantly revised and improved and finally published after his death. In 1830 he became rector of the university and was decorated by Frederick William III of Prussia.

On the 7th of November, 1831, Hegel finished the preface to a second edition of his *Logic.* In closing he recalled the legend that Plato revised the *Republic* seven times, and remarked that, despite this illustrious example, "the writer must content himself with what he has been allowed to achieve under the pressure of circumstances, the unavoidable waste caused by the extent and many-sidedness of the interests of the time, and the haunting doubt whether, amid the loud clamor of the day and the deafening babble of opinion . . . there is left any room for sympathy with the passionless stillness of a science of pure thought." Seven days later he died of cholera, and was buried, as he had wished, between Fichte and Solger.

GENERAL CONTENTS

CONTENTS: PHILOSOPHY OF RIGHT

ABBREVIATIONS

HEGEL'S WORKS

Aesthetic . . . . . . = *Hegel's Philosophy of Fine Art,* translated by F. P. B. Osmaston, 4 vols., London, 1916.

Enc. . . . . = *Encyclopaedia of the Philosophical Sciences.*

Hegels e. R. . . . . . = *Hegels eigenhändige Randbemerkungen zu seiner Rechtsphilosophie,* hrsg. von G. Lasson, Leipzig, 1930.

History of Philosophy . . = *Hegel's History of Philosophy,* translated by E. S. Haldane, 3 vols., London, 1892.

Phenomenology . . . . = *Hegel's Phenomenology of Mind,* translated by Sir J. B. Baillie, 2nd edn., London, 1931.

Philosophy of History . . = *Hegel's Philosophy of History,* translated by J. Sibree, pp. 153–369 in this volume.

Philosophy of Religion . . = *Hegel's Philosophy of Religion,* translated by the Rev. E. B. Speirs and J. Burdon Sanderson, 3 vols., London, 1895.

Science of Logic . . . . = *Hegel's Science of Logic,* translated by W. H. Johnston and L. G. Struthers, 2. vols., London, 1929.

Werke[1] or[2] . . . . . . = *Hegels sämtliche Werke,* neu hrsg. von H. Glockner, Stuttgart, 1927 ff. The pagination quoted is that of the original edition, which is given in the margin of Glockner's reprint.

EDITIONS AND TRANSLATIONS OF THE PHILOSOPHY OF RIGHT

Bolland . . . . = *Hegels Grundlinien der Philosophie des Rechts,* hrsg. von G. J. P. J. Bolland, Leyden, 1902.

Gans . . . . = *Hegels sämtliche Werke,* vol. viii, Berlin, 1st edn. 1833, 3rd edn. 1854.

Lasson . . . . = *Hegels Grundlinien der Philosophie des Rechts,* neu hrsg. von G. Lasson, 2nd edn., Leipzig, 1921.

Messineo . . . . . . = *Hegel: Lineamenti di filosofia del diritto,* tradotti da Francesco Messineo, Bari, 1913.

Sterrett . . . . = *The Ethics of Hegel, translated selections from his Rechtsphilosophie,* with an introduction by J. Macbride Sterrett, D.D., Boston, 1893.

OTHER WORKS

Science of Knowledge . . = *Fichte's Science of Knowledge (Wissenschaftslehre),* translated by A. E. Kroeger, London, 1889.

Science of Rights . . . . = *Fichte's Science of Rights (Grundlage des Naturrechts),* translated by A. E. Kroeger, London, 1889. References to numbered sections are omitted in Kroeger's translation, and they are inserted here from J. G. Fichte, *Werke,* hrsg. von F. Medicus, Leipzig, 1908, vol. ii.

Philosophy of Law . . . = *Kant's Philosophy of Law* (the *Science of Right* in vol. 42 of this set, pp. 395–458), translated by W. Hastie.

Kant's Theory of Ethics . = *Kant's Theory of Ethics,* translated by T. K. Abbott, 6th edn., London, 1923.

In quoting from translations of Hegel, the translator in his Notes has made modifications here and there in order to bring the terminology into accordance with that used here.

PREFACE

THE immediate inducement to publish this manual is the need for putting into the hands of my audience a text-book for the lectures on the Philosophy of Right which I deliver in the course of my professional duties. This compendium is an enlarged and especially a more systematic exposition of the same fundamental concepts which in relation to this part of philosophy are already contained in a book of mine designed previously for my lectures—the *Encyclopaedia of Philosophical Sciences* (Heidelberg, 1817).[1]

But this manual was to appear in print and therefore it now comes before the general public; and this was my inducement to amplify here a good many of the Remarks which were primarily meant in a brief compass to indicate ideas akin to my argument or at variance with it, further inferences from it, and the like, i.e. material which would receive its requisite elucidation in my lectures. The object of amplifying them here was to clarify occasionally the more abstract parts of the text and to take a more comprehensive glance at current ideas widely disseminated at the present time. Hence the result has been a number of Remarks rather more extensive than is usually consistent with the style and aim of a compendium. Apart from that, however, a compendium proper has as its subject-matter what is taken to be the closed circle of a science; and what is appropriate in it, except perhaps for a small addition here and there, is principally the assembly and arrangement of the essential factors in a content which has long been familiar and accepted, just as the form in which it is arranged has its rules and artifices which have long been settled. *Philosophical* manuals are perhaps not now expected to conform to such a pattern, for it is supposed that what philosophy puts together is a work as ephemeral as Penelope's web, one which must be begun afresh every morning.

I need hardly say that the chief difference between this manual and an ordinary compendium lies in the method which constitutes their guiding principle. But in this book I am presupposing that philosophy's mode of progression from one topic to another and its mode of scientific proof—this whole speculative way of knowing—is essentially distinct from any other way of knowing. It is only insight into the necessity of such a difference that can rescue philosophy from the shameful decay in which it is immersed at the present time. It is true that the forms and rules of the old logic, of definition, classification, and syllogism, which include the rules of discursive thinking, have become recognized as inadequate for speculative science; or rather their inadequacy has not been recognized; it has only been felt, and then these rules have been thrown off as if they were mere fetters in order to allow the heart, the imagination, and casual intuition to say what they pleased. And since reflection and connexions of thought have after all to come on the scene as well, there is an unconscious relapse into the despised method of commonplace deduction and argumentation.

Since I have fully expounded the nature of speculative knowing in my *Science of Logic*,[2] in this manual I have only added an explanatory note here and there about procedure and method. In dealing with a topic which is concrete and intrinsically of so varied a character, I have omitted to bring out and demonstrate the chain of logical argument in each and every detail. For one thing, to have done this might have been regarded as superfluous where acquaintance with philosophical method is presupposed; for another, it will be obvious from the work itself that the whole, like the formation of its parts, rests on the logical spirit. It is also from this point of view above all that I should like my book to be taken and judged. What we have to do with here is philosophical *science*, and in such science content is essentially bound up with form.

We may of course hear from those who seem to be taking a profound view that the form is something external and indifferent to the subject-matter, that the latter alone is important; further, the task of a writer, especially a writer

[1] Where Hegel has cited in the *Philosophy of Right* paragraphs of the first edition, the translator has appended in square brackets references to the corresponding passages of the third edition.

[2] Cf. Kant, *Critique of Pure Reason*, p. 196.—ED.

I

on philosophy, may be said to lie in the discovery of truth, the statement of truth, the dissemination of truth and sound concepts. But if we consider how this task is as a rule actually discharged, what we find in the first place is that the same old stew is continually warmed up again and again and served round to everybody —a task that will even be meritorious in educating and stimulating men's hearts, though it might preferably be regarded as the superfluous labour of a busybody—"They have Moses and the Prophets, let them hear them." In particular, we have ample opportunity to marvel at the pretentious tone recognizable in these busybodies when they talk as if the world had wanted for nothing except their energetic dissemination of truths, or as if their *réchauffé* were productive of new and unheard-of truths and was to be specially taken to heart before everything else "to-day" and every day. But in this situation we also find one party giving out truths of this sort only to have them dislodged and brushed aside by truths of just the same sort purveyed by other parties. In this press of truths, there is something neither new nor old but perennial; yet how else is this to be lifted out of these reflections which oscillate from this to that without method, how else is it to be separated from them and proved, if not by philosophic science?

After all, the truth about Right, Ethics, and the state is as old as its public recognition and formulation in the law of the land, in the morality of everyday life, and in religion. What more does this truth require—since the thinking mind is not content to possess it in this ready fashion? It requires to be grasped in thought as well; the content which is already rational in principle must win the *form* of rationality and so appear well-founded to untrammelled thinking. Such thinking does not remain stationary at the given, whether the given be upheld by the external positive authority of the state or the *consensus hominum*, or by the authority of inward feeling and emotion and by the "witness of the spirit" which directly concurs with it. On the contrary, thought which is free starts out from itself and thereupon claims to know itself as united in its innermost being with the truth.

The unsophisticated heart takes the simple line of adhering with trustful conviction to what is publicly accepted as true and then building on this firm foundation its conduct and its set position in life. Against this simple line of conduct there may at once be raised the alleged difficulty of how it is possible, in an infinite variety of opinions, to distinguish and discover what is universally recognized and valid. This perplexity may at first sight be taken for a right and really serious attitude to the thing, but in fact those who boast of this perplexity are in the position of not being able to see the wood for the trees; the only perplexity and difficulty they are in is one of their own making. Indeed, this perplexity and difficulty of theirs is proof rather that they want as the substance of the right and the ethical not what is universally recognized and valid, but something else. If they had been serious with what is universally accepted instead of busying themselves with the vanity and particularity of opinions and things, they would have clung to what is substantively right, namely to the commands of the ethical order and the state, and would have regulated their lives in accordance with these.

A more serious difficulty arises, however, from the fact that man thinks and tries to find in thinking both his freedom and the basis of ethical life. But however lofty, however divine, the right of thought may be, it is perverted into wrong if it is only this [opining] which passes for thinking and if thinking knows itself to be free only when it diverges from what is *universally* recognized and valid and when it has discovered how to invent for itself some *particular* character.

At the present time, the idea that freedom of thought, and of mind generally, evinces itself only in divergence from, indeed in hostility to, what is publicly recognized, might seem to be most firmly rooted in connexion with the state, and it is chiefly for this reason that a philosophy of the state might seem essentially to have the task of discovering and promulgating still another theory, and a special and original one at that. In examining this idea and the activity in conformity with it, we might suppose that no state or constitution had ever existed in the world at all or was even in being at the present time, but that nowadays—and this "nowadays" lasts for ever—we had to start all over again from the beginning, and that the ethical world had just been waiting for such present-day projects, proofs, and investigations. So far as nature is concerned, people grant that it is nature as it is which philosophy has to bring within its ken, that the philosopher's stone lies concealed somewhere, somewhere within nature itself, that nature is inherently rational, and that what knowledge has to investigate and grasp in concepts is this actual reason present in it; not the formations and accidents evident to the superficial observer, but nature's eternal harmony, its harmony, however, in the sense of the law and essence immanent within it. The ethical world, on the other hand, the state (i.e. reason as it actualizes itself in the element of self-consciousness), is not allowed to enjoy the good fortune which springs from the fact that it is reason which has achieved power and mastery within that element and which maintains itself and has its home there. [A.] [1] The universe of mind is supposed rather to be left to the mercy of chance and caprice, to be God-forsaken, and the result is that if the ethical world is Godless, truth lies outside it, and at the same time, since even so reason is supposed to be in it as well, truth becomes nothing but a problem. But it is this also that is to authorize, nay to oblige, every thinker to take his own road, though not in search of the philosopher's stone, for he is saved this search by the philosophizing of our contemporaries, and everyone nowadays is assured that he has this stone in his grasp as his birthright. Now admittedly it is the case that those who live their lives in the state as it actually exists here and now and find satisfaction there for their knowledge and volition (and of these there are many, more in fact than think or know it, because ultimately this is the position of everybody), or those at any rate who *consciously* find their satisfaction in the state, laugh at these operations and affirmations and regard them as an empty game, sometimes rather funny, sometimes rather serious, now amusing, now dangerous. Thus this restless activity of empty reflection, together with its popularity and the welcome it has received, would be a thing on its own, developing in privacy in its own way, were it not that it is philosophy itself which has earned all kinds of scorn and discredit by its indulgence in this occupation. The worst of these kinds of scorn is this, that, as I said just now, everyone is convinced that his mere birthright puts him in a position to pass judgement on philosophy in general and to condemn it. No other art or science is subjected to this last degree of scorn, to the supposition that we are masters of it without ado.

In fact, what we have seen recent philosophical publications proclaiming with the maximum of pretension about the state has really justified anybody who cared to busy himself with the subject in this conviction that he could manufacture a philosophy of this kind himself without ado and so give himself proof of his possession of philosophy. Besides, this self-styled "philosophy"

has expressly stated that "truth itself cannot be known," that that only is true which each individual allows to rise out of his heart, emotion, and inspiration about ethical institutions, especially about the state, the government, and the constitution. In this connexion what a lot of flattery has been talked, especially to the young! Certainly the young have listened to it willingly enough. "He giveth to his own in sleep" has been applied to science and hence every sleeper has numbered himself among the elect, but the concepts he has acquired in sleep are themselves of course only the wares of sleep.

A ringleader of these hosts of superficiality, of these self-styled "philosophers," Herr Fries,[2] did not blush, on the occasion of a public festival[3] which has become notorious, to express the following ideas in a speech on "The state and the constitution": "In the people ruled by a genuine communal spirit, life for the discharge of all public business would come from below, from the people itself; living associations, indissolubly united by the holy chain of friendship, would be dedicated to every single project of popular education and popular service," and so on. This is the quintessence of shallow thinking, to base philosophic science not on the development of thought and the concept but on immediate sense-perception and the play of fancy; to take the rich inward articulation of ethical life, i.e. the state, the architectonic of that life's rationality —which sets determinate limits to the different circles of public life and their rights, uses the strict accuracy of measurement which holds together every pillar, arch, and buttress and thereby produces the strength of the whole out of the harmony of the parts—to take this structure and confound the completed fabric in the broth of "heart, friendship, and inspiration." According to a view of this kind, the world of ethics (Epicurus, holding a similar view, would have said the "world in general") should be given over —as in fact of course it is not—to the subjective accident of opinion and caprice. By the simple family remedy of ascribing to feeling the labour, the more than millenary labour, of reason and its intellect, all the trouble of rational insight and knowledge directed by speculative thinking is of course saved. On this point, Goethe's Mephistopheles, a good authority!, says some-

---

[1] [A.] Additions (PP. 115-150), culled from notes taken at Hegel's lectures by Edward Gans.

[2] I have borne witness before to the superficiality of his philosophy—see *Science of Logic* (Nuremberg, 1812), Introduction, p. xvii [Eng. tr. vol. i, p. 63].
[3] See Paragraph 126 and Remark (d) to Paragraph 140. Note that Hegel subjoins to many of his paragraphs explanatory notes which are here printed in smaller type and referred to throughout as "remarks" in order to distinguish them from the translators "Notes."—ED.

thing like this, a quotation I have used elsewhere [1] already: "Do but despise intellect and knowledge, the highest of all man's gifts, and thou hast surrendered thyself to the devil and to perdition art doomed." The next thing is that such sentiments assume even the guise of piety, for this bustling activity has used any and every expedient in its endeavour to give itself authority. With godliness and the Bible, however, it has arrogated to itself the highest of justifications for despising the ethical order and the objectivity of law, since it is piety too which envelops in the simpler intuition of feeling the truth which is articulated in the world into an organic realm. But if it is piety of the right sort, it sheds the form of this emotional region so soon as it leaves the inner life, enters upon the daylight of the Idea's development and revealed riches, and brings with it, out of its inner worship of God, reverence for law and for an absolute truth exalted above the subjective form of feeling.

The particular form of guilty conscience revealed by the type of eloquence in which such superficiality flaunts itself may be brought to your attention here and above all if you notice that when it is furthest from mind, superficiality speaks most of mind, when its talk is the most tedious dead-and-alive stuff, its favourite words are "life" and "vitalize," and when it gives evidence of the pure selfishness of baseless pride, the word most on its lips is "people." But the special mark which it carries on its brow is the hatred of law. Right and ethics, and the actual world of justice and ethical life, are understood through thoughts; through thoughts they are invested with a rational form, i.e. with universality and determinacy. This form is law; and this it is which the feeling that stipulates for its own whim, the conscience that places right in subjective conviction, has reason to regard as its chief foe. The formal character of the right as a duty and a law it feels as the letter, cold and dead, as a shackle; for it does not recognize itself in the law and so does not recognize itself as free there, because law is the reason of the thing, and reason refuses to allow feeling to warm itself at its own private hearth. Hence law, as I have remarked somewhere [2] in the course of this textbook, is *par excellence* the shibboleth which marks out these false friends and comrades of what they call the "people."

At the present time, the pettifoggery of caprice has usurped the name of philosophy and succeeded in giving a wide public the opinion that such triflings are philosophy. The result of this is that it has now become almost a disgrace to go on speaking in philosophical terms about the nature of the state, and law-abiding men cannot be blamed if they become impatient so soon as they hear mention of a philosophical science of the state. Still less is it a matter for surprise that governments have at last directed their attention to this kind of philosophy, since, apart from anything else, philosophy with us is not, as it was with the Greeks for instance, pursued in private like an art, but has an existence in the open, in contact with the public, and especially, or even only, in the service of the state. Governments have proved their trust in their scholars who have made philosophy their chosen field by leaving entirely to them the construction and contents of philosophy—though here and there, if you like, it may not have been so much confidence that has been shown as indifference to learning itself, and professorial chairs of philosophy have been retained only as a tradition (in France, for instance, to the best of my knowledge, chairs of metaphysics at least have been allowed to lapse). Their confidence, however, has very often been ill repaid, or alternatively, if you preferred to see indifference, you would have to regard the result, the decay of thorough knowledge, as the penalty of this indifference. Prima facie, superficiality seems to be extremely accommodating, one might say, at least in relation to public peace and order, because it fails to touch or even to guess at the substance of the things; no action, or at least no police action,[3] would thus have been taken against it in the first instance, had it not been that there still existed in the state a need for a deeper education and insight, a need which the state required philosophical science to satisfy. On the other hand, superficial thinking about the ethical order, about right and duty in general, starts automatically from the maxims which constitute superficiality in this sphere, i.e. from the principles of the Sophists which are so clearly outlined for our information in Plato.[4] What is right these principles locate in subjective aims and opinions, in subjective feeling and particular conviction, and from them there follows the ruin of the inner ethical life and a good conscience, of love and right dealing between private persons, no less than the ruin of public order and the law of the land. The significance

---

[1] Cf. Goethe, *Faust*, I. iv. 322-3, 337-8.—ED.
[2] In the footnote to Paragraph 258.—ED.

[3] See Paragraphs 231-49.—ED.
[4] Cf. Plato, *Protagoras* and *Republic*, 493 ff., where the sophist is contrasted with the true philosopher.—ED.

which such phenomena must acquire for governments is not likely to suffer any diminution as a result of the pretentiousness which has used that very grant of confidence and the authority of a professorial chair to support the demand that the state should uphold and give scope to what corrupts the ultimate source of achievement, namely universal principles, and so even to the defiance of the state as if such defiance were what it deserved. "If God gives a man an office, he also gives him brains" is an old joke which in these days surely no one will take wholly in earnest.

In the fresh importance which circumstances have led governments to attach to the character of philosophical work, there is one element which we cannot fail to notice; this is the protection and support which the study of philosophy now seems to have come to need in several other directions. Think of the numerous publications in the field of the positive sciences, as well as edifying religious works and vague literature of other kinds, which reveal to their readers the contempt for philosophy I have already mentioned, in that, although the thought in them is immature to the last degree and philosophy is entirely alien to them, they treat it as something over and done with. More than this, they expressly rail against it and pronounce its content, namely the speculative knowledge of God, nature, and mind, the knowledge of truth, to be a foolish and even sinful presumptuousness, while reason, and again reason, and reason repeated *ad infinitum* is arraigned, disparaged, and condemned. At the very least such writings reveal to us that, to a majority of those engaged in activities supposedly scientific, the claims of the concept are an embarrassment which none the less they cannot escape. I venture to say that anyone with such phenomena before him may very well begin to think that, if they alone are considered, tradition is now neither worthy of respect nor sufficient to secure for the study of philosophy either tolerance or existence as a public institution.[1] The arrogant declamations current in our time against philosophy present the singular spectacle, on the one hand of

deriving their justification from the superficiality to which that study has been degraded, and, on the other, of being themselves rooted in this element against which they turn so ungratefully. For by pronouncing the knowledge of truth a wild-goose chase, this self-styled philosophizing has reduced all thoughts and all topics to the same level, just as the despotism of the Roman Empire abolished the distinction between free men and slaves, virtue and vice, honour and dishonour, learning and ignorance. The result of this levelling process is that the concepts of what is true, the laws of ethics, likewise become nothing more than opinions and subjective convictions. The maxims of the worst of criminals, since they too are convictions, are put on the same level of value as those laws; and at the same time any object, however sorry, however accidental, any material however insipid, is put on the same level of value as what constitutes the interest of all thinking men and the bonds of the ethical world.

It is therefore to be taken as a piece of *luck* for philosophic science—though in actual fact, as I have said, it is the *necessity* of the thing— that this philosophizing which like an exercise in scholasticism might have continued to spin its web in seclusion, has now been put into closer touch and so into open variance with actuality, in which the principles of rights and duties are a serious matter, and which lives in the light of its consciousness of these.

It is just this placing of philosophy in the actual world which meets with misunderstandings, and so I revert to what I have said before, namely that, since philosophy is the exploration of the rational, it is for that very reason the apprehension of the present and the actual, not the erection of a beyond, supposed to exist, God knows where, or rather which exists, and we can perfectly well say where, namely in the error of a one-sided, empty, ratiocination. In the course of this book,[2] I have remarked that even Plato's *Republic*, which passes proverbially as an empty ideal, is in essence nothing but an interpretation of the nature of Greek ethical life. Plato was conscious that there was breaking into that life in his own time a deeper principle which could appear in it directly only as a longing still unsatisfied, and so only as something corruptive. To combat it, he needs must have sought aid from that very longing itself. But this aid had to come from on High and all that Plato could do was to seek it in the first place in a particular external form of that same Greek ethical life. By

---

[1] I came across a similar view in a letter of Joh. von Müller (*Werke*, Part vii, p. 57). In talking of the state of Rome in 1803 when the city was under French control, he says: "Asked how the public educational institutions were faring, a professor replied *On les tolère comme les bordels.*" The so-called "Doctrine of Reason," logic namely, we can indeed still hear recommended, perhaps with the conviction that it is such a dry and profitless science that nobody will busy himself with it, or that if here and there a man does take it up, he will thereby acquire mere empty formulae, unproductive and innocuous, and that therefore in either case the recommendation will do no harm, even if it does no good.

[2] In the Remark to Paragraph 185.—ED.

that means he thought to master this corruptive invader, and thereby he did fatal injury to the deeper impulse which underlay it, namely free infinite personality. Still, his genius is proved by the fact that the principle on which the distinctive character of his Idea of the state turns is precisely the pivot on which the impending world revolution turned at that time.[1]

What is rational is actual and what is actual is rational.[2] On this conviction the plain man like the philosopher takes his stand, and from it philosophy starts in its study of the universe of mind as well as the universe of nature. If reflection, feeling, or whatever form subjective consciousness may take, looks upon the present as something vacuous and looks beyond it with the eyes of superior wisdom, it finds itself in a vacuum, and because it is actual only in the present, it is itself mere vacuity. If on the other hand the Idea passes for "only an Idea," for something represented in an opinion, philosophy rejects such a view and shows that nothing is actual except the Idea. Once that is granted, the great thing is to apprehend in the show of the temporal and transient the substance which is immanent and the eternal which is present. For since rationality (which is synonymous with the Idea) enters upon external existence simultaneously with its actualization, it emerges with an infinite wealth of forms, shapes, and appearances. Around its heart it throws a motley covering with which consciousness is at home to begin with, a covering which the concept has first to penetrate before it can find the inward pulse and feel it still beating in the outward appearances. But the infinite variety of circumstance which is developed in this externality by the light of the essence glinting in it—this endless material and its organization—this is not the subject matter of philosophy. To touch this at all would be to meddle with things to which philosophy is unsuited; on such topics it may save itself the trouble of giving good advice. Plato[3] might have omitted his recommendation to nurses to keep on the move with infants and to rock them continually in their arms. And Fichte too need not have carried what has been called the "construction" of his passport regulations to such a pitch of perfection as to require suspects not merely to sign their passports but to have their likenesses painted on them. Along

such tracks all trace of philosophy is lost, and such super-erudition it can the more readily disclaim since its attitude to this infinite multitude of topics should of course be most liberal. In adopting this attitude, philosophic science shows itself to be poles apart from the hatred with which the folly of superior wisdom regards a vast number of affairs and institutions, a hatred in which pettiness takes the greatest delight because only by venting it does it attain a feeling of its self-hood.

This book, then, containing as it does the science of the state, is to be nothing other than the endeavour to apprehend and portray the state as something inherently rational. As a work of philosophy, it must be poles apart from an attempt to construct a state as it ought to be. The instruction which it may contain cannot consist in teaching the state what it ought to be; it can only show how the state, the ethical universe, is to be understood.

'Ιλού 'Ρόλος ιλού καὶ τὸ πήλημα.
Hic Rhodus, *hic* saltus.

To comprehend what is, this is the task of philosophy, because what is, is reason. Whatever happens, every individual is a child of his time; so philosophy too is its own time apprehended in thoughts.[4] It is just as absurd to fancy that a philosophy can transcend its contemporary world as it is to fancy that an individual can overleap his own age, jump over Rhodes. If his theory really goes beyond the world as it is and builds an ideal one as it ought to be, that world exists indeed, but only in his opinions, an unsubstantial element where anything you please may, in fancy, be built.

With hardly an alteration, the proverb just quoted would run:

Here is the rose, dance thou here.

What lies between reason as self-conscious mind and reason as an actual world before our eyes, what separates the former from the latter and prevents it from finding satisfaction in the latter, is the fetter of some abstraction or other which has not been liberated [and so transformed] into the concept. To recognize reason as the rose in the cross of the present and thereby to enjoy the present, this is the rational insight which reconciles us to the actual, the reconciliation which philosophy affords to those in whom there has once arisen an inner voice bidding them to comprehend, not only to dwell in what is substantive while still retaining subjec-

---

[1] See the Remark to Paragraph 140. See Paragraphs 185 and 206. "Free infinite personality"—See Paragraphs 5, 21, and 35.—ED.

[2] See the Addition to Paragraph 270 and the closing pages of the *Philosophy of History*.—ED.

[3] Cf. Plato, *Laws*, vii. 789.—ED.

[4] Cf. Bacon. *Novum Organum*, i. 84.—ED.

tive freedom, but also to possess subjective freedom while standing not in anything particular and accidental but in what exists absolutely.

It is this too which constitutes the more concrete meaning of what was described above[1] rather abstractly as the unity of form and content; for form in its most concrete signification is reason as speculative knowing, and content is reason as the substantial essence of actuality, whether ethical or natural. The known identity of these two is the philosophical Idea. It is a sheer obstinacy, the obstinacy which does honour to mankind, to refuse to recognize in conviction anything not ratified by thought. This obstinacy is the characteristic of our epoch, besides being the principle peculiar to Protestantism. What Luther[2] initiated as faith in feeling and in the witness of the spirit, is precisely what spirit, since become more mature, has striven to apprehend in the concept in order to free and so to find itself in the world as it exists to-day. The saying has become famous that "a half-philosophy leads away from God"—and it is the same half-philosophy that locates knowledge in an "approximation" to truth[3]—"while true philosophy leads to God"; and the same is true of philosophy and the state. Just as reason is not content with an approximation which, as something "neither cold nor hot," it will "spue out of its mouth," so it is just as little content with the cold despair which submits to the view that in this earthly life things are truly bad or at best only tolerable, though here they cannot be improved and that this is the only reflection which can keep us at peace with the world. There is less chill in the peace with the world which knowledge supplies.

One word more about giving instruction as to what the world ought to be. Philosophy in any case always comes on the scene too late to give it. As the thought of the world, it appears only when actuality is already there cut and dried after its process of formation has been completed. The teaching of the concept, which is also history's inescapable lesson, is that it is only when actuality is mature that the ideal first appears over against the real and that the ideal apprehends this same real world in its substance and builds it up for itself into the shape of an intellectual realm. When philosophy paints its grey in grey,[4] then has a shape of life grown old. By philosophy's grey in grey it cannot be rejuvenated but only understood. The owl of Minerva spreads its wings only with the falling of the dusk.

But it is time to close this preface. After all, as a preface, its only business has been to make some external and subjective remarks about the standpoint of the book it introduces. If a topic is to be discussed philosophically, it spurns any but a scientific and objective treatment, and so too if criticisms of the author take any form other than a scientific discussion of the thing itself, they can count only as a personal epilogue and as capricious assertion, and he must treat them with indifference.

BERLIN, *June 25th,* 1820.

---

[1] See p. 1.—ED.
[2] See Remark to Paragraph 270.—ED.
[3] Cf. Kant, *Critique of Pure Reason,* p. 194.—ED.

[4] Cf. Goethe, *Faust,* Part I. ll. 2039–40.—ED.

INTRODUCTION

[Concept of the Philosophy of Right, of the Will, Freedom, and Right.]

1. The subject-matter of the philosophical science of right is the Idea of right, i.e. the concept of right together with the actualization of that concept.

Philosophy has to do with Ideas, and therefore not with what are commonly dubbed "mere concepts." On the contrary, it exposes such concepts as one-sided and false, while showing at the same time that it is the concept alone (not the mere abstract category of the understanding which we often hear called by the name) which has actuality, and further that it gives this actuality to itself. All else, apart from this actuality established through the working of the concept itself, is ephemeral existence, external contingency, opinion, unsubstantial appearance, falsity, illusion, and so forth. The shapes which the concept assumes in the course of its actualization are indispensable for the knowledge of the concept itself. They are the second essential moment of the Idea, in distinction from the first, i.e. from its form, from its mode of being as concept alone.[1] [A.]

2. The science of right is a section of philosophy. Consequently, its task is to develop the Idea—the Idea being the rational factor in any object of study—out of the concept, or, what is the same thing, to look on at the proper immanent development of the thing itself. As a section, it has a definite starting-point, i.e. the result and the truth of what has preceded, and it is what has preceded which constitutes the so-called "proof" of the starting-point. Hence the concept of right, so far as its coming to be is concerned, falls outside the science of right; it is to be taken up here as given and its deduction is presupposed.[2]

According to the abstract, non-philosophical, method of the sciences, the first thing sought and demanded is a definition, or at any rate this demand is made for the sake of preserving the external form of scientific procedure. (But the science of positive law at least cannot be very intimately concerned with definitions since it begins in the first place by stating what is legal, i.e. what the particular legal provisions are, and for this reason the warning has been given: *omnis definitio in jure civili periculosa.*[3] In fact, the more disconnected and inherently contradictory are the provisions giving determinate character to a right, the less are any definitions in its field possible, for definitions should be stated in universal terms, while to use these immediately exposes in all its nakedness what contradicts them—the wrong in this instance. Thus in Roman law, for example, there could be no definition of "man," since "slave" could not be brought under it—the very status of slave indeed is an outrage on the conception of man; it would appear just as hazardous to attempt a definition of "property" and "proprietor" in many cases.) But the deduction of the definition is derived, it may be, from etymology, or especially by abstraction from particular cases, so that it is based on human feelings and ideas. The correctness of the definition is then made to lie in its correspondence with current ideas. This method neglects what is all-essential for science—i.e. in respect of content, the absolute necessity of the thing (right, in this instance), and, in respect of form, the nature of the concept.

The truth is that in philosophical knowledge the necessity of a concept is the principal thing; and the process of its production as a result is its proof and deduction. Then, once its content has been shown in this way to be necessary on its own account, the second step is to look round for what corresponds to it in our ideas and language. But this concept as it actually is in its truth not only may be different from our common idea of it, but in fact must be different from it in form and outline. If, however, the common idea of it is not false in content also, the concept may be exhibited as implied in it and as essentially present in it. In other words, the common idea may be raised to assume the form of the concept. But the common idea is so far from being the standard or criterion of the concept (which is necessary and true on its own account) that it must rather derive its truth from the latter, adjust itself to it, and recognize its own nature by its aid.

But while the above-mentioned abstract way of knowing with its formal definitions, syllogisms, proofs, and the like, is more or less a thing of the past, still it is a poor substitute which a different artifice has provided, namely to adopt and uphold Ideas in general (and in particular the Idea of right and its further specifications) as immediate "facts of

[1] See Paragraph 32.—Ed.
[2] See Paragraphs 29 and 4.—Ed.
[3] "In civil law, definition is always hazardous."—Ed.

consciousness" and to make into the source of right
our natural or our worked up feelings and the inspirations of our own hearts. This method may be
the handiest of all, but it is also the most unphilo-
sophical—not to mention here other aspects of such
an outlook, which has a direct bearing on action and
not simply on knowledge.[1] While the old method,
abstract as it is, does at least insist on the *form* of
the concept in its definition and the *form* of necessary knowledge in its demonstration, the artifice of
feeling and immediate awareness elevates into a
guiding principle the subjectivity, contingency, and
arbitrariness of sapience. What constitutes scientific
procedure in philosophy is expounded in philosophical logic and is here presupposed.[2] [A.]

3. Right is positive[3] in general (*a*) when it has
the *form* of being valid in a particular state, and
this legal authority is the guiding principle for
the knowledge of right in this positive form, i.e.
for the science of positive law. (*b*) Right in this
positive form acquires a positive element in its
content

(*a*) through the particular national character
of a people, its stage of historical development,
and the whole complex of relations connected
with the necessities of nature;[4]

(*β*) because a system of positive law must necessarily involve the application of the universal
concept to particular, externally given, characteristics of objects and cases.[5] This application lies outside speculative thought and the development of the concept, and is the subsumption by the Understanding [of the particular
under the universal];

(*γ*) through the finally detailed provisions requisite for actually pronouncing judgement in
court.

If inclination, caprice, and the sentiments of the
heart are set up in opposition to positive right and
the laws, philosophy at least cannot recognize authorities of that sort.—That force and tyranny may
be an element in law is accidental to law and has
nothing to do with its nature. Later on in this book,
in Paragraphs 211-14, it will be shown at what point
right must become positive. The details to be expounded there are being mentioned here only to indicate the limits of the philosophical study of law
and to obviate at once any possible supposition, let
alone demand, that the outcome of its systematic
development should be a code of positive law, i.e.
a code like the one an actual state requires.

Natural law, or law from the philosophical point
of view, is distinct from positive law; but to pervert

their difference into an opposition and a contradiction would be a gross misunderstanding. The relation between them is much more like that between
Institutes and Pandects.

As for the historical element in positive law, mentioned above in Paragraph 3, Montesquieu[6] proclaimed the true historical view, the genuinely philosophical position, namely that legislation both in
general and in its particular provisions is to be
treated not as something isolated and abstract but
rather as a subordinate moment in a whole, interconnected with all the other features which make
up the character of a nation and an epoch. It is in
being so connected that the various laws acquire
their true meaning and therewith their justification.
To consider particular laws as they appear and
develop in time is a purely historical task. Like acquaintance with what can be logically deduced from
a comparison of these laws with previously existing
legal principles, this task is appreciated and re-
warded in its own sphere and has no relation whatever to the philosophical study of the subject—unless of course the derivation of particular laws from
historical events is confused with their derivation
from the concept, and the historical explanation and
justification is stretched to become an absolutely
valid justification. This difference, which is very important and should be firmly adhered to, is also very
obvious. A particular law may be shown to be
wholly grounded in and consistent with the circumstances and with existing legally established institutions, and yet it may be wrong and irrational in its
essential character, like a number of provisions in
Roman private law which followed quite logically
from such institutions as Roman matrimony and
Roman *patria potestas*.[7] But even if particular laws
are both right and reasonable, still it is one thing
to *prove* that they have that character—which cannot be truly done except by means of the concept—
and quite another to describe their appearance in
history or the circumstances, contingencies, needs,
and events which brought about their enactment.
That kind of exposition and (pragmatic) knowledge, based on proximate or remote historical causes,
is frequently called "explanation" or preferably
"comprehension" by those who think that to expound history in this way is the only thing, or rather the essential thing, the only important thing, to
be done in order to comprehend law or an established institution; whereas what is really essential,
the concept of the thing, they have not discussed at
all. From the same point of view, reference is commonly made also to the Roman or the German "concepts" of law, i.e. concepts of law as they might be
defined in this or that legal code, whereas what is
meant is not concepts but only general legal principles, propositions of the Understanding, maxims,
positive laws, and the like.

By dint of obscuring the difference between the

[1] See e.g., Remarks to Paragraphs 126 and 140.—ED.
[2] See Preface, p. 1.—ED.
[3] For the distinction between *Recht* and *Gesetz* see Paragraphs 211 ff.—ED.
[4] See the section on the "Geographical Basis of History" in the *Philosophy of History*, pp. 190 ff.—ED.
[5] See Remarks to Paragraphs 69, 212, 214.—ED.

[6] Cf. Montesquieu, *The Spirit of Laws*, Book i, Chap.
3.—ED.
[7] See Remark and Addition to Paragraph 180.—ED.

historical and the philosophical study of law, it becomes possible to shift the point of view and slip over from the problem of the true justification of a thing to a justification by appeal to circumstances, to deductions from presupposed conditions which in themselves may have no higher validity, and so forth. To generalize, by this means the relative is put in place of the absolute and the external appearance in place of the true nature of the thing. When those who try to justify things on historical grounds confound an origin in external circumstances with one in the concept, they unconsciously achieve the very opposite of what they intend. Once the origination of an institution has been shown to be wholly to the purpose and necessary in the circumstances of the time, the demands of history have been fulfilled. But if this is supposed to pass for a general justification of the thing itself, it turns out to be the opposite, because, since those circumstances are no longer present, the institution so far from being justified has by their disappearance lost its meaning and its right. Suppose, for example, that we accept as a vindication of the monasteries their service in cultivating wildernesses and populating them, in keeping learning alive by transcribing manuscripts and giving instruction, &c., and suppose further that this service has been deemed to be the ground and the purpose of their continued existence, then what really follows from considering this past service is that, since circumstances have now entirely altered, the monasteries are at least in this respect superfluous and inappropriate.

Now that the historical meaning of coming to be —the historical method of portraying it and making it comprehensible—is at home in a different sphere from the philosophical survey of the concept of the thing and of a thing's coming to be too,[1] philosophy and history are able to that extent to preserve an attitude of mutual indifference. But they are not always at peace in this way, even in scientific circles, and so I quote something, relevant to their contact, which appears in Herr Hugo's *Lehrbuch der Geschichte des römischen Rechts*,[2] and which will at the same time cast further light on the affectation that they are opposed. Herr Hugo says [3] that "Cicero praises the Twelve Tables with a side-glance at the philosophers . . . but the philosopher Favorinus treats them exactly as many a great philosopher since his day has treated positive law." In the same context Herr Hugo makes the final retort to a treatment of the subject like Favorinus' when he gives as the reason for it that "Favorinus understood the Twelve Tables just as little as these philosophers have understood positive law."

The correction of the philosopher Favorinus by the jurist Sextus Caecilius in Aulus Gellius [4] is primarily an expression of the permanent and true principle

for justifying what is purely positive in its intrinsic worth. *Non . . . ignoras,* Caecilius happily retorts to Favorinus, *legum opportunitates et medelas pro temporum moribus et pro rerum publicarum generibus, ac pro utilitatum praesentium rationibus, proque vitiorum, quibus medendum est, fervoribus, mutari ac flecti, neque uno statu consistere, quin, ut facies coeli et maris, ita rerum atque fortunae tempestatibus varientur. Quid salubrius visum est rogatione illa Stolonis . . ., quid utilius plebiscito Voconio . . .? Quid tam necessarium existimatum est . . . quam Lex Licinia . . .? Omnia tamen haec obliterata et operta sunt civitatis opulentia.*[5] These laws are positive in so far as they have their meaning and appropriateness in contemporary conditions, and therefore their sole value is historical and they are of a transitory nature. The wisdom of what legislators and administrators did in their day or settled to meet the needs of the hour is a separate matter and one properly to be assessed by history. History's recognition of it will be all the deeper the more its assessment is supported by a philosophical outlook.

Of Caecilius's further arguments in justification of the Twelve Tables against Favorinus, however, I will give an example, because he introduces in them the eternally deceptive method and argumentation of the Understanding, I mean the production of a good reason for a bad thing and the supposition that the bad thing has thereby been justified. Caecilius is discussing the horrible law that gave a creditor the right after a fixed period of time to kill his debtor or sell him into slavery, or, if there were several creditors, to cut pieces off their debtor and divide him up amongst themselves; and there was even a further proviso that if one of them cut off too much or too little, no action was for that reason to lie against him—a clause which would have benefited Shakespeare's Shylock in the *Merchant of Venice* and of which he would most gratefully have availed himself. For this law Caecilius adduces the good reason that it rendered trust and credit all the more secure and that because of its horrible character there was never to have been any question of its application. In his thoughtlessness not only does the reflection escape him that if the law could never have been applied, then the aim of securing trust and credit by it was frustrated, but he even goes on directly afterwards to give an example of how the law concerning false witness was made ineffective owing to its immoderate penalties.

There is no knowing, however, what Herr Hugo

---

[1] For some of Hegel's criticisms of Savigny, see Paragraph 211.—ED.
[2] Gustav, Ritter von Hugo, *Text-book of the History of Roman Law.*—ED.
[3] 5th edn., § 53.
[4] *Noctes Atticae,* xx. 1.

[5] "You must be aware that the advantages and remedies offered by the laws vary and fluctuate in accordance with contemporary customs, types of constitution, considerations of immediate advantage, and the violence of the ills to be remedied. Laws do not persist unchanged in character; on the contrary, the storms of circumstance and chance alter them as storms change the face of the sea and the sky. Has anything ever seemed more salutary than Stolo's proposal . . ., more advantageous than the decree . . . carried by Voconius as tribune? What has been taken to be so necessary . . . as the Licinian law? Yet, now that the state has grown wealthy, all these regulations have been blotted out and buried."—ED.

means when he says that Favorinus did not understand the law. Any schoolboy is perfectly capable of understanding it, and Shylock would have understood better than anyone else the clause, cited above, which would have been so advantageous to him. By "understand" Herr Hugo must have meant only that level of understanding which in the case of such a law is content if it can find a good reason for it.

Still, another misunderstanding of which Favorinus was convicted by Caecilius in the same context is one to which a philosopher may surely confess without exactly blushing; I mean the failure to understand that *jumentum* (which "as distinct from *arcera*" is, according to the law, the only conveyance to be provided for a sick man who has to appear in court) is to be interpreted to mean not only a horse but also a carriage or wagon. From this legal proviso Caecilius was able to derive a further proof of the excellence and precision of the old laws by pointing out that, in fixing the terms of a summons to a sick man to appear in court, they even carried precision so far as to distinguish not only between a horse and a wagon, but even between one wagon and another, between one covered in and "upholstered," according to Caecilius' interpretation, and one not so comfortable. Here we would have the choice between the severity of the original law and the triviality of such distinctions, but to describe such things, and still more their learned interpretation, as "trivial" would be one of the worst of insults to erudition of this kind and others!

But in the same *Lehrbuch* Herr Hugo goes on to speak of rationality in connexion with Roman law, and what has struck me in his remarks is the following. In his treatment of the "period from the origin of the state to the Twelve Tables" he says [1] that (in Rome) "men had many wants and were compelled to work and hence needed the assistance of draught and pack animals, such as we are familiar with ourselves; that in Roman territory hills and valleys alternated and that the city was built on a hill" and so forth—disquisitions which were perhaps intended to carry out Montesquieu's ideas, but in which one will hardly find that his spirit has been caught. Then he goes on to say [2] that "the legal position was still very far from satisfying the highest demands of reason." That is quite right, Roman law in respect of the family, slavery, &c., fails even to satisfy reason's most modest demands. But in dealing with later periods of Roman history, Herr Hugo forgets to tell us whether in any of them, and if so in which, Roman law did "satisfy the highest demands of reason." However, of the classical jurists in the period of the "highest maturity of Roman law as a science," Herr Hugo writes: [3] "It has long since been observed that the classical jurists were educated through philosophy," yet "few know" (though more know now, thanks to the numerous editions of Herr Hugo's *Lehrbuch*) "that no class of writers is so well en-

titled as these same Roman jurists to be compared with mathematicians in respect of the rigorous logic of their deductive reasoning or with the new founder of metaphysics in respect of their quite strikingly distinctive method of developing their concepts—a contention supported by the curious fact that nowhere are there to be found so many trichotomies as there are in the classical jurists and in Kant." Logical deduction, a method commended by Leibniz, is certainly an essential characteristic of the study of positive law, as of mathematics and any other science of the Understanding, but this deductive method of the Understanding has nothing whatever to do with the satisfaction of the demands of reason or with philosophical science. But apart from that it is the *il*logicality of the Roman jurists and praetors that must be regarded as one of their chief virtues, for by dint of being illogical they evaded unjust and detestable laws, though in the process they found themselves compelled *callide* [4] to devise empty verbal distinctions (e.g. to call *bonorum possessio* what was nevertheless *hereditas*) and downright foolish subterfuges (and folly also is illogicality) in order to preserve the letter of the Twelve Tables (e.g. by the *fictio*, ὑπόκρισις, that a *filia* was a *filius*).[5] It is ludicrous though to see the classical jurists compared with Kant because of a few trichotomous divisions, especially those cited as examples in the fifth note to Herr Hugo's paragraph, and to see that kind of thing called "development of concepts."

4. The basis of right is, in general, mind; its precise place and point of origin is the will. The will is free, so that freedom is both the substance of right and its goal, while the system of right is the realm of freedom made actual, the world of mind brought forth out of itself like a second nature.

In considering the freedom of the will, we may recall the old method of cognition. The procedure was to presuppose the idea of the will and to attempt to establish a definition of the will by deriving it from that idea; then the so-called "proof" of the will's freedom was extracted, in the manner of the old empirical psychology, from the various feelings and phenomena of the ordinary consciousness, such as remorse, guilt, and the like, by maintaining that they were to be explained only in the light of a will that was free. But it is more convenient of course to arrive at the same point by taking the short cut of supposing that freedom is given as a "fact of consciousness" and that we must simply *believe* in it!

The proof that the will is free and the proof of the nature of the will and freedom can be established (as has already been pointed out in Paragraph 2) only as a link in the whole chain [of philosophy]. The fundamental premisses of this proof are that mind

[1] §§ 38–9 [*op. cit.* in 7th edn.].
[2] § 40 [*ibid.* in 7th edn.]
[3] § 289 [§ 314 in 7th edn.].
[4] *Callide*—"artfully" or "on the sly" (see Remark to Paragraph 180).—ED.
[5] J. G. Heineccius: *Antiquitatum Romanarum jurisprudentiam illustrantium Syntagma* [Basel, 1752], lib. i, tit. ii, § 24.

to start with is intelligence, that the phases through which it passes in its development from feeling, through representative thinking, to thinking proper, are the road along which it produces itself as will, and that will, as practical mind in general, is the truth of intelligence, the stage next above it. These premisses I have expounded in my *Encyclopaedia of the Philosophical Sciences*[1] and I hope by and by to be able to elaborate them still further. There is all the more need for me by so doing to make my contribution to what I hope is the deeper knowledge of the nature of mind in that, as I have said in the *Encyclopaedia*,[2] scarcely any philosophical science is so neglected and so ill off as the theory of mind, usually called "psychology." The moments in the concept of the will which are dealt with in this and the following Paragraphs of the Introduction result from the premisses to which I have just referred, but in addition anyone may find help towards forming an idea of them by calling on his own self-consciousness. In the first place, anyone can discover in himself ability to abstract from everything whatever, and in the same way to determine himself, to posit any content in himself by his own effort; and similarly the other specific characteristics of the will are exemplified for him in his own consciousness. [A.]

5. The will contains (α) the element of pure indeterminacy or that pure reflection of the ego into itself which involves the dissipation of every restriction and every content either immediately presented by nature, by needs, desires, and impulses, or given and determined by any means whatever. This is the unrestricted infinity of absolute abstraction or universality, the pure thought of oneself.

Those who regard thinking as one special faculty, distinct from the will as another special faculty, and who even proceed to contend that thinking is prejudicial to the will, especially the good will, reveal at the very outset their complete ignorance of the nature of the will—a remark we shall have to make rather often when dealing with this same subject.

In Paragraph 5, it is only one side of the will which is described, namely this unrestricted possibility of abstraction from every determinate state of mind which I may find in myself or which I may have set up in myself, my flight from every content as from a restriction. When the will's self-determination consists in this alone, or when representative thinking regards this side by itself as freedom and clings fast to it, then we have negative freedom, or freedom as the Understanding conceives it. This is the freedom of the void which rises to a passion and takes shape in the world; while still remaining theoretical, it takes shape in religion as the Hindu fanaticism of pure contemplation, but when it turns to actual practice, it takes shape in religion and politics alike as the fanaticism of destruction—the destruction of the whole subsisting social order—as the elimination of individuals who are objects of suspicion to any social order, and the annihilation of any organization which tries to rise anew from the ruins. Only in destroying something does this negative will possess the feeling of itself as existent. Of course it imagines that it is willing some positive state of affairs, such as universal equality or universal religious life, but in fact it does not will that this shall be positively actualized, and for this reason: such actuality leads at once to some sort of order, to a particularization of organizations and individuals alike; while it is precisely out of the annihilation of particularity and objective characterization that the self-consciousness of this negative freedom proceeds. Consequently, what negative freedom intends to will can never be anything in itself but an abstract idea, and giving effect to this idea can only be the fury of destruction. [A.]

6. (β) At the same time, the ego is also the transition from undifferentiated indeterminacy to the differentiation, determination, and positing of a determinacy as a content and object. Now further, this content may either be given by nature or engendered by the concept of mind. Through this positing of itself as something determinate, the ego steps in principle into determinate existence. This is the absolute moment, the finitude or particularization of the ego.

This second moment—determination—is negativity and cancellation like the first, i.e. it cancels the abstract negativity of the first. Since it is the general rule that the particular is contained in the universal, it follows that this second moment is already contained in the first and is simply an explicit positing of what the first already was implicitly. The first moment, I mean—because by itself it is only the first—is not true infinity or concrete universality, not the concept, but only something determinate, one-sided; i.e., being abstraction from all determinacy, it is itself not without determinacy; and to be something abstract and one-sided constitutes its determinacy, its defectiveness, and its finitude.

The determination and differentiation of the two moments which have been mentioned is to be found in the philosophies of Fichte, Kant, and others; only, in Fichte—to confine ourselves to his exposition—the ego, as that which is without limitation, is taken (in the first proposition of his *Science of Knowledge*) purely and simply as something positive and so as the universality and identity of the Understanding. The result is that this abstract ego by itself is supposed to be the whole truth, and therefore the restriction—the negative in general, whether as a given external barrier or as an activity of the ego itself—appears (in the second proposition) as an addition merely.

To apprehend the negativity immanent in the universal or self-identical, e.g. in the ego, was the

---

[1] Heidelberg, 1817, §§ 363–99 [3rd edn. §§ 440–82].
[2] [1st edn.] Remark to § 367 [3rd edn. § 444 and cf. § 378].

next step which speculative philosophy had to take
—a step of whose necessity they have no inkling who
hold to the dualism of infinite and finite and do not
even grasp it in that immanence and abstraction in
which Fichte did. [A.]

7. (γ) The will is the unity of both these moments. It is particularity reflected into itself and
so brought back to universality, i.e. it is individuality. It is the *self*-determination of the ego,
which means that at one and the same time the
ego posits itself as its own negative, i.e. as restricted and determinate, and yet remains by itself, i.e. in its self-identity and universality. It
determines itself and yet at the same time binds
itself together with itself. The ego determines
itself in so far as it is the relating of negativity
to itself. As this self-relation, it is indifferent to
this determinacy; it knows it as something which
is its own, something which is only ideal, a mere
possibility by which it is not constrained and in
which it is confined only because it has put itself in it.—This is the freedom of the will and
it constitutes the concept or substantiality of the
will, its weight, so to speak, just as weight constitutes the substantiality of a body.

Every self-consciousness knows itself (i) as universal, as the potentiality of abstracting from everything
determinate, and (ii) as particular, with a determinate object, content, and aim. Still, both these moments are only abstractions; what is concrete and
true (and everything true is concrete) is the universality which has the particular as its opposite, but
the particular which by its reflection into itself has
been equalized with the universal. This unity is individuality, not individuality in its immediacy as a
unit, our first idea of individuality, but individuality
in accordance with its concept;[1] indeed, individuality in this sense is just precisely the concept itself.
The first two moments—(i) that the will can abstract from everything, and (ii) that it is also determined in some specific way either by itself or by
something else—are readily admitted and grasped
because, taken independently, they are false and
moments of the Understanding. But the third moment, which is true and speculative (and everything
true must be thought speculatively if it is to be comprehended) is the one into which the Understanding
declines to advance, for it is precisely the concept
which it persists in calling the inconceivable. It is
the task of logic as purely speculative philosophy to
prove and explain further this innermost secret of
speculation, of infinity as negativity relating itself
to itself, this ultimate spring of all activity, life, and
consciousness. Here attention can only be drawn to
the fact that if you say "the will is universal, the
will determines itself," the words you use to describe
the will presuppose it to be a subject or substratum
from the start. But the will is not something com-

plete and universal prior to its determining itself
and prior to its superseding and idealizing this determination. The will is not a will until it is this
self-mediating activity, this return into itself. [A.]

8. The more detailed process of particularization (see Paragraph 6) constitutes the difference
between the forms of the will: (*a*) If the will's
determinate character lies in the abstract opposition of its subjectivity to the objectivity of external immediate existence, then this is the formal will of mere self-consciousness which finds
an external world confronting it. As individuality returning in its determinacy into itself, it is
the process of translating the subjective purpose
into objectivity through the use of its own activity and some external means. Once mind has
developed its potentialities to actuality (*wie er
an und für sich ist*), its determinate character
is true and simply its own.[2] At that stage, the relation of consciousness constitutes only the *appearance* of the will,[3] an aspect which is not separately considered any further here. [A.]

9. (*b*) In so far as the specific determinations
of the will are its own or, in general, its particularization reflected into itself, they are its content. This content, as content of the will, is, in
accordance with the form of will described in
(*a*), its purpose, either its inward or subjective
purpose when the will merely images its object,
or else its purpose actualized and achieved by
means of its activity of translating its subjective
purpose into objectivity.

10. This content, or the will's determination on
something specific, is in the first place immediate. Consequently the will is then free only *in*
itself or *for* an external observer, or, to speak
generally, it is the will in its concept. It is not
until it has itself as its object that the will is for
itself what it is in itself.

Finitude consists therefore in this, that what something is *in* itself or in accordance with its concept is
one phenomenon or exists in one way, while what it
is *for* itself is a different phenomenon or exists in another way; so, for example, *in* itself the abstract reciprocal externality characteristic of nature is space,
but *for* itself it is time.[4] In this connexion, two things
are to be noticed: (i) The true is the Idea and the
Idea alone, and hence if you take an object or a category only as it is in itself or in its concept, you have
not yet grasped it in its truth. (ii) A thing which is
in itself or as concept is also existent in some way
and its existence in such a way is a shape proper to
the thing itself (as space is in the example just given).

[1] *Enc.*, [1st edn.] §§ 112–14 [3rd edn. §§ 163–5].

[2] *Enc.*, [1st edn.] § 363 [3rd edn. § 440].
[3] With this Paragraph compare the references to it in
Paragraphs 25, 28, 108, and 109.—ED.
[4] See Addition to Paragraph 42.—ED.

The gulf present in the sphere of the finite between "in-itself-ness" and "for-itself-ness" constitutes at the same time that sphere's mere existential or phenomenal character. (Examples of this—the natural will and then formal rights, &c.—will be forthcoming directly.)[1]

The Understanding goes no further than the purely implicit character of a thing and consequently calls the freedom which accords with this implicit character a "potency," because if freedom is only implicit it is indeed mere potentiality. But the Understanding looks upon this implicit character as absolute and perennial; and it takes the relation of freedom to what it wills, or in general to the object in which it is realized, as merely a matter of its application to a given material, not belonging to the essence of freedom itself. Thus it has to do with the abstract only, not with its Idea and its truth. [A.]

11. The will which is but implicitly free is the immediate or natural will. The specific characteristics of the difference which the self-determining concept sets up within the will appear in the natural will as an immediately existing content, i.e. as the impulses, desires, inclinations, whereby the will finds itself determined in the course of nature. This content, together with the specific differences developed within it, arises from the rationality of the will and so is implicitly rational; but, poured out in this way into the mould of immediacy, it still lacks the form of rationality. It is true that this content has for me the general character of being mine; but this form is still different from the content, and hence the will is still a will finite in character.

Empirical psychology details and describes these impulses and inclinations, and the needs arising from them, as it finds them, or presumes it finds them, in experience, and it proceeds in the usual way to classify this given material. Consideration is given below[2] to the objective element in these impulses, both to its true character stripped of the form of irrationality which it possesses as impulse and also to the manner in which at the same time it is shaped externally. [A.]

12. The whole of this content, as we light upon it in its immediacy in the will, is there only as a medley and multiplicity of impulses, each of which is merely "my desire" but exists alongside other desires which are likewise all "mine," and each of which is at the same time something universal and indeterminate, aimed at all kinds of objects and satiable in all kinds of ways. When, in this twofold indeterminacy, the will gives itself the form of individuality (see Paragraph 7), this constitutes the resolution of the will, and it is only in so far as it resolves that the will is an actual will at all.

To resolve on something is to cancel the state of indeterminacy in which one content is prima facie just as much of a possibility as any other. As an alternative to *etwas beschliessen* (to resolve on something) the German language also contains the expression *sich entschliessen*. This expresses the fact that the indeterminate character of the will itself, as itself neutral yet infinitely prolific, the original seed of all determinate existence, contains its determinations and aims within itself and simply brings them forth out of itself.

13. By resolving, the will posits itself as the will of a specific individual and as a will separating itself off against another individual. But apart from this finitude as consciousness (see Paragraph 8), the immediate will is on account of the difference between its form and its content (see Paragraph 11) a will only in form. The decision which belongs to it as such is only abstract and its content is not yet the content and product of its freedom.

In so far as intelligence thinks,[3] its object and content remains something universal, while its own behaviour consists of a universal activity. In the will, "the universal" also means in essence "mine," "individuality"; and in the immediate will—the will which is will in form only—it means abstract individuality, individuality not yet filled with its free universality. Hence it is in the will that the intrinsic finitude of intelligence has its beginning; and it is only by raising itself to become thought again,[4] and endowing its aims with immanent universality, that the will cancels the difference of form and content and makes itself the objective, infinite, will. Thus they understand little of the nature of thinking and willing who suppose that while, in willing as such, man is infinite, in thinking, he, or even reason itself, is restricted. In so far as thinking and willing are still distinguished, the opposite is rather the truth, and will is thinking reason resolving itself to finitude. [A.]

14. The finite will as, in respect of its form, though only its form, the self-reflecting, independent, and infinite ego (see Paragraph 5), stands over its content, i.e. its various impulses, and also over the further separate ways in which these are actualized and satisfied. At the same time, since it is infinite in form only, it is tied to this content (see Paragraphs 6 and 11) as to the specific determinations of its nature and its external actuality; though since it is indeterminate, it is not tied to this or that specific content. From the point of view of the ego reflected into itself, this content is only a possible one,

---

[1] See Paragraphs 11-18 and 21 ff.—Ed.
[2] i.e., in Paragraphs 19 and 150 with the Remarks thereto.—Ed.

[3] See Paragraph 4.—Ed.
[4] See Part III.—Ed.

i.e. it may be mine or it may not; and the ego similarly is the possibility of determining myself to this or to something else, of *choosing* between these specific determinations, which at this point I regard as external to me.

15. At this stage, the freedom of the will is arbitrariness (*Willkür*) and this involves two factors: (*a*) free reflection, abstracting from everything, and (*b*) dependence on a content and material given either from within or from without. Because this content, implicitly necessary as purpose,[1] is at the same time qualified in the face of free reflection as possible, it follows that arbitrariness is contingency manifesting itself as will.[2]

The idea which people most commonly have of freedom is that it is arbitrariness—the mean, chosen by abstract reflection, between the will wholly determined by natural impulses, and the will free absolutely. If we hear it said that the definition of freedom is ability to do what we please, such an idea can only be taken to reveal an utter immaturity of thought, for it contains not even an inkling of the absolutely free will, of right, ethical life, and so forth. Reflection, the formal universality and unity of self-consciousness, is the will's abstract certainty of its freedom, but it is not yet the truth of freedom, because it has not yet got *itself* as its content and aim, and consequently the subjective side is still other than the objective; the content of this self-determination, therefore, also remains purely and simply finite. Instead of being the will in its truth, arbitrariness is more like the will as contradiction. In the controversy carried on especially at the time of Wolff's metaphysic[3] as to whether the will were really free or whether the conviction of its freedom were only a delusion, it was arbitrariness which was in view. In opposition to the certitude of this abstract self-determination, determinism has rightly pointed to the content which, as something met with, is not contained in that certitude and so comes to it from outside, although "outside" in this case means impulses, ideas, or, in general, consciousness so filled in one way or another that its content is not intrinsic to its self-determining activity as such. Since, then, arbitrariness has immanent in it only the formal element in willing, i.e. free self-determination, while the other element is something given to it, we may readily allow that, if it is arbitrariness which is supposed to be freedom, it may indeed be called an illusion. In every philosophy of reflection, like Kant's, and Kant's deprived of all its depth by Fries, freedom is nothing else but this empty self-activity. [A.]

16. What the will has decided to choose (see Paragraph 14) it can equally easily renounce (see Paragraph 5). But its ability to go beyond

any other choice which it may substitute, and so on *ad infinitum*, never enables it to get beyond its own finitude, because the content of every such choice is something other than the form of the will and therefore something finite, while the opposite of determinacy, namely indeterminacy, i.e. indecision or abstraction from any content, is only the other, equally one-sided, moment of the will.

17. The contradiction which the arbitrary will is (see Paragraph 15), comes into appearance as a dialectic of impulses and inclinations; each of them is in the way of every other—the satisfaction of one is unavoidably subordinated or sacrificed to the satisfaction of another, and so on. An impulse is simply a uni-directional urge and thus has no measuring-rod in itself, and so this determination of its subordination or sacrifice is the contingent decision of the arbitrary will which, in deciding, may proceed either by using intelligence to calculate which impulse will give most satisfaction, or else in accordance with any other optional consideration. [A.]

18. In connexion with the *judgement* of impulses, this dialectic appears in the following form: (*a*) As immanent and so positive, the determinations of the immediate will are good; thus man is said to be by nature good. (*b*) But, in so far as these determinations are natural and thus are in general opposed to freedom and the concept of mind, and hence negative, they must be uprooted, and so man is said to be by nature evil.—At this point a decision in favour of either thesis depends equally on subjective arbitrariness. [A.]

19. In the demand for the *purification*[4] of impulses there lies the general notion that they should be freed both from their form as immediate and natural determinations, and also from the subjectivity and contingency of their content, and so brought back to their substantial essence. The truth behind this vague demand is that the impulses should become the rational system of the will's volitions. To grasp them like that, proceeding out of the concept of the will, is the content of the philosophical science of right.

The content of this science through every single one of its moments, e.g. right, property, morality, family, state, and so forth, may be expounded in the form: man has by nature the impulse towards right, also the impulse to property and morality, also the impulse of love between the sexes, the impulse to sociability, &c. This form is to be found in empirical psychology. But if in its stead the greater

---

[1] See Paragraph 19 and the Remark thereto.—ED.
[2] See Paragraph 5.—ED.
[3] See Remark to Paragraph 4.—ED.
[4] See Paragraph 139.—ED.

dignity of a philosophical dress is desired, then according to what, as was remarked before,[1] has passed in recent times, and still passes, for philosophy, this dress may be had cheap by the simple device of saying that man discovers within himself as a "fact of his consciousness" that right, property, the state, &c., are objects of his volition. Later in the text,[2] this same subject-matter, which appears here in the shape of impulses, will come on the scene in another form, i.e. in the shape of duties.

20. When reflection is brought to bear on impulses, they are imaged, estimated, compared with one another, with their means of satisfaction and their consequences, &c., and with a sum of satisfaction (i.e. with happiness). In this way reflection invests this material with abstract universality and in this external manner purifies it from its crudity and barbarity. This growth of the universality of thought is the absolute value in education[3] (compare Paragraph 187). [A.]

21. The truth, however, of this abstract universality, which is indeterminate in itself and finds its determinacy in the material mentioned in Paragraph 20, is self-determining universality, the will, freedom. In having universality, or itself *qua* infinite form,[4] for its object, content, and aim, the will is free not only *in* itself but *for* itself also; it is the Idea in its truth.

(i) When the will's self-consciousness takes the form of desire and impulse, this consciousness is sense-consciousness, just as sensation in general denotes externality and therefore the condition in which self-consciousness is self-external. (ii) When the will is reflective, it contains two elements—this sense-consciousness and the universality of thought. (iii) When the will's potentialities have become fully explicit, then it has for its object the will itself as such, and so the will in its sheer universality—a universality which is what it is simply because it has absorbed in itself the immediacy of instinctive desire and the particularity which is produced by reflection and with which such desire *eo ipso* becomes imbued. But this process of absorption in or elevation to universality is what is called the activity of thought. The self-consciousness which purifies its object, content, and aim, and raises them to this universality effects this as thinking getting its own way in the will. Here is the point at which it becomes clear that it is only as thinking intelligence that the will is genuinely a will and free. The slave does not know his essence, his infinity, his freedom; he does not know himself as human in essence; and he lacks this knowledge of himself because he does not think

himself. This self-consciousness which apprehends itself through thinking as essentially human, and thereby frees itself from the contingent and the false, is the principle of right, morality, and all ethical life. Philosophic utterances about right, morality, and ethical life from those who would banish thought and have recourse instead to feeling, enthusiasm, the heart and the breast, are expressive of the utterly contemptible position into which thought and philosophic science have fallen, because what this amounts to is that even philosophic science itself, plunged in self-despair and extreme exhaustion, is taking as its principle barbarity and absence of thought, and would do its best to rob mankind of all truth, worth, and dignity. [A.]

22. It is the will whose potentialities have become fully explicit which is truly infinite, because its object is itself and so is not in its eyes an "other" or a barrier; on the contrary, in its object this will has simply turned backward into itself. Further this will is not mere potentiality, capacity, potency (*potentia*), but the infinite in actuality (*infinitum actu*), since the concept's existence or its objective externality is inwardness itself.

Thus, if anyone speaks simply of the "free will" as such, without specifically referring to the will which is free absolutely, he is speaking only of the capacity for freedom, or of the natural and finite will (see Paragraph 11), and not by any means therefore of the free will, despite his intention and the words he uses.

Since the Understanding takes the infinite only as something negative and so as something "beyond," it supposes that it is doing all the more honour to the infinite, the more it pushes it into the distance away from itself and removes it from itself as something alien. In the free will, the truly infinite becomes actual and present; the free will itself is this Idea whose nature it is to be present here and now. [A.]

23. Only in freedom of this kind is the will by itself without qualification, because then it is related to nothing except itself and so is released from every tie of dependence on anything else. The will is then true, or rather truth itself, because its self-determination consists in a correspondence between what it is in its existence (i.e. what it is as objective to itself) and its concept; or in other words, the pure concept of the will has the intuition of itself for its goal and its reality.

24. The will is then universal, because all restriction and all particular individuality have been absorbed within it. These lie only in the difference between the concept and its content or object, or, to put it otherwise, in the differ-

[1] e.g., Remarks to Paragraphs 2 and 4.—ED.
[2] See Paragraphs 148 ff. and especially Remark to Paragraph 150.—ED.
[3] See Paragraphs 123, 268, and 315.—ED.
[4] See Paragraph 5.—ED.

ence between its implicit character and its subjective awareness of itself, or between its universality and its exclusive individuality, the individuality which resolves.

The various types of universality develop in logic.[1] In connexion with this word "universality," what strikes representative thinking first is the idea of abstract and external universality; but in connexion with absolute universality—and the universality here in question is of this character—we have to think neither of the universality of reflection, i.e. "all-ness" or the universal as a common characteristic, nor of the abstract universality which stands outside and over against the individual, the abstract identity of the Understanding (see Remark to Paragraph 6). It is the universality concrete in character and so explicitly universal which is the substance of self-consciousness, its immanent generic essence, or its immanent Idea. This—the concept of the free will—is the universal which overlaps its object, penetrates its particular determination through and through and therein remains identical with itself. The absolutely universal is definable as what is called the "rational," and it can be apprehended only in this speculative way.

25. The subjective, in relation to the will in general, means the will's self-conscious side, its individuality (see Paragraph 7) in distinction from its implicit concept. The subjectivity of the will means therefore

(a) the pure form of the will, the absolute unity of self-consciousness with itself (a unity in which self-consciousness, as I=I, is purely and simply inward and abstractly self-dependent), the pure certainty, as distinguished from the truth, of individuality;

(β) the particular will as the arbitrary will and the contingent content of optional aims;

(γ) in general, the one-sided form of the will (see Paragraph 8) for which the thing willed, whatever its content, is but a content belonging to self-consciousness and an aim unfulfilled.

26. (a) The will is purely and simply objective in so far as it has itself for its determination and so is in correspondence with its concept and genuinely a will;

(β) but the objective will, being without the infinite form of self-consciousness, is the will absorbed in its object or condition, whatever the content of these may be; it is the will of the child, the ethical will, also the will of the slave, the superstitious man, &c.;

(γ) objectivity, finally, is the one-sided form opposed to the subjective volition, and hence it is the immediacy of existence as external reality; the will first becomes objective to itself in this

sense through the fulfilment of its aims.

These logical categories—subjectivity and objectivity—have been set forth in detail here primarily with a view to pointing out expressly in relation to them, since they are often used in the sequel, that they, like other distinctions and opposed categories of reflection, pass over into their opposites as a result of their finitude and their dialectical character. In other cases of opposition between two categories, each opposite retains a hard and fast meaning for representative thinking and the Understanding, because the identity of the opposites is still only something inward. In the will, on the other hand, these opposed aspects are supposed to be at one and the same time abstractions and yet determinations of the *will,* which can be known only as something concrete, and they lead automatically to their identity and to the confusion of their meanings—a confusion into which the Understanding slips quite unconsciously. Thus, for example, the will as inward freedom is subjectivity itself; subjectivity therefore is the concept of the will and so its objectivity. But it is its subjectivity, contrasted with objectivity, which is finitude, and yet, because of this very contrast, the will is not by itself but is entangled with its object, and so its finitude consists quite as much in the fact that it is not subjective—and so on. Hence the meaning to be attributed in what follows to "subjective" or "objective" in respect of the will must each time appear from the context, which supplies the data for inferring their position in relation to the will as a whole. [A.]

27. The absolute goal, or, if you like, the absolute impulse, of free mind (see Paragraph 21) is to make its freedom its object, i.e. to make freedom objective as much in the sense that freedom shall be the rational system of mind, as in the sense that this system shall be the world of immediate actuality (see Paragraph 26). In making freedom its object, mind's purpose is to be explicitly, as Idea, what the will is implicitly. The definition of the concept of the will in abstraction from the Idea of the will is "the free will which wills the free will." [2]

28. The will's activity consists in annulling the contradiction between subjectivity and objectivity and giving its aims an objective instead of a subjective character, while at the same time remaining by itself even in objectivity. Outside the formal mode of willing (i.e. consciousness, see Paragraph 8) where objectivity is present only as immediate actuality, this activity is in essence the development of the substantive content of the Idea (see Paragraph 21)—a development through which the concept determines the Idea, itself at first abstract, until it becomes a

---

[1] *Enc.,* [1st edn.] §§ 118-26 [3rd edn. §§ 169-78].

[2] See Paragraph 28.—Ed.

systematized whole. This whole, as what is substantive, is independent of the opposition between a merely subjective aim and its realization and is the same in both despite their difference in form.

29. An existent of any sort embodying the free will, this is what right is. Right therefore is by definition freedom as Idea.

The crucial point in both the Kantian and the generally accepted definition of right (see the Introduction to Kant's *Philosophy of Law*) is the *"restriction which makes it possible for my freedom or self-will to co-exist with the self-will of each and all according to a universal law."* On the one hand, this definition contains only a negative category, restriction, while on the other hand the positive factor—the universal law or the so-called "law of reason," the correspondence of the self-will of one individual with that of another—is tantamount to the principle of contradiction and the familiar notion of abstract identity. The definition of right which I have quoted involves that way of looking at the matter, especially popular since Rousseau,[1] according to which what is fundamental, substantive, and primary is supposed to be the will of a single person in his own private self-will, not the absolute or rational will, and mind as a particular individual, not mind as it is in its truth. Once this principle is adopted, of course the rational can come on the scene only as a restriction on the type of freedom which this principle involves, and so also not as something immanently rational but only as an external abstract universal. This view is devoid of any speculative thinking and is repudiated by the philosophic concept. And the phenomena which it has produced both in men's heads and in the world are of a frightfulness parallel only to the superficiality of the thoughts on which they are based.

30. It is only because right is the embodiment of the absolute concept or of self-conscious freedom that it is something sacrosanct. But the exclusively formal character of right (and duty also, as we shall see)[2] arises at a distinct stage in the development of the concept of freedom. By contrast with the right which is comparatively formal (i.e. abstract) and so comparatively restricted, a higher right belongs to the sphere and stage of mind in which mind has determined and actualized within itself the further moments contained in its Idea; and it belongs to this sphere as the sphere which is concreter, intrinsically richer, and more genuinely universal.

Every stage in the development of the Idea of freedom has its own special right, since it is the embodiment of freedom in one of its proper specific forms. When there is said to be a clash between the moral or the ethical and the right, the right in question is only the elementary, formal, right of abstract personality. Morality, ethical life, the interest of the state, each of these is a right of a special character because each of them is a specific form and embodiment of freedom. They can come into collision with each other only in so far as they are all on the same footing as rights. If mind's moral attitude were not also a right, or freedom in one of its forms, it could not possibly come into collision with the right of personality or with any other right, because any right whatever has inherent in it the concept of freedom, i.e. the highest category of mind, in contrast with which any other thing is without substance. Yet at the same time collision involves another moment, namely the fact that it is restrictive, and so if two rights collide one is subordinated to the other. It is only the right of the world-mind which is absolute without qualification.

31. The method whereby, in philosophic science, the concept develops itself out of itself is expounded in logic and is here likewise presupposed.[3] Its development is a purely immanent progress, the engendering of its determinations. Its advance is not effected by the assertion that various things exist and then by the application of the universal to extraneous material of that sort culled from elsewhere.

The concept's moving principle, which alike engenders and dissolves the particularizations of the universal, I call "dialectic," though I do not mean that dialectic which takes an object, proposition, &c., given to feeling or, in general, to immediate consciousness, and explains it away, confuses it, pursues it this way and that, and has as its sole task the deduction of the contrary of that with which it starts —a negative type of dialectic commonly appearing even in Plato. Dialectic of this kind may regard as its final result either the contrary of the idea with which it begins, or, if it is as incisive as the scepticism of the ancients, the contradictory of this idea, or again, it may be feeble enough to be content with an "approximation" to the truth, a modern half-measure.[4] The loftier dialectic of the concept consists not simply in producing the determination as a contrary and a restriction, but in producing and seizing upon the positive content and outcome of the determination, because it is this which makes it solely a development and an immanent progress. Moreover, this dialectic is not an activity of subjective thinking applied to some matter externally, but is rather the matter's very soul putting forth its branches and fruit organically. This development of the Idea is the proper activity of its rationality, and thinking, as something subjective, merely looks on at it without for its part adding to it any ingredient of its own. To consider a thing rationally means not to

---

[1] Cf. Rousseau, *The Social Contract,* i. 6.—ED.
[2] Paragraphs 133 ff.—ED.

[3] See Paragraph 2.—ED.
[4] Plato—it is usually the second half of the *Parmenides* which Hegel has in mind.—ED.

bring reason to bear on the object from the outside and so to tamper with it, but to find that the object is rational on its own account; here it is mind in its freedom, the culmination of self-conscious reason, which gives itself actuality and engenders itself as an existing world. The sole task of philosophic science is to bring into consciousness this proper work of the reason of the thing itself.

32. The determinations of the concept in the course of its development are from one point of view themselves concepts, but from another they take the form of existents, since the concept is in essence Idea. The series of concepts which this development yields is therefore at the same time a series of shapes of experience, and philosophic science must treat them accordingly.

In a more speculative sense, a concept's determinacy and its mode of existence are one and the same thing. But it is to be noticed that the moments, whose result is a further determined form of the concept, precede it in the philosophical development of the Idea as determinations of the concept, but they do not go in advance of it in the temporal development as shapes of experience. Thus, for instance, the Idea determined as the family, presupposes the determinations of the concept from which the family will later on in this work be shown to result. But the explicit existence of these inner presuppositions as shapes of experience also, e.g. as the right of property, contract, morality, and so forth, is the other aspect of the development, and it is only in a higher and more complete civilization that the development has gone so far as to endow its moments with this appropriately shaped existence. [A.]

Division of the Subject

33. In correspondence with the stages in the development of the Idea of the absolutely free will, the will is

A. immediate; its concept therefore is abstract, namely personality, and its embodiment is an immediate external thing—the sphere of *Abstract* or *Formal Right;*

B. reflected from its external embodiment into itself—it is then characterized as subjective individuality in opposition to the universal. The universal here is characterized as something inward, the good, and also as something outward, a world presented to the will; both these sides of the Idea are here mediated only by each other. This is the Idea in its division or in its existence as particular; and here we have the right of the subjective will in relation to the right of the world and the right of the Idea, though only the

Idea implicit—the sphere of *Morality;*

C. the unity and truth of both these abstract moments—the Idea of the good not only apprehended in thought but so realized both in the will reflected into itself and in the external world that freedom exists as substance, as actuality and necessity, no less than as subjective will; this is the Idea in its absolutely universal existence—*Ethical Life.*

But on the same principle the ethical substance is

(*a*) natural mind, the *Family;*

(*b*) in its division and appearance, *Civil Society;*

(*c*) the *State* as freedom, freedom universal and objective even in the free self-subsistence of the particular will. This actual and organic mind(a) of a single nation (β) reveals and actualizes itself through the inter-relation of the particular national minds until (γ) in the process of world-history it reveals and actualizes itself as the universal world-mind whose right is supreme.

The fact that when a thing or a content is posited first of all in accordance with its concept or as it is implicitly, it then has the form of immediacy or pure being, is the doctrine of speculative logic, here presupposed; the concept which confronts itself in the form of the concept is a different thing and no longer something immediate.

The principle which determines the division of the subject is likewise here presupposed. The division may also be looked upon as a predeclaration in historical form of the parts of the book, since the various stages must engender themselves out of the subject-matter itself as moments in the development of the Idea. A philosophical division is far from being an external one, i.e. it is not an external classification of a given material in accordance with one or more borrowed bases of division, but, on the contrary, is the immanent self-differentiation of the concept.

"Morality" and "ethical life," [1] which perhaps usually pass current as synonyms, are taken here in essentially different senses. Yet even commonplace thinking seems to be distinguishing them; Kant generally prefers to use the word "morality" and, since the principles of action in his philosophy are always limited to this conception, they make the standpoint of ethical life completely impossible, in fact they explicitly nullify and spurn it. But even if "moral" and "ethical" meant the same thing by derivation, that would in no way hinder them, once they had become different words, from being used for different conceptions. [A.]

[1] See Paragraph 141.—ED.

FIRST PART

ABSTRACT RIGHT

34. The absolutely free will, at the stage when its concept is abstract, has the determinate character of immediacy. Accordingly this stage is its negative actuality, and actuality contrasted with the real world, only an abstractly self-related actuality—the inherently single will of a subject. Pursuant to the moment of the particularity of the will, it has in addition a content consisting of determinate aims and, as exclusive individuality, it has this content at the same time as an external world directly confronting it.[1] [A.]

35. The universality of this consciously free will is abstract universality, the self-conscious but otherwise contentless and simple relation of itself to itself in its individuality, and from this point of view the subject is a person. Personality implies that as *this* person: (i) I am completely determined on every side (in my inner caprice, impulse, and desire, as well as by immediate external facts) and so finite, yet (ii) none the less I am simply and solely self-relation, and therefore in finitude I know myself as something infinite, universal, and free.

Personality begins not with the subject's mere general consciousness of himself as an ego concretely determined in some way or other, but rather with his consciousness of himself as a completely abstract ego in which every concrete restriction and value is negated and without validity. In personality, therefore, knowledge is knowledge of oneself as an object, but an object raised by thinking to the level of simple infinity and so an object purely self-identical. Individuals and nations have no personality until they have achieved this pure thought and knowledge of themselves. Mind fully explicit differs from the phenomenal mind in this, that at the same level at which the latter is only self-consciousness—a consciousness of self but only one pursuant to the natural will and its still external oppositions [2]—the former has itself, as the abstract and free ego, for its object and aim, and so is personality. [A.]

36. (1) Personality essentially involves the ca-

pacity for rights and constitutes the concept and the basis (itself abstract) of the system of abstract and therefore formal right. Hence the imperative of right is: "Be a person and respect others as persons."

37. (2) The particularity of the will is a moment in the consciousness of the will as a whole (see Paragraph 34), but it is not yet contained in abstract personality as such. Therefore, it is present at this point, but as still sundered from personality, from the character of freedom, present as desire, need, impulse, casual whim, and so forth. In formal right, therefore, there is no question of particular interests, of my advantage or my welfare, any more than there is of the particular motive behind my volition, of insight and intention.[3] [A.]

38. In relation to action in the concrete and to moral and ethical ties, abstract right is, in contrast with the further content which these involve, only a possibility, and to have a right is therefore to have only a permission or a warrant. The unconditional commands of abstract right are restricted, once again because of its abstractness, to the negative: "Do not infringe personality and what personality entails." The result is that there are only prohibitions in the sphere of right, and the positive form of any command in this sphere is based in the last resort, if we examine its ultimate content, on prohibition.

39. (3) As *immediate* individuality, a person in making decisions is related to a world of nature directly confronting him, and thus the personality of the will stands over against this world as something subjective. For personality, however, as inherently infinite and universal, the restriction of being only subjective is a contradiction and a nullity. Personality is that which struggles to lift itself above this restriction and to give itself reality, or in other words to claim that external world as its own.

40. Right is in the first place the immediate

[1] See Paragraph 5.—Ed.
[2] See *Phenomenology* (Bamberg and Würzburg, 1807), pp. 101 ff. [Eng. tr. pp. 218 ff.], and *Enc.* [1st edn.], § 344 [3rd edn. § 424].
[3] See Paragraphs 119 ff. and Paragraph 132.—Ed.

embodiment which freedom gives itself in an immediate way, i.e. (*a*) possession, which is *property*-ownership. Freedom is here the freedom of the abstract will in general or, *eo ipso*, the freedom of a single person related only to himself. (*b*) A person by distinguishing himself from himself relates himself to another person,[1] and it is only as owners that these two persons really exist for each other. Their implicit identity is realized through the transference of property from one to the other in conformity with a common will and without detriment to the rights of either. This is *contract*. (*c*) The will which is differentiated not in the sense of (*b*) as being contrasted with another person, but in the sense of (*a*) as related to itself, is as a particular will at variance with and opposed to itself as an absolute will. This opposition is wrongdoing and *crime*.

The classification of the system of rights into *jus ad personam* and *jus ad rem* on the one hand, and *jus ad actiones* on the other, like the many other similar classifications, has as its primary aim the imposition of an external order on the mass of unorganized material confronting the classifier. The striking thing about this classification is the confusion in it due to the disorderly intermixture of rights which presuppose substantial ties, e.g. those of family and political life, and rights which only concern abstract personality as such. This confusion is exemplified in the classification of rights (adopted by Kant and since favoured by others) into *jus reale, jus personale,* and *jus realiter personale.*

To develop the perversity and lack of speculative thought in the classification of rights into *jus ad personam* and *jus ad rem*, which lies at the root of Roman law (*jus ad actiones* concerns the administration of justice and is of a different order altogether), would take us too far afield. Here this much at least is clear: it is personality alone which can confer a right to things and therefore *jus ad personam* in its essence is *jus ad rem, rem* being taken here in its general sense as anything external to my freedom, including even my body and my life. In this sense, *jus ad rem* is the right of personality as such. But from the point of view of what is called *jus ad personam* in Roman law, a man is reckoned a person only when he is treated as possessing a certain status.[2] Hence in Roman law, even personality itself is only a certain standing or status contrasted with slavery. The so-called Roman law of "personal" rights, then, is concerned with family relationships, though it excludes the right over slaves (and "slaves" almost includes children too)as well as the status (called *capitis diminutio*) of having lost one's rights.[3] (In Kant, by the way, family relationships are the *jura realiter personalia.*) The Roman *jus ad personam* is therefore not the right of the person as person but at most the right of a person in his particular capacity. (Later on in this book,[4] it will be shown that the substantial basis of family relationships is rather the sacrifice of personality.) Now it must be obvious that it is perverse to treat the right of a specific person in his particular capacity before the universal right of personality as such.

Kant's *jura personalia* are the rights issuing from a contract whereby I undertake to give something or to perform something—the *jus ad rem* conferred by an *obligatio* in Roman law. To be sure, it is only a person who is required to execute the covenants of a contract, just as it is also only a person who acquires the right to their execution. But a right of this sort cannot for this reason be called a "personal" right; rights of whatever sort belong to a person alone. Objectively considered, a right arising from a contract is never a right over a person, but only a right over something external to a person or something which he can alienate, always a right over a thing.

Sub-section I

PROPERTY

41. A person must translate his freedom into an external sphere in order to exist as Idea. Personality is the first, still wholly abstract, determination of the absolute and infinite will, and therefore this sphere distinct from the person, the sphere capable of embodying his freedom, is likewise determined as what is immediately different and separable from him. [A.]

42. What is immediately different from free mind is that which, both for mind and in itself, is the external pure and simple, a thing, something not free, not personal, without rights.

"Thing," like "the objective," has two opposed meanings. If we say "that's the thing" or "the thing is what matters, not the person," "thing" means what is substantive. On the other hand, when "thing" is contrasted with "person" as such, not with the particular subject, it means the opposite of what is substantive, i.e. that whose determinate character lies in its pure externality. From the point of view of free mind, which must, of course, be distinguished from mere consciousness, the external is external absolutely, and it is for this reason that the determinate character assigned to nature by the concept is inherent externality. [A.]

43. As the concept in its *immediacy,* and so as in essence a unit, a person has a *natural* existence partly within himself and partly of such a kind that he is related to it as to an external world.—It is only these things in their immediacy as things, not what they are capable of be-

---

[1] See Paragraphs 323 and 331.—ED.
[2] J. G. Heineccius: *Elementa juris civilis* [Bonn, 1763], § lxxv.
[3] See Remarks to Paragraphs 175, 180.—ED.
[4] Paragraphs 163, 167-8.—ED.

coming through the mediation of the will, i.e. things with determinate characteristics, which are in question here where the topic under discussion is personality, itself at this point still in its most elementary immediacy.

Mental aptitudes, erudition, artistic skill, even things ecclesiastical (like sermons, masses, prayers, consecration of votive objects), inventions, and so forth, become subjects of a contract, brought on to a parity, through being bought and sold, with things recognized as things. It may be asked whether the artist, scholar, &c., is from the legal point of view in possession of his art, erudition, ability to preach a sermon, sing a mass, &c., that is, whether such attainments are "things." We may hesitate to call such abilities, attainments, aptitudes, &c., "things," for while possession of these may be the subject of business dealings and contracts, as if they were things, there is also something inward and mental about it, and for this reason the Understanding may be in perplexity about how to describe such possession in legal terms, because its field of vision is as limited to the dilemma that this is "either a thing or not a thing" as to the dilemma "either finite or infinite." Attainments, erudition, talents, and so forth, are, of course, owned by free mind and are something internal and not external to it, but even so, by expressing them it may embody them in something external and alienate them (see below),[1] and in this way they are put into the category of "things." Therefore they are not immediate at the start but only acquire this character through the mediation of mind which reduces its inner possessions to immediacy and externality.

It was an unjustifiable and unethical proviso of Roman law that children were from their father's point of view "things." Hence he was legally the owner of his children, although, of course, he still also stood to them in the ethical relation of love (though this relation must have been much weakened by the injustice of his legal position). Here, then, the two qualities "being a thing" and "not being a thing" were united, though quite wrongly.

In the sphere of abstract right, we are concerned only with the person as person, and therefore with the particular (which is indispensable if the person's freedom is to have scope and reality) only in so far as it is something separable from the person and immediately different from him, no matter whether this separability constitutes the essential nature of the particular, or whether the particular receives it only through the mediation of the subjective will. Hence in this sphere we are concerned with mental aptitudes, erudition, &c., only in so far as they are possessions in a legal sense; we have not to treat here the possession of our body and mind which we can achieve through education, study, habit, &c., and which exists as an *inward* property of mind. But it is not until we come to deal with alienation [2] that we

need begin to speak of the *transition* of such mental property into the external world where it falls under the category of property in the legal sense.

44. A person has as his substantive end the right of putting his will into any and every thing and thereby making it his, because it has no such end in itself and derives its destiny and soul from his will. This is the absolute right of appropriation which man has over all "things."

The so-called "philosophy" which attributes reality in the sense of self-subsistence and genuine independent self-enclosed existence to unmediated single things, to the non-personal, is directly contradicted by the free will's attitude to these things. The same is true of the other philosophy which assures us that mind cannot apprehend the truth or know the nature of the thing-in-itself. While so-called "external" things have a show of self-subsistence for consciousness, intuition, and representative thinking, the free will idealizes that type of actuality and so is its truth. [A.]

45. To have power over a thing *ab extra* constitutes possession. The particular aspect of the matter, the fact that I make something my own as a result of my natural need, impulse, and caprice, is the particular interest satisfied by possession. But I as free will am an object to myself in what I possess and thereby also for the first time am an actual will, and this is the aspect which constitutes the category of *property*, the true and right factor in possession.

If emphasis is placed on my needs, then the possession of property appears as a means to their satisfaction, but the true position is that, from the standpoint of freedom, property is the first embodiment of freedom and so is in itself a substantive end.

46. Since my will, as the will of a person, and so as a single will, becomes objective to me in property, property acquires the character of private property; and common property of such a nature that it may be owned by separate persons acquires the character of an inherently dissoluble partnership in which the retention of my share is explicitly a matter of my arbitrary preference.

The nature of the elements makes it impossible for the use of them to become so particularized as to be the private possession of anyone.

In the Roman agrarian laws there was a clash between public and private ownership of land. The latter is the more rational and therefore had to be given preference even at the expense of other rights.

One factor in family testamentary trusts contravenes the right of personality and so the right of private property. But the specific characteristics pertaining to private property may have to be subordinated to a higher sphere of right (e.g. to a society or the state),

[1] Paragraphs 65 ff.—ED.
[2] Paragraphs 65 ff.—ED.

as happens, for instance, when private property is put into the hands of a so-called "artificial" person and into mortmain. Still, such exceptions to private property cannot be grounded in chance, in private caprice, or private advantage, but only in the rational organism of the state.

The general principle that underlies Plato's ideal state violates the right of personality by forbidding the holding of private property.[1] The idea of a pious or friendly and even a compulsory brotherhood of men holding their goods in common and rejecting the principle of private property may readily present itself to the disposition which mistakes the true nature of the freedom of mind and right and fails to apprehend it in its determinate moments. As for the moral or religious view behind this idea, when Epicurus's friends proposed to form such an association holding goods in common, he forbade them, precisely on the ground that their proposal betrayed distrust and that those who distrusted each other were not friends.[2] [A.]

47. As a person, I am myself an *immediate* individual; if we give further precision to this expression, it means in the first instance that I am alive in this bodily organism which is my external existence, universal in content and undivided, the real pre-condition of every further determined mode of existence. But, all the same, as person, I possess my life and my body, like other things, only in so far as my will is in them.

The fact that, considered as existing not as the concept explicit but only as the concept in its immediacy, I am alive and have a bodily organism, depends on the concept of life and on the concept of mind as soul—on moments which are taken over here from the Philosophy of Nature [3] and from Anthropology.[4]

I possess the members of my body, my life, only so long as I will to possess them. An animal cannot maim or destroy itself, but a man can. [A.]

48. In so far as the body is an immediate existent, it is not in conformity with mind. If it is to be the willing organ and soul-endowed instrument of mind, it must first be taken into possession by mind (see Paragraph 57). But from the point of view of others, I am in essence a free entity in my body while my possession of it is still immediate.

It is only because I am alive as a free entity in my body that this living existent ought not to be misused by being made a beast of burden. While I am alive, my soul (the concept and, to use a higher term, the free entity) and my body are not separated; my body is the embodiment of my freedom and it is with my body that I feel. It is therefore only abstract sophistical reasoning which can so distinguish body and soul as to hold that the "thing-in-itself," the soul, is not touched or attacked if the body is maltreated and the existent embodiment of personality is subjected to the power of another. I can withdraw into myself out of my bodily existence and make my body something external to myself; particular feelings I can regard as something outside me and in chains I can still be free. But this is *my* will; so far as *others* are concerned, I am in my body. To be free from the point of view of others is identical with being free in my determinate existence.[5] If another does violence to my body, he does violence to me.

If my body is touched or suffers violence, then, because I feel, I am touched myself actually, here and now. This creates the distinction between personal injury and damage to my external property, for in such property my will is not actually present in this direct fashion.

49. In relation to external things, the rational aspect is that I possess property, but the particular aspect comprises subjective aims, needs, arbitrariness, abilities, external circumstances, and so forth (see Paragraph 45). On these mere possession as such depends, but this particular aspect has in this sphere of abstract personality not yet been established as identical with freedom. What and how much I possess, therefore, is a matter of indifference so far as rights are concerned.

If at this stage we may speak of more persons than one, although no such distinction has yet been made, then we may say that in respect of their personality persons are equal. But this is an empty tautology, for the person, as something abstract, has not yet been particularized or established as distinct in some specific way.

"Equality" is the abstract identity of the Understanding; reflective thought and all kinds of intellectual mediocrity stumble on it at once when they are confronted by the relation of unity to a difference. At this point, equality could only be the equality of abstract persons as such, and therefore the whole field of possession, this terrain of inequality, falls outside it.

The demand sometimes made for an equal division of land, and other available resources too, is an intellectualism all the more empty and superficial in that at the heart of particular differences there lies not only the external contingency of nature but also the whole compass of mind, endlessly particularized and differentiated, and the rationality of mind developed into an organism.

We may not speak of the injustice of nature in the unequal distribution of possessions and resources, since nature is not free and therefore is neither just

---

[1] Cf. Plato, *Laws*, v. 739.—Ed.
[2] Diogenes Laertius, x. 6.
[3] *Enc.* [1st edn.], §§ 259 ff. Cf. §§ 161, 164, 298. [3rd edn. §§ 336 ff. Cf. §§ 213, 216, 376].
[4] *Enc.* [1st edn.], § 318 [3rd edn. §§ 388 ff.].

[5] See my *Science of Logic* [1st edn.], vol. i, pp. 49 ff. [Eng. tr. vol. i, pp. 127-35, but this is a translation of the second edition, in which the passage in question was much altered, as Lasson points out].

nor unjust. That everyone ought to have subsistence enough for his needs is a moral wish and thus vaguely expressed is well enough meant, but like anything that is only well meant it lacks objectivity. On the other hand, subsistence is not the same as possession and belongs to another sphere, i.e. to civil society.[1] [A.]

50. The principle that a thing belongs to the person who happens to be the first in time to take it into his possession is immediately self-explanatory and superfluous, because a second person cannot take into his possession what is already the property of another. [A.]

51. Since property is the *embodiment* of personality, my inward idea and will that something is to be mine is not enough to make it my property; to secure this end occupancy is requisite. The embodiment which my willing thereby attains involves its recognizability by others.— The fact that a thing of which I can take possession is a *res nullius* is (see Paragraph 50) a self-explanatory negative condition of occupancy, or rather it has a bearing on the anticipated relation to others. [A.]

52. Occupancy makes the matter of the thing my property, since matter in itself does not belong to itself.

Matter offers resistance to me—and matter is nothing except the resistance it offers to me—that is, it presents itself to my mind as something abstractly independent only when my mind is taken abstractly as sensation. (Sense-perception perversely takes mind as sensation for the concrete and mind as reason for the abstract.) In relation to the will and property, however, this independence of matter has no truth. Occupancy, as an external activity whereby we actualize our universal right of appropriating natural objects, comes to be conditioned by physical strength, cunning, dexterity, the means of one kind or another whereby we take physical possession of things. Owing to the qualitative differences between natural objects, mastery and occupancy of these has an infinite variety of meanings and involves a restriction and contingency that is just as infinite. Apart from that, a "kind" of thing, or an element as such, is not the correlative object of an individual person. Before it can become such and be appropriated, it must first be individualized into single parts, into a breath of air or a drink of water. In the fact that it is impossible to take possession of an external "kind" of thing as such, or of an element, it is not the external physical impossibility which must be looked on as ultimate, but the fact that a person, as will, is characterized as individual, while as person he is at the same time *immediate* individuality; hence as person he is related to the external world

as to single things (see Remark to Paragraph 13 and Paragraph 43).

Thus the mastery and external possession of things becomes, in ways that again are infinite, more or less indeterminate and incomplete. Yet matter is never without an essential form of its own and only because it has one is it anything. The more I appropriate this form, the more do I enter into actual possession of the thing. The consumption of food is an out and out alteration of its qualitative character, the character on the strength of which it was what it was before it was eaten. The training of my body in dexterity, like the training of my mind, is likewise a more or less complete occupancy and penetration of it. It is my mind which of all things I can make most completely my own. Yet this actual occupancy is different from property as such because property is complete as the work of the free will alone.[2] In face of the free will, the thing retains no property in itself even though there still remains in possession, as an external relation to an object, something external. The empty abstraction of a matter without properties which, when a thing is my property, is supposed to remain outside me and the property of the thing, is one which thought must master. [A.]

53. Property has its modifications determined in the course of the will's relation to the thing. This relation is
(A) *taking possession* of the thing directly (here it is in the thing *qua* something positive that the will has its embodiment);
(B) *use* (the thing is negative in contrast with the will and so it is in the thing as something to be negated that the will has its embodiment);
(C) *alienation*, the reflection of the will back from the thing into itself.
These three are respectively the positive, negative, and infinite judgements of the will on the thing.

A. *Taking Possession*

54. We take possession of a thing (α) by directly grasping it physically, (β) by forming it, and (γ) by merely marking it as ours. [A.]

55. (α) From the point of view of sensation, to grasp a thing physically is the most complete of these modes, because then I am directly present in this possession, and therefore my will is recognizable in it. But at bottom this mode is only subjective, temporary, and seriously restricted in scope, as well as by the qualitative nature of the things grasped.—As a result of the connexion which I may effect between something and things which have already become my property in other ways, or into which something may otherwise be accidentally brought, the scope of this method

---

[1] See Paragraphs 199 ff., 230, 237 ff.—Ed.

[2] Cf. end of the Remark to Paragraph 43.—Ed.

is somewhat enlarged, and the same result is produced by other means also.

Mechanical forces, weapons, tools, extend the range of my power. Connexions between my property and something else may be regarded as making it more easily possible for me than for another owner, or sometimes possible for me alone, to take possession of something or to make use of it. Instances of such connexions are that my land may be on the seashore, or on a river bank; or my estate may march with hunting country or pasture or land useful for some other purpose; stone or other mineral deposits may be under my fields; there may be treasure in or under my ground, and so on. The same is true of connexions made by chance and subsequent to possession, like some of what are called "natural accessions," such as alluvial deposits, &c., and jetsam. (*Fetura* is an accession to my wealth too, but the connexion here is an organic one, it is not a case of a thing being added *ab extra* to another thing already in my possession; and therefore *fetura* is of a type quite different from the other accessions.) Alternatively, the addition to my property may be looked upon as a non-self-subsistent accident of the thing to which it has been added. In every case, however, these are *external* conjunctions whose bond of connexion is neither life nor the concept. It devolves, therefore, on the Understanding to adduce and weigh their pros and cons, and on positive legislation to make decisions about them in accordance with the extent to which the relation between the things conjoined has or has not any essentiality. [A.]

56. (β) When I impose a form on something, the thing's determinate character as mine acquires an independent externality and ceases to be restricted to my presence here and now and to the direct presence of my awareness and will.

To impose a form on a thing is the mode of taking possession most in conformity with the Idea to this extent, that it implies a union of subject and object, although it varies endlessly with the qualitative character of the objects and the variety of subjective aims.

Under this head there also falls the formation of the organic. What I do to the organic does not remain external to it but is assimilated by it. Examples are the tilling of the soil, the cultivation of plants, the taming and feeding of animals, the preservation of game, as well as contrivances for utilizing raw materials or the forces of nature and processes for making one material produce effects on another, and so forth. [A.]

57. Man, pursuant to his *immediate* existence within himself, is something natural, external to his concept. It is only through the development of his own body and mind, essentially through his self-consciousness's apprehension of itself as free, that he takes possession of himself and becomes his own property and no one else's. This taking possession of oneself, looked at from the opposite point of view, is the translation into actuality of what one is according to one's concept, i.e. a potentiality, capacity, potency. In that translation one's self-consciousness for the first time becomes established as one's own, as one's object also and distinct from self-consciousness pure and simple, and thereby capable of taking the form of a "thing" (compare Remark to Paragraph 43).

The alleged justification of slavery (by reference to all its proximate beginnings through physical force, capture in war, saving and preservation of life, upkeep, education, philanthropy, the slave's own acquiescence, and so forth), as well as the justification of a slave-ownership as simple lordship in general, and all historical views of the justice of slavery and lordship, depend on regarding man as a natural entity pure and simple, as an existent not in conformity with its concept (an existent also to which arbitrariness is appropriate). The argument for the absolute injustice of slavery, on the other hand, adheres to the concept of man as mind, as something inherently free. This view is one-sided in regarding man as free by nature, or in other words it takes the concept as such in its immediacy, not the Idea, as the truth. This antinomy rests, like all others, on the abstract thinking which asserts both the moments of an Idea in separation from one another and clings to each of them in its independence and so in its inadequacy to the Idea and in its falsity. Free mind consists precisely (see Paragraph 21) in its being no longer implicit or as concept alone, but in its transcending this formal stage of its being, and *eo ipso* its immediate natural existence, until the existence which it gives to itself is one which is solely its own and free. The side of the antinomy which asserts the concept of freedom therefore has the merit of implying the absolute starting-point, though only the starting-point, for the discovery of truth, while the other side goes no further than existence without the concept and therefore excludes the outlook of rationality and right altogether. The position of the free will, with which right and the science of right begin, is already in advance of the false position at which man, as a natural entity and only the concept implicit, is for that reason capable of being enslaved. This false, comparatively primitive, phenomenon of slavery is one which befalls mind when mind is only at the level of consciousness. The dialectic of the concept and of the purely immediate consciousness of freedom brings about at that point the fight for recognition and the relationship of master and slave.[1] But that objective mind, the content of the right, should no longer be apprehended in its subjective concept alone, and consequently that man's absolute unfitness for slavery should no long-

---

[1] See *Phenomenology* [1st edn.], pp. 115 ff. [Eng. tr. pp. 229 ff.], and *Enc.* [1st edn.], §§ 352 ff. [3rd edn. §§ 430 ff.].

er be apprehended as a mere "ought to be," is something which does not come home to our minds until we recognize that the Idea of freedom is genuinely actual only as the state. [A.]

58. (γ) The mode of taking possession which in itself is not actual but is only *representative* of my will is to mark the thing, and the meaning of the mark is supposed to be that I have put my will into the thing. In its objective scope and its meaning, this mode of taking possession is very indeterminate. [A.]

B. *Use of the Thing*

59. By being taken into possession, the thing acquires the predicate "mine" and my will is related to it positively. Within this identity, the thing is equally established as something negative, and my will in this situation is a particular will, i.e. need, inclination, and so forth. Yet my need, as the particular aspect of a single will, is the positive element which finds satisfaction, and the thing, as something negative in itself, exists only for my need and is at its service.— The use of the thing is my need being externally realized through the change, destruction, and consumption of the thing. The thing thereby stands revealed as naturally self-less and so fulfils its destiny.[1]

The fact that property is realized and actualized only in use floats before the minds of those who look upon property as derelict and a *res nullius* if it is not being put to any use, and who excuse its unlawful occupancy on the ground that it has not been used by its owner. But the owner's will, in accordance with which a thing is his, is the primary substantive basis of property; use is a further modification of property, secondary to that universal basis, and is only its manifestation and particular mode. [A.]

60. To use a thing by grasping it directly is in itself to take possession of a *single* thing here and now. But if my use of it is grounded on a persistent need, and if I make repeated use of a product which continually renews itself, restricting my use if necessary to safeguard that renewal, then these and other circumstances transform the direct single grasp of the thing into a mark, intended to signify that I am taking it into my possession in a universal way, and thereby taking possession of the elemental or organic basis of such products, or of anything else that conditions them.

61. Since the substance of the thing which is my property is, if we take the thing by itself,

its externality, i.e. its non-substantiality [2]—in contrast with me it is not an end in itself (see Paragraph 42)—and since in my use or employment of it this externality is realized, it follows that my full use or employment of a thing is the thing in its entirety, so that if I have the full use of the thing I am its owner. Over and above the entirety of its use, there is nothing left of the thing which could be the property of another. [A.]

62. My merely partial or temporary use of a thing, like my partial or temporary possession of it (a possession which itself is simply the partial or temporary possibility of using it) is therefore to be distinguished from ownership of the thing itself. If the whole and entire use of a thing were mine, while the abstract ownership was supposed to be someone else's, then the thing as mine would be penetrated through and through by my will (see Paragraphs 52 and 61), and at the same time there would remain in the thing something impenetrable by me, namely the will, the empty will, of another. As a positive will, I would be at one and the same time objective and not objective to myself in the thing —an absolute contradiction. Ownership therefore is in essence free and complete.

To distinguish between the right to the whole and entire use of a thing and ownership in the abstract is the work of the empty Understanding for which the Idea—i.e. in this instance the unity of (*a*) ownership (or even the person's will as such) and (*b*) its realization—is not the truth, but for which these two moments in their separation from one another pass as something which is true. This distinction, then, as a relation in the world of fact, is that of an overlord to nothing, and this might be called an "insanity of personality" (if we may mean by "insanity" not merely the presence of a direct contradiction between a man's purely subjective ideas and the actual facts of his life), because "mine" as applied to a single object would have to mean the direct presence in it of both my single exclusive will and also the single exclusive will of someone else. In the *Institutes* [3] we read: "*ususfructus est jus alienis rebus utendifruendi salva rerum substantia. . . . Ne tamen in universum inutiles essent proprietates, semper abscedente usufructu, placuit certis modis extingui usumfructum et ad proprietatem reverti.*" [4] *Placuit!* As if it were in the first instance a whim

---

[1] See Paragraph 42.—Ed.

[2] See Paragraph 44.—Ed.
[3] [Of Justinian] ii. 4.
[4] "Usufruct is the right of using another's property, of enjoying its fruits short of waste of its substance. . . . Nevertheless, in order that properties should not remain wholly unused through the entire cessation of usufruct, the law has been pleased to ordain that in certain circumstances the right of usufruct shall be annulled and that the owner proper shall resume the land."—Ed.

or a fiat to make this proviso and thereby give some sense to that empty distinction! A *proprietas* SEM-PER *abscedente usufructu* would not merely be *inutilis,* it would be no *proprietas* at all.

To examine other distinctions in property itself, e.g. between *res mancipi* and *nec mancipi, dominium quiritarium* and *bonitarium,* &c., is inappropriate here since they have no bearing on any of the modifications of property determined by the concept and are merely tit-bits culled from the history of the right of property. The empty distinction discussed above, however, is in a way contained in the relations of *dominium directum* and *dominium utile,* in the *contractus emphyteuticus,* in the further relations involved in estates in fee with the ground rents and other rents, dues, villeinage, &c., entailed in their sundry modifications, in cases where such burdens are irredeemable. But from another point of view, these relations preclude that distinction. They preclude it in so far as burdens are entailed in *dominium utile,* with the result that *dominium directum* becomes at the same time a *dominium utile.* Were there nothing in these two relationships except that distinction in its rigid abstraction, then in them we would not have two overlords (*domini*) in the strict sense, but an owner on the one hand and an overlord who was the overlord of nothing on the other. But on the score of the burdens imposed there are two owners standing in relation to each other. Although their relation is not that of being common owners of a property, still the transition from it to common ownership is very easy—a transition which has already begun in *dominium directum* when the yield of the property is calculated and looked upon as the essential thing, while that incalculable factor in the overlordship of a property, the factor which has perhaps been regarded as the honourable thing about property, is subordinated to the *utile* which here is the rational factor.

It is about a millennium and a half since the freedom of personality began through the spread of Christianity to blossom and gain recognition as a universal principle from a part, though still a small part, of the human race. But it was only yesterday, we might say, that the principle of the freedom of property became recognized in some places. This example from history may serve to rebuke the impatience of opinion and to show the length of time that mind requires for progress in its self-consciousness.

63. A thing in use is a single thing determined quantitatively and qualitatively and related to a specific need. But its specific utility, being quantitatively determinate, is at the same time comparable with [the specific utility of] other things of like utility. Similarly, the specific need which it satisfies is at the same time need in general and thus is comparable on its particular side with other needs, while the thing in virtue of the same considerations is comparable with things

meeting other needs. This, the thing's universality, whose simple determinate character arises from the particularity of the thing, so that it is *eo ipso* abstracted from the thing's specific quality, is the thing's *value,* wherein its genuine substantiality becomes determinate and an object of consciousness.[1] As full owner of the thing, I am *eo ipso* owner of its value as well as of its use.

The distinctive character of the property of a feudal tenant is that he is supposed to be the owner of the use only, not of the value of the thing. [A.]

64. The form given to a possession and its mark are themselves externalities but for the subjective presence of the will which alone constitutes the meaning and value of externalities. This presence, however, which is use, employment, or some other mode in which the will expresses itself, is an event in time, and what is objective in time is the continuance of this expression of the will. Without this the thing becomes a *res nullius,* because it has been deprived of the actuality of the will and possession. Therefore I gain or lose possession of property through prescription.

Prescription, therefore, has not been introduced into law solely from an external consideration running counter to right in the strict sense, i.e. with a view to truncating the disputes and confusions which old claims would introduce into the security of property. On the contrary, prescription rests at bottom on the specific character of property as "real," on the fact that the will to possess something must express itself.

Public memorials are national property, or, more precisely, like works of art in general so far as their enjoyment is concerned, they have life and count as ends in themselves so long as they enshrine the spirit of remembrance and honour. If they lose this spirit, they become in this respect *res nullius* in the eyes of a nation and the private possession of the first comer, like e.g. the Greek and Egyptian works of art in Turkey.

The right of private property which the family of an author has in his publications dies out for a similar reason; such publications become *res nullius* in the sense that like public memorials, though in an opposite way, they become public property, and, by having their special handling of their topic copied, the private property of anyone.

Vacant land consecrated for a burial ground, or even to lie unused in perpetuity, embodies an empty absent arbitrary will. If such a will is infringed, nothing actual is infringed, and hence respect for it cannot be guaranteed. [A.]

C. *Alienation of Property*

65. The reason I can alienate my property is that it is mine only in so far as I put my will into

---

[1] See Paragraph 44.—ED.

it. Hence I may abandon (*derelinquere*) as a *res nullius* anything that I have or yield it to the will of another and so into his possession, provided always that the thing in question is a thing external by nature. [A.]

66. Therefore those goods, or rather substantive characteristics, which constitute my own private personality and the universal essence of my self-consciousness are inalienable and my right to them is imprescriptible. Such characteristics are my personality as such, my universal freedom of will, my ethical life, my religion.

The fact that what mind is in accordance with its concept or implicitly it also should be explicitly and existentially (the fact that thus mind should be a person, be capable of holding property, should have an ethical life, a religion) is the Idea which is itself the concept of mind. As *causa sui,* i.e. as free causality, mind is that *cuius natura non potest concipi nisi existens.*[1]

It is just in this concept of mind as that which is what it is only through its own free causality and through its endless return into itself out of the natural immediacy of its existence, that there lies the possibility of a clash: i.e. what it is potentially it may not be actually (see Paragraph 57), and vice versa what it is actually (e.g. evil, in the case of the will) may be other than what it is potentially. Herein lies the possibility of the alienation of personality and its substantive being, whether this alienation occurs unconsciously or intentionally. Examples of the alienation of personality are slavery, serfdom, disqualification from holding property, encumbrances on property, and so forth. Alienation of intelligence and rationality, of morality, ethical life, and religion, is exemplified in superstition, in ceding to someone else full power and authority to fix and prescribe what actions are to be done (as when an individual binds himself expressly to steal or to murder, &c., or to a course of action that may involve crime), or what duties are binding on one's conscience or what religious truth is, &c.

The right to what is in essence inalienable is imprescriptible, since the act whereby I take possession of my personality, of my substantive essence, and make myself a responsible being, capable of possessing rights and with a moral and religious life, takes away from these characteristics of mine just that externality which alone made them capable of passing into the possession of someone else. When I have thus annulled their externality, I cannot lose them through lapse of time or from any other reason drawn from my prior consent or willingness to alienate them. This return of mine into myself, whereby I make myself existent as Idea, as a person with rights and moral principles, annuls the previous position and the wrong done to my concept and my reason by others and myself when the infinite embodiment of self-consciousness has been treated as

[1] Spinoza: *Ethics,* Part I, Definition i.

something external, and that with my consent. This return into myself makes clear the contradiction in supposing that I have given into another's possession my capacity for rights, my ethical life and religious feeling; for either I have given up what I myself did not possess, or I am giving up what, so soon as I possess it, exists in essence as mine alone and not as something external. [A.]

67. Single products of my particular physical and mental skill and of my power to act I can alienate to someone else and I can give him the use of my abilities for a restricted period, because, on the strength of this restriction, my abilities acquire an external relation to the totality and universality of my being. By alienating the whole of my time, as crystallized in my work, and everything I produced, I would be making into another's property the substance of my being, my universal activity and actuality, my personality.

The relation here between myself and the exercise of my abilities is the same as that between the substance of a thing and its use (see Paragraph 61). It is only when use is restricted that a distinction between use and substance arises. So here, the use of my powers differs from my powers and therefore from myself, only in so far as it is quantitatively restricted. Force is the totality of its manifestations, substance of its accidents, the universal of its particulars. [A.]

68. What is peculiarly mine in a product of my mind may, owing to the method whereby it is expressed, turn at once into something external like a "thing" which *eo ipso* may then be produced by other people. The result is that by taking possession of a thing of this kind, its new owner may make his own the thoughts communicated in it or the mechanical invention which it contains, and it is ability to do this which sometimes (i.e. in the case of books) constitutes the value of these things and the only purpose of possessing them. But besides this, the new owner at the same time comes into possession of the universal methods of so expressing himself and producing numerous other things of the same sort.

In the case of works of art, the form—the portrayal of thought in an external medium—is, regarded as a thing, so peculiarly the property of the individual artist that a copy of a work of art is essentially a product of the copyist's own mental and technical ability. In the case of a literary work, the form in virtue of which it is an external thing is of a mechanical kind, and the same is true of the invention of a machine; for in the first case the thought is presented not *en bloc,* as a statue is, but in a series of separable abstract symbols, while in the second case the thought has a mechanical content throughout. The ways and means of producing things of that mechanical kind as things are commonplace accomplishments.

But between the work of art at one extreme and the mere journeyman production at the other there are transitional stages which to a greater or less degree partake of the character of one or other of the extremes.

69. Since the owner of such a product, in owning a copy of it, is in possession of the entire use and value of that copy *qua* a single thing, he has complete and free ownership of that copy *qua* a *single* thing, even if the author of the book or the inventor of the machine remains the owner of the *universal* ways and means of multiplying such books and machines, &c. *Qua* universal ways and means of expression, he has not necessarily alienated them, but may reserve them to himself as means of expression which belong to him.

The substance of an author's or an inventor's right cannot in the first instance be found in the supposition that when he disposes of a single copy of his work, he arbitrarily makes it a condition that the power to produce facsimiles as things, a power which thereupon passes into another's possession, should not become the property of the other but should remain his own. The first question is whether such a separation between ownership of the thing and the power to produce facsimiles which is given with the thing is compatible with the concept of property, or whether it does not cancel the complete and free ownership (see Paragraph 62) on which there originally depends the option of the original producer of intellectual work to reserve to himself the power to reproduce, or to part with this power as a thing of value, or to attach no value to it at all and surrender it together with the single exemplar of his work. I reply that this power to reproduce has a special character, viz. it is that in virtue of which the thing is not merely a possession but a capital asset (see Paragraphs 170 ff.) ; the fact that it is such an asset depends on the particular external kind of way in which the thing is used, a way distinct and separable from the use to which the thing is directly destined (the asset here is not, as has been said, an *accessio naturalis* like *fetura*). Since then this distinction falls into the sphere of that whose nature entails its divisibility, into the sphere of *external* use, the retention of part of a thing's [external] use and the alienation of another part is not the retention of a proprietorship without *utile*.

The purely negative, though the primary, means of advancing the sciences and arts is to guarantee scientists and artists against theft and to enable them to benefit from the protection of their property, just as it was the primary and most important means of advancing trade and industry to guarantee it against highway robbery.

Moreover, the purpose of a product of mind is that people other than its author should understand it and make it the possession of their ideas, memory, thinking, &c. Their mode of expression, whereby in turn they make what they have *learnt* (for "learning" means more than "learning things by heart," "memorizing them"; the thoughts of others can be apprehended only by thinking, and this re-thinking the thoughts of others is learning too) into a "thing" which they can alienate, very likely has some special form of its own in every case. The result is that they may regard as their own property the capital asset accruing from their learning and may claim for themselves the right to reproduce their learning in books of their own. Those engaged in the propagation of knowledge of all kinds, in particular those whose appointed task is teaching, have as their specific function and duty (above all in the case of the positive sciences, the doctrine of a church, the study of positive law, &c.) the repetition of well-established thoughts, taken up *ab extra* and all of them given expression already. The same is true of writings devised for teaching purposes and the spread and propagation of the sciences. Now to what extent does the new form which turns up when something is expressed again and again transform the available stock of knowledge, and in particular the thoughts of others who still retain *external* property in those intellectual productions of theirs, into a private mental property of the individual reproducer and thereby give him or fail to give him the right to make them his *external* property as well ? To what extent is such repetition of another's material in one's book a plagiarism ? There is no precise principle of determination available to answer these questions, and therefore they cannot be finally settled either in principle or by positive legislation. Hence plagiarism would have to be a matter of honour and be held in check by honour.

Thus copyright legislation attains its end of securing the property rights of author and publisher only to a very restricted extent, though it does attain it within limits. The ease with which we may deliberately change something in the form of what we are expounding or invent a trifling modification in a large body of knowledge or a comprehensive theory which is another's work, and even the impossibility of sticking to the author's words in expounding something we have learnt, all lead of themselves (quite apart from the particular purposes for which such repetitions are required) to an endless multiplicity of alterations which more or less superficially stamp someone else's property as our own. For instance, the hundreds and hundreds of compendia, selections, anthologies, &c., arithmetics, geometries, religious tracts, &c., show how every new idea in a review or annual or encyclopaedia, &c., can be forthwith repeated over and over again under the same or a different title, and yet may be claimed as something peculiarly the writer's own. The result of this may easily be that the profit promised to the author, or the projector of the original undertaking, by his work or his original idea becomes negligible or reduced for both parties or lost to all concerned.

But as for the effectiveness of honour in checking plagiarism, what has happened is that nowadays we scarcely hear the word "plagiarism," nor are scholars accused of stealing each other's results. It may be that honour has been effective in abolishing plagiarism, or perhaps plagiarism has ceased to be dishonourable and feeling against it is a thing of the past; or possibly an ingenious and trivial idea, and a change in external form, is rated so highly as originality and a product of independent thinking that the thought of plagiarism becomes wholly insufferable.

70. The comprehensive sum of external activity, i.e. life, is not external to personality as that which itself is immediate and a *this*. The surrender or the sacrifice of life is not the existence of *this* personality but the very opposite. There is therefore no unqualified right to sacrifice one's life. To such a sacrifice nothing is entitled except an ethical Idea[1] as that in which *this* immediately single personality has vanished and to whose power it is actually subjected. Just as life as such is immediate, so death is its immediate negation and hence must come from without, either by natural causes, or else, in the service of the Idea, by the hand of a foreigner. [A.]

Transition from Property to Contract

71. Existence as determinate being is in essence being for another (see Remark to Paragraph 48). One aspect of property is that it is an existent as an external thing, and in this respect property exists for other external things and is connected with their necessity and contingency. But it is also an existent as an embodiment of the will, and from this point of view the "other" for which it exists can only be the will of another person. This relation of will to will is the true and proper ground in which freedom is existent. —The sphere of contract is made up of this mediation whereby I hold property not merely by means of a thing and my subjective will, but by means of another person's will as well and so hold it in virtue of my participation in a common will.

Reason makes it just as necessary for men to enter into contractual relationships—gift, exchange, trade, &c.—as to possess property (see Remark to Paragraph 45). While all they are conscious of is that they are led to make contracts by need in general, by benevolence, advantage, &c., the fact remains that they are led to do this by reason implicit within them, i.e. by the Idea of the real existence of free personality, "real" here meaning "present in the will alone." [2]

[1] See Paragraphs 257 and 323 ff.—Ed.
[2] Cf. Paragraph 344 and Aristotle, *Ethics*, 1153^{b}25 ff. and *On the Soul*, 415^{a}26 ff.—Ed.

Contract presupposes that the parties entering it recognize each other as persons and property owners. It is a relationship at the level of mind objective, and so contains and presupposes from the start the moment of recognition (compare Remarks to Paragraphs 35 and 57). [A.]

Sub-section II
CONTRACT

72. Contract brings into existence the property whose external side, its side as an existent, is no longer a mere "thing" but contains the moment of a will (and consequently the will of a second person also). Contract is the process in which there is revealed and mediated the contradiction that I am and remain the independent owner of something from which I exclude the will of another only in so far as in identifying my will with the will of another I cease to be an owner.

73. I have power to alienate a property as an external thing (see Paragraph 65); but more than this, the concept compels me to alienate it *qua* property in order that thereby my will may become objective to me as determinately existent. In this situation, however, my will as alienated is at the same time another's will.[3] Consequently this situation wherein this compulsion of the concept is realized is the unity of different wills and so a unity in which both surrender their difference and their own special character. Yet this identity of their wills implies also (at this stage) that each will still is and remains *not* identical with the other but retains from its own point of view a special character of its own.

74. This contractual relationship, therefore, is the means whereby one identical will can persist within the absolute difference between independent property owners. It implies that each, in accordance with the common will of both, ceases to be an owner and yet is and remains one. It is the mediation of the will to give up a property, a single property, and the will to take up another, i.e. another belonging to someone else; and this mediation takes place when the two wills are associated in an identity in the sense that one of them comes to its decision only in the presence of the other.

75. The two contracting parties are related to each other as *immediate* self-subsistent persons. Therefore (*a*) contract arises from the arbitrary

[3] See Paragraph 71 with the Remark and the note thereto.—Ed.

will. (β) The identical will which is brought into existence by the contract is only one *posited* by the parties, and so is only a will shared in common and not an absolutely universal will. (γ) The object about which a contract is made is a single external thing, since it is only things of that kind which the parties' purely arbitrary will has it in its power to alienate (see Paragraphs 65 ff.).

To subsume marriage under the concept of contract is thus quite impossible; this subsumption—though shameful is the only word for it—is propounded in Kant's *Philosophy of Law*.[1] It is equally far from the truth to ground the nature of the state on the contractual relation, whether the state is supposed to be a contract of all with all, or of all with the monarch and the government.

The intrusion of this contractual relation, and relationships concerning private property generally, into the relation between the individual and the state has been productive of the greatest confusion in both constitutional law and public life. Just as at one time[2] political rights and duties were considered and maintained to be an unqualified private property of particular individuals, something contrasted with the right of the monarch and the state, so also in more recent times the rights of the monarch and the state have been regarded as the subjects of a contract and as grounded in contract, as something embodying merely a common will and resulting from the arbitrariness of parties united into a state. However different these two points of view may be, they have this in common, that they have transferred the characteristics of private property into a sphere of a quite different and higher nature. (See below,[3] Ethical Life and the State.) [A.]

76. Contract is *formal* when the double consent whereby the common will is brought into existence is apportioned between the two contracting parties so that one of them has the negative moment—the alienation of a thing—and the other the positive moment—the appropriation of the thing. Such a contract is *gift*. But contract may be called *real* when each of the two contracting wills is the sum of these mediating moments and therefore in such a contract becomes a property owner and remains so. This is a contract of *exchange*. [A.]

77. Since in real contract each party retains the same property with which he enters the contract and which at the same time he surrenders, what thus remains identical throughout as the property implicit in the contract is distinct from the external things whose owners alter when the ex-

change is made. What remains identical is the value, in respect of which the subjects of the contract are equal to one another whatever the qualitative external differences of the things exchanged. Value is the universal in which the subjects of the contract participate (see Paragraph 63).

The legal provision that *laesio enormis*[4] annuls the obligation arising out of the making of a contract has its source, therefore, in the concept of contract, particularly in this moment of it, that the contracting party by alienating his property still remains a property owner and, more precisely, an owner of the quantitative equivalent of what he alienates. But a *laesio* is not merely *enormis* (as it is taken to be if it exceeds one-half of the value) but infinite, if someone has entered on a contract or made a stipulation of any sort for the alienation of inalienable goods (see Paragraph 66).

A stipulation, moreover, differs from a contract, first, in its *content*, because it signifies only some single part or moment of the whole contract, and secondly, because it is the *form* in which the contract is settled (a point on which more will be said later).[5] So far as its content is concerned, it comprises only the formal character of contract, i.e. the willingness of one party to give something and the willingness of the other to accept it; for this reason, the stipulation has been enumerated amongst so-called "unilateral" contracts. The distinction between unilateral and bilateral contracts, and distinctions in Roman law between other types of contract, are sometimes superficial juxtapositions made from an isolated and often external point of view such as that of the different types of contractual forms; or sometimes they confuse characteristics intrinsic to contract itself with others which only arise later in connexion with the administration of justice (*actiones*) and the legal processes giving effect to positive laws, and which are often derived from quite external circumstances and contravene the concept of right.

78. The distinction between property and possession, the substantive and external aspects of ownership (see Paragraph 45), appears in the sphere of contract as the distinction between a common will and its actualization, or between a covenant and its performance. Once made, a covenant taken by itself in distinction from its performance is something held before the mind, something therefore to which a particular determinate existence must be given in accordance with the appropriate mode of giving determinate existence to ideas by symbolizing them.[6] This is done, therefore, by expressing the stipulation in formalities such as gestures and other symbolic actions, particularly by declaring it with preci-

---

[1] [§§ 24-7.].
[2] See Paragraphs 277-8.—ED.
[3] i.e., Part III; see especially Paragraphs 258, 278, 294.—ED.

[4] *Laesio enormis,* excessive damage.
[5] See Paragraph 217.—ED.
[6] *Enc.* [1st edn.] §§ 379 ff. [3rd edn. §§ 458 ff.].

sion in language, the most worthy medium for the expression of our mental ideas.

The stipulation accordingly is the form given to the content of a contract, i.e. to what is agreed in it, and thereby this content, previously only an idea, attains its determinate existence. But the idea which we have of the content is itself only a form which the content takes; to have an idea of the content does not mean that the content is still something subjective, a desire or a wish for so and so. On the contrary, the content is the will's ultimate decision on such subjective wishes. [A.]

79. In contract it is the will, and therefore the substance of what is right in contract, that the stipulation enshrines. In contrast with this substance, the possession which is still being retained while the contract remains unfulfilled is in itself only something external, dependent for its character as a possession on the will alone. By making the stipulation, I have given up a property and withdrawn my particular arbitrary will from it, and it has *eo ipso* become the property of another. If then I agree to stipulated terms, I am by rights at once bound to carry them out.

The difference between a mere promise and a contract lies in the fact that a promise is a statement that I will give or do or perform something in the *future,* and a promise still remains a subjective volition which because it is subjective I can still alter. A stipulation in a contract, on the other hand, is itself already the embodiment of the will's decision in the sense that by making the stipulation I have alienated my property, it has *now* ceased to be mine, and I already recognize it as the property of another. The distinction in Roman law between *pactum* and *contractus* is one of a false type.

Fichte at one time maintained that my obligation to keep a contract begins only when the other party starts fulfilling his side of it; his reason was that up to that point I am uncertain whether the other party's declarations are seriously meant. In that case it would follow that the obligation to keep a contract before it was carried out would only be a moral one, not an obligation by *rights*.—But the expression of the stipulation is not simply a declaration of a general character; it embodies a common will which has been brought into existence and which has superseded the arbitrary and alterable dispositions of the parties. The question therefore is not whether the other party *could* have had different private intentions when the contract was made or afterwards, but whether he had any *right* to have them. Even if the other party begins to fulfil his side of the contract, it is equally open to me to do wrong if I like. The nullity of Fichte's view is also shown by the fact that it would base contractual rights on the false infinite, i.e. on the progress *ad infinitum* involved in the infinite divisibility of time, things, action, &c. The embodiment of the will in formal gestures or in explicit and precise language is already the complete

embodiment of the will as an intelligent entity, and the performance of the covenant so embodied is only the mechanical consequence.

It is true that in positive law there are so-called "real" contracts as distinguished from "consensual" contracts, in the sense that the former are looked upon as fully valid only when the actual performance (*res, traditio rei*) of the undertaking supervenes upon willingness to perform it; but this has nothing to do with the thing at issue. For one thing, these "real" contracts cover particular cases where it is only this delivery by the other party which puts me in a position to fulfil my side of the bargain, and where my obligation to do my part relates only to the thing after it has come into my hands, as happens for instance in loans, pawning, or deposits. (The same may also be the case in other contracts.) But this is a matter which concerns not the nature of the relation of the stipulation to performance but only the manner of performance.—For another thing, it is always open to the parties at their discretion to stipulate in any contract that the obligation of one party to perform his side shall not lie in the making of the contract itself as such, but shall arise only from the performance by the other party of his side.

80. The classification of contracts and an intelligent treatment of their various species once classified is not here to be derived from external circumstances but from distinctions lying in the very nature of contract. These distinctions are those between formal and real[1] contracts, between ownership and possession and use, between value and specific thing, and they yield contracts of the following sorts:[2]

A. *Gift.*

(1) Gift of a thing— gift properly so called.

(2) Loan of a thing—i.e. the gift of a portion of it or of restricted use and enjoyment of it; here the lender remains the owner of the thing (*mutuum* and *commodatum* without interest). Here the thing lent is either a specific thing or else, even if it be such, it may none the less be looked on as universal, or it may be a thing which counts (like money) as a thing universal in itself.

(3) Gift of service of any sort, e.g. the mere safe-keeping of a property (*depositum*). The gift of a thing on the special condition that its recipient shall not become its owner until the date of the donor's death, i.e. the date at which he ceases in any case to be an owner of property, is testamentary disposition; this is not contained

---

[1] See Paragraph 76.—ED.

[2] The classification given here agrees on the whole with Kant's (*Philosophy of Law* [§ 31.]). One would have expected that the usual humdrum classification of contracts as real and consensual, nominate and innominate, &c., would have been long since abandoned in favour of a rational classification.

in the concept of contract but presupposes civil society and positive legislation.[1]

B. *Exchange.*

(1) Exchange as such:

(*a*) exchange of a thing pure and simple, i.e. exchange of one specific thing for another of the same kind.

(*β*) purchase or sale (*emtio, venditio*); exchange of a specific thing for one characterized as universal, one which counts as value alone and which lacks the other specific character, utility—i.e. for money.

(2) Letting (*locatio, conductio*); alienation of the temporary use of a property in return for rent:

(*a*) letting of a specific thing—letting strictly so called, or

(*β*) letting of a universal thing, so that the lessor remains only the owner of this universal, or in other words of the value—loan (*mutuum*, or even *commodatum,* if interest is charged). The additional empirical characteristics of the thing (which may be, e.g., a flat, furniture, a house, *res fungibilis* or *non fungibilis,* &c.) entail (as in A. 2 above) other particular though unimportant subdivisions.

(3) Contract for wages (*locatio operae*)— alienation of my productive capacity or my services so far, that is, as these are alienable, the alienation being restricted in time or in some other way (see Paragraph 67).

Counsel's acceptance of a brief is akin to this, and so are other contracts whose fulfilment depends on character, good faith, or superior gifts, and where an incommensurability arises between the services rendered and a value in terms of cash. (In such cases the cash payment is called not "wages" but "honorarium.")

C. *Completion of a contract* (cautio)
through giving a pledge.

In the contracts whereby I part with the *use* of a thing, I am no longer in possession of the thing though I am still its owner, as for example when I let a house. Further, in gifts or contracts for exchange or purchase, I may have become the owner of a thing without as yet being in possession of it, and the same cleavage between ownership and possession arises in respect of the implementing of any undertaking which is not simply a cash or barter transaction. Now what the pledge effects is that in the one case I remain, and in the other case I am put, in actual possession of the value as that which is still or has already become my property, without in either case being in possession of the specific thing

which I am renouncing or which is to be mine. The pledge is a specific thing but one which is my property only to the extent of the value of the property which I have renounced into another's possession or which is due to me; its specific character as a thing and any excess value it may have still belong to the person who gave the pledge. Giving a pledge, therefore, is not itself a contract but only a stipulation (see [Remark to] Paragraph 77), i.e. it is the moment which brings a contract to completion so far as the *possession* of the property is concerned. Mortgage and surety are particular forms of pledge. [A.]

81. In the bare relation of *immediate* persons to one another, their wills while implicitly identical, and in contract posited by them as common, are yet particular. Because they are *immediate* persons, it is a matter of chance whether or not their particular wills actually correspond with the implicit will, although it is only through the former that the latter has its real existence. If the particular will is explicitly at variance with the universal, it assumes a way of looking at things and a volition which are capricious and fortuitous and comes on the scene in opposition to the principle of rightness. This is *wrong*.

The transition to wrong is made by the logical higher necessity that the moments of the concept—here the principle of rightness or the will as universal, and right in its real existence, which is just the particularity of the will—should be posited as explicitly different, and this happens when the concept is realized abstractly. But this particularity of the will, taken by itself, is arbitrariness and contingency, and in contract I have surrendered these only as arbitrariness in the case of a single thing and not as the arbitrariness and contingency of the will itself. [A.]

Sub-section III
WRONG

82. In contract the principle of rightness is present as something posited, while its inner universality is there as something common in the arbitrariness and particular will of the parties. This *appearance* of right, in which right and its essential embodiment, the particular will, correspond immediately, i.e. fortuitously, proceeds in wrong to become a *show*,[2] an opposition between the principle of rightness and the particular will as that in which right becomes particularized. But the truth of this show is its nullity and the fact that right reasserts itself by negating this negation of itself. In this process the right is mediated by returning into itself out of the negation of itself; thereby it makes itself actual and valid, while at the start it was only implicit and something immediate. [A.]

[1] See Paragraphs 179 ff.—Ed.

[2] See Paragraphs 97 ff.—Ed.

83. When right is something particular and therefore manifold in contrast with its implicit universality and simplicity, it acquires the form of a show. (*a*) This show of right is implicit or immediate—non-malicious wrong or a civil offence; (*b*) right is made a show by the agent himself—fraud; (*c*) the agent makes it a nullity altogether—crime. [A.]

A. *Non-malicious Wrong*

84. Taking possession (see Paragraph 54) and contract—both in themselves and in their particular species—are in the first instance different expressions and consequences of my willing pure and simple; but since the will is the inherently universal, they are, through their recognition by others, grounds of title. Such grounds are external to one another and multiple, and this implies that different persons may have them in relation to one and the same thing. Each person may look upon the thing as his property on the strength of the particular ground on which he bases his title. It is in this way that one man's right may clash with another's.

85. This clash which arises when a thing has been claimed on some single ground, and which comprises the sphere of civil suits at law, entails the recognition of rightness as the universal and decisive factor, so that it is common ground that the thing in dispute should belong to the party who has the right to it. The suit is concerned only with the subsumption of the thing under the property of one or other of the parties —a straightforward negative judgement, where, in the predicate "mine," only the particular is negated.

86. The recognition of rightness by the parties is bound up with their opposed particular interest and point of view. In opposition to this show of rightness, yet within this show itself (see the preceding Paragraph), the principle of rightness arises as something kept in view and demanded by the parties. But at first it arises only as an "ought-to-be" because the will is not yet present here as a will so freed from the immediacy of interest as, despite its particularity, to have the universal will for its aim; nor is it yet at this point characterized as a recognized actuality of such a sort that in face of it the parties would have to renounce their particular interest and point of view. [A.]

B. *Fraud*

87. The principle of rightness, when distinguished from the right as particular and as de-

terminately existent, is characterized as something demanded, as the essential thing; yet in this situation it is still only something *demanded* and from that point of view something purely subjective, and so inessential—something merely showing there. Thus we have *fraud* when the universal is set aside by the particular will and reduced to something only showing in the situation, primarily in contract, when the universal will is reduced to a will which is common only from the outsider's point of view. [A.]

88. In contract I acquire a property for the sake of its particular characteristics, and at the same time my acquisition of it is governed by the inner universality which it possesses partly in respect of its value and partly because it has been the *property* of another. If the other likes, a false disguise may be given to the thing I acquire, so that the contract is right enough so far as it is an exchange, voluntary on both sides, of *this* thing in its immediacy and uniqueness, but still the aspect of implicit universality is lacking. (Here we have an infinite judgement expressed positively or as a tautology.[1])

89. Here again it is in the first instance only a demand that, in contrast with this acceptance of the thing simply as *this* thing and with the mere intentions and arbitrariness of the will, objectivity or universality should be recognizable as value and should prevail as right, and equally a demand only that the subjective arbitrary will, opposing itself to the right, should be superseded. [A.]

C. *Coercion and Crime*

90. In owning property I place my will in an external thing, and this implies that my will, just by being thus reflected in the object, may be seized in it and brought under compulsion. It may simply be forced in the thing unconditionally, or it may be constrained to sacrifice something or to do some action as a condition of retaining one or other of its possessions or embodiments—it may be coerced. [A.]

91. As a living thing man may be coerced, i.e. his body or anything else external about him may be brought under the power of others; but the free will cannot be coerced at all (see Paragraph 5), except in so far as it fails to withdraw itself out of the external object in which it is held fast, or rather out of its idea of that object (see Paragraph 7). Only the will which allows itself to be coerced can in any way be coerced.

92. Since it is only in so far as the will has an ex-

1 *Enc.* [1st edn.], § 121 [3rd edn. § 173].

istence in something determinate that it is Idea or actually free, and since the existent in which it has laid itself is freedom in being, it follows that force or coercion is in its very conception directly self-destructive because it is an expression of a will which annuls the expression or determinate existence of a will. Hence force or coercion, taken abstractly, is wrong.

93. That coercion is in its conception self-destructive is exhibited in the world of reality by the fact that coercion is annulled by coercion; coercion is thus shown to be not only right under certain conditions but necessary, i.e. as a second act of coercion which is the annulment of one that has preceded.

Breaking a contract by failing to carry out its stipulated terms, or neglect of duty rightly owed to family or state, or action in defiance of that duty, is the first act of coercion or at least force, in that it involves depriving another of his property or evading a service due to him.

Coercion by a schoolmaster, or coercion of savages and brutes, seems at first sight to be an initial act of coercion, not a second, following on one that has preceded. But the merely natural will is implicitly a force against the implicit Idea of freedom which must be protected against such an uncivilized will and be made to prevail in it. Either an ethical institution has already been established in family or government, and the natural will is a mere display of force against it; or else there is only a state of nature, a state of affairs where mere force prevails and against which the Idea establishes a right of Heroes.[1] [A.]

94. Abstract right is a right to coerce, because the wrong which transgresses it is an exercise of force against the existence of my freedom in an external thing. The maintenance of this existent against the exercise of force therefore itself takes the form of an external act and an exercise of force annulling the force originally brought against it.

To define abstract right, or right in the strict sense, at the very outset as a right in the name of which coercion may be used, means to fasten on it in a result which first comes on the scene by the indirect route of wrong. [A.]

95. The initial act of coercion as an exercise of force by the free agent, an exercise of force which infringes the existence of freedom in its concrete sense, infringes the right as right, is crime—a negatively infinite judgement in its full sense,[2] whereby not only the particular (i.e. the subsumption under my will of a single thing—

see Paragraph 85) is negated, but also the universality and infinity in the predicate "mine" (i.e. my capacity for rights). Here the negation does not come about with the co-operation of my thinking (as it does in fraud—see Paragraph 88) but in defiance of it. This is the sphere of criminal law.

Right, the infringement of which is crime, has so far only those formations which we have seen in the preceding Paragraphs; hence crime also, to begin with, has its more precise significance in relation to these specific rights. But the substance of these forms is the universal which remains the same throughout its further development and formation, and consequently its infringement, crime, also remains the same and accords with its concept. Thus the specific characteristic of crime [in general] to be noticed in the next Paragraph is characteristic also of the particular, more determinate, content in e.g. perjury, treason, forgery, coining, &c.

96. It is only the will existent in an object that can suffer injury. In becoming existent in something, however, the will enters the sphere of quantitative extension and qualitative characteristics, and hence varies accordingly. For this reason, it makes a difference to the objective aspect of crime whether the will so objectified and its specific quality is injured throughout its entire extent, and so in the infinity which is equivalent to its concept (as in murder, slavery, enforced religious observance, &c.), or whether it is injured only in a single part or in one of its qualitative characteristics, and if so, in which of these.

The Stoic view that there is only one virtue and one vice, the laws of Draco which prescribe death as a punishment for every offence,[3] the crude formal code of Honour which takes any insult as an offence against the infinity of personality, all have this in common, that they go no further than the abstract thought of the free will and personality and fail to apprehend it in the concrete and determinate existence which it must possess as Idea.

The distinction between robbery and theft is qualitative; when I am robbed, personal violence is done to me and I am injured in my character as consciousness existing here and now and so as *this* infinite subject.

Many qualitative characteristics of crime, e.g. its danger to public safety,[4] have their basis in more concrete circumstances, although in the first instance they also are often fastened on by the indirect route as consequences instead of from the concept of the thing. For instance, the crime which taken by itself is the more dangerous in its immediate character is

---

[1] Cf. Hegel, *Philosophy of History*, pp. 166, 344.—ED.
[2] See my [*Science of*] *Logic* [1st edn.], vol. ii, p. 99 [Eng. tr. vol. 11, pp. 277-8].

[3] Cf. Plutarch, *Lives*, life of Solon.—ED.
[4] See Paragraph 218 and Remark to Paragraph 319. —ED.

an injury of a more serious type in its range or its quality.

The subjective, moral, quality of crime rests on the higher distinction implied in the question of how far an event or fact pure and simple is an action, and concerns the subjective character of the action itself, on which see below.[1] [A.]

97. The infringement of right as right is something that happens and has positive existence in the external world, though inherently it is nothing at all. The manifestation of its nullity is the appearance, also in the external world, of the annihilation of the infringement. This is the right actualized, the necessity of the right mediating itself with itself by annulling what has infringed it. [A.]

98. In so far as the infringement of the right is only an injury to a possession or to something which exists externally, it is a *malum* or damage to some kind of property or asset. The annulling of the infringement, so far as the infringement is productive of damage, is the satisfaction given in a civil suit, i.e. compensation for the wrong done, so far as any such compensation can be found.

Apropos of such satisfaction, the universal character of the damage, i.e. its "value," must here again take the place of its specific qualitative character in cases where the damage done amounts to destruction and is quite irreparable.

99. But the injury which has befallen the *implicit* will (and this means the implicit will of the *injuring* party as well as that of the injured and everyone else) has as little positive existence in this implicit will as such as it has in the mere state of affairs which it produces. In itself this implicit will (i.e. the right or law implicit) is rather that which has no external existence and which for that reason cannot be injured. Consequently, the injury from the point of view of the particular will of the injured party and of onlookers is only something negative. The sole positive existence which the injury possesses is that it is the particular will of the criminal.[2] Hence to injure [or penalize] this particular will as a will determinately existent is to annul the crime, which otherwise would have been held valid, and to restore the right.

The theory of punishment is one of the topics which have come off worst in the recent study of the positive science of law, because in this theory the Understanding is insufficient; the essence of the matter depends on the concept. If crime and its annulment (which later [3] will ac-

quire the specific character of punishment) are treated as if they were unqualified evils, it must, of course, seem quite unreasonable to will an evil merely because "another evil is there already." [4] To give punishment this superficial character of an evil is, amongst the various theories of punishment, the fundamental presupposition of those which regard it as a preventive, a deterrent, a threat, as reformative, &c., and what on these theories is supposed to result from punishment is characterized equally superficially as a good. But it is not merely a question of an evil or of this, that, or the other good; the precise point at issue is wrong and the righting of it. If you adopt that superficial attitude to punishment, you brush aside the objective treatment of the righting of wrong, which is the primary and fundamental attitude in considering crime; and the natural consequence is that you take as essential the moral attitude, i.e. the subjective aspect of crime, intermingled with trivial psychological ideas of stimuli, impulses too strong for reason, and psychological factors coercing and working on our ideas (as if freedom were not equally capable of thrusting an idea aside and reducing it to something fortuitous!). The various considerations which are relevant to punishment as a phenomenon and to the bearing it has on the particular consciousness, and which concern its effects (deterrent, reformative, &c.) on the imagination, are an essential topic for examination in their place, especially in connexion with modes of punishment, but all these considerations presuppose as their foundation the fact that punishment is inherently and actually just. In discussing this matter the only important things are, first, that crime is to be annulled, not because it is the producing of an evil, but because it is an infringement of the right as right, and secondly, the question of what that positive existence is which crime possesses and which must be annulled; it is this existence which is the real evil to be removed, and the essential point is the question of where it lies. So long as the concepts here at issue are not clearly apprehended, confusion must continue to reign in the theory of punishment. [A.]

100. The injury [the penalty] which falls on the criminal is not merely *implicitly* just—as just, it is *eo ipso* his implicit will, an embodiment of his freedom, his right; on the contrary, it is also a right *established* within the criminal himself, i.e. in his objectively embodied will, in his action. The reason for this is that his action is the action of a rational being and this implies that it is something universal and that by doing it the criminal has laid down a law which he has explicitly recognized in his action and under which in consequence he should be brought as under his right.

As is well known, Beccaria denied to the state the

---

[1] See Paragraphs 113 ff.—Ed.
[2] See Paragraphs 97 and 99.—Ed.
[3] See Paragraph 220.—Ed.

[4] [E. F.] Klein: *Grundsätze des peinlichen Rechts* [Halle, 1796], §§ 9 ff.

right of inflicting capital punishment. His reason was that it could not be presumed that the readiness of individuals to allow themselves to be executed was included in the social contract, and that in fact the contrary would have to be assumed. But the state is not a contract at all (see [Remark to] Paragraph 75) nor is its fundamental essence the unconditional protection and guarantee of the life and property of members of the public as individuals. On the contrary, it is that higher entity which even lays claim to this very life and property and demands its sacrifice. Further, what is involved in the action of the criminal is not only the concept of crime, the rational aspect present in crime as such whether the individual wills it or not, the aspect which the state has to vindicate, but also the abstract rationality of the individual's *volition*. Since that is so, punishment is regarded as containing the criminal's right and hence by being punished he is honoured as a rational being. He does not receive this due of honour unless the concept and measure of his punishment are derived from his own act. Still less does he receive it if he is treated either as a harmful animal who has to be made harmless, or with a view to deterring and reforming him.

Moreover, apart from these considerations, the form in which the righting of wrong exists in the state, namely punishment, is not its only form, nor is the state a pre-condition of the principle of righting wrong. [A.]

101. The annulment of the crime is retribution in so far as (*a*) retribution in *conception* is an "injury of the injury," and (*b*) since as existent a crime is something determinate in its scope both qualitatively and quantitatively, its negation as *existent* is similarly determinate. This identity rests on the concept, but it is not an equality between the specific character of the crime and that of its negation; on the contrary, the two injuries are equal only in respect of their implicit character, i.e. in respect of their "value."

Empirical science requires that the definition of a class concept (punishment in this case) shall be drawn from ideas universally present to conscious psychological experience. This method would prove that the universal feeling of nations and individuals about crime is and has been that it deserves punishment, that as the criminal has done, so should it be done to him. (There is no understanding how these sciences, which find the source of their class concepts in ideas universally shared, come on other occasions to take for granted propositions contradictory of like "facts of consciousness" also styled "universal.")

But a point of great difficulty has been introduced into the idea of retribution by the category of equality, though it is still true that the justice of specific types or amounts of punishment is a further matter, subsequent to the substance of the thing itself. Even if to determine the later question of specific punishments we had to look round for principles other than those determining the universal character of punishment, still the latter remains what it is. The only thing is that the concept itself must in general contain the *fundamental* principle for determining the particular too. But the determinate character given by the concept to punishment is just that necessary connexion between crime and punishment already mentioned; crime, as the will which is implicitly null, *eo ipso* contains its negation in itself and this negation is manifested as punishment. It is this inner identity whose reflection in the external world appears to the Understanding as "equality." The qualitative and quantitative characteristics of crime and its annulment fall, then, into the sphere of externality. In any case, no absolute determinacy is possible in this sphere (compare Paragraph 49) ; in the field of the finite, absolute determinacy remains only a demand, a demand which the Understanding has to meet by continually increasing delimitation— a fact of the greatest importance—but which continues *ad infinitum* and which allows only of perennially approximate satisfaction.

If we overlook this nature of the finite and then into the bargain refuse to go beyond abstract and specific equality, we are faced with the insuperable difficulty of fixing punishments (especially if psychology adduces in addition the strength of sensual impulses and consequentially either the greater strength of the evil will or the greater weakness, or the restricted freedom, of the will as such—we may choose which we please). Furthermore, it is easy enough from this point of view to exhibit the retributive character of punishment as an absurdity (theft for theft, robbery for robbery, an eye for an eye, a tooth for a tooth—and then you can go on to suppose that the criminal has only one eye or no teeth). But the concept has nothing to do with this absurdity, for which indeed the introduction of this specific equality is solely to blame. Value, as the inner equality of things which in their outward existence are specifically different from one another in every way, is a category which has appeared already in connexion with contracts (see Paragraph 77), and also in connexion with injuries that are the subject of civil suits (see Remark to Paragraph 98) ;[1] and by means of it our idea of a thing is raised above its immediate character to its universality. In crime, as that which is characterized at bottom by the infinite aspect[2] of the deed, the purely external specific character vanishes all the more obviously, and equality remains the fundamental regulator of the essential thing, to wit the deserts of the criminal, though not for the specific external form which the payment of those deserts may take. It is only in respect of that form that there is a plain inequality between theft and robbery on the one hand, and fines, imprisonment, &c., on the other. In respect of their "value," however, i.e. in respect of their universal

---

[1] All editions have "Paragraph 95."—ED.
[2] See Paragraph 22.—ED.

property of being injuries, they are comparable. Thus, as was said above, it is a matter for the Understanding to look for something approximately equal to their "value" in this sense. If the implicit interconnexion of crime and its negation, and if also the thought of value and the comparability of crime and punishment in respect of their value are not apprehended, then it may become possible to see in a punishment proper only an "arbitrary"[1] connexion of an evil with an unlawful action. [A.]

102. The annulling of crime in this sphere where right is immediate is principally revenge, which is just in its content in so far as it is retributive. But in its form it is an act of a subjective will which can place its infinity in every act of transgression and whose justification, therefore, is in all cases contingent, while to the other party too it appears as only particular. Hence revenge, because it is a positive action of a particular will, becomes a new transgression; as thus contradictory in character, it falls into an infinite progression and descends from one generation to another *ad infinitum*.

In cases where crimes are prosecuted and punished not as *crimina publica* but as *crimina privata* (e.g. in Jewish law and Roman law, theft and robbery; in English law to this day, certain crimes, &c.) punishment is in principle, at least to some extent, revenge. There is a difference between private revenge and the revenge of heroes, knights-errant, &c., which is part of the founding of states. [A.]

103. The demand that this contradiction, which is present here in the manner in which wrong is annulled, be resolved like contradictions in the case of other types of wrong (see Paragraphs 86, 89), is the demand for a justice freed from subjective interest and a subjective form and no longer contingent on might, i.e. it is the demand for justice not as revenge but as punishment. Fundamentally, this implies the demand for a will which, though particular and subjective, yet wills the universal as such. But this concept of *Morality* is not simply something demanded; it has emerged in the course of this movement itself.

Transition from Right to Morality

104. That is to say, crime, and justice in the form of revenge, display (i) the shape which the

[1] Klein: *op. cit.,* § 9.

will's development takes when it has passed over into the distinction between the universal implicit will and the single will explicitly in opposition to the universal; and (ii) the fact that the universal will, returning into itself through superseding this opposition, has now itself become actual and explicit. In this way, the right, upheld in face of the explicitly independent single will, is and is recognized as actual on the score of its necessity. At the same time, however, this external formation which the will has here is *eo ipso* a step forward in the inner determination of the will by the concept. The will's immanent actualization in accordance with its concept is the process whereby it supersedes its implicit stage and the form of immediacy in which it begins and which is the shape it assumes in abstract right (see [Remark to] Paragraph 21); this means that it first puts itself in the opposition between the implicit universal will and the single explicitly independent will; and then, through the supersession of this opposition (through the negation of the negation), it determines itself in its *existence* as a will, so that it is a free will not only in itself but for itself also, i.e. it determines itself as self-related negativity. Its personality—and in abstract right the will is personality and no more—it now has for its object; the infinite subjectivity of freedom, a subjectivity become explicit in this way, is the principle of the *moral* standpoint.[2]

Let us look back more closely over the moments through which the concept of freedom develops itself from the will's determinate character as originally abstract to its character as self-related, and so at this point to its self-determination as subjectivity. In property this determinate character is the abstract one, "mine," and is therefore found in an external thing. In contract, "mine" is mediated by the wills of the parties and means only something common. In wrong the will of the sphere of right has its abstract character of implicit being or immediacy posited as contingency through the act of a single will, itself a contingent will. At the moral standpoint, the abstract determinacy of the will in the sphere of right has been so far overcome that this contingency itself is, as reflected in upon itself and self-identical, the inward infinite contingency of the will, i.e. its subjectivity. [A.]

[2] See Paragraphs 7, 34, 15, and Addition to Paragraph 35.—ED.

SECOND PART

MORALITY

105. The standpoint of morality is the standpoint of the will which is infinite not merely in itself but for itself (see Paragraph 104). In contrast with the will's implicit being, with its immediacy and the determinate characteristics developed within it at that level, this reflection of the will into itself and its explicit awareness of its identity makes the person into the subject.

106. It is as subjectivity that the concept has now been determined, and since subjectivity is distinct from the concept as such, i.e. from the implicit principle of the will, and since furthermore it is at the same time the will of the subject as a single individual aware of himself (i.e. still has immediacy in him), it constitutes the determinate *existence* of the concept. In this way a higher ground has been assigned to freedom; the Idea's existential aspect, or its moment of reality, is now the subjectivity of the will. Only in the will as subjective can freedom or the implicit principle of the will be actual.[1]

The second sphere, Morality, therefore throughout portrays the real aspect of the concept of freedom, and the movement of this sphere is as follows: the will, which at the start is aware only of its independence and which before it is mediated is only implicitly identical with the universal will or the principle of the will, is raised beyond its [explicit] difference from the universal will, beyond this situation in which it sinks deeper and deeper into itself, and is established as explicitly identical with the principle of the will. This process is accordingly the cultivation of the ground in which freedom is now set, i.e. subjectivity. What happens is that subjectivity, which is abstract at the start, i.e. distinct from the concept, becomes likened to it, and thereby the Idea acquires its genuine realization. The result is that the subjective will determines itself as objective too and so as truly concrete. [A.]

107. The self-determination of the will is at the same time a moment in the concept of the will, and subjectivity is not merely its existential aspect but its own determinate character (see Paragraph 104). The will aware of its freedom

[1] See Paragraph 90.—ED.

and determined as subjective is at the start concept alone, but itself has determinate existence in order to exist as Idea. The moral standpoint therefore takes shape as the right of the subjective will.[2] In accordance with this right, the will recognizes something and is something, only in so far as the thing is its own and as the will is present to itself there as something subjective.

The same process through which the moral attitude develops (see the Remark to the preceding Paragraph) has from this point of view the form of being the development of the right of the subjective will, or of the mode of its existence. In this process the subjective will further determines what it recognizes as its own in its object (*Gegenstand*), so that this object becomes the will's own true concept, becomes objective (*objektiv*) as the expression of the will's own universality.[3] [A.]

108. The subjective will, directly aware of itself, and distinguished from the principle of the will (see Remark to Paragraph 106), is therefore abstract, restricted, and formal. But not merely is subjectivity itself formal; in addition, as the infinite self-determination of the will, it constitutes the form of all willing. In this, its first appearance in the single will, this form has not yet been established as identical with the concept of the will, and therefore the moral point of view is that of relation, of ought-to-be, or demand. And since the self-difference of subjectivity involves at the same time the character of being opposed to objectivity as external fact, it follows that the point of view of consciousness comes on the scene here too (see Paragraph 8). The general point of view here is that of the will's self-difference, finitude, and appearance.[4]

The moral is not characterized primarily by its having already been opposed to the immoral, nor is right directly characterized by its opposition to wrong. The point is rather that the general characteristics of morality and immorality alike rest on the subjectivity of the will. [A.]

[2] See Paragraph 29.—ED.
[3] See Paragraphs 125, 26, and 112.—ED.
[4] See Paragraph 7.—ED.

40

109. This form of all willing primarily involves in accordance with its general character (*a*) the opposition of subjectivity and objectivity, and (*b*) the activity (see Paragraph 8) related to this opposition. Now existence and specific determinacy are identical in the concept of the will (see Paragraph 104), and the will as subjective is itself this concept.[1] Hence the moments of this activity consist more precisely in (*a*) distinguishing between objectivity and subjectivity and even ascribing independence to them both, and (*b*) establishing them as identical. In the will which is self-determining, (α) its specific determinacy is in the first place established in the will itself by itself as its inner particularization, as a content which it gives to itself. This is the first negation, and the formal limitation (*Grenze*) of this negation is that of being only something posited, something subjective. (β) As infinitely reflected into itself, this limitation exists for the will, and the will is the struggle to transcend this barrier (*Schranke*), i.e. it is the activity of translating this content in some way or other from subjectivity into objectivity, into an immediate existence. (γ) The simple identity of the will with itself in this opposition is the content which remains self-identical in both these opposites and indifferent to this formal distinction of opposition. In short, it is my aim [the purpose willed].[2]

110. But, at the standpoint of morality, where the will is aware of its freedom, of this identity of the will with itself (see Paragraph 105), this identity of content acquires the more particularized character appropriate to itself.

(*a*) The content as "mine" has for me this character: by virtue of its identity in subject and object it enshrines for me my subjectivity, not merely as my inner purpose, but also inasmuch as it has acquired outward existence. [A.]

111. (*b*) Though the content does have in it something particular, whencesoever it may be derived, still it is the content of the will reflected into itself in its determinacy and thus of the self-identical and universal will; and therefore:

(*a*) the content is inwardly characterized as adequate to the principle of the will or as possessing the objectivity of the concept;

(β) since the subjective will, as aware of itself, is at the same time still formal (see Paragraph 108), the content's adequacy to the concept is still only something demanded, and hence this entails the possibility that the content may

not be adequate to the concept.

112. (*c*) Since in carrying out my aims I retain my subjectivity (see Paragraph 110), during this process of objectifying them I simultaneously supersede the immediacy of this subjectivity as well as its character as this my individual subjectivity. But the external subjectivity which is thus identical with me is the will of others (see Paragraph 73). The will's ground of existence is now subjectivity (see Paragraph 106) and the will of others is that existence which I give to my aim and which is at the same time to me an other. The achievement of my aim, therefore, implies this identity of my will with the will of others, it has a positive bearing on the will of others.

The objectivity of the aim achieved thus involves three meanings, or rather it has three moments present within it at once; it is:

(α) something existing externally and immediately (see Paragraph 109);

(β) adequate to the concept (see Paragraph 111);[3]

(γ) *universal* subjectivity.

The subjectivity which maintains itself in this objectivity consists:

(α) in the fact that the objective aim is mine, so that in it I maintain myself as *this* individual (see Paragraph 110);

(β) and (γ), in moments which coincide with the moments (β) and (γ) above.

At the standpoint of morality, subjectivity and objectivity are distinct from one another, or united only by their mutual contradiction; it is this fact more particularly which constitutes the finitude of this sphere or its character as mere appearance (see Paragraph 108), and the development of this standpoint is the development of these contradictions and their resolutions, resolutions, however, which within this field can be no more than relative. [A.]

113. The externalization of the subjective or moral will is action. Action implies the determinate characteristics here indicated:

(*a*) in its externality it must be known to me as *my* action;

(β) it must bear essentially on the concept as an "ought" [see Paragraph 131];

(γ) it must have an essential bearing on the will of others.

It is not until we come to the externalization of the moral will that we come to action. The existence which the will gives to itself in the sphere of formal rights is existence in an immediate thing and is itself immediate; to start with, it neither has in itself any express bearing on the concept, which is at that point not yet contrasted with the subjective will and so is not distinguished from it, nor has it a positive bearing on the will of others; in the sphere of right, com-

---

[1] See Remark to Paragraph 32.—ED.
[2] See Addition to Paragraph 110.—ED.
[3] All editions read "112."—ED.

mand in its fundamental character is only prohibition (see Paragraph 38). In contract and wrong, there is the beginning of a bearing on the will of others; but the correspondence established in contract between one will and another is grounded in arbitrariness, and the essential bearing which the will has there on the will of the other is, as a matter of rights, something negative, i.e. one party retains his property (the value of it) and allows the other to retain his. On the other hand, crime in its aspect as issuing from the subjective will, and the question of the mode of its existence in that will, come before us now for consideration for the first time.

The content of an action at law (*actio*), as something determined by legal enactment, is not imputable to me. Consequently, such an action contains only some of the moments of a moral action proper, and contains them only incidentally. The aspect of an action in virtue of which it is properly moral is therefore distinct from its aspect as legal.

114. The right of the moral will involves three aspects:

(*a*) The abstract or formal right of action, the right that the content of the action as carried out in immediate existence, shall be in principle mine, that thus the action shall be the *Purpose* of the subjective will.

(*b*) The particular aspect of the action is its inner content (*a*) as I am aware of it in its general character; my awareness of this general character constitutes the worth of the action and the reason I think good to do it—in short my *Intention*. (*β*) Its content is my special aim, the aim of my particular, merely individual, existence, i.e. *Welfare*.

(*c*) This content (as something which is inward and which yet at the same time is raised to its universality as to absolute objectivity) is the absolute end of the will, the *Good*—with the opposition in the sphere of reflection, of *subjective* universality, which is now wickedness and now conscience.[1] [A.]

Sub-section I

PURPOSE AND RESPONSIBILITY

115. The finitude of the subjective will in the immediacy of acting consists directly in this, that its action *presupposes* an external object with a complex environment. The deed sets up an alteration in this state of affairs confronting the will, and my will has responsibility in general for its deed in so far as the abstract predicate "mine" belongs to the state of affairs so altered.

An event, a situation which has been produced, is a concrete external actuality which because of its

[1] See Remark to Paragraph 112.—Ed.

concreteness has in it an indeterminable multiplicity of factors. Any and every single element which appears as the condition, ground, or cause of one such factor, and so has contributed its share to the event in question, may be looked upon as responsible for the event, or at least as sharing the responsibility for it. Hence, in the case of a complex event (e.g. the French Revolution) it is open to the abstract Understanding to choose which of an endless number of factors it will maintain to be responsible for it. [A.]

116. It is, of course, not my own doing if damage is caused to others by things whose owner I am and which as external objects stand and are effective in manifold connexions with other things (as may also be the case with my self as a bodily mechanism or as a living thing). This damage, however, is to some extent chargeable to me because the things that cause it are in principle mine, although it is true that they are subject to my control, vigilance, &c., only to an extent varying with their special character.

117. The freely acting will, in directing its aim on the state of affairs confronting it, has an idea of the attendant circumstances. But because the will is finite, since this state of affairs is presupposed, the objective phenomenon is contingent so far as the will is concerned, and may contain something other than what the will's idea of it contains. The will's right, however, is to recognize as its action, and to accept responsibility for, only those presuppositions of the deed of which it was conscious in its aim and those aspects of the deed which were contained in its purpose. The deed can be imputed to me only if my will is responsible for it—this is the right to know. [A.]

118. Further, action is translated into external fact, and external fact has connexions in the field of external necessity through which it develops itself in all directions. Hence action has a multitude of consequences. These consequences are the outward form whose inner soul is the aim of the action, and thus they are the consequences *of the action*, they belong to the action. At the same time, however, the action, as the aim posited in the external world, has become the prey of external forces which attach to it something totally different from what it is explicitly and drive it on into alien and distant consequences. Thus the will has the right to repudiate the imputation of all consequences except the first, since it alone was purposed.

To determine which results are accidental and which necessary is impossible, because the necessity implicit in the finite comes into determinate existence as an external necessity, as a relation of single things to one another, things which as self-subsistent are conjoined in indifference to one another and externally. The maxim: "Ignore the consequences of actions" and the other: "Judge actions by their consequences and make these the criterion of right and good" are both alike maxims of the abstract Understanding. The consequences, as the shape proper to the action and immanent within it, exhibit nothing but its nature and are simply the action itself; therefore the action can neither disavow nor ignore them. On the other hand, however, among the consequences there is also comprised something interposed from without and introduced by chance, and this is quite unrelated to the nature of the action itself.

The development in the external world of the contradiction involved in the *necessity* of the *finite* is just the conversion of necessity into contingency and vice versa. From this point of view, therefore, acting means surrendering oneself to this law.[1] It is because of this that it is to the advantage of the criminal if his action has comparatively few bad consequences (while a good action must be content to have had no consequences or very few), and that the fully developed consequences of a crime are counted as part of the crime.

The self-consciousness of heroes (like that of Oedipus and others in Greek tragedy) had not advanced out of its primitive simplicity either to reflection on the distinction between act and action, between the external event and the purpose and knowledge of the circumstances, or to the subdivision of consequences. On the contrary, they accepted responsibility for the whole compass of the deed. [A.]

Sub-section II

INTENTION AND WELFARE

119. An action as an external event is a complex of connected parts which may be regarded as divided into units *ad infinitum,* and the action may be treated as having touched in the first instance only one of these units. The truth of the single, however, is the universal; and what explicitly gives action its specific character is not an isolated content limited to an external unit, but a universal content, comprising in itself the complex of connected parts. Purpose, as issuing from a thinker, comprises more than the mere unit; essentially it comprises that universal side of the action, i.e. the intention.

Etymologically, *Absicht* (intention) implies abstraction, either the form of universality or the extraction of a particular aspect of the concrete thing. The endeavour to justify an action by the intention behind it involves the isolation of one or other of its single aspects which is alleged to be the essence of

[1] See Remark to Paragraph 26.—ED.

the action on its subjective side.

To judge an action as an external deed without yet determining its rightness or wrongness is simply to bestow on it a universal predicate, i.e. to describe it as burning, killing, &c.

The discrete character of the external world shows what the nature of that world is, namely a chain of external relations. Actuality is touched in the first instance only at a single point (arson, for instance, *directly* concerns only a tiny section of the firewood, i.e. is describable in a proposition, not a judgement), but the universal nature of this point entails its expansion. In a living thing, the single part is there in its immediacy not as a mere part, but as an organ in which the universal is really present as the universal; hence in murder, it is not a piece of flesh, as something isolated, which is injured, but life itself which is injured in that piece of flesh. It is subjective reflection, ignorant of the logical nature of the single and the universal, which indulges *ad libitum* in the subdivision of single parts and consequences; and yet it is the nature of the finite deed itself to contain such separable contingencies.—The device of *dolus indirectus* has its basis in these considerations. [A.]

120. The right of intention is that the universal quality of the action shall not merely be implicit but shall be known by the agent, and so shall have lain from the start in his subjective will. Vice versa, what may be called the right of the objectivity of action is the right of the action to evince itself as known and willed by the subject as a *thinker*.

This right to insight of this kind entails the complete, or almost complete, irresponsibility of children, imbeciles, lunatics, &c., for their actions.—But just as actions on their external side as events include accidental consequences, so there is involved in the subjective agent an indeterminacy whose degree depends on the strength and force of his self-consciousness and circumspection. This indeterminacy, however, may not be taken into account except in connexion with childhood or imbecility, lunacy, &c., since it is only such well marked states of mind that nullify the trait of thought and freedom of will, and permit us to treat the agent as devoid of the dignity of being a thinker and a will.

121. The universal quality of the action is the manifold content of the action as such, reduced to the simple form of universality. But the subject, an entity reflected into himself and so particular in correlation with the particularity of his object, has in his end his own particular content, and this content is the soul of the action and determines its character. The fact that this moment of the particularity of the agent is contained and realized in the action constitutes subjective freedom in its more concrete sense, the right of the subject to find his satisfaction in the action. [A.]

122. It is on the strength of this particular aspect that the action has subjective worth or interest for me. In contrast with this *end*—the content of the intention—the direct character of the action in its further content is reduced to a *means*. In so far as such an end is something finite, it may in its turn be reduced to a means to some further intention and so on *ad infinitum*.

123. For the content of these ends nothing is available at this point except (*a*) pure activity itself, i.e. the activity present owing to the fact that the subject puts himself into whatever he is to look upon and promote as his end. Men are willing to be *active* in pursuit of what interests them, or should interest them, as something which is their own. (*β*) A more determinate content, however, the still abstract and formal freedom of subjectivity possesses only in its natural subjective embodiment, i.e. in needs, inclinations, passions, opinions, fancies, &c. The satisfaction of these is welfare or happiness, both in general and in its particular species—the ends of the whole sphere of finitude.

Here—the standpoint of relation (see Paragraph 108), when the subject is characterized by his self-difference and so counts as a particular—is the place where the content of the natural will (see Paragraph 11) comes on the scene. But the will here is not as it is in its immediacy; on the contrary, this content now belongs to a will reflected into itself and so is elevated to become a universal end, the end of welfare or happiness;[1] this happens at the level of the thinking which does not yet apprehend the will in its freedom but reflects on its content as on one natural and given—the level, for example, of the time of Croesus and Solon.[2] [A.]

124. Since the subjective satisfaction of the individual himself (including the recognition which he receives by way of honour and fame) is also part and parcel of the achievement of ends of absolute worth, it follows that the demand that such an end alone shall appear as willed and attained, like the view that, in willing, objective and subjective ends are mutually exclusive, is an empty dogmatism of the abstract Understanding. And this dogmatism is more than empty, it is pernicious if it passes into the assertion that because subjective satisfaction is present, as it always is when any task is brought to completion, it is what the agent intended in essence to secure and that the objective end was in his eyes only a means to that.— What the subject is, is the series of his actions.

If these are a series of worthless productions, then the subjectivity of his willing is just as worthless. But if the series of his deeds is of a substantive nature, then the same is true also of the individual's inner will.

The right of the subject's particularity, his right to be satisfied, or in other words the right of subjective freedom, is the pivot and centre of the difference between antiquity and modern times. This right in its infinity is given expression in Christianity and it has become the universal effective principle of a new form of civilization. Amongst the primary shapes which this right assumes are love, romanticism, the quest for the eternal salvation of the individual, &c.; next come moral convictions and conscience; and, finally, the other forms, some of which come into prominence in what follows as the principle of civil society and as moments in the constitution of the state, while others appear in the course of history, particularly the history of art, science, and philosophy.[3]

Now this principle of particularity is, to be sure, one moment of the antithesis, and in the first place at least it is just as much identical with the universal as distinct from it. Abstract reflection, however, fixes this moment in its distinction from and opposition to the universal and so produces a view of morality as nothing but a bitter, unending, struggle against self-satisfaction, as the command: "Do with abhorrence what duty enjoins."

It is just this type of ratiocination which adduces that familiar psychological view of history which understands how to belittle and disparage all great deeds and great men by transforming into the main intention and operative motive of actions the inclinations and passions which likewise found their satisfaction from the achievement of something substantive, the fame and honour, &c., consequential on such actions, in a word their particular aspect, the aspect which it has decreed in advance to be something in itself pernicious. Such ratiocination assures us that, while great actions and the efficiency which has subsisted through a series of them have produced greatness in the world and have had as their consequences for the individual agent power, honour, and fame, still what belongs to the individual is not the greatness itself but what has accrued to him from it, this purely particular and external result; because this result is a consequence, it is therefore supposed to have been the agent's end and even his sole end. Reflection of this sort stops short at the subjective side of great men, since it itself stands on purely subjective ground, and consequently it overlooks what is substantive in this emptiness of its own making. This is the view of those valet psychologists "for whom there are no heroes, not because there are no heroes, but because these psychologists are only valets."[4] [A.]

125. The subjective element of the will, with its

---

[1] *Enc.* [1st edn.], §§ 395 ff. [3rd edn. §§ 478 ff.].
[2] Cf. Herodotus, i. 30–3.—ED.

[3] See Paragraphs 120 ff.—ED.
[4] *Phenomenology* [1st edn.], p. 616 [Eng. tr. p. 673].

particular content—welfare, is reflected into itself and infinite and so stands related to the universal element, to the principle of the will. This moment of universality, posited first of all within this particular content itself, is the welfare of others also, or, specified completely, though quite emptily, the welfare of all. The welfare of many other unspecified particulars is thus also an essential end and right of subjectivity. But since the absolutely universal, in distinction from such a particular content, has not so far been further determined than as "the right," it follows that these ends of particularity, differing as they do from the universal, may be in conformity with it, but they also may not.

126. My particularity, however, like that of others, is only a right at all in so far as I am a free entity. Therefore it may not make claims for itself in contradiction to this its substantive basis, and an intention to secure my welfare or that of others (and it is particularly in this latter case that such an intention is called "moral") cannot justify an action which is wrong.

It is one of the most prominent of the corrupt maxims of our time to enter a plea for the so-called "moral" intention behind wrong actions and to imagine bad men with well-meaning hearts, i.e. hearts willing their own welfare and perhaps that of others also. This doctrine is rooted in the "benevolence" (*guten Herzens*) of the pre-Kantian philosophers and constitutes, e.g., the quintessence of well-known touching dramatic productions; but to-day it has been resuscitated in a more extravagant form, and inner enthusiasm and the heart, i.e. the form of particularity as such, have been made the criterion of right, rationality, and excellence. The result is that crime and the thoughts that lead to it, be they fancies however trite and empty, or opinions however wild, are to be regarded as right, rational, and excellent, simply because they issue from men's hearts and enthusiasms. (See the Remark to Paragraph 140, where more details are given.)

Incidentally, however, attention must be paid to the point of view from which right and welfare are being treated here. We are considering right as abstract right and welfare as the particular welfare of the single agent. The so-called "general good," the welfare of the state, i.e. the right of mind actual and concrete, is quite a different sphere, a sphere in which abstract right is a subordinate moment like particular welfare and the happiness of the individual. As was remarked above,[1] it is one of the commonest blunders of abstract thinking to make private rights and private welfare count as *absolute* in opposition to the universality of the state. [A.]

127. The particularity of the interests of the natural will, taken in their entirety as a single

[1] See the Remark to Paragraph 29.—ED.

whole, is personal existence or life. In extreme danger and in conflict with the rightful property of someone else, this life may claim (as a right, not a mercy) a right of distress, because in such a situation there is on the one hand an infinite injury to a man's existence and the consequent loss of rights altogether, and on the other hand only an injury to a single restricted embodiment of freedom, and this implies a recognition both of right as such and also of the injured man's capacity for rights, because the injury affects only *this* property of his.

The right of distress is the basis of *beneficium competentiae* whereby a debtor is allowed to retain of his tools, farming implements, clothes, or, in short, of his resources, i.e. of his creditor's property, so much as is regarded as indispensable if he is to continue to support life—to support it, of course, on his own social level. [A.]

128. This distress reveals the finitude and therefore the contingency of both right and welfare, of right as the abstract embodiment of freedom without embodying the particular person, and of welfare as the sphere of the particular will without the universality of right. In this way they are *established* as one-sided and ideal, the character which in *conception* they already possessed. Right has already (see Paragraph 106) determined its embodiment as the particular will; and subjectivity, in its particularity as a comprehensive whole, is itself the *embodiment* of freedom (see Paragraph 127), while as the infinite relation of the will to itself, it is implicitly the *universal* element in freedom. The two moments present in right and subjectivity, thus integrated and attaining their truth, their identity, though in the first instance still remaining *relative* to one another, are (*a*) the good (as the concrete, absolutely determinate, universal), and (*b*) conscience (as infinite subjectivity inwardly conscious and inwardly determining its content).

Sub-section III

GOOD AND CONSCIENCE

129. The good is the Idea as the unity of the concept of the will with the particular will. In this unity, abstract right, welfare, the subjectivity of knowing and the contingency of external fact, have their independent self-subsistence superseded, though at the same time they are still contained and retained within it in their essence. The good is thus freedom realized the absolute end and aim of the world. [A.]

130. In this Idea, welfare has no independent validity as the embodiment of a single particular will but only as universal welfare and essentially as universal in principle, i.e. as according with freedom. Welfare without right is not a good. Similarly, right without welfare is not the good; *fiat justitia* should not be followed by *pereat mundus*. Consequently, since the good must of necessity be actualized through the particular will and is at the same time its substance, it has absolute right in contrast with the abstract right of property and the particular aims of welfare. If either of these moments becomes distinguished from the good, it has validity only in so far as it accords with the good and is subordinated to it.

131. For the subjective will, the good and the good alone is the essential, and the subjective will has value and dignity only in so far as its insight and intention accord with the good. Inasmuch as the good is at this point still only this *abstract* Idea of good, the subjective will has not yet been caught up into it and established as according with it. Consequently, it stands in a *relation* to the good, and the relation is that the good *ought* to be substantive for it, i.e. it ought to make the good its aim and realize it completely, while the good on its side has in the subjective will its only means of stepping into actuality. [A.]

132. The right of the subjective will is that whatever it is to recognize as valid shall be seen by it as good, and that an action, as its aim entering upon external objectivity, shall be imputed to it as right or wrong, good or evil, legal or illegal, in accordance with its *knowledge* of the worth which the action has in this objectivity.

The good is in principle the essence of the will in its substantiality and universality, i.e. of the will in its truth, and therefore it exists simply and solely in thinking and by means of thinking. Hence assertions such as "man cannot know the truth but has to do only with phenomena," or "thinking injures the good will" are dogmas depriving mind not only of intellectual but also of all ethical worth and dignity.

The right of giving recognition only to what my insight sees as rational is the highest right of the subject, although owing to its subjective character it remains a formal right; against it the right which reason *qua* the objective possesses over the subject remains firmly established.

On account of its formal character, insight is capable equally of being true and of being mere opinion and error. The individual's acquisition of this right of insight is, on the principles of the sphere which is still moral only, part and parcel of his particular

subjective education. I may demand from myself, and regard it as one of my subjective rights, that my insight into an obligation shall be based on good reasons, that I shall be convinced of the obligation and even that I shall apprehend it from its concept and fundamental nature. But whatever I may claim for the satisfaction of my conviction about the character of an action as good, permitted, or forbidden, and so about its imputability in respect of this character, this in no way detracts from the right of objectivity.

This right of insight into the good is distinct from the right of insight in respect of action as such (see Paragraph 117); the form of the right of objectivity which corresponds to the latter is this, that since action is an alteration which is to take place in an actual world and so will have recognition in it, it must in general accord with what has validity there. Whoever wills to act in this world of actuality has *eo ipso* submitted himself to its laws and recognized the right of objectivity.

Similarly, in the state as the objectivity of the concept of reason, legal responsibility cannot be tied down to what an individual may hold to be or not to be in accordance with his reason, or to his subjective insight into what is right or wrong, good or evil, or to the demands which he makes for the satisfaction of his conviction. In this objective field, the right of insight is valid as insight into the legal or illegal, *qua* into what is recognized as right, and it is restricted to its elementary meaning, i.e. to knowledge in the sense of acquaintance with what is legal and to that extent obligatory. By means of the publicity of the laws and the universality of manners,[1] the state removes from the right of insight its formal aspect and the contingency which it still retains for the subject at the level of morality. The subject's right to know action in its specific character as good or evil, legal or illegal, has the result of diminishing or cancelling in this respect too[2] the responsibility of children, imbeciles, and lunatics, although it is impossible to delimit precisely either childhood, imbecility, &c., or their degree of irresponsibility. But to turn momentary blindness, the goad of passion, intoxication, or, in a word, what is called the strength of sensual impulse (excluding impulses which are the basis of the right of distress—see Paragraph 127) into *reasons* when the imputation, specific character, and culpability of a crime are in question, and to look upon such circumstances as if they took away the criminal's guilt, again means (compare Paragraph 100 and the Remark to Paragraph 120)[3] failing to treat the criminal in accordance with the right and honour due to him as a man; for the nature of man consists precisely in the fact that he is essentially something universal, not a being whose knowledge is an abstractly momentary and piecemeal affair.

Just as what the incendiary really sets on fire is not the isolated square inch of wooden surface to which

---

[1] See Paragraph 151.—ED.
[2] See Remark to Paragraph 120.—ED.
[3] All editions read "119."—ED.

he applies his torch, but the universal in that square inch, e.g. the house as a whole, so, as subject, he is neither the single existent of this moment of time nor this isolated hot feeling of revenge. If he were, he would be an animal which would have to be knocked on the head as dangerous and unsafe because of its liability to fits of madness.

The claim is made that the criminal in the moment of his action must have had a "clear idea" of the wrong and its culpability before it can be imputed to him as a crime. At first sight, this claim seems to preserve the right of his subjectivity, but the truth is that it deprives him of his indwelling nature as intelligent, a nature whose effective presence is not confined to the "clear ideas" of Wolff's psychology, and only in cases of lunacy is it so deranged as to be divorced from the knowing and doing of isolated things.

The sphere in which these extenuating circumstances come into consideration as grounds for the mitigation of punishment is a sphere other than that of rights, the sphere of pardon.[1]

133. The particular subject is related to the good as to the essence of his will, and hence his will's obligation arises directly in this relation.[2] Since particularity is distinct from the good and falls within the subjective will, the good is characterized to begin with only as the universal abstract essentiality of the will, i.e. as duty. Since duty is thus abstract and universal in character, it should be done for duty's sake. [A.]

134. Because every action explicitly calls for a particular content and a specific end, while duty as an abstraction entails nothing of the kind, the question arises: what is my duty? As an answer nothing is so far available except: (a) to do the right, and (b) to strive after welfare, one's own welfare, and welfare in universal terms, the welfare of others (see Paragraph 119).[3] [A.]

135. These specific duties, however, are not contained in the definition of duty itself; but since both of them are conditioned and restricted, they eo ipso bring about the transition to the higher sphere of the unconditioned, the sphere of duty. Duty itself in the moral self-consciousness is the essence or the universality of that consciousness, the way in which it is inwardly related to itself alone; all that is left to it, therefore, is abstract universality, and for its determinate character it has identity without content, or the abstractly positive, the indeterminate.

However essential it is to give prominence to the pure unconditioned self-determination of the will as the root of duty, and to the way in which knowl-edge of the will, thanks to Kant's philosophy, has won its firm foundation and starting-point for the first time owing to the thought of its infinite autonomy, still to adhere to the exclusively moral position, without making the transition to the conception of ethics, is to reduce this gain to an empty formalism, and the science of morals to the preaching of duty for duty's sake. From this point of view, no immanent doctrine of duties is possible; of course, material may be brought in from outside and particular duties may be arrived at accordingly, but if the definition of duty is taken to be the absence of contradiction, formal correspondence with itself— which is nothing but abstract indeterminacy stabilized—then no transition is possible to the specification of particular duties nor, if some such particular content for acting comes under consideration, is there any criterion in that principle for deciding whether it is or is not a duty. On the contrary, by this means any wrong or immoral line of conduct may be justified.

Kant's further formulation,[4] the possibility of visualizing an action as a *universal* maxim, does lead to the more concrete visualization of a situation, but in itself it contains no principle beyond abstract identity and the "absence of contradiction" already mentioned.

The absence of property contains in itself just as little contradiction as the non-existence of this or that nation, family, &c., or the death of the whole human race. But if it is already established on other grounds and presupposed that property and human life are to exist and be respected, then indeed it is a contradiction to commit theft or murder; a contradiction must be a contradiction of something, i.e. of some content presupposed from the start as a fixed principle. It is to a principle of that kind alone, therefore, that an action can be related either by correspondence or contradiction. But if duty is to be willed simply for duty's sake and not for the sake of some content, it is only a formal identity whose nature it is to exclude all content and specification.

The further antinomies and configurations of this never-ending ought-to-be, in which the exclusively moral way of thinking—thinking in terms of *relation*—just wanders to and fro without being able to resolve them and get beyond the ought-to-be, I have developed in my *Phenomenology of Mind*.[5] [A.]

136. Because of the abstract characterization of the good, the other moment of the Idea— particularity in general—falls within subjectivity. Subjectivity in its universality reflected into itself is the subject's absolute inward certainty (*Gewissheit*) of himself, that which establishes the particular and is the determining and decisive element in him, his conscience (*Gewissen*). [A.]

[1] See Paragraph 282.—Ed.
[2] See Paragraph 131.—Ed.
[3] Together with Paragraph 125.—Ed.
[4] Cf. Kant, *Critique of Practical Reason,* Analytic, Chap. i, sections 1-6.—Ed.
[5] [1st edn.] pp. 550 ff. [Eng. tr. pp. 615 ff.]. Cf *Enc.* [1st edn.], §§ 420 ff. [3rd edn. §§ 507 ff.].

137. True conscience is the disposition to will what is absolutely good. It therefore has fixed principles and it is aware of these as its explicitly objective determinants and duties. In distinction from this its content (i.e. truth), conscience is only the formal side of the activity of the will, which as *this* will has no special content of its own. But the objective system of these principles and duties, and the union of subjective knowing with this system, is not present until we come to the standpoint of ethical life. Here at the abstract standpoint of morality, conscience lacks this objective content and so its explicit character is that of infinite abstract self-certainty, which at the same time is for this very reason the self-certainty of *this* subject.

Conscience is the expression of the absolute title of subjective self-consciousness to know in itself and from within itself what is right and obligatory, to give recognition only to what it thus knows as good, and at the same time to maintain that whatever in this way it knows and wills is in truth right and obligatory. Conscience as this unity of subjective knowing with what is absolute is a sanctuary which it would be sacrilege to violate. But whether the conscience of a specific individual corresponds with this Idea of conscience, or whether what it takes or declares to be good is actually so, is ascertainable only from the content of the good it seeks to realize. What is right and obligatory is the absolutely rational element in the will's volitions and therefore it is not in essence the *particular* property of an individual, and its form is not that of feeling or any other private (i.e. sensuous) type of knowing, but essentially that of universals determined by thought, i.e. the form of laws and principles. Conscience is therefore subject to the judgement of its truth or falsity, and when it appeals only to itself for a decision, it is directly at variance with what it wishes to be, namely the rule for a mode of conduct which is rational, absolutely valid, and universal. For this reason, the state cannot give recognition to conscience in its private form as subjective knowing, any more than science can grant validity to subjective opinion, dogmatism, and the appeal to a subjective opinion. In true conscience, its elements are not different, but they may become so, and it is the determining element, the subjectivity of willing and knowing, which can sever itself from the true content of conscience, establish its own independence, and reduce that content to a form and a show. The ambiguity in connexion with conscience lies therefore in this: it is presupposed to mean the *identity* of subjective knowing and willing with the true good, and so is claimed and recognized to be something sacrosanct; and yet at the same time, as the mere subjective reflection of self-consciousness into itself, it still claims for itself the title due, solely on the strength of its absolutely valid rational *content*, to that identity alone.

At the level of morality, distinguished as it is in this book from the level of ethics, it is only formal conscience that is to be found. True conscience has been mentioned only to indicate its distinction from the other and to obviate the possible misunderstanding that here, where it is only formal conscience that is under consideration, the argument is about true conscience. The latter is part of the ethical disposition which comes before us for the first time in the following section.[1]—The religious conscience, however, does not belong to this sphere at all. [A.]

138. This subjectivity, *qua* abstract self-determination and pure certainty of oneself alone, as readily evaporates into itself the whole determinate character of right, duty, and existence, as it remains both the power to judge, to determine from within itself alone, what is good in respect of any content, and also the power to which the good, at first only an ideal and an ought-to-be, owes its actuality.

The self-consciousness which has attained this absolute reflection into itself knows itself in this reflection to be the kind of consciousness which is and should be beyond the reach of every existent and given specific determination. As one of the commoner features of history (e.g. in Socrates,[2] the Stoics, and others), the tendency to look deeper into oneself and to know and determine from within oneself what is right and good appears in ages when what is recognized as right and good in contemporary manners cannot satisfy the will of better men. When the existing world of freedom has become faithless to the will of better men, that will fails to find itself in the duties there recognized and must try to find in the ideal world of the inner life alone the harmony which actuality has lost. Once self-consciousness has grasped and secured its formal right in this way, everything depends on the character of the content which it gives to itself. [A.]

139. Once self-consciousness has reduced all otherwise valid duties to emptiness and itself to the sheer inwardness of the will, it has become the potentiality of either making the absolutely universal its principle, or equally well of elevating above the universal the self-will of private particularity, taking that as its principle and realizing it through its actions, i.e. it has become potentially evil.

To have a conscience, if conscience is only formal subjectivity, is simply to be on the verge of slipping into evil; in independent self-certainty, with its independence of knowledge and decision, both morality and evil have their common root.

The origin of evil in general is to be found in the mystery of freedom (i.e. in the speculative aspect of freedom), the mystery whereby freedom of ne-

---

[1] See Paragraph 268.—ED.
[2] See Paragraphs 279 and 343.—ED.

cessity arises out of the natural level of the will and is something inward in comparison with that level.[1] It is this natural level of the will which comes into existence as a self-contradiction, as incompatible with itself in this opposition, and so it is just this particularity of the will which later makes itself evil. That is to say, particularity is always duality; here it is the opposition of the natural level and the inwardness of the will. In this opposition, the latter is only a relative and abstract subjectivity which can draw its content only from the determinate content of the natural will, from desire, impulse, inclination, &c. Now it is said of these desires, impulses, &c., that they may be either good or evil. But since the will here makes into a determinant of its content both these impulses in this contingent character which they possess as natural, and also, therefore, the form which it has at this point, the form of particularity itself, it follows that it is set in opposition to the universal as inner objectivity, to the good, which comes on the scene as the opposite extreme to immediate objectivity, the natural pure and simple, as soon as the will is reflected into itself and consciousness is a *knowing* consciousness. It is in this opposition that this inwardness of the will is evil. Man is therefore evil by a conjunction between his natural or undeveloped character and his reflection into himself; and therefore evil belongs neither to nature as such by itself—unless nature were supposed to be the natural character of the will which rests in its particular content—nor to introverted reflection by itself, i.e. cognition in general, unless this were to maintain itself in that opposition to the universal.

With this facet of evil, its necessity, there is inevitably combined the fact that this same evil is condemned to be that which of necessity ought not to be, i.e. the fact that evil ought to be annulled. It is not that there ought never to be a diremption of any sort in the will—on the contrary, it is just this level of diremption which distinguishes man from the unreasoning animal; the point is that the will should not rest at that level and cling to the particular as if that and not the universal were the essential thing; it should overcome the diremption as a nullity. Further, as to this necessity of evil, it is subjectivity, as infinite self-reflection, which is present in and confronted by this opposition of universal and particular; if it rests in this opposition, i.e. if it is evil, then it is *eo ipso* independent, regarding itself as isolated, and is itself this self-will.[2] Therefore if the individual subject as such does evil, the evil is purely and simply his own responsibility. [A.]

140. In every end of a self-conscious subject, there is a *positive* aspect (see Paragraph 135) necessarily present because the end is what is purposed in an actual concrete action. This aspect he knows how to elicit and emphasize, and he may then proceed to regard it as a duty or a fine intention. By so interpreting it, he is enabled to pass off his action as good in the eyes both of himself and others, despite the fact that, owing to his reflective character and his knowledge of the universal aspect of the will, he is aware of the contrast between this aspect and the essentially *negative* content of his action. To impose in this way on others is hypocrisy; while to impose on oneself is a stage beyond hypocrisy, a stage at which subjectivity claims to be absolute.[3]

This final, most abstruse, form of evil, whereby evil is perverted into good and good into evil, and consciousness, in being aware of its power to effect this perversion, is also made aware of itself as absolute, is the highwater mark of subjectivity at the level of morality; it is the form into which evil has blossomed in our present epoch, a result due to philosophy, i.e. to a shallowness of thought which has twisted a profound concept into this shape and usurped the name of philosophy, just as it has arrogated to evil the name of good.

In this Remark I will indicate briefly the chief forms of this subjectivity which have become current.

(*a*) In hypocrisy the following moments are contained: (α) knowledge of the true universal, whether knowledge in the form merely of a feeling for right and duty, or of a deeper cognition and apprehension of them; (β) volition of the particular which conflicts with this universal; (γ) conscious comparison of both moments (α) and (β), so that the conscious subject is aware in willing that his particular volition is evil in character.

These points are descriptive of acting with a bad conscience; hypocrisy proper involves something more.

At one time great importance was attached to the question whether an action was evil only in so far as it was done with a bad conscience, i.e. with explicit knowledge of the three moments just specified. The inference from an affirmative answer is admirably drawn by Pascal: *Ils seront tous damnés ces demi-pécheurs, qui ont quelque amour pour la vertu. Mais pour ces franc-pécheurs, pécheurs endurcis, pécheurs sans mélange, pleins et achevés, l'enfer ne les tient pas; ils ont trompé le diable à force de s'y abandonner.*[4]

---

[1] See Paragraphs 11-15 and the Remark to Paragraph 132.—Ed.

[2] i.e., the self-will mentioned in Paragraph 139.—Ed.

[3] See Paragraphs 120 ff.—Ed.

[4] *Provincial Letters*, iv. In the same context, Pascal also quotes Christ's intercession on the Cross for his enemies: "Father, forgive them, for they know not what they do"—a superfluous prayer if the fact that they did not know what they did made their action innocent and so took away the need of forgiveness. Pascal quotes there too Aristotle's distinction (*Ethics*, 1110^b24) between the man who acts οὐκ εἰδώς and the one who acts ἀγνοῶν in the former type of ignorance, his action is not freely willed (here the ignorance depends on external circumstances, see above, Paragraph 117) and his action is not imputable to him. But of the latter Aristotle says: "Every wicked man is ignorant of what he ought to do and what he ought to refrain from doing; and it is this kind of failure (ἁμαρτία) which makes men unjust and in

The subjective right of self-consciousness to know whether an action is truly good or evil in character must not be thought of as so colliding with the absolute right of the objectivity of this character that the two rights are represented as separable, indifferent to one another, and related only accidentally. It was such a conception of their relation that lay in particular at the root of the old questions about efficacious grace. On its formal side, evil is most peculiarly the individual's own, since (a) it is precisely his subjectivity establishing itself purely and simply for itself, and for that reason it is purely and simply the individual's own responsibility (see Paragraph 139 and the Remark thereto); (b) on his objective side man accords with his concept inasmuch as he is mind, in a word a rational entity, and has in his own nature as such the character of self-knowing universality. Therefore it means failing to treat him with the respect due to his concept if his good side is divorced from him, so that the character of his evil action as evil is divorced from him too and is not imputed to him as evil. How determinate is the consciousness of these moments in distinction from one another, or to what extent it has developed or failed to develop in clarity so as to become a recognition of them, and to what degree an evil action has been done with a conscience more or less downright evil—all these questions are the more trivial aspect of the matter, the aspect mainly concerned with the empirical.

(b) Evil and doing evil with a bad conscience, however, is not quite hypocrisy. Into hypocrisy there enters in addition the formal character of falsity, first the falsity of holding up evil as good in the eyes of others, of setting oneself up to all appearance as good, conscientious, pious, and so on— conduct which in these circumstances is only a trick to deceive others. Secondly, however, the bad man may find in his good conduct on other occasions, or in his piety, or, in a word, in good reasons, a justification in his own eyes for the evil he does, because he can use these reasons to pervert its apparent character from evil into good. His ability to do this depends on the subjectivity which, as abstract negativity, knows that all determinations are subordinate to itself and issue from its own will.

(c) In this perversion of evil into good we may prima facie include the form of subjectivism known as Probabilism. Its guiding principle is that an action is permissible, and may be done with an easy conscience, provided that the agent can hunt out any single good reason for it, be it only the authority of a single theologian, and even if other theologians are known by the agent to dissent ever so widely from that authority. Even in this idea there is still

present the correct apprehension that authority and a reason based on authority gives probability only, although this is supposed to be enough to produce an easy conscience; it is granted in Probabilism that a good reason is inevitably of such a character that there may exist along with it different reasons at least as good. Even here we must recognize a vestige of objectivity in the admission that it is a reason which should be the determining factor. But since the discrimination between good and evil is made to depend on all those good reasons, including theological authorities too, despite the fact that they are so numerous and contradictory, the implication is that it is not this objectivity of the thing, but subjectivity, which has the last word. This means that caprice and self-will are made the arbiters of good and evil, and the result is that ethics as well as religious feeling is undermined. But the fact that it is private subjectivity to which the decision falls is one which Probabilism does not openly avow as its principle; on the contrary, as has already been stated, it gives out that it is some reason or other which is decisive, and Probabilism is to that extent still a form of hypocrisy.

(d) In the stages of subjectivism, the next in ascending order is the view that the goodness of the will consists in its willing the good; this *willing* of the abstract good is supposed to suffice, in fact to be the sole requisite, to make its action good. As the willing of something determinate, action has a content, but good in the abstract determines nothing, and hence it devolves on particular subjectivity to give this content its character and constituents. Just as in Probabilism anyone who is not himself a learned *Révérend Père* may have the subsumption of a determinate content under the universal predicate "good" effected for him by the sole authority of one such theologian, so here every subject, without any further qualification, is invested with this honour of giving a content to good in the abstract, or in other words subsuming a content under a universal. This content is only one of the many elements in an action as a concrete whole, and the others may perhaps entail its description as "criminal" and "bad." That determinate content which I, as subject, give to the good, however, is the good known to me in the action, i.e. it is my good intention (see Paragraph 114).[1] Thus there arises a contradiction between descriptions: according to one the action is good, according to the other it is criminal. Hence also there seems to arise, in connexion with a concrete action, the question whether in such circumstances the intention behind it is actually good. It may generally be the case that the good is what is actually intended; but this in fact must always be the case if it is held that good in the abstract is the subject's determining motive. Where wrong is done through an action which is well intentioned but in other respects criminal and bad, the wrong so done must, of course, also be good, and the important question

general bad. . . . An ignorant choice" between good and evil "is the cause not of the action's being involuntary" (of being nonimputable) "but only of its being wicked." Aristotle evidently had a deeper insight into the connexion between knowing and willing than has become common in a superficial philosophy which teaches that the opposite of knowledge, the heart and enthusiasm, are the true principles of ethical action.

[1] So Hegel's first edition. All other editions read "111." Sterrett reads "119."—ED.

would seem to be: which of these sides of the action is really the essential one? This objective question, however, is here out of place, or rather it is the subjective consciousness alone whose decision constitutes objectivity at this point. Besides, "essential" and "good" mean the same thing; one is just as much an abstraction as the other. Good is that which is essential in respect of the will; and the essential in this respect should be precisely this, that my action be characterized as good in my eyes. But the subsumption under the good of any content one pleases is the direct and explicit result of the fact that this abstract good is totally devoid of content and so is simply reduced to meaning anything positive, i.e. to something which is valid from some single point of view and which in its immediate character may even be valid as an essential end, as for example to do good to the poor, to take thought for myself, my life, my family, and so forth. Further, just as the good is the abstract, so the bad too must be without content and derive its specification from my subjectivity; and it is in this way also that there arises the moral end of hating and uprooting the bad, the nature of the bad being left unspecified.

Theft, cowardice, murder, and so forth, as actions, i.e. as achievements of a subjective will, have the immediate character of being satisfactions of such a will and therefore of being something positive. In order to make the action a good one, it is only a question of recognizing this positive aspect of the action as my intention, and this then becomes the essential aspect in virtue of which the action is made good, simply because I recognize it as the good in my intention. Theft in order to do good to the poor, theft or flight from battle for the sake of fulfilling one's duty to care for one's life or one's family (a poor family perhaps into the bargain), murder out of hate or revenge (i.e. in order to satisfy one's sense of one's own rights or of right in general, or one's sense of another's wickedness, of wrong done by him to oneself or to others or to the world or the nation at large, by extirpating this wicked individual who is wickedness incarnate, and thereby contributing at least one's quota to the project of uprooting the bad)—all these actions are made well intentioned and therefore good by this method of taking account of the positive aspect of their content. Only the bare minimum of intelligence is required to discover in any action, as those learned theologians can, a positive side and so a good reason for it and a good intention behind it. Hence it has been said that in the strict sense there are no wicked men, since no one wills evil for the sake of evil, i.e. no one wills a pure negative as such. On the contrary, everyone always wills something positive, and therefore, on the view we are considering, something good. In this abstract good the distinction between good and evil has vanished together with all concrete duties; for this reason, simply to will the good and to have a good intention in acting is more like evil than good, because the good willed is only this abstract form of good and therefore to make it

concrete devolves on the arbitrary will of the subject.

To this context there also belongs the notorious maxim: "The end justifies the means." In itself and prima facie this expression is trivial and pointless. Quite so, one may retort in terms equally general, a just end of course justifies the means, while an unjust end does not. The phrase: "If the end is right, so is the means" is a tautology, since the means is precisely that which is nothing in itself but is for the sake of something else, and therein, i.e. in the end, has its purpose and worth—provided of course it be truly a means.

But when someone says that the end justifies the means, his purport is not confined to this bare tautology; he understands by the words something more specific, namely that to use as means to a good end something which in itself is simply not a means at all, to violate something in itself sacrosanct, in short to commit a crime as a means to a good end, is permissible and even one's bounden duty. (i) There floats before the minds of those who say that the end justifies the means a vague consciousness of the dialectic of the aforesaid "positive" element in isolated legal or ethical principles, or of such equally vague general maxims as: "Thou shalt not kill," or "Thou shalt take thought for thy welfare and the welfare of thy family." Executioners and soldiers have not merely the right but the duty to kill men, though there it has been precisely laid down what kind of men and what circumstances make the killing permissible and obligatory. So also my welfare and the welfare of my family must be subordinated to higher ends and so reduced to means to their attainment. (ii) And yet what bears the mark of crime is not a general maxim of that kind, left vague and still subject to a dialectic; on the contrary, its specific character is already objectively fixed. Now what is set up against such a determinate crime, what is supposed to have deprived the crime of its criminal nature, is the justifying end, and this is simply subjective opinion about what is good and better. What happens here is the same as what happens when the will stops at willing good in the abstract, i.e. the absolute and valid determinate character assigned to good and evil, right and wrong, is entirely swept away and the determination of them is ascribed instead to the individual's feeling, imagination, and caprice.

(e) Subjective opinion is at last expressly given out as the measuring-rod of right and duty and it is supposed that the conviction which holds something to be right is to decide the ethical character of an action. Since the good we will to do is here still without content, the principle of conviction only adds the information that the subsumption of an action under the category of good is purely a personal matter. If this be so, the very pretence of an ethical objectivity has totally disappeared. A doctrine like this is directly connected with the self-styled philosophy, often mentioned already, which denies that the truth is knowable—and the truth of mind *qua* will, the rationality of mind in its self-actualizing process, is the laws of ethics. Asserting, as such philosophizing does, that the knowledge of the true is an empty vanity, transcending the territory of science (which is supposed to be mere appearance), it must in the matter of action at once find its principle also in the apparent; thereby ethics is reduced to the special theory of life held by the individual and to his private conviction. The degradation into which philosophy has thus sunk appears doubtless at a first glance to be only an affair of supreme indifference, an occurrence confined to the trivial field of academic futilities; but the view necessarily makes itself a home in ethics, an essential part of philosophy; and it is then that the true meaning of these theories makes its first appearance in and is apprehended by the world of actuality.

The result of the dissemination of the view that subjective conviction, and it alone, decides the ethical character of an action is that the charge of hypocrisy, once so frequent, is now rarely heard; you can only qualify wickedness as hypocrisy on the assumption that certain actions are inherently and actually misdeeds, vices, and crimes, and that the defaulter is necessarily aware of them as such, because he is aware of and recognizes the principles and outward acts of piety and honesty even in the pretence to which he misapplies them. In other words, it was generally assumed as regards evil that it is a duty to know the good and to be aware of its distinction from evil. In any case, however, it was an absolute injunction which forbade the commission of vicious and criminal actions and which insisted on such actions being imputed to the agent, so far as he was a man and not a beast. But if a good heart, a good intention, a subjective conviction are set forth as the sources from which conduct derives its worth, then there is no longer any hypocrisy or immorality at all; for whatever a man does, he can always justify by the reflection on it of good intentions and motives, and by the influence of that conviction it is good.[1] Thus there is no longer anything absolutely vicious or criminal; and instead of the above-mentioned [2] frank and free, hardened and unperturbed sinner, we have the man who is conscious of being fully justified by intention and conviction. My good intention in my action and my conviction of its goodness make it good. We speak

[1] "That he feels completely *convinced* I have not the least doubt. But how many men are led by such feelings of conviction into the worst of misdeeds! Besides, if everything may be excused on this ground, then that terminates the rational judgement of good and wicked, honourable and shameful, resolutions. Lunacy in that case would have equal rights with reason; or in other words reason would have no rights whatever, its judgement would cease to have any validity. Its voice would be a minus quantity; truth would be the possession of the man with no doubts! I tremble at the results of such toleration, for it would be exclusively to the advantage of unreason." (F. H. Jacobi to Count Holmer, on Count Stolberg's change of faith, Eutin, August 5th, 1800. *Brennus,* Berlin, August 1802.)

[2] In the quotation from Pascal in Remark (a) to this Paragraph.—Ed.

of judging and estimating an *action;* but on this principle it is only the intention and conviction of the agent, his faith, by which he ought to be judged. Not, however, his faith in the sense in which Christ requires faith in objective truth, so that on one who has a false faith, i.e. a conviction bad in its content, the judgement to be pronounced must be a condemnation, i.e. one in conformity with this content. On the contrary, faith here means fidelity to conviction, and the question to be asked about action is: "Has the agent in his acting kept true to his conviction?" Fidelity to formal subjective conviction is thus made the sole measuring-rod of duty.

This principle, under which conviction is expressly made something subjective, cannot but thrust upon us the thought of possible error, with the further implied presupposition of an absolute law. But the law is no agent; it is only the actual human being who acts. And, on the aforesaid principle, the only question, in estimating the worth of human actions, is how far he has taken up the law into his conviction. But if on this theory it is not actions which are to be judged, i.e. measured generally, by that law, it is impossible to see what the law is for and what end it is to serve. Such a law is degraded to a mere external letter, in fact to an empty word, if it is only my conviction which makes it a law and invests it with obligatory force.

Such a law may claim its authority from God or the state. It may even have behind it the authority of tens of centuries during which it was the bond which gave men, with all their deeds and destiny, coherence and subsistence. And these are authorities which enshrine the convictions of countless individuals. Now if I set against these the authority of my single conviction—for as my subjective conviction its sole validity is authority—that at first seems a piece of monstrous self-conceit, but in virtue of the principle that subjective conviction is to be the measuring-rod, it is pronounced not to be self-conceit at all.

Even if reason and conscience—which shallow science and bad sophistry can never altogether expel —admit with a noble illogicality that error is possible, still by describing crime, and evil generally, as only an error, we minimize the fault. To err is human—who has not been mistaken on one point or another, whether he had fresh or pickled cabbage for dinner yesterday, and about innumerable other things of more or less importance? But the difference between importance and triviality vanishes if everything turns on the subjectivity of conviction and on persistence in it. The said noble illogicality which admits the possibility of error is inevitable then in the nature of the case, but when it comes round to say that a wrong conviction is only an error, it only falls into a further illogicality, the illogicality of dishonesty. At one moment conviction is made the basis of ethics and of man's supreme value, and is thus pronounced the supreme and the sacrosanct; at another, all we have to do with is error, and my conviction is something trivial and casual, in fact something strictly external, which may turn out this way or that. Really, my being convinced *is* something supremely trivial if I cannot *know* the truth; for then it is a matter of indifference how I think, and all that is left to my thinking is that empty good, the abstraction to which the Understanding reduces the good.

One other point. It follows further, on this principle of justification by conviction, that logic requires me, in dealing with the way others act against my action, to admit that they are quite in the right—so far at any rate as they maintain with faith and conviction that my action is criminal. On such logic, not merely do I gain nothing, I am even deposed from the post of liberty and honour into a situation of slavery and dishonour. Justice, which in the abstract is mine as well as theirs, I feel only as a foreign subjective conviction, and when it is executed on me, I fancy myself to be treated only by an external force.

(*f*) Finally, the supreme form in which this subjectivism is completely comprised and expressed is the phenomenon which has been called by a name borrowed from Plato—"Irony." The name alone, however, is taken from Plato; he used it to describe a way of speaking which Socrates employed in conversation when defending the Idea of truth and justice against the conceit of the Sophists and the uneducated.[1] What he treated ironically, however, was only their type of mind, not the Idea itself. Irony is only a manner of talking against *people*. Except as directed against persons, the essential movement of thought is dialectic, and Plato was so far from regarding the dialectical in itself, still less irony, as the last word in thought and a substitute for the Idea, that he terminated the flux and reflux of thinking, let alone of a subjective opinion, and submerged it in the substantiality of the Idea.[2]

[1] Cf. Plato, *The Republic*, 337.—ED.
[2] My colleague, the late Professor Solger, adopted the word "irony" which Friedrich von Schlegel brought into use at a comparatively early period of his literary career and enhanced to equivalence with the said principle of subjectivity knowing itself as supreme. But Solger's finer mind was above such an exaggeration; he had philosophic insight and so seized upon, emphasized, and retained only that part of Schlegel's view which was dialectic in the strict sense, i.e. dialectic as the pulsating drive of speculative inquiry. His last publication, a solid piece of work, a thorough *Kritik über die Vorlesungen des Herrn August Wilhelm von Schlegel über dramatische Kunst und Literatur* (Wiener Jahrbuch, vol. vii, pp. 90 ff.), I find somewhat obscure, however, and I cannot agree with the argument which he develops. "True irony," he says (p. 92), "arises from the view that so long as man lives in this present world, it is only in this world that he can fulfil his 'appointed task' no matter how elevated a sense we give to this expression. Any hope we may have of transcending finite ends is foolish and empty conceit. Even the highest is existent for our conduct only in a shape that is limited and finite." Rightly understood, this is Platonic doctrine, and a true remark in rejection of what he has referred to earlier, the empty striving towards the (abstract) infinite. But to say that the highest is existent in a limited and finite shape, like the ethical order (and that order is in essence actual life and action), is very different from saying that the highest thing is a *finite* end. The outward shape, the form of finitude, in no way deprives the content of

The culminating form of this subjectivity which conceives itself as the final court of appeal—our topic here—can be nothing except what was implicitly present already in its preceding forms, namely subjectivity knowing itself as the arbiter and judge of truth, right, and duty. It consists then in this, that it knows the objective ethical principles, but fails in self-forgetfulness and self-renunciation to immerse itself in their seriousness and to base action upon them. Although related to them, it holds itself aloof from them and knows itself as that which wills and decides thus, although it may equally well will and decide otherwise. You actually accept a law, it says, and respect it as absolute. So do I, but I go further than you, because I am beyond this law and can make it to suit myself. It is not the thing that is excellent, but I who am so; as the master of law and thing alike, I simply play with them as with my caprice; my consciously ironical attitude lets the highest perish and I merely hug myself at the thought.

ethical life of its substantiality and the infinity inherent within it. Solger continues: "And just for this reason the highest is in *us* as negligible as the lowest and perishes of necessity with us and our nugatory thoughts and feelings. The highest is truly existent in God alone, and as it perishes in us it is transfigured into something divine, a divinity in which we would have had no share but for its immediate presence revealed in the very disappearance of our actuality; now the mood to which this process directly comes home in human affairs is tragic irony." The arbitrary name "irony" would be of no importance, but there is an obscurity here when it is said that it is "the highest" which perishes with our nothingness and that it is in the disappearance of our actuality that the divine is first revealed; e.g. again (*ibid.*, p. 91): "We see heroes beginning to wonder whether they have erred in the noblest and finest elements of their feelings and sentiments, not only in regard to their successful issue, but also to their source and their worth; indeed, what elevates us is the destruction of the best itself." (The *just* destruction of utter scoundrels and criminals who flaunt their villainy—the hero of a modern tragedy, *Die Schuld*, is one—has an interest for criminal law, but none at all for art proper which is what is in question here.) The *tragic* destruction of figures whose ethical life is on the highest plane can interest and elevate us and reconcile us to its occurrence only in so far as they come on the scene in opposition to one another together with equally justified but different ethical powers which have come into collision through misfortune, because the result is that then these figures acquire guilt through their opposition to an ethical law. Out of this situation there arises the right and wrong of both parties and therefore the true ethical Idea, which, purified and in triumph over this one-sidedness, is thereby reconciled in *us*. Accordingly, it is not the highest in us which perishes; we are elevated not by the destruction of the best but by the triumph of the true. This it is which constitutes the true, purely ethical, interest of ancient tragedy (in romantic tragedy the character of the interest undergoes a certain modification). All this I have worked out in detail in my *Phenomenology of Mind* (1st edn., pp. 404 ff. Cf. pp. 683 ff. [Eng. tr. pp. 484 ff. Cf. pp. 736 ff.]). But the ethical Idea is actual and present in the world of social institutions without the misfortune of tragic clashes and the destruction of individuals overcome by this misfortune. And this Idea's (the highest's) revelation of itself in its actuality as anything but a nullity is what the external embodiment of ethical life, the state, purposes and effects, and what the ethical self-consciousness possesses, intuits, and knows in the state and what the thinking mind comprehends there.

This type of subjectivism not merely substitutes a void for the whole content of ethics, right, duties, and laws—and so is evil, in fact evil through and through and universally—but in addition its form is a subjective void, i.e. it knows itself as this contentless void and in this knowledge knows itself as absolute.

In my *Phenomenology of Mind*,[1] I have shown how this absolute self-complacency fails to rest in a solitary worship of itself but builds up a sort of community whose bond and substance is, e.g., the "mutual asseveration of conscientiousness and good intentions, the enjoyment of this mutual purity," but is above all "the refreshment derived from the glory of this self-knowledge and self-expression, from the glory of fostering and cherishing this experience." I have shown also how what has been called a "beautiful soul"—that still nobler type of subjectivism which empties the objective of all content and so fades away until it loses all actuality— is a variation of subjectivism like other forms of the same phenomenon akin to the series of them here considered. What is said here may be compared with the entire section (C), "Conscience," in the *Phenomenology,* especially the part dealing with the transition to a higher stage—a stage, however, there different in character. [A.]

Transition from Morality to Ethical Life

141. For the good as the substantial universal of freedom, but as something still abstract, there are therefore required determinate characteristics of some sort and the principle for determining them, though a principle identical with the good itself. For conscience similarly, as the purely abstract principle of determination, it is required that its decisions shall be universal and objective. If good and conscience are each kept abstract and thereby elevated to independent totalities, then both become the indeterminate which ought to be determined.—But the integration of these two relative totalities into an absolute identity has already been implicitly achieved in that this very subjectivity of pure self-certainty, aware in its vacuity of its gradual evaporation, is identical with the abstract universality of the good. The identity of the good

[1] [1st edn.] pp. 605 ff. [Eng. tr. pp. 663 ff.].

with the subjective will, an identity which therefore is concrete and the truth of them both, is Ethical Life.

The details of such a transition of the concept are made intelligible in logic. Here, however, it need only be said that it is the nature of the restricted and the finite (i.e. here the abstract good which only ought to be [but is not], and the equally abstract subjectivity which only *ought* to be good [but is not]) to have its opposite implicit within it, the good its actuality, and subjectivity (the moment in which ethical life is actual) the good; but since they are one-sided they are not yet posited in accordance with their implicit nature. They become so posited in their negation. That is to say, in their one-sidedness, when each is bent on declining to have in it what is in it implicitly—when the good is without subjectivity and a determinate character, and the determining principle, subjectivity, is without what is implicit within it—and when both build themselves into independent totalities, they are annulled and thereby reduced to moments, to moments of the concept which becomes manifest as their unity and, having acquired reality precisely through this positing of its moments, is now present as Idea—as the concept which has matured its determinations to reality and at the same time is present in their identity as their implicit essence.

The embodiment of freedom which was (α) first of all immediate as right, is (β) characterized in the reflection of self-consciousness as good. (γ) The third stage, originating here, in its transition from (β) to ethical life, as the truth of good and subjectivity, is therefore the truth both of subjectivity and right. Ethical life is a subjective disposition, but one imbued with what is inherently right. The fact that this Idea is the truth of the concept of freedom is something which, in philosophy, must be proved, not presupposed, not adopted from feeling or elsewhere. This demonstration is contained only in the fact that right and the moral self-consciousness both display in themselves their regression to this Idea as their outcome. Those who hope to be able to dispense with proof and demonstration in philosophy show thereby that they are still far from knowing the first thing about what philosophy is. On other topics argue they may, but in philosophy they have no right to join in the argument if they wish to argue without the concept. [A.]

THIRD PART

ETHICAL LIFE

142. Ethical life is the Idea of freedom in that on the one hand it is the good become alive—the good endowed in self-consciousness with knowing and willing and actualized by self-conscious action—while on the other hand self-consciousness has in the ethical realm its absolute foundation and the end which actuates its effort.[1] Thus ethical life is the concept of freedom developed into the existing world and the nature of self-consciousness.

143. Since this unity of the concept of the will with its embodiment—i.e. the particular will—is knowing, consciousness of the distinction between these two moments of the Idea is present, but present in such a way that now each of these moments is in its own eyes the totality of the Idea and has that totality as its foundation and content.[2]

144. (a) The objective ethical order, which comes on the scene in place of good in the abstract, is substance made concrete by subjectivity as infinite form.[3] Hence it posits within itself distinctions whose specific character is thereby determined by the concept,[4] and which endow the ethical order with a stable content independently necessary and subsistent in exaltation above subjective opinion and caprice. These distinctions are absolutely valid laws and institutions. [A.]

145. It is the fact that the ethical order is the system of these specific determinations of the Idea which constitutes its rationality. Hence the ethical order is freedom or the absolute will as what is objective, a circle of necessity whose moments are the ethical powers which regulate the life of individuals. To these powers individuals are related as accidents to substance, and it is in individuals that these powers are represented, have the shape of appearance, and become actualized.[5] [A.]

146. (β) The substantial order, in the self-consciousness which it has thus actually attained in individuals, knows itself and so is an object of knowledge. This ethical substance and its laws and powers are on the one hand an object over against the subject, and from his point of view they *are*—"are" in the highest sense of self-subsistent being. This is an absolute authority and power infinitely more firmly established than the being of nature.[6]

The sun, the moon, mountains, rivers, and the natural objects of all kinds by which we are surrounded, *are*. For consciousness they have the authority not only of mere being but also of possessing a particular nature which it accepts and to which it adjusts itself in dealing with them, using them, or in being otherwise concerned with them. The authority of ethical laws is infinitely higher, because natural objects conceal rationality under the cloak of contingency and exhibit it only in their utterly external and disconnected way.

147. On the other hand, they are not something alien to the subject. On the contrary, his spirit bears witness to them as to its own essence, the essence in which he has a feeling of his selfhood, and in which he lives as in his own element which is not distinguished from himself. The subject in thus directly linked to the ethical order by a relation which is more like an identity than even the relation of faith or trust.

Faith and trust emerge along with reflection; they presuppose the power of forming ideas and making distinctions. For example, it is one thing to be a pagan, a different thing to believe in a pagan religion. This relation or rather this absence of relation, this identity in which the ethical order is the actual living soul of self-consciousness, can no doubt pass over into a relation of faith and conviction and into a relation produced by means of further reflection, i.e. into an *insight* due to reasoning starting perhaps

---

[1] See Paragraphs 258 and 146-7.—Ed.
[2] See Paragraphs 109, 144-5, and 146-7.—Ed.
[3] See Paragraph 156.—Ed.
[4] See Paragraphs 7, 262, 269-70, and 272.—Ed.

[5] See Remark to Paragraph 163.—Ed.
[6] See Addition to Paragraph 44.—Ed.

from some particular purposes, interests, and considerations, from fear or hope, or from historical conditions. But adequate *knowledge* of this identity depends on thinking in terms of the concept.

148. As substantive in character, these laws and institutions are duties binding on the will of the individual, because as subjective, as inherently undetermined, or determined as particular, he distinguishes himself from them and hence stands related to them as to the substance of his own being.

The "doctrine of duties" in moral philosophy (I mean the objective doctrine, not that which is supposed to be contained in the empty principle of moral subjectivity, because that principle determines nothing—see Paragraph 134) is therefore comprised in the systematic development of the circle of ethical necessity [1] which follows in this Third Part. The difference between the exposition in this book and the form of a "doctrine of duties" [2] lies solely in the fact that, in what follows, the specific types of ethical life turn up as necessary relationships; there the exposition ends, without being supplemented in each case by the addition that "therefore men have a duty to conform to this institution."

A "doctrine of duties" which is other than a philosophical science takes its material from existing relationships and shows its connexion with the moralist's personal notions or with principles and thoughts, purposes, impulses, feelings, &c., that are forthcoming everywhere; and as reasons for accepting each duty in turn, it may tack on its further consequences in their bearing on the other ethical relationships or on welfare and opinion. But an immanent and logical "doctrine of duties" can be nothing except the serial exposition of the relationships which are necessitated by the Idea of freedom and are therefore actual in their entirety, to wit in the state.

149. The bond of duty can appear as a restriction only on indeterminate subjectivity or abstract freedom, and on the impulses either of the natural will or of the moral will which determines its indeterminate good arbitrarily. The truth is, however, that in duty the individual finds his liberation; first, liberation from dependence on mere natural impulse and from the depression which as a particular subject he cannot escape in his moral reflections on what ought to be and what might be; secondly, liberation from the indeterminate subjectivity which, never reaching reality or the objective determinacy of action, remains self-enclosed and devoid of actuality. In duty the individual acquires his substantive freedom. [A.]

---

[1] See Addition to Paragraph 2.—ED.
[2] See Remark to Paragraph 150.—ED.

150. Virtue is the ethical order reflected in the individual character so far as that character is determined by its natural endowment. When virtue displays itself solely as the individual's simple conformity with the duties of the station to which he belongs, it is rectitude.

In an *ethical* community, it is easy to say what man must do, what are the duties he has to fulfil in order to be virtuous: he has simply to follow the well-known and explicit rules of his own situation. Rectitude is the general character which may be demanded of him by law or custom. But from the standpoint of *morality,* rectitude often seems to be something comparatively inferior, something beyond which still higher demands must be made on oneself and others, because the craving to be something special is not satisfied with what is absolute and universal; it finds consciousness of peculiarity only in what is exceptional.

The various facets of rectitude may equally well be called virtues, since they are also properties of the individual, although not specially of him in contrast with others. Talk about virtue, however, readily borders on empty rhetoric, because it is only about something abstract and indeterminate; and furthermore, argumentative and expository talk of the sort is addressed to the individual as to a being of caprice and subjective inclination. In an existing ethical order in which a complete system of ethical relations has been developed and actualized, virtue in the strict sense of the word is in place and actually appears only in exceptional circumstances or when one obligation clashes with another. The clash, however, must be a genuine one, because moral reflection can manufacture clashes of all sorts to suit its purpose and give itself a consciousness of being something special and having made sacrifices. It is for this reason that the phenomenon of virtue proper is commoner when societies and communities are uncivilized, since in those circumstances ethical conditions and their actualization are more a matter of private choice or the natural genius of an exceptional individual. For instance, it was especially to Hercules that the ancients ascribed virtue. In the states of antiquity, ethical life had not grown into this free system of an objective order self-subsistently developed, and consequently it was by the personal genius of individuals that this defect had to be made good. It follows that if a "doctrine of virtues" is not a mere "doctrine of duties," and if therefore it embraces the particular facet of character, the facet grounded in natural endowment, it will be a natural history of mind.

Since virtues are ethical principles applied to the particular, and since in this their subjective aspect they are something indeterminate, there turns up here for determining them the quantitative principle of more or less. The result is that consideration of them introduces their corresponding defects or vices, as in Aristotle, who defined each particular virtue as strictly a mean between an excess and a deficiency.

The content which assumes the form of duties and then virtues is the same as that which also has the form of impulses (see Remark to Paragraph 19). Impulses have the same basic content as duties and virtues, but in impulses this content still belongs to the immediate will and to instinctive feeling; it has not been developed to the point of becoming ethical. Consequently, impulses have in common with the content of duties and virtues only the abstract object on which they are directed, an object indeterminate in itself, and so devoid of anything to discriminate them as good or evil. Or in other words, impulses, considered abstractly in their positive aspect alone, are good, while, considered abstractly in their negative aspect alone, they are evil (see Paragraph 18). [A.]

151. But when individuals are simply identified with the actual order, ethical life (*das Sittliche*) appears as their general mode of conduct, i.e. as custom[1] (*Sitte*), while the habitual practice of ethical living appears as a second nature which, put in the place of the initial, purely natural will, is the soul of custom permeating it through and through, the significance and the actuality of its existence. It is mind living and present as a world, and the substance of mind thus exists now for the first time as mind. [A.]

152. In this way the ethical substantial order has attained its right, and its right its validity. That is to say, the self-will of the individual has vanished together with his private conscience which had claimed independence and opposed itself to the ethical substance. For, when his character is ethical, he recognizes as the end which moves him to act the universal which is itself unmoved but is disclosed in its specific determinations as rationality actualized. He knows that his own dignity and the whole stability of his particular ends are grounded in this same universal, and it is therein that he actually attains these. Subjectivity is itself the absolute form and existent actuality of the substantial order, and the distinction between subject on the one hand and substance on the other, as the object, end, and controlling power of the subject, is the same as, and has vanished directly along with, the distinction between them in form.

Subjectivity is the ground wherein the concept of freedom is realized (see Paragraph 106). At the level of morality, subjectivity is still distinct from freedom, the concept of subjectivity; but at the level of ethical life it is the realization of the concept in a way adequate to the concept itself.

[1] Cf. Pascal, *Pensée* 93.—ED.

153. The right of individuals to be subjectively destined to freedom is fulfilled when they belong to an actual ethical order, because their conviction of their freedom finds its truth in such an objective order, and it is in an ethical order that they are actually in possession of their own essence or their own inner universality (see Paragraph 147).

When a father inquired about the best method of educating his son in ethical conduct, a Pythagorean replied: "Make him a citizen of a state with good laws." (The phrase has also been attributed to others.) [A.]

154. The right of individuals to their *particular* satisfaction is also contained in the ethical substantial order, since particularity is the outward appearance of the ethical order—a mode in which that order is existent.

155. Hence in this identity of the universal will with the particular will, right and duty coalesce, and by being in the ethical order a man has rights in so far as he has duties, and duties in so far as he has rights. In the sphere of abstract right, I have the right and another has the corresponding duty. In the moral sphere, the right of my private judgement and will, as well as of my happiness, has not, but only ought to have, coalesced with duties and become objective. [A.]

156. The ethical substance, as containing independent self-consciousness united with its concept, is the actual mind of a family and a nation. [A.]

157. The concept of this Idea has being only as mind, as something knowing itself and actual, because it is the objectification of itself, the movement running through the form of its moments. It is therefore

(A) ethical mind in its natural or immediate phase—the *Family*. This substantiality loses its unity, passes over into division, and into the phase of relation, i.e. into

(B) *Civil Society*—an association of members as self-subsistent individuals in a universality which, because of their self-subsistence, is only abstract. Their association is brought about by their needs, by the legal system—the means to security of person and property—and by an external organization for attaining their particular and common interests. This external state

(C) is brought back to and welded into unity in the *Constitution of the State* which is the end and actuality of both the substantial universal order and the public life devoted thereto.

Sub-section I
THE FAMILY

158. The family, as the immediate substantiality of mind, is specifically characterized by love, which is mind's feeling of its own unity. Hence in a family, one's frame of mind is to have self-consciousness of one's individuality within this unity as the absolute essence of oneself, with the result that one is in it not as an independent person but as a member. [A.]

159. The right which the individual enjoys on the strength of the family unity and which is in the first place simply the individual's life within this unity, takes on the *form* of right (as the abstract moment of determinate individuality) only when the family begins to dissolve. At that point those who should be family-members both in their inclination and in actuality begin to be self-subsistent persons, and whereas they formerly constituted one specific moment within the whole, they now receive their share separately and so only in an external fashion by way of money, food, educational expenses, and the like. [A.]

160. The family is completed in these three phases:
(a) *Marriage*, the form assumed by the concept of the family in its immediate phase;
(b) *Family Property and Capital* (the external embodiment of the concept) and attention to these;
(c) *The Education of Children and the Dissolution of the Family.*

A. *Marriage*

161. Marriage, as the immediate type of ethical relationship, contains first, the moment of physical life; and since marriage is a *substantial* tie, the life involved in it is life in its totality, i.e. as the actuality of the race and its life-process.[1] But, secondly, in self-consciousness the natural sexual union—a union purely inward or implicit and for that very reason *existent* as purely external—is changed into a union on the level of mind, into self-conscious love. [A.]

162. On the subjective side, marriage may have a more obvious source in the particular inclination of the two persons who are entering upon the marriage tie, or in the foresight and contrivance of the parents, and so forth. But its objective source lies in the free consent of the persons, especially in their consent to make them-selves one person, to renounce their natural and individual personality to this unity of one with the other. From this point of view, their union is a self-restriction, but in fact it is their liberation, because in it they attain their substantive self-consciousness.

Our objectively appointed end and so our ethical duty is to enter the married state. The external origin of any *particular* marriage is in the nature of the case contingent, and it depends principally on the extent to which reflective thought has been developed. At one extreme, the first step is that the marriage is arranged by the contrivance of benevolent parents; the appointed end of the parties is a union of mutual love, and their inclination to marry arises from the fact that each grows acquainted with the other from the first as a destined partner. At the other extreme, it is the inclination of the parties which comes first, appearing in them as *these* two infinitely particularized individuals. The more ethical way to matrimony may be taken to be the former extreme or any way at all whereby the decision to marry comes first and the inclination to do so follows, so that in the actual wedding both decision and inclination coalesce. In the latter extreme, it is the uniqueness of the infinitely particularized which makes good its claims in accordance with the subjective principle of the modern world (see Remark to Paragraph 124).

But those works of modern art, dramatic and other, in which the love of the sexes is the main interest, are pervaded by a chill despite the heat of passion they portray, for they associate the passion with accident throughout and represent the entire dramatic interest as if it rested solely on the characters as *these individuals;* what rests on them may indeed be of infinite importance to *them,* but is of none whatever in itself.[2] [A.]

163. The ethical aspect of marriage consists in the parties' consciousness of this unity as their substantive aim, and so in their love, trust, and common sharing of their entire existence as individuals. When the parties are in this frame of mind and their union is actual, their physical passion sinks to the level of a physical moment, destined to vanish in its very satisfaction. On the other hand, the spiritual bond of union secures its rights as the substance of marriage and thus rises, inherently indissoluble, to a plane above the contingency of passion and the transience of particular caprice.

It was noted above (in Paragraph 75) that marriage, so far as its essential basis is concerned, is not a contractual relation. On the contrary, though marriage begins in contract, it is precisely a contract to transcend the standpoint of contract, the standpoint from which persons are regarded in their individ-

---

[1] Cf. *Enc.* [1st edn.], §§ 167 ff. and §§ 288 ff. [3rd edn. §§ 220 ff. and §§ 366ff.].

[2] See the footnote to Remark (*f*) to Paragraph 140.—ED.

uality as self-subsistent units. The identification of personalities, whereby the family becomes one person and its members become its accidents (though substance is in essence the relation of accidents to itself[1]), is the ethical mind. Taken by itself and stripped of the manifold externals of which it is possessed owing to its embodiment in *these* individuals and the interests of the phenomenal realm, interests limited in time and numerous other ways, this mind emerges in a shape for representative thinking and has been revered as *Penates,* &c.; and in general it is in this mind that the religious character of marriage and the family, or *pietas,* is grounded. It is a further abstraction still to separate the divine, or the substantive, from its body, and then to stamp it, together with the feeling and consciousness of mental unity, as what is falsely called "Platonic" love. This separation is in keeping with the monastic doctrine which characterizes the moment of physical life as purely negative and which, precisely by thus separating the physical from the mental, endows the former by itself with infinite importance. [A.]

164. Mere agreement to the stipulated terms of a contract in itself involves the genuine transfer of the property in question (see Paragraph 79). Similarly, the solemn declaration by the parties of their consent to enter the ethical bond of marriage, and its corresponding recognition and confirmation by their family and community,[2] constitutes the formal completion and actuality of marriage. The knot is tied and made ethical only after this ceremony, whereby through the use of signs, i.e. of language (the most mental embodiment of mind—see Paragraph 78), the substantial thing in the marriage is brought completely into being. As a result, the sensuous moment, the one proper to physical life, is put into its ethical place as something only consequential and accidental, belonging to the external embodiment of the ethical bond, which indeed can subsist exclusively in reciprocal love and support.

If with a view to framing or criticizing legal enactments, the question is asked: what should be regarded as the chief end of marriage?, the question may be taken to mean: which single facet of marriage in its actuality is to be regarded as the most essential one? No one facet by itself, however, makes up the whole range of its implicit and explicit content, i.e. of its ethical character, and one or other of its facets may be lacking in an existing marriage without detriment to the essence of marriage itself. It is in the actual conclusion of a marriage, i.e. in the wedding, that the essence of the tie is expressed and established beyond dispute as something ethical,

[1] See *Enc.* [1st edn.], § 98 [3rd edn. § 150].
[2] The fact that the church comes in in this connexion is a further point, but not one for discussion here. See footnote 2, p. 85.

raised above the contingency of feeling and private inclination. If this ceremony is taken as an external formality, a mere so-called "civil requirement," it is thereby stripped of all significance except perhaps that of serving the purpose of edification and attesting the civil relation of the parties. It is reduced indeed to a mere *fiat* of a civil or ecclesiastical authority. As such it appears as something not merely indifferent to the true nature of marriage, but actually alien to it. The heart is constrained by the law to attach a value to the formal ceremony and the latter is looked upon merely as a condition which must precede the complete mutual surrender of the parties to one another. As such it appears to bring disunion into their loving disposition and, like an alien intruder, to thwart the inwardness of their union. Such a doctrine pretentiously claims to afford the highest conception of the freedom, inwardness, and perfection of love; but in fact it is a travesty of the ethical aspect of love, the higher aspect which restrains purely sensual impulse and puts it in the background. Such restraint is already present at the instinctive level in shame, and it rises to chastity and modesty as consciousness becomes more specifically intelligent. In particular, the view just criticized casts aside marriage's specifically ethical character, which consists in this, that the consciousness of the parties is crystallized out of its physical and subjective mode and lifted to the thought of what is substantive; instead of continually reserving to itself the contingency and caprice of bodily desire, it removes the marriage bond from the province of this caprice, surrenders to the substantive, and swears allegiance to the *Penates;* the physical moment it subordinates until it becomes something wholly conditioned by the true and ethical character of the marriage relation and by the recognition of the bond as an ethical one. It is effrontery and its buttress, the Understanding, which cannot apprehend the speculative character of the substantial tie; nevertheless, with this speculative character there correspond both ethical purity of heart and the legislation of Christian peoples. [A.]

165. The difference in the physical characteristics of the two sexes has a rational basis and consequently acquires an intellectual and ethical significance. This significance is determined by the difference into which the ethical substantiality, as the concept, internally sunders itself in order that its vitality may become a concrete unity consequent upon this difference.

166. Thus one sex is mind in its self-diremption into explicit personal self-subsistence and the knowledge and volition of free universality, i.e. the self-consciousness of conceptual thought and the volition of the objective final end. The other sex is mind maintaining itself in unity as knowledge and volition of the substantive, but knowledge and volition in the form of concrete indi-

viduality and feeling. In relation to externality, the former is powerful and active, the latter passive and subjective. It follows that man has his actual substantive life in the state, in learning, and so forth, as well as in labour and struggle with the external world and with himself so that it is only out of his diremption that he fights his way to self-subsistent unity with himself. In the family he has a tranquil intuition of this unity, and there he lives a subjective ethical life on the plane of feeling. Woman, on the other hand, has her substantive destiny in the family, and to be imbued with family piety is her ethical frame of mind.

For this reason, family piety is expounded in Sophocles' *Antigone*—one of the most sublime presentations of this virtue—as principally the law of woman, and as the law of a substantiality at once subjective and on the plane of feeling, the law of the inward life, a life which has not yet attained its full actualization; as the law of the ancient gods, "the gods of the underworld"; as "an everlasting law, and no man knows at what time it was first put forth." [1] This law is there displayed as a law opposed to public law, to the law of the land. This is the supreme opposition in ethics and therefore in tragedy; and it is individualized in the same play in the opposing natures of man and woman. [2] [A.]

167. In essence marriage is monogamy because it is personality—immediate exclusive individuality—which enters into this tie and surrenders itself to it; and hence the tie's truth and inwardness (i.e. the subjective form of its substantiality) proceeds only from the mutual, wholehearted, surrender of this personality. Personality attains its right of being conscious of itself in another only in so far as the other is in this identical relationship as a person, i.e. as an atomic individual.

Marriage, and especially monogamy, is one of the absolute principles on which the ethical life of a community depends. Hence marriage comes to be recorded as one of the moments in the founding of states by gods or heroes.

168. Further, marriage results from the free surrender by both sexes of their personality—a personality in every possible way unique in each of the parties. Consequently, it ought not to be entered by two people identical in stock who are already acquainted and perfectly known to one another; for individuals in the same circle of relationship have no special personality of their own in contrast with that of others in the same circle. On the contrary, the parties should be

drawn from separate families and their personalities should be different in origin. Since the very conception of marriage is that it is a freely undertaken ethical transaction, not a tie directly grounded in the physical organism and its desires, it follows that the marriage of blood-relations runs counter to this conception and so also to genuine natural feeling.

Marriage itself is sometimes said to be grounded not in natural rights but simply in instinctive sexual impulses; or again it is treated as a contract with an arbitrary basis. External arguments in support of monogamy have been drawn from physical considerations such as the number of men and women. Dark feelings of repulsion are advanced as the sole ground for prohibiting consanguineous marriage. The basis of all these views is the fashionable idea of a state of nature and a natural origin for rights, and the lack of the concept of rationality and freedom. [A.]

169. The family, as person, has its real external existence in property; and it is only when this property takes the form of capital that it becomes the embodiment of the substantial personality of the family.

B. *The Family Capital*

170. It is not merely property which a family possesses; as a universal and enduring person, it requires possessions specifically determined as permanent and secure, i.e. it requires capital. The arbitrariness of a single owner's particular needs is one moment in property taken abstractly; but this moment, together with the selfishness of desire, is here transformed into something ethical, into labour and care for a common possession.

In the sagas of the founding of states, or at least of a social and orderly life, the introduction of permanent property is linked with the introduction of marriage. The nature of this capital, however, and the proper means of its consolidation will appear in the section on civil society. [3]

171. The family as a legal entity in relation to others must be represented by the husband as its head. Further, it is his prerogative to go out and work for its living, to attend to its needs, and to control and administer its capital. This capital is common property so that, while no member of the family has property of his own, each has his right in the common stock. This right, however, may come into collision with the head of the family's right of administration owing to the fact that the ethical temper of the family is still only at the level of immediacy (see Paragraph

[1] Cf. Sophocles, *Antigone*, ll. 450-7.—Ed.
[2] Cf. *Phenomenology* [1st edn.], pp. 383 ff., 417 ff. [Eng. tr. pp. 466 ff., 495 ff.]
[3] See Paragraphs 199 ff. and 253.—Ed.

158) and so is exposed to partition and contingency.

172. A marriage brings into being a new family which is self-subsistent and independent of the clans or "houses" from which its members have been drawn. The tie between these and the new family has a natural basis—consanguinity, but the new family is based on love of an ethical type. Thus an individual's property too has an essential connexion with his conjugal relationship and only a comparatively remote one with his relation to his clan or "house."

The significance of marriage settlements which impose a restriction on the couple's common ownership of their goods, of arrangements to secure continued legal assistance for the woman, and so forth, lies in their being provisions in case of the dissolution of the marriage, either naturally by death, or by divorce, &c. They are also safeguards for securing that in such an eventuality the different members of the family shall secure their share of the common stock. [A.]

C. *The Education of Children and the Dissolution of the Family*

173. In substance marriage is a unity, though only a unity of inwardness or disposition; in outward existence, however, the unity is sundered in the two parties. It is only in the children that the unity itself exists externally, objectively, and explicitly as a unity, because the parents love the children as their love, as the embodiment of their own substance. From the physical point of view, the presupposition—persons immediately existent (as parents)—here becomes a result, a process which runs away into the infinite series of generations, each producing the next and presupposing the one before. This is the mode in which the single mind of the *Penates* reveals its existence in the finite sphere of nature as a race. [A.]

174. Children have the right to maintenance and education at the expense of the family's common capital. The right of the parents to the service as service of their children is based upon and is restricted by the common task of looking after the family generally. Similarly, the right of the parents over the wishes of their children is determined by the object in view—discipline and education. The punishment of children does not aim at justice as such; the aim is more subjective and moral in character, i.e. to deter them from exercising a freedom still in the toils of nature and to lift the universal into their consciousness and will. [A.]

175. Children are potentially free and their life directly embodies nothing save potential freedom. Consequently they are not things and cannot be the property either of their parents or others. In respect of his relation to the family, the child's education has the positive aim of instilling ethical principles into him in the form of an immediate feeling for which differences are not yet explicit, so that thus equipped with the foundation of an ethical life, his heart may live its early years in love, trust, and obedience. In respect of the same relation, this education has the negative aim of raising children out of the instinctive, physical, level on which they are originally, to self-subsistence and freedom of personality and so to the level on which they have power to leave the natural unity of the family.

One of the blackest marks against Roman legislation is the law whereby children were treated by their fathers as slaves. This gangrene of the ethical order at the tenderest point of its innermost life is one of the most important clues for understanding the place of the Romans in the history of the world and their tendency towards legal formalism.[1]

The necessity for education is present in children as their own feeling of dissatisfaction with themselves as they are, as the desire to belong to the adult world whose superiority they divine, as the longing to grow up. The play theory of education assumes that what is childish is itself already something of inherent worth and presents it as such to the children; in their eyes it lowers serious pursuits, and education itself, to a form of childishness for which the children themselves have scant respect. The advocates of this method represent the child, in the immaturity in which he feels himself to be, as really mature and they struggle to make him satisfied with himself as he is. But they corrupt and distort his genuine and proper need for something better, and create in him a blind indifference to the substantial ties of the intellectual world, a contempt of his elders because they have thus posed before him, a child, in a contemptible and childish fashion, and finally a vanity and conceit which feeds on the notion of its own superiority. [A.]

176. Marriage is but the ethical Idea in its *immediacy* and so has its objective actuality only in the inwardness of subjective feeling and disposition. In this fact is rooted the fundamental contingency of marriage in the world of existence. There can be no compulsion on people to marry; and, on the other hand, there is no merely legal or positive bond which can hold the parties together once their dispositions and actions have become hostile and contrary. A third ethical authority, however, is called for to maintain the right of marriage—an ethical

[1] Cf. Hegel, *Philosophy of History,* pp. 288 ff. Also see below, Paragraph 180.—ED.

substantiality—against the mere whims of hostile disposition or the accident of a purely passing mood, and so forth. Such an authority distinguishes these from the total estrangement of the two parties and may not grant divorce until it is satisfied that the estrangement is total. [A.]

177. The ethical dissolution of the family consists in this, that once the children have been educated to freedom of personality, and have come of age, they become recognized as persons in the eyes of the law and as capable of holding free property of their own and founding families of their own, the sons as heads of new families, the daughters as wives. They now have their substantive destiny in the new family; the old family on the other hand falls into the background as merely their ultimate basis and origin, while a fortiori the clan is an abstraction, devoid of rights.

178. The natural dissolution of the family by the death of the parents, particularly the father, has inheritance as its consequence so far as the family capital is concerned. The essence of inheritance is the transfer to private ownership of property which is in principle common. When comparatively remote degrees of kinship are in question, and when persons and families are so dispersed in civil society that they have begun to gain self-subsistence, this transfer becomes the less hard and fast as the sense of family unity fades away and as every marriage becomes the surrender of previous family relationships and the founding of a new self-subsistent family.

It has been suggested that the basis of inheritance lies in the fact that, by a man's death, his property becomes wealth without an owner, and as such falls to the first person who takes possession of it, because of course it is the relatives who are normally nearest a man's death-bed and so they are generally the first to take possession. Hence it is supposed that this customary occurrence is made a rule by positive legislation in the interests of orderliness. This ingenious idea disregards the nature of family relationship.

179. The result of this disintegration of the family is that a man may at will either squander his capital altogether, mainly in accordance with his private caprices, opinions, and ends, or else look upon a circle of friends and acquaintances, &c., as if they were his family and make a will embodying a declaration to that effect, with the result that they become his legal heirs.

The ethical justification of freedom to dispose of one's property by will to a circle of friends would depend on the formation of such a circle; but there goes to its formation so much accident, arbitrariness, and shrewd self-seeking, &c.—especially since testamentary hopes have a bearing on readiness to enter it—that the ethical moment in it is only something very vague. Further, the recognition of a man's competence to bequeath his property arbitrarily is much more likely to be an occasion for breach of ethical obligations and for mean exertions and equally mean subservience; and it also provides opportunity and justification for the folly, caprice, and malice of attaching to professed benefactions and gifts vain, tyrannical, and vexatious conditions operative after the testator's death and so in any case after his property ceases to be his.

180. The principle that the members of the family grow up to be self-subsistent persons in the eyes of the law (see Paragraph 177) lets into the circle of the family something of the same arbitrariness and discrimination among the natural heirs, though its exercise there must be restricted to a minimum in order to prevent injury to the basic family relationship.

The mere downright arbitrariness of the deceased cannot be made the principle underlying the right to make a will, especially if it runs counter to the substantive right of the family. For after all no respect would be forthcoming for his wishes after his death, if not from the family's love and veneration for its deceased fellow-member. Such arbitrariness by itself contains nothing worthy of higher respect than the right of the family as such—on the contrary.

The other ground for the validity of testamentary disposition would consist simply in its arbitrary recognition by others. But such an argument may prima facie be admitted only when family ties, to which testamentary disposition is intrinsic, become remoter and more ineffective. If they are actually present, however, without being effective, the situation is unethical; and to give extended validity to arbitrary dispositions at the expense of family ties eo ipso weakens the ethical character of the latter.

To make the father's arbitrary will within the family the main principle of inheritance was part of the harsh and unethical legal system of Rome to which reference has been made already. That system even gave a father power to sell his son, and if the son was manumitted by a third party, he came under his father's potestas once more. Not until he was manumitted a third time was he actually and finally free. The son never attained his majority de jure nor did he become a person in law; the only property he could hold was booty won in war (peculium castrense). If he passed out of his father's potestas after being thrice sold and manumitted, he did not inherit along with those who had continued in bondage to the head of the family, unless the will specifically so provided. Similarly, a wife[1] remained

---

[1] i.e. a matrona, not a wife who in manum convenit, in mancipio est, and whose marriage was a slavery to her husband.

attached to her family of origin rather than to the new family which by her marriage she had helped to found, and which was now properly her own, and she was therefore precluded from inheriting any share of the goods of what was properly her own family, for neither wife nor mother shared in the distribution of an estate.

Later, with the growing feeling for rationality, the unethical provisions of laws such as these and others were evaded in the course of their administration, for example with the help of the expression *bonorum possessio* [1] instead of *hereditas*, and through the fiction of nicknaming a *filia* a *filius*. This was referred to above (see Remark to Paragraph 3) as the sad necessity to which the judge was reduced in the face of bad laws—the necessity of smuggling reason into them on the sly, or at least into some of their consequences. Connected with this were the terrible instability of the chief political institutions and a riot of legislation to stem the outbreak of resulting evils.

From Roman history and the writings of Lucian and others, we are sufficiently familiar with the unethical consequences of giving the head of a Roman family the right to name whom he pleased as his heir.

Marriage is ethical life at the level of immediacy; in the very nature of the case, therefore, it must be a mixture of a substantial tie with natural contingency and inner arbitrariness. Now when by the slave-status of children, by legal provisions such as those mentioned above as well as others consequential upon them, and in addition by the ease of Roman divorce, pride of place is given to arbitrariness instead of to the right of the substantial (so that even Cicero—and what fine writing about the *Honestum* and *Decorum* there is in his *De Officiis* and in all sorts of other places!—even Cicero divorced his wife as a business speculation in order to pay his debts with his new wife's dowry), then a legal road is paved to the corruption of manners, or rather the laws themselves necessitate such corruption.

The institution of heirs-at-law with a view to preserving the family and its *splendor* by means of *fideicommissa* and *substitutiones* (in order to favour sons by excluding daughters from inheriting, or to favour the eldest son by excluding the other children) is an infringement of the principle of the freedom of property (see Paragraph 62), like the admission of any other inequality in the treatment of heirs. And besides, such an institution depends on an arbitrariness which in and by itself has no right to recognition, or more precisely on the thought of wishing to preserve intact not so much *this* family but rather *this* clan or "house." Yet it is not this clan or "house," but the family proper which is the Idea and which therefore possesses the right to recognition, and both the ethical disposition and family trees are much more likely to be preserved by free-

dom of property and equality of inheritance than by the reverse of these.

Institutions of this kind, like the Roman, wholly ignore the right due to marriage, because by a marriage the foundation of a unique actual family is *eo ipso* completed (see Paragraph 172), and because what is called, in contrast with the new family, the family in the wide sense, i.e. the *stirps* or *gens*, becomes only an abstraction (see Paragraph 177) growing less and less actual the further it recedes into the background as one generation succeeds another. Love, the ethical moment in marriage, is by its very nature a feeling for actual living individuals, not for an abstraction. This abstraction of the Understanding [the *gens*] appears in history as the principle underlying the contribution of the Roman Empire to world history (see Paragraph 357).[2] In the higher sphere of the state, a right of primogeniture arises together with estates rigidly entailed; it arises, however, not arbitrarily but as the inevitable outcome of the Idea of the state. On this point see below, Paragraph 306. [A.]

Transition of the Family into Civil Society

181. The family disintegrates (both essentially, through the working of the principle of personality, and also in the course of nature) into a plurality of families, each of which conducts itself as in principle a self-subsistent concrete person and therefore as externally related to its neighbours. In other words, the moments bound together in the unity of the family, since the family is the ethical Idea still in its concept, must be released from the concept to self-subsistent objective reality. This is the stage of difference. This gives us, to use abstract language in the first place, the determination of particularity which is related to universality but in such a way that universality is its basic principle, though still only an inward principle; for that reason, the universal merely shows in the particular as its form. Hence this relation of reflection prima facie portrays the disappearance of ethical life or, since this life as the essence necessarily shows itself,[3] this relation constitutes the world of ethical appearance—civil society.

The expansion of the family, as its transition into a new principle, is in the external world sometimes its peaceful expansion until it becomes a people, i.e. a nation, which thus has a common natural origin, or sometimes the federation of scattered groups of families under the influence of an overlord's power or as a result of a voluntary association produced by the tie of needs and the reciprocity of their satisfaction. [A.]

---

[1] The fact that there is a further distinction between this and *possessio bonorum* is a piece of the erudition which constitutes the juristic expert.

[2] All editions read "356."—ED.
[3] Cf. *Enc.* [1st. edn.], §§ 64 ff., §§ 81 ff. [3rd edn. §§ 115 ff., §§ 131 ff.].

Sub-section II
CIVIL SOCIETY

182. The concrete person,[1] who is himself the object of his particular aims, is, as a totality of wants and a mixture of caprice and physical necessity, one principle of civil society. But the particular person is essentially so related to other particular persons that each establishes himself and finds satisfaction by means of the others, and at the same time purely and simply by means of the form of universality, the second principle here. [A.]

183. In the course of the actual attainment of selfish ends—an attainment conditioned in this way by universality—there is formed a system of complete interdependence, wherein the livelihood, happiness, and legal status of one man is interwoven with the livelihood, happiness, and rights of all. On this system, individual happiness, &c., depend, and only in this connected system are they actualized and secured. This system may be prima facie regarded as the external state, the state based on need, the state as the Understanding envisages it.

184. The Idea in this its stage of division imparts to each of its moments a characteristic embodiment; to particularity it gives the right to develop and launch forth in all directions; and to universality the right to prove itself not only the ground and necessary form of particularity, but also the authority standing over it and its final end. It is the system of the ethical order, split into its extremes and lost, which constitutes the Idea's abstract moment, its moment of reality. Here the Idea is present only as a relative totality and as the inner necessity behind this outward appearance. [A.]

185. Particularity by itself, given free rein in every direction to satisfy its needs, accidental caprices, and subjective desires, destroys itself and its substantive concept in this process of gratification. At the same time, the satisfaction of need, necessary and accidental alike, is accidental because it breeds new desires without end, is in thoroughgoing dependence on caprice and external accident, and is held in check by the power of universality. In these contrasts and their complexity, civil society affords a spectacle of extravagance and want as well as of the physical and ethical degeneration common to them both.

[1] See Paragraphs 230 ff.—Ed.

The development of particularity to self-subsistence (compare Remark to Paragraph 124) is the moment which appeared in the ancient world as an invasion of ethical corruption and as the ultimate cause of that world's downfall. Some of these ancient states were built on the patriarchal and religious principle, others on the principle of an ethical order which was more explicitly intellectual, though still comparatively simple; in either case they rested on primitive unsophisticated intuition. Hence they could not withstand the disruption of this state of mind when self-consciousness was infinitely reflected into itself; when this reflection began to emerge, they succumbed to it, first in spirit and then in substance, because the simple principle underlying them lacked the truly infinite power to be found only in that unity which allows both sides of the antithesis of reason to develop themselves separately in all their strength and which has so overcome the antithesis that it maintains itself in it and integrates it in itself.

In his *Republic*, Plato displays the substance of ethical life in its ideal beauty and truth; but he could only cope with the principle of self-subsistent particularity, which in his day had forced its way into Greek ethical life, by setting up in opposition to it his purely substantial state. He absolutely excluded it from his state, even in its very beginnings in private property (see Remark to Paragraph 46) and the family, as well as in its more mature form as the subjective will, the choice of a social position, and so forth. It is this defect which is responsible both for the misunderstanding of the deep and substantial truth of Plato's state and also for the usual view of it as a dream of abstract thinking, as what is often called a "mere ideal." The principle of the self-subsistent inherently infinite personality of the individual, the principle of subjective freedom, is denied its right in the purely substantial form which Plato gave to mind in its actuality. This principle dawned in an inward form in the Christian religion and in an external form (and therefore in one linked with abstract universality) in the Roman world. It is historically subsequent to the Greek world, and the philosophic reflection which descends to its depth is likewise subsequent to the substantial Idea of Greek philosophy. [A.]

186. But in developing itself independently to totality, the principle of particularity passes over into universality, and only there does it attain its truth and the right to which its positive actuality is entitled. This unity is not the identity which the ethical order requires, because at this level, that of division (see Paragraph 184), both principles are self-subsistent. It follows that this unity is present here not as freedom but as necessity, since it is by compulsion that the particular rises to the form of universality and seeks and gains its stability in that form.

187. Individuals in their capacity as burghers[1] in this state are private persons whose end is their own interest. This end is *mediated* through the universal which thus *appears* as a *means* to its realization. Consequently, individuals can attain their ends only in so far as they themselves determine their knowing, willing, and acting in a universal way and make themselves links in this chain of social connexions. In these circumstances, the interest of the Idea—an interest of which these members of civil society are as such unconscious—lies in the process whereby their singularity and their natural condition are raised, as a result of the necessities imposed by nature as well as of arbitrary needs, to formal freedom and formal universality of knowing and willing—the process whereby their particularity is educated up to subjectivity.

The idea that the state of nature is one of innocence and that there is a simplicity of manners in uncivilized (*ungebildeter*) peoples, implies treating education (*Bildung*) as something purely external, the ally of corruption. Similarly, the feeling that needs, their satisfaction, the pleasures and comforts of private life, and so forth, are absolute ends, implies treating education as a mere means to these ends. Both these views display lack of acquaintance with the nature of mind and the end of reason. Mind attains its actuality only by creating a dualism within itself, by submitting itself to physical needs and the chain of these external necessities, and so imposing on itself this barrier and this finitude, and finally by maturing (*bildet*) itself inwardly even when under this barrier until it overcomes it and attains its objective reality in the finite. The end of reason, therefore, is neither the manners of an unsophisticated state of nature, nor, as particularity develops, the pleasure for pleasure's sake which education procures. On the contrary, its end is to banish natural simplicity, whether the passivity which is the absence of the self, or the crude type of knowing and wiling, i.e. immediacy and singularity, in which mind is absorbed. It aims in the first instance at securing for this, its external condition, the rationality of which it is capable, i.e. the form of universality or the Understanding (*Verständigkeit*). By this means alone does mind become at home with itself within this pure externality. There, then, mind's freedom is existent and mind becomes objective to itself in this element which is implicitly inimical to mind's appointed end, freedom; it has to do there only with what it has itself produced and stamped with its seal. It is in this way then that the form of universality comes explicitly into existence in thought, and this form is the only worthy element for the existence of the Idea. The final purpose of education, therefore, is liberation and the struggle for a higher liberation still; education is the absolute transition from an ethical substantiality which is immediate and natural to the one which is intellectual and so both infinitely subjective and lofty enough to have attained universality of form. In the individual subject, this liberation is the hard struggle against pure subjectivity of demeanour, against the immediacy of desire, against the empty subjectivity of feeling and the caprice of inclination. The disfavour showered on education is due in part to its being this hard struggle; but it is through this educational struggle that the subjective will itself attains objectivity within, an objectivity in which alone it is for its part capable and worthy of being the actuality of the Idea.

Moreover, this form of universality—the Understanding, to which particularity has worked its way and developed itself, brings it about at the same time that particularity becomes individuality genuinely existent in its own eyes. And since it is from this particularity that the universal derives the content which fills it as well as its character as infinite self-determination, particularity itself is present in ethical life as infinitely independent free subjectivity. This is the position which reveals education as a moment immanent in the Absolute and which makes plain its infinite value. [A.]

188. Civil society contains three moments:

(A) The mediation of need and one man's satisfaction through his work and the satisfaction of the needs of all others—the *System of Needs*.

(B) The actuality of the universal principle of freedom therein contained—the protection of property through the *Administration of Justice*.

(C) Provision against contingencies still lurking in systems (A) and (B), and care for particular interests as a common interest, by means of the *Police* and the *Corporation*.

A. *The System of Needs*

189. Particularity is in the first instance characterized in general by its contrast with the universal principle of the will and thus is subjective need (see Paragraph 59).[2] This attains its objectivity, i.e. its satisfaction, by means of (*a*) external things, which at this stage are likewise the property and product of the needs and wills of others, and (*β*) work and effort, the middle term between the subjective and the objective. The aim here is the satisfaction of subjective particularity, but the universal asserts itself in the bearing which this satisfaction has on the needs of others and their free arbitrary wills. The show of rationality thus produced in this sphere of finitude is the Understanding, and this is the aspect which is of most importance in considering this sphere and which itself constitutes the reconciling element within it.

Political economy is the science which starts from

---

[1] See Remark to Paragraph 190.—ED.

[2] All editions read "60."—ED.

this view of needs and labour but then has the task of explaining mass-relationships and mass-movements in their complexity and their qualitative and quantitative character. This is one of the sciences which have arisen out of the conditions of the modern world. Its development affords the interesting spectacle (as in Smith, Say, and Ricardo) of thought working upon the endless mass of details which confront it at the outset and extracting therefrom the simple principles of the thing, the Understanding effective in the thing and directing it. It is to find reconciliation here to discover in the sphere of needs this show of rationality lying in the thing and effective there; but if we look at it from the opposite point of view, this is the field in which the Understanding with its subjective aims and moral fancies vents its discontent and moral frustration. [A.]

(a) The Kind of Need and Satisfaction [typical of civil society]

190. An animal's needs and its ways and means of satisfying them are both alike restricted in scope. Though man is subject to this restriction too, yet at the same time he evinces his transcendence of it and his universality, first by the multiplication of needs and means of satisfying them, and secondly by the differentiation and division of concrete need into single parts and aspects which in turn become different needs, particularized and so more abstract.

In [abstract] right, what we had before us was the person; in the sphere of morality, the subject; in the family, the family-member; in civil society as a whole, the burgher or *bourgeois*. Here at the standpoint of needs (compare Remark to Paragraph 123) what we have before us is the composite idea which we call *man*. Thus this is the first time, and indeed properly the only time, to speak of *man* in this sense.[1] [A.]

191. Similarly, the means to particularized needs and all the various ways of satisfying these are themselves divided and multiplied and so in turn become proximate ends and abstract needs. This multiplication goes on *ad infinitum*; taken as a whole, it is refinement, i.e. a discrimination between these multiplied needs, and judgement on the suitability of means to their ends. [A.]

192. Needs and means, as things existent *realiter*, become something which has being for others by whose needs and work satisfaction for all alike is conditioned. When needs and means become abstract in quality (see Paragraph 191), abstraction is also a character of the reciprocal relation of individuals to one another.[2] This abstract character, universality, is the character

of being recognized and is the moment which makes concrete, i.e. social, the isolated and abstract needs and their ways and means of satisfaction. [A.]

193. This social moment thus becomes a particular end-determinant for means in themselves and their acquisition, as well as for the manner in which needs are satisfied. Further, it directly involves the demand for equality of satisfaction with others. The need for this equality and for emulation, which is the equalizing of oneself with others, as well as the other need also present here, the need of the particular to assert itself in some distinctive way, become themselves a fruitful source of the multiplication of needs and their expansion.

194. Since in social needs, as the conjunction of immediate or natural needs with mental needs arising from ideas, it is needs of the latter type which because of their universality make themselves preponderant, this social moment has in it the aspect of liberation, i.e. the strict natural necessity of need is obscured and man is concerned with his own opinion, indeed with an opinion which is universal, and with a necessity of his own making alone, instead of with an external necessity, an inner contingency, and mere caprice.

The idea has been advanced that in respect of his needs man lived in freedom in the so-called "state of nature" when his needs were supposed to be confined to what are known as the simple necessities of nature, and when he required for their satisfaction only the means which the accidents of nature directly assured to him. This view takes no account of the moment of liberation intrinsic to work, on which see the following Paragraphs. And apart from this, it is false, because to be confined to mere physical needs as such and their direct satisfaction would simply be the condition in which the mental is plunged in the natural and so would be one of savagery and unfreedom, while freedom itself is to be found only in the reflection of mind into itself, in mind's distinction from nature, and in the reflex of mind in nature.

195. This liberation is abstract since the particularity of the ends remains their basic content. When social conditions tend to multiply and subdivide needs, means, and enjoyments indefinitely—a process which, like the distinction between natural and refined needs, has no qualitative limits—this is luxury. In this same process, however, dependence and want increase *ad infinitum*, and the material to meet these is permanently barred to the needy man because it consists of external objects with the special char-

[1] See Remark to Paragraph 209.—ED.
[2] See Paragraphs 48, 49, and 71.—ED.

acter of being property, the embodiment of the free will of others, and hence from his point of view its recalcitrance is absolute.[1] [A.]

(β) The Kind of Work [typical of civil society]

196. The means of acquiring and preparing the particularized means appropriate to our similarly particularized needs is work. Through work the raw material directly supplied by nature is specifically adapted to these numerous ends by all sorts of different processes. Now this formative change confers value on means and gives them their utility, and hence man in what he consumes is mainly concerned with the products of men. It is the products of human effort which man consumes. [A.]

197. The multiplicity of objects and situations which excite interest is the stage on which theoretical education develops. This education consists in possessing not simply a multiplicity of ideas and facts, but also a flexibility and rapidity of mind, ability to pass from one idea to another, to grasp complex and general relations, and so on. It is the education of the understanding in every way, and so also the building up of language. Practical education, acquired through working, consists first in the automatically recurrent need for something to do and the habit of simply being busy; next, in the strict adaptation of one's activity according not only to the nature of the material worked on, but also, and especially, to the pleasure of other workers; and finally, in a habit, produced by this discipline, of objective activity and universally recognized aptitudes. [A.]

198. The universal and objective element in work, on the other hand, lies in the abstracting process which effects the subdivision of needs and means and thereby *eo ipso* subdivides production and brings about the division of labour. By this division, the work of the individual becomes less complex, and consequently his skill at his section of the job increases, like his output. At the same time, this abstraction of one man's skill and means of production from another's completes and makes necessary everywhere the dependence of men on one another and their reciprocal relation in the satisfaction of their other needs. Further, the abstraction of one man's production from another's makes work more and more mechanical, until finally man is able to step aside and install machines in his place.

[1] See Paragraphs 241-2.—ED.

(γ) Capital [and class-divisions] [2]

199. When men are thus dependent on one another and reciprocally related to one another in their work and the satisfaction of their needs, subjective self-seeking turns into a contribution to the satisfaction of the needs of everyone else. That is to say, by a dialectical advance, subjective self-seeking turns into the mediation of the particular through the universal, with the result that each man in earning, producing, and enjoying on his own account is *eo ipso* producing and earning for the enjoyment of everyone else. The compulsion which brings this about is rooted in the complex interdependence of each on all, and it now presents itself to each as the universal permanent capital (see Paragraph 170) which gives each the opportunity, by the exercise of his education and skill, to draw a share from it and so be assured of his livelihood, while what he thus earns by means of his work maintains and increases the general capital.

200. A particular man's resources, or in other words his opportunity of sharing in the general resources, are conditioned, however, partly by his own unearned principal (his capital), and partly by his skill; this in turn is itself dependent not only on his capital, but also on accidental circumstances whose multiplicity introduces differences in the development of natural, bodily, and mental characteristics, which were already in themselves dissimilar. In this sphere of particularity, these differences are conspicuous in every direction and on every level, and, together with the arbitrariness and accident which this sphere contains as well, they have as their inevitable consequence disparities of individual resources and ability.

The objective right of the particularity of mind is contained in the Idea. Men are made unequal by nature, where inequality is in its element, and in civil society the right of particularity is so far from annulling this natural inequality that it produces it out of mind and raises it to an inequality of skill and resources, and even to one of moral and intellectual attainment. To oppose to this right a demand for equality is a folly of the Understanding which takes as real and rational its abstract equality and its "ought-to-be."

This sphere of particularity, which fancies itself the universal, is still only relatively identical with the universal, and consequently it still retains in itself the particularity of nature, i.e. arbitrariness, or in other words the relics of the state of nature. Further, it is reason, immanent in the restless system of human needs, which articulates it into an organic

[2] See Remark to Paragraph 326 and to 303.—ED.

whole with different members (see the following Paragraph).

201. The infinitely complex, criss-cross, movements of reciprocal production and exchange, and the equally infinite multiplicity of means therein employed, become crystallized, owing to the universality inherent in their content, and distinguished into general groups. As a result, the entire complex is built up into particular systems of needs, means, and types of work relative to these needs, modes of satisfaction and of theoretical and practical education, i.e. into systems, to one or other of which individuals are assigned—in other words, into class-divisions. [A.]

202. The classes are specifically determined in accordance with the concept as (a) the *substantial* or immediate [or agricultural] class; (b) the reflecting or *formal* [or business] class; and finally, (c) the *universal* class [the class of civil servants].

203. (a) The substantial [or agricultural] class has its capital in the natural products of the soil which it cultivates—soil which is capable of exclusively private ownership and which demands formation in an objective way and not mere haphazard exploitation. In face of the connexion of [agricultural] work and its fruits with separate and fixed times of the year, and the dependence of harvests on the variability of natural processes, the aim of need in this class turns into provision for the future; but owing to the conditions here, the agricultural mode of subsistence remains one which owes comparatively little to reflection and independence of will, and this mode of life is in general such that this class has the substantial disposition of an ethical life which is immediate, resting on family relationship and trust.

The real beginning and original foundation of states has been rightly ascribed to the introduction of agriculture along with marriage, because the principle of agriculture brings with it the formation of the land and consequentially exclusively private property (compare Remark to Paragraph 170); the nomadic life of savages, who seek their livelihood from place to place, it brings back to the tranquillity of private rights and the assured satisfaction of their needs. Along with these changes, sexual love is restricted to marriage, and this bond in turn grows into an enduring league, inherently universal, while needs expand into care for a family, and personal possessions into family goods. Security, consolidation, lasting satisfaction of needs, and so forth—things which are the most obvious recommendations of marriage and agriculture—are nothing but forms of universality, modes in which rationality, the final end and aim, asserts itself in these spheres.

In this matter, nothing is of more interest than the ingenious and learned explanations which my distinguished friend, Herr Creuzer, has given [1] of the agrarian festivals, images, and sanctuaries of the ancients. He shows that it was because the ancients themselves had become conscious of the divine origin of agriculture and other institutions associated with it that they held them in such religious veneration.

In course of time, the character of this class as "substantial" undergoes modifications through the working of the civil law, in particular the administration of justice, as well as through the working of education, instruction, and religion. These modifications, which occur in the other classes also, do not affect the substantial content of the class but only its form and the development of its power of reflection. [A.]

204. (b) The business class has for its task the adaptation of raw materials, and for its means of livelihood it is thrown back on its work, on reflection and intelligence, and essentially on the mediation of one man's needs and work with those of others. For what this class produces and enjoys, it has mainly itself, its own industry, to thank. The task of this class is subdivided into

(a) work to satisfy single needs in a comparatively concrete way and to supply single orders—craftsmanship;

(β) work of a more abstract kind, mass-production to satisfy single needs, but needs in more universal demand—manufacture;

(γ) the business of exchange, whereby separate utilities are exchanged the one for the other, principally through the use of the universal medium of exchange, money, which actualizes the abstract value of all commodities—trade. [A.]

205. (c) The universal class [the class of civil servants] has for its task the universal interests of the community. It must therefore be relieved from direct labour to supply its needs, either by having private means or by receiving an allowance from the state which claims its industry, with the result that private interest finds its satisfaction in its work for the universal.

206. It is in accordance with the concept that class-organization, as particularity become objective to itself, is split in this way into its general divisions. But the question of the particular class to which an individual is to belong is one on which natural capacity, birth, and other circumstances have their influence, though the es-

[1] Notably in the fourth volume of his *Mythologie und Symbolik*.

sential and final determining factors are subjective opinion and the individual's arbitrary will, which win in this sphere their right, their merit, and their dignity. Hence what happens here by inner necessity occurs at the same time by the mediation of the arbitrary will, and to the conscious subject it has the shape of being the work of his own will.

In this respect too there is a conspicuous difference, in relation to the principle of particularity and the subject's arbitrary will, between the political life of the east and the west, and also between that of the ancient and the modern world. In the former, the division of the whole into classes came about objectively of itself, because it is inherently rational; but the principle of subjective particularity was at the same time denied its rights, in that, for example, the allotment of individuals to classes was left to the ruling class, as in Plato's *Republic*,[1] or to the accident of birth, as in the Indian caste-system. Thus subjective particularity was not incorporated into the organization of society as a whole; it was not reconciled in the whole, and therefore—since as an essential moment it emerges there in any event—it shows itself there as something hostile, as a corruption of the social order (see Remark to Paragraph 185). Either it overthrows society, as happened in the Greek states and in the Roman Republic; or else, should society preserve itself in being as a force or as a religious authority, for instance, it appears as inner corruption and complete degeneration, as was the case to some extent in Sparta and is now altogether the case in India.

But when subjective particularity is upheld by the objective order in conformity with it and is at the same time allowed its rights, then it becomes the animating principle of the entire civil society, of the development alike of mental activity, merit, and dignity. The recognition and the right that what is brought about by reason of necessity in civil society and the state shall at the same time be effected by the mediation of the arbitrary will is the more precise definition of what is primarily meant by freedom in common parlance (see Paragraph 121).

207. A man actualizes himself only in becoming something definite, i.e. something specifically particularized; this means restricting himself exclusively to one of the particular spheres of need. In this class system, the ethical frame of mind therefore is rectitude and *esprit de corps*, i.e. the disposition to make oneself a member of one of the moments of civil society by one's own act, through one's energy, industry, and skill, to maintain oneself in this position, and to fend for oneself only through this process of mediating oneself with the universal, while in this way gaining recognition both in one's own eyes and in the eyes of others. Morality has its

proper place in this sphere where the paramount thing is reflection on one's doings, and the quest of happiness and private wants, and where the contingency in satisfying these makes into a duty even a single and contingent act of assistance.

At first (i.e. especially in youth) a man chafes at the idea of resolving on a particular social position, and looks upon this as a restriction on his universal character and as a necessity imposed on him purely *ab extra*. This is because his thinking is still of that abstract kind which refuses to move beyond the universal and so never reaches the actual. It does not realize that if the concept is to be determinate, it must first of all advance into the distinction between the concept and its real existence and thereby into determinacy and particularity (see Paragraph 7). It is only thus that the concept can win actuality and ethical objectivity. [A.]

208. As the private particularity of knowing and willing, the principle of this system of needs contains absolute universality, the universality of freedom, only abstractly and therefore as the right of property. At this point, however, this right is no longer merely implicit but has attained its recognized actuality as the protection of property through the administration of justice.

B. *The Administration of Justice*

209. The relatedness arising from the reciprocal bearing on one another of needs and work to satisfy these is first of all reflected into itself as infinite personality, as abstract right.[2] But it is this very sphere of relatedness—a sphere of education—which gives abstract right the determinate existence of being something universally recognized, known, and willed, and having a validity and an objective actuality mediated by this known and willed character.

It is part of education, of thinking as the consciousness of the single in the form of universality, that the ego comes to be apprehended as a universal person in which all are identical. A man counts as a man in virtue of his manhood alone, not because he is a Jew, Catholic, Protestant, German, Italian, &c. This is an assertion which thinking ratifies and to be conscious of it is of infinite importance. It is defective only when it is crystallized, e.g. as a cosmopolitanism in opposition to the concrete life of the state. [A.]

210. The objective actuality of the right consists, first, in its existence for consciousness, in its being known in some way or other; secondly, in its possessing the power which the actual possesses, in its being valid, and so also in its be-

---

[1] Book iii [415].

[2] See Paragraph 187.—ED.

coming known as universally valid.

(a) Right as Law

211. The principle of rightness becomes the law (*Gesetz*) when, in its objective existence, it is posited (*gesetzt*), i.e. when thinking makes it determinate for consciousness and makes it known as what is right and valid; and in acquiring this determinate character, the right becomes positive law in general.

To posit something as universal, i.e. to bring it before consciousness as universal, is, I need hardly say, to think (compare Remarks to Paragraphs 13 and 21). Thereby its content is reduced to its simplest form and so is given its final determinacy. In becoming law, what is right acquires for the first time not only the torm proper to its universality, but also its true determinacy. Hence making a law is not to be represented as merely the expression of a rule of behaviour valid for everyone, though that is one moment in legislation; the more important moment, the inner essence of the matter, is knowledge of the content of the law in its determinate universality.

Since it is only animals which have their law as instinct, while it is man alone who has law as custom, even systems of customary law contain the moment of being thoughts and being known. Their difference from positive law consists solely in this, that they are known only in a subjective and accidental way, with the result that in themselves they are less determinate and the universality of thought is less clear in them. (And apart from this, knowledge of a system of law either in general or in its details, is the accidental possession of a few.) The supposition that it is customary law, on the strength of its character as custom, which possesses the privilege of having become part of life is a delusion, since the valid laws of a nation do not cease to be its customs by being written and codified—and besides, it is as a rule precisely those versed in the deadest of topics and the deadest of thoughts who talk nowadays of "life" and of "becoming part of life." When a nation begins to acquire even a little culture, its customary law must soon come to be collected and put together. Such a collection is a legal code, but one which, as a mere collection, is markedly formless, indeterminate, and fragmentary. The main difference between it and a code properly so-called is that in the latter the principles of jurisprudence in their universality, and so in their determinacy, have been apprehended in terms of thought and expressed. English national law or municipal law is contained, as is well known, in statutes (written laws) and in so-called "unwritten" laws. This unwritten law, however, is as good as written, and knowledge of it may, and indeed must, be acquired simply by reading the numerous quartos which it fills. The monstrous confusion, however, which prevails both in English law and its administration is graphically portrayed by those acquainted with the matter. In particular, they comment on the fact that, since this unwritten law is contained in court verdicts and judgements, the judges are continually legislators. The authority of precedent is binding on them, since their predecessors have done nothing but give expression to the unwritten law; and yet they are just as much exempt from its authority, because they are themselves repositories of the unwritten law and so have the right to criticize previous judgements and pronounce whether they accorded with the unwritten law or not.

A similar confusion might have arisen in the legal system of the later Roman Empire owing to the different but authoritative judgements of all the famous jurists. An Emperor met the situation, however, by a sensible expedient when, by what was called the Law of Citations, he set up a kind of College of the jurists who were longest deceased. There was a President, and the majority vote was accepted.[1]

No greater insult could be offered to a civilized people or to its lawyers than to deny them ability to codify their law; for such ability cannot be that of constructing a legal system with a novel content, but only that of apprehending, i.e. grasping in thought, the content of existing laws in its determinate universality and then applying them to particular cases. [A.]

212. It is only because of this identity between its implicit and its posited character that positive law has obligatory force in virtue of its rightness. In being posited in positive law, the right acquires determinate existence. Into such existence there may enter the contingency of self-will and other particular circumstances and hence there may be a discrepancy between the content of the law and the principle of rightness.

In positive law, therefore, it is the legal which is the source of our knowledge of what is right, or, more exactly, of our legal rights (*Rechtens*). Thus the science of positive law is to that extent an historical science with authority as its guiding principle. Anything over and above this historical study is matter for the Understanding and concerns the collection of laws, their classification on external principles, deductions from them, their application to fresh details, &c. When the Understanding meddles with the nature of the thing itself, its theories, e.g. of criminal law, show what its deductive argumentation can concoct.

The science of positive law has not only the right, but even the inescapable duty, to study given laws, to deduce from its positive data their progress in history, their applications and subdivisions, down to the last detail, and to exhibit their implications. On the other hand, if, after all these deductions have been proved, the further question about the rationality of a specific law is still raised, the question may

[1] Hugo: *Lehrbuch der Geschichte des römischen Rechts,* § 354 [§ 385 in the 7th edn.].

seem perverse to those who are busied with these pursuits, but their astonishment at it should at least stop short of dismay.

With this Remark, compare what was said in the Remark to Paragraph 3 about "understanding" the law.

213. Right becomes determinate in the first place when it has the form of being posited as positive law; it also becomes determinate in content by being applied both to the material of civil society (i.e. to the endlessly growing complexity and subdivision of social ties and the different species of property and contract within the society) and also to ethical ties based on the heart, on love and trust, though only in so far as these involve abstract right as one of their aspects (see Paragraph 159). Morality and moral commands concern the will on its most private, subjective, and particular side, and so cannot be a matter for positive legislation. Further material for the determinate content of law is provided by the rights and duties which have their source in the administration of justice itself, in the state, and so forth. [A.]

214. But apart from being applied to particular instances, right by being embodied in positive law becomes applicable to the single case. Hence it enters the sphere where quantity, not the concept, is the principle of determination. This is the sphere of the quantitative as such, of the quantitative as that which determines the relative value in exchange of *qualia*. In this sphere, the concept merely lays down a general limit, within which vacillation is still allowed. This vacillation must be terminated, however, in the interest of getting something done, and for this reason there is a place within that limit for contingent and arbitrary decisions.

The purely positive side of law lies chiefly in this focusing of the universal not merely on a particular instance, but on an isolated case, i.e. in its *direct* application. Reason cannot determine, nor can the concept provide any principle whose application could decide whether justice requires for an offence (i) a corporal punishment of forty lashes or thirty-nine, or (ii) a fine of five dollars or four dollars ninety-three, four, &c., cents, or (iii) imprisonment of a year or three hundred and sixty-four, three, &c., days, or a year and one, two, or three days. And yet injustice is done at once if there is one lash too many, or one dollar or one cent, one week in prison or one day, too many or too few.

Reason itself requires us to recognize that contingency, contradiction, and show have a sphere and a right of their own, restricted though it be, and it is irrational to strive to resolve and rectify contradictions within that sphere. Here the only interest present is that something be actually done, that the matter be settled and decided somehow, no matter how (within a certain limit). This decision pertains to abstract subjectivity, to formal self-certainty, which may decide either by simply holding to its power (within that limit) of settling the matter by merely terminating deliberation and thereby dismissing it out of hand, or else by adopting some reason for decision such as keeping to round numbers or always adopting, say thirty-nine.

It is true that the law does not settle these ultimate decisions required by actual life; it leaves them instead to the judge's discretion, merely limiting him by a maximum and minimum. But this does not affect the point at issue, because the maximum and minimum are themselves in every instance only round numbers once more. To fix them, therefore, does not exempt the judge from making a finite, purely positive, decision, since on the contrary such a decision is still left to him by the necessities of the case. [A.]

(β) Law determinately existent

215. If laws are to have a binding force, it follows that, in view of the right of self-consciousness (see Paragraph 132 and the Remark thereto) they must be made universally known.

To hang the laws so high that no citizen could read them (as Dionysius the Tyrant did) is injustice of one and the same kind as to bury them in row upon row of learned tomes, collections of dissenting judgements and opinions, records of customs, &c., and in a dead language too, so that knowledge of the law of the land is accessible only to those who have made it their professional study. Rulers who have given a national law to their peoples in the form of a well-arranged and clear-cut legal code—or even a mere formless collection of laws, like Justinian's—have been the greatest benefactors of their peoples and have received thanks and praise for their beneficence. But the truth is that their work was at the same time a great act of justice. [A.]

216. For a public legal code, simple general laws are required, and yet the nature of the *finite* material to which law is applied leads to the further determining of general laws *ad infinitum*. On the one hand, the law ought to be a comprehensive whole, closed and complete; and yet, on the other hand, the need for further determinations is continual. But since this antinomy arises only when universal principles, which remain fixed and unchanged, are applied to particular types of case, the right to a complete legal code remains unimpaired, like the right that these simple general principles should be capable of being laid down and understood apart and in distinction from their application to such particular types.

A fruitful source of complexity in legislation is the

gradual intrusion of reason, of what is inherently and actually right, into primitive institutions which have something wrong at their roots and so are purely historical survivals. This occurred in Roman law, as was remarked above (see Remark to Paragraph 180), in medieval feudal law, &c. It is essential to notice, however, that the very nature of the finite material to which law is applied necessarily entails an infinite progress in the application to it of principles universal in themselves and inherently and actually rational.

It is misunderstanding which has given rise alike to the demand—a morbid craving of German scholars chiefly—that a legal code should be something absolutely complete, incapable of any fresh determination in detail, and also to the argument that because a code is incapable of such completion, therefore we ought not to produce something "incomplete," i.e. we ought not to produce a code at all. The misunderstanding rests in both cases on a misconception of the nature of a finite subject-matter like private law, whose so-called "completeness" is a perennial approximation to completeness, on a misconception of the difference between the universal of reason and the universal of the Understanding, and also on the application of the latter to the material of finitude and atomicity which goes on for ever.—*Le plus grand ennemi du Bien, c'est le Meilleur* is the utterance of true common sense against the common sense of idle argumentation and abstract reflection. [A.]

217. The principle of rightness passes over in civil society into law. My individual right, whose embodiment has hitherto been immediate and abstract, now similarly becomes embodied in the existent will and knowledge of everyone, in the sense that it becomes recognized. Hence property acquisitions and transfers must now be undertaken and concluded only in the form which that embodiment gives to them. In civil society, property rests on contract and on the formalities which make ownership capable of proof and valid in law.

Original, i.e. direct, titles and means of acquisition (see Paragraphs 54 ff.) are simply discarded in civil society and appear only as isolated accidents or as subordinated factors of property transactions. It is either feeling, refusing to move beyond the subjective, or reflection, clinging to its abstract essences, which casts formalities aside, while the dry-as-dust Understanding may for its part cling to formalities instead of the real thing and multiply them indefinitely.

Apart from this, however, the march of mental development is the long and hard struggle to free a content from its sensuous and immediate form, endow it with its appropriate form of thought, and thereby give it simple and adequate expression. It is because this is the case that when the development of law is just beginning, ceremonies and formalities are more circumstantial and count rather as the thing itself than as its symbol. Thus even in Roman law, a number of forms and especially phrases were retained from old-fashioned ceremonial usages, instead of being replaced by intelligible forms and phrases adequately expressing them. [A.]

218. Since property and personality have legal recognition and validity in civil society, wrongdoing now becomes an infringement, not merely of what is subjectively infinite, but of the universal thing which is existent with inherent stability and strength. Hence a new attitude arises: the action is seen as a danger to society and thereby the magnitude of the wrongdoing is increased.[1] On the other hand, however, the fact that society has become strong and sure of itself diminishes the external importance of the injury and so leads to a mitigation of its punishment.

The fact that an injury to one member of society is an injury to all others does not alter the conception of wrongdoing, but it does alter it in respect of its outward existence as an injury done, an injury which now affects the mind and consciousness of civil society as a whole, not merely the external embodiment of the person directly injured. In heroic times, as we see in the tragedy of the ancients, the citizens did not feel themselves injured by wrongs which members of the royal houses did to one another.

Implicitly, crime is an infinite injury; but as an existent fact it must be measured in quantity and quality (see Paragraph 96), and since its field of existence here has the essential character of affecting an idea and consciousness of the validity of the laws, its danger to civil society is a determinant of the magnitude of a crime, or even *one* of its qualitative characteristics.

Now this quality or magnitude varies with the state of civil society; and this is the justification for sometimes attaching the penalty of death to a theft of a few pence or a turnip, and at other times a light penalty to a theft of a hundred or more times that amount. If we consider its danger to society, this seems at first sight to aggravate the crime; but in fact it is just this which has been the prime cause of the mitigation of its punishment. A penal code, then, is primarily the child of its age and the state of civil society at the time. [A.]

(γ) The Court of Justice

219. By taking the form of law, right steps into a determinate mode of being. It is then something on its own account, and in contrast with particular willing and opining of the right, it is self-subsistent and has to vindicate itself as something universal. This is achieved by recognizing it and making it actual in a particular case without the subjective feeling of private interest; and this is the business of a public au-

[1] Compare Remarks to Paragraphs 96 and 319.—Ed.

thority—the court of justice.

The historical origin of the judge and his court may have had the form of a patriarch's gift to his people or of force or free choice; but this makes no difference to the concept of the thing. To regard the introduction of a legal system as no more than an optional act of grace or favour on the part of monarchs and governments (as Herr von Haller[1] does in his *Restauration der Staatswissenschaft*) is a piece of the mere thoughtlessness which has no inkling of the point at issue in a discussion of law and the state. The point is that legal and political institutions are rational in principle and therefore absolutely necessary, and the question of the form in which they arose or were introduced is entirely irrelevant to a consideration of their rational basis.

At the other extreme from Herr von Haller's point of view is the barbarous notion that the administration of justice is now, as it was in the days when might was right, an improper exercise of force, a suppression of freedom, and a despotism. The administration of justice must be regarded as the fulfilment of a duty by the public authority, no less than as the exercise of a right; and so far as it is a right, it does not depend upon an optional delegation to one authority by the individual members of society.

220. When the right against crime has the form of revenge (see Paragraph 102), it is only right implicit, not right in the form of right, i.e. no *act* of revenge is justified. Instead of the injured party, the injured *universal* now comes on the scene, and this has its proper actuality in the court of law. It takes over the pursuit and the avenging of crime, and this pursuit consequently ceases to be the subjective and contingent retribution of revenge and is transformed into the genuine reconciliation of right with itself, i.e. into punishment. Objectively, this is the reconciliation of the law with itself; by the annulment of the crime, the law is restored and its authority is thereby actualized. Subjectively, it is the reconciliation of the criminal with himself, i.e. with the law known by him as his own and as valid for him and his protection; when this law is executed upon him, he himself finds in this process the satisfaction of justice and nothing save his own act.

221. A member of civil society has the right *in judicio stare* and, correspondingly, the duty of acknowledging the jurisdiction of the court and accepting its decision as final when his own rights are in dispute. [A.]

222. In court the specific character which rightness acquires is that it must be demonstrable. When parties go to law, they are put in the posi-

[1] See Hegel's footnote to Paragraph 258.—ED.

tion of having to make good their evidence and their claims and to make the judge acquainted with the facts. These steps in a legal process are themselves rights, and their course must therefore be fixed by law. They also constitute an essential part of jurisprudence. [A.]

223. These steps in a legal process are subdivided continually within no fixed limits into more and more actions, each being distinct in itself and a right. Hence a legal process, in itself in any case a means, now begins to be something external to its end and contrasted with it. This long course of formalities is a right of the parties at law and they have the right to traverse it from beginning to end. Still, it may be turned into an evil, and even an instrument of wrong, and for this reason it is by law made the duty of the parties to submit themselves to the simple process of arbitration (before a tribunal of arbitrators) and to the attempt to reconcile their differences out of court, in order that they—and right itself, as the substance of the thing and so the thing really at issue—may be protected against legal processes and their misuse.

Equity involves a departure from formal rights owing to moral or other considerations and is concerned primarily with the content of the lawsuit. A court of equity, however, comes to mean a court which decides in a single case without insisting on the formalities of a legal process or, in particular, on the objective evidence which the letter of the law may require. Further, it decides on the merits of the single case as a unique one, not with a view to disposing of it in such a way as to create a binding legal precedent for the future.

224. Amongst the rights of the subjective consciousness are not only the publication of the laws (see Paragraph 215) but also the possibility of ascertaining the actualization of the law in a particular case (the course of the proceedings, the legal argument, &c.)—i.e. the publicity of judicial proceedings. The reason for this is that a trial is implicitly an event of universal validity, and although the particular content of the action affects the interests of the parties alone, its universal content, i.e. the right at issue and the judgement thereon, affects the interests of everybody.

If the members of the bench deliberate amongst themselves about the judgement which they are to deliver, such deliberations express opinions and views still personal and so naturally are not public. [A.]

225. By the judgement of the court, the law is applied to a single case, and the work of judgement has two distinct aspects: first, ascertain-

ment of the nature of the case as a unique, single, occurrence (e.g. whether a contract, &c., &c., has been made, whether a trespass has been committed, and if so by whom) and, in criminal cases, reflection to determine the essential, criminal, character of the deed (see Remark to Paragraph 119); secondly, the subsumption of the case under the law that right must be restored. Punishment in criminal cases is a conception falling under this law. Decisions on these two different aspects are given by different functionaries.

In the Roman judicial system, this distinction of functions appeared in that the Praetor pronounced judgement on the assumption that the facts were so and so, and then appointed a special *judex* to inquire into the facts.

In English law, it is left to the insight or option of the prosecutor to determine the precise character of a criminal act (e.g. whether it is murder or manslaughter) and the court is powerless to alter the indictment if it finds the prosecutor's choice wrong.

226. First, the conduct of the entire process of inquiry, secondly, the detailed stages of the action between the parties (these stages themselves being rights—see Paragraph 222), and then also the second of the aspects of the work of judgement mentioned in the previous Paragraph, are all a task which properly belongs to the judge at law. He is the organ of the law, and the case must be prepared for him in such a way as to make possible its subsumption under some principle; that is to say, it must be stripped of its apparent, empirical, character and exalted into a recognized fact of a general type.

227. The first aspect of the work of judgement, i.e. the knowledge of the facts of the case as a unique, single, occurrence, and the description of its general character, involves in itself no pronouncement on points of law. This is knowledge attainable by any educated man. In settling the character of an action, the subjective moment, i.e. the agent's insight and intention (see the Second Part[1]), is the essential thing; and apart from this, the proof depends not on objects of reason or abstractions of the Understanding, but only on single details and circumstances, objects of sensuous intuition and subjective certainty, and therefore does not contain in itself any absolute, objective, probative factor. It follows that judgement on the facts lies in the last resort with subjective conviction and conscience (*animi sententia*[2]),

[1] Especially Paragraph 119.—ED.
[2] "I swear to the best of my belief," or "on my conscience."—ED.

while the proof, resting as it does on the statements and affidavits of others, receives its final though purely subjective verification from the oath.

In this matter it is of the first importance to fix our eyes on the type of proof here in question and to distinguish it from knowledge and proof of another sort. To establish by proof a rational category, like the concept of right itself, means to apprehend its necessity, and so demands a method other than that requisite for the proof of a geometrical theorem. Further, in this latter case, the figure is determined by the Understanding and made abstract in advance according to a rule. But in the case of something empirical in content, like a fact, the material of knowledge is a given sensuous intuition and subjective sense-certainty, and statements and affidavits about such material. It is then a question of drawing conclusions and putting two and two together out of depositions of that kind, attestations and other details, &c. The objective truth which emerges from material of this kind and the method appropriate to it leads, when attempts are made to determine it rigidly and objectively, to half-proofs and then, by further sincere deductions from these—deductions which at the same time involve formal illogicality—to extraordinary punishments. But such objective truth means something quite different from the truth of a rational category or a proposition whose content the Understanding has determined for itself abstractly in advance. To show that, since the strictly legal character of a court covers competence to ascertain this sort of truth about empirical events, it thereby properly qualifies a court for this task and so gives it an inherent exclusive right to perform it and lays on it the necessity of performing it—that is the best approach to settling the question of how far decisions on points of fact, as well as on points of law, should be ascribed to courts as strictly juristic bodies. [A.]

228. When judgement is pronounced—so far as the function of judgement is the subsumption under the law of the case whose nature has been settled—the right due to the parties on the score of their self-consciousness is preserved in relation to the *law* because the law is known and so is the law of the parties themselves, and in relation to the *subsumption,* because the trial is public. But when a verdict is given on the particular, subjective, and external facts of the case (knowledge of which falls under the first of the aspects described in Paragraph 225), this right is satisfied by the confidence which the parties feel in the subjectivity of those who give the verdict. This confidence is based primarily on the similarity between them and the parties in respect of their particularity, i.e. their social position, &c.

The right of self-consciousness, the moment of

subjective freedom, may be regarded as the fundamental thing to keep before us in considering the necessity for publicity in legal proceedings and for the so-called jury-courts, and this in the last resort is the essence of whatever may be advanced in favour of these institutions on the score of their utility. Other points of view and reasoning about their several advantages and disadvantages may give rise to an argumentative exchange, but reasoning of this kind, like all deductive reasoning, is either secondary and inconclusive, or else drawn from other and perhaps higher spheres than that of advantage. It may be the case that if the administration of justice were entirely in the hands of professional lawyers, and there were no lay institutions like juries, it would in theory be managed just as well, if not better. It may be so, but even if this possibility rises by general consent to probability, or even certainty, it still does not matter, for on the other side there is always the right of self-consciousness, insisting on its claims and dissatisfied if laymen play no part.

Owing to the character of the entire body of the laws, knowledge both of what is right and also of the course of legal proceedings may become, together with the capacity to prosecute an action at law, the property of a class which makes itself an exclusive clique by the use of a terminology like a foreign tongue to those whose rights are at issue. If this happens, the members of civil society, who depend for their livelihood on their industry, on their own knowledge and will, are kept strangers to the law, not only to those parts of it affecting their most personal and intimate affairs, but also to its substantive and rational basis, the right itself, and the result is that they become the wards, or even in a sense the bondsmen, of the legal profession. They may indeed have the right to appear in court in person and to "stand" there (*in judicio stare*), but their bodily presence is a trifle if their minds are not to be there also, if they are not to follow the proceedings with their own knowledge, and if the justice they receive remains in their eyes a doom pronounced *ab extra*.

229. In civil society, the Idea is lost in particularity and has fallen asunder with the separation of inward and outward. In the administration of justice, however, civil society returns to its concept, to the unity of the implicit universal with the subjective particular, although here the latter is only that present in single cases and the universality in question is that of *abstract* right. The actualization of this unity through its extension to the whole ambit of particularity is (i) the specific function of the Police, though the unification which it effects is only relative; (ii) it is the Corporation which actualizes the unity completely, though only in a whole which, while concrete, is restricted.[1] [A.]

[1] See Paragraph 235.—Ed.

C. *The Police and the Corporation*

230. In the system of needs, the livelihood and welfare of every single person is a possibility whose actual attainment is just as much conditioned by his caprices and particular endowment as by the objective system of needs. Through the administration of justice, offences against property or personality are annulled. But the right actually present in the particular requires, first, that accidental hindrances to one aim or another be removed, and undisturbed safety of person and property be attained; and secondly, that the securing of every single person's livelihood and welfare be treated and actualized as a right, i.e. that particular welfare as such be so treated.

(*a*) Police [or the public authority]

231. Inasmuch as it is still the particular will which governs the choice of this or that end, the universal authority by which security is ensured remains in the first instance, (*a*) restricted to the sphere of contingencies, and (*b*) an external organization.

232. Crime is contingency as subjective willing of evil, and this is what the universal authority must prevent or bring to justice. But, crime apart, the subjective willing which is permissible in actions lawful *per se* and in the private use of property, also comes into external relation with other single persons, as well as with public institutions, other than law-courts, established for realizing a common end. This universal aspect makes private actions a matter of contingency which escapes the agent's control and which either does or may injure others and wrong them.

233. There is here only a possibility of injury; but the actual non-occurrence of injury is at this stage not just another contingency. The point is that the actions of individuals may always be wrongful, and this is the ultimate reason for police control and penal justice.

234. The relations between external existents fall into the infinite of the Understanding; there is, therefore, no inherent line of distinction between what is and what is not injurious, even where crime is concerned, or between what is and what is not suspicious, or between what is to be forbidden or subjected to supervision and what is to be exempt from prohibition, from surveillance and suspicion, from inquiry and the demand to render an account of itself. These details are determined by custom, the spirit of the

rest of the constitution, contemporary conditions, the crisis of the hour, and so forth. [A.]

235. In the indefinite multiplication and interconnexion of day-to-day needs, (a) the acquisition and exchange of the means to their satisfaction—a satisfaction which everyone confidently expects to be possible of attainment without hindrance, and (b) the endeavours made and the transactions carried out in order to shorten the process of attainment as much as possible, give rise to factors which are a common interest, and when one man occupies himself with these his work is at the same time done for all. The situation is productive too of contrivances and organizations which may be of use to the community as a whole. These universal activities and organizations of general utility call for the oversight and care of the public authority.

236. The differing interests of producers and consumers may come into collision with each other; and although a fair balance between them on the whole may be brought about automatically, still their adjustment also requires a control which stands above both and is consciously undertaken. The right to the exercise of such control in a single case (e.g. in the fixing of the prices of the commonest necessaries of life) depends on the fact that, by being publicly exposed for sale, goods in absolutely universal daily demand are offered not so much to an individual as such but rather to a universal purchaser, the public; and thus both the defence of the public's right not to be defrauded, and also the management of goods inspection, may lie, as a common concern, with a public authority. But public care and direction are most of all necessary in the case of the larger branches of industry, because these are dependent on conditions abroad and on combinations of distant circumstances which cannot be grasped as a whole by the individuals tied to these industries for their living.

At the other extreme to freedom of trade and commerce in civil society is public organization to provide for everything and determine everyone's labour —take for example in ancient times the labour on the pyramids and the other huge monuments in Egypt and Asia which were constructed for public ends, and the worker's task was not mediated through his private choice and particular interest. This interest invokes freedom of trade and commerce against control from above; but the more blindly it sinks into self-seeking aims, the more it requires such control to bring it back to the universal. Control is also necessary to diminish the danger of upheavals arising from clashing interests and to

abbreviate the period in which their tension should be eased through the working of a necessity of which they themselves know nothing. [A.]

237. Now while the possibility of sharing in the general wealth is open to individuals and is assured to them by the public authority, still it is subject to contingencies on the subjective side (quite apart from the fact that this assurance must remain incomplete), and the more it presupposes skill, health, capital, and so forth as its conditions, the more is it so subject.

238. Originally the family is the substantive whole whose function it is to provide for the individual on his particular side by giving him either the means and the skill necessary to enable him to earn his living out of the resources of society, or else subsistence and maintenance in the event of his suffering a disability. But civil society tears the individual from his family ties, estranges the members of the family from one another, and recognizes them as self-subsistent persons. Further, for the paternal soil and the external inorganic resources of nature from which the individual formerly derived his livelihood, it substitutes its own soil and subjects the permanent existence of even the entire family to dependence on itself and to contingency. Thus the individual becomes a son of civil society which has as many claims upon him as he has rights against it. [A.]

239. In its character as a universal family, civil society has the right and duty of superintending and influencing education, inasmuch as education bears upon the child's capacity to become a member of society. Society's right here is paramount over the arbitrary and contingent preferences of parents, particularly in cases where education is to be completed not by the parents but by others. To the same end, society must provide public educational facilities so far as is practicable. [A.]

240. Similarly, society has the right and duty of acting as trustee to those whose extravagance destroys the security of their own subsistence or their families'. It must substitute for extravagance the pursuit of the ends of society and the individuals concerned. [A.]

241. Not only caprice, however, but also contingencies, physical conditions, and factors grounded in external circumstances (see Paragraph 200) may reduce men to poverty. The poor still have the needs common to civil society, and yet since society has withdrawn from them the natural means of acquisition (see Para-

graph 217) and broken the bond of the family—in the wider sense of the clan (see Paragraph 181)—their poverty leaves them more or less deprived of all the advantages of society, of the opportunity of acquiring skill or education of any kind, as well as of the administration of justice, the public health services, and often even of the consolations of religion, and so forth. The public authority takes the place of the family where the poor are concerned in respect not only of their immediate want but also of laziness of disposition, malignity, and the other vices which arise out of their plight and their sense of wrong.

242. Poverty and, in general, the distress of every kind to which every individual is exposed from the start in the cycle of his natural life has a subjective side which demands similarly subjective aid, arising both from the special circumstances of a particular case and also from love and sympathy. This is the place where morality finds plenty to do despite all public organization. Subjective aid, however, both in itself and in its operation, is dependent on contingency and consequently society struggles to make it less necessary, by discovering the general causes of penury and general means of its relief, and by organizing relief accordingly.

Casual almsgiving and casual endowments, e.g. for the burning of lamps before holy images, &c., are supplemented by public alms-houses, hospitals, street-lighting, and so forth. There is still quite enough left over and above these things for charity to do on its own account. A false view is implied both when charity insists on having this poor relief reserved solely to private sympathy and the accidental occurrence of knowledge and a charitable disposition, and also when it feels injured or mortified by universal regulations and ordinances which are *obligatory*. Public social conditions are on the contrary to be regarded as all the more perfect the less (in comparison with what is arranged publicly) is left for an individual to do by himself as his private inclination directs.

243. When civil society is in a state of unimpeded activity, it is engaged in expanding internally[1] in population and industry. The amassing of wealth is intensified by generalizing (a) the linkage of men by their needs, and (b) the methods of preparing and distributing the means to satisfy these needs, because it is from this double process of generalization that the largest profits are derived. That is one side of the picture. The other side is the subdivision and restriction of particular jobs. This results in the

[1] See Paragraph 246.—ED.

dependence and distress of the class tied to work of that sort, and these again entail inability to feel and enjoy the broader freedoms and especially the intellectual benefits of civil society.

244. When the standard of living of a large mass of people falls below a certain subsistence level—a level regulated automatically as the one necessary for a member of the society—and when there is a consequent loss of the sense of right and wrong, of honesty and the self-respect which makes a man insist on maintaining himself by his own work and effort, the result is the creation of a rabble of paupers. At the same time this brings with it, at the other end of the social scale, conditions which greatly facilitate the concentration of disproportionate wealth in a few hands. [A.]

245. When the masses begin to decline into poverty, (a) the burden of maintaining them at their ordinary standard of living might be directly laid on the wealthier classes, or they might receive the means of livelihood directly from other public sources of wealth (e.g. from the endowments of rich hospitals, monasteries, and other foundations). In either case, however, the needy would receive subsistence directly, not by means of their work, and this would violate the principle of civil society and the feeling of individual independence and self-respect in its individual members. (b) As an alternative, they might be given subsistence indirectly through being given work, i.e. the opportunity to work. In this event the volume of production would be increased, but the evil consists precisely in an excess of production and in the lack of a proportionate number of consumers who are themselves also producers, and thus it is simply intensified by both of the methods (a) and (b) by which it is sought to alleviate it. It hence becomes apparent that despite an excess of wealth civil society is not rich enough, i.e. its own resources are insufficient to check excessive poverty and the creation of a penurious rabble.

In the example of England we may study these phenomena on a large scale and also in particular the results of poor-rates, immense foundations, unlimited private beneficence, and above all the abolition of the Guild Corporations. In Britain, particularly in Scotland, the most direct measure against poverty and especially against the loss of shame and self-respect—the subjective bases of society—as well as against laziness and extravagance, &c., the begetters of the rabble, has turned out to be to leave the poor to their fate and instruct them to beg in the streets.

246. This inner dialectic of civil society thus drives it—or at any rate drives a specific civil society—to push beyond its own limits and seek markets, and so its necessary means of subsistence, in other lands which are either deficient in the goods it has over-produced, or else generally backward in industry, &c.

247. The principle of family life is dependence on the soil, on land, *terra firma*. Similarly, the natural element for industry, animating its outward movement, is the sea. Since the passion for gain involves risk, industry though bent on gain yet lifts itself above it; instead of remaining rooted to the soil and the limited circle of civil life with its pleasures and desires, it embraces the element of flux, danger, and destruction. Further, the sea is the greatest means of communication,[1] and trade by sea creates commercial connexions between distant countries and so relations involving contractual rights. At the same time, commerce of this kind is the most potent instrument of culture, and through it trade acquires its significance in the history of the world.

Rivers are not natural boundaries of separation, which is what they have been accounted to be in modern times. On the contrary, it is truer to say that they, and the sea likewise, link men together. Horace is wrong when he says:

> *deus abscidit*
> *prudens Oceano dissociabili*
> *terras.*[2]

The proof of this lies not merely in the fact that the basins of rivers are inhabited by a single clan or tribe, but also, for example, in the ancient bonds between Greece, Ionia, and Magna Graecia, between Brittany and Britain, between Denmark and Norway, Sweden, Finland, Livonia, &c., bonds, further, which are especially striking in contrast with the comparatively slight intercourse between the inhabitants of the littoral and those of the hinterland. To realize what an instrument of culture lies in the link with the sea, consider countries where industry flourishes and contrast their relation to the sea with that of countries which have eschewed sea-faring and which, like Egypt and India, have become stagnant and sunk in the most frightful and scandalous superstition. Notice also how all great progressive peoples press onward to the sea.

248. This far-flung connecting link affords the means for the colonizing activity—sporadic or systematic—to which the mature civil society is driven and by which it supplies to a part of its population a return to life on the family basis in a new land and so also supplies itself with a new demand and field for its industry. [A.]

249. While the public authority must also undertake the higher directive function of providing for the interests which lead beyond the borders of its society (see Paragraph 246), its primary purpose is to actualize and maintain the universal contained within the particularity of civil society, and its control takes the form of an external system and organization for the protection and security of particular ends and interests *en masse,* inasmuch as these interests subsist only in this universal. This universal is immanent in the interests of particularity itself and, in accordance with the Idea, particularity makes it the end and object of its own willing and activity. In this way ethical principles circle back and appear in civil society as a factor immanent in it; this constitutes the specific character of the Corporation.

(β) The Corporation

250. In virtue of the substantiality of its natural and family life, the agricultural class has directly within itself the concrete universal in which it lives. The class of civil servants is universal in character and so has the universal explicitly as its ground and as the aim of its activity. The class between them, the business class, is essentially concentrated on the particular, and hence it is to it that Corporations are specially appropriate.

251. The labour organization of civil society is split, in accordance with the nature of its particulars, into different branches. The implicit likeness of such particulars to one another becomes really existent in an association, as something common to its members. Hence a selfish purpose, directed towards its particular self-interest, apprehends and evinces itself at the same time as universal; and a member of civil society is in virtue of his own particular skill a member of a Corporation, whose universal purpose is thus wholly concrete and no wider in scope than the purpose involved in business, its proper task and interest.

252. In accordance with this definition of its functions, a Corporation has the right, under the surveillance of the public authority, (*a*) to look after its own interests within its own sphere, (*b*) to co-opt members, qualified objectively by the requisite skill and rectitude, to a

---

[1] Cf. Kant, *Critique of Aesthetic Judgment,* § 29. Also, Hegel, *Philosophy of History,* the section on the "Geographical Basis of History," especially pp. 195 ff.—ED.

[2] *Odes,* I. iii [ll. 21-3. "God of set purpose has sundered the lands by the estranging sea"].

number fixed by the general structure of society, (*c*) to protect its members against particular contingencies, (*d*) to provide the education requisite to fit others to become members. In short, its right is to come on the scene like a second family for its members, while civil society can only be an indeterminate sort of family because it comprises everyone and so is farther removed from individuals and their special exigencies.

The Corporation member is to be distinguished from a day labourer or from a man who is prepared to undertake casual employment on a single occasion. The former who is, or will become, master of his craft, is a member of the association not for casual gain on single occasions but for the whole range, the universality, of his personal livelihood.

Privileges, in the sense of the rights of a branch of civil society organized into a Corporation, are distinct in meaning from privileges proper in the etymological sense. The latter are casual exceptions to universal rules; the former, however, are only the crystallization, as regulations, of characteristics inherent in an essential branch of society itself owing to its nature as particular.

253. In the Corporation, the family has its stable basis in the sense that its livelihood is assured there, conditionally upon capability, i.e. it has a stable capital (see Paragraph 170). In addition, this nexus of capability and livelihood is a *recognized* fact, with the result that the Corporation member needs no external marks beyond his own membership as evidence of his skill and his regular income and subsistence, i.e. as evidence that he is a somebody.[1] It is also recognized that he belongs to a whole which is itself an organ of the entire society, and that he is actively concerned in promoting the comparatively disinterested end of this whole. Thus he commands the respect due to one in his social position.

The institution of Corporations corresponds, on account of its assurance of capital, to the introduction of agriculture and private property in another sphere (see Remark to Paragraph 203).

When complaints are made about the luxury of the business classes and their passion for extravagance—which have as their concomitant the creation of a rabble of paupers (see Paragraph 244)—we must not forget that besides its other causes (e.g. increasing mechanization of labour) this phenomenon has an ethical ground, as was indicated above.[2] Unless he is a member of an authorized Corporation (and it is only by being authorized that an association becomes a Corporation), an individual is without rank or dignity, his isolation reduces his business to mere self-seeking, and his livelihood and

satisfaction become insecure. Consequently, he has to try to gain recognition for himself by giving external proofs of success in his business, and to these proofs no limits can be set. He cannot live in the manner of his class, for no class really exists for him, since in civil society it is only something common to particular persons which really exists, i.e. something legally constituted and recognized. Hence he cannot achieve for himself a way of life proper to his class and less idiosyncratic.

Within the Corporation the help which poverty receives loses its accidental character and the humiliation wrongfully associated with it. The wealthy perform their duties to their fellow associates and thus riches cease to inspire either pride or envy, pride in their owners, envy in others. In these conditions rectitude obtains its proper recognition and respect.

254. The so-called "natural" right of exercising one's skill and thereby earning what there is to be earned is restricted within the Corporation only in so far as it is therein made rational instead of natural. That is to say, it becomes freed from personal opinion and contingency, saved from endangering either the individual workman or others, recognized, guaranteed, and at the same time elevated to conscious effort for a common end.

255. As the family was the first, so the Corporation is the second ethical root of the state, the one planted in civil society. The former contains the moments of subjective particularity and objective universality in a substantial unity. But these moments are sundered in civil society to begin with; on the one side there is the particularity of need and satisfaction, reflected into itself, and on the other side the universality of abstract rights. In the Corporation these moments are united in an inward fashion, so that in this union particular welfare is present as a right and is actualized.

The sanctity of marriage and the dignity of Corporation membership are the two fixed points round which the unorganized atoms of civil society revolve. [A.]

256. The end of the Corporation is restricted and finite, while the public authority was an external organization involving a separation and a merely relative identity of controller and controlled. The end of the former and the externality and relative identity of the latter find their truth in the absolutely universal end and its absolute actuality. Hence the sphere of civil society passes over into the state.

The town is the seat of the civil life of business. There reflection arises, turns in upon itself, and pursues its atomizing task; each man maintains himself

---

[1] See Addition to Paragraph 207.—ED.
[2] See Paragraphs 184, 185, and 243.—ED.

in and through his relation to others who, like himself, are persons possessed of rights. The country, on the other hand, is the seat of an ethical life resting on nature and the family. Town and country thus constitute the two moments, still ideal[1] moments, whose true ground is the state, although it is from them that the state springs.

The philosophic proof of the concept of the state is this development of ethical life from its immediate phase through civil society, the phase of division, to the state, which then reveals itself as the true ground of these phases. A proof in philosophic science can only be a development of this kind.

Since the state appears as a result in the advance of the philosophic concept through displaying itself as the true ground [of the earlier phases], that show of mediation is now cancelled and the state has become directly present before us. Actually, therefore, the state as such is not so much the result as the beginning. It is within the state that the family is first developed into civil society, and it is the Idea of the state itself which disrupts itself into these two moments. Through the development of civil society, the substance of ethical life acquires its infinite form, which contains in itself these two moments: (1) infinite differentiation down to the inward experience of independent self-consciousness, and (2) the form of universality involved in education, the form of thought whereby mind is objective and actual to itself as an organic totality in laws and institutions which are its will in terms of thought.

Sub-section III

THE STATE

257. The state is the actuality of the ethical Idea. It is ethical mind *qua* the substantial will manifest and revealed to itself, knowing and thinking itself, accomplishing what it knows and in so far as it knows it. The state exists immediately in custom, mediately in individual self-consciousness, knowledge, and activity, while self-consciousness in virtue of its sentiment towards the state finds in the state, as its essence and the end and product of its activity, its substantive freedom.

The *Penates* are inward gods, gods of the underworld; the mind of a nation[2] (Athene for instance) is the divine, knowing and willing itself. Family piety is feeling, ethical behaviour directed by feeling; political virtue is the willing of the absolute end in terms of thought.

258. The state is absolutely rational inasmuch as it is the actuality of the substantial will which it possesses in the particular self-consciousness once that consciousness has been raised to con-

sciousness of its universality. This substantial unity is an absolute unmoved end in itself, in which freedom comes into its supreme right. On the other hand this final end has supreme right against the individual, whose supreme duty is to be a member of the state.

If the state is confused with civil society, and if its specific end is laid down as the security and protection of property and personal freedom, then the interest of the individuals as such becomes the ultimate end of their association, and it follows that membership of the state is something optional. But the state's relation to the individual is quite different from this. Since the state is mind objectified, it is only as one of its members that the individual himself has objectivity, genuine individuality, and an ethical life. Unification pure and simple is the true content and aim of the individual, and the individual's destiny is the living of a universal life. His further particular satisfaction, activity, and mode of conduct have this substantive and universally valid life as their starting point and their result.

Rationality, taken generally and in the abstract, consists in the thoroughgoing unity of the universal and the single. Rationality, concrete in the state, consists (*a*) so far as its content is concerned, in the unity of objective freedom (i.e. freedom of the universal or substantial will) and subjective freedom (i.e. freedom of everyone in his knowing and in his volition of particular ends) ; and consequently, (*b*) so far as its form is concerned, in self-determining action on laws and principles which are thoughts and so universal. This Idea is the absolutely eternal and necessary being of mind.[3]

But if we ask what is or has been the historical origin of the state in general, still more if we ask about the origin of any particular state, of its rights and institutions, or again if we inquire whether the state originally arose out of patriarchal conditions or out of fear or trust, or out of Corporations, &c., or finally if we ask in what light the basis of the state's rights has been conceived and consciously established, whether this basis has been supposed to be positive divine right, or contract, custom, &c.—all these questions are no concern of the Idea of the state. We are here dealing exclusively with the philosophic science of the state, and from that point of view all these things are mere appearance and therefore matters for history. So far as the authority of any existing state has anything to do with reasons, these reasons are culled from the forms of the law authoritative within it.

The philosophical treatment of these topics is concerned only with their inward side, with the thought of their concept. The merit of Rousseau's contribution to the search for this concept is that, by adducing the will as the principle of the state, he is adducing a principle which has thought both for its form and its content, a principle indeed which is thinking itself, not a principle, like gregarious in-

---

[1] See Paragraph 278.—ED.
[2] With this Remark, compare Remarks to Paragraphs 163 and 166.—ED.

[3] See Paragraphs 302-4.—ED.

stinct, for instance, or divine authority, which has thought as its form only. Unfortunately, however, as Fichte did later, he takes the will only in a determinate form as the individual will, and he regards the universal will not as the absolutely rational element in the will, but only as a "general" will which proceeds out of this individual will as out of a conscious will. The result is that he reduces the union of individuals in the state to a contract and therefore to something based on their arbitrary wills, their opinion, and their capriciously given express consent; and abstract reasoning proceeds to draw the logical inferences which destroy the absolutely divine principle of the state, together with its majesty and absolute authority. For this reason, when these abstract conclusions came into power, they afforded for the first time in human history the prodigious spectacle of the overthrow of the constitution of a great actual state and its complete reconstruction *ab initio* on the basis of pure thought alone, after the destruction of all existing and given material. The will of its re-founders was to give it what they alleged was a purely rational basis, but it was only abstractions that were being used; the Idea was lacking; and the experiment ended in the maximum of frightfulness and terror.

Confronted with the claims made for the individual will, we must remember the fundamental conception that the objective will is rationality implicit or in conception, whether it be recognized or not by individuals, whether their whims be deliberately for it or not. We must remember that its opposite, i.e. knowing and willing, or subjective freedom (the *only* thing contained in the principle of the individual will) comprises only one moment, and therefore a one-sided moment, of the Idea of the rational will, i.e. of the will which is rational solely because what it is implicitly, that it also is explicitly.

The opposite to thinking of the state as something to be known and apprehended as explicitly rational is taking external appearances—i.e. contingencies such as distress, need for protection, force, riches, &c.—not as moments in the state's historical development, but as its substance. Here again what constitutes the guiding thread of discovery is the individual in isolation—not, however, even so much as the *thought* of this individuality, but instead only empirical individuals, with attention focused on their accidental characteristics, their strength and weakness, riches and poverty, &c. This ingenious idea of ignoring the absolute infinity and rationality in the state and excluding thought from apprehension of its inward nature has assuredly never been put forward in such an unadulterated form as in Herr von Haller's *Restauration der Staatswissenschaft.* I say "unadulterated," because in all other attempts to grasp the essence of the state, no matter on what one-sided or superficial principles, this very intention of comprehending the state rationally has brought with it thoughts, i.e. universal determinations. Herr von Haller, however, with his eyes open, has not merely renounced the rational material of

which the state consists, as well as the form of thought, but he has even gone on with passionate fervour to inveigh against the form and the material so set aside. Part of what Herr von Haller assures us is the "wide-spread" effect of his principles, this *Restauration* undoubtedly owes to the fact that, in his exposition, he has deliberately dispensed with thought altogether, and has deliberately kept his whole book all of a piece with its lack of thought. For in this way he has eliminated the confusion and disorder which lessen the force of an exposition where the accidental is treated along with hints of the substantial, where the purely empirical and external are mixed with a reminiscence of the universal and rational, and where in the midst of wretched inanities the reader is now and again reminded of the loftier sphere of the infinite. For the same reason again his exposition is consistent. He takes as the essence of the state, not what is substantive but the sphere of accident, and consistency in dealing with a sphere of that kind amounts to the complete inconsistency of utter thoughtlessness which jogs along without looking behind, and is just as much at home now with the exact opposite of what it approved a moment ago.[1] [A.]

[1] I have described the book sufficiently to show that it is of an original kind. There might be something noble in the author's indignation by itself, since it was kindled by the false theories, mentioned above, emanating principally from Rousseau, and especially by the attempt to realize them in practice. But to save himself from these theories, Herr von Haller has gone to the other extreme by dispensing with thought altogether and consequently it cannot be said that there is anything of intrinsic value in his virulent hatred of all laws and legislation, of all expressly and legally determinate rights. The hatred of law, of right made determinate in law, is the shibboleth whereby fanaticism, flabby-mindedness, and the hypocrisy of good intentions are clearly and infallibly recognized for what they are, disguise themselves as they may.

Originality like Herr von Haller's is always a curious phenomenon, and for those of my readers who are not yet acquainted with his book I will quote a few specimen passages. This is how he lays down (vol. i, pp. 342 ff. [pp. 361 ff.]) his most important basic proposition: "Just as, in the inorganic world, the greater dislodges the less and the mighty the weak . . . , so in the animal kingdom, and then amongst human beings, the same law appears in nobler" (often, too, surely in ignobler?) "forms," and [p. 375] "this, therefore, is the eternal, unalterable, ordinance of God, that the mightier rules, must rule, and will always rule." It is clear enough from this, let alone from what follows, in what sense "might" is taken here. It is not the might of justice and ethics, but only the irrational power of brute force. Herr von Haller then goes on (*ibid.*, pp. 365 ff. [pp. 380 ff.]) to support this doctrine on various grounds, amongst them that "nature with amazing wisdom has so ordered it that the mere sense of personal superiority irresistibly ennobles the character and encourages the development of just those virtues which are most necessary for dealing with subordinates." He asks with a great elaboration of undergraduate rhetoric [*ibid.*] "whether it is the strong or the weak in the kingdom of science who more misuse their trust and their authority in order to achieve their petty selfish ends and the ruin of the credulous; whether to be a past master in legal learning is not to be a pettifogger, a *leguleius*, one who cheats the hopes of unsuspecting clients, who makes white black and black white, who misapplies the law and makes it a vehicle for wrongdoing, who brings to beggary those who need his assistance and rends them as the hungry vulture rends

259. The Idea of the state

(*a*) has immediate actuality and is the individual state as a self-dependent organism—the *Constitution* or *Constitutional Law;*

(*b*) passes over into the relation of one state to other states—*International Law;*

(*c*) is the universal Idea as a genus and as an absolute power over individual states—the mind which gives itself its actuality in the process of *World-History.* [A.]

A. *Constitutional Law*

260. The state is the actuality of concrete freedom. But concrete freedom consists in this, that personal individuality and its particular inter-

ests not only achieve their complete development and gain explicit recognition for their right (as they do in the sphere of the family and civil society) but, for one thing, they also pass over of their own accord into the interest of the universal, and, for another thing, they know and will the universal; they even recognize it as their own substantive mind; they take it as their end and aim and are active in its pursuit. The result is that the universal does not prevail or achieve completion except along with particular interests and through the co-operation of particular knowing and willing; and individuals likewise do not live as private persons for their own ends alone, but in the very act of willing these they

---

the innocent lamb," &c., &c. Herr von Haller forgets here that the point of this rhetoric is to support his proposition that the rule of the mightier is an everlasting ordinance of God; so presumably it is by the same ordinance that the vulture rends the innocent lamb, and that hence the mighty are quite right to treat their unsuspecting clients as the weak and to make use of knowledge of the law to empty their pockets. It would be too much, however, to ask that two thoughts should be put together where there is really not a single one.

It goes without saying that Herr von Haller is an enemy of codes of law. In his view, the laws of the land, are on the one hand, in principle "unnecessary, because they spring self-explanatory from the laws of nature." If men had remained satisfied with "self-explanatory" as the basis of their thinking, then they would have been spared the endless labour devoted, since ever there were states, to legislation and legal codes, and which is still devoted thereto and to the study of positive law. "On the other hand, laws are not exactly promulgated for private individuals, but as instructions to puisne judges, acquainting them with the will of the high court" [vol. ii, part i, chap. 32]. Apart from that, the provision of law-courts is (vol. i, p. 297 [pp. 309 ff.], vol. ii, part i, p. 254 [pp. 264-9] and all over the place) not a state duty, but a favour, help rendered by the authorities, and "quite supererogatory"; it is not the most perfect method of guaranteeing men's rights; on the contrary, it is an insecure and uncertain method, "the only one left to us by our modern lawyers. They have reft us of the other three methods, of just those which lead most swiftly and surely to the goal, those which, unlike law-courts, friendly nature has given to man for the safeguarding of his rightful freedom." And these three methods are—what do you suppose?— "(1) Personal acceptance and inculcation of the law of nature; (2) Resistance to wrong; (3) Flight, when there is no other remedy." Lawyers are unfriendly indeed, it appears, in comparison with the friendliness of nature! "But" (vol. i, p. 292 [p. 305]) "the natural, divine, law, given to everyone by nature the all-bountiful, is: Honour everyone as thine equal" (on the author's principles this should read "Honour not the man who is thine equal, but the one who is mightier"); "hurt no man who hurts thee not; demand from him nothing but what he owes" (but what does he owe?); "nay more, love thy neighbour and serve him when thou canst." The "implanting of this law" is to make a legislator and a constitution superfluous. It would be curious to see how Herr von Haller makes it intelligible why legislators and constitutions have appeared in the world despite this "implanting."

In vol. iii, pp. 362 [361] ff., the author comes to the "so-called national liberties," by which he means the laws and constitutions of nation states. Every legally constituted right is in this wide sense of the word a "liberty." Of these laws he says, *inter alia*, that "their content is usually very insignificant, although in books a

high value may be placed on documentary liberties of that kind." When we then realize that the author is speaking here of the national liberties of the German Estates, of the English people (e.g. Magna Carta [p. 367] "which is little read, and on account of its archaic phraseology still less understood," the Bill of Rights, and so forth), of the people of Hungary, &c., we are surprised to find that these possessions, formerly so highly prized, are only insignificant; and no less surprised to learn that it is only in books that these nations place a value on laws whose co-operation has entered into every coat that is worn and every crust that is eaten, and still enters into every day and hour of the lives of everyone.

To carry quotation further, Herr von Haller speaks particularly ill (vol. i, pp. 185 ff. [pp. 192-3]) of the Prussian General Legal Code, because of the "incredible" influence on it of the errors of false philosophy (though in this instance at any rate the fault cannot be ascribed to Kant's philosophy, a topic on which Herr von Haller is at his angriest), especially where it speaks of the state, the resources of the state, the end of the state, the head of the state, his duties, and those of civil servants, and so forth. Herr von Haller finds particularly mischievous [vol. i, pp. 198-9] "the right of defraying the expenses of the state by levying taxes on the private wealth of individuals, on their businesses, on goods produced or consumed. Under those circumstances, neither the king himself (since the resources of the state belong to the state and are not the private property of the king), nor the Prussian citizens can call anything their own, neither their person nor their property; and all subjects are bondslaves to the law, since they may not withdraw themselves from the service of the state."

In this welter of incredible crudity, what is perhaps most comical of all is the emotion with which Herr von Haller describes his unspeakable pleasure in his discoveries (vol. i, Preface [pp. xxv-xxvii])—"a joy such as only the friend of truth can feel when after honest search he has become confident that he has found as it were" (yes indeed! "as it were" is right!) "the voice of nature, the very word of God." (The truth is that the word of God very clearly distinguishes its revelations from the voices of nature and unregenerate man.) "The author could have sunk to the ground in open amazement, a stream of joyful tears burst from his eyes, and living religious feeling sprang up in him there and then." Herr von Haller might have discovered by his "religious feeling" that he should rather bewail his condition as the hardest chastisement of God. For the hardest thing which man can experience is to be so far excluded from thought and reason, from respect for the laws, and from knowing how infinitely important and divine it is that the duties of the state and the rights of the citizens, as well as the rights of the state and the duties of the citizens, should be defined by law—to be so far excluded from all this that absurdity can foist itself upon him as the word of God.

will the universal in the light of the universal, and their activity is consciously aimed at none but the universal end. The principle of modern states has prodigious strength and depth because it allows the principle of subjectivity to progress to its culmination in the extreme of self-subsistent personal particularity, and yet at the same time brings it back to the substantive unity and so maintains this unity in the principle of subjectivity itself. [A.]

261. In contrast with the spheres of private rights and private welfare (the family and civil society), the state is from one point of view an external necessity and their higher authority; its nature is such that their laws and interests are subordinate to it and dependent on it. On the other hand, however, it is the end immanent within them, and its strength lies in the unity of its own universal end and aim with the particular interest of individuals, in the fact that individuals have duties to the state in proportion as they have rights against it (see Paragraph 155).

In the Remark to Paragraph 3 above, reference was made to the fact that it was Montesquieu above all who, in his famous work *The Spirit of Laws,* kept in sight and tried to work out in detail both the thought of the dependence of laws—in particular, laws concerning the rights of persons—on the specific character of the state, and also the philosophic notion of always treating the part in its relation to the whole.

Duty is primarily a relation to something which from my point of view is substantive, absolutely universal. A right, on the other hand, is simply the embodiment of this substance and thus is the particular aspect of it and enshrines my particular freedom. Hence at abstract levels, right and duty appear parcelled out on different sides or in different persons. In the state, as something ethical, as the interpenetration of the substantive and the particular, my obligation to what is substantive is at the same time the embodiment of my particular freedom. This means that in the state duty and right are united in one and the same relation. But further, since none the less the distinct moments acquire in the state the shape and reality peculiar to each, and since therefore the distinction between right and duty enters here once again, it follows that while implicitly, i.e. in form, identical, they at the same time differ in content. In the spheres of personal rights and morality, the necessary bearing of right and duty on one another falls short of actualization; and hence there is at that point only an abstract similarity of content between them, i.e. in those abstract spheres, what is one man's right ought also to be another's, and what is one man's duty ought also to be another's. The absolute identity of right and duty in the state is present in these spheres not as a

genuine identity but only as a similarity of content, because in them this content is determined as quite general and is simply the fundamental principle of both right and duty, i.e. the principle that men, as persons, are free. Slaves, therefore, have no duties because they have no rights, and vice versa. (Religious duties are not here in point.[1])

In the course of the inward development of the concrete Idea, however, its moments become distinguished and their specific determinacy becomes at the same time a difference of content. In the family, the content of a son's duties to his father differs from the content of his rights against him; the content of the rights of a member of civil society is not the same as the content of his duties to his prince and government.

This concept of the union of duty and right is a point of vital importance and in it the inner strength of states is contained.

Duty on its abstract side goes no farther than the persistent neglect and proscription of a man's particular interest, on the ground that it is the inessential, even the discreditable, moment in his life. Duty, taken concretely as Idea, reveals the moment of particularity as itself essential and so regards its satisfaction as indisputably necessary. In whatever way an individual may fulfil his duty, he must at the same time find his account therein and attain his personal interest and satisfaction. Out of his position in the state, a right must accrue to him whereby public affairs shall be his own particular affair. Particular interests should in fact not be set aside or completely suppressed; instead, they should be put in correspondence with the universal, and thereby both they and the universal are upheld. The *isolated* individual, so far as his duties are concerned, is in subjection; but as a member of *civil society* he finds in fulfilling his duties to it protection of his person and property, regard for his private welfare, the satisfaction of the depths of his being, the consciousness and feeling of himself as a member of the whole; and, in so far as he completely fulfils his duties by performing tasks and services for the *state,* he is upheld and preserved. Take duty abstractly, and the universal's interest would consist simply in the completion as duties of the tasks and services which it exacts. [A.]

262. The actual Idea is mind, which, sundering itself into the two ideal spheres of its concept, family and civil society, enters upon its finite phase, but it does so only in order to rise above its ideality and become explicit as infinite actual mind. It is therefore to these ideal spheres that the actual Idea assigns the material of this its finite actuality, viz. human beings as a mass, in such a way that the function assigned to any given individual is visibly mediated by circumstances, his caprice and his personal

[1] See Hegel's second footnote to the Remark to Paragraph 270.—ED.

choice of his station in life (see Paragraph 185 and the Remark thereto). [A.]

263. In these spheres in which its moments, particularity and individuality, have their immediate and reflected reality, mind is present as their objective universality glimmering in them as the power of reason in necessity (see Paragraph 184), i.e. as the institutions considered above. [A.]

264. Mind is the nature of human beings *en masse* and their nature is therefore twofold: (i) at one extreme, explicit individuality of consciousness and will, and (ii) at the other extreme, universality which knows and wills what is substantive. Hence they attain their right in both these respects only in so far as both their private personality and its substantive basis are actualized. Now in the family and civil society they acquire their right in the first of these respects directly and in the second indirectly, in that (i) they find their substantive self-consciousness in social institutions which are the universal implicit in their particular interests, and (ii) the Corporation supplies them with an occupation and an activity directed on a universal end.

265. These institutions are the components of the constitution (i.e. of rationality developed and actualized) in the sphere of particularity. They are, therefore, the firm foundation not only of the state but also of the citizen's trust in it and sentiment towards it. They are the pillars of public freedom since in them particular freedom is realized and rational, and therefore there is *implicitly* present even in them the union of freedom and necessity. [A.]

266. But mind is objective and actual to itself not merely as this necessity and as a realm of appearance, but also as the ideality and the heart of this necessity. Only in this way is this substantive universality *aware* of itself as its own object and end, with the result that the necessity appears to itself in the shape of freedom as well.

267. This necessity in ideality is the inner self-development of the Idea. As the substance of the individual subject, it is his political sentiment [patriotism]; in distinction therefrom, as the substance of the objective world, it is the organism of the state, i.e. it is the strictly political state[1] and its constitution. [A.]

[1] See Paragraphs 273, 276.—ED.

268. The political sentiment, patriotism pure and simple, is assured conviction with truth as its basis—mere subjective assurance is not the outcome of truth but is only opinion—and a volition which has become habitual. In this sense it is simply a product of the institutions subsisting in the state, since rationality is *actually* present in the state, while action in conformity with these institutions gives rationality its practical proof. This sentiment is, in general, trust (which may pass over into a greater or lesser degree of educated insight), or the consciousness that my interest, both substantive and particular, is contained and preserved in another's (i.e. in that state's) interest and end, i.e. in the other's relation to me as an individual. In this way, this very other is immediately not an other in my eyes, and in being conscious of this fact, I am free.

Patriotism is often understood to mean only a readiness for exceptional sacrifices and actions. Essentially, however, it is the sentiment which, in the relationships of our daily life and under ordinary conditions, habitually recognizes that the community is one's substantive groundwork and end. It is out of this consciousness, which during life's daily round stands the test in all circumstances, that there subsequently also arises the readiness for extraordinary exertions. But since men would often rather be magnanimous than law-abiding, they readily persuade themselves that they possess this exceptional patriotism in order to be sparing in the expression of a genuine patriotic sentiment or to excuse their lack of it. If again this genuine patriotism is looked upon as that which may begin of itself and arise from subjective ideas and thoughts, it is being confused with opinion, because so regarded patriotism is deprived of its true ground, objective reality. [A.]

269. The patriotic sentiment acquires its specifically determined content from the various members of the organism of the state. This organism is the development of the Idea to its differences and their objective actuality. Hence these different members are the various powers of the state with their functions and spheres of action, by means of which the universal continually engenders itself, and engenders itself in a necessary way because their specific character is fixed by the nature of the concept. Throughout this process the universal maintains its identity, since it is itself the presupposition of its own production. This organism is the constitution of the state. [A.]

270. (1) The abstract actuality or the substantiality of the state consists in the fact that its end is the universal interest as such and the conservation therein of particular interests since

the universal interest is the substance of these. (2) But this substantiality of the state is also its *necessity,* since its substantiality is divided into the distinct spheres of its activity which correspond to the moments of its concept, and these spheres, owing to this substantiality, are thus actually fixed determinate characteristics of the state, i.e. its *powers.* (3) But this very substantiality of the state is mind knowing and willing itself after passing through the forming process of education. The state, therefore, knows what it wills and knows it in its universality, i.e. as something thought. Hence it works and acts by reference to consciously adopted ends, known principles, and laws which are not merely implicit but are actually present to consciousness; and further, it acts with precise knowledge of existing conditions and circumstances, inasmuch as its actions have a bearing on these.

This is the place to allude to the relation of the state to religion, because it is often reiterated nowadays that religion is the basis of the state, and because those who make this assertion even have the impertinence to suggest that, once it is made, political science has said its last word. No doctrine is more fitted to produce so much confusion, more fitted indeed to exalt confusion itself to be the constitution of the state and the proper form of knowledge.

In the first place, it may seem suspicious that religion is principally sought and recommended for times of public calamity, disorder, and oppression, and that people are referred to it as a solace in face of wrong or as a hope in compensation for loss. Then further, while the state is mind on earth (*der Geist der in der Welt steht*), religion may sometimes be looked upon as commanding downright indifference to earthly interests, the march of events, and current affairs, and so to turn men's attention to religion does not seem to be the way to exalt the interest and business of the state into the fundamental and serious aim of life. On the contrary, this suggestion seems to assert that politics is wholly a matter of caprice and indifference, either because this way of talking merely amounts to saying that it is only the aims of passion and lawless force, &c., which bear sway in the state, or because this recommendation of religion is supposed to be of self-sufficient validity, and religion is to claim to decide the law and administer it. While it might seem a bitter jest to stifle all animus against tyranny by asserting that the oppressed find their consolation in religion, it still must not be forgotten that religion may take a form leading to the harshest bondage in the fetters of superstition and man's degraded subservience to animals. (The Egyptians and the Hindus, for instance, revere animals as beings higher than themselves.) This phenomenon may at least make it evident that we ought not to speak of religion at all in general terms and that we really need a power to protect us from it in some of its forms and to espouse against them the rights of reason and self-consciousness.

The essence of the relation between religion and the state can be determined, however, only if we recall the concept of religion. The content of religion is absolute truth, and consequently the religious is the most sublime of all dispositions. As intuition, feeling, representative knowledge, its task is concentrated upon God as the unrestricted principle and cause on which everything hangs. It thus involves the demand that everything else shall be seen in this light and depend on it for corroboration, justification, and verification. It is in being thus related to religion that state, laws, and duties all alike acquire for consciousness their supreme confirmation and their supreme obligatoriness, because even the state, laws, and duties are in their actuality something determinate which passes over into a higher sphere and so into that on which it is grounded.[1] It is for this reason that in religion there lies the place where man is always assured of finding a consciousness of the unchangeable, of the highest freedom and satisfaction, even within all the mutability of the world and despite the frustration of his aims and the loss of his interests and possessions.[2] Now if religion is in this way the groundwork which includes the ethical realm in general, and the state's fundamental nature—the divine will—in particular, it is at the same time only a groundwork; and it is at this point that state and religion begin to diverge. The state is the divine will, in the sense that it is mind present on earth, unfolding itself to be the actual shape and organization of a world. Those who insist on stopping at the form of *religion,* as opposed to the state, are acting like those logicians who think they are right if they continually stop at the essence and refuse to advance beyond that abstraction to existence, or like those moralists (see Remark to Paragraph 140) who will only good in the abstract and leave it to caprice to decide what is good. Religion is a relation to the Absolute, a relation which takes the form of feeling, representative thinking, faith; and, brought within its all-embracing circumference, everything becomes only accidental and transient. Now if, in relation to the state, we cling to this form of experience and make it the authority for the state and its essential determinant, the state must become a prey to weakness, insecurity, and

[1] See *Enc.* [1st edn.], § 453 [3rd edn. § 553].

[2] Religion, knowledge, and science have as their principle a form peculiar to each and different from that of the state. They therefore enter the state partly as *means* —means to education and [a higher] mentality—partly in so far as they are in essence *ends* in themselves, for the reason that they are embodied in existent institutions. In both these respects the principles of the state have, in their application, a bearing on them. A comprehensive, concrete treatise on the state would also have to deal with those spheres of life as well as with art and such things as mere geographical matters, and to consider their place in the state and their bearing on it. In this book, however, it is the principle of the state in its own special sphere which is being fully expounded in accordance with the Idea, and it is only in passing that reference can be made to the principles of religion, &c., and to the application of the right of the state to them.

disorder, because it is an organism in which firmly fixed distinct powers, laws, and institutions have been developed. In contrast with the form of religion, a form which draws a veil over everything determinate, and so comes to be purely subjective, the objective and universal element in the state, i.e. the laws, acquires a negative instead of a stable and authoritative character, and the result is the production of maxims of conduct like the following: "To the righteous man no law is given; only be pious, and for the rest, practise what thou wilt; yield to thine own caprice and passion, and if thereby others suffer wrong, commend them to the consolations and hopes of religion, or better still, call them irreligious and condemn them to perdition." This negative attitude, however, may not confine itself to an inner disposition and attitude of mind; it may turn instead to the outside world and assert its authority there, and then there is an outbreak of the religious fanaticism which, like fanaticism in politics, discards all government and legal order as barriers cramping the inner life of the heart and incompatible with its infinity, and at the same time proscribes private property, marriage, the ties and work involved in civil society, &c., &c., as degrading to love and the freedom of feeling. But since even then decisions must somehow be made for everyday life and practice, the same doctrine which we had before (see Remark to Paragraph 140, where we dealt generally with the subjectivity of the will which knows itself to be absolute) turns up again here, namely that subjective ideas, i.e. opinion and capricious inclination, are to do the deciding.

In contrast with the truth thus veiled behind subjective ideas and feelings, the genuine truth is the prodigious transfer of the inner into the outer, the building of reason into the real world, and this has been the task of the world during the whole course of its history. It is by working at this task that civilized man has actually given reason an embodiment in law and government and achieved consciousness of the fact. Those who "seek guidance from the Lord" and are assured that the whole truth is directly present in their unschooled opinions, fail to apply themselves to the task of exalting their subjectivity to consciousness of the truth and to knowledge of duty and objective right. The only possible fruits of their attitude are folly, abomination, and the demolition of the whole ethical order, and these fruits must inevitably be reaped if the religious disposition holds firmly and exclusively to its intuitive form and so turns against the real world and the truth present in it in the form of the universal, i.e. of the laws. Still, there is no necessity for this disposition to turn outward and actualize itself in this way. With its negative standpoint, it is of course also open to it to remain something inward, to accommodate itself to government and law, and to acquiesce in these with sneers and idle longings, or with a sigh of resignation. It is not strength but weakness which has turned religious feeling nowadays into piety of a polemical kind, whether the

polemic be connected with some genuine need or simply with unsatisfied vanity. Instead of subduing one's opinions by the labour of study, and subjecting one's will to discipline and so elevating it to free obedience, the line of least resistance is to renounce knowledge of objective truth. Along this line we may preserve a feeling of abject humility and so also of self-conceit, and claim to have ready to hand in godliness everything requisite for seeing into the heart of law and government, for passing sentence on them, and laying down what their character should and must be; and of course if we take this line, the source of our claims is a pious heart, and they are therefore infallible, and unimpeachable, and the upshot is that since we make religion the basis of our intentions and assertions, they cannot be criticized on the score of their shallowness or their immorality.

But if religion be religion of a genuine kind, it does not run counter to the state in a negative or polemical way like the kind just described. It rather recognizes the state and upholds it, and furthermore it has a position and an external organization of its own. The practice of its worship consists in ritual and doctrinal instruction, and for this purpose possessions and property are required, as well as individuals dedicated to the service of the flock. There thus arises a relation between the state and the church. To determine this relation is a simple matter. In the nature of the case, the state discharges a duty by affording every assistance and protection to the church in the furtherance of its religious ends; and, in addition, since religion is an integrating factor in the state, implanting a sense of unity in the depths of men's minds, the state should even require all its citizens to belong to a church—a church is all that can be said, because since the content of a man's faith depends on his private ideas, the state cannot interfere with it. A state which is strong because its organization is mature may be all the more liberal in this matter; it may entirely overlook details of religious practice which affect it, and may even tolerate a sect (though, of course, all depends on its numbers) which on religious grounds declines to recognize even its direct duties to the state. The reason for the state's liberal attitude here is that it makes over the members of such sects to civil society and its laws, and is content if they fulfil their direct duties to the state passively, for instance by such means as commutation or the performance of a different service.[1]

[1] Quakers, Anabaptists, &c., may be said to be active members only of civil society, and they may be regarded as private persons standing in merely private relations to others. Even when this position has been allowed them, they have been exempted from taking the oath. They fulfil their direct duties to the state in a passive way; one of the most important of these duties, the defence of the state against its enemies, they refuse outright to fulfil, and their refusal may perhaps be admitted provided they perform some other service instead. To sects of this kind, the state's attitude is toleration in the strict sense of the word, because since they decline to recognize their duty to the state, they may not claim the rights of citizenship. On one occasion when the abo-

But since the church owns property and carries on besides the practice of worship, and since therefore it must have people in its service, it forsakes the inner for the worldly life and therefore enters the domain of the state, and *eo ipso* comes under its laws. The oath and ethical ties generally, like the marriage bond, entail that inner permeation and elevation of *sentiment* which acquires its deepest confirmation through religion. But since ethical ties are in essence ties within the actual *rational* order, the first thing is to affirm within that order the rights which it involves. Confirmation of these rights by the church is secondary and is only the inward, comparatively abstract, side of the matter.

As for the other ways in which an ecclesiastical communion gives expression to itself, so far as doctrine is concerned the inward preponderates over the outward to a greater extent than is the case with acts of worship and other lines of conduct connected with these, in which the legal side at least seems at once to be a matter for the state. (It is true, of course, that churches have managed to exempt their ministers and property from the power and jurisdiction of the state, and they have even arrogated to themselves jurisdiction over laymen as well in matters in which religion co-operates, such as divorce and the taking of the oath, &c.) Public control of actions of this kind is indeterminate in extent, but this is due to the nature of public control itself and obtains similarly in purely civil transactions (see Paragraph 234). When individuals, holding religious views in common, form themselves into a church, a Corporation, they fall under the general control and

lition of the slave-trade was being pressed with great vigour in the American Congress, a member from one of the Southern States made the striking retort: "Give us our slaves, and you may keep your Quakers." Only if the state is otherwise strong can it overlook and suffer such anomalies, because it can then rely principally on the strength of custom and the inner rationality of its institutions to diminish and close the gap between the existence of anomalies and the full assertion of its own strict rights. Thus technically it may have been right to refuse a grant of even civil rights to the Jews on the ground that they should be regarded as belonging not merely to a religious sect but to a foreign race. But the fierce outcry raised against the Jews, from that point of view and others, ignores the fact that they are, above all, *men;* and manhood, so far from being a mere superficial, abstract quality (see Remark to Paragraph 209), is on the contrary itself the basis of the fact that what civil rights rouse in their possessors is the feeling of oneself as counting in civil society as a person with rights, and this feeling of selfhood, infinite and free from all restrictions, is the root from which the desired similarity in disposition and ways of thinking comes into being. To exclude the Jews from civil rights, on the other hand, would rather be to confirm the isolation with which they have been reproached—a result for which the state refusing them rights would be blamable and reproachable, because by so refusing, it would have misunderstood its own basic principle, its nature as an objective and powerful institution (compare the end of the Remark to Paragraph 268). The exclusion of the Jews from civil rights may be supposed to be a right of the highest kind and may be demanded on that ground; but experience has shown that so to exclude them is the silliest folly, and the way in which governments now treat them has proved itself to be both prudent and dignified.

oversight of the higher state officials. Doctrine as such, however, has its domain in conscience and falls within the right of the subjective freedom of self-consciousness, the sphere of the inner life, which as such is not the domain of the state. Yet the state, too, has a doctrine, since its organization and whatever rights and constitution are authoritative within it exist essentially in the form of thought as law. And since the state is not a mechanism but the rational life of self-conscious freedom, the system of the ethical world, it follows that an essential moment in the actual state is the mental attitude of the citizens, and so their consciousness of the *principles* which this attitude implies. On the other hand, the doctrine of the church is not purely and simply an inward concern of conscience. As doctrine it is rather the expression of something, in fact the expression of a subject-matter which is most closely linked, or even directly concerned, with ethical principles and the law of the land. Hence at this point the paths of church and state either coincide or diverge at right angles. The difference of their two domains may be pushed by the church into sheer antagonism since, by regarding itself as enshrining the content of religion—a content which is absolute—it may claim as its portion mind in general and so the whole ethical sphere, and conceive the state as a mere mechanical scaffolding for the attainment of external, non-mental, ends. It may take itself to be the Kingdom of God, or at least as the road to it or its vestibule, while it regards the state as the kingdom of this world, i.e. of the transient and the finite. In a word, it may think that it is an end in itself, while the state is a mere means. These claims produce the demand, in connexion with doctrinal instruction, that the state should not only allow the church to do as it likes with complete freedom, but that it should pay unconditional respect to the church's doctrines as doctrines, whatever their character, because their determination is supposed to be the task of the church alone. The church bases this claim on the wide ground that the whole domain of mind (*Geist*) is its property. But science and all types of knowledge also have a footing in that domain and, like a church, they build themselves into a whole with a guiding principle of its own, and, with even better justification, may regard themselves as occupying the position which the church claims. Hence science also may in the same way demand to be independent of the state, which is then supposed to be a mere means with the task of providing for science as though science were an end in itself.

Further, for determining the relation between church and state, it makes no difference whether the leaders of congregations or individuals ordained to the service of the church feel impelled to withdraw from the state and lead a sort of secluded life of their own, so that only the other church members are subject to the state's control, or whether they remain within the state except in their capacity as ecclesiastics, a capacity which they take to be but one side of their life. The most striking thing about such a conception of the church's relation to the state is that it implies the idea that the state's specific function consists in protecting and securing everyone's life, property, and caprice, in so far as these do not encroach upon the life, property, and caprice of others.[1] The state from this point of view is treated simply as an organization to satisfy men's necessities. In this way the element of absolute truth, of mind in its higher development, is placed, as subjective religious feeling or theoretical science, beyond the reach of the state. The state, as the laity pure and simple, is confined to paying its respects to this element and so is entirely deprived of any strictly ethical character. Now it is, of course, a matter of history that in times and under conditions of barbarism, all higher forms of intellectual life had their seat only in the church, while the state was a mere mundane rule of force, caprice, and passion. At such times it was the abstract opposition of state and church which was the main underlying principle of history (see Paragraph 359).[2] But it is far too blind and shallow a proceeding to declare that this situation is the one which truly corresponds with the Idea. The development of this Idea has proved this rather to be the truth, that mind, as free and rational, is implicitly ethical, while the Idea in its truth is rationality actualized; and this it is which exists as the state. Further, this Idea has made it no less clearly evident that the ethical truth in it is present to conscious thought as a content worked up into the form of universality, i.e. as law—in short, that the state *knows* its aims, apprehends and gives practical proof of them with a clear-cut consciousness and in accordance with principles. Now, as I said earlier, religion has the truth as its universal subject-matter, but it possesses it only as a *given* content which has not been apprehended in its fundamental characteristics as a result of thinking and the use of concepts. Similarly, the relation of the individual to this subject-matter is an obligation grounded on authority, while the "witness of his own spirit and heart," i.e. that wherein the moment of freedom resides, is faith and feeling. It is philosophic insight which sees that while church and state differ in form, they do not stand opposed in content, for truth and rationality are the content of both. Thus when the church begins to teach doctrines (though there are and have been some churches with a ritual only, and others in which ritual is the chief thing, while doctrine and a more educated consciousness are only secondary), and when these doctrines touch on objective principles, on thoughts of the ethical and the rational, then their expression *eo ipso* brings the church into the domain of the state. In contrast with the church's faith and authority in matters affecting ethical principles, rightness, laws, institutions, in contrast with the church's subjective conviction, the state is that which knows. Its principle is such that its content is in essence no longer clothed with the form of feeling and faith but is determinate thought.

If the content of absolute truth appears in the form of religion as a particular content, i.e. as the doctrines peculiar to the church as a religious community, then these doctrines remain out of the reach of the state (in Protestantism they are out of the reach of priests too because, as there is no laity there, so there is no priesthood to be an exclusive depository of church doctrine).[3] Since ethical principles and the organization of the state in general are drawn into the domain of religion and not only may, but also should, be established by reference thereto, this reference gives religious credentials to the state itself. On the other hand, however, the state retains the right and the form of self-conscious, objective, rationality, the right to make this form count and to maintain it against pretensions springing from truth in a subjective dress, no matter how such truth may girdle itself with certitude and authority.

The state is universal in form, a form whose essential principle is thought. This explains why it was in the state that freedom of thought and science had their origin. It was a church, on the other hand, which burnt Giordano Bruno, forced Galileo to recant on his knees his exposition of the Copernican view of the solar system, and so forth.[4] Science too,

[3] Cf. Hegel, *Philosophy of History*, p. 350.—Ed.

[4] "When Galileo published the discoveries" about the phases of Venus, &c., which he had made with the aid of the telescope, "he showed that they incontestably proved the motion of the earth. But this idea of the motion of the earth was declared heretical by an assembly of Cardinals, and Galileo, its most famous advocate, was haled before the Inquisition and compelled to recant it, under pain of severe imprisonment. One of the strongest of passions is the love of truth in a man of genius. . . . Convinced of the motion of the earth as a result of his own observations, Galileo meditated a long while on a new work in which he had resolved to develop all the proofs in its favour. But in order at the same time to escape from the persecution of which otherwise he would inevitably have been the victim, he hit upon the device of expounding them in the form of dialogues between three speakers. . . . It is obvious enough in them that the advantage lies with the advocate of the Copernican system; but since Galileo did not decide between the speakers, and gave as much weight as possible to the objections raised by the partisans of Ptolemy, he might well have expected to be left to enjoy undisturbed the peace to which his advanced age and his labours had entitled him. . . . In his seventieth year he was haled once more before the tribunal of the Inquisition. . . . He was imprisoned and required to recant his opinions a second time under threat of the penalty fixed for a relapse into heresy. . . . He was made to sign an abjuration in the following terms: "I, Galileo, appearing in person before the court in my seventieth year, kneeling, and with my eyes on the holy Gospels which I hold in my hands, abjure, damn, and execrate with my whole heart and true belief the absurd, false, and heretical doctrine of the motion of the earth. . . ." What a spectacle! An aged, venerable man, famous throughout a long life exclusively devoted to the study of nature, abjuring on his knees, against the witness of his own conscience, the truth which he had demonstrated so convincingly! By the judgement of the Inquisition he was condemned to perpetual imprisonment. A year later he was set at

[1] This is a reference to the dictum quoted from Kant in the Remark to Paragraph 29 (Messineo).—Ed.

[2] All editions read "358." The reference a few sentences below to the "witness of his own spirit and heart" is a reference to the Lutheran doctrine mentioned towards the end of the Preface. Cf. Paragraph 147.—Ed.

therefore, has its place on the side of the state since it has one element, its form, in common with the state, and its aim is knowledge, knowledge of objective truth and rationality in terms of thought. Such knowledge may, of course, fall from the heights of science into opinion and deductive argumentation, and, turning its attention to ethical matters and the organization of the state, set itself against their basic principles. And it may perhaps do this while making for this opining—as if it were reason and the right of subjective self-consciousness—the same pretentious claim as the church makes for its own sphere, the claim, namely, to be free from restraint in its opinions and convictions.

This principle of the subjectivity of knowing has been dealt with above (see Remark to Paragraph 140). It is here only necessary to add a note on the twofold attitude of the state to this opining. On the one hand, in so far as opining is mere opining, a purely subjective matter, it is without any genuine inherent force or power, plume itself as it may ; and from this point of view the state may be as totally indifferent to it as the painter who sticks to the three primary colours on his palette is indifferent to the academic wisdom which tells him there are seven. On the other hand, however, when this opining of bad principles embodies itself in a general organization corrosive of the actual order, the state has to set its face against it and protect objective truth and the principles of ethical life (and it must do the same in face of the formulae of unconditioned subjectivity if these have proposed to take the starting point of science as their basis, and turn state educational institutions against the state by encouraging them to make against it claims as pretentious as those of a church) ; while, vice versa, in face of a church claiming unrestricted and unconditional authority, the state has in general to make good the formal right of self-consciousness to its own insight, its own conviction, and, in short, its own thought of what is to hold good as objective truth.

Mention may also be made of the "unity of state and church"—a favourite topic of modern discussion and held up by some as the highest of ideals.[1] While state and church are essentially one in truth of principle and disposition, it is no less essential that, despite this unity, the distinction between their forms of consciousness should be externalized as a distinction between their special modes of existence. This often desired unity of church and state is found under oriental despotisms, but an oriental despotism is not a state, or at any rate not the self-conscious form of state which is alone worthy of mind, the form which is organically developed and where there are rights and a free ethical life. Further, if the state is to come into existence as the self-*knowing* ethical

actuality of mind, it is essential that its form should be distinct from that of authority and faith. But this distinction emerges only in so far as the church is subjected to inward divisions. It is only thereafter that the state, in contrast with the particular sects, has attained to universality of thought—its formal principle—and is bringing this universality into existence. (In order to understand this, it is necessary to know not only what universality is in itself, but also what its existence is.[2]) Hence so far from its being or its having been a misfortune for the state that the church is disunited, it is only as a result of that disunion that the state has been able to reach its appointed end as a self-consciously rational and ethical organization. Moreover, this disunion is the best piece of good fortune which could have befallen either the church or thought so far as the freedom and rationality of either is concerned. [A.]

271. The constitution of the state is, in the first place, the organization of the state and the self-related process of its organic life, a process whereby it differentiates its moments within itself and develops them to self-subsistence. Secondly, the state is an individual, unique and exclusive, and therefore related to others. Thus it turns its differentiating activity outward and accordingly establishes within itself the ideality of its subsisting inward differentiations. [A.]

1. *The Constitution (on its internal side only)*

272. The constitution is rational[3] in so far as the state inwardly differentiates and determines its activity in accordance with the nature of the concept. The result of this is that each of these powers is in itself the totality of the constitution, because each contains the other moments and has them effective in itself, and because the moments, being expressions of the differentiation of the concept, simply abide in their ideality and constitute nothing but a single individual whole.

In our day there has come before the public an endless amount of babble about the constitution, as about reason itself, and the stalest babble of all has been produced in Germany, thanks to those who have persuaded themselves that they have the best, or even the sole, understanding of what a constitution is. Elsewhere, particularly in governments, misunderstanding is supposed to reign. And these gentlemen are convinced that they have an unassailable justification for what they say because they claim that religion and piety are the basis of all this shallow thinking of theirs. It is no wonder that this babble has made reasonable men just as sick of the words "reason," "enlightenment," "right," &c., as of the words "constitution" and "freedom," and a man might well be ashamed now to go on discussing the

liberty through the intercession of the Grand Duke of Florence. . . . He died in 1642. . . . Europe mourned his loss. It had been enlightened by his labours and was exasperated by the judgement passed by a detested tribunal on a man of his greatness." (Laplace: *Exposition du système du monde*, Book V, chap. 4.)

[1] See Addition to Paragraph 141.—Ed.

[2] Cf. Hegel, *Philosophy of History*, pp. 348 ff.—Ed.
[3] See Paragraphs 275, 300, and 269.—Ed.

constitution of the state at all! However, we may
at least hope that this surfeit will be effective in producing the general conviction that philosophical
knowledge of such topics cannot arise from argumentation, deduction, calculations of purpose and
utility, still less from the heart, love, and inspiration, but only from the concept. We may also hope
that those who hold that the divine is inconceivable
and the knowledge of truth a wild-goose chase will
feel themselves bound to refrain from taking part
in the discussion. The products of their hearts and
their inspirations are either undigested chatter or
mere edification, and whatever the worth of these
neither can pretend to notice from philosophy.

Amongst current ideas, mention may be made (in
connexion with Paragraph 269) of the necessity for
a division of powers within the state.[1] This point is
of the highest importance and, if taken in its true
sense, may rightly be regarded as the guarantee of
public freedom. It is an idea, however, with which
the very people who pretend to talk out of their inspiration and love neither have, nor desire to have,
any acquaintance, since it is precisely there that the
moment of rational determinacy lies. That is to say,
the principle of the division of powers contains the
essential moment of difference, of rationality *realized*. But when the abstract Understanding handles
it, it reads into it the false doctrine of the absolute
self-subsistence of each of the powers against the
others, and then one-sidedly interprets their relation
to each other as negative, as a mutual restriction.
This view implies that the attitude adopted by each
power to the others is hostile and apprehensive, as
if the others were evils, and that their function is to
oppose one another and as a result of this counterpoise to effect an equilibrium on the whole, but never a living unity. It is only the inner self-determination of the concept, not any other consideration,
whether of purpose or advantage, that is the absolute source of the division of powers, and in virtue
of this alone is the organization of the state something inherently rational and the image of eternal
reason.

How the concept and then, more concretely, how
the Idea, determine themselves inwardly and so
posit their moments—universality, particularity, and
individuality—in abstraction from one another, is
discoverable from my logic, though not of course
from the logic current elsewhere. To take the merely negative as a starting-point and to exalt to the
first place the volition of evil and the mistrust of
this volition, and then on the basis of this presupposition slyly to construct dikes whose efficiency
simply necessitates corresponding dikes over against
them, is characteristic in thought of the negative
Understanding and in sentiment of the outlook of
the rabble (see Paragraph 244).

If the powers (e.g. what are called the "Executive"
and the "Legislature") become self-subsistent, then
as we have recently seen on a grand scale, the destruction of the state is forthwith a *fait accompli*.

Alternatively, if the state is maintained in essentials,
it is strife which through the subjection by one power of the others, produces unity at least, however
defective, and so secures the bare essential, the maintenance of the state. [A.]

273. The state as a political entity is thus cleft
into three substantive divisions:

(*a*) the power to determine and establish the
universal—the Legislature;

(*b*) the power to subsume single cases and the
spheres of particularity under the universal—
the Executive;

(*c*) the power of subjectivity, as the will with
the power of ultimate decision—the Crown. In
the crown, the different powers are bound into
an individual unity which is thus at once the
apex and basis of the whole, i.e. of constitutional monarchy.

The development of the state to constitutional
monarchy is the achievement of the modern world,
a world in which the substantial Idea has won the
infinite form [of subjectivity—see Paragraph 144].
The history of this inner deepening of the world
mind—or in other words this free maturation in
course of which the Idea, realizing rationality in the
external, releases its moments (and they are only its
moments) from itself as totalities, and just for that
reason still retains them in the ideal unity of the concept—the history of this genuine formation of ethical life is the content of the whole course of world-
history.

The ancient division of constitutions into monarchy, aristocracy, and democracy, is based upon
the notion of substantial, still undivided, unity, a
unity which has not yet come to its inner differentiation (to a matured, internal organization) and
which therefore has not yet attained depth or concrete rationality. From the standpoint of the ancient world, therefore, this division is the true and
correct one, since for a unity of that still substantial
type, a unity inwardly too immature to have attained its absolutely complete development, difference is essentially an external difference and appears
at first as a difference in the number [2] of those in
whom that substantial unity is supposed to be immanent.[3] These forms, which on this principle belong to different wholes, are given in limited monarchy the humbler position of moments in a whole.
The monarch is a *single* person; the *few* come on the
scene with the executive, and the *many* en masse
with the legislative. But, as has been indicated,[4]
purely quantitative distinctions like these are only
superficial and do not afford the concept of the
thing. Equally inadequate is the mass of contemporary talk about the democratic and aristocratic elements in monarchy, because when the elements specified in such talk are found in a monarchy there is

[1] Cf. Montesquieu, *The Spirit of Laws*, xi. 6.—ED.

[2] See *Enc.* [1st edn.], § 52 [3rd edn. § 99].
[3] Cf. Aristotle, *Politics*, 1279ª26 ff.—ED.
[4] In, e.g., Paragraph 214.—ED.

no longer anything democratic or aristocratic about them. There are notions of constitutions in which the state is portrayed from top to bottom as an abstraction which is supposed to rule and command, and how many individuals are at the head of such a state, whether one or a few or all, is a question left undecided and regarded as a matter of indifference. [E.g.:] "All these forms," says Fichte, ". . . are justified, provided there be an ephorate" (a scheme devised by Fichte to be a counterpoise to the chief power in the state) "and may . . . be the means of introducing universal rights into the state and maintaining them there." [1] A view of this kind—and the device of the ephorate also—is begotten by the superficial conception of the state to which reference has just been made. It is true enough that in quite simple social conditions these differences of constitutional form have little or no meaning. For instance, in the course of his legislation Moses prescribed that, in the event of his people's desiring a king, its institutions should remain unchanged except for the new requirement that the king should not "multiply horses to himself . . . nor wives . . . nor silver and gold." [2] Besides, in a sense one may of course say that the Idea too is indifferent to these forms (including monarchy, but only when it is restricted in meaning by being defined as an *alternative* on a parity with aristocracy and democracy). But the Idea is indifferent to them, not in Fichte's but in the opposite sense, because every one of them is inadequate to it in its rational development (see Paragraph 272) and in none of them, taken singly, could the Idea attain its right and its actuality. Consequently, it is quite idle to inquire which of the three is most to be preferred. Such forms must be discussed historically or not at all.

Still, here again, as in so many other places, we must recognize the depth of Montesquieu's insight in his now famous treatment of the basic principles of these forms of government. To recognize the accuracy of his account, however, we must not misunderstand it. As is well known, he held that "virtue" [3] was the principle of democracy [and rightly], since it is in fact the case that that type of constitution rests on sentiment, i.e. on the purely substantial form in which the rationality of the absolute will still exists in democracy. But Montesquieu goes on to say that in the seventeenth century England provided "a fine spectacle of the way in which efforts to found a democracy were rendered ineffective by a lack of virtue in the leaders." And again he adds "when virtue vanishes from the republic, ambition enters hearts which are capable of it and greed masters everyone . . . so that the state becomes everyone's booty and its strength now consists only in the power of a few citizens and the licence of all alike." These quotations call for the comment that in more mature social conditions and when the powers of particularity have developed and become free, a form of rational law other than the form of sentiment is required, because virtue in the heads of the state is not enough if the state as a whole is to gain the power to resist disruption and to bestow on the powers of particularity, now become mature, both their positive and their negative rights. Similarly, we must remove the misunderstanding of supposing that because the sentiment of virtue is the substantial form of a democratic republic, it is evidently superfluous in monarchy or even absent from it altogether, [4] and, finally, we may not suppose that there is an opposition and an incompatibility between virtue and the legally determinate agency of a state whose organization is fully articulated.

The fact that "moderation" [5] is cited as the principle of aristocracy implies the beginning at this point of a divorce between public authority and private interest. And yet at the same time these touch each other so directly that this constitution by its very nature stands on the verge of lapsing forthwith into tyranny or anarchy—the harshest of political conditions—and so into self-annihilation. See Roman history, for example.

The fact that Montesquieu discerns "honour" [6] as the principle of monarchy at once makes it clear that by "monarchy" he understands, not the patriarchal or any ancient type, nor, on the other hand, the type organized into an objective constitution, [7] but only feudal monarchy, the type in which the relationships recognized in its constitutional law are crystallized into the rights of private property and the privileges of individuals and Corporations. In this type of constitution, political life rests on privileged persons and a great part of what must be done for the maintenance of the state is settled at their pleasure. The result is that their services are the objects not of duty but only of ideas and opinions. Thus it is not duty but only honour which holds the state together.

Another question readily presents itself here: "Who is to frame the constitution?" This question seems clear, but closer inspection shows at once that it is meaningless, for it presupposes that there is no constitution there, but only an agglomeration of atomic individuals. How an agglomeration of individuals could acquire a constitution, whether automatically or by someone's aid, whether as a present or by force or by thought, it would have to be allowed to settle for itself, since with an agglomeration the concept has nothing to do. But if the question presupposes an already existent constitution, then it is not about framing, but only about altering the constitution, and the very presupposition of a constitution directly implies that its alteration may come about only by constitutional means. In any case, however, it is absolutely essential that the constitution should not be regarded as something made, even though it has come into being in time. It must be treated rather as something simply existent in and by itself,

---

[1] *Science of Rights* [§ 16, sub-section 6, p. 248].
[2] Deut. 17. 16 ff.
[3] Cf. Montesquieu, *The Spirit of Laws*, iii. 3. See Remark to Paragraph 185.—ED.

[4] Cf. Montesquieu, *The Spirit of Laws*, iii. 5.—ED.
[5] *ibid.*, iii. 4.—ED.
[6] *ibid.*, iii. 7.—ED.
[7] See Paragraph 272.—ED.

as divine therefore, and constant, and so as exalted above the sphere of things that are made. [A.]

274. Mind is actual only as that which it knows itself to be, and the state, as the mind of a nation, is both the law permeating all relationships within the state and also at the same time the manners and consciousness of its citizens. It follows, therefore, that the constitution of any given nation depends in general on the character and development of its self-consciousness.[1] In its self-consciousness its subjective freedom is rooted and so, therefore, is the actuality of its constitution.

The proposal to give a constitution—even one more or less rational in content—to a nation a priori would be a happy thought overlooking precisely that factor in a constitution which makes it more than an ens rationis. Hence every nation has the constitution appropriate to it and suitable for it. [A.]

(a) The Crown

275. The power of the crown contains in itself the three moments of the whole (see Paragraph 272), viz. (a) the universality of the constitution and the laws; (β) counsel, which refers the particular to the universal; and (γ) the moment of ultimate decision, as the self-determination to which everything else reverts and from which everything else derives the beginning of its actuality. This absolute self-determination constitutes the distinctive principle of the power of the crown as such, and with this principle our exposition is to begin. [A.]

276. (1) The fundamental characteristic of the state as a political entity is the substantial unity, i.e. the ideality, of its moments. (a) In this unity, the particular powers and their activities are dissolved and yet retained. They are retained, however, only in the sense that their authority is no independent one but only one of the order and breadth determined by the Idea of the whole; from its might they originate, and they are its flexible limbs while it is their single self. [A.]

277. (β) The particular activities and agencies of the state are its essential moments and therefore are proper to it. The individual functionaries and agents are attached to their office not on the strength of their immediate personality, but only on the strength of their universal and objective qualities. Hence it is in an external and contingent way that these offices are linked with particular persons, and therefore the func-

tions and powers of the state cannot be private property. [A.]

278. These two points (a) and (β) constitute the sovereignty of the state. That is to say, sovereignty depends on the fact that the particular functions and powers of the state are not self-subsistent or firmly grounded either on their own account or in the particular will of the individual functionaries, but have their roots ultimately in the unity of the state as their single self.

This is the sovereignty of the state at home. Sovereignty has another side, i.e. sovereignty vis-à-vis foreign states, on which see below.[2]

In feudal times, the state was certainly sovereign vis-à-vis other states; at home however, not only was the monarch not sovereign at all, but the state itself was not sovereign either. For one thing, the particular functions and powers of the state and civil society were arranged (compare Remark to Paragraph 273) into independent Corporations and societies, so that the state as a whole was rather an aggregate than an organism; and, for another thing, office was the private property of individuals, and hence what they were to do in their public capacity was left to their own opinion and caprice.

The idealism which constitutes sovereignty is the same characteristic as that in accordance with which the so-called "parts" of an animal organism are not parts but members, moments in an organic whole, whose isolation and independence spell disease.[3] The principle here is the same as that which came before us (see Paragraph 7) in the abstract concept of the will (see Remark to Paragraph 279) as self-related negativity, and therefore as the universality of the will determining itself to individuality and so cancelling all particularity and determinacy, as the absolute self-determining ground of all volition. To understand this, one must have mastered the whole conception of the substance and genuine subjectivity of the concept.

The fact that the sovereignty of the state is the ideality of all particular authorities within it gives rise to the easy and also very common misunderstanding that this ideality is only might and pure arbitrariness while "sovereignty" is a synonym for "despotism." But despotism means any state of affairs where law has disappeared and where the particular will as such, whether of a monarch or a mob (ochlocracy), counts as law or rather takes the place of law; while it is precisely in legal, constitutional, government that sovereignty is to be found as the moment of ideality—the ideality of the particular spheres and functions. That is to say, sovereignty brings it about that each of these spheres is not something independent, self-subsistent in its aims and modes of working, something immersed solely in itself, but that instead, even in these aims and modes of working, each is determined by and de-

---

[1] Cf. Montesquieu, The Spirit of Laws, i. 3.—Ed.

[2] Paragraphs 321 ff.—Ed.
[3] See Enc. [1st edn.], § 293 [3rd edn. § 371].

pendent on the aim of the whole (the aim which has been denominated in general terms by the rather vague expression "welfare of the state").

This ideality manifests itself in a twofold way:

(i) In times of peace, the particular spheres and functions pursue the path of satisfying their particular aims and minding their own business, and it is in part only by way of the unconscious necessity of the thing that their self-seeking is turned into a contribution to reciprocal support and to the support of the whole (see Paragraph 183). In part, however, it is by the direct influence of higher authority that they are not only continually brought back to the aims of the whole and restricted accordingly (see Paragraph 289), but are also constrained to perform direct services for the support of the whole.

(ii) In a situation of exigency, however, whether in home or foreign affairs, the organism of which these particular spheres are members fuses into the single concept of sovereignty. The sovereign is entrusted with the salvation of the state at the sacrifice of these particular authorities whose powers are valid at other times, and it is then that that ideality comes into its proper actuality (see Paragraph 321).

279. (2) Sovereignty, at first simply the universal *thought* of this ideality, comes into *existence* only as subjectivity sure of itself, as the will's abstract and to that extent ungrounded self-determination in which finality of decision is rooted. This is the strictly individual aspect of the state, and in virtue of this alone is the state *one*. The truth of subjectivity, however, is attained only in a subject, and the truth of personality only in a person; and in a constitution which has become mature as a realization of rationality, each of the three moments of the concept has its explicitly actual and separate formation. Hence this absolutely decisive moment of the whole is not individuality in general, but a single individual, the monarch.

The immanent development of a science, the derivation [1] of its entire content from the concept in its simplicity (a science otherwise derived, whatever its merit, does not deserve the name of a philosophical science) exhibits this peculiarity, that one and the same concept—the will in this instance—which begins by being abstract (because it is at the beginning), maintains its identity even while it consolidates its specific determinations, and that too solely by its own activity, and in this way gains a concrete content. Hence it is the basic moment of personality, abstract at the start in immediate rights, which has matured itself through its various forms of subjectivity, and now—at the stage of absolute rights, of the state, of the completely concrete objectivity of the will—has become the personality of the state, its certainty of itself. This last reabsorbs all particu-

[1] Hegel emphatically repudiates apriorism in the Preface to the *Philosophy of Right*.—ED.

larity into its single self, cuts short the weighing of pros and cons between which it lets itself oscillate perpetually now this way and now that, and by saying "I will" makes its decision and so inaugurates all activity and actuality.

Further, however, personality, like subjectivity in general, as infinitely self-related, has its truth (to be precise, its most elementary, immediate, truth) only in a person, in a subject existing "for" himself, and what exists "for" itself is just simply a unit. It is only as a person, the monarch, that the personality of the state is actual. Personality expresses the concept as such; but the person enshrines the actuality of the concept, and only when the concept is determined as person is it the Idea or truth. A so-called "artificial person," be it a society, a community, or a family, however inherently concrete it may be, contains personality only abstractly, as one moment of itself. In an "artificial person," personality has not achieved its true mode of existence. The state, however, is precisely this totality in which the moments of the concept have attained the actuality correspondent to their degree of truth. All these categories, both in themselves and in their external formations, have been discussed in the whole course of this treatise. They are repeated here, however, because while their existence in their particular external formations is readily granted, it does not follow at all that they are recognized and apprehended again when they appear in their true place, not isolated, but in their truth as moments of the Idea.

The conception of the monarch is therefore of all conceptions the hardest for ratiocination, i.e. for the method of reflection employed by the Understanding. This method refuses to move beyond isolated categories and hence here again knows only *raisonnement*, finite points of view, and deductive argumentation. Consequently it exhibits the dignity of the monarch as something deduced, not only in its form, but in its essence. The truth is, however, that to be something not deduced but purely self-originating is precisely the conception of monarchy. Akin, then, to this reasoning is the idea of treating the monarch's right as grounded in the authority of God, since it is in its divinity that its unconditional character is contained. We are familiar, however, with the misunderstandings connected with this idea, and it is precisely this "divine" element which it is the task of a philosophic treatment to comprehend.

We may speak of the "sovereignty of the people" in the sense that any people whatever is self-subsistent *vis-à-vis* other peoples, and constitutes a state of its own, like the British people for instance. But the peoples of England, Scotland, or Ireland, or the peoples of Venice, Genoa, Ceylon, &c., are not sovereign peoples at all now that they have ceased to have rulers or supreme governments of their own.

We may also speak of sovereignty in home affairs residing in the people, provided that we are speaking generally about the whole state and meaning only what was shown above (see Paragraphs 277,

278), namely that it is to the state that sovereignty belongs.

The usual sense, however, in which men have recently begun to speak of the "sovereignty of the people" is that it is something opposed to the sovereignty existent in the monarch. So opposed to the sovereignty of the monarch, the sovereignty of the people is one of the confused notions based on the wild idea of the "people." Taken without its monarch and the articulation of the whole which is the indispensable and direct concomitant of monarchy, the people is a formless mass and no longer a state. It lacks every one of those determinate characteristics—sovereignty, government, judges, magistrates, class-divisions, &c.,—which are to be found only in a whole which is inwardly organized. By the very emergence into a people's life of moments of this kind which have a bearing on an organization, on political life, a people ceases to be that indeterminate abstraction which, when represented in a quite general way, is called the "people."

If by "sovereignty of the people" is understood a republican form of government, or to speak more specifically (since under "republic" are comprised all sorts of other mixed forms of government, which are purely empirical, let alone irrelevant in a philosophical treatise) a democratic form, then all that is needed in reply has been said already (in the Remark to Paragraph 273) ; and besides, such a notion cannot be further discussed in face of the Idea of the state in its full development.

If the "people" is represented neither as a patriarchal clan, nor as living under the simple conditions which make democracy or aristocracy possible as forms of government (see Remark to Paragraph 273), nor as living under some other unorganized and haphazard conditions, but instead as an inwardly developed, genuinely organic, totality, then sovereignty is there as the personality of the whole, and this personality is there, in the real existence adequate to its concept, as the person of the monarch.

At the stage at which constitutions are divided, as above mentioned,[1] into democracy, aristocracy, and monarchy, the point of view taken is that of a still substantial unity, abiding in itself, without having yet embarked on its infinite differentiation and the plumbing of its own depths. At that stage, the moment of the final, self-determining, decision of the will does not come on the scene explicitly in its own proper actuality as an organic moment immanent in the state. None the less, even in those comparatively immature constitutional forms, there must always be individuals at the head. Leaders must either be available already, as they are in monarchies of that type, or, as happens in aristocracies, but more particularly in democracies, they may rise to the top, as statesmen or generals, by chance and in accordance with the particular needs of the hour. This must happen, since everything done and everything actual is inaugurated and brought to completion by the single decisive act of a leader. But comprised in a union of

[1] In the Remark to Paragraph 273.—ED.

powers which remains undifferentiated, this subjectivity of decision is inevitably either contingent in its origin and appearance, or else is in one way or another subordinate to something else. Hence in such states, the power of the leaders was conditioned, and only in something beyond them could there be found a pure unambiguous decision, a *fatum*, determining affairs from without. As a moment of the Idea, this decision had to come into existence, though rooted in something outside the circle of human freedom with which the state is concerned. Herein lies the origin of the need for deriving the last word on great events and important affairs of state from oracles, a "divine sign" (in the case of Socrates), the entrails of animals, the feeding and flight of birds, &c. It was when men had not yet plumbed the depths of self-consciousness or risen out of their undifferentiated unity of substance to their independence that they lacked strength to look within their own being for the final word.

In the "divine sign" of Socrates [2] (compare Remark to Paragraph 138) we see the will which formerly had simply transferred itself beyond itself now beginning to apply itself to itself and so to recognize its own inward nature. This is the beginning of a self-knowing and so of a genuine freedom. This realized freedom of the Idea consists precisely in giving to each of the moments of rationality its own self-conscious actuality here and now. Hence it is this freedom which makes the ultimate self-determining certitude—the culmination of the concept of the will—the function of a single consciousness. This ultimate self-determination, however, can fall within the sphere of human freedom only in so far as it has the position of a pinnacle, explicitly distinct from, and raised above, all that is particular and conditional, for only so is it actual in a way adequate to its concept. [A.]

280. (3) This ultimate self in which the will of the state is concentrated is, when thus taken in abstraction, a single self and therefore is *immediate* individuality.[3] Hence its "natural" character is implied in its very conception. The monarch, therefore, is essentially characterized as *this* individual, in abstraction from all his other characteristics, and *this* individual is raised to the dignity of monarchy in an immediate, natural, fashion, i.e. through his birth in the course of nature.

This transition of the concept of pure self-determination into the immediacy of being and so into the realm of nature is of a purely speculative character, and apprehension of it therefore belongs to logic. Moreover, this transition is on the whole the same as that familiar to us in the nature of willing, and there the process is to translate something from

[2] Cf. Plato, *Apology*, 31 ff.—ED.
[3] See the end of the Remark to Paragraph 279. For the connection between "immediacy" and "nature," see Paragraphs 11, 34, 43, 158, and the Additions to Paragraphs 10 and 18.—ED.

subjectivity (i.e. some purpose held before the mind) into existence (see Paragraph 8). But the proper form of the Idea and of the transition here under consideration is the immediate conversion of the pure self-determination of the will (i.e. of the simple concept itself) into a single and natural existent without the mediation of a particular content (like a purpose in the case of action).

In the so-called "ontological" proof of the existence of God, we have the same conversion of the absolute concept into existence. This conversion has constituted the depth of the Idea in the modern world, although recently it has been declared inconceivable,[1] with the result that knowledge of truth has been renounced, since truth is simply the unity of concept and existence (see Paragraph 23). Since the Understanding has no inner consciousness of this unity and refuses to move beyond the separation of these two moments of the truth, it may perhaps, so far as God is concerned, still permit a "faith" in this unity. But since the idea of the monarch is regarded as being quite familiar to ordinary consciousness, the Understanding clings here all the more tenaciously to its separatism and the conclusions which its astute ratiocination deduces therefrom. As a result, it denies that the moment of ultimate decision in the state is linked implicitly and actually (i.e. in the rational concept) with the immediate birthright of the monarch. Consequently it infers, first, that this link is a matter of accident, and further—since it has claimed that the absolute diversity of these moments is the rational thing—that such a link is irrational, and then there follow the other deductions disruptive of the Idea of the state.[2] [A.]

281. Both moments in their undivided unity— (a) the will's ultimate ungrounded self, and (b) therefore its similarly ungrounded objective existence (existence being the category which is at home in nature)—constitute the Idea of something against which caprice is powerless,[3] the "majesty" of the monarch. In this unity lies the actual unity of the state, and it is only through this, its inward and outward immediacy, that the unity of the state is saved from the risk of being drawn down into the sphere of particularity and its caprices, ends, and opinions, and saved too from the war of factions round the throne and from the enfeeblement and overthrow of the power of the state.

The rights of birth and inheritance constitute the basis of legitimacy, the basis of a right not purely positive but contained in the Idea.

If succession to the throne is rigidly determined, i.e. if it is hereditary, then faction is obviated at a demise of the crown; this is one aspect of hereditary succession and it has long been rightly stressed as a

point in its favour. This aspect, however, is only consequential, and to make it the reason for hereditary succession is to drag down the majesty of the throne into the sphere of argumentation, to ignore its true character as ungrounded immediacy and ultimate inwardness, and to base it not on the Idea of the state immanent within it, but on something external to itself, on some extraneous notion such as the "welfare of the state" or the "welfare of the people." Once it has been so based, its hereditary character may of course be deduced by the use of *medii termini*. But other *medii termini* are equally available, and so therefore are different conclusions, and it is only too well known what conclusions have in fact been drawn from this "welfare of the people" (*salut du peuple*). Hence the majesty of the monarch is a topic for thoughtful treatment by philosophy alone, since every method of inquiry, other than the speculative method of the infinite Idea which is purely self-grounded, annuls the nature of majesty altogether.

An elective monarchy seems of course to be the most natural idea, i.e. the idea which superficial thinking finds handiest. Because it is the concerns and interests of his people for which a monarch has to provide, so the argument runs, it must be left to the people to entrust with its welfare whomsoever it pleases, and only with the grant of this trust does his right to rule arise. This view, like the notion of the monarch as the highest executive official in the state, or the notion of a contractual relation between him and his people, &c., &c., is grounded on the will interpreted as the whim, opinion, and caprice of the Many.[4] A will of this character counts as the first thing in civil society (as was pointed out long ago)[5] or rather it tries to count as the only thing there, but it is not the guiding principle of the family, still less of the state, and in short it stands opposed to the Idea of ethical life.

It is truer to say that elective monarchy is the worst of institutions, and its results suffice to reveal this to ratiocination. To ratiocination, however, these results have the appearance of something merely possible and probable, though they are in fact inherent in the very essence of this institution. In an elective monarchy, I mean, the nature of the relation between king and people implies that the ultimate decision is left with the particular will, and hence the constitution becomes a Compact of Election, i.e. a surrender of the power of the state at the discretion of the particular will. The result of this is that the particular offices of state turn into private property, the sovereignty of the state is enfeebled and lost, and finally the state disintegrates within and is overthrown from without.[6] [A.]

282. The right to pardon criminals arises from the sovereignty of the monarch, since it is this alone which is empowered to actualize mind's

[1] Cf. Kant, *Critique of Pure Reason*, p. 10.—ED.
[2] See the reference to *salut du peuple* in the Remark to the next Paragraph.—ED.
[3] See Paragraph 283.—ED.

[4] See Remark to Paragraph 301.—ED.
[5] In the section on Civil Society; see, e.g., Paragraphs 183 and 206.—ED.
[6] Cf. Hegel, *Philosophy of History*, p. 355.—ED.

power of making undone what has been done and wiping out a crime by forgiving and forgetting it.

The right of pardon is one of the highest recognitions of the majesty of mind. Moreover it is one of those cases where a category which belongs to a higher sphere is applied to or reflected in the sphere below.[1] Applications of higher categories to a lower sphere, however, concern the particular science which has to handle its subject-matter in all its empirical details (see [the second] footnote to the Remark to Paragraph 270). Another instance of the same kind of thing is the subsumption under the concept of crime (which came before us earlier—see Paragraphs 95-102) of injuries against the state in general, or against the sovereignty, majesty, and person of the prince. In fact these acquire the character of crime of the worst kind, requiring a special procedure, &c. [A.]

283. The second moment in the power of the crown is the moment of particularity, or the moment of a determinate content and its subsumption under the universal. When this acquires a special objective existence, it becomes the supreme council and the individuals who compose it. They bring before the monarch for his decision the content of current affairs of state or the legal provisions required to meet existing needs, together with their objective aspects, i.e. the grounds on which decision is to be based, the relative laws, circumstances, &c. The individuals who discharge these duties are in direct contact with the person of the monarch and therefore their choice and dismissal alike rest with his unrestricted caprice.

284. It is only for the *objective* side of decision, i.e. for knowledge of the problem and the attendant circumstances, and for the legal and other reasons which determine its solution, that men are answerable; in other words, it is these alone which are capable of objective proof. It is for this reason that these may fall within the province of a council which is distinct from the personal will of the monarch as such. Hence it is only councils or their individual members that are made answerable. The personal majesty of the monarch, on the other hand, as the final *subjectivity* of decision, is above all answerability for acts of government.

285. The third moment in the power of the crown concerns the absolute universality which subsists subjectively in the conscience of the monarch and objectively in the whole of the constitution and the laws. Hence the power of the crown presupposes the other moments in the state just as it is presupposed by each of them.

286. The *objective* guarantee of the power of the crown, of the hereditary right of succession to the throne, and so forth, consists in the fact that just as monarchy has its own actuality in distinction from that of the other rationally determined moments in the state, so these others explicitly possess the rights and duties appropriate to their own character. In the rational organism of the state, each member, by maintaining itself in its own position, *eo ipso* maintains the others in theirs.

One of the results of more recent history is the development of a monarchical constitution with succession to the throne firmly fixed on hereditary principles in accordance with primogeniture. With this development, monarchy has been brought back to the patriarchal principle in which it had its historical origin, but its determinate character is now higher, because the monarch is the absolute apex of an organically developed state. This historical result is of the utmost importance for public freedom and for rationality in the constitution, but, as was remarked above,[2] it is often grossly misunderstood despite the respect paid to it.

The history of despotisms, as of the now obsolete, purely feudal, monarchies, is a tale of the vicissitudes of revolt, monarchical tyranny, civil war, the ruin of princes of the blood and whole dynasties, and, consequentially, the general devastation and overthrow of the state in both its home and foreign concerns. This is all due to the fact that, in monarchies of that type, the division of the business of the state is purely mechanical, the various sections being merely handed over to pashas, vassals, &c. The difference between the departments is simply one of greater or lesser power instead of being one of form and specific character. Hence each department maintains itself and in doing so is productive only of itself and not of the others at the same time; each is independent and autonomous and completely incorporates in itself all the moments of the concept. When there is an *organic* relation subsisting between members, not parts, then each member by fulfilling the functions of its own sphere is *eo ipso* maintaining the others; what each fundamentally aims at and achieves in maintaining itself is the maintenance of the others.

The guarantees in question here for the maintenance of the succession to the throne or for the power of the crown generally, or for justice, public freedom, &c., are modes of securing these things by means of institutions. For *subjective* guarantees we may look to the affection of the people, to character, oaths of allegiance, power, and so forth, but, when the constitution is being discussed, it is only objective guarantees that are relevant. And such guarantees are institutions, i.e. mutually conditioning moments, organically interconnected. Hence public freedom in general and an hereditary monarchy guarantee each other; they stand or fall together of neces-

[1] See the end of the Remark to Paragraph 137.—ED.

[2] See Remarks to Paragraphs 279 and 281.—ED.

sity, because public freedom means a rational constitution, while the hereditary character of the power of the crown is, as has been shown,[1] the moment lying in the concept of that power.

(β) The Executive

287. There is a distinction between the monarch's decisions and their execution and application, or in general between his decisions and the continued execution or maintenance of past decisions, existing laws, regulations, organizations for the securing of common ends, and so forth. This task of merely subsuming the particular under the universal is comprised in the executive power, which also includes the powers of the judiciary and the police. The latter have a more immediate bearing on the particular concerns of civil society and they make the universal interest authoritative over its particular aims.

288. Particular interests which are common to everyone fall within civil society and lie outside the absolutely universal interest of the state proper (see Paragraph 256). The administration of these is in the hands of Corporations (see Paragraph 251, commercial and professional as well as municipal, and their officials, directors, managers, and the like. It is the business of these officials to manage the private property and interests of these particular spheres and, from that point of view, their authority rests on the confidence of their commonalties and professional equals. On the other hand, however, these circles of particular interests must be subordinated to the higher interests of the state, and hence the filling of positions of responsibility in Corporations, &c., will generally be effected by a mixture of popular election by those interested with appointment and ratification by higher authority.

289. The maintenance of the state's universal interest, and of legality, in this sphere of particular rights, and the work of bringing these rights back to the universal, require to be superintended by holders of the executive power, by (a) the executive civil servants, and (b) the higher advisory officials (who are organized into committees). These converge in their supreme heads who are in direct contact with the monarch.

Just as civil society is the battlefield where everyone's individual private interest meets everyone else's, so here we have the struggle (a) of private interests against particular matters of common concern and (b) of both of these together against the organization of the state and its higher outlook. At the same time the corporation mind, engendered when the particular spheres gain their title to rights, is now inwardly converted into the mind of the state, since it finds in the state the means of maintaining its particular ends. This is the secret of the patriotism of the citizens in the sense that they know the state as their substance, because it is the state that maintains their particular spheres of interest together with the title, authority, and welfare of these. In the corporation mind the rooting of the particular in the universal is directly entailed, and for this reason it is in that mind that the depth and strength which the state possesses in sentiment is seated.

The administration of a Corporation's business by its own officials is frequently clumsy, because although they keep before their minds and are acquainted with its special interests and affairs, they have a far less complete appreciation of the connexion of those affairs with more remote conditions and the outlook of the state. In addition, other circumstances contribute to the same result, e.g. close private relationships and other factors putting officials on a footing of equality with those who should be their subordinates, the rather numerous ways in which officials lack independence, and so on. This sphere of private interests, however, may be regarded as the one left to the moment of formal freedom,[2] the one which affords a playground for personal knowledge, personal decisions and their execution, petty passions and conceits. This is all the more permissible, the more trivial, from the point of view of the more universal affairs of state, is the intrinsic worth of the business which in this way comes to ruin or is managed less well or more laboriously, &c. And further, it is all the more permissible, the more this laborious or foolish management of such trivial affairs stands in direct relation with the self-satisfaction and vanity derived therefrom.

290. Division of labour (see Paragraph 198) occurs in the business of the executive also. For this reason, the organization of officials has the abstract though difficult task of so arranging that (a) civil life shall be governed in a concrete manner from below where it is concrete, but that (b) none the less the business of government shall be divided into its abstract branches manned by special officials as different centres of administration, and further that (c) the operations of these various departments shall converge again when they are directed on civil life from above, in the same way as they converge into a general supervision in the supreme executive.[3] [A.]

291. The nature of the executive functions is that they are objective and that in their substance they have been explicitly fixed by pre-

---

[1] See Paragraph 280.—ED.

[2] See Paragraphs 182 ff.—ED.
[3] Cf. Hegel, *Philosophy of History*, p. 367. See Remark to Paragraph 288 and Paragraph 295.—ED.

vious decisions (see Paragraph 287); these functions have to be fulfilled and carried out by individuals. Between an individual and his office there is no immediate natural link. Hence individuals are not appointed to office on account of their birth or native personal gifts. The *objective* factor in their appointment is knowledge and proof of ability. Such proof guarantees that the state will get what it requires; and since it is the sole condition of appointment, it also guarantees to every citizen the chance of joining the class of civil servants.

292. Since the objective qualification for the civil service is not genius (as it is for work as an artist, for example), there is of necessity an indefinite plurality of eligible candidates whose relative excellence is not determinable with absolute precision. The selection of one of the candidates, his nomination to office, and the grant to him of full authority to transact public business—all this, as the linking of two things, a man and his office, which in relation to each other must always be fortuitous, is the *subjective* aspect of election to office, and it must lie with the crown as the power in the state which is sovereign and has the last word.

293. The particular public functions which the monarch entrusts to officials constitute one part of the objective aspect of the sovereignty residing in the crown. Their specific discrimination is therefore given in the nature of the thing. And while the actions of the officials are the fulfilment of their duty, their office is also a right exempt from contingency.

294. Once an individual has been appointed to his official position by the sovereign's act (see Paragraph 292), the tenure of his post is conditional on his fulfilling its duties. Such fulfilment is the very essence of his appointment, and it is only consequential that he finds in his office his livelihood and the assured satisfaction of his particular interests (see Paragraph 264), and further that his external circumstances and his official work are freed from other kinds of subjective dependence and influence.

The state does not count on optional, discretionary, services (e.g. on justice administered by knights errant). It is just because such services are optional and discretionary that the state cannot rely on them, for casual servants may fail for private reasons to fulfil their duties completely, or they may arbitrarily decide not to fulfil them at all but pursue their private ends instead. The opposite extreme to a knight errant, so far as the service of the state goes, would be an official who clung to his office purely and simply to make a living without any real sense of duty and so without any real right to go on holding it.

What the service of the state really requires is that men shall forgo the selfish and capricious satisfaction of their subjective ends; by this very sacrifice, they acquire the right to find their satisfaction in, but only in, the dutiful discharge of their public functions. In this fact, so far as public business is concerned, there lies the link between universal and particular interests which constitutes both the concept of the state and its inner stability (see Paragraph 260).

It follows that a man's tenure of his civil service post is not contractual (see Paragraph 75), although his appointment involves a consent and an undertaking on both sides. A civil servant is not appointed, like an agent, to perform a single casual act of service; on the contrary, he concentrates his main interests (not only his particular interests but his mental interests also) on his relation to his work. Similarly, the work imposed upon him and entrusted to him is not merely a particular thing, external in character; the value of such a thing is something inward and therefore distinct from its outward character, so that it is in no way impaired if what has been stipulated is not fulfilled (see Paragraph 77). The work of a civil servant, however, is as such a value in and for itself. Hence the wrong committed through its non-performance, or positive misperformance (i.e. through an action contrary to official duty, and both of these are of that type), is an infringement of the universal content itself (i.e. is a negatively infinite judgement—see Paragraph 95) and so is a trespass or even a crime.

The assured satisfaction of particular needs removes the external compulsion which may tempt a man to seek ways and means of satisfying them at the expense of his official duties. Those who are entrusted with affairs of state find in its universal power the protection they need against another subjective phenomenon, namely the personal passions of the governed, whose private interests, &c., suffer injury as the interest of the state is made to prevail against them.

295. The security of the state and its subjects against the misuse of power by ministers and their officials lies directly in their hierarchical organization and their answerability; but it lies too in the authority given to societies and Corporations, because in itself this is a barrier against the intrusion of subjective caprice into the power entrusted to a civil servant, and it completes from below the state control which does not reach down as far as the conduct of individuals.

The conduct and culture of officials is the sphere where the laws and the government's decisions come into contact with individuals and are actually made good. Hence it is on the conduct of officials that there depend not only the contentment of citizens and their confidence in the government, but also the execution—or alternatively the distortion and frustration—of state projects; at any rate, this is the case in the sense that feeling and sentiment may easily rate the manner of execution as highly as the very content of the command to be executed, even though the content may in fact be the imposition of a tax. Owing to the direct and personal nature of this contact with individuals, control from above can attain its ends in this respect only to a rather incomplete extent. Moreover, its ends may also be hindered by interests common to officials who form a clique over against their inferiors on one side and their superiors on the other. In states whose institutions may perhaps be imperfectly developed in other respects also, the removal of hindrances like these requires and justifies the higher intervention of the sovereign (as for example of Frederick the Great in the notorious affair of Arnold the miller).

296. But the fact that a dispassionate, upright, and polite demeanour becomes customary [in civil servants] is (i) partly a result of direct education in thought and ethical conduct. Such an education is a mental counterpoise to the mechanical and semi-mechanical activity involved in acquiring the so-called "sciences" of matters connected with administration, in the requisite business training, in the actual work done, &c. (ii) The size of the state, however, is an important factor in producing this result, since it diminishes the stress of family and other personal ties, and also makes less potent and so less keen such passions as hatred, revenge, &c. In those who are busy with the important questions arising in a great state, these subjective interests automatically disappear, and the habit is generated of adopting universal interests, points of view, and activities.

297. Civil servants and the members of the executive constitute the greater part of the middle class, the class in which the consciousness of right and the developed intelligence of the mass of the people is found. The sovereign working on the middle class at the top, and Corporation rights working on it at the bottom, are the institutions which effectually prevent it from acquiring the isolated position of an aristocracy and using its education and skill as means to an arbitrary tyranny.

At one time the administration of justice, which is concerned with the private interests of all members of the state, was in this way turned into an instrument of profit and tyranny, when the knowledge of the law was buried in pedantry and a foreign tongue, and knowledge of legal processes was similarly buried in involved formalities. [A.]

(γ) The Legislature

298. The legislature is concerned (a) with the laws as such in so far as they require fresh and extended determination; and (b) with the content of home affairs affecting the entire state. The legislature is itself a part of the constitution which is presupposed by it and to that extent lies absolutely outside the sphere directly determined by it; none the less, the constitution becomes progressively more mature in the course of the further elaboration of the laws and the advancing character of the universal business of government. [A.]

299. Legislative business is more precisely determined, in relation to private individuals, under these two heads: (a) provision by the state for their well-being and happiness, and (β) the exaction of services from them. The former comprises the laws dealing with all sorts of private rights, the rights of communities, Corporations, and organizations affecting the entire state, and further it indirectly (see Paragraph 298) comprises the whole of the constitution. As for the services to be exacted, it is only if these are reduced to terms of money, the really existent and universal value of both things and services, that they can be fixed justly and at the same time in such a way that any particular tasks and services which an individual may perform come to be mediated through his own arbitrary will.

The proper object of universal legislation may be distinguished in a general way from the proper function of administrative officials or of some kind of state regulation, in that the content of the former is wholly universal, i.e. determinate laws, while it is what is particular in content which falls to the latter, together with ways and means of enforcing the law. This distinction, however, is not a hard and fast one, because a law, by being a law, is *ab initio* something more than a mere command in general terms (such as "Thou shalt not kill"—compare Remark (d) to Paragraph 140). A law must in itself be something determinate, but the more determinate it is, the more readily are its terms capable of being carried out as they stand. At the same time, however, to give to laws such a fully detailed determinacy would give them empirical features subject inevitably to alteration in the course of their being actually carried out, and this would contravene their character as laws. The organic unity of the powers of the state itself implies that it is one single mind which both firmly establishes the universal and also brings it into its determinate actuality and carries it out.

In the state it may happen, to begin with,[1] that the numerous aptitudes, possessions, pursuits, and

[1] i.e., before war breaks out. War-time services are considered in Paragraphs 324 ff.—Ed.

talents of its members, together with the infinitely varied richness of life intrinsic to these—all of which are at the same time linked with their owner's mentality—are not subject to direct levy by the state. It lays claim only to a single form of riches, namely money. (Services requisitioned for the defence of the state in war arise for the first time in connexion with the duty considered in the next subdivision of this book.) In fact, however, money is not one particular type of wealth amongst others, but the universal form of all types so far as they are expressed in an external embodiment and so can be taken as "things." [1] Only by being translated into terms of this extreme culmination of externality can services exacted by the state be fixed quantitatively and so justly and equitably.

In Plato's *Republic,* the Guardians are left to allot individuals to their particular classes and impose on them their particular tasks (compare Remark to Paragraph 185). Under the feudal monarchies the services required from vassals were equally indeterminate, but they had also to serve in their *particular* capacity, e.g. as judges. The same particular character pertains to tasks imposed in the East and in Egypt in connexion with colossal architectural undertakings, and so forth. In these circumstances the principle of subjective freedom is lacking, i.e. the principle that the individual's substantive activity—which in any case becomes something particular in content in services like those mentioned—shall be mediated through his particular volition. This is a right which can be secured only when the demand for service takes the form of a demand for something of universal value, and it is this right which has brought with it this conversion of the state's demands into demands for cash. [A.]

300. In the legislature as a whole the other powers are the first two moments which are effective, (i) the monarchy as that to which ultimate decisions belong; (ii) the executive as the advisory body since it is the moment possessed of (a) a concrete knowledge and oversight of the whole state in its numerous facets and the actual principles firmly established within it, and (β) a knowledge in particular of what the state's power needs. The last moment in the legislature is the Estates. [2] [A.]

301. The Estates have the function of bringing public affairs into existence not only implicitly, but also actually, i.e. of bringing into existence the moment of subjective formal freedom, the public consciousness as an empirical universal, of which the thoughts and opinions of the Many are particulars.

The phrase "the Many" ($o\iota$ $\pi o\lambda\lambda o\iota$) denotes empirical universality more strictly than "All," which is in current use. If it is said to be obvious that this

[1] See Paragraphs 42 ff.—ED.
[2] See Remark to Paragraph 303.

"all" prima facie excludes at least children, women, &c., then it is surely still more obvious that the quite definite word "all" should not be used when something quite indefinite is meant.

Current opinion has put into general circulation such a host of perverse and false ideas and ways of speaking about "People," "Constitution," and "Estates" that it would be a waste of energy to try to specify, expound, and correct them. The idea uppermost in men's minds when they speak about the necessity or the expediency of "summoning the Estates" is generally something of this sort: (i) The deputies of the people, or even the people themselves, must know best what is in their best interest, and (ii) their will for its promotion is undoubtedly the most disinterested. So far as the first of these points is concerned, however, the truth is that if "people" means a particular section of the citizens, then it means precisely that section which does *not* know what it wills. To know what one wills, and still more to know what the absolute will, Reason, wills, is the fruit of profound apprehension and insight, precisely the things which are *not* popular.

The Estates are a guarantee of the general welfare and public freedom. A little reflection will show that this guarantee does not lie in their particular power of insight, because the highest civil servants necessarily have a deeper and more comprehensive insight into the nature of the state's organization and requirements. They are also more habituated to the business of government and have greater skill in it, so that even without the Estates they are *able* to do what is best, just as they also continually *have* to do while the Estates are in session. No, the guarantee lies on the contrary (a) in the *additional* insight of the deputies, insight in the first place into the activity of such officials as are not immediately under the eye of the higher functionaries of state, and in particular into the more pressing and more specialized needs and deficiencies which are directly in their view; (β) in the fact that the anticipation of criticism from the Many, particularly of public criticism, has the effect of inducing officials to devote their best attention beforehand to their duties and the schemes under consideration, and to deal with these only in accordance with the purest motives. This same compulsion is effective also on the members of the Estates themselves.

As for the conspicuously good will for the general welfare which the Estates are supposed to possess, it has been pointed out already (in the Remark to Paragraph 272) that to regard the will of the executive as bad, or as less good [than that of the ruled] is a presupposition characteristic of the rabble or of the negative outlook generally. This presupposition might at once be answered on its own ground by the counter-charge that the Estates start from isolated individuals, from a private point of view, from particular interests, and so are inclined to devote their activities to these at the expense of the general interests, while *per contra* the other moments in the power of the state explicitly take up the standpoint of the state from the start and devote themselves to the universal end.

As for the general guarantee which is supposed to lie peculiarly in the Estates, each of the other political institutions shares with the Estates in being a guarantee of public welfare and rational freedom, and some of these institutions, as for instance the sovereignty of the monarch, hereditary succession to the throne, the judicial system, &c., guarantee these things far more effectively than the Estates can.

Hence the specific function which the concept assigns to the Estates is to be sought in the fact that in them the subjective moment in universal freedom—the private judgement and private will of the sphere called "civil society" in this book—comes into existence integrally related to the state. This moment is a determination of the Idea once the Idea has developed to totality, a moment arising as a result of an inner necessity not to be confused with external necessities and expediencies. The proof of this follows, like all the rest of our account of the state, from adopting the philosophical point of view. [A.]

302. Regarded as a mediating organ, the Estates stand between the government in general on the one hand and the nation broken up into particulars (people and associations) on the other. Their function requires them to possess a political and administrative sense and temper, no less than a sense for the interests of individuals and particular groups. At the same time the significance of their position is that, in common with the organized executive, they are a middle term preventing both the extreme isolation of the power of the crown, which otherwise might seem a mere arbitrary tyranny, and also the isolation of the particular interests of persons, societies, and Corporations. Further, and more important, they prevent individuals from having the appearance of a mass or an aggregate and so from acquiring an unorganized opinion and volition and from crystallizing into a powerful *bloc* in opposition to the organized state.

It is one of the most important discoveries of logic that a specific moment which, by standing in an opposition, has the position of an extreme, ceases to be such and is a moment in an organic whole by being at the same time a mean. In connexion with our present topic it is all the more important to emphasize this aspect of the matter because of the popular, but most dangerous, prejudice which regards the Estates principally from the point of view of their opposition to the executive, as if that were their essential attitude. If the Estates become an organ in the whole by being taken up into the state, they evince themselves solely through their mediating function. In this way their opposition to the executive is reduced to a show. There may indeed be an appearance of opposition between them, but if they were opposed, not merely superficially, but actually

and in substance, then the state would be in the throes of destruction. That the clash is not of this kind is evident in the nature of the thing, because the Estates have to deal, not with the essential elements in the organism of the state, but only with rather specialized and trifling matters, while the passion which even these arouse spends itself in party cravings in connexion with purely subjective interests such as appointments to the higher offices of state. [A.]

303. The universal class, or, more precisely, the class of civil servants, must, purely in virtue of its character as universal, have the universal as the end of its essential activity. In the Estates, as an element in the legislative power, the unofficial class acquires its political significance and efficacy; it appears, therefore, in the Estates neither as a mere indiscriminate multitude nor as an aggregate dispersed into its atoms, but as what it already is, namely a class subdivided into two, one sub-class [the agricultural class] being based on a tie of substance between its members, and the other [the business class] on particular needs and the work whereby these are met (see Paragraph 201 ff.). It is only in this way that there is a genuine link between the particular which is effective in the state and the universal.

This runs counter to another prevalent idea, the idea that since it is in the legislature that the unofficial class rises to the level of participating in matters of state, it must appear there in the form of individuals, whether individuals are to choose representatives for this purpose, or whether every single individual is to have a vote in the legislature himself. This atomistic and abstract point of view vanishes at the stage of the family, as well as that of civil society where the individual is in evidence only as a member of a general group. The state, however, is essentially an organization each of whose members is in itself a group of this kind, and hence no one of its moments should appear as an unorganized aggregate. The Many, as units—a congenial interpretation of "people," are of course something connected, but they are connected only as an aggregate, a formless mass whose commotion and activity could therefore only be elementary, irrational, barbarous, and frightful. When we hear speakers on the constitution expatiating about the "people"—this unorganized collection—we know from the start that we have nothing to expect but generalities and perverse declamations.

The circles of association in civil society are already communities. To picture these communities as once more breaking up into a mere conglomeration of individuals as soon as they enter the field of politics, i.e. the field of the highest concrete universality, is *eo ipso* to hold civil and political life apart from one another and as it were to hang the latter in the air, because its basis could then only be the abstract individuality of caprice and opinion, and hence it would be grounded on chance and not on what is absolutely stable and justified.

So-called "theories" of this kind involve the idea that the classes (*Stände*) of civil society and the Estates (*Stände*), which are the "classes" given a political significance, stand wide apart from each other. But the German language, by calling them both *Stände* has still maintained the unity which in any case they actually possessed in former times.

304. The Estates, as an element in political life, still retain in their own function the class distinctions already present in the lower spheres of civil life. The position of the classes is abstract to begin with, i.e. in contrast with the whole principle of monarchy or the crown, their position is that of an extreme—empirical universality. This extreme opposition implies the possibility, though no more, of harmonization, and the equally likely possibility of set hostility. This abstract position changes into a rational relation (into a syllogism, see Remark to Paragraph 302) only if the middle term between the opposites comes into existence. From the point of view of the crown, the executive already has this character (see Paragraph 300). So, from the point of view of the classes, one moment in them must be adapted to the task of existing as in essence the moment of mediation.

305. The principle of one of the classes of civil society is in itself capable of adaptation to this political position. The class in question is the one whose ethical life is natural, whose basis is family life, and, so far as its livelihood is concerned, the possession of land. Its particular members attain their position by birth, just as the monarch does, and, in common with him, they possess a will which rests on itself alone.[1]

306. This class is more particularly fitted for political position and significance in that its capital is independent alike of the state's capital, the uncertainty of business, the quest for profit, and any sort of fluctuation in possessions. It is likewise independent of favour, whether from the executive or the mob. It is even fortified against its own wilfulness, because those members of this class who are called to political life are not entitled, as other citizens are, either to dispose of their entire property at will, or to the assurance that it will pass to their children, whom they love equally, in similarly equal divisions. Hence their wealth becomes inalienable, entailed, and burdened by primogeniture. [A.]

307. The right of this section of the agricultural class is thus based in a way on the natural

[1] See Paragraph 199.—ED.

principle of the family. But this principle is at the same time reversed owing to hard sacrifices made for political ends, and thereby the activity of this class is essentially directed to those ends. As a consequence of this, this class is summoned and entitled to its political vocation by birth without the hazards of election. It therefore has the fixed, substantive position between the subjective wilfulness or contingency of both extremes; and while it mirrors in itself (see Paragraph 305) the moment of the monarchical power, it also shares in other respects the needs and rights of the other extreme [i.e. civil society] and hence it becomes a support at once of the throne and society.

308. The second section of the Estates comprises the fluctuating element in civil society. This element can enter politics only through its deputies; the multiplicity of its members is an external reason for this, but the essential reason is the specific character of this element and its activity. Since these deputies are the deputies of civil society, it follows as a direct consequence that their appointment is made by the society as a society. That is to say, in making the appointment, society is not dispersed into atomic units, collected to perform only a single and temporary act, and kept together for a moment and no longer. On the contrary, it makes the appointment as a society, articulated into associations, communities, and Corporations, which although constituted already for other purposes, acquire in this way a connexion with politics. The existence of the Estates and their assembly finds a constitutional guarantee of its own in the fact that this class is entitled to send deputies at the summons of the crown, while members of the former class are entitled to present themselves in person in the Estates (see Paragraph 307).

To hold that every single person should share in deliberating and deciding on political matters of general concern on the ground that all individuals are members of the state, that its concerns are their concerns, and that it is their right that what is done should be done with their knowledge and volition, is tantamount to a proposal to put the democratic element without any rational form into the organism of the state, although it is only in virtue of the possession of such a form that the state is an organism at all. This idea comes readily to mind because it does not go beyond the abstraction of "being a member of the state," and it is superficial thinking which clings to abstractions. The rational consideration of a topic, the consciousness of the Idea, is concrete, and to that extent coincides with a genuine practical sense. Such a sense is itself nothing but the sense of rationality or the Idea, though it is not to be confused with mere business routine or the horizon of a restricted sphere. The concrete state is the whole, articulated into its particular groups. The member of a state is a member of such a group, i.e. of a social class, and it is only as characterized in this objective way that he comes under consideration when we are dealing with the state. His mere character as universal implies that he is at one and the same time both a private person and also a thinking consciousness, a will which wills the universal. This consciousness and will, however, lose their emptiness and acquire a content and a living actuality only when they are filled with particularity, and particularity means determinacy as particular and a particular class-status; or, to put the matter otherwise, abstract individuality is a generic essence, but has its immanent universal actuality as the generic essence next higher in the scale. Hence the single person attains his actual and living destiny for universality only when he becomes a member of a Corporation, a society, &c. (see Paragraph 251), and thereby it becomes open to him, on the strength of his skill, to enter any class for which he is qualified, the class of civil servants included.

Another presupposition of the idea that all should participate in the business of the state is that everyone is at home in this business—a ridiculous notion, however commonly we may hear it sponsored. Still, in public opinion (see Paragraph 316) a field is open to everyone where he can express his purely personal political opinions and make them count.

309. Since deputies are elected to deliberate and decide on *public* affairs, the point about their election is that it is a choice of individuals on the strength of confidence felt in them, i.e. a choice of such individuals as have a better understanding of these affairs than their electors have and such also as essentially vindicate the universal interest, not the particular interest of a society or a Corporation in preference to that interest. Hence their relation to their electors is not that of agents with a commission or specific instructions. A further bar to their being so is the fact that their assembly is meant to be a living body in which all members deliberate in common and reciprocally instruct and convince each other. [A.]

310. The guarantee that deputies will have the qualifications and disposition that accord with this end—since independent means attains its right in the first section of the Estates—is to be found so far as the second section is concerned —the section drawn from the fluctuating and changeable element in civil society—above all in the knowledge (of the organization and interests of the state and civil society), the temperament, and the skill which a deputy acquires as a result of the actual transaction of business in managerial or official positions, and then evinces in his actions. As a result, he also acquires and develops a managerial and political sense, tested by his experience, and this is a further guarantee of his suitability as a deputy.

Subjective opinion, naturally enough, finds superfluous and even perhaps offensive the demand for such guarantees, if the demand is made with reference to what is called the "people." The state, however, is characterized by objectivity, not by a subjective opinion and its self-confidence. Hence it can recognize in individuals only their objectively recognizable and tested character, and it must be all the more careful on this point in connexion with the second section of the Estates, since this section is rooted in interests and activities directed towards the particular, i.e. in the sphere where chance, mutability, and caprice enjoy their right of free play.

The external guarantee, a property qualification, is, if taken by itself, evidently just as one-sided in its externality as, at the other extreme, are purely subjective confidence and the opinion of the electorate. Both alike are abstractions in contrast with the concrete qualifications requisite for deliberation on affairs of state and comprised in the points indicated in Paragraph 302. This apart, however, a property qualification has a sphere, where it may work effectively, in the choice of the heads and other officers of the associations and societies, especially if many of these posts are honorary, and in direct reference to Estates business if the members draw no salary.

311. A further point about the election of deputies is that, since civil society is the electorate, the deputies should themselves be conversant with and participate in its special needs, difficulties, and particular interests. Owing to the nature of civil society, its deputies are the deputies of the various Corporations (see Paragraph 308), and this simple mode of appointment obviates any confusion due to conceiving the electorate abstractly and as an agglomeration of atoms. Hence the deputies *eo ipso* adopt the point of view of society, and their actual election is therefore either something wholly superfluous or else reduced to a trivial play of opinion and caprice.

It is obviously of advantage that the deputies should include representatives of each particular main branch of society (e.g. trade, manufactures, &c., &c.) —representatives who are thoroughly conversant with it and who themselves belong to it. The idea of free unrestricted election leaves this important consideration entirely at the mercy of chance. All such branches of society, however, have equal rights of representation. Deputies are sometimes regarded as "representatives"; but they are representatives in an organic, rational sense only if they are representatives not of individuals or a conglomeration of them, but of one of the essential spheres of society and its large-scale interests. Hence representation cannot now be taken to mean simply the substitution of one man for another; the point is rather that the interest itself is actually present in its representative, while he himself is there to represent the objective element of his own being.

As for popular suffrage, it may be further remarked that especially in large states it leads inevitably to electoral indifference, since the casting of a single vote is of no significance where there is a multitude of electors. Even if a voting qualification is highly valued and esteemed by those who are entitled to it, they still do not enter the polling booth. Thus the result of an institution of this kind is more likely to be the opposite of what was intended; election actually falls into the power of a few, of a caucus, and so of the particular and contingent interest which is precisely what was to have been neutralized.

312. Each class in the Estates (see Paragraphs 305-8) contributes something peculiarly its own to the work of deliberation. Further, one moment in the class-element has in the sphere of politics the special function of mediation,[1] mediation between two existing things. Hence this moment must likewise acquire a separate existence of its own. For this reason the assembly of the Estates is divided into two houses.

313. This division, by providing chambers of the first and second instance, is a surer guarantee for ripeness of decision and it obviates the accidental character which a snap division has and which a numerical majority may acquire. But the principal advantage of this arrangement is that there is less chance of the Estates being in direct opposition to the executive; or that, if the mediating element is at the same time on the side of the lower house, the weight of the lower house's opinion is all the stronger, because it appears less partisan and its opposition appears neutralized.

314. The purpose of the Estates as an institution is not to be an inherent *sine qua non* of maximum efficiency in the consideration and dispatch of state business, since in fact it is only an *added* efficiency that they can supply (see Paragraph 301). Their distinctive purpose is that in their pooled political knowledge, deliberations, and decisions, the moment of formal freedom shall come into its right in respect of those members of civil society who are without any share in the executive. Consequently, it is knowledge of public business above all which is extended by the publicity of Estates debates.

[1] See Paragraphs 301, 304, 305, 313, and the Remark to Paragraph 24.—Ed.

315. The opening of this opportunity to know has a more universal aspect because by this means public opinion first reaches thoughts that are true and attains insight into the situation and concept of the state and its affairs, and so first acquires ability to estimate these more rationally. By this means also, it becomes acquainted with and learns to respect the work, abilities, virtues, and dexterity of ministers and officials. While such publicity provides these abilities with a potent means of development and a theatre of higher distinction, it is at the same time another antidote to the self-conceit of individuals singly and *en masse,* and another means—indeed one of the chief means—of their education. [A.]

316. The formal subjective freedom of individuals consists in their having and expressing their own private judgements, opinions, and recommendations on affairs of state. This freedom is collectively manifested as what is called "public opinion," in which what is absolutely universal, the substantive and the true, is linked with its opposite, the purely particular and private opinions of the Many. Public opinion as it exists is thus a standing self-contradiction, knowledge as appearance, the essential just as directly present as the inessential. [A.]

317. Public opinion, therefore, is a repository not only of the genuine needs and correct tendencies of common life, but also, in the form of common sense (i.e. all-pervasive fundamental ethical principles disguised as prejudices), of the eternal, substantive principles of justice, the true content and result of legislation, the whole constitution, and the general position of the state. At the same time, when this inner truth emerges into consciousness and, embodied in general maxims, enters representative thinking —whether it be there on its own account or in support of concrete arguments about felt wants, public affairs, the organization of the state, and relations of parties within it—it becomes infected by all the accidents of opinion, by its ignorance and perversity, by its mistakes and falsity of judgement. Since in considering such opinion we have to do with the consciousness of an insight and conviction peculiarly one's own, the more peculiarly one's own an opinion may be the worse its content is, because the bad is that which is wholly private and personal in its content; the rational, on the other hand, is the absolutely universal, while it is on peculiarity that opining prides itself.

Hence it is not simply due to a subjective difference of view that we find it said that *vox populi, vox Dei,* and on the other hand, as Ariosto has it,

Che 'l volgare ignorante ogn' un riprenda
E parli più di quel che meno intenda

or, as Goethe puts it, "the masses are respectable hands at fighting, but miserable hands at judging."

Both types of assertion are true at one and the same time of public opinion, and since it is such a hotch-potch of truth and endless error, it cannot be genuinely serious about both of these. But about which *is* it serious? The question may seem hard to answer and it will actually be hard if we cling simply to the words in which public opinion is directly expressed. The substantial, however, is the heart of public opinion, and therefore it is with that alone that it is truly serious. What the substantial is, though, is not discoverable from public opinion, because its very substantiality implies that it is known in and from itself alone. The passion with which an opinion is urged or the seriousness with which it is maintained or attacked and disputed is no criterion of its real content; and yet the last thing which opinion could be made to see is that its seriousness is nothing serious.

A great genius propounded as a problem for a public essay competition the question "whether it be permissible to deceive a people." The answer must have been that a people does not allow itself to be deceived about its substantive basis, the essence and specific character of its mind. On the other hand, it is *self-*deceived about the manner of its knowledge of these things and about its corresponding judgement of its actions, experiences, &c. [A.]

318. Public opinion therefore deserves to be as much respected as despised—despised for its concrete expression and for the concrete consciousness it expresses, respected for its essential basis, a basis which only glimmers more or less dimly in that concrete expression. But in itself it has no criterion of discrimination, nor has it the ability to extract the substantive element it contains and raise it to precise knowledge. Thus to be independent of public opinion is the first formal condition of achieving anything great or rational whether in life or in science. Great achievement is assured, however, of subsequent recognition and grateful acceptance by public opinion, which in due course will make it one of its own prejudices. [A.]

319. Freedom of public communication—of the two modes of communication, the press and the spoken word, the first exceeds the second in range of contact but lags behind it in vivacity— satisfaction of the goading desire to say one's say and to have said it, is directly assured by the laws and by-laws which control or punish its excesses. But it is assured indirectly by the innocuous character which it acquires as a result principally of the rationality of the constitution, the stability of government, and secondly of the publicity of Estates Assemblies. The reason why the latter makes free speech harmless is that what is voiced in these Assemblies is a sound and mature insight into the concerns of the state, with the result that members of the general public are left with nothing of much importance to say, and above all are deprived of the opinion that what they say is of peculiar importance and efficacy. A further safeguard of free speech is the indifference and contempt speedily and necessarily visited on shallow and cantankerous talking.

To define freedom of the press as freedom to say and write whatever we please is parallel to the assertion that freedom as such means freedom to do as we please. Talk of this kind is due to wholly uneducated, crude, and superficial ideas. Moreover, it is in the very nature of the thing that abstract thinking should nowhere be so stubborn, so unintelligent, as in this matter of free speech, because what it is considering is the most fleeting, the most contingent, and the most personal side of opinion in its infinite diversity of content and tergiversation. Beyond the direct incitation to theft, murder, rebellion, &c., there lies its artfully constructed expression—an expression which seems in itself quite general and vague, while all the time it conceals a meaning anything but vague or else is compatible with inferences which are not actually expressed, and it is impossible to determine whether they rightly follow from it, or whether they were meant to be inferred from it. This vagueness of matter and form precludes laws on these topics from attaining the requisite determinacy of law, and since the trespass, wrong, and injury here are so extremely personal and subjective in form, judgement on them is reduced equally to a wholly subjective verdict. Such an injury is directed against the thoughts, opinions, and wills of others, but apart from that, these form the element in which alone it is actually anything. But this element is the sphere of the freedom of others, and it therefore depends on them whether the injurious expression of opinion is or is not actually an effective act.

Laws then [against libel, &c.] may be criticized by exhibiting their indeterminacy as well as by arguing that they leave it open to the speaker or writer to devise turns of phrase or tricks of expression, and so evade the laws or claim that judicial decisions are mere subjective verdicts. Further, however, against the view that the expression of opinion is an act with injurious effects, it may be maintained that it is not an act at all, but only opining and thinking, or only talking. And so we have before us a claim that mere opining and talking is to go unpunished because it is of a purely subjective character both in form and content, because it does not mean anything and is of no importance. And yet in the same breath we have the claim that this same opining and talking should be held in high esteem and respect—the opining because it is personal property and in fact pre-eminently the property of mind; the talking because it is only this same property being expressed and used.

But the substance of the matter is and remains that traducing the honour of anyone, slander, abuse, the contemptuous caricature of government, its ministers, officials, and in particular the person of the monarch, defiance of the laws, incitement to rebellion, &c., &c., are all crimes or misdemeanours in one or other of their numerous gradations. The rather high degree of indeterminability which such actions acquire on account of the element in which they are expressed does not annul this fundamental character of theirs. Its only effect is that the subjective field in which they are committed also determines the nature and form of the reaction to the offence. It is the field in which the offence was committed which itself necessitates subjectivity of view, contingency, &c., in the reaction to the offence, whether the reaction takes the form of punishment proper or of police action to prevent crimes. Here, as always, abstract thinking sets itself to explain away the fundamental and concrete nature of the thing by concentrating on isolated aspects of its external appearance and on abstractions drawn therefrom.

The sciences, however, are not to be found anywhere in the field of opinion and subjective views, provided of course that they be sciences in other respects. Their exposition is not a matter of clever turns of phrase, allusiveness, half-utterances, and semi-reticences, but consists in the unambiguous, determinate, and open expression of their meaning and purport. It follows that they do not fall under the category of public opinion (see Paragraph 316). Apart from this, however, as I said just now, the element in which views and their expression become actions in the full sense and exist effectively, consists of the intelligence, principles, and opinions of others. Hence this aspect of these actions, i.e. their effectiveness proper and their danger to individuals, society, and the state (compare Paragraph 218), depends on the character of the ground on which they fall, just as a spark falling on a heap of gunpowder is more dangerous than if it falls on hard ground where it vanishes without trace. Thus, just as the right of science to express itself depends on and is safeguarded by its subject-matter and content, so an illegitimate expression may also acquire a measure of security, or at least sufferance, in the scorn which it has brought upon itself. An offence of this sort is punishable on its own account too, but part of it may be accounted that kind of nemesis which inner impotence, feeling itself oppressed by the preponderating abilities and virtues of others, is impelled to vent in order to come to itself again in face of such superiority, and to restore some self-consciousness to its own nullity. It was a nemesis of a more harmless type which Roman soldiers vented against their generals when they sang scurrilous songs about them in triumphal processions

in order in a way to get even with them for all the hard service and discipline they had undergone, and especially for the omission of their names from the triumphal honours. The former type of nemesis, the bad and hateful type, is deprived of its effect by being treated with scorn, and hence, like the public, which perhaps forms a circle of spectators of scurrility, it is restricted to futile malice and to the self-condemnation which it implicitly contains.

320. Subjectivity is manifested in its most external form as the undermining of the established life of the state by opinion and ratiocination when they endeavour to assert the authority of their own fortuitous character and so bring about their own destruction. But its true actuality is attained in the opposite of this, i.e. in the subjectivity identical with the substantial will of the state, the subjectivity which constitutes the concept of the power of the crown and which, as the ideality of the whole state, has not up to this point attained its right or its existence. [A.]

2. Sovereignty vis-à-vis foreign States

321. Sovereignty at home (see Paragraph 278) is this ideality in the sense that the moments of mind and its actuality, the state, have become developed in their necessity and subsist as the organs of the state. Mind in its freedom is an infinitely negative relation to itself and hence its essential character from its own point of view is its singleness, a singleness which has incorporated these subsistent differences into itself and so is a unit, exclusive of other units. So characterized, the state has individuality, and individuality is in essence an individual, and in the sovereign an actual, immediate individual (see Paragraph 279).

322. Individuality is awareness of one's existence as a unit in sharp distinction from others. It manifests itself here in the state as a relation to other states, each of which is autonomous vis-à-vis the others. This autonomy embodies mind's actual awareness of itself as a unit and hence it is the most fundamental freedom which a people possesses as well as its highest dignity.

Those who talk of the "wishes" of a collection of people constituting a more or less autonomous state with its own centre, of its "wishes" to renounce this centre and its autonomy in order to unite with others to form a new whole, have very little knowledge of the nature of a collection or of the feeling of selfhood which a nation possesses in its independence.

Thus the dominion which a state has at its first entry into history is this bare autonomy, even if it be quite abstract and without further inner development. For this reason, to have an individual at its head—a patriarch, a chieftain, &c.—is appropriate to this original appearance of the state.

323. This negative relation of the state to itself is embodied in the world as the relation of one state to another and as if the negative were something external. In the world of existence, therefore, this negative relation has the shape of a happening and an entanglement with chance events coming from without. But in fact this negative relation is that moment in the state which is most supremely its own, the state's actual infinity as the ideality of everything finite within it. It is the moment wherein the substance of the state—i.e. its absolute power against everything individual and particular, against life, property, and their rights, even against societies and associations—makes the nullity of these finite things an accomplished fact and brings it home to consciousness.

324. This destiny whereby the rights and interests of individuals are established as a passing phase, is at the same time the positive moment, i.e. the positing of their absolute, not their contingent and unstable, individuality. This relation and the recognition of it is therefore the individual's substantive duty, the duty to maintain this substantive individuality, i.e. the independence and sovereignty of the state, at the risk and the sacrifice of property and life, as well as of opinion and everything else naturally comprised in the compass of life.

An entirely distorted account of the demand for this sacrifice results from regarding the state as a mere civil society and from regarding its final end as only the security of individual life and property. This security cannot possibly be obtained by the sacrifice of what is to be secured—on the contrary.

The ethical moment in war is implied in what has been said in this Paragraph. War is not to be regarded as an absolute evil and as a purely external accident, which itself therefore has some accidental cause, be it injustices, the passions of nations or the holders of power, &c., or in short, something or other which ought not to be. It is to what is by nature accidental that accidents happen, and the fate whereby they happen is thus a necessity. Here as elsewhere, the point of view from which things seem pure accidents vanishes if we look at them in the light of the concept and philosophy, because philosophy knows accident for a show and sees in it its essence, necessity. It is necessary that the finite—property and life —should be definitely established as accidental, because accidentality is the concept of the finite. From one point of view this necessity appears in the form of the power of nature, and everything is mortal and transient. But in the ethical substance, the state, nature is robbed of this power, and the necessity is ex-

alted to be the work of freedom, to be something ethical. The transience of the finite becomes a willed passing away, and the negativity lying at the roots of the finite becomes the substantive individuality proper to the ethical substance.

War is the state of affairs which deals in earnest with the vanity of temporal goods and concerns—a vanity at other times a common theme of edifying sermonizing. This is what makes it the moment in which the ideality of the particular attains its right and is actualized. War has the higher significance that by its agency, as I have remarked elsewhere, "the ethical health of peoples is preserved in their indifference to the stabilization of finite institutions; just as the blowing of the winds preserves the sea from the foulness which would be the result of a prolonged calm, so also corruption in nations would be the product of prolonged, let alone 'perpetual,' peace." This, however, is said to be only a philosophic idea, or, to use another common expression, a "justification of Providence," and it is maintained that actual wars require some other justification. On this point, see below.[1]

The ideality which is in evidence in war, i.e. in an accidental relation of a state to a foreign state, is the same as the ideality in accordance with which the domestic powers of the state are organic moments in a whole. This fact appears in history in various forms, e.g. successful wars have checked domestic unrest and consolidated the power of the state at home. Other phenomena illustrate the same point: e.g. peoples unwilling or afraid to tolerate sovereignty at home have been subjugated from abroad, and they have struggled for their independence with the less glory and success the less they have been able previously to organize the powers of the state in home affairs—their freedom has died from the fear of dying; states whose autonomy has been guaranteed not by their armed forces but in other ways (e.g. by their disproportionate smallness in comparison with their neighbours) have been able to subsist with a constitution of their own which by itself would not have assured peace in either home or foreign affairs. [A.]

325. Sacrifice on behalf of the individuality of the state is the substantial tie between the state and all its members and so is a universal duty. Since this tie is a *single* aspect of the ideality, as contrasted with the reality, of subsistent particulars, it becomes at the same time a *particular* tie, and those who are in it form a class of their own with the characteristic of courage.[2]

326. The matter at issue in disputes between states may be only one particular aspect of their relation to each other, and it is for such disputes that the particular class devoted to the state's defence is principally appointed. But if the state as such, if its autonomy, is in jeopardy, all its

---

[1] Paragraphs 334-7 and 343.—ED.
[2] Cf. Plato, *Republic*, 429.—ED.

citizens are in duty bound to answer the summons to its defence. If in such circumstances the entire state is under arms and is torn from its domestic life at home to fight abroad, the war of defence turns into a war of conquest.

The armed force of the state becomes a standing army, while its appointment to the particular task of state defence makes it a class. This happens from the same necessity as compels other particular moments, interests, and activities in the state to crystallize into a given status or class, e.g. into the status of marriage or into the business or civil servant class, or into the Estates of the Realm. Ratiocination, running hither and thither from ground to consequent, launches forth into reflections about the relative advantages and disadvantages of standing armies. Opinion readily decides that the latter preponderate, partly because the concept of a thing is harder to grasp than its single and external aspects, but also because particular interests and ends (the expense of a standing army, and its result, higher taxation, &c.) are rated in the consciousness of civil society more highly than what is necessary in and by itself. In this way the latter comes to count only as a means to particular ends.

327. In itself, courage is a *formal* virtue, because (i) it is a display of freedom by radical abstraction from all particular ends, possessions, pleasure, and life; but (ii) this negation is a negation of externalities, and their alienation, the culmination of courage, is not intrinsically of a spiritual (*geistiger*) character; (iii) the courageous man's inner motive need only be some particular reason or other, and even the actual result of what he does need be present solely to the minds of others and not to his own.[1] [A.]

328. The intrinsic worth of courage as a disposition of mind is to be found in the genuine, absolute, final end, the sovereignty of the state. The work of courage is to actualize this final end, and the means to this end is the sacrifice of personal actuality. This form of experience thus contains the harshness of extreme contradictions: a self-sacrifice which yet is the real existence of one's freedom; the maximum self-subsistence of individuality, yet only as a cog playing its part in the mechanism of an external organization; absolute obedience, renunciation of personal opinions and reasonings, in fact complete *absence* of mind, coupled with the most intense and comprehensive *presence* of mind and decision in the moment of acting; the most hostile and so most personal action against individuals, coupled with an attitude of complete indifference or even liking towards them as individuals.

[1] See Paragraph 328 and the Remark thereto.—ED.

To risk one's life is better than merely fearing death, but is still purely negative and so indeterminate and without value in itself. It is the positive aspect, the end and content, which first gives significance to this spiritedness. Robbers and murderers bent on crime as their end, adventurers pursuing ends planned to suit their own whims, &c., these too have spirit enough to risk their lives.

The principle of the modern world—thought and the universal—has given courage a higher form, because its display now seems to be more mechanical, the act not of this particular person, but of a member of a whole. Moreover, it seems to be turned not against single persons, but against a hostile group, and hence personal bravery appears impersonal. It is for this reason that thought has invented the gun, and the invention of this weapon, which has changed the purely personal form of bravery into a more abstract one, is no accident.

329. The state's tendency to look abroad lies in the fact that it is an individual subject. Its relation to other states therefore falls to the power of the crown. Hence it directly devolves on the monarch, and on him alone, to command the armed forces, to conduct foreign affairs through ambassadors &c., to make war and peace, and to conclude treaties of all kinds. [A.]

B. *International Law*

330. International law springs from the relations between autonomous states. It is for this reason that what is absolute in it retains the form of an ought-to-be, since its actuality depends on different wills each of which is sovereign. [A.]

331. The nation state is mind in its substantive rationality and immediate actuality and is therefore the absolute power on earth. It follows that every state is sovereign and autonomous against its neighbours. It is entitled in the first place and without qualification to be sovereign from their point of view, i.e. to be recognized by them as sovereign. At the same time, however, this title is purely formal, and the demand for this recognition of the state, merely on the ground that it is a state, is abstract. Whether a state is in fact something absolute depends on its content, i.e. on its constitution and general situation; and recognition, implying as it does an identity of both form and content, is conditional on the neighbouring state's judgement and will.

A state is as little an actual individual without relations to other states (see Paragraph 322) as an individual is actually a person without *rapport* with other persons (see Paragraph 71 and elsewhere[2]).

[2] e.g., Paragraph 40. On "recognition" see Remark to Paragraph 349.—ED.

The legitimate authority of a state and, more particularly, so far as its foreign relations are concerned, of its monarch also, is partly a purely domestic matter (one state should not meddle with the domestic affairs of another). On the other hand, however, it is no less essential that this authority should receive its full and final legitimation through its recognition by other states, although this recognition requires to be safeguarded by the proviso that where a state is to be recognized by others, it shall likewise recognize them, i.e. respect their autonomy; and so it comes about that they cannot be indifferent to each other's domestic affairs.

The question arises how far a nomadic people, for instance, or any people on a low level of civilization, can be regarded as a state. As once was the case with the Jews and the Mohammedan peoples, religious views may entail an opposition at a higher level between one people and its neighbours and so preclude the general identity which is requisite for recognition. [A.]

332. The immediate actuality which any state possesses from the point of view of other states is particularized into a multiplicity of relations which are determined by the arbitrary will of both autonomous parties and which therefore possess the formal nature of contracts pure and simple. The subject-matter of these contracts, however, is infinitely less varied than it is in civil society, because in civil society individuals are reciprocally interdependent in the most numerous respects, while autonomous states are principally wholes whose needs are met within their own borders.

333. The fundamental proposition of international law (i.e. the universal law which ought to be absolutely valid between states, as distinguished from the particular content of positive treaties) is that treaties, as the ground of obligations between states, ought to be kept. But since the sovereignty of a state is the principle of its relations to others, states are to that extent in a state of nature in relation to each other. Their rights are actualized only in their particular wills and not in a universal will with constitutional powers over them. This universal proviso of international law therefore does not go beyond an ought-to-be, and what really happens is that international relations in accordance with treaty alternate with the severance of these relations.

There is no Praetor to judge between states; at best there may be an arbitrator or a mediator, and even he exercises his functions contingently only, i.e. in dependence on the particular wills of the disputants. Kant had an idea for securing "perpetual peace" by a League of Nations to adjust every dispute. It was to be a power recognized by each individual state, and was to arbitrate in all cases of dissension in order to make it impossible for disputants to resort to war in order to settle them. This idea presupposes an accord between states; this would rest on moral or religious or other grounds and considerations, but in any case would always depend ultimately on a particular sovereign will and for that reason would remain infected with contingency.

334. It follows that if states disagree and their particular wills cannot be harmonized, the matter can only be settled by war. A state through its subjects has widespread connexions and many-sided interests, and these may be readily and considerably injured; but it remains inherently indeterminable which of these injuries is to be regarded as a specific breach of treaty or as an injury to the honour and autonomy of the state. The reason for this is that a state may regard its infinity and honour as at stake in each of its concerns, however minute, and it is all the more inclined to susceptibility to injury the more its strong individuality is impelled as a result of long domestic peace to seek and create a sphere of activity abroad.

335. Apart from this, the state is in essence mind and therefore cannot be prepared to stop at just taking notice of an injury *after* it has actually occurred. On the contrary, there arises in addition as a cause of strife the *idea* of such an injury as the idea of a danger *threatening* from another state, together with calculations of degrees of probability on this side and that, guessing at intentions, &c., &c.

336. Since states are related to one another as autonomous entities and so as particular wills on which the very validity of treaties depends, and since the particular will of the whole is in content a will for its own welfare pure and simple, it follows that welfare is the highest law governing the relation of one state to another. This is all the more the case since the Idea of the state is precisely the supersession of the clash between right (i.e. empty abstract freedom) and welfare (i.e. the particular content which fills that void), and it is when states become *concrete* wholes that they first attain recognition (see Paragraph 331).

337. The substantial welfare of the state is its welfare as a particular state in its specific interest and situation and its no less special foreign affairs, including its particular treaty relations. Its government therefore is a matter of particular wisdom, not of universal Providence (compare Remark to Paragraph 324). Similarly, its

aim in relation to other states and its principle for justifying wars and treaties is not a universal thought (the thought of philanthropy) but only its actually injured or threatened welfare as something specific and peculiar to itself.

At one time the opposition between morals and politics, and the demand that the latter should conform to the former, were much canvassed. On this point only a general remark is required here. The welfare of a state has claims to recognition totally different from those of the welfare of the individual. The ethical substance, the state, has its determinate being, i.e. its right, directly embodied in something existent, something not abstract but concrete, and the principle of its conduct and behaviour can only be this concrete existent and not one of the many universal thoughts supposed to be moral commands. When politics is alleged to clash with morals and so to be always wrong, the doctrine propounded rests on superficial ideas about morality, the nature of the state, and the state's relation to the moral point of view.

338. The fact that states reciprocally recognize each other as states remains, even in war—the state of affairs when rights disappear and force and chance hold sway—a bond wherein each counts to the rest as something absolute. Hence in war, war itself is characterized as something which ought to pass away. It implies therefore the proviso of the *jus gentium* that the possibility of peace be retained (and so, for example, that envoys must be respected), and, in general, that war be not waged against domestic institutions, against the peace of family and private life, or against persons in their private capacity. [A.]

339. Apart from this, relations between states (e.g. in war-time, reciprocal agreements about taking prisoners; in peace-time, concessions of rights to subjects of other states for the purpose of private trade and intercourse, &c.) depend principally upon the customs of nations, custom being the inner universality of behaviour maintained in all circumstances. [A.]

340. It is as particular entities that states enter into relations with one another. Hence their relations are on the largest scale a maelstrom of external contingency and the inner particularity of passions, private interests and selfish ends, abilities and virtues, vices, force, and wrong. All these whirl together, and in their vortex the ethical whole itself, the autonomy of the state, is exposed to contingency. The principles of the national minds [1] are wholly restricted on account of their particularity, for it is in this par-

ticularity that, as existent individuals, they have their objective actuality and their self-consciousness. Their deeds and destinies in their reciprocal relations to one another are the dialectic of the finitude of these minds, and out of it arises the universal mind, the mind of the world, free from all restriction, producing itself as that which exercises its right—and its right is the highest right of all—over these finite minds in the "history of the world which is the world's court of judgement."

C. *World History*

341. The element in which the universal mind exists in art is intuition and imagery, in religion feeling and representative thinking, in philosophy pure freedom of thought. In world history this element is the actuality of mind in its whole compass of internality and externality alike. World history is a court of judgement because in its absolute universality, the particular—i.e. the *Penates,* civil society, and the national minds in their variegated actuality—is present as only ideal, and the movement of mind in this element is the exhibition of that fact. [2]

342. Further, world history is not the verdict of mere might, i.e. the abstract and non-rational inevitability of a blind destiny. On the contrary, since mind is implicitly and actually reason, and reason is explicit to itself in mind as knowledge, world history is the necessary development, out of the concept of mind's freedom alone, of the moments of reason and so of the self-consciousness and freedom of mind. This development is the interpretation and actualization of the universal mind.

343. The history of mind is its own act. Mind is only what it does, and its act is to make itself the object of its own consciousness. In history its act is to gain consciousness of itself as mind, to apprehend itself in its interpretation of itself to itself. This apprehension is its being and its principle, and the completion of apprehension at one stage is at the same time the rejection of that stage and its transition to a higher. To use abstract phraseology, the mind apprehending this apprehension anew, or in other words returning to itself again out of its rejection of this lower stage of apprehension, is the mind of the stage higher than that on which it stood in its earlier apprehension.

The question of the perfectibility and *Education of the Human Race* arises here. Those who have maintained this perfectibility have divined something of

---

[1] Cf. Montesquieu, *The Spirit of Laws,* xix. 4-5.—Ed.

[2] Paragraphs 341-60 are a very compressed summary of Hegel's *Philosophy of History.*—Ed.

the nature of mind, something of the fact that it is its nature to have γνῶθι σεαυτόν as the law of its being, and, since it apprehends that which it is, to have a form higher than that which constituted its mere being. But to those who reject this doctrine, mind has remained an empty word, and history a superficial play of casual, so-called "merely human," strivings and passions. Even if, in connexion with history, they speak of Providence and the plan of Providence, and so express a faith in a higher power, their ideas remain empty because they expressly declare that for them the plan of Providence is inscrutable and incomprehensible.

344. In the course of this work of the world mind, states, nations, and individuals arise animated by their particular determinate principle which has its interpretation and actuality in their constitutions and in the whole range of their life and condition. While their consciousness is limited to these and they are absorbed in their mundane interests, they are all the time the unconscious tools and organs of the world mind at work within them. The shapes which they take pass away, while the absolute mind prepares and works out its transition to its next higher stage.

345. Justice and virtue, wrongdoing, power and vice, talents and their achievements, passions strong and weak, guilt and innocence, grandeur in individual and national life, autonomy, fortune and misfortune of states and individuals, all these have their specific significance and worth in the field of known actuality; therein they are judged and therein they have their partial, though only partial justification. World-history, however, is above the point of view from which these things matter. Each of its stages is the presence of a necessary moment in the Idea of the world mind, and that moment attains its absolute right in that stage. The nation whose life embodies this moment secures its good fortune and fame, and its deeds are brought to fruition.

346. History is mind clothing itself with the form of events or the immediate actuality of nature. The stages of its development are therefore presented as immediate natural principles. These, because they are natural, are a plurality external to one another, and they are present therefore in such a way that each of them is assigned to one nation in the external form of its geographical and anthropological conditions.

347. The nation to which is ascribed a moment of the Idea in the form of a natural principle is entrusted with giving complete effect to it in the advance of the self-developing self-consciousness of the world mind. This nation is dominant in world history during this one epoch, and it is only once (see Paragraph 345)[1] that it can make its hour strike. In contrast with this its absolute right of being the vehicle of this present stage in the world mind's development, the minds of the other nations are without rights, and they, along with those whose hour has struck already, count no longer in world history.

The history of a single world-historical nation contains (a) the development of its principle from its latent embryonic stage until it blossoms into the self-conscious freedom of ethical life and presses in upon world history; and (b) the period of its decline and fall, since it is its decline and fall that signalizes the emergence in it of a higher principle as the pure negative of its own. When this happens, mind passes over into the new principle and so marks out another nation for world-historical significance. After this period, the declining nation has lost the interest of the absolute; it may indeed absorb the higher principle positively and begin building its life on it, but the principle is only like an adopted child, not like a relative to whom its ties are immanently vital and vigorous. Perhaps it loses its autonomy, or it may still exist, or drag out its existence, as a particular state or a group of states and involve itself without rhyme or reason in manifold enterprises at home and battles abroad.

348. All actions, including world-historical actions, culminate with individuals as subjects giving actuality to the substantial (see Remark to Paragraph 279). They are the living instruments of what is in substance the deed of the world mind and they are therefore directly at one with that deed though it is concealed from them and is not their aim and object (see Paragraph 344). For the deeds of the world mind, therefore, they receive no honour or thanks either from their contemporaries (see Paragraph 344) or from public opinion in later ages. All that is vouchsafed to them by such opinion is undying fame in respect of the subjective form of their acts.

349. A nation does not begin by being a state. The transition from a family, a horde, a clan, a multitude, &c., to political conditions is the realization of the Idea in the form of that nation. Without this form, a nation, as an ethical substance—which is what it is implicitly, lacks the objectivity of possessing in its own eyes and in the eyes of others, a universal and universally valid embodiment in laws, i.e. in determinate thoughts, and as a result it fails to secure recognition from others. So long as it lacks objective

[1] All editions read "346."—Ed.

law and an explicitly established rational constitution, its autonomy is formal only and is not sovereignty.

It would be contrary even to commonplace ideas to call patriarchal conditions a "constitution" or a people under patriarchal government a "state" or its independence "sovereignty." Hence, before history actually begins, we have on the one hand dull innocence, devoid of interest, and, on the other, the courage of revenge and of the struggle for formal recognition (see Paragraph 331 and Remark to Paragraph 57).

350. It is the absolute right of the Idea to step into existence in clear-cut laws and objective institutions, beginning with marriage and agriculture (see Remark to Paragraph 203), whether this right be actualized in the form of divine legislation and favour, or in the form of force and wrong. This right is the right of heroes to found states.

351. The same consideration justifies civilized nations in regarding and treating as barbarians those who lag behind them in institutions which are the essential moments of the state. Thus a pastoral people may treat hunters as barbarians, and both of these are barbarians from the point of view of agriculturists, &c. The civilized nation is conscious that the rights of barbarians are unequal to its own and treats their autonomy as only a formality.

When wars and disputes arise in such circumstances, the trait which gives them a significance for world history is the fact that they are struggles for recognition in connexion with something of specific intrinsic worth.

352. The concrete Ideas, the minds of the nations, have their truth and their destiny in the concrete Idea which is absolute universality, i.e. in the world mind. Around its throne they stand as the executors of its actualization and as signs and ornaments of its grandeur. As mind, it is nothing but its active movement towards absolute knowledge of itself and therefore towards freeing its consciousness from the form of natural immediacy and so coming to itself. Therefore the principles of the formations of this self-consciousness in the course of its liberation—the world-historical realms—are four in number.

353. In its *first* and immediate revelation, mind has as its principle the shape of the substantial mind, i.e. the shape of the identity in which individuality is absorbed in its essence and its claims are not explicitly recognized.

The *second* principle is this substantial mind endowed with knowledge so that mind is both the positive content and filling of mind and also the individual self-awareness which is the living form of mind. This principle is ethical individuality as beauty.

The *third* principle is the inward deepening of this individual self-awareness and knowledge until it reaches abstract universality and therefore infinite opposition to the objective world which in the same process has become mind-forsaken.

The principle of the *fourth* formation is the conversion of this opposition so that mind receives in its inner life its truth and concrete essence, while in objectivity it is at home and reconciled with itself. The mind which has thus reverted to the substantiality with which it began is the mind which has returned out of the infinite opposition, and which consequently engenders and knows this its truth as thought and as a world of actual laws.

354. In accordance with these four principles, the world-historical realms are the following: (1) the Oriental, (2) the Greek, (3) the Roman, (4) the Germanic.

355. (1) The Oriental realm.
The world-view of this first realm is substantial, without inward division, and it arises in natural communities patriarchically governed. According to this view, the mundane form of government is theocratic, the ruler is also a high priest or God himself; constitution and legislation are at the same time religion, while religious and moral commands, or usages rather, are at the same time natural and positive law. In the magnificence of this régime as a whole, individual personality loses its rights and perishes; the external world of nature is either directly divine or else God's ornament, and the history of the actual is poetry. Distinctions are developed in customs, government, and state on their many sides, and in default of laws and amidst the simplicity of manners, they become unwieldy, diffuse, and superstitious ceremonies, the accidents of personal power and arbitrary rule, and class differences become crystallized into hereditary castes. Hence in the Oriental state nothing is fixed, and what is stable is fossilized; it lives therefore only in an outward movement which becomes in the end an elemental fury and desolation. Its inner calm is merely the calm of non-political life and immersion in feebleness and exhaustion.

A still substantial, natural, mentality is a moment in the development of the state, and the point at

which any state takes this form is the absolute beginning of its history. This has been emphasized and
demonstrated with learning and profound insight
in connexion with the history of particular states by
Dr. Stuhr in his book *Der Untergang der Natur-
staaten*—a work in which he leads the way to a rational treatment of constitutional history and of history generally. The principle of subjectivity and self-
conscious freedom is there too shown to be the
principle of the Germanic people, but the book
goes no further than the decline of natural states,
and consequently the principle is only brought to
the point where it appears either as a restless mobility, as human caprice and corruption, or in
its particular form as emotion, and where it has
not yet developed to the objectivity of the self-
conscious substantiality or to an organized legal
system.

356. (2) The Greek realm.

This realm possesses this substantial unity of
finite and infinite, but only as a mysterious background, suppressed in dim recesses of the memory, in caves and traditional imagery. This background, reborn out of the mind which differentiates itself to individual mentality, emerges into
the daylight of knowing and is tempered and
transfigured into beauty and a free and unruffled
ethical life. Hence it is in a world of this character that the principle of personal individuality
arises, though it is still not self-enclosed but
kept in its ideal unity. The result is that the
whole is divided into a group of particular national minds; ultimate decision is ascribed not
to the subjectivity of explicitly independent self-
consciousness but to a power standing above
and outside it (see Remark to Paragraph 279);
on the other hand, the due satisfaction of particular needs is not yet comprised in the sphere
of freedom but is relegated exclusively to a class
of slaves.

357. (3) The Roman realm.

In this realm, differentiation is carried to its
conclusion, and ethical life is sundered without end into the extremes of the private self-
consciousness of persons on the one hand, and abstract universality on the other. This opposition
begins in the clash between the substantial intuition of an aristocracy and the principle of free
personality in democratic form. As the opposition grows, the first of these opponents develops
into superstition and the maintenance of heartless self-seeking power, while the second becomes more and more corrupt until it sinks into
a rabble. Finally, the whole is dissolved and the
result is universal misfortune and the destruction of ethical life. National heroes die away

into the unity of a Pantheon, all individuals are
degraded to the level of private persons equal
with one another, possessed of formal rights,
and the only bond left to hold them together is
abstract insatiable self-will.

358. (4) The Germanic realm.

Mind and its world are thus both alike lost and
plunged in the infinite grief of that fate for
which a people, the Jewish people, was held in
readiness. Mind is here pressed back upon itself
in the extreme of its absolute negativity. This is
the absolute turning point; mind rises out of
this situation and grasps the infinite positivity
of this its inward character, i.e. it grasps the
principle of the unity of the divine nature and
the human, the reconciliation of objective truth
and freedom as the truth and freedom appearing
within self-consciousness and subjectivity, a
reconciliation with the fulfilment of which the
principle of the north, the principle of the Germanic peoples, has been entrusted.

359. This principle is first of all inward and abstract; it exists in feeling as faith, love, and
hope, the reconciliation and resolution of all
contradiction. It then discloses its content, raising it to become actuality and self-conscious
rationality, to become a mundane realm proceeding from the heart, fidelity, and comrade-
ship of free men, a realm which in this its subjectivity is equally a realm of crude individual
caprice and barbarous manners. This realm it
sets over against a world of beyond, an intellectual realm, whose content is indeed the truth
of its (the principle's) mind, but a truth not yet
thought and so still veiled in barbarous imagery.
This world of beyond, as the power of mind
over the mundane heart, acts against the latter
as a compulsive and frightful force.

360. These two realms stand distinguished from
one another though at the same time they are
rooted in a single unity and Idea. Here their
distinction is intensified to absolute opposition
and a stern struggle ensues in the course of
which the realm of mind lowers the place of its
heaven to an earthly here and now, to a common worldliness of fact and idea. The mundane
realm, on the other hand, builds up its abstract
independence into thought and the principle of
rational being and knowing, i.e. into the rationality of right and law. In this way their opposition implicitly loses its marrow and disappears.
The realm of fact has discarded its barbarity
and unrighteous caprice, while the realm of
truth has abandoned the world of beyond and

its arbitrary force, so that the true reconciliation which discloses the state as the image and actuality of reason has become objective. In the state, self-consciousness finds in an organic development the actuality of its substantive knowing and willing; in religion, it finds the feeling and the representation of this its own truth as an ideal essentiality; while in philosophic science, it finds the free comprehension and knowledge of this truth as one and the same in its mutually complementary manifestations, i.e. in the state, in nature, and in the ideal world.

ADDITIONS

1. Preface, p. 1

Laws are of two kinds—laws of nature and laws of the land. The laws of nature simply are what they are and are valid as they are; they are not liable to encroachment, though in certain cases man may transgress them. To know the law of nature, we must learn to know nature, since its laws are rigid and it is only our ideas about them that can be false. The measure of these laws is outside us; knowing them adds nothing to them and does not assist their operation; our knowledge of them can expand, that is all. Knowledge of the laws of the land is in one way similar, but in another way not. These laws too we learn to know just as they exist; the citizen's knowledge of them is more or less of this sort, and the student of positive law equally stops at what is given. But the difference in the case of laws of the land is that they arouse the spirit of reflection, and their diversity at once draws attention to the fact that they are not absolute. Positive laws are something posited, something originated by men. Between what is so originated and man's inner voice there may be an inevitable clash or there may be agreement. Man does not stop short at the existent, but claims to have in himself the measure of what is right. He may be subjected to the compulsion and dominion of an external authority, though never as he is to the compulsion of nature, because his inner self always tells him how things ought to be and he finds within himself the confirmation or denial of what passes as valid. In nature, the highest truth is that there is a *law*; in the law of the land, the thing is not valid simply because it exists; on the contrary, everyone demands that it shall comply with his private criterion. Here then an antagonism is possible between what ought to be and what is, between the absolutely right which stands unaltered and the arbitrary determination of what is to be recognized as right. A schism and a conflict of this sort is to be found only in the territory of mind, and because mind's privilege seems therefore to lead to discontent and unhappiness, men are often thrown back from the arbitrariness of life to the contemplation of nature and set themselves to take nature as an example. But it is precisely in these clashes between what is absolutely right and what arbitrariness makes pass as right that there lies the need for studying the fundamentals of right. In the right, man must meet with his own reason; consequently, he must consider the rationality of the right, and this is the task of our science in contrast with the positive study of law which often has to do only with contradictions.[1] The world of to-day has in addition a more urgent need to make this study because while amongst the ancients the existing laws were still respected and reverenced, nowadays the civilization of the age has taken a new turning and thought has placed itself at the head of everything which is to have validity. Theories are set over against the existent and are intended to appear as absolutely correct and necessary. At present there is a rather special need for becoming acquainted with, and understanding, the thoughts of the right. Since thought has risen to be the essential form of things, we must try to grasp the right too as thought. It seems to be opening wide the door to casual opinions to hold that thought is to be pre-eminent over the right, yet true thought is not an opinion about the thing but the concept of the thing itself. The concept of the thing does not come our way by nature. Anyone has fingers and may take a brush and colours, but that does not make him a painter. The same is true about thinking. The thought of the right is surely not the thought that everybody possesses at first hand; on the contrary, exact thinking is cognizing and apprehending the thing, and our apprehension should therefore be scientific.

2. Paragraph 1.

The concept and its objective existence are two sides of the same thing, distinct and united, like soul and body. The body is the same life as the soul and yet both may be spoken of as lying outside one another. A soul without a body would not be a living thing, nor would a body without a soul. Hence the determinate existence of the concept is its body, while its body obeys the soul which brought it into being. The seeds have the tree implicit within them and contain the tree's whole strength, although they are not yet the tree itself. The tree corresponds in detail with the simple construction of the seed. If the body does not match the soul, it is a poor sort of thing. The unity of determinate existence and the concept, of body and soul, is the Idea. The unity is not a mere harmony, but rather a complete interpenetration. Nothing is alive which is not in some way or other Idea. The Idea of right is freedom, and if it is to be truly understood, it must be known both in its concept and in the determinate existence of that concept.

[1] [i.e. with the inconsistencies in any system of positive law (see, e.g., Hegel's comments on fictions in Roman law in the Remarks to Paragraphs 3 and 180) as well as with contradictory judgements, see, e.g., Remark to Paragraph 211.]

3. *Paragraph 2.*

Philosophy forms a circle. It has a beginning, an immediate factor (for it must somehow make a start), something unproved which is not a result. But the *terminus a quo* of philosophy is simply relative, since it must appear in another terminus as a *terminus ad quem*. Philosophy is a sequence which does not hang in the air; it is not something which begins from nothing at all; on the contrary, it circles back into itself.[1]

4. *Paragraph 4.*

The freedom of the will is best explained by a reference to the physical world. Freedom, I mean, is just as fundamental a character of the will as weight is of bodies. If we say: matter is "heavy," we might mean that this predicate is only contingent; but it is nothing of the kind, for nothing in matter is without weight. Matter is rather weight itself. Heaviness constitutes the body and is the body. The same is the case with freedom and the will, since the free entity is the will. Will without freedom is an empty word, while freedom is actual only as will, as subject.

The following points should be noted about the connexion between the will and thought. Mind is in principle thinking, and man is distinguished from beast in virtue of thinking. But it must not be imagined that man is half thought and half will, and that he keeps thought in one pocket and will in another, for this would be a foolish idea. The distinction between thought and will is only that between the theoretical attitude and the practical. These, however, are surely not two faculties; the will is rather a special way of thinking, thinking translating itself into existence, thinking as the urge to give itself existence.

This distinction between thought and will may be described as follows. In thinking an object, I make it into thought and deprive it of its sensuous aspect; I make it into something which is directly and essentially mine. Since it is in thought that I am first by myself, I do not penetrate an object until I understand it; it then ceases to stand over against me and I have taken from it the character of its own which it had in opposition to me. Just as Adam said to Eve: "Thou art flesh of my flesh and bone of my bone," [2] so mind says: "This is mind of my mind and its foreign character has disappeared." An idea is always a generalization, and generalization is a property of thinking. To generalize means to think. The ego is thought and so the universal. When I say "I," I *eo ipso* abandon all my particular characteristics, my disposition, natural endowment, knowledge, and age. The ego is quite empty, a mere point, simple, yet active in this simplicity. The variegated canvas of the world is before me; I stand over against it; by my theoretical attitude to it I overcome its opposition to me and make its content my own. I am at home in the world when I know it, still more so when I have understood it. So much for the theoretical attitude.

[1] [See *Science of Logic*, i. 79–90.]
[2] [Genesis, 2.23]

The practical attitude, on the other hand, begins in thinking, in the ego itself, and it appears first as though opposed to thinking because, I mean, it sets up a sort of diremption. In so far as I am practical or active, i.e. in so far as I do something, I determine myself, and to determine myself simply means to posit a difference. But these differences which I posit are still mine all the same; the determinate volitions are mine and the aims which I struggle to realize belong to me. If I now let these determinations and differences go, i.e. if I posit them in the so-called external world, they none the less still remain mine. They are what I have done, what I have made; they bear the trace of my mind.

Such is the distinction between the theoretical attitude and the practical, but now the tie between them must be described. The theoretical is essentially contained in the practical; we must decide against the idea that the two are separate, because we cannot have a will without intelligence. On the contrary, the will contains the theoretical in itself. The will determines itself and this determination is in the first place something inward, because what I will I hold before my mind as an idea; it is the object of my thought. An animal acts on instinct, is driven by an inner impulse and so it too is practical, but it has no will, since it does not bring before its mind the object of its desire. A man, however, can just as little be theoretical or think without a will, because in thinking he is of necessity being active. The content of something thought has the form of being; but this being is something mediated, something established through our activity. Thus these distinct attitudes cannot be divorced; they are one and the same; and in any activity, whether of thinking or willing, both moments are present.

5. *Paragraph 5.*

In this element of the will is rooted my ability to free myself from everything, abandon every aim, abstract from everything. Man alone can sacrifice everything, his life included; he can commit suicide. An animal cannot; it always remains merely negative, in an alien destiny to which it merely accustoms itself. Man is the pure thought of himself, and only in thinking has he this power to give himself universality, i.e. to extinguish all particularity, all determinacy. This negative freedom, or freedom as the Understanding conceives it, is one-sided; but a one-sided view always contains one essential factor and therefore is not to be discarded. But the Understanding is defective in exalting a single one-sided factor to be the sole and the supreme one.

In history this form of freedom is a frequent phenomenon. Amongst the Hindus, for instance, the highest life is held to be persistence in the bare knowledge of one's simple identity with oneself, fixation in this empty space of one's inner life, as light remains colourless in pure vision, and the sacrifice of every activity in life, every aim, and every project. In this way man becomes Brahma; there is no longer any distinciton between the finite man and

Brahma. In fact in this universality every difference has disappeared.

This form of freedom appears more concretely in the active fanaticism of both political and religious life. For instance, during the Terror in the French Revolution all differences of talent and authority were supposed to have been superseded. This period was an upheaval, an agitation, an irreconcilable hatred of everything particular. Since fanaticism wills an abstraction only, nothing articulated, it follows that, when distinctions appear, it finds them antagonistic to its own indeterminacy and annuls them. For this reason, the French Revolutionaries destroyed once more the institutions which they had made themselves, since any institution whatever is antagonistic to the abstract self-consciousness of equality.

6. *Paragraph 6.*

This second moment appears as the moment opposed to the first; it is to be grasped in its general character; it is intrinsic to freedom, although it does not constitute the whole of freedom. Here the ego leaves undifferentiated indeterminacy and proceeds to differentiate itself, to posit a content or object and so to give itself determinacy. My willing is not pure willing but the willing of something. A will which, like that expounded in Paragraph 5, wills only the abstract universal, wills nothing and is therefore no will at all. The particular volition is a restriction, since the will, in order to be a will, must restrict itself in some way or other. The fact that the will wills *something* is restriction, negation. Thus particularization is what as a rule is called finitude. Reflective thinking usually takes the first moment, i.e. indeterminacy, as the higher and absolute moment, while it regards restriction as a mere negation of this indeterminacy.[1] But this indeterminacy is itself only a negation in contrast with the determinate, with finitude; the ego is this solitude and absolute negation.[2] The indeterminate will is to this extent just as one-sided as the will rooted in sheer determinacy.

7. *Paragraph 7.*

What is properly called the will includes in itself both the preceding moments. The ego as such is in the first place pure activity, the universal which is by itself. But this universal determines itself and to that extent is no longer by itself but posits itself as an other and ceases to be the universal. Now the third moment is that, in its restriction, in this other, the will is by itself; in determining itself it still remains by itself and does not cease to keep hold of the universal. This moment, then, is the concrete concept of freedom, while the two previous moments have been found to be through and through abstract and one-sided.

Freedom in this sense, however, we already possess

[1] [Hegel is thinking e.g. of Spinoza's view that all determination is negation and that only the indeterminate, or the infinite, is real.]

[2] [i.e. the pure ego of Paragraph 5. It is "alone" and negative because it is the renunciation of everything determinate and is simply turned in upon itself.]

in the form of feeling—in friendship and love, for instance. Here we are not inherently one-sided; we restrict ourselves gladly in relating ourselves to another, but in this restriction know ourselves as ourselves. In this determinacy a man should not feel himself determined; on the contrary, since he treats the other as other, it is there that he first arrives at the feeling of his own selfhood. Thus freedom lies neither in indeterminacy nor in determinacy; it is both of these at once. The will which restricts itself simply to a *this* is the will of the capricious man who supposes that he is not free unless he has *this* will. But the will is not tied to something restricted; it must go beyond the restriction, since the nature of the will is other than this one-sidedness and constraint. Freedom is to will something determinate, yet in this determinacy to be by oneself and to revert once more to the universal.

8. *Paragraph 8.*

The consideration of the will's determinacy properly belongs to the Understanding and is in the first instance not speculative. The will is determined in two senses, i.e. in both content and form. Its determinacy in form is its purpose and the fulfilment of its purpose. My purpose is at first only something inward, something subjective, but it should also become objective and cast aside the defect of mere subjectivity. At this point you may ask the why of this defect. If what has a defect does not at the same time stand above its defect, it cannot recognize the defect as a defect. An animal is a defective thing from our point of view, not from its own. My purpose, so far as it is still only mine, is felt by me as a defect since freedom and will are for me the unity of the subjective and objective. Hence the purpose must be established objectively and thereby it attains not a new one-sided character but only its realization.

9. *Paragraph 10.*

The will which is a will only in accordance with its concept is implicitly free but at the same time it is also unfree, for it would first become truly free as truly determinate content. At that point it is free in its own eyes, has freedom as its object, and *is* freedom. What is still only in accordance with its concept, what is merely implicit, is only immediate, only natural. In our ordinary ways of thinking we are familiar with this. The child is man implicit. At first it possesses reason only implicitly; it begins by being the potentiality of reason and freedom, and so is free only in accordance with its concept. Now what exists purely implicitly in this way does not yet exist in its actuality. Man is implicitly rational, but he must also become explicitly so by struggling to create himself, not only by going forth from himself but also by building himself up within.

10. *Paragraph 11.*

An animal too has impulses, desires, inclinations, but it has no will and must obey its impulse if nothing external deters it. Man, however, the wholly undetermined, stands above his impulses and may make them his own, put them in himself as his own. An impulse is something natural, but to put it into my ego depends on my will which thus cannot fall back on the plea that the impulse has its basis in nature.

11. *Paragraph 13.*

A will which resolves on nothing is no actual will; a characterless man never reaches a decision. The reason for indecision may also lie in a faint-heartedness which knows that, in willing something determinate, it is engaging with finitude, imposing a barrier on itself and sacrificing the infinite; yet it will not renounce the totality after which it hankers. However "beautiful"[1] such a disposition may be, it is nevertheless dead. As Goethe says: "Whoever wills great achievement must be able to restrict himself."[2] Only by resolving can a man step into actuality, however bitter to him his resolve may be. Inertia lacks the will to abandon the inward brooding which[3] allows it to retain everything as a possibility. But possibility is still less than actuality. The will which is sure of itself does not *eo ipso* lose itself in its determinate volition.

12. *Paragraph 15.*

Since it is possible for me to determine myself in this way or that, or in other words since I can choose, I possess the arbitrary will, and to possess this is what is usually called freedom. The choice which I have is grounded in the universality of the will, in the fact that I can make this or that mine. This thing that is mine is particular in content and therefore not adequate to me and so is separate from me; it is only potentially mine, while I am the potentiality of linking myself to it. Choice, therefore, is grounded in the indeterminacy of the ego and the determinacy of a content. Thus the will, on account of this content, is not free, although it has an infinite aspect in virtue of its form. No single content is adequate to it and in no single content is it really at grips with itself. Arbitrariness implies that the content is made mine not by the nature of my will but by chance. Thus I am dependent on this content, and this is the contradiction lying in arbitrariness. The man in the street thinks he is free if it is open to him to act as he pleases but his very arbitrariness implies that he is not free. When I will what is rational, then I am acting not as a particular individual but in accordance with the concepts of ethics in general. In an ethical action, what I vindicate is not myself but the thing. But in doing a perverse action, it is my singularity that I bring on to the centre of the stage. The rational is the high road where everyone travels, where no one is conspicuous. When great artists complete a masterpiece, we may speak of its inevitability, which means that the artist's idiosyncrasy has completely disappeared and no mannerism is detectable in it. Pheidias

has no mannerisms; his figures themselves live and declare themselves. But the worse the artist is, the more we see in his work the artist, his singularity, his arbitrariness. If you stop at the consideration that, having an arbitrary will, a man can will this or that, then of course his freedom consists in that ability. But if you keep firmly in view that the content of his willing is a given one, then he is determined thereby and in that respect at all events is free no longer.

13. *Paragraph 17.*

Impulses and inclinations are in the first instance a content of the will, and reflection alone stands above them. But these impulses begin to impel themselves, they drive one another, stir each other, and all of them demand satisfaction. Now if I neglect all the others and put myself in one of them by itself, I find myself under a restriction which destroys me, since just by so doing I have surrendered my universality, which is a system of all impulses. But it is just as little help to make a mere hierarchy of impulses—a device to which the Understanding usually resorts—since no criterion for so ordering them is available here, and therefore the demand for such a hierarchy runs out in the tedium of generalities.

14. *Paragraph 18.*

The Christian doctrine that man is by nature evil is loftier than the other which takes him to be by nature good. This doctrine is to be understood as follows in accordance with the philosophical exegesis of it:[4] As mind, man is a free substance which is in the position of not allowing itself to be determined by natural impulse. When man's condition is immediate and mentally undeveloped, he is in a situation in which he ought not to be and from which he must free himself. This is the meaning of the doctrine of original sin without which Christianity would not be the religion of freedom.

15. *Paragraph 20.*

In happiness thought has already a mastery over the natural force of impulses, since the thinker is not content with the momentary but requires happiness in a whole. This requirement is connected with education in that it is education which vindicates a universal. In the ideal of happiness, however, there are two moments: (i) a universal which is above all particularity; but (ii) since the content of this universal is still only universal *pleasure,* there appears here once again the singular, the particular, i.e. something finite, and a return must therefore be made to impulse. Since the content of happiness lies in everyone's subjectivity and feeling, this universal end is for its part particular, and consequently there is still not present in it any genuine unity of form and content.

16. *Paragraph 21.*

Truth in philosophy means that concept and external reality correspond. For example, the body is the external reality, while the soul is the concept; but

---

[1] [An allusion to the "beautiful soul" of the Moravians, for which see Remark (*f*) to Paragraph 140.]

[2] [From the sonnet *Natur und Kunst* (Lasson). Hegel quotes inaccurately. Goethe's actual words may be translated: "Whoever wills great achievement must first collect his energies; it is in restriction that a man first shows his mastery."]

[3] [Taking *der* as a misprint for *dem.*]

[4] [For Hegel's exegesis of this doctrine, see Addition 90, Paragraph 139 below and the Addition to *Enc.* § 24.]

soul and body ought to be adequate to one another. Therefore a corpse is still an existent, but its existence is no true existence; the concept has left it; and for this reason a dead body putrefies. So a will is truly a will only when what it wills, its content, is identical with itself, when, that is to say, freedom wills freedom.

17. Paragraph 22.

Infinity has rightly been represented figuratively as a circle, because a straight line goes on and on forever and denotes the purely negative and false infinite which, unlike the true infinite, has no return into itself. The free will is truly infinite, since it is not just a potentiality and a capacity. On the contrary, its external existence is its own inwardness, is itself.

18. Paragraph 26.

It is usually supposed that subjective and objective stand rigidly in opposition to one another. But this is not the case; it would be truer to say that they pass over into each other, since they are not abstract categories like positive and negative but already have a more concrete significance.

Consider first the word "subjective." We may call "subjective" an end which is only the end of one specific individual subject. In this sense a very bad work of art, one which is not quite the thing, is purely "subjective." The word may also be applied, however, to the content of the will, and it is then almost synonymous with "arbitrary"; a "subjective" content is that which belongs to the subject alone. Hence bad actions, for example, are purely "subjective." But, further, it is just that pure empty ego which may be called "subjective," the ego which has itself alone for its object and possesses the power to abstract from any other content. Thus subjectivity sometimes means something wholly idiosyncratic, and at other times something with the highest of claims, since everything which I am to recognize has also the task of becoming mine and attaining its validity in me. Subjectivity is insatiably greedy to concentrate and drown everything in this single spring of the pure ego.

No less varied are the ways in which we may take "objective." We may understand by it everything which we make an object to ourselves, whether objective actualities or pure thoughts which we bring before our minds. We also include under this category the immediacy of existence in which the end is to be realized; even if the end is itself wholly singular and subjective, we none the less call it "objective" on its appearance. But the "objective" will is also that in which truth lies, and thus God's will, the ethical will, is an "objective" one. Finally, we may also call "objective" the will which is entirely absorbed in its object, as for example the will of the child, which is rooted in trust and lacks subjective freedom, and the will of the slave, which does not yet know itself as free and on that account is a will-less will. In this sense any will is "objective" which acts under the guidance of an alien authority and

has not yet completed its endless return into itself.

19. Paragraph 32.

The Idea must further determine itself within itself continually, since in the beginning it is no more than an abstract concept. But this original abstract concept is never abandoned. It merely becomes continually richer in itself and the final determination is therefore the richest. In this process its earlier, merely implicit, determinations attain their free self-subsistence but in such a way that the concept remains the soul which holds everything together and attains its own proper differentiation only through an immanent process. It therefore cannot be said that the concept reaches anything new; on the contrary, its final determination coincides with its first. Even if the concept seems in its existence to have become decomposed, this is nothing but a semblance revealing itself in due course as a semblance, because every single detail reverts at last to the concept of the universal. The empirical sciences are usually analyses of the content of our ideas, and when the single instance has been brought back to the common character, the latter is then called the concept. This is not our procedure; we only wish to look on at the way in which the concept determines itself and to restrain ourselves from adding thereto anything of our thoughts and opinions. What we acquire in this way, however, is a series of thoughts and another series of existent shapes of experience; to which I may add that the time order in which the latter actually appear is other than the logical order. Thus, for example, we cannot say that property *existed* before the family, yet, in spite of that, property must be dealt with first.

Consequently you might raise here the question why we do not begin at the highest point, i.e. with the concretely true. The answer is that it is precisely the truth in the form of a result that we are looking for, and for this purpose it is essential to start by grasping the abstract concept itself. What is actual, the shape in which the concept is embodied, is for us therefore the secondary thing and the sequel, even if it were itself first in the actual world. The development we are studying is that whereby the abstract forms reveal themselves not as self-subsistent but as false.

20. Paragraph 33.

In speaking of Right [*Recht*, i.e. *jus*] in this book, we mean not merely what is generally understood by the word, namely civil law, but also morality, ethical life, and world-history; these belong just as much to our topic, because the concept brings thoughts together into a true system. If the free will is not to remain abstract, it must in the first place give itself an embodiment, and the material primarily available to sensation for such an embodiment is things, i.e. objects outside us. This primary mode of freedom is the one which we are to become acquainted with as property, the sphere of formal and abstract right. To this sphere there also belong property in its mediated form as contract, and right in its infringement as crime and punishment. The freedom which we have here is what is called a person, i.e. the subject who is free, free indeed in his own eyes, and who gives himself an embodiment in things.

The sheer immediacy of external fact, however, is not an adequate embodiment of freedom, and the negation of this immediacy is the sphere of morality. I am now free, not merely in this immediate thing, but also after the immediacy has been superseded, i.e. I am free in myself, in my subjectivity. In this sphere the main thing is my insight, my intention, my purpose, because externality has now been established as of no importance. Good, however, which here is the universal end, should not simply remain in my inner life; it should be realized. That is to say, the subjective will demands that what is internal to it, i.e. its end, shall acquire an external existence, that the good shall in this way be consummated in the external world.

Morality and formal right are two abstract moments whose truth is ethical life alone. Hence ethical life is the unity of the will in its concept with the will of the individual, i.e. of the subject. Its first embodiment is again something natural, whose form is love and feeling—the family. Here the individual has transcended his shyness of personality and finds himself and his consciousness of himself in a whole. At the next stage, however, we see substantial unity disappearing along with ethical life proper; the family falls asunder and its members relate themselves to each other as self-subsistent, since their only bond of connexion is reciprocal need. This stage—civil society—has often been looked upon as the state, but the state is first present at the third stage, the stage of ethical life and the stage of mind in which the prodigious unification of self-subsistent individuality with universal substantiality has been achieved. The right of the state therefore stands above the preceding stages; it is freedom in its most concrete shape and as such is subordinate to one thing alone—the supreme absolute truth of the world-mind.

21. Paragraph 34.

When I say that "the absolutely free will at the stage when its concept is abstract has the determinate character of immediacy," what I mean is this: when the concept had fully realized itself and when the embodiment of the concept had become nothing but the unfolding of its own self, then that state of affairs would be the fully developed Idea of the will. But at the start the concept is abstract, which means that all its determinations are contained within it, but still only contained within it; they are only implicit and not yet developed to be a totality in themselves. If I say "I am free," the ego is still this inwardness, not confronted by an opposite. In morality, on the other hand, there is opposition from the start, since I stand in the moral sphere as a *single* will while the good is the *universal* even though it is within myself. Thus at that level, the will has in itself the different factors of singularity and univer-

sality, and this gives it its specific character. But, to begin with, no such difference is present, since at the first stage, that of abstract unity, there is no advance and no mediation and so the will has the form of immediacy, of mere being. The essential point of view to be taken here then is that this original indeterminacy is itself a determinacy. The indeterminacy lies in the fact that there is as yet no difference between the will and its content; but indeterminacy, opposed to the determinate, acquires the character of being something determinate. It is abstract identity which here constitutes determinacy; the will therefore becomes a single will, a person.

22. Paragraph 35.

The abstract will, consciously self-contained, is personality. Man's chief glory is to be a person, and yet in spite of that the bare abstraction, "person," is somewhat contemptuous in its very expression. "Person" is essentially different from "subject," since "subject" is only the possibility of personality; every living thing of any sort is a subject. A person, then, is a subject aware of this subjectivity, since in personality it is of myself alone that I am aware. A person is a unit of freedom aware of its sheer independence. As *this* person, I know myself to be free in myself. I can abstract from everything, since nothing confronts me save pure personality, and yet as *this* person I am something wholly determinate, e.g. I am of a certain age, a certain stature, I occupy this space, and so on through whatever other details you like. Thus personality is at once the sublime and the trivial. It implies this unity of the infinite with the purely finite, of the wholly limitless with determinate limitation. It is the sublimity of personality that is able to sustain this contradiction, a contradiction which nothing merely natural contains or could endure.

23. Paragraph 37.

Since, in personality, particularity is not present as freedom, everything which depends on particularity is here a matter of indifference. To have no interest except in one's formal right may be pure obstinacy, often a fitting accompaniment of a cold heart and restricted sympathies. It is uncultured people who insist most on their rights, while noble minds look on other aspects of the thing. Thus abstract right is nothing but a bare possibility and, at least in contrast with the whole range of the situation, something formal. On that account, to have a right gives one a warrant, but it is not absolutely necessary that one should insist on one's rights, because that is only one aspect of the whole situation. That is to say, possibility is being which has the significance of also not being.

24. Paragraph 41.

The rationale of property is to be found not in the satisfaction of needs but in the supersession of the pure subjectivity of personality. In his property a person exists for the first time as reason. Even if my freedom is here realized first of all in an external thing, and so falsely realized, nevertheless abstract personality in its immediacy can have no other embodiment save one characterized by immediacy.

25. Paragraph 42.

Since a thing lacks subjectivity, it is external not merely to the subject but to itself. Space and time are external in this way. As sentient, I am myself external, spatial, and temporal. As receptive of sensuous intuitions, I receive them from something which is external to itself. An animal can intuit, but the soul of an animal has for its object not its soul, itself, but something external.

26. Paragraph 44.

All things may become man's property, because man is free will and consequently is absolute, while what stands over against him lacks this quality. Thus everyone has the right to make his will the thing or to make the thing his will, or in other words to destroy the thing and transform it into his own; for the thing, as externality, has no end in itself; it is not infinite self-relation but something external to itself. A living thing too (an animal) is external to itself in this way and is so far itself a thing. Only the will is the infinite, absolute in contrast with everything other than itself, while that other is on its side only relative. Thus "to appropriate" means at bottom only to manifest the pre-eminence of my will over the thing and to prove that it is not absolute, is not an end in itself. This is made manifest when I endow the thing with some purpose not directly its own. When the living thing becomes my property, I give to it a soul other than the one it had before, I give to it my soul. The free will, therefore, is the idealism which does not take things as they are to be absolute, while realism pronounces them to be absolute, even if they only exist in the form of finitude. Even an animal has gone beyond this realist philosophy since it devours things and so proves that they are not absolutely self-subsistent.

27. Paragraph 46.

In property my will is the will of a person; but a person is a unit and so property becomes the personality of this unitary will. Since property is the means whereby I give my will an embodiment, property must also have the character of being "this" or "mine." This is the important doctrine of the necessity of private property. While the state may cancel private ownership in exceptional cases, it is nevertheless only the state that can do this; but frequently, especially in our day, private property has been re-introduced by the state. For example, many states have dissolved the monasteries, and rightly, for in the last resort no community has so good a right to property as a person has.

28. Paragraph 47.

Animals are in possession of themselves; their soul is in possession of their body. But they have no right to their life, because they do not will it.

29. Paragraph 49.

The equality which might be set up, e.g. in connexion with the distribution of goods, would all the same soon be destroyed again, because wealth depends on diligence. But if a project cannot be executed, it ought not to be executed. Of course men are equal, but only *qua* persons, that is, with respect only to the source from which possession springs; the inference from this is that everyone must have property. Hence, if you wish to talk of equality, it is this equality which you must have in view. But this equality is something apart from the fixing of particular amounts, from the question of how much I own. From this point of view it is false to maintain that justice requires everyone's property to be equal, since it requires only that everyone shall own property. The truth is that particularity is just the sphere where there is room for inequality and where equality would be wrong. True enough, men often lust after the goods of others, but that is just doing wrong, since right is that which remains indifferent to particularity.

30. Paragraph 50.

The points made so far have been mainly concerned with the proposition that personality must be embodied in property. Now the fact that the first person to take possession of a thing should also be its owner is an inference from what has been said. The first is the rightful owner, however, not because he is the first but because he is a free will, for it is only by another's succeeding him that he becomes the first.

31. Paragraph 51.

A person puts his will into a thing—that is just the concept of property, and the next step is the *realization* of this concept. The inner act of will which consists in saying that something is mine must also become recognizable by others. If I make a thing mine, I give to it a predicate, "mine," which must appear in it in an external form and must not simply remain in my inner will. It often happens that children lay stress on their prior willing in preference to the seizure of a thing by others. But for adults this willing is not sufficient, since the form of subjectivity must be removed and must work its way beyond the subjective to objectivity.

32. Paragraph 52.

Fichte [1] has raised the question whether the matter too belongs to me if I impose a form on it. On his argument, after I had made a golden cup, it would have to be open to someone else to take the gold provided that in so doing he did no damage to my work. However separable the matter may be in thought, still in reality this distinction is an empty

[1] [*Science of Rights*, § 19 A, pp. 298 ff. (so Lasson and Reyburn). Fichte is there maintaining that the farmer has no right to his land as such but only to its products, to its "accidents," not to its "substance"; he may not prevent others from grazing cattle on it after harvest, unless, in addition to cultivation rights, he has grazing rights for cattle of his own.]

subtlety, because, if I take possession of a field and plough it, it is not only the furrow that is my property, but the rest as well, the furrowed earth. That is to say, I will to take this matter, the whole thing, into my possession; the matter therefore does not remain a *res nullius* nor does it remain its own property. Further, even if the matter remains external to the form which I have given to the object, the form is precisely a sign that I claim the thing as mine. The thing therefore does not remain external to my will or outside what I have willed. Hence there is nothing left to be taken into possession by someone else.

33. *Paragraph 54.*

These modes of taking possession involve the advance from the category of singularity to that of universality. It is only of a single thing that we can take possession physically, while marking a thing as mine is taking possession of it in idea. In the latter case I have an idea of the thing and mean that the thing as a whole is mine, not simply the part which I can take into my possession physically.

34. *Paragraph 55.*

Taking possession is always piece-meal in type; I take into possession no more than what I touch with my body. But here comes the second point: external objects extend further than I can grasp. Therefore, whatever I have in my grasp is linked with something else. It is with my hand that I manage to take possession of a thing, but its reach can be extended. What I hold in my hand—that magnificent tool which no animal possesses—can itself be a means to gripping something else. If I am in possession of something, the intellect immediately draws the inference that it is not only the immediate object in my grasp which is mine but also what is connected with it. At this point positive law must enact its statutes since nothing further on this topic can be deduced from the concept.

35. *Paragraph 56.*

This forming of an object may in practice assume the most various guises. In farming land I impose a form on it. Where inorganic objects are concerned, the imposition of a form is not always direct. For example, if I build a windmill, I have not imposed a form on the air, but I have formed something for utilizing the air, though I am not on that account at liberty to call the air mine, since I have not formed the air itself. Further, the preserving of game may be regarded as a way of forming game, for we preserve it with a view to maintaining the species. [The same is true of] the taming of animals, only of course that is a more direct way of forming them and it depends on me to a greater extent.

36. *Paragraph 57.*

To adhere to man's absolute freedom—one aspect of the matter—is *eo ipso* to condemn slavery. Yet if a man is a slave, his own will is responsible for his slavery, just as it is its will which is responsible if a people is subjugated. Hence the wrong of slavery lies at the door not simply of enslavers or conquerors but of the slaves and the conquered themselves. Slavery occurs in man's transition from the state of nature to genuinely ethical conditions; it occurs in a world where a wrong is still right. At that stage wrong has validity and so is necessarily in place.

37. *Paragraph 58.*

To take possession by marking a thing is of all sorts of taking possession the most complete, since the mark is implicitly at work to some extent in the other sorts too. When I grasp a thing or form it, this also means in the last resort that I mark it, and mark it for others, in order to exclude them and show that I have put my will into the thing. The notion of the mark, that is to say, is that the thing does not count as the thing which it is but as what it is supposed to signify. A cockade, for instance, signifies citizenship of a state, though the colour has no connexion with the nation and represents not itself but the nation. By being able to give a mark to things and thereby to acquire them, man just shows his mastery over things.

38. *Paragraph 59.*

While in marking a thing I am taking possession in a universal way of the thing as such, the use of it implies a still more universal relation to the thing, because, when it is used, the thing in its particularity is not recognized but is negated by the user.[1] The thing is reduced to a means to the satisfaction of my need. When I and the thing meet, an identity is established and therefore one or other must lose its qualitative character. But I am alive, a being who wills and is truly affirmative; the thing on the other hand is something physical. Therefore the thing must be destroyed while I preserve myself. This, in general terms, is the prerogative and the principle of the organic.

39. *Paragraph 61.*

The relation of use to property is the same as that of substance to accident, inner to outer, force to its manifestation. Just as force exists only in manifesting itself, so arable land is arable land only in bearing crops. Thus he who has the use [2] of arable land is the owner of the whole, and it is an empty abstraction to recognize still another property in the object itself.

40. *Paragraph 63.*

The qualitative disappears here in the form of the quantitative; that is to say, when I speak of "need," I use a term under which the most various things may be brought; they share it in common and become commensurable. The advance of thought

---

[1] [When I mark a thing as mine, I attribute to it the universal predicate "mine" and "recognize" its particular characteristics in the sense that I do not interfere with them. But when I use it I "negate" its particular characteristics in the sense that I change them to suit my purpose. To mark land as mine by fencing it does not change its character, but to use it, e.g. by planting it, does.]

[2] [i.e. the entire and permanent use of it—see Paragraph 62.]

here therefore is from a thing's specific quality to a character which is indifferent to quality, i.e. quantity. A similar thing occurs in mathematics. The definition of a circle, an ellipse, and a parabola reveals their specific difference. But, in spite of this, the distinction between these different curves is determined purely quantitatively, i.e. in such a way that the only important thing is a purely quantitative difference which rests on their coefficients alone, on purely empirical magnitudes. In property, the quantitative character which emerges from the qualitative is value. Here the qualitative provides the quantity with its quantum and in consequence is as much preserved in the quantity as superseded by it. If we consider the concept of value, we must look on the thing itself only as a symbol; it counts not as itself but as what it is worth. A bill of exchange, for instance, does not represent what it really is—paper; it is only a symbol of another universal—value. The value of a thing may be very heterogeneous; it depends on need. But if you want to express the value of a thing not in a specific case but in the abstract, then it is money which expresses this. Money represents any and every thing, though since it does not portray the need itself but is only a symbol of it, it is itself controlled by the specific value [of the commodity]. Money, as an abstraction, merely expresses this value.[1] It is possible in principle to be the owner of a thing without at the same time being the owner of its value. If a family can neither sell nor pawn its goods, it is not the owner of their value. But since this form of property is not in accordance with the concept of property, such restrictions on ownership (feudal tenure, testamentary trusts) are mostly in course of disappearing.

41. *Paragraph 64.*

Prescription rests on the presumption that I have ceased to regard the thing as mine. If a thing is to remain mine, my will must continue in it, and using it or keeping it safe shows this continuance. That public memorials may lose their value were frequently shown during the Reformation in the case of foundations, endowments, &c., for the Mass. The spirit of the old faith, i.e. of these foundations, had fled, and consequently they could be seized as private property.

42. *Paragraph 65.*

While prescription is an alienation with no direct expression of the will to alienate, alienation proper is an expression of my will, of my will no longer to regard the thing as mine. The whole matter may also be so viewed that alienation is seen to be a true mode of taking possession. To take possession of the thing directly is the first moment in property. Use is likewise a way of acquiring property. The third

moment then is the unity of these two, taking possession of the thing by alienating it.[2]

43. *Paragraph 66.*

It is in the nature of the case that a slave has an absolute right to free himself and that if anyone has prostituted his ethical life by hiring himself to thieve and murder, this is an absolute nullity and everyone has a warrant to repudiate this contract. The same is the case if I hire my religious feeling to a priest who is my confessor, for such an inward matter a man has to settle with himself alone. A religious feeling which is partly in control of someone else is no proper religious feeling at all. The spirit is always one and single and should dwell in me. I am entitled to the union of my potential and my actual being.

44. *Paragraph 67.*

The distinction here explained is that between a slave and a modern domestic servant or day labourer. The Athenian slave perhaps had an easier occupation and more intellectual work than is usually the case with our servants, but he was still a slave, because he had alienated to his master the whole range of his activity.

45. *Paragraph 70.*

A single person, I need hardly say, is something subordinate, and as such he must dedicate himself to the ethical whole. Hence if the state claims life, the individual must surrender it. But may a man take his own life? Suicide may at a first glance be regarded as an act of courage, but only the false courage of tailors and servant girls. Or again it may be looked upon as a misfortune, since it is inward distraction which leads to it. But the fundamental question is: Have I a *right* to take my life? The answer will be that I, as *this* individual, am not master of my life, because life, as the comprehensive sum of my activity, is nothing external to personality, which itself is this immediate personality. Thus when a person is said to have a right over his life, the words are a contradiction, because they mean that a person has a right over himself. But he has no such right, since he does not stand over himself and he cannot pass judgement on himself. When Hercules destroyed himself by fire and when Brutus fell on his sword, this was the conduct of a hero against his personality. But as for an unqualified right to suicide, we must simply say that there is no such thing, even for heroes.

46. *Paragraph 71.*

In a contract I hold property on the strength of a common will; that is to say, it is the interest of reason that the subjective will should become universal and raise itself to this degree of actualization. Thus

---

[1] ["Prices are regulated by an average price; this in the last resort means that they are regulated by the value of the commodities. I say 'in the last resort' because average prices do not (as Adam Smith, Ricardo, and others believed) directly coincide with the value of commodities." Karl Marx: *Capital,* tr. by E. and C. Paul, London, 1929, p. 153.]

[2] [Taking possession is *positive* acquisition. Use is the *negation* of a thing's particular characteristics (see Paragraph 59). Alienation is the synthesis of positive and negative; it is negative in that it involves spurning the thing altogether; it is positive because it is only a thing completely mine which I can so spurn.]

in contract my will still has the character "this," though it has it in community with another will. The universal will, however, still appears here only in the form and guise of community.

47. Paragraph 75.

It has recently become very fashionable to regard the state as a contract of all with all. Everyone makes a contract with the monarch, so the argument runs, and he again with his subjects. This point of view arises from thinking superficially of a mere unity of different wills. In contract, however, there are two identical wills who are both persons and wish to remain property owners. Thus contract springs from a person's arbitrary will, an origin which marriage too has in common with contract. But the case is quite different with the state; it does not lie with an individual's arbitrary will to separate himself from the state, because we are already citizens of the state by birth. The rational end of man is life in the state, and if there is no state there, reason at once demands that one be founded. Permission to enter a state or leave it must be given by the state; this then is not a matter which depends on an individual's arbitrary will and therefore the state does not rest on contract, for contract presupposes arbitrariness. It is false to maintain that the foundation of the state is something at the option of all its members. It is nearer the truth to say that it is absolutely necessary for every individual to be a citizen. The great advance of the state in modern times is that nowadays all the citizens have one and the same end, an absolute and permanent end; it is no longer open to individuals, as it was in the Middle Ages, to make private stipulations in connexion with it.

48. Paragraph 76.

Contract implies two consenting parties and two things. That is to say, in a contract my purpose is both to acquire property and to surrender it. Contract is real when the action of both parties is complete, i.e. when both surrender and both acquire property, and when both remain property owners even in the act of surrender. Contract is formal where only one of the parties acquires property or surrenders it.

49. Paragraph 78.

Just as in the theory of property we had the distinction between ownership and possession, between the substance of the matter and its purely external side, so here in contract we have the difference between a common will—covenant—and a particular will—performance. It lies in the nature of contract that it should be an expression of both the common and the particular will of the parties, because in it will is related to will. The covenant, made manifest in a symbol, and its performance are quite distinct from each other amongst civilized peoples, though amongst savages they may coincide. In the forests of Ceylon there is a tribe of traders who put down their property and wait quietly until others come to put

theirs down opposite. Here there is no difference between the dumb declaration of will and the performance of what is willed.

50. Paragraph 80.

In contract we drew the distinction between the covenant or stipulation (which made the property mine though it did not give me possession) and performance (which first gave me possession). Now if I am already the out-and-out owner of the property, the object of the pledge is to put me simultaneously in possession of the value of the property and thereby to guarantee the covenant's performance at the very time the covenant is made. Surety is a particular kind of pledge whereby someone gives his promise or pledges his credit as a guarantee for another's performance. Here a person fulfils the function which is fulfilled by a mere thing in the case of a pledge proper.

51. Paragraph 81.

In contract we had the relation of two wills as a common will. But this identical will is only relatively universal, posited as universal, and so is still opposed to the particular will. In contract, to be sure, making a covenant entails the right to require its performance. But this performance is dependent again on the particular will which *qua* particular may act in contravention of the principle of rightness. At this point then the negation, which was implicitly present in the principle of the will at the start, comes into view, and this negation is just what wrong is. In general terms, the course of events is that the will is freed from its immediacy and thus there is evoked out of the common will the particularity which then comes on the scene as opposed to the common will. In contract the parties still retain their particular wills; contract therefore is not yet beyond the stage of arbitrariness, with the result that it remains at the mercy of wrong.

52. Paragraph 82.

The principle of rightness, the universal will, receives its essential determinate character through the particular will, and so is in relation with something which is inessential. This is the relation of essence to its appearance. Even if the appearance corresponds with the essence, still, looked at from another point of view, it fails to correspond with it, since appearance is the stage of contingency, essence related to the inessential. In wrong, however, appearance proceeds to become a show. A show is a determinate existence inadequate to the essence, the empty disjunction and positing of the essence, so that in both essence and show the distinction of the one from the other is present as sheer difference. The show, therefore, is the falsity which disappears in claiming independent existence; and in the course of the show's disappearance the essence reveals itself as essence, i.e. as the authority of the show. The essence has negated that which negated it and so is corroborated. Wrong is a show of this kind, and, when it disappears, right acquires the character of something fixed and valid. What is here called the essence is just the principle of rightness, and in contrast with it the particular will annuls itself as a falsity. Hitherto the being of the right has been immediate only, but now it is actual because it returns out of its negation. The actual is the effectual; in its otherness it still holds fast to itself, while anything immediate remains susceptible of negation.

53. Paragraph 83.

Wrong is thus the show of the essence, putting itself as self-subsistent. If the show is only implicit and not explicit also, i.e. if the wrong passes in my eyes as right, the wrong is nonmalicious. The show here is a show from the point of view of the right but not from my point of view.

The second type of wrong is fraud. Here the wrong is not a show from the point of view of the principle of rightness. The position is that I am making a show to deceive the other party. In fraud the right is in my eyes only a show. In the first case, the wrong was a show from the point of view of the right. In the second case, from my own point of view, from the point of view of wrong, right is only a show.

Finally, the third type of wrong is crime. This is wrong both in itself and from my point of view. But here I will the wrong and make no use of even a show of right. I do not intend the other against whom the crime is committed to regard the absolutely wrong as right. The distinction between crime and fraud is that in the latter the form of acting still implies a recognition of the right, and this is just what is lacking in crime.

54. Paragraph 86.

There is a specific ground for what is inherently right, and the wrong which I hold to be right I also defend on some ground or other. The nature of the finite and particular is to allow room for accidents. Thus here collisions must occur, because here we are on the level of the finite. This first type of wrongdoing negates the particular will only, while universal rightness is respected. Consequently this is the most venial of the types of wrong-doing. If I say "a rose is not red," I still recognize that it has a colour. Hence I do not deny the genus; all that I negate is the particular colour, red. Similarly, right is recognized here. Each of the parties wills the right and what is supposed to result to each is the right alone. The wrong of each consists simply in his holding that what he wants is right.

55. Paragraph 87.

At this second level of wrong-doing, the particular will is respected, but universal rightness is not. In fraud, the particular will is not infringed, because the party defrauded is saddled with what he is asked to believe is right. Thus the right which he demands is posited as something subjective, as a mere show, and it is this which constitutes fraud.

56. Paragraph 89.

In the case of nonmalicious wrong and civil suits at law, no punishment is imposed, because in such cases the wrongdoer has willed nothing in opposition to the right. In the case of fraud, on the other hand, punishments come in, because here it *is* an infringement of right which is in question.

57. Paragraph 90.

Wrong in the full sense of the word is crime, where there is no respect either for the principle of rightness or for what seems right to me, where, then, both sides, the objective and the subjective, are infringed.

58. Paragraph 93.

Once the state has been founded, there can no longer be any heroes. They come on the scene only in uncivilized conditions. Their aim is right, necessary, and political, and this they pursue as their own affair. The heroes who founded states, introduced marriage and agriculture, did not do this as their recognized right, and their conduct still has the appearance of being their particular will. But as the higher right of the Idea against nature, this heroic coercion is a rightful coercion. Mere goodness can achieve little against the power of nature.

59. Paragraph 94.

Special attention must be paid at this point to the difference between the right and the moral. In morality, i.e. when I am reflected into myself, there is also a duality, because the good is my aim and I ought to determine myself by reference to that Idea. The good is embodied in my decision and I actualize the good in myself. But this embodiment is purely inward and therefore cannot be coerced. The law of the land therefore cannot possibly wish to reach as far as a man's disposition, because, so far as his moral convictions are concerned, he exists for himself alone, and force in that context is meaningless.

60. Paragraph 96.

How any given crime is to be punished cannot be settled by mere thinking; positive laws are necessary. But with the advance of education, opinions about crime become less harsh, and to-day a criminal is not so severely punished as he was a hundred years ago. It is not exactly crimes or punishments which change but the relation between them.

61. Paragraph 97.

A crime alters something in some way, and the thing has its existence in this alteration. Yet this existence is a self-contradiction and to that extent is inherently a nullity. The nullity is that the crime has set aside right as such. That is to say, right as something absolute cannot be set aside, and so committing a crime is in principle a nullity: and this nullity is the essence of what a crime effects. A nullity, however, must reveal itself to be such, i.e. manifest itself as vulnerable. A crime, as an act, is not something positive, not a first thing, on which punishment would supervene as a negation. It is something negative, so that its punishment is only a negation of the negation. Right in its actuality, then, annuls what infringes it and therein displays its validity and proves itself to be a necessary, mediated, reality.

62. *Paragraph 99.*

Feuerbach [1] bases his theory of punishment on threat and thinks that if anyone commits a crime despite the threat, punishment must follow because the criminal was aware of it beforehand. But what about the justification of the threat? A threat presupposes that a man is not free, and its aim is to coerce him by the idea of an evil. But right and justice must have their seat in freedom and the will, not in the lack of freedom on which a threat turns. To base a justification of punishment on threat is to liken it to the act of a man who lifts his stick to a dog. It is to treat a man like a dog instead of with the freedom and respect due to him as a man. But a threat, which after all may rouse a man to demonstrate his freedom in spite of it, discards justice altogether.— Coercion by psychological factors can concern only differences of quantity and quality in crime, not the nature of crime itself, and therefore any legal codes that may be products of the doctrine that crime is due to such coercion lack their proper foundation.

63. *Paragraph 100.*

Beccaria's requirement that men should give their consent to being punished is right enough, but the criminal gives his consent already by his very act. The nature of the crime, no less than the private will of the criminal, requires that the injury initiated by the criminal should be annulled. However that may be, Beccaria's endeavour to have capital punishment abolished has had beneficial effects. Even if neither Joseph II nor the French ever succeeded in entirely abolishing it, still we have begun to see which crimes deserve the death penalty and which do not. Capital punishment has in consequence become rarer, as in fact should be the case with this most extreme punishment.

64. *Paragraph 101.*

Retribution is the inner connexion and the identity of two conceptions which are different in appearance and which also exist in the world as two distinct and opposed events. Retribution is inflicted on the criminal and so it has the look of an alien destiny, not intrinsically his own. Nevertheless punishment, as we have seen, is only crime made manifest, i.e. is the second half which necessarily presupposes the first. Prima facie, the objection to retribution is that it looks like something immoral, i.e. like revenge, and that thus it may pass for something personal. Yet it is not something personal, but the concept itself, which carries out retribution. "Vengeance is mine, saith the Lord," as the Bible says.[2] And if something in the word *"repay"* calls up the idea of a particular caprice of the subjective will, it must be pointed out that what is meant is only that the form which crime takes is turned round against itself. The Eumenides sleep, but crime awakens them,

[1] [P. J. A. Feuerbach (1775–1833). See his *Lehrbuch des gemeinen peinlichen Rechts* (1801). (Messineo).]
[2] [Romans, 12.19]

and hence it is the very act of crime itself which vindicates itself.—Now although requital cannot simply be made specifically equal to the crime, the case is otherwise with murder, which is of necessity liable to the death penalty; the reason is that since life is the full compass of a man's existence, the punishment here cannot simply consist in a "value," for none is great enough, but can consist only in taking away a second life.

65. *Paragraph 102.*

In that condition of society when there are neither magistrates nor laws, punishment always takes the form of revenge; revenge remains defective inasmuch as it is the act of a subjective will and therefore does not correspond with its content. Those who administer justice are persons, but their will is the universal will of the law and they intend to import into the punishment nothing except what is implied in the nature of the thing. The person wronged, however, views the wrong not as something qualitatively and quantitatively limited but only as wrong pure and simple, and in requiting the injury he may go too far, and this would lead to a new wrong. Amongst uncivilized peoples, revenge is deathless; amongst the Arabs, for instance, it can be checked only by superior force or by the impossibility of its satisfaction. A residue of revenge still lingers in comparatively modern legislation in those cases where it is left to the option of individuals whether to prosecute or not.

66. *Paragraph 104.*

Truth entails that the concept shall be, and that this existence shall correspond with the concept. In the sphere of right, the will is existent in something external, but the next requirement is that the will should be existent in something inward, in itself. It must in its own eyes be subjectivity, and have itself as its own object. This relation to itself is the moment of affirmation, but it can attain it only by superseding its immediacy. The immediacy superseded in crime leads, then, through punishment, i.e. through the nullity of this nullity, to affirmation, i.e. to morality.

67. *Paragraph 106.*

So far as right in the strict sense was concerned, it was of no importance what my intention or my principle was. This question about the self-determination and motive of the will, like the question about its purpose, now enters at this point in connexion with morality. Since man wishes to be judged in accordance with his own self-determined choices, he is free in this relation to himself whatever the external situation may impose upon him. No one can break in upon this inner conviction of mankind, no violence can be done to it, and the moral will, therefore, is inaccessible. Man's worth is estimated by reference to his inward action and hence the standpoint of morality is that of freedom aware of itself.

68. *Paragraph 107.*

This entire category of the subjectivity of the will is once again a whole which, as subjectivity, must also have objectivity. It is in a subject that freedom can first be realized, since the subjective is the true material for this realization. But this embodiment of the will which we have called subjectivity is different from the will which has developed all its potentialities to actuality. That is to say, the will must free itself from this second one-sidedness of pure subjectivity in order to become the fully actualized will. In morality, it is man's private interest that comes into question, and the high worth of this interest consists precisely in the fact that man knows himself as absolute and is self-determined. The uneducated man allows himself to be constrained in everything by brute force and natural factors; children have no moral will but leave their parents to decide things for them. The educated man, however, develops an inner life and wills that he himself shall be in everything he does.

69. *Paragraph 108.*

In morality, self-determination is to be thought of as the pure restlessness and activity which can never arrive at anything that *is*. It is in the sphere of ethical life that the will is for the first time identical with the concept of the will and has this concept alone as its content. In the moral sphere the will still relates itself to its *implicit* principle and consequently its position is that of difference. The process through which this position develops is that whereby the subjective will becomes identified with its concept. Therefore the "ought-to-be" which is never absent from the moral sphere becomes an "is" only in ethical life. Further, this "other" in relation to which the subjective will stands is two-sided: first, it is what is substantive, the concept; secondly, it is external fact. Even if the good were posited in the subjective will, that still would not give it complete realization.

70. *Paragraph 110.*

The content of the subjective or moral will has a specific character of its own, i.e. even if it has acquired the form of objectivity, it must still continue to enshrine my subjectivity, and my act is to count as mine only if on its inward side it has been determined by me, if it was my purpose, my intention. Beyond what lay in my subjective will I recognize nothing in its expression as mine. What I wish to see in my deed is my subjective consciousness over again.

71. *Paragraph 112.*

In dealing with formal right, I said [see Paragraph 38] that it contained prohibitions only, that hence a right action, strictly so called, was purely negative in character in respect of the will of others. In morality, on the other hand, my will has a positive character in relation to the will of others, i.e. the universal will is implicitly present within what the subjective will effects. To effect something is to produce something or to alter what already exists, and such changes have a bearing on the will of others. The concept of morality is the inner relation of the will to itself. But here it is not only *one* will; on

the contrary its objectification implies at the same time the cancellation of the single will, and therefore, in addition, just because the character of one-sidedness vanishes, the positing of two wills and a positive bearing of each on the other. So far as rights are concerned, it makes no difference whether someone else's will may do something in relation to mine when I give my will an embodiment in property. In morality, however, the welfare of others too is in question, and this positive bearing cannot come on the scene before this point.

72. *Paragraph 114.*

If an action is to be moral, it must in the first place correspond with my purpose, since the moral will has the right to refuse to recognize in the resulting state of affairs what was not present inwardly as purpose. Purpose concerns only the formal principle that the external will shall be within me as something inward. On the other hand, in the second moment of the moral sphere, questions may be asked about the intention behind the action, i.e. about the relative worth of the action in relation to me. The third and last moment is not the relative worth of the action but its universal worth, the good.

In a moral action, then, there may be a breach first between what is purposed and what is really effected and achieved; secondly, between what is there externally as a universal will and the particular inner determination which I give to it. The third and last point is that the intention should be in addition the universal content of the action. The good is the intention raised to be the concept of the will.

73. *Paragraph 115.*

I am chargeable with what lay in my purpose and this is the most important point in connexion with crime. But responsibility contains only the quite external judgement whether I have or have not done some thing. It does not follow that, because I am responsible, the thing done may be imputed to me.

74. *Paragraph 117.*

The will has confronting it a state of affairs upon which it acts. But in order to know what this state of affairs is I must have an idea of it, and the responsibility is truly mine only in so far as I had knowledge of the situation confronting me. Such a situation is a presupposition of my volition and my will is therefore finite, or rather, since my will is finite, it has a presupposition of this kind. As soon as my thinking and willing is rational, I am no longer at this level of finitude, since the object on which I act is no longer an "other" to me. Finitude, however, implies fixed limits and restrictions. I have confronting me an "other" which is only contingent, something necessary in a purely external way; its path and mine may meet or diverge. Nevertheless, I am nothing except in relation to my freedom, and my will is responsible for the deed only in so far as I know what I am doing. Oedipus, who killed his father without knowing it, cannot be accused of parricide. The ancient penal codes, however, attached less weight to the subjective side of action, to imputability, than we do nowadays. That is why sanctuaries were instituted in ancient times for harbouring and protecting the fugitive from vengeance.

75. *Paragraph 118.*

The transition to intention depends on the fact that I accept responsibility only for what my idea of the situation was. That is to say, there can be imputed to me only what I knew of the circumstances. On the other hand, there are inevitable consequences linked with every action, even if I am only bringing about some single, immediate, state of affairs. The consequences in such a case represent the universal implicit within that state of affairs. Of course I cannot foresee the consequences—they might be preventable—but I must be aware of the universal character of my isolated act. The important point here is not the isolated thing but the whole, and that depends not on the differentia of the particular action, but on its universal nature. Now the transition from purpose to intention lies in the fact that I ought to be aware not simply of my single action but also of the universal which is conjoined with it. The universal which comes on the scene here in this way is what I have willed, my intention.

76. *Paragraph 119.*

It happens of course that circumstances may make an action miscarry to a greater or lesser degree. In a case of arson, for instance, the fire may not catch or alternatively it may take hold further than the incendiary intended. In spite of this, however, we must not make this a distinction between good and bad luck, since in acting a man must lay his account with externality. The old proverb is correct: "A flung stone is the devil's." To act is to expose oneself to bad luck. Thus bad luck has a right over me and is an embodiment of my own willing.

77. *Paragraph 121.*

In my own eyes, reflected into myself, I am a particular in correlation with the externality of my action. My end constitutes the content of the action, the content determinant of the action. Murder and arson, for example, are universals and so are not the positive content of my action *qua* the action of a subject. If one of these crimes has been committed, its perpetrator may be asked why he committed it. The murder was not done for the sake of murdering; the murderer had in view some particular positive end. But if we were to say that he murdered for the mere pleasure of murdering, then the purely positive content of the subject would surely be pleasure, and if that is the case then the deed is the satisfaction of the subject's will. Thus the motive of an act is, more particularly, what is called the "moral" factor, and this has in that case the double meaning of the *universal* implicit in the purpose and the *particular* aspect of the intention. It is a striking modern innovation to inquire continually about the motives of men's actions. Formerly, the question was simply: "Is he an honest man? Does he do his duty?"

Nowadays we insist on looking into men's hearts and so we presuppose a gulf between the objectivity of actions and their inner side, the subjective motives. To be sure, the subject's volition must be considered; he wills something and the reason for what he wills lies within himself; he wills the satisfaction of his desire, the gratification of his passion. None the less, the good and the right are also a content of action, a content not purely natural but put there by my rationality. To make my freedom the content of what I will is a plain goal of my freedom itself. Therefore it is to take higher moral ground to find satisfaction *in* the action and to advance beyond the gulf between the self-consciousness of a man and the objectivity of his deed, even though to treat action as if it involved such a gulf is a way of looking at the matter characteristic of certain epochs in world history and in individual biography.

78. *Paragraph 123.*

Since the specifications of happiness are *given,* they are not true specifications of freedom, because freedom is not genuinely free in its own eyes except in the good, i.e. except when it is its own end. Consequently we may raise the question whether a man has the right to set before himself ends not freely chosen but resting solely on the fact that the subject is a living being. The fact that man is a living being, however, is not fortuitous, but in conformity with reason, and to that extent he has a right to make his needs his end. There is nothing degrading in being alive, and there is no mode of intelligent being higher than life in which existence would be possible. It is only the raising of the given to something self-created which yields the higher orbit of the good, although this distinction implies no incompatibility between the two levels.

79. *Paragraph 124.*

In magnis . . . voluisse sat est [1] is right in the sense that we ought to will something great. But we must also be able to achieve it, otherwise the willing is nugatory. The laurels of mere willing are dry leaves that never were green.

80. *Paragraph 126.*

The famous answer: [2] *Je n'en vois pas la nécessité,* given to the lampooner who excused himself with the words: *Il faut donc que je vive,* is apposite at this point. Life ceases to be necessary in face of the higher realm of freedom. When St. Crispin stole leather to make shoes for the poor, his action was moral but wrong and so inadmissible.

81. *Paragraph 127.*

Life as the sum of ends has a right against abstract right. If for example it is only by stealing bread that the wolf can be kept from the door, the action is of course an encroachment on someone's property, but it would be wrong to treat this action as an ordinary theft. To refuse to allow a man in

---

[1] ["In great things to have willed is enough" (Propertius, II. x. 6).]
[2] [By Richelieu (Bolland).]

jeopardy of his life to take such steps for self-preservation would be to stigmatize him as without rights, and since he would be deprived of his life, his freedom would be annulled altogether. Many diverse details have a bearing on the preservation of life, and when we have our eyes on the future we have to engage ourselves in these details. But the only thing that is necessary is to live *now*, the future is not absolute but ever exposed to accident. Hence it is only the necessity of the immediate present which can justify a wrong action, because not to do the action would in turn be to commit an offence, indeed the most wrong of all offences, namely the complete destruction of the embodiment of freedom. *Beneficium competentiae* is relevant here, because kinship and other close relationships imply the right to demand that no one shall be sacrificed altogether on the altar of right.

82. *Paragraph 129.*

Every stage is really the Idea, but the earlier stages contain it only in rather an abstract form. Thus for example, even the ego, as personality, is already the Idea, though in its most abstract shape. The good, therefore, is the Idea further determined, the unity of the concept of the will with the particular will. It is not something abstractly right, but something concrete whose contents are made up of both right and welfare alike.

83. *Paragraph 131.*

The good is the truth of the particular will, but the will is only that into which it puts itself; it is not good by nature but can become what it is only by its own labour. On the other hand, the good itself, apart from the subjective will, is only an abstraction without that real existence which it is to acquire for the first time through the efforts of that will. Accordingly, the development of the good has three stages: (i) The good should present itself to my volition as a particular will and I should know it. (ii) I should myself say what is good and should develop its particular specifications. (iii) Finally, the specification of the good on its own account, the particularization of the good as infinite subjectivity aware of itself. This inward specifying of what good is, is conscience.

84. *Paragraph 133.*

From my point of view the essence of the will is duty. Now if my knowledge stops at the fact that the good is my duty, I am still going no further than the abstract character of duty. I should do my duty for duty's sake, and when I do my duty it is in a true sense my own objectivity which I am bringing to realization. In doing my duty, I am by myself and free. To have emphasized this meaning of duty has constituted the merit of Kant's moral philosophy and its loftiness of outlook.

85. *Paragraph 134.*

This is the same question as was put to Jesus when someone wished to learn from him what he should do to inherit eternal life.[1] Good as a universal is abstract and cannot be accomplished so long as it remains abstract. To be accomplished it must acquire in addition the character of particularity.

86. *Paragraph 135.*

While we laid emphasis above on the fact that the outlook of Kant's philosophy is a high one in that it propounds a correspondence between duty and rationality, still we must notice here that this point of view is defective in lacking all articulation. The proposition: "Act as if the maxim of thine action could be laid down as a universal principle," would be admirable if we already had determinate principles of conduct. That is to say, to demand of a principle that it shall be able to serve in addition as a determinant of universal legislation is to presuppose that it already possesses a content. Given the content, then of course the application of the principle would be a simple matter. In Kant's case, however, the principle itself is still not available and his criterion of non-contradiction is productive of nothing, since where there is nothing, there can be no contradiction either.

87. *Paragraph 136.*

We may speak in a very lofty strain about duty, and talk of the kind is uplifting and broadens human sympathies, but if it never comes to anything specific it ends in being wearisome. Mind demands particularity and is entitled to it. But conscience is this deepest inward solitude with oneself where everything external and every restriction has disappeared—this complete withdrawal into oneself. As conscience, man is no longer shackled by the aims of particularity, and consequently in attaining that position he has risen to higher ground, the ground of the modern world, which for the first time has reached this consciousness, reached this sinking into oneself. The more sensuous consciousness[2] of earlier epochs had something external and given confronting it, either religion or law. But conscience knows itself as thinking and knows that what alone has obligatory force for me is this that I think.

88. *Paragraph 137.*

When we speak of conscience, it may easily be thought that, in virtue of its form, which is abstract inwardness, conscience is at this point without more ado true conscience. But true conscience determines itself to will what is absolutely good and obligatory and is this self-determination. So far, however, it is only with good in the abstract that we have to do and conscience is still without this objective content and is but the infinite certainty of oneself.

89. *Paragraph 138.*

If we look more closely at this process of evaporation and see how all specific determinations disappear into this simple concept and then have to be

---

[1] [Luke, 10.25]
[2] [For the distinction between sense-consciousness and more highly developed types of consciousness, see Remarks to Paragraphs 21 and 35.]

condensed out of it again, what we find is that it is primarily due to the fact that everything recognized as right and duty may be proved by discursive thinking to be nugatory, restricted, and in all respects not absolute. On the other hand, just as subjectivity evaporates every content into itself, so it may develop it out of itself once more. Everything which arises in the ethical sphere is produced by this activity of mind. The moral point of view, however, is defective because it is purely abstract. When I am aware of my freedom as the *substance* of my being, I am inactive and do nothing. But if I proceed to act and look for principles on which to act, I grope for something determinate and then demand its deduction from the concept of the free will. While, therefore, it is right enough to evaporate right and duty into subjectivity, it is wrong if this abstract groundwork is not then condensed out again. It is only in times when the world of actuality is hollow, spiritless, and unstable, that an individual may be allowed to take refuge from actuality in his inner life. Socrates lived at the time of the ruin of the Athenian democracy. His thought vaporized the world around him and he withdrew into himself to search there for the right and the good. Even in our day there are cases when reverence for the established order is more or less lacking; man insists on having the authoritative as his *will*, as that to which he has granted recognition.

90. *Paragraph 139.*

The abstract self-certainty which knows itself as the basis of everything has in it the potentiality either of willing the universality of the concept or alternatively of taking a particular content as a principle and realizing that. The second alternative is evil, which therefore always includes the abstraction of self-certainty. It is only man who is good, and he is good only because he can also be evil. Good and evil are inseparable, and their inseparability is rooted in the fact that the concept becomes an object to itself, and as object it *eo ipso* acquires the character of difference. The evil will wills something opposed to the universality of the will, while the good will acts in accordance with its true concept.

The difficulty of the question as to how the will can be evil as well as good usually arises because we think of the will as related to itself purely positively and because we represent its volition as something determinate [1] confronting it, as the good. But the problem of the origin of evil may be more precisely put in the form: "How does the negative come into the positive?" If we begin by presupposing that in the creation of the world God is the absolutely positive, then, turn where we will, we shall never discover the negative within that positive, since to talk of God's "permitting" evil is to ascribe to him a passive relation to evil which is unsatisfactory and meaningless. In the representative thinking of religious mythology there is no comprehension of the origin of evil; i.e. the positive and the negative are not dis-covered in one another, there is only a representation of their succession and juxtaposition, so that it is from outside that the negative comes to the positive. But this cannot satisfy thought, which demands a reason and a necessity and insists on apprehending the negative as itself rooted in the positive. Now the solution of the problem, the way the concept treats the matter, is already contained in the concept, since the concept, or to speak more concretely, the Idea, has it in its essence to differentiate itself and to posit itself negatively. If we adhere to the purely positive, i.e. if we rest in the unmixed good which is supposed to be good at its source, then we are accepting an empty category of the Understanding which clings to abstractions and one-sided categories of this kind and by the very asking of this question makes it a difficult one. If we begin with the standpoint of the concept, however, we apprehend the positive as activity and as self-distinction. Evil and good alike have their origin in the will and the will in its concept is both good and evil.

The natural will is implicitly the contradiction of self-distinction, of being both inwardness and also self-awareness. [2] To maintain then that evil implies the further point that man is evil in so far as his will is natural would be to contradict the usual idea that it is just the natural will which is guiltless and good. But the natural will stands in opposition to the content of freedom, and the child and the uneducated man, whose wills are only natural, are for that very reason liable to be called to account for their actions only in a less degree. Now when we speak of man, we mean not the child but the self-conscious adult, and when we speak of good, we mean the knowledge of it. It is doubtless true that the natural is inherently innocent, neither good nor bad, but when it is drawn into the orbit of the will which is free and knows that it is free, it acquires the character of not being free and is therefore evil. When man *wills* the natural, it is no longer merely natural, but the negative opposed to the good, i.e. to the concept of the will.

On the other hand, if it is now objected that since evil is rooted in the concept and inevitable, man would be guiltless if he committed it, our reply must be that a man's decision is his own act, and his own act is freely chosen and his own responsibility. In the religious legend it is said that man is as God when he knows good and evil; [3] and it is true that this likeness to God is present in such knowledge in that the inevitability here is no natural inevitability since on the contrary the decision is really the transcendence of this duality of good and evil. When both good and evil are placed before me, I have a choice between the two; I can decide between them and endow my subjective character with either. Thus the nature of evil is that man may will it but need not.

---

[1] [Reading *und sein Wollen als ein Bestimmtes,* with Lasson.]

[2] [i.e. both universal inner principle and also awareness of self as particular, as opposed to the universal.]

[3] [Genesis, 3.5, i.e. after doing what had been forbidden.]

91. *Paragraph 140.*

Representative thinking may go further and pervert the evil will into a show of goodness. Although it cannot alter the nature of evil, it can invest it with a show of goodness. Since every action has a positive aspect, and since the category of good as opposed to evil is likewise reduced to positivity, I may claim that my action in its bearing on my intention is good. Thus evil has good linked with it not only in my consciousness but also if we look at my action on its positive side. When self-consciousness gives out, to others only, that its action is good, this form of subjectivism is hypocrisy. But if it goes so far as to claim that the deed is good in its own eyes also, then we have a still higher peak of the subjectivism which knows itself as absolute. For this type of mind absolute good and absolute evil have both vanished, and the subject is therefore at liberty to pass himself off at discretion as anything he likes. This is the position of the absolute sophistry which usurps the office of lawgiver and rests the distinction between good and evil on its own caprice. The chief hypocrites are the pious ones (the Tartuffes) who are punctilious in every ritual observance and may even be religious to all appearance, while yet they do just as they please. There is little mention of hypocrites nowadays, partly because the accusation of hypocrisy seems to be too harsh; partly, however, because hypocrisy in its naïve form has more or less disappeared. This downright falsehood, this veneer of goodness, has now become too transparent not to be seen through, and the divorce between doing good with one hand and evil with the other no longer occurs, since advancing culture has weakened the opposition between these categories.

Instead, hypocrisy has now assumed the subtler form of Probabilism, which involves the agent's attempt to represent a transgression as something good from the point of view of his private conscience. This doctrine can only arise when the moral and the good are determined by authority, with the result that there are as many reasons as there are authorities for supposing that evil is good. Casuist theologians, Jesuits especially, have worked up these cases of conscience and multiplied them *ad infinitum.*

These cases have now been elaborated to such a high degree of subtlety that numerous clashes have arisen between them, and the opposition between good and evil has become so weak that in single instances they appear to turn into one another. The only desideratum now is probability, i.e. something approximately good, something which may be supported by any single reason or authority. Thus the special characteristic of this attitude is that its content is purely abstract; it sets up the concrete content as something inessential or rather abandons it to bare opinion. On this principle, anyone may have committed a crime and yet have willed the good. For example, if a bad character is murdered, the positive side of the action may be given out to be the withstanding of evil and the will to diminish it. Now the next step beyond Probabilism is that it

is no longer a question of someone else's statement or authority; it is a question only of the subject himself, i.e. of his own conviction—a conviction which alone is able to make a thing good. The defect here is that everything is supposed to fall within the orbit of conviction alone and that the absolutely right, for which this conviction should be only the form, no longer exists. It is certainly not a matter of indifference whether I do something by habit and custom or because I am actuated throughout by the truth which underlies these. But objective truth is still different from my conviction, because conviction lacks the distinction between good and evil. Conviction always remains conviction, and the bad could only be that of which I am not convinced.

Now while this obliteration of good and evil implies a very lofty attitude, there is involved in this attitude the admission that it is subject to error, and to that extent it is brought down from its pedestal into mere fortuitousness and seems undeserving of respect. Now this form of subjectivism is irony, the consciousness that this principle of conviction is not worth much and that, lofty criterion though it be, it is only caprice that governs it. This attitude is really a product of Fichte's philosophy, which proclaims that the Ego is absolute, i.e. is absolute certainty, the "universal self-hood" which advances through a course of further development to objectivity.[1] Of Fichte himself it cannot properly be said that he made subjective caprice a guiding principle in ethics, but, later on, this principle of the mere particular, in the sense of "particular self-hood," was deified by Friedrich von Schlegel with reference to the good and the beautiful. As a result, he made objective goodness only an image of my conviction, receiving support from my efforts alone, and dependent for its appearance and disappearance on me as its lord and master. If I relate myself to something objective, it vanishes at the same moment before my eyes, and so I hover over a pit of nothingness, summoning shapes from the depths and annihilating them. This supreme type of subjectivism can emerge only in a period of advanced culture when faith has lost its seriousness, and its essence is simply "all is vanity."

92. *Paragraph 141.*

Each of the two principles hitherto discussed, namely good in the abstract and conscience, is defective in lacking its opposite. Good in the abstract evaporates into something completely powerless, into which I may introduce any and every content, while the subjectivity of mind becomes just as worthless because it lacks any objective significance. Thus a longing may arise for an objective order in which man gladly degrades himself to servitude and total subjection, if only to escape the torment of vacuity and negation. Many Protestants have recently gone over to the Roman Catholic Church, and they have done so because they found their inner life worthless and grasped at something fixed,

[1] [For further comments on Fichte's views, with references, see e.g. *History of Philosophy*, iii. 481 ff.]

at a support, an authority, even if it was not exactly the stability of thought which they caught.

The unity of the subjective with the objective and absolute good is ethical life, and in it we find the reconciliation which accords with the concept. Morality is the form of the will in general on its subjective side. Ethical life is more than the subjective form and the self-determination of the will; in addition it has as its content the concept of the will, namely freedom. The right and the moral cannot exist independently; they must have the ethical as their support and foundation, for the right lacks the moment of subjectivity, while morality in turn possesses that moment alone, and consequently both the right and the moral lack actuality by themselves. Only the infinite, the Idea, is actual. Right exists only as a branch of a whole or like the ivy which twines itself round a tree firmly rooted on its own account.

93. *Paragraph 144.*

Throughout ethical life the objective and subjective moments are alike present, but both of them are only its forms. Its substance is the good, i.e. the objective is filled with subjectivity. If we consider ethical life from the objective standpoint, we may say that in it we are ethical unselfconsciously. In this sense, Antigone proclaims that "no one knows whence the laws come; they are everlasting," [1] i.e. their determinate character is absolute and has its source in the nature of the thing. None the less, however, the substance of ethical life has a consciousness also, though the status of this consciousness is never higher than that of being one moment.

94. *Paragraph 145.*

Since the laws and institutions of the ethical order make up the concept of freedom, they are the substance or universal essence of individuals, who are thus related to them as accidents only. Whether the individual exists or not is all one to the objective ethical order. It alone is permanent and is the power regulating the life of individuals. Thus the ethical order has been represented by mankind as eternal justice, as gods absolutely existent, in contrast with which the empty business of individuals is only a game of see-saw.

95. *Paragraph 149.*

Duty is a restriction only on the self-will of subjectivity. It stands in the way only of that abstract good to which subjectivity adheres. When we say: "We want to be free," the primary meaning of the words is simply: "We want abstract freedom," and every institution and every organ of the state passes as a restriction on freedom of that kind. Thus duty is not a restriction on freedom, but only on freedom in the abstract, i.e. on unfreedom. Duty is the attainment of our essence, the winning of *positive* freedom.

[1] [This misquotation of Sophocles: *Antigone*, ll. 450-7, may be due to the transcriber of Hegel's lecture, because the lines are quoted correctly in the Remark to Paragraph 166.]

96. *Paragraph 150.*

To conform to the ethical order on this or that particular occasion is hardly enough to make a man virtuous; he is virtuous only when this mode of behaviour is a fixed element in his character. Virtue is rather like ethical virtuosity,[2] and the reason why we speak of virtue less nowadays than formerly is that ethical living is less like the form of a particular individual's character. The French are *par excellence* the people who speak most of virtue, and the reason is that amongst them ethical life in the individual[3] is more a matter of his own idiosyncrasies or a natural mode of conduct. The Germans, on the other hand, are more thoughtful, and amongst them the same content acquires the form of universality.

97. *Paragraph 151.*

Just as nature has its laws, and as animals, trees, and the sun fulfil their law, so custom (*Sitte*) is the law appropriate to free mind. Right and morality are not yet what ethics (*Sitte*) is, namely mind. In right, particularity is still not the particularity of the concept, but only that of the natural will. So, too, at the standpoint of morality, self-consciousness is not yet *mind's* consciousness of itself. At that level it is only the worth of the subject in himself that is in question, i.e. the subject who determines himself by reference to good in contrast with evil, who still has self-will as the form of his willing. Here, however, at the standpoint of ethics, the will is mind's will and it has a content which is substantive and in conformity with itself.

Education is the art of making men ethical. It begins with pupils whose life is at the instinctive level and shows them the way to a second birth, the way to change their instinctive nature into a second, intellectual, nature, and makes this intellectual level habitual to them. At this point the clash between the natural and the subjective will disappears, the subject's internal struggle dies away. To this extent, habit is part of ethical life as it is of philosophic thought also, since such thought demands that mind be trained against capricious fancies, and that these be destroyed and overcome to leave the way clear for rational thinking. It is true that a man is killed by habit, i.e. if he has once come to feel completely at home in life, if he has become mentally and physically dull, and if the clash between subjective consciousness and mental activity has disappeared; for man is active only in so far as he has not attained his end and wills to develop his potentialities and vindicate himself in struggling to attain it. When this has been fully achieved, activity and vitality are at an end, and the result—loss of interest in life—

[2] [Heroes ("ethical virtuosi") lived in uncivilized conditions (see Addition to Paragraph 93) and there was no ethical life in society as they found it; but since they introduced ethical institutions for the first time (see Remarks to Paragraphs 167 and 203), they displayed virtue as a kind of virtuosity. Nowadays, ethical life is common to everyone and consists in conformity to the existing order, not in divergence from it.]

[3] [Reading *das Sittliche am Individuum*, with Lasson.]

is mental or physical death.

98. *Paragraph 153.*

The educational experiments, advocated by Rousseau in *Émile,* of withdrawing children from the common life of every day and bringing them up in the country, have turned out to be futile, since no success can attend an attempt to estrange people from the laws of the world. Even if the young have to be educated in solitude, it is still useless to hope that the fragrance of the intellectual world will not ultimately permeate this solitude or that the power of the world mind is too feeble to gain the mastery of those outlying regions. It is by becoming a citizen of a good state that the individual first comes into his right.

99. *Paragraph 155.*

A slave can have no duties; only a free man has them. If all rights were put on one side and all duties on the other, the whole would be dissolved, since their identity alone is the fundamental thing, and it is to this that we have here to hold fast.

100. *Paragraph 156.*

Ethical life is not abstract like the good, but is intensely actual. Mind has actuality, and individuals are accidents of this actuality. Thus in dealing with ethical life, only two views are possible: either we start from the substantiality of the ethical order, or else we proceed atomistically and build on the basis of single individuals. This second point of view excludes mind because it leads only to a juxtaposition. Mind, however, is not something single, but is the unity of the single and the universal.

101. *Paragraph 158.*

Love means in general terms the consciousness of my unity with another, so that I am not in selfish isolation but win my self-consciousness only as the renunciation of my independence and through knowing myself as the unity of myself with another and of the other with me. Love, however, is feeling, i.e. ethical life in the form of something natural. In the state, feeling disappears; there we are conscious of unity as law; there the content must be rational and known to us. The first moment in love is that I do not wish to be a self-subsistent and independent person and that, if I were, then I would feel defective and incomplete. The second moment is that I find myself in another person, that I count for something in the other, while the other in turn comes to count for something in me. Love, therefore, is the most tremendous contradiction; the Understanding cannot resolve it since there is nothing more stubborn than this point (*Punktualität*) of self-consciousness which is negated and which nevertheless I ought to possess as affirmative. Love is at once the propounding and the resolving of this contradiction. As the resolving of it, love is unity of an ethical type.

102. *Paragraph 159.*

The right of the family properly consists in the fact that its substantiality should have determinate existence. Thus it is a right against externality and against secessions from the family unity. On the other hand, to repeat, love is a feeling, something subjective, against which unity cannot make itself effective. The demand for unity can be sustained, then, only in relation to such things as are by nature external and not conditioned by feeling.

103. *Paragraph 161.*

Marriage is in essence an ethical tie. Formerly, especially in most systems of natural law, attention was paid only to the physical side of marriage or to its natural character. Consequently, it was treated only as a sex relationship, and this completely barred the way to its other characteristics. This is crude enough, but it is no less so to think of it as only a civil contract, and even Kant does this. On this view, the parties are bound by a contract of mutual caprice, and marriage is thus degraded to the level of a contract for reciprocal use. A third view of marriage is that which bases it on love alone, but this must be rejected like the other two, since love is only a feeling and so is exposed in every respect to contingency, a guise which ethical life may not assume. Marriage, therefore, is to be more precisely characterized as ethico-legal (*rechtlich sittliche*) love, and this eliminates from marriage the transient, fickle, and purely subjective aspects of love.

104. *Paragraph 162.*

Amongst peoples who hold the female sex in scant respect, marriages are arranged by the parents at will without consulting the young people. The latter raise no objection, since at that level of culture the particularity of feeling makes no claims for itself. For the woman it is only a matter of getting a husband, for the man, of getting a wife. In other social conditions, considerations of wealth, connexions, political ends, may be the determining factor. In such circumstances, great hardships may arise through making marriage a means to other ends. Nowadays, however, the subjective origin of marriage, the state of being in love, is regarded as the only important originating factor. Here the position is represented to be that a man must wait until his hour has struck and that he can bestow his love only on one specific individual.

105. *Paragraph 163.*

The distinction between marriage and concubinage is that the latter is chiefly a matter of satisfying natural desire, while this satisfaction is made secondary in the former. It is for this reason that physical experiences may be mentioned in married life without a blush, although outside the marriage tie their mention would produce a sense of shame. But it is on this account, too, that marriage must be regarded as in principle indissoluble, for the end of marriage is the ethical end, an end so lofty that everything else is manifestly powerless against it and made subject to it. Marriage is not to be dissolved because of passion, since passion is subordinate to it. But it is not indissoluble except in principle, since as Christ says, only "for the hardness of your heart"[1] is divorce established. Since marriage has feeling for one of its moments, it is not absolute but weak and potentially dissoluble. Legislators, however, must make its dissolution as difficult as possible and uphold the right of the ethical order against caprice.

106. *Paragraph 164.*

Friedrich von Schlegel in his *Lucinde,*[2] and a follower of his in the *Briefe eines Ungenannten,*[3] have put forward the view that the wedding ceremony is superfluous and a formality which might be discarded. Their reason is that love is, so they say, the substance of marriage and that the celebration therefore detracts from its worth. Surrender to sensual impulse is here represented as necessary to prove the freedom and inwardness of love—an argument not unknown to seducers.

It must be noticed in connexion with sex-relations that a girl in surrendering her body loses her honour. With a man, however, the case is otherwise, because he has a field for ethical activity outside the family. A girl is destined in essence for the marriage tie and for that only; it is therefore demanded of her that her love shall take the form of marriage and that the different moments in love shall attain their true rational relation to each other.

107. *Paragraph 166.*

Women are capable of education, but they are not made for activities which demand a universal faculty such as the more advanced sciences, philosophy, and certain forms of artistic production. Women may have happy ideas, taste, and elegance, but they cannot attain to the ideal.[4] The difference between men and women is like that between animals and plants. Men correspond to animals, while women correspond to plants because their development is more placid and the principle that underlies it is the rather vague unity of feeling. When women hold the helm of government, the state is at once in jeopardy, because women regulate their actions not by the demands of universality but by arbitrary inclinations and opinions. Women are educated—who knows how?—as it were by breathing in ideas, by living rather than by acquiring knowledge. The status of manhood, on the other hand, is attained only by the stress of thought and much technical exertion.

108. *Paragraph 168.*

A sense of shame—to go no farther—is a bar to consanguineous marriage. But this repugnance finds justification in the concept of the thing. What is already united, I mean, cannot be united for the first time by marriage. It is a commonplace of stockbreeding that the offspring is comparatively weak when animals of the same stock are mated, since if

there is to be unification there must first be division. The force of generation, as of mind, is all the greater, the greater the oppositions out of which it is reproduced. Familiarity, close acquaintance, the habit of common pursuits, should not precede marriage; they should come about for the first time within it. And their development has all the more value, the richer it is and the more facets it has.

109. *Paragraph 172.*

In many legal codes the wider circle of the clan is adhered to, and this is regarded as the essential bond, while the other bond, that of each particular family, appears less important in comparison. Thus in the older Roman law, the wife in the easily dissolved type of marriage stood in a closer relation to her kinsfolk than to her husband and children. Under feudal law, again, the maintenance of the *splendor familiae* made it necessary for only the males of the family to be reckoned members and for the clan as a whole to count as the important thing, while the newly founded family disappeared in comparison. Nevertheless, each new family is the essential thing in contrast with the more remote connexions of clan-kinship, and parents and children form the nucleus proper as opposed to the clan, which is also in certain sense called a "family." Hence an individual's relation to his wealth must have a more essential connexion with his marriage than with the wider circle of his kin.

110. *Paragraph 173.*

The relation of love between husband and wife is in itself not objective, because even if their feeling is their substantial unity, still this unity has no objectivity. Such an objectivity parents first acquire in their children, in whom they can see objectified the entirety of their union. In the child, a mother loves its father and he its mother. Both have their love objectified for them in the child. While in their goods their unity is embodied only in an external thing, in their children it is embodied in a spiritual one in which the parents are loved and which they love.

111. *Paragraph 174.*

Man has to acquire for himself the position which he ought to attain; he is not already in possession of it by instinct. It is on this fact that the child's right to education is based. Peoples under patriarchal government are in the same position as children; they are fed from central stores and not regarded as self-subsistent and adults. The services which may be demanded from children should therefore have education as their sole end and be relevant thereto; they must not be ends in themselves, since a child in slavery is in the most unethical of all situations whatever. One of the chief factors in education is discipline, the purport of which is to break down the child's self-will and thereby eradicate his purely natural and sensuous self. We must not expect to achieve this by mere goodness, since it is just the immediate will which acts on immediate fancies and caprices, not on reasons and representative thinking. If we

---

[1] [Matthew, 19.8; Mark, 10.5]
[2] [Berlin, 1799.]
[3] Lübeck and Leipzig, 1800. ["*Anonymous Letters*," i.e. Schleiermacher's anonymously published defence of *Lucinde* against the charge of immorality.]
[4] [*Ideale.* By this word Hegel means "the Beautiful and whatever tends thither" (*Science of Logic,* i. 163, footnote).]

advance reasons to children, we leave it open to them to decide whether the reasons are weighty or not, and thus we make everything depend on their whim. So far as children are concerned, universality and the substance of things reside in their parents, and this implies that children must be obedient. If the feeling of subordination, producing the longing to grow up, is not fostered in children, they become forward and impertinent.

112. Paragraph 175.

As a child, man must have lived with his parents encircled by their love and trust, and rationality must appear in him as his very own subjectivity. In the early years it is education by the mother especially which is important, since ethical principles must be implanted in the child in the form of feeling. It is noteworthy that on the whole children love their parents less than their parents love them. The reason for this is that they are gradually increasing in strength, and are learning to stand on their own feet, and so are leaving their parents behind them. The parents, on the other hand, possess in their children the objective embodiment of their union.

113. Paragraph 176.

It is because marriage depends entirely on feeling, something subjective and contingent, that it may be dissolved. The state, on the other hand, is not subject to partition, because it rests on law. To be sure, marriage *ought* to be indissoluble, but here again we have to stop at this "ought"; yet, since marriage is an ethical institution, it cannot be dissolved at will but only by an ethical authority, whether the church or the law court. If the parties are completely estranged, e.g. owing to adultery, then even the ecclesiastical authority must permit divorce.

114. Paragraph 180.

In earlier times, a Roman father had the right to disinherit his children and even kill them. Later he lost both these rights. Attempts were made to forge into a legal system this incoherence between unethical institutions and devices to rob them of that character, and it is the retention of this incoherence which constitutes the deficiency and difficulty of the German law of inheritance. To be sure, the right to make a will must be conceded; but in conceding it our point of view must be that this right of free choice arises or is magnified with the dispersion and estrangement of the members of the family. Further, the so-called "family of friends" which testamentary disposition brings with it may be admitted only in defect of members of the family proper, i.e. of spouse and children. To make a will at all entails something obnoxious and disagreeable, because in making it I reveal the names of my favourites. Favour, however, is arbitrary; it may be gained surreptitiously by a variety of expedients, it may depend on all sorts of foolish reasons, and as a condition of having his name included in a will, a beneficiary may be required to subject himself to the most abject servilities. In England, the home of all sorts of eccentricity, there is no end to the folly and whimsicality of bequests.

115. Paragraph 181.

The starting-point for the universal here is the self-subsistence of the particular, and the ethical order seems therefore to be lost at this point, since it is precisely the identity of the family which consciousness takes to be the primary thing, the divine, and the source of obligation. Now, however, a situation arises in which the particular is to be my primary determining principle, and thus my determinacy by ethical factors has been annulled. But this is nothing but a pure mistake, since, while I suppose that I am adhering to the particular, the universal and the necessity of the link between particulars remains the primary and essential thing. I am thus altogether on the level of show, and while my particularity remains my determining principle, i.e. my end, I am for that very reason the servant of the universal which properly retains power over me in the last resort.

116. Paragraph 182.

Civil society is the [stage of] difference which intervenes between the family and the state, even if its formation follows later in time than that of the state, because, as [the stage of] difference, it presupposes the state; to subsist itself, it must have the state before its eyes as something self-subsistent. Moreover, the creation of civil society is the achievement of the modern world which has for the first time given all determinations of the Idea their due. If the state is represented as a unity of different persons, as a unity which is only a partnership, then what is really meant is only civil society. Many modern constitutional lawyers have been able to bring within their purview no theory of the state but this. In civil society each member is his own end, everything else is nothing to him. But except in contact with others he cannot attain the whole compass of his ends, and therefore these others are means to the end of the particular member. A particular end, however, assumes the form of universality through this relation to other people, and it is attained in the simultaneous attainment of the welfare of others. Since particularity is inevitably conditioned by universality, the whole sphere of civil society is the territory of mediation where there is free play for every idiosyncrasy, every talent, every accident of birth and fortune, and where waves of every passion gush forth, regulated only by reason glinting through them. Particularity, restricted by universality, is the only standard whereby each particular member promotes his welfare.

117. Paragraph 184.

Here ethical life is split into its extremes and lost; the immediate unity of the family has fallen apart into a plurality. Reality here is externality, the decomposing of the concept, the self-subsistence of its moments which have now won their freedom and their determinate existence. Though in civil society universal and particular have fallen apart, yet both are still reciprocally bound together and conditioned. While each of them seems to do just the opposite to the other and supposes that it can exist only by keeping the other at arm's length, none the less each still conditions the other. Thus, for example, most people regard the paying of taxes as injurious to their particular interest, as something inimical and obstructive of their own ends. Yet, however true this *seems,* particular ends cannot be attained without the help of the universal, and a country where no taxes were paid could not be singled out as invigorating its citizens. Similarly, it might seem that universal ends would be more readily attainable if the universal absorbed the strength of the particulars in the way described, for instance, in Plato's *Republic.* But this, too, is only an illusion, since both universal and particular turn into one another and exist only for and by means of one another. If I further my ends, I further the ends of the universal, and this in turn furthers my end.

118. *Paragraph 185.*

Particularity by itself is measureless excess, and the forms of this excess are themselves measureless. By means of his ideas and reflections man expands his desires, which are not a closed circle like animal instinct, and carries them on to the false infinite. At the other end of the scale, however, want and destitution are measureless too, and the discord of this situation can be brought into a harmony only by the state which has powers over it. Plato wished to exclude particularity from his state, but this is no help, since help on these lines would contravene the infinite right of the Idea to allow freedom to the particular. It was in the Christian religion in the first place that the right of subjectivity arose, together with the infinity of self-awareness, and while granting this right, the whole order must at the same time retain strength enough to put particularity in harmony with the unity of ethical life.

119. *Paragraph 187.*

By educated men, we may prima facie understand those who without the obtrusion of personal idiosyncrasy can do what others do. It is precisely this idiosyncrasy, however, which uneducated men display, since their behaviour is not governed by the universal characteristics of the situation. Similarly, an uneducated man is apt to hurt the feelings of his neighbours. He simply lets himself go and does not reflect on the susceptibilities of others. It is not that he intends to hurt them, but his conduct is not consonant with his intention. Thus education rubs the edges off particular characteristics until a man conducts himself in accordance with the nature of the thing. Genuine originality, which produces the real thing, demands genuine education, while bastard originality adopts eccentricities which only enter the heads of the uneducated.

120. *Paragraph 189.*

There are certain universal needs such as food, drink, clothing, &c., and it depends entirely on ac-

cidental circumstances how these are satisfied. The fertility of the soil varies from place to place, harvests vary from year to year, one man is industrious, another indolent. But this medley of arbitrariness generates universal characteristics by its own working; and this apparently scattered and thoughtless sphere is upheld by a necessity which automatically enters it. To discover this necessary element here is the object of political economy, a science which is a credit to thought because it finds laws for a mass of accidents. It is an interesting spectacle here to see all chains of activity leading back to the same point; particular spheres of action fall into groups, influence others, and are helped or hindered by others. The most remarkable thing here is this mutual interlocking of particulars, which is what one would least expect because at first sight everything seems to be given over to the arbitrariness of the individual, and it has a parallel in the solar system which displays to the eye only irregular movements, though its laws may none the less be ascertained.

121. *Paragraph 190.*

An animal is restricted to particularity. It has its instincts and means of satisfying them, means which are limited and which it cannot overstep. Some insects are parasitic on a certain kind of plant; some animals have a wider range and can live in different climates, but there is always a restriction preventing them from having the range open to man. The need of shelter and clothing, the necessity of cooking his food to make it fit to eat and to overcome its natural rawness, both mean that man has less comfort than an animal, and indeed, as mind, he ought to have less. Intelligence, with its grasp of distinctions, multiplies these human needs, and since taste and utility become criteria of judgement, even the needs themselves are affected thereby. Finally, it is no longer need but opinion which has to be satisfied, and it is just the educated man who analyses the concrete into its particulars. The very multiplication of needs involves a check on desire, because when many things are in use, the urge to obtain any one thing which might be needed is less strong, and this is a sign that want altogether is not so imperious.

122. *Paragraph 191.*

What the English call "comfort" is something inexhaustible and illimitable. [Others can discover to you that what you take to be] comfort at any stage is discomfort, and these discoveries never come to an end. Hence the need for greater comfort does not exactly arise within you directly; it is suggested to you by those who hope to make a profit from its creation.

123. *Paragraph 192.*

The fact that I must direct my conduct by reference to others introduces here the form of universality. It is from others that I acquire the means of satisfaction and I must accordingly accept their views. At the same time, however, I am compelled to produce means for the satisfaction of others. We play into each other's hands and so hang together. To this extent everything private becomes something social. In dress fashions and hours of meals, there are certain conventions which we have to accept because in these things it is not worth the trouble to insist on displaying one's own discernment. The wisest thing here is to do as others do.

124. *Paragraph 195.*

The entire Cynical mode of life adopted by Diogenes was nothing more or less than a product of Athenian social life, and what determined it was the way of thinking against which his whole manner protested. Hence it was not independent of social conditions but simply their result; it was itself a rude product of luxury. When luxury is at its height, distress and depravity are equally extreme, and in such circumstances Cynicism is the outcome of opposition to refinement.

125. *Paragraph 196.*

There is hardly any raw material which does not need to be worked on before use. Even air has to be worked for because we have to warm it. Water is perhaps the only exception, because we can drink it as we find it. It is by the sweat of his brow and the toil of his hands that man obtains the means to satisfy his needs.

126. *Paragraph 197.*

The savage is lazy and is distinguished from the educated man by his brooding stupidity, because practical education is just education in the need and habit of being busy. A clumsy man always produces a result he does not intend; he is not master of his own job. The skilled worker, on the other hand, may be said to be the man who produces the thing as it ought to be and who hits the nail on the head without shrinking (*keine Sprödigkeit in seinem subjektiven Tun gegen den Zweck findet*).

127. *Paragraph 201.*

The ways and means of sharing in the capital of society are left to each man's particular choice, but the subdivision of civil society into different general branches is a necessity. The family is the first precondition of the state, but class divisions are the second. The importance of the latter is due to the fact that although private persons are self-seeking, they are compelled to direct their attention to others. Here then is the root which connects self-seeking to the universal, i.e. to the state, whose care it must be that this tie is a hard and fast one.

128. *Paragraph 203.*

In our day agriculture is conducted on methods devised by reflective thinking, i.e. like a factory.[1] This has given it a character like that of industry and contrary to its natural one. Still, the agricultural class will always retain a mode of life which is patriarchal and the substantial frame of mind prop-

[1] [On the authority of Arthur Young's *Lincolnshire* (1799), Halévy remarks that, if you were in the offices of a certain farm there, "you could not tell whether you were on a farm or in the heart of a large factory" (*History of the English People in 1815*, Bk. ii, Chap. i).]

er to such a life. The member of this class accepts unreflectively what is given him and takes what he gets, thanking God for it and living in faith and confidence that this goodness will continue. What comes to him suffices him; once it is consumed, more comes again. This is the simple attitude of mind not concentrated on the struggle for riches. It may be described as the attitude of the old nobility which just ate what there was. So far as this class is concerned, nature does the major part, while individual effort is secondary. In the business class, however, it is intelligence which is the essential thing, and natural products can be treated only as raw materials.

129. *Paragraph 204.*

In the business class, the individual is thrown back on himself, and this feeling of self-hood is most intimately connected with the demand for law and order. The sense of freedom and order has therefore arisen above all in towns. The agricultural class, on the other hand, has little occasion to think of itself; what it obtains is the gift of a stranger, of nature. Its feeling of dependence is fundamental to it, and with this feeling there is readily associated a willingness to submit to whatever may befall it at other men's hands. The agricultural class is thus more inclined to subservience, the business class to freedom.

130. *Paragraph 207.*

When we say that a man must be a "somebody," we mean that he should belong to some specific social class, since to be a somebody means to have substantive being. A man with no class is a mere private person and his universality is not actualized. On the other hand, the individual in his particularity may take himself as the universal and presume that by entering a class he is surrendering himself to an indignity. This is the false idea that in attaining a determinacy necessary to it, a thing is restricting and surrendering itself.

131. *Paragraph 209.*

From one point of view, it is through the working of the system of particularity that right becomes an external compulsion as a protection of particular interests. Even though this result is due to the concept, right none the less only becomes something existent because this is useful for men's needs. To become conscious in thought of his right, man must be trained to think and give up dallying with mere sensation. We must invest the objects of our thought with the form of universality and similarly we must direct our willing by a universal principle. It is only after man has devised numerous needs and after their acquisition has become intertwined with his satisfaction, that he can frame laws for himself.

132. *Paragraph 211.*

The sun and the planets have their laws too, but they do not know them. Savages are governed by impulses, customs, and feelings, but they are unconscious of this. When right is posited as law and is known, every accident of feeling vanishes together with the form of revenge, sympathy, and selfishness, and in this way the right attains for the first time its true determinacy and is given its due honour. It is as a result of the discipline of comprehending the right that the right first becomes capable of universality. In the course of applying the laws, clashes occur, and in dealing with these the judge's intelligence has its proper scope; this is quite inevitable, because otherwise carrying out the law would be something mechanical from start to finish. But to go so far as to get rid of clashes altogether by leaving much to the judge's discretion is a far worse solution, because even the clash is intrinsic to thought, to conscious thinking and its dialectic, while the mere fiat of a judge would be arbitrary.

It is generally alleged in favour of customary law that it is "living," but this vitality, i.e. the identity between the subject and what the law provides, is not the whole essence of the matter. Law (*Recht*) must be known by thought, it must be a system in itself, and only as such can it be recognized in a civilized country. The recent denial that nations "have a vocation to codify their laws" is not only an insult; it also implies the absurdity of supposing that not a single individual has been endowed with skill enough to bring into a coherent system the endless mass of existing laws. The truth is that it is just systematization, i.e. elevation to the universal, which our time is pressing for without any limit. A similar view is that collections of judgements, like those available in a *Corpus Juris,* are far superior to a code worked out in the most general way. The reason alleged is that such judgements always retain a certain particularity and a certain reminiscence of history which men are unwilling to sacrifice. But the mischievousness of such collections is made clear enough by the practice of English law.

133. *Paragraph 213.*

In the higher relationships of marriage, love, religion, and the state, the only aspects which can become the subject of legislation are those of such a nature as to permit of their being in principle external. Still, in this respect there is a wide difference between the laws of different peoples. The Chinese, for instance, have a law requiring a husband to love his first wife more than his other wives. If he is convicted of doing the opposite, corporal punishment follows. Similarly, the legislation of the ancients in earlier times was full of precepts about uprightness and integrity which are unsuited by nature to legal enactment because they fall wholly within the field of the inner life. It is only in the case of the oath, whereby things are brought home to conscience, that uprightness and integrity must be taken into account as the substance of the matter.

134. *Paragraph 214.*

There is one essential element in law and the administration of justice which contains a measure of contingency and which arises from the fact that the law is a universal prescription which has to be applied to the single case. If you wished to declare yourself against this contingency, you would be talking in abstractions. The measure of a man's punishment, for example, cannot be made equivalent to any determination of the concept of punishment, and the decision made, whatever it be, is from this point of view arbitrary always. But this contingency is itself necessary, and if you argue against having a code at all on the ground that any code is incomplete, you are overlooking just that element of law in which completion is not to be achieved and which therefore must just be accepted as it stands.

135. *Paragraph 215.*

The legal profession, possessed of a special knowledge of the law, often claims this knowledge as its monopoly and refuses to allow any layman to discuss the subject. Physicists similarly have taken amiss Goethe's theory about colours [1] because he did not belong to their craft and was a poet into the bargain. But we do not need to be shoemakers to know if our shoes fit, and just as little have we any need to be professionals to acquire knowledge of matters of universal interest. Law is concerned with freedom, the worthiest and holiest thing in man, the thing man must know if it is to have obligatory force for him.

136. *Paragraph 216.*

Completeness means the exhaustive collection of every single thing pertaining to a given field, and no science or branch of knowledge can be complete in this sense. Now if we say that philosophy or any one of the sciences is incomplete, we are not far from holding that we must wait until the deficiency is made up, since the best part may still be wanting. But take up this attitude and advance is impossible, either in geometry, which seems to be a closed science although new propositions do arise, or in philosophy, which is always capable of freshness in detail even though its subject is the universal Idea. In the past, the universal law always consisted of the ten commandments; now we can see at once that not to lay down the law "Thou shalt not kill," on the ground that a legal code cannot be complete, is an obvious absurdity. Any code could be still better—no effort of reflection is required to justify this affirmation; we can think of the best, finest, and noblest as still better, finer, and nobler. But a big old tree puts forth more and more branches without thereby becoming a new tree; though it would be silly to refuse to plant a tree at all simply because it might produce new branches.

137. *Paragraph 217.*

Law and the right are identical in the sense that what is implicitly right is posited in the law. I possess something, own a property, which I occupied when it was ownerless. This possession must now further be recognized and posited as mine. Hence in civil society formalities arise in connexion with property. Boundary stones are erected as a symbol for

[1] [Hegel's acceptance of this anti-Newtonian theory, e.g. in *Enc.,* § 320, gave great pleasure to Goethe. For a summary and criticism of the theory, see e.g. G. H. Lewes: *Life of Goethe,* Book V, chap. ix.]

others to recognize. Entries are made in mortgage and property registers. Most property in civil society is held on contract, and contractual forms are fixed and determinate. Now we may have an antipathy to formalities of this kind and we may suppose that they only exist to bring in money to the authorities; we may even regard them as something offensive and a sign of mistrust because they impair the validity of the saying: "A man is as good as his word." But the formality is essential because what is inherently right must also be posited as right. My will is a rational will; it has validity, and its validity should be recognized by others. At this point, then, my subjectivity and that of others must be set aside and the will must achieve the security, stability, and objectivity which can be attained only through such formalities.

138. *Paragraph 218.*

It seems to be a contradiction that a crime committed in society appears more heinous and yet is punished more leniently. But while it would be impossible for society to leave a crime unpunished, since that would be to posit it as right, still since society is sure of itself, a crime must always be something idiosyncratic in comparison, something unstable and exceptional. The very stability of society gives a crime the status of something purely subjective which seems to be the product rather of natural impulse than of a prudent will. In this light, crime acquires a milder status, and for this reason its punishment too becomes milder. If society is still internally weak, then an example must be made by inflicting punishments, since punishment is itself an example over against the example of crime. But in a society which is internally strong, the commission of crime is something so feeble that its annulment must be commensurable with its feebleness. Harsh punishments, therefore, are not unjust in and by themselves; they are related to contemporary conditions. A criminal code cannot hold good for all time, and crimes are only shows of reality which may draw on themselves a greater or lesser degree of disavowal.

139. *Paragraph 221.*

Since any individual has the right *in judicio stare,* he must also know what the law is or otherwise this privilege would be useless to him. But it is also his *duty* to stand his trial. Under the feudal system, the nobles often refused to stand their trial. They defied the court and alleged that the court was wrong to demand their appearance. Feudal conditions, however, contravened the very idea of a court. Nowadays monarchs have to recognize the jurisdiction of the court in their private affairs, and in free states they commonly lose their case.

140. *Paragraph 222.*

A man may be indignant if a right which he knows he has is refused him because he cannot prove it. But if I have a right, it must at the same time be a right posited in law. I must be able to explain and prove it, and its validity can only be recognized in society if its rightness in principle is also made a posited rightness in law.

141. *Paragraph 224.*

It is straightforward common sense to hold that the publicity of legal proceedings is right and just. A strong reason against such publicity has always been the rank [1] of justices; they are unwilling to sit in public and they regard themselves as a sanctuary of law which laymen are not to enter. But an integral part of justice is the confidence which citizens have in it, and it is this which requires that proceedings shall be public. The right of publicity depends on the fact that (i) the aim of the court is justice, which as universal falls under the cognizance of everyone, and (ii) it is through publicity that the citizens become convinced that the judgement was actually just.

142. *Paragraph 227.*

No grounds can be adduced for supposing that the judge, i.e. the legal expert, should be the only person to establish how the facts lie, for ability to do so depends on general, not on purely legal, education. Determination of the facts of the case depends on empirical details, on depositions about what happened, and on similar perceptual data, or again on facts from which inferences can be drawn about the deed in question and which make it probable or improbable. Here then, it is an assurance which should be required, not truth in the higher sense in which it is always something eternal. Here such assurance is subjective conviction, or conscience, and the problem is: What form should this assurance take in a court of law? The demand, commonly made in German law, that a criminal should confess his guilt, has this to be said for it, that the right of self-consciousness thereby attains a measure of satisfaction; consciousness must chime in with the judge's sentence, and it is only when the criminal has confessed that the judgement loses its alien character so far as he is concerned. But a difficulty arises here, because the criminal may lie, and the interest of justice may be jeopardized. If, on the other hand, the subjective conviction of the judge is to hold good, some hardship is once more involved, because the accused is no longer being treated as a free man. Now the middle term between these extremes is trial by jury, which meets the demand that the declaration of guilt or innocence shall spring from the soul of the accused.[2]

143. *Paragraph 229.*

In civil society, universality is necessity only. When we are dealing with human needs, it is only right as such which is steadfast. But this right—only a restricted sphere—has a bearing simply on the protec-

---

[1] [In the eighteenth century, judicial authority was often still vested in Lords of the Manor.]

[2] [The verdict of his peers is the verdict of the criminal's own soul or reason because reason is universal and so common to them and to him alike. His crime is his subjective defiance of his reason or his inner universality —see Part i, subsection 3 (c).]

tion of property; welfare is something external to
right as such. This welfare, however, is an essential
end in the system of needs. Hence the universal,
which in the first instance is the right only, has to
be extended over the whole field of particularity.
Justice is a big thing in civil society. Given good
laws, a state can flourish, and freedom of property is
a fundamental condition of its prosperity. Still, since
I am inextricably involved in particularity, I have
a right to claim that in this association with other
particulars, my particular welfare too shall be promoted. Regard should be paid to my welfare, to my
particular interest, and this is done through the police and the Corporation.

144. *Paragraph 234.*

Here nothing hard and fast can be laid down and
no absolute lines can be drawn. Everything here is
personal; subjective opinion enters in, and the spirit
of the constitution and the crisis of the day have to
provide precision of detail. In time of war, for instance, many a thing, harmless at other times, has to
be regarded as harmful. As a result of this presence
of accident, of personal arbitrariness, the public authority acquires a measure of odium. When reflective thinking is very highly developed, the public
authority may tend to draw into its orbit everything
it possibly can, for in everything some factor may be
found which might make it dangerous in one of its
bearings. In such circumstances, the public authority
may set to work very pedantically and embarrass
the day-to-day life of people. But however great
this annoyance, no objective line can be drawn here
either.

145. *Paragraph 236.*

The oversight and care exercised by the public authority aims at being a middle term between an individual and the universal possibility, afforded by
society, of attaining individual ends. It has to undertake street-lighting, bridge-building, the pricing
of daily necessaries, and the care of public health. In
this connexion, two main views predominate at the
present time. One asserts that the superintendence
of everything properly belongs to the public authority, the other that the public authority has nothing
at all to settle here because everyone will direct his
conduct according to the needs of others. The individual must have a right to work for his bread as
he pleases, but the public also has a right to insist
that essential tasks shall be properly done. Both
points of view must be satisfied, and freedom of
trade should not be such as to jeopardize the general
good.

146. *Paragraph 238.*

To be sure, the family has to provide bread for its
members, but in civil society the family is something
subordinate and only lays the foundations; its effective range is no longer so comprehensive. Civil society is rather the tremendous power which draws
men into itself and claims from them that they work
for it, owe everything to it, and do everything by its

means. If man is to be a member of civil society in
this sense, he has rights and claims against it just as
he had rights and claims in the family. Civil society
must protect its members and defend their rights,
while its rights impose duties on every one of its
members.

147. *Paragraph 239.*

The line which demarcates the rights of parents
from those of civil society is very hard to draw here.
Parents usually suppose that in the matter of education they have complete freedom and may arrange
everything as they like. The chief opposition to any
form of public education usually comes from parents and it is they who talk and make an outcry
about teachers and schools because they have a fad-
dish dislike of them. None the less, society has a
right to act on principles tested by its experience and
to compel parents to send their children to school, to
have them vaccinated, and so forth. The disputes
that have arisen in France [1] between the advocates
of state supervision and those who demand that education shall be free, i.e. at the option of the parents, are relevant here.

148. *Paragraph 240.*

There was an Athenian law compelling every citizen to give an account of his source of livelihood.[2]
Nowadays we take the view that this is nobody's
business but his own. Of course every individual is
from one point of view independent, but he also
plays his part in the system of civil society, and
while every man has the right to demand subsistence
from it, it must at the same time protect him from
himself. It is not simply starvation which is at issue;
the further end in view is to prevent the formation
of a pauperized rabble. Since civil society is responsible for feeding its members, it also has the right
to press them to provide for their own livelihood.

149. *Paragraph 244.*

The lowest subsistence level, that of a rabble of
paupers, is fixed automatically, but the minimum
varies considerably in different countries. In England, even the very poorest believe that they have
rights; this is different from what satisfies the poor
in other countries. Poverty in itself does not make
men into a rabble; a rabble is created only when
there is joined to poverty a disposition of mind, an
inner indignation against the rich, against society,
against the government, &c. A further consequence
of this attitude is that through their dependence on
chance men become frivolous and idle, like the Ne-
apolitan *lazzaroni* for example. In this way there is
born in the rabble the evil of lacking self-respect
enough to secure subsistence by its own labour and

[1] [Rousseau's *Émile*, published in 1762, is the classic
demand for freedom in education. State supervision was
advocated by La Chalotais in his *Essai d' Éducation na-
tionale*, published a year later. The Jesuits, the chief
educators in France, were expelled in 1764. The revival
of family life also helped to stimulate French interest in
education in the second half of the eighteenth century.]
[2] [Herodotus, *History*, ii. 177. Plutarch: *Life of
Solon.*]

yet at the same time of claiming to receive subsistence as its right. Against nature man can claim no right, but once society is established, poverty immediately takes the form of a wrong done to one class by another. The important question of how poverty is to be abolished is one of the most disturbing problems which agitate modern society.

150. Paragraph 248.

Civil society is thus driven to found colonies. Increase of population alone has this effect, but it is due in particular to the appearance of a number of people who cannot secure the satisfaction of their needs by their own labour once production rises above the requirements of consumers. Sporadic colonization is particularly characteristic of Germany. The emigrants withdraw to America or Russia and remain there with no home ties, and so prove useless to their native land. The second and entirely different type of colonization is the systematic; the state undertakes it, is aware of the proper method of carrying it out and regulates it accordingly. This type was common amongst the ancients, particularly the Greeks. Hard work was not the business of the citizens in Greece, since their energy was directed rather to public affairs. So if the population increased to such an extent that there might be difficulty in feeding it, the young people would be sent away to a new district, sometimes specifically chosen, sometimes left to chance discovery. In modern times, colonists have not been allowed the same rights as those left at home, and the result of this situation has been wars and finally independence, as may be seen in the history of the English and Spanish colonies. Colonial independence proves to be of the greatest advantage to the mother country, just as the emancipation of slaves turns out to the greatest advantage of the owners.

151. Paragraph 255.

The consideration behind the abolition of Corporations in recent times is that the individual should fend for himself. But we may grant this and still hold that corporation membership does not alter a man's obligation to earn his living. Under modern political conditions, the citizens have only a restricted share in the public business of the state, yet it is essential to provide men—ethical entities—with work of a public character over and above their private business. This work of a public character, which the modern state does not always provide, is found in the Corporation. We saw earlier [Addition to Paragraph 184] that in fending for himself a member of civil society is also working for others. But this unconscious compulsion is not enough; it is in the Corporation that it first changes into a known and thoughtful ethical mode of life. Of course Corporations must fall under the higher surveillance of the state, because otherwise they would ossify, build themselves in, and decline into a miserable system of castes. In and by itself, however, a Corporation is not a closed caste; its purpose is rather to bring an isolated trade into the social order and elevate it to a sphere in which it gains strength and respect.

152. Paragraph 258.

The state in and by itself is the ethical whole, the actualization of freedom; and it is an absolute end of reason that freedom should be actual. The state is mind on earth and consciously realizing itself there. In nature, on the other hand, mind actualizes itself only as its own other, as mind asleep. Only when it is present in consciousness, when it knows itself as a really existent object, is it the state. In considering freedom, the starting-point must be not individuality, the single self-consciousness, but only the essence of self-consciousness; for whether man knows it or not, this essence is externally realized as a self-subsistent power in which single individuals are only moments. The march of God in the world, that is what the state is. The basis of the state is the power of reason actualizing itself as will. In considering the Idea of the state, we must not have our eyes on particular states or on particular institutions. Instead we must consider the Idea, this actual God, by itself. On some principle or other, any state may be shown to be bad, this or that defect may be found in it; and yet, at any rate if one of the mature states of our epoch is in question, it has in it the moments essential to the existence of the state. But since it is easier to find defects than to understand the affirmative, we may readily fall into the mistake of looking at isolated aspects of the state and so forgetting its inward organic life. The state is no ideal work of art; it stands on earth and so in the sphere of caprice, chance, and error, and bad behaviour may disfigure it in many respects. But the ugliest of men, or a criminal, or an invalid, or a cripple, is still always a living man. The affirmative, life, subsists despite his defects, and it is this affirmative factor which is our theme here.

153. Paragraph 259.

The state in its actuality is essentially an individual state, and beyond that a particular state. Individuality is to be distinguished from particularity. The former is a moment in the very Idea of the state, while the latter belongs to history. States as such are independent of one another, and therefore their relation to one another can only be an external one, so that there must be a third thing standing above them to bind them together. Now this third thing is the mind which gives itself actuality in world-history and is the absolute judge of states. Several states may form an alliance to be a sort of court with jurisdiction over others, there may be confederations of states, like the Holy Alliance for example, but these are always relative only and restricted, like "perpetual peace." [1] The one and only absolute judge, which makes itself authoritative against the particular and at all times, is the absolute mind which manifests itself in the history of the world as the universal and as the genus there operative.

[1] [See Paragraphs 324, 333, and the Addition thereto.]

154. *Paragraph 260.*

The Idea of the state in modern times has a special character in that the state is the actualization of freedom not in accordance with subjective whim but in accordance with the concept of the will, i.e. in accordance with its universality and divinity. Immature states are those in which the Idea of the state is still veiled and where its particular determinations have not yet attained free self-subsistence. In the states of classical antiquity, universality was present, but particularity had not then been released, given free scope, and brought back to universality, i.e. to the universal end of the whole. The essence of the modern state is that the universal be bound up with the complete freedom of its particular members and with private well-being, that thus the interests of family and civil society must concentrate themselves on the state, although the universal end cannot be advanced without the personal knowledge and will of its particular members, whose own rights must be maintained. Thus the universal must be furthered, but subjectivity on the other hand must attain its full and living development. It is only when both these moments subsist in their strength that the state can be regarded as articulated and genuinely organized.

155. *Paragraph 261.*

In the state everything depends on the unity of universal and particular. In the states of antiquity, the subjective end simply coincided with the state's will. In modern times, however, we make claims for private judgement, private willing, and private conscience. The ancients had none of these in the modern sense; the ultimate thing with them was the will of the state. Whereas under the despots of Asia the individual had no inner life and no justification in himself, in the modern world man insists on respect being paid to his inner life. The conjunction of duty and right has a twofold aspect: what the state demands from us as a duty is *eo ipso* our right as individuals, since the state [1] is nothing but the articulation of the concept of freedom. The determinations of the individual will are given an objective embodiment through the state and thereby they attain their truth and their actualization for the first time. The state is the one and only prerequisite of the attainment of particular ends and welfare.

156. *Paragraph 262.*

In Plato's state, subjective freedom does not count, because people have their occupations assigned to them by the Guardians. In many oriental states, this assignment is determined by birth. But subjective freedom, which must be respected, demands that individuals should have free choice in this matter.

157. *Paragraph 263.*

The state, as mind, sunders itself into the particular determinations of its concept, of its mode of being. We might use here an illustration drawn from nature. The nervous system is the sensitive system

[1] [Reading *er*, with Lasson.]

proper; it is the abstract moment, the moment of being by oneself and so of having identity with oneself. But analysis of sensation reveals that it has two aspects and these are distinct in such a way that each of them seems to be a whole system by itself. The first is feeling in the abstract, keeping oneself self-enclosed, the dull movement which goes on internally, reproduction, internal self-nutrition, growth, and digestion. The second moment is that this self-related existence has over against it the moment of difference, a movement outwards. This is irritability, sensation moving outwards. This constitutes a system of its own, and there are some of the lower types of animals which have developed this system alone, while they lack the soul-charged unity of inner sensation. If we compare these natural features with those of mind, then the family must be paralleled with sensibility and civil society with irritability. Now the third is the state, the nervous system as a whole, something inwardly organized; but this lives only in so far as both moments (in this case family and civil society) are developed within it. The laws regulating family and civil society are the institutions of the rational order which glimmers in them. But the ground and final truth of these institutions is mind, their universal end and known objective. The family too is ethical, only its end is not known as such, while it is the separation between one man and another which makes civil society what it is.

158. *Paragraph 265.*

As was remarked earlier on, [2] the sanctity of marriage and the institutions in which civil society is an appearance of ethical life constitute the stability of the whole, i.e. stability is secured when universal affairs are the affairs of each member in his particular capacity. What is of the utmost importance is that the law of reason should be shot through and through by the law of particular freedom, and that my particular end should become identified with the universal end, or otherwise the state is left in the air. The state is actual only when its members have a feeling of their own self-hood and it is stable only when public and private ends are identical. It has often been said that the end of the state is the happiness of the citizens. That is perfectly true. If all is not well with them, if their subjective aims are not satisfied, if they do not find that the state as such is the means to their satisfaction, then the footing of the state itself is insecure.

159. *Paragraph 267.*

The unity of the freedom which knows and wills itself is present first of all as necessity. Here substance is present as the subjective existence of individuals. Necessity's other mode of being, however, is the organism, i.e. mind is a process internal to itself, it articulates itself within, posits differences in itself, and thereby completes the cycle of its life.

160. *Paragraph 268.*

Immature minds delight in argumentation and

[2] [The reference is probably to Paragraph 255.]

fault-finding, because it is easy enough to find fault, though hard to see the good and its inner necessity. The learner always begins by finding fault, but the scholar sees the positive merit in everything. In religion, this or that is quickly dismissed as superstitious, but it is infinitely harder to apprehend the truth underlying the superstition. Hence men's apparent sentiment towards the state is to be distinguished from what they really will; inwardly they really will the thing, but they cling to details and take delight in the vanity of pretending to know better. We are confident that the state must subsist and that in it alone can particular interests be secured. But habit blinds us to that on which our whole existence depends. When we walk the streets at night in safety, it does not strike us that this might be otherwise. This habit of feeling safe has become second nature, and we do not reflect on just how this is due solely to the working of special institutions. Commonplace thinking often has the impression that force holds the state together, but in fact its only bond is the fundamental sense of order which everybody possesses.

161. *Paragraph 269.*

The state is an organism, i.e. the development of the Idea to the articulation of its differences. Thus these different sides of the state are its various powers with their functions and spheres of action, by means of which the universal continually engenders itself in a necessary way; in this process it maintains its identity since it is presupposed even in its own production. This organism is the constitution of the state; it is produced perpetually by the state, while it is through it that the state maintains itself. If the state and its constitution fall apart, if the various members of the organism free themselves, then the unity produced by the constitution is no longer an accomplished fact. This tallies with the fable[1] about the belly and the other members. The nature of an organism is such that unless each of its parts is brought into identity with the others, unless each of them is prevented from achieving autonomy, the whole must perish. By listing attributes, axioms, &c., no progress can be made in assessing the nature of the state; it must be apprehended as an organism. One might as well try to understand the nature of God by listing his attributes, while the truth is that we must intuit God's life in that life itself.

162. *Paragraph 270.*

The state is actual, and its actuality consists in this, that the interest of the whole is realized in and through particular ends. Actuality is always the unity of universal and particular, the universal dismembered in the particulars which seem to be self-subsistent, although they really are upheld and contained only in the whole. Where this unity is not present, a thing is not actual even though it may have acquired existence. A bad state is one which

---

[1] [The fable recounted by Menenius Agrippa to dissuade the Roman *plebs* from secession. Livy, ii. 32. Shakespeare, *Coriolanus*, Act I, Sc. i.]

merely exists; a sick body exists too, but it has no genuine reality. A hand which is cut off still looks like a hand, and it exists, but without being actual.[2] Genuine actuality is necessity; what is actual is inherently necessary. Necessity consists in this, that the whole is sundered into the differences of the concept and that this divided whole yields a fixed and permanent determinacy, though one which is not fossilized but perpetually recreates itself in its dissolution.

To a mature state thought and consciousness essentially belong. Therefore the state knows what it wills and knows it as something thought. Now since knowing has its seat in the state, the seat of science must be there too and not in the church. Despite this, it is often said nowadays that the state must grow out of religion. The state is mind fully mature and it exhibits its moments in the daylight of consciousness. Now the fact that what is hidden in the Idea steps forth into objective existence gives the state the appearance of something finite, and so the state reveals itself as a domain of worldliness, while religion displays itself as a domain of the infinite. If this be so, the state seems to be the subordinate, and since what is finite cannot stand on its own feet, the state is therefore said to need the church as its basis. As finite, it lacks justification, and it is only through religion that it can become sacrosanct and pertain to the infinite. This handling of the matter, however, is supremely one-sided. Of course the state is essentially worldly and finite; it has particular ends and particular powers; but its worldly character is only one of its aspects, and it is only to an unintelligent superficial glance that it is finite and nothing more. For the state has a life-giving soul, and the soul which animates it is subjectivity, which creates differences and yet at the same time holds them together in unity. In the realm of religion too there are distinctions and limitations. God, it is said, is triune; thus there are three persons whose unity alone is Spirit (*Geist*). Therefore to apprehend the nature of God concretely is to apprehend it through distinctions alone. Hence in the kingdom of God there are limitations, just as there are in the world, and to hold that mind (*Geist*) on earth, i.e. the state, is only a finite mind, is a one-sided view, since there is nothing irrational about actuality. Of course a bad state is worldly and finite and nothing else, but the rational state is inherently infinite.

Secondly, it is averred that the state must derive its justification from religion. In religion, the Idea is mind in the inwardness of the heart, but it is this same Idea which gives itself a worldly form as the state and fashions for itself an embodiment and an actuality in knowing and willing. Now if you say that the state must be grounded on religion, you may mean that it should rest on rationality and arise out of it; but your statement may also be misunderstood to mean that men are most adroitly schooled to obedience if their minds are shackled

---

[2] [The illustration is from Aristotle's *Politics* 1253[a] 19 ff.]

by a slavish religion. (The Christian religion, however, is the religion of freedom, though it must be admitted that this religion may become changed in character and perverted from freedom to bondage when it is infected with superstition.) Now if you mean that men must have religion so that their minds, already shackled, may the more easily be oppressed by the state, then the purport of your statement is bad. But if you mean that men ought to respect the state, this whole whose limbs they are, then of course the best means of effecting this is to give them philosophical insight into the essence of the state, though, in default of that, a religious frame of mind may lead to the same result. For this reason, the state may have need of religion and faith. But the state remains essentially distinct from religion, since whatever it claims, it claims in the form of a legal duty, and it is a matter of indifference to it in what spirit that duty is performed. The field of religion, on the other hand, is the inner life, and just as the state would jeopardize the right of that life if, like religion, it made claims on it, so also when the church acts like a state and imposes penalties, it degenerates into a religion of tyranny.

A third difference which is connected with the foregoing is that the content of religion is and remains veiled, and consequently religion's place is in the field of the heart, feeling, and representative thinking. In this field everything has the form of *subjectivity*. The state, on the other hand, actualizes itself and gives its specific institutions a stable, *objective,* existence. Now if religious feeling wished to assert itself in the state in the same way as it is wont to do in its own field, it would overturn the organization of the state, because the different organs of the state have latitude to pursue their several distinct paths, while in religion everything is always referred back to the whole. If this whole, then, wished to engulf all the concerns of the state, this would be tantamount to fanaticism; the wish to have the whole in every particular could be fulfilled only by the destruction of the particular, and fanaticism is just the refusal to give scope to particular differences. Hence to say: "To the pious man no law is given" is nothing but an expression of this same fanaticism. Once piety usurps the place of the state, it cannot tolerate the determinate but simply shatters it. It is quite consistent with this if piety leaves decisions to conscience, to the inner life, and is not governed by reasons. This inner life does not develop into reasoned argument or give an account of itself. Hence if piety is to pass for the actuality of the state, all laws are cast to the winds and subjective feeling is the legislator. This feeling may be pure caprice, and whether it is or not can only be learnt from its actions. But by becoming actions and precepts, its actions assume the guise of laws, and this is just the very opposite of the subjective feeling with which we started. This feeling has God for its object, and we might make him the determinant of everything. But God is the universal Idea and this feeling can regard him only as the indeterminate,

which is too immature to determine what is existent in the state in a developed form. It is precisely the fact that everything in the state is fixed and secure which is the bulwark against caprice and dogmatic opinion. Religion as such, then, ought not to be the governor.

163. *Paragraph 271.*

Just as irritability in the living organism is itself from one point of view something inward, something pertaining to the organism as such, so here again the outward reference is an inward tendency. The inner side of the state as such is the civil power, while its outward tendency is the military power, although this has a fixed place inside the state itself. Now to have both these powers in equilibrium constitutes an important factor in the spirit of the state. Sometimes the civil power is wholly effaced and rests entirely on the military power, as was the case, for instance, in the time of the Roman Emperors and the Praetorians.[1] At other times, nowadays for example, the military power is a mere by-product of the civil power once all the citizens are conscriptable.

164. *Paragraph 272.*

We should desire to have in the state nothing except what is an expression of rationality. The state is the world which mind has made for itself; its march, therefore, is on lines that are fixed and absolute. How often we talk of the wisdom of God in nature! But we are not to assume for that reason that the physical world of nature is a loftier thing than the world of mind. As high as mind stands above nature, so high does the state stand above physical life. Man must therefore venerate the state as a secular deity,[2] and observe that if it is difficult to comprehend nature, it is infinitely harder to understand the state. It is a fact of the highest importance that nowadays we have gained a clear-cut intuition into the state in general and have been so much engaged in discussing and making constitutions. But by getting so far we have not yet settled everything. In addition, it is necessary to bring to bear on a rational topic the reason underlying intuition, to know what the essence of the matter is and to realize that the obvious is not always the essential.

The powers of the state, then, must certainly be distinguished, but each of them must build itself inwardly into a whole and contain in itself the other moments. When we speak of the distinct activities of these powers, we must not slip into the monstrous error of so interpreting their distinction as to suppose that each power should subsist independently in abstraction from the others. The truth is that the

---

[1] [Under the reforms instituted by Diocletian and Constantine, the Praetorian Prefects, who were originally exclusively military officials, had supreme authority, under the Emperor, in both civil and military affairs. See e.g. Gibbon, chap. xvii—perhaps Hegel's source.]

[2] [*Irdisch-Göttliches*. Hegel here follows Kant who, e.g. at the end of his essay on Theory and Practice, refers to nation states as *Erden-Götter*.]

powers are to be distinguished only as moments of the concept. If instead they subsist independently in abstraction from one another, then it is as clear as day that two independent units cannot constitute a unity but must of course give rise to strife, whereby either the whole is destroyed or else unity is restored by force. Thus in the French Revolution, the legislative power sometimes engulfed the so-called "executive," the executive sometimes engulfed the legislative, and in such a case it must be stupid to formulate e.g. the moral demand for harmony.

Leave the thing to the heart if you like and be saved all trouble; but even if ethical feeling is indispensable, it has no right to determine the powers of the state by reference to itself alone. The vital point, then, is that since the fixed characters of the powers are implicitly the whole, so also all the powers as existents constitute the concept as a whole. Mention is usually made of three powers, the legislative, the executive, and the judiciary; of these the first corresponds to universality and the second to particularity, but the judiciary is not the third moment of the concept, since the individuality intrinsic to the concept lies outside these spheres.

165. *Paragraph 273.*

The principle of the modern world is freedom of subjectivity, the principle that all the essential factors present in the intellectual whole are now coming into their right in the course of their development. Starting from this point of view, we can hardly raise the idle question: Which is the better form of government, monarchy or democracy? We may only say that all constitutional forms are one-sided unless they can sustain in themselves the principle of free subjectivity and know how to correspond with a matured rationality.

166. *Paragraph 274.*

The state in its constitution must permeate all relationships within the state. Napoleon, for instance, wished to give the Spaniards a constitution *a priori*,[1] but the project turned out badly enough. A constitution is not just something manufactured; it is the work of centuries, it is the Idea, the consciousness of rationality so far as that consciousness is developed in a particular nation. No constitution, therefore, is just the creation of its subjects. What Napoleon gave to the Spaniards was more rational than what they had before, and yet they recoiled from it as from something alien, because they were not yet educated up to its level. A nation's constitution must embody its feeling for its rights and its position, otherwise there may be a constitution there in an external way, but it is meaningless and valueless. Isolated individuals may often feel the need and the

longing for a better constitution, but it is quite another thing, and one that does not arise till later, for the mass of the people to be animated by such an idea. The principle of morality, of the inner life of Socrates, was a necessary product of his age, but time was required before it could become part and parcel of the self-consciousness of everyone.

167. *Paragraph 275.*

We begin with the power of the crown, i.e. with the moment of individuality, since this includes the state's three moments as a totality in itself. The ego, that is to say, is at once the most individual thing and the most universal. Prima facie, individuality occurs in nature too, but reality, the opposite of ideality, and reciprocal externality are not the same as self-enclosed existence. On the contrary, in nature the various individual things subsist alongside one another. In mind, on the other hand, variety exists only as something ideal and as a unity. The state, then, as something mental, is the exhibition of all its moments, but individuality is at the same time the bearer of its soul and its life-giving principle, i.e. the sovereignty which contains all differences in itself.

168. *Paragraph 276.*

Much the same thing as this ideality of the moments in the state occurs with life in the physical organism. Life is present in every cell. There is only one life in all the cells and nothing withstands it. Separated from that life, every cell dies. This is the same as the ideality of every single class, power, and Corporation as soon as they have the impulse to subsist and be independent. It is with them as it is with the belly in the organism. It, too, asserts its independence, but at the same time its independence is set aside and it is sacrificed and absorbed into the whole.

169. *Paragraph 277.*

The business of the state is in the hands of individuals. But their authority to conduct its affairs is based not on their birth but on their objective qualities. Ability, skill, character, all belong to a man in his *particular* capacity. He must be educated and be trained to a particular task. Hence an office may not be saleable or hereditary. In France, seats in parliament were formerly saleable, and in the English army commissions up to a certain rank are saleable to this day.[2] This saleability of office, however, was or is still connected with the medieval constitution of certain states, and such constitutions are nowadays gradually disappearing.

170. *Paragraph 279.*

In the organization of the state—which here means in constitutional monarchy—we must have nothing before our minds except the inherent necessity of the Idea. All other points of view must vanish. The state must be treated as a great architectonic struc-

[1] [When he expelled the Bourbons from Spain and put Joseph Bonaparte on the throne under the Constitution of Bayonne in 1808. With the breakdown of the Napoleonic régime in 1812–13, the Bourbons were restored together with the old constitution. A liberal document, the Constitution of Cadiz, was drawn up in 1812, but it remained a dead letter. Note that Hegel regards a more *liberal* constitution as a more rational one.]

[2] [In Hegel's day, all officers' commissions from an ensign's to a lieutenant-colonel's were on sale, but there were restrictions on both purchaser and price.]

ture, as a hieroglyph of the reason which reveals itself in actuality. Everything to do with mere utility, externality, and so forth, must be eliminated from the philosophical treatment of the subject. Now our ordinary ideas can quite well grasp the conception of the state as a self-determining and completely sovereign will, as final decision. What is more difficult is to apprehend this "I will" as a person. To do so is not to say that the monarch may act capriciously. As a matter of fact, he is bound by the concrete decisions of his counsellors, and if the constitution is stable, he has often no more to do than sign his name. But this name is important. It is the last word beyond which it is impossible to go. It might be said that an organic, articulated, constitution was present even in the beautiful democracy of Athens, and yet we cannot help noticing that the Greeks derived their final decisions from the observation of quite external phenomena such as oracles, the entrails of sacrificial animals, and the flight of birds. They treated nature as a power which in those ways revealed and expressed what was good for men. At that time, self-consciousness had not yet advanced to the abstraction of subjectivity, not even so far as to understand that, when a decision is to be made, an "I will" must be pronounced by man himself. This "I will" constitutes the great difference between the ancient world and the modern, and in the great edifice of the state it must therefore have its appropriate objective existence. Unfortunately, however, this requirement is regarded as only external and optional.

171. *Paragraph 280.*

It is often alleged against monarchy that it makes the welfare of the state dependent on chance, for, it is urged, the monarch may be ill-educated, he may perhaps be unworthy of the highest position in the state, and it is senseless that such a state of affairs should exist because it is supposed to be rational. But all this rests on a presupposition which is nugatory, namely that everything depends on the monarch's *particular* character. In a completely organized state, it is only a question of the culminating point of formal decision (and a natural bulwark against passion. It is wrong therefore to demand objective qualities in a monarch) ; [1] he has only to say "yes" and dot the "i," because the throne should be such that the significant thing in its holder is not his particular make-up. (Monarchy in this sense is rational because it corresponds with the concept, but since this is hard to grasp, we often fail to notice the rationality of monarchy. Monarchy must be inherently stable and) whatever else the monarch may have in addition to this power of final decision is part and parcel of his private character and should be of no consequence. Of course there may be circumstances in which it is this private character alone which has prominence, but in that event the state is either not fully developed, or else is badly con-

structed. In a well-organized monarchy, the objective aspect belongs to law alone, and the monarch's part is merely to set to the law the subjective "I will."

172. *Paragraph 281.*

If we are to grasp the Idea of the monarch, we cannot be content with saying that God has appointed kings to rule over us, since God has made everything, even the worst of things. The point of view of utility does not get us very far either, and it is always possible to point out counterbalancing disadvantages. Still less does it help to regard monarchy as a *positive* right. That I should hold property is necessary, but my holding of this particular property is contingent; and in the same way, the right that there must be one man at the head of affairs seems contingent too if it is treated as abstract and as posited. This right, however, is inevitably present both as a felt want and as a requirement of the situation. Monarchs are not exactly distinguished for bodily prowess or intellectual gifts, and yet millions submit to their rule. Now to say that men allow themselves to be ruled counter to their own interests, ends, and intentions is preposterous. Men are not so stupid. It is their need, it is the inner might of the Idea, which, even against what they appear to think, constrains them to obedience and keeps them in that relation.

If then the monarch comes on the scene as the head and a part of the constitution, we are compelled to hold that there is no constitutional identity between a conquered people and its prince. A rebellion in a province conquered in war is a different thing from a rising in a well-organized state. It is not against their prince that the conquered are in rebellion, and they are committing no crime against the state, because their connexion with their master is not a connexion within the Idea or one within the inner necessity of the constitution. In such a case, there is only a contract, no political tie. *Je ne suis pas votre prince, je suis votre maître,* Napoleon retorted to the envoys at Erfurt.[2]

173. *Paragraph 282.*

Pardon is the remission of punishment, but it does not annul the law (*Recht*). On the contrary, the law stands and the pardoned man remains a criminal as before. Pardon does not mean that he has not committed a crime. This annulment of punishment may take place through religion, since something done may by spirit (*Geist*) be made undone in spirit. But the power to accomplish this on earth resides in the king's majesty alone and must belong solely to his self-determined decision.

174. *Paragraph 290.*

The point of special importance in the executive is the division of functions. The executive is concerned with the transition from the universal to the partic-

---

[1] [The passages in parentheses are translated from Gans's third edition; they did not appear in the first.]

[2] [When Napoleon met Tsar Alexander at Erfurt in 1808, he was visited by representatives of many German states. This is one of the many stories of his rudeness on that occasion.]

ular and the individual, and its functions must be divided in accordance with the differences between its branches. The difficulty, however, is that these different branches meet again at both the top and the bottom. The police and the judiciary, for instance, move at right angles to one another, but in each particular case they coincide again. The usual expedient adopted to meet this difficulty is to appoint a Chancellor, a Prime Minister, or a Président du Conseil des Ministres to unify control at the top. But the result of this is that once more everything may have its source in the Minister's power, and the business of the state is, as we say, centralized. This entails the maximum of simplification, speed, and efficiency in meeting state requirements. A system of this kind was introduced by the French revolutionaries, elaborated by Napoleon, and still exists in France to-day. On the other hand, France lacks Corporations and local government, i.e. associations wherein particular and universal interests meet. It is true that these associations won too great a measure of self-subsistence in the Middle Ages, when they were states within states and obstinately persisted in behaving like independent corporate bodies. But while that should not be allowed to happen, we may none the less affirm that the proper strength of the state lies in these associations. In them the executive meets with legitimate interests which it must respect, and since the administration cannot be other than helpful to such interests, though it must also supervise them, the individual finds protection in the exercise of his rights and so links his private interest with the maintenance of the whole. For some time past organizations have been framed with a view to controlling these particular spheres from above,[1] and effort has chiefly been expended on organizations of that type, while the lower classes, the mass of the population, have been left more or less unorganized. And yet it is of the utmost importance that the masses should be organized, because only so do they become mighty and powerful. Otherwise they are nothing but a heap, an aggregate of atomic units. Only when the particular associations are organized members of the state are they possessed of legitimate power.

175. *Paragraph 297.*

The middle class, to which civil servants belong, is politically conscious and the one in which education is most prominent. For this reason it is also the pillar of the state so far as honesty and intelligence are concerned. A state without a middle class must therefore remain on a low level. Russia, for instance, has a mass of serfs on the one hand and a mass of rulers on the other. It is a prime concern of the state that a middle class should be developed, but this can be done only if the state is an organic unity like the one described here, i.e. it can be done only by giving authority to spheres of particular interests, which are relatively independent, and by appointing

[1] [Hegel is thinking of his own experience in Bavaria in 1807. See *Briefe von und an Hegel*, vol. i, p. 130. (Lasson).]

an army of officials whose personal arbitrariness is broken against such authorized bodies. Action in accordance with everyone's rights, and the habit of such action, is a consequence of the counterpoise to officialdom which independent and self-subsistent bodies create.

176. *Paragraph 298.*

The constitution must in and by itself be the fixed and recognized ground on which the legislature stands, and for this reason it must not first be constructed. Thus the constitution *is,* but just as essentially it *becomes,* i.e. it advances and matures. This advance is an alteration which is imperceptible and which lacks the form of alteration. For example, the wealth of the German princes and their families began by being private property but then without any struggle or opposition it was converted into crown lands, i.e. into public property. This came about because the princes felt the need of integrating their possessions and demanded property guarantees from their country and Estates; and these guarantees were intertwined with such a mode of stabilizing property that it ceased to be at the sole disposal of the princes. An analogous case is that [in the Holy Roman Empire] the Emperor was formerly a judge and travelled the Empire on circuit, and then, owing to the purely superficial results of cultural progress, external reasons made it necessary for him to delegate more and more of his judicial functions to others, with the result that the judicial power was transferred from the person of the monarch to groups of judges. Hence the advance from one state of affairs to another is tranquil in appearance and unnoticed. In this way a constitution changes over a long period of time into something quite different from what it was originally.

177. *Paragraph 299.*

The two sides of the constitution bear respectively on the rights and the services of individuals. Services are now almost entirely reduced to money payments, and military service is now almost the only personal one exacted. In the past, far more claims were made directly on a man's own person, and he used to be called upon for work according to his ability. In our day, the state purchases what it requires. This may at first sight seem an abstract, heartless, and dead state of affairs, and for the state to be satisfied with indirect services may also look like decadence in the state. But the principle of the modern state requires that the whole of an individual's activity shall be mediated through his will. By means of money, however, the justice of equality can be achieved much more efficiently. Otherwise, if assessment depended on concrete ability, a talented man would be more heavily taxed than an untalented one. But nowadays respect for subjective freedom is publicly recognized precisely in the fact that the state lays hold of a man only by that which is capable of being held.[2]

178. *Paragraph 300.*

The proposal to exclude members of the executive

[2] [i.e. external goods. See Paragraph 299.]

from legislative bodies, as for instance the Constituent Assembly[1] did, is a consequence of false views
of the state. In England, ministers must be members
of parliament, and this is right, because executive
officers should be linked with and not opposed to the
legislature. The idea[2] of the so-called "independence
of powers" contains the fundamental error of supposing that the powers, though independent, are to
check one another. This independence, however, destroys the unity of the state, and unity is the chief
of all desiderata.

179. *Paragraph 301.*

The attitude of the executive to the Estates should
not be essentially hostile, and a belief in the necessity of such hostility is a sad mistake. The executive
is not a party standing over against another party
in such a way that each has continually to steal a
march on the other and wrest something from the
other. If such a situation arises in the state, that is a
misfortune, but it cannot be called health. The taxes
voted by the Estates, moreover, are not to be regarded as a present given to the state. On the contrary,
they are voted in the best interests of the voters themselves. The real significance of the Estates lies in the
fact that it is through them that the state enters the
subjective consciousness of the people and that the
people begins to participate in the state.

180. *Paragraph 302.*

The constitution is essentially a system of mediation. In despotisms where there are only rulers and
people, the people is effective, if at all, only as a
mass destructive of the organization of the state.
When the multitude enters the state as one of its
organs, it achieves its interests by legal and orderly
means. But if these means are lacking, the voice of
the masses is always for violence. Hence, in despotic
states, the despot always indulges the mob and keeps
his wrath for his entourage. For the same reason too
the mob in such states pays only a few taxes. Taxes
rise in a constitutionally governed state simply owing to the people's own consciousness. In no country
are so many taxes paid as in England.

181. *Paragraph 306.*

This class has a volition of a more independent
character. On the whole, the class of landed property
owners is divided into an educated section and a section of farmers. But over against both of these sorts
of people there stands the business class, which is dependent on needs and concentrated on their satisfaction, and the civil servant class, which is essentially
dependent on the state. The security and stability of
the agricultural class may be still further increased
by the institution of primogeniture, though this institution is desirable only from the point of view of
politics, since it entails a sacrifice for the political end
of giving the eldest son a life of independence. Primogeniture is grounded on the fact that the state
should be able to reckon not on the bare possibility

of political inclinations, but on something necessary.
Now an inclination for politics is of course not bound
up with wealth, but there is a relatively necessary
connexion between the two, because a man with independent means is not hemmed in by external circumstances and so there is nothing to prevent him
from entering politics and working for the state.
Where political institutions are lacking, however,
the foundation and encouragement of primogeniture
is nothing but a chain on the freedom of private
rights, and either political meaning must be given to
it, or else it will in due course disappear.

182. *Paragraph 309.*

The introduction of representation implies that
consent is to be given not directly by all but only
by plenipotentiaries, since under a representative
system the individual, *qua* infinite person, no longer
comes into the picture. Representation is grounded
on trust, but trusting another is something different
from giving my vote myself in my own personal capacity. Hence majority voting runs counter to the
principle that I should be personally present in anything which is to be obligatory on me. We have confidence in a man when we take him to be a man of
discretion who will manage our affairs conscientious-
ly and to the best of his knowledge, just as if they
were his own. Thus the principle of the individual
subjective will disappears, since confidence is given
to a thing, to a man's principles, or his demeanour
or his conduct or his concrete mentality generally.
The important thing, then, is that a member of the
Estates shall have a character, insight, and will adequate to his task of concentrating on public business. In other words there is no question of an individual's talking as an abstract single person. The
point is rather that his interests are made good in an
assembly whose business is with the general interest.
The electors require a guarantee that their deputy
will further and secure this general interest.

183. *Paragraph 315.*

Estates Assemblies, open to the public, are a great
spectacle and an excellent education for the citizens,
and it is from them that the people learns best how
to recognize the true character of its interests. The
idea usually dominant is that everyone knows from
the start what is best for the state and that the Assembly debate is a mere discussion of this knowledge. In fact, however, the precise contrary is the
truth. It is here that there first begin to develop the
virtues, abilities, dexterities, which have to serve as
examples to the public. Of course such debates are
irksome to ministers, who have to equip themselves
with wit and eloquence to meet the criticisms there
directed against them. None the less, publicity here
is the chief means of educating the public in national affairs. A nation which has such public sittings is
far more vitally related to the state than one which
has no Estates Assembly or one which meets in private. It is only because their every step is made
known publicly in this way that the two Houses keep
pace with the advance of public opinion, and it then

---

[1] [In France.]
[2] [Montesquieu's. See *The Spirit of Laws*, xi. 6.]

becomes clear that a man's castle building at his fireside with his wife and his friends is one thing, while what happens in a great Assembly, where one shrewd idea devours another, is something quite different.

184. Paragraph 316.

Public opinion is the unorganized way in which a people's opinions and wishes are made known. What is actually made authoritative in the state must operate in an organized manner as the parts of the constitution do. But at all times public opinion has been a great power and it is particularly so in our day when the principle of subjective freedom has such importance and significance. What is to be authoritative nowadays derives its authority, not at all from force, only to a small extent from habit and custom, really from insight and argument.

185. Paragraph 317.

The principle of the modern world requires that what anyone is to recognize shall reveal itself to him as something entitled to recognition. Apart from that, however, everyone wishes to have some share in discussion and deliberation. Once he has had his say and so his share of responsibility, his subjectivity has been satisfied and he puts up with a lot. In France freedom of speech has turned out far less dangerous than enforced silence, because with the latter the fear is that men bottle up their objections to a thing, whereas argument gives them an outlet and a measure of satisfaction, and this is in addition a means whereby the thing can be pushed ahead more easily.

186. Paragraph 318.

Public opinion contains all kinds of falsity and truth, but it takes a great man to find the truth in it. The great man of the age is the one who can put into words the will of his age, tell his age what its will is, and accomplish it.[1] What he does is the heart and the essence of his age, he actualizes his age. The man who lacks sense enough to despise public opinion expressed in gossip will never do anything great.

187. Paragraph 320.

Subjectivity has been treated once already [Paragraphs 279 ff.] as the apex of the state, as the crown. Its other aspect is its arbitrary manifestation in public opinion, its most external mode of appearance. The subjectivity of the monarch is inherently abstract, but it should be something concrete and so be the ideality which diffuses itself over the whole state. The state at peace is that in which all branches of civil life subsist, but they possess their subsistence outside and alongside one another as something which issues from the Idea of the whole. The fact that it so issues must also come into appearance as the ideality of the whole.

188. Paragraph 324.

In peace civil life continually expands; all its departments wall themselves in, and in the long run men stagnate. Their idiosyncrasies become continual-

ly more fixed and ossified. But for health the unity of the body is required, and if its parts harden themselves into exclusiveness, that is death. Perpetual peace is often advocated as an ideal towards which humanity should strive. With that end in view, Kant proposed a league of monarchs to adjust differences between states, and the Holy Alliance[2] was meant to be a league of much the same kind. But the state is an individual, and individuality essentially implies negation. Hence even if a number of states make themselves into a family, this group as an individual must engender an opposite and create an enemy. As a result of war, nations are strengthened, but peoples involved in civil strife also acquire peace at home through making wars abroad. To be sure, war produces insecurity of property, but this insecurity of things is nothing but their transience—which is inevitable. We hear plenty of sermons from the pulpit about the insecurity, vanity, and instability of temporal things, but everyone thinks, however much he is moved by what he hears, that he at least will be able to retain his own. But if this insecurity now comes on the scene in the form of hussars with shining sabres and they actualize in real earnest what the preachers have said, then the moving and edifying discourses which foretold all these events turn into curses against the invader. Be that as it may, the fact remains that wars occur when the necessity of the case requires. The seeds burgeon once more, and harangues are silenced by the solemn cycles of history.

189. Paragraph 327.

The military class is that universal class which is charged with the defence of the state, and its duty is to make real the ideality implicit within itself, i.e. to sacrifice itself. Courage to be sure is multiform. The mettle of an animal or a brigand, courage for the sake of honour, the courage of a knight, these are not true forms of courage. The true courage of civilized nations is readiness for sacrifice in the service of the state, so that the individual counts as only one amongst many. The important thing here is not personal mettle but aligning oneself with the universal. In India five hundred men conquered twenty thousand who were not cowards, but who only lacked this disposition to work in close co-operation with others.[3]

190. Paragraph 329.

In almost all European countries the individual head of the state is the monarch, and foreign affairs are his business. Where the Estates have constitutional powers, the question may arise whether they

---

[1] [Reading Wer, was seine Zeit will, ausspricht, ihr sagt und vollbringt, with Ziegler in Kant-Studien, 1909.]

[2] [1815, between Russia, Austria, and Prussia; formed on the initiative of Tsar Alexander in the professed endeavour "to regulate future conduct by the principles of the Gospel."]

[3] [In 1751 Clive "led five hundred men to Arcot . . . and there held a crumbling fortress against ten thousand Indians with a stiffening of French troops." At Plassey "he brought 3,000 men into action of whom 900 only were Europeans, against a force of 40,000 infantry and 15,000 cavalry and . . . routed his opponents" (Fisher, History of Europe, London, 1936, p. 764).]

should not decide on war and peace, and in any case they have their influence on the question, particularly in connexion with ways and means. In England, for example, no unpopular war can be waged. If, however, it is supposed that monarchs and cabinets are more subject to passion than parliaments are, and if for this reason an attempt is made to juggle the decision on war and peace into the hands of the latter, then we must point out that whole peoples may often be a prey to excitement or be carried away by passion to a greater extent than their leaders. In England the whole nation has frequently pressed for war and to a certain extent compelled ministers to wage it. The popularity of Pitt was due to his knowing how to fall in with what the people wanted at the time.[1] It was only later[2] that the people cooled down and so began to reflect that the war was useless and unnecessary and had been undertaken without counting the cost. Moreover, a state stands in relation not with one other state only, but with many. And the complexities of their relations become so delicate that they can be handled only by the head of the state.

191. *Paragraph 330.*

States are not private persons but completely autonomous totalities in themselves, and so the relation between them differs from a moral relation and a relation involving private rights. Attempts have often been made to regard the state as a person with the rights of persons and as a moral entity. But the position with private persons is that they are under the jurisdiction of a court which gives effect to what is right in principle. Now a relation between states ought also to be right in principle, but in mundane affairs a principle ought also to have power. Now

[1] [1793.]
[2] [1797.]

since there is no power in existence which decides in face of the state what is right in principle and actualizes this decision, it follows that so far as international relations are concerned we can never get beyond an "ought." The relation between states is a relation between autonomous entities which make mutual stipulations but which at the same time are superior to these stipulations.

192. *Paragraph 331.*

When Napoleon said before the Peace of Campoformio[3] that "the French Republic needs recognition as little as the sun requires it," what his words implied was simply the thing's *strength* which carries with it, without any verbal expression, the guarantee of recognition.

193. *Paragraph 338.*

Modern wars are therefore humanely waged, and person is not set over against person in hatred. At most, personal enmities appear in the vanguard, but in the main body of the army hostility is something vague and gives place to each side's respect for the duty of the other.

194. *Paragraph 339.*

The European peoples form a family in accordance with the universal principle underlying their legal codes, their customs, and their civilization. This principle has modified their international conduct accordingly in a state of affairs [i.e. war] otherwise dominated by the mutual infliction of evils. The relations of state to state are uncertain, and there is no Praetor available to adjust them. The only higher judge is the universal absolute mind, the world mind.

[3] [1797, at the close of Napoleon's first Italian campaign.]

CONTENTS: PHILOSOPHY OF HISTORY

INTRODUCTION

The subject of this course of lectures is the philosophical history of the world. And by this must be understood, not a collection of general observations respecting it, suggested by the study of its records, and proposed to be illustrated by its facts, but universal history itself.[1] To gain a clear idea, at the outset, of the nature of our task, it seems necessary to begin with an examination of the other methods of treating history. The various methods may be ranged under three heads:

    I. Original history.
    II. Reflective history.
    III. Philosophical history.

I.

Of the first kind, the mention of one or two distinguished names will furnish a definite type. To this category belong Herodotus, Thucydides, and other historians of the same order, whose descriptions are for the most part limited to deeds, events, and states of society, which they had before their eyes, and whose spirit they shared. They simply transferred what was passing in the world around them, to the realm of representative intellect. An external phenomenon is thus translated into an internal conception. In the same way, the poet operates upon the material supplied him by his emotions; projecting it into an image for the conceptive faculty. These original historians did, it is true, find statements and narratives of other men ready to hand. One person cannot be an eye or ear witness of everything. But they make use of such aids only as the poet does of that heritage of an already-formed language, to which he owes so much; merely as an ingredient. Historiographers bind together the fleeting elements of story, and treasure them up for immortality in the temple of Mnemosyne. Legends, ballad-stories, traditions, must be excluded from such original history. These are but

dim and hazy forms of historical apprehension, and therefore belong to nations whose intelligence is but half awakened. Here, on the contrary, we have to do with people fully conscious of what they were and what they were about. The domain of reality—actually seen, or capable of being so—affords a very different basis in point of firmness from that fugitive and shadowy element, in which were engendered those legends and poetic dreams whose historical prestige vanishes, as soon as nations have attained a mature individuality.

Such original historians, then, change the events, the deeds, and the states of society with which they are conversant, into an object for the conceptive faculty. The narratives they leave us cannot, therefore, be very comprehensive in their range. Herodotus, Thucydides, Guicciardini, may be taken as fair samples of the class in this respect. What is present and living in their environment is their proper material. The influences that have formed the writer are identical with those which have moulded the events that constitute the matter of his story. The author's spirit, and that of the actions he narrates, is one and the same. He describes scenes in which he himself has been an actor, or at any rate an interested spectator. It is short periods of time, individual shapes of persons and occurrences, single, unreflected traits, of which he makes his picture. And his aim is nothing more than the presentation to posterity of an image of events as clear as that which he himself possessed in virtue of personal observation, or life-like descriptions. Reflections are none of his business, for he lives in the spirit of his subject; he has not attained an elevation above it. If, as in Cæsar's case, he belongs to the exalted rank of generals or statesmen, it is the prosecution of *his own aims* that constitutes the history.

Such speeches as we find in Thucydides (for example) of which we can positively assert that they are not *bona fide* reports, would seem to make against our statement that a historian of his class presents us no reflected picture; that persons and people appear in his works in *propria persona*. Speeches, it must be allowed, are veri-

---

[1] I cannot mention any work that will serve as a compendium of the course, but I may remark that in my *Philosophy of Right*, §§ 341-360, I have already given a definition of such a universal history as it is proposed to develop, and a syllabus of the chief elements or periods into which it naturally divides itself.

table transactions in the human commonwealth; in fact, very gravely influential transactions. It is, indeed, often said, "Such and such things are only talk"; by way of demonstrating their harmlessness. That for which this excuse is brought may be mere "talk"; and talk enjoys the important privilege of being harmless. But addresses of peoples to peoples, or orations directed to nations and to princes, are integrant constituents of history. Granted that such orations as those of Pericles—that most profoundly accomplished, genuine, noble statesman—were elaborated by Thucydides, it must yet be maintained that they were not foreign to the character of the speaker. In the orations in question, these men proclaim the maxims adopted by their countrymen, and which formed their own character; they record their views of their political relations, and of their moral and spiritual nature; and the principles of their designs and conduct. What the historian puts into their mouths is no supposititious system of ideas, but an uncorrupted transcript of their intellectual and moral habitudes.

Of these historians, whom we must make thoroughly our own, with whom we must linger long, if we would live with their respective nations, and enter deeply into their spirit: of these historians, to whose pages we may turn not for the purposes of erudition merely, but with a view to deep and genuine enjoyment, there are fewer than might be imagined. Herodotus, the Father, *i.e.*, the Founder of History, and Thucydides have been already mentioned. Xenophon's account of the retreat of the Ten Thousand is a work equally original. Cæsar's *Commentaries* is the simple masterpiece of a mighty spirit. Among the ancients, these annalists were necessarily great captains and statesmen. In the Middle Ages, if we except the bishops, who were placed in the very centre of the political world, the monks monopolize this category as naïve chroniclers who were as decidedly isolated from active life as those elder annalists had been connected with it. In modern times the relations are entirely altered. Our culture is essentially comprehensive, and immediately changes all events into historical representations. Belonging to the class in question, we have vivid, simple, clear narrations—especially of military transactions —which might fairly take their place with those of Cæsar. In richness of matter and fulness of detail as regards strategic appliances, and attendant circumstances, they are even more instructive. The French *Mémoires*, also, fall under this category. In many cases these are written by men

of mark, though relating to affairs of little note. They not unfrequently contain a large proportion of anecdotal matter, so that the ground they occupy is narrow and trivial. Yet they are often veritable masterpieces in history; as those of Cardinal de Retz, which in fact trench on a larger historical field. In Germany such masters are rare. Frederick the Great (*Histoire de mon temps*) is an illustrious exception. Writers of this order must occupy an elevated position. Only from such a position is it possible to take an extensive view of affairs—to see everything. This is out of the question for him, who from below merely gets a glimpse of the great world through a miserable cranny.

II.

The second kind of history we may call the *reflective*. It is history whose mode of representation is not really confined by the limits of the time to which it relates, but whose spirit transcends the present. In this second order a strongly marked variety of species may be distinguished.

1. It is the aim of the investigator to gain a view of the entire history of a people or a country, or of the world, in short, what we call *universal history*. In this case the working up of the historical material is the main point. The workman approaches his task with *his own* spirit; a spirit distinct from that of the element he is to manipulate. Here a very important consideration will be the principles to which the author refers the bearing and motives of the actions and events which he describes, and those which determine the form of his narrative. Among us Germans this reflective treatment and the display of ingenuity which it occasions assume a manifold variety of phases. Every writer of history proposes to himself an original method. The English and French confess to general principles of historical composition. Their standpoint is more that of cosmopolitan or of national culture. Among us each labors to invent a purely individual point of view. Instead of writing history, we are always beating our brains to discover how history ought to be written. This first kind of reflective history is most nearly akin to the preceding, when it has no farther aim than to present the annals of a country complete. Such compilations (among which may be reckoned the works of Livy, Diodorus Siculus, Johannes von Müller's *History of Switzerland*) are, if well performed, highly meritorious. Among the best of the kind may be reckoned such annalists as approach those of the first class; who give so vivid a transcript of events that the reader may well

fancy himself listening to contemporaries and eye-witnesses. But it often happens that the individuality of tone which must characterize a writer belonging to a different culture, is not modified in accordance with the periods such a record must traverse. The spirit of the writer is quite other than that of the times of which he treats. Thus Livy puts into the mouths of the old Roman kings, consuls, and generals, such orations as would be delivered by an accomplished advocate of the Livian era, and which strikingly contrast with the genuine traditions of Roman antiquity (e. g., the fable of Menenius Agrippa). In the same way he gives us descriptions of battles, as if he had been an actual spectator; but whose features would serve well enough for battles in any period, and whose distinctness contrasts on the other hand with the want of connection and the inconsistency that prevail elsewhere, even in his treatment of chief points of interest. The difference between such a compiler and an original historian may be best seen by comparing Polybius himself with the style in which Livy uses, expands, and abridges his annals in those periods of which Polybius' account has been preserved. Johannes von Müller has given a stiff, formal, pedantic aspect to his history, in the endeavor to remain faithful in his portraiture to the times he describes. We much prefer the narratives we find in old Tschudy. All is more naïve and natural than it appears in the garb of a fictitious and affected archaism.

A history which aspires to traverse long periods of time, or to be universal, must indeed forego the attempt to give individual representations of the past as it actually existed. It must foreshorten its pictures by abstractions; and this includes not merely the omission of events and deeds, but whatever is involved in the fact that thought is, after all, the most trenchant epitomist. A battle, a great victory, a siege, no longer maintains its original proportions, but is put off with a bare mention. When Livy, e. g., tells us of the wars with the Volsci, we sometimes have the brief announcement: "This year war was carried on with the Volsci."

2. A second species of reflective history is what we may call the *pragmatical*. When we have to deal with the past, and occupy ourselves with a remote world, a present rises into being for the mind, produced by its own activity, as the reward of its labor. The occurrences are, indeed, various; but the idea which pervades them— their deeper import and connection—is *one*. This takes the occurrence out of the category of the past and makes it virtually present. Pragmatical

(didactic) reflections, though in their nature decidedly abstract, are truly and indefeasibly of the present, and quicken the annals of the dead past with the life of to-day. Whether, indeed, such reflections are truly interesting and enlivening, depends on the writer's own spirit. Moral reflections must here be specially noticed—the moral teaching expected from history, which latter has not infrequently been treated with a direct view to the former. It may be allowed that examples of virtue elevate the soul, and are applicable in the moral instruction of children for impressing excellence upon their minds. But the destinies of peoples and states, their interests, relations, and the complicated tissue of their affairs, present quite another field. Rulers, statesmen, nations, are wont to be emphatically commended to the teaching which experience offers in history. But what experience and history teach is this—that peoples and governments never have learned anything from history, or acted on principles deduced from it. Each period is involved in such peculiar circumstances, exhibits a condition of things so strictly idiosyncratic, that its conduct must be regulated by considerations connected with itself, and itself alone. Amid the pressure of great events, a general principle gives no help. It is useless to revert to similar circumstances in the past. The pallid shades of memory struggle in vain with the life and freedom of the present. Looked at in this light, nothing can be shallower than the oft-repeated appeal to Greek and Roman examples during the French Revolution. Nothing is more diverse than the genius of those nations and that of our times. Johannes von Müller, in his *Universal History,* as also in his *History of Switzerland,* had such moral aims in view. He designed to prepare a body of political doctrines for the instruction of princes, governments, and peoples (he formed a special collection of doctrines and reflections—frequently giving us in his correspondence the exact number of apophthegms which he had compiled in a week); but he cannot reckon on this part of his labor as among the best that he accomplished. It is only a thorough, liberal, comprehensive view of historical relations (such, e. g., as we find in Montesquieu's *Esprit des lois*), that can give truth and interest to reflections of this order. One reflective history, therefore, supersedes another. The materials are patent to every writer: each is likely enough to believe himself capable of arranging and manipulating them; and we may expect that each will insist upon his own spirit as that of the age in question. Disgusted by such reflective histories, readers have often returned with pleasure to a narrative adopting no particular point of view. These certainly have their value; but for the most part they offer only material for history. We Germans are content with such. The French, on the other hand, display great genius in reanimating bygone times, and in bringing the past to bear upon the present condition of things.

3. The third form of reflective history is the *critical*. This deserves mention as pre-eminently the mode of treating history now current in Germany. It is not history itself that is here presented. We might more properly designate it as a history of history; a criticism of historical narratives and an investigation of their truth and credibility. Its peculiarity, in point of fact and of intention, consists in the acuteness with which the writer extorts something from the records which was not in the matters recorded. The French have given us much that is profound and judicious in this class of composition, but they have not endeavored to pass a merely critical procedure for substantial history. They have duly presented their judgments in the form of critical treatises. Among us, the so-called "higher criticism," which reigns supreme in the domain of philology, has also taken possession of our historical literature. This "higher criticism" has been the pretext for introducing all the antihistorical monstrosities that a vain imagination could suggest. Here we have the other method of making the past a living reality; putting subjective fancies in the place of historical data; fancies whose merit is measured by their boldness, that is, the scantiness of the particulars on which they are based, and the peremptoriness with which they contravene the best established facts of history.

4. The last species of reflective history announces its fragmentary character on the very face of it. It adopts an abstract position; yet, since it takes general points of view (*e.g.,* as the history of art, of law, of religion), it forms a transition to the Philosophical History of the World. In our time this form of the history of ideas has been more developed and brought into notice. Such branches of national life stand in close relation to the entire complex of a people's annals; and the question of chief importance in relation to our subject is, whether the connection of the whole is exhibited in its truth and reality, or referred to merely external relations. In the latter case, these important phenomena (art, law, religion, etc.) appear as purely accidental national peculiarities. It must be remarked that, when reflective history has advanced to the adoption of general points of view, if the position taken is a true one, these are found to constitute—not a merely external thread, a superficial series—but are the inward guiding soul of the occurrences and actions that occupy a nation's annals. For, like the soul-conductor Mercury, the idea is in truth, the leader of peoples and of the world; and spirit, the rational and necessitated will of that conductor, is and has been the director of the events of the world's history. To become acquainted with spirit in this its office of guidance, is the object of our present undertaking. This brings us to

III.

The third kind of history—the *philosophical*. No explanation was needed of the two previous classes; their nature was self-evident. It is otherwise with this last, which certainly seems to require an exposition or justification. The most general definition that can be given is: that the philosophy of history means nothing but the *thoughtful consideration of it*. Thought is, indeed, essential to humanity. It is this that distinguishes us from the brutes. In sensation, cognition, and intellection; in our instincts and volitions, as far as they are truly human, thought is an invariable element. To insist upon thought in this connection with history may, however, appear unsatisfactory. In this science it would seem as if thought must be subordinate to what is given, to the realities of fact; that this is its basis and guide: while philosophy dwells in the region of self-produced ideas, without reference to actuality. Approaching history thus prepossessed, speculation might be expected to treat it as a mere passive material; and, so far from leaving it in its native truth, to force it into conformity with a tyrannous idea, and to construe it, as the phrase is, "*a priori*." But as it is the business of history simply to adopt into its records what is and has been, actual occurrences and transactions; and since it remains true to its character in proportion as it strictly adheres to its data, we seem to have in philosophy, a process diametrically opposed to that of the historiographer. This contradiction, and the charge consequently brought against speculation, shall be explained and confuted. We do not, however, propose to correct the innumerable special misrepresentations, trite or novel, that are current respecting the aims, the interests, and the modes of treating history, and its relation to philosophy.

The only thought which philosophy brings with it to the contemplation of history, is the simple conception of *reason;* that reason is the sovereign of the world; that the history of the world, therefore, presents us with a rational process. This conviction and intuition is a hypothesis in the domain of history as such. In that of philosophy it is no hypothesis. It is there proved by speculative cognition, that reason—and this term may here suffice us, without investigating the relation sustained by the universe to the divine being—is *substance*, as well as *infinite power*; its own *infinite material* underlying all the natural and spiritual life which it originates, as also the *infinite form*—that which sets this material in motion. On the one hand, reason is the *substance* of the universe; *viz.*, that by which and in which all reality has its being and subsistence. On the other hand, it is the *infinite energy* of the universe; since reason is not so powerless as to be incapable of producing anything but a mere ideal, a mere intention, having its place outside reality, nobody knows where; something separate and abstract, in the heads of certain human beings. It is *the infinite complex of things*, their entire essence and truth. It is its own material which it commits to its own active energy to work up; not needing, as finite action does, the conditions of an external material of given means from which it may obtain its support, and the objects of its activity. It supplies its own nourishment, and is the object of its own operations. While it is exclusively its own basis of existence, and absolute final aim, it is also the energizing power realizing this aim; developing it not only in the phenomena of the natural, but also of the spiritual universe—the history of the world. That this "idea" or "reason" is the *true*, the *eternal*, the absolutely *powerful* essence; that it reveals itself in the world, and that in that world nothing else is revealed but this and its honour and glory—is the thesis which, as we have said, has been proved in philosophy, and is here regarded as demonstrated.

In those of my hearers who are not acquainted with philosophy, I may fairly presume, at least, the existence of a *belief* in reason, a desire, a thirst for acquaintance with it, in entering upon this course of lectures. It is, in fact, the wish for rational insight, not the ambition to amass a mere heap of acquirements, that should be presupposed in every case as possessing the mind of the learner in the study of science. If the clear idea of reason is not already developed in our minds, in beginning the study of universal history, we should at least have the firm, unconquerable faith that reason *does* exist there; and that the world of intelligence and conscious volition is not abandoned to chance, but must

show itself in the light of the self-cognizant idea. Yet I am not obliged to make any such preliminary demand upon your faith. What I have said thus provisionally, and what I shall have further to say, is, even in reference to *our* branch of science, not to be regarded as hypothetical, but as a summary view of the whole; the *result of the investigation* we are about to pursue; a result which happens to be known to *me*, because I have traversed the entire field. It is only an inference from the history of the world, that its development has been a rational process; that the history in question has constituted the rational necessary course of the world-spirit—that spirit whose nature is always one and the same, but which unfolds this its one nature in the phenomena of the world's existence. This must, as before stated, present itself as the ultimate *result* of history. But we have to take the latter as it is. We must proceed historically—empirically. Among other precautions we must take care not to be misled by professed historians who (especially among the Germans, and enjoying a considerable authority), are chargeable with the very procedure of which they accuse the philosopher—introducing *a priori* inventions of their own into the records of the past. It is, for example, a widely current fiction, that there was an original primeval people, taught immediately by God, endowed with perfect insight and wisdom, possessing a thorough knowledge of all natural laws and spiritual truth; that there have been such or such sacerdotal peoples; or, to mention a more specific averment, that there was a Roman epos, from which the Roman historians derived the early annals of their city, etc. Authorities of this kind we leave to those talented historians by profession, among whom (in Germany at least) their use is not uncommon. We might then announce it as the first condition to be observed, that we should faithfully adopt all that is historical. But in such general expressions themselves, as "faithfully" and "adopt," lies the ambiguity. Even the ordinary, the "impartial" historiographer, who believes and professes that he maintains a simply receptive attitude; surrendering himself only to the data supplied him—is by no means passive as regards the exercise of his thinking powers. He brings his categories with him, and sees the phenomena presented to his mental vision, exclusively through these media. And, especially in all that pretends to the name of science, it is indispensable that reason should not sleep—that reflection should be in full play. To him who looks upon the world rationally, the world in its turn presents a rational aspect. The relation is mutual. But the various exercises of reflection, the different points of view, the modes of deciding the simple question of the relative importance of events (the first category that occupies the attention of the historian), do not belong to this place.

I will only mention two phases and points of view that concern the generally diffused conviction that reason has ruled, and is still ruling in the world, and consequently in the world's history; because they give us, at the same time, an opportunity for more closely investigating the question that presents the greatest difficulty, and for indicating a branch of the subject, which will have to be enlarged on in the sequel.

I. One of these points is that passage in history which informs us that the Greek Anaxagoras was the first to enunciate the doctrine that νοῦς, understanding generally, or reason, governs the world. It is not intelligence as self-conscious reason—not a spirit as such that is meant; and we must clearly distinguish these from each other. The movement of the solar system takes place according to unchangeable laws. These laws are reason, implicit in the phenomena in question. But neither the sun nor the planets, which revolve around it according to these laws, can be said to have any consciousness of them.

A thought of this kind—that nature is an embodiment of reason, that it is unchangeably subordinate to universal laws—appears nowise striking or strange to us. We are accustomed to such conceptions, and find nothing extraordinary in them. And I have mentioned this extraordinary occurrence, partly to show how history teaches, that ideas of this kind, which may seem trivial to us, have not always been in the world; that, on the contrary, such a thought makes an epoch in the annals of human intelligence. Aristotle says of Anaxagoras, as the originator of the thought in question, that he appeared as a sober man among the drunken. Socrates adopted the doctrine from Anaxagoras, and it forthwith became the ruling idea in philosophy—except in the school of Epicurus, who ascribed all events to chance. "I was delighted with the sentiment" —Plato makes Socrates say—"and hoped I had found a teacher who would show me nature in harmony with reason, who would demonstrate in each particular phenomenon its specific aim, and in the whole, the grand object of the universe. I would not have surrendered this hope for a great deal. But how very much was I disappointed, when, having zealously applied myself to the writings of Anaxagoras, I found that he adduces only external causes, such as atmosphere, ether, water, and the like." It is evident that the defect which Socrates complains of, respecting Anaxagoras' doctrine, does not concern the principle itself, but the shortcoming of the propounder in applying it to nature in the concrete. Nature is not deduced from that principle: the latter remains in fact a mere abstraction, inasmuch as the former is not comprehended and exhibited as a development of it— an organization produced by and from reason. I wish, at the very outset, to call your attention to the important difference between a conception, a principle, a truth limited to an *abstract* form and its determinate application, and concrete development. This distinction affects the whole fabric of philosophy; and among other bearings of it there is one to which we shall have to revert at the close of our view of universal history, in investigating the aspect of political affairs in the most recent period.

We have next to notice the rise of this idea— that reason directs the world—in connection with a further application of it, well known to us—in the form, *viz.,* of the *religious truth,* that the world is not abandoned to chance and external contingent causes, but that a *Providence* controls it. I stated above, that I would not make a demand on your faith, in regard to the principle announced. Yet I might appeal to your belief in it, *in this religious aspect,* if, as a general rule, the nature of philosophical science allowed it to attach authority to presuppositions. To put it in another shape—this appeal is forbidden, because the science of which we have to treat, proposes itself to furnish the proof (not indeed of the abstract *truth* of the doctrine, but) of its correctness as compared with facts. The truth, then, that a Providence (that of God) presides over the events of the world—consorts with the proposition in question; for *Divine* Providence is wisdom, endowed with an infinite power, which realizes its aim, *viz.,* the absolute rational design of the world. Reason is thought conditioning itself with perfect freedom. But a difference, rather a contradiction, will manifest itself, between this belief and our principle, just as was the case in reference to the demand made by Socrates in the case of Anaxagoras' dictum. For that belief is similarly indefinite; it is what is called a belief in a general providence, and is not followed out into definite application, or displayed in its bearing on the grand total—the entire course of human history. But to *explain* history is to depict the passions of mankind, the genius, the active powers, that play their part on the great stage; and the providentially determined process which these exhibit, constitutes what is generally called the "plan" of providence. Yet it is this very plan which is supposed to be concealed from our view: which it is deemed presumption, even to wish to recognize. The ignorance of Anaxagoras, as to how intelligence reveals itself in actual existence, was ingenuous. Neither in his consciousness, nor in that of Greece at large, had that thought been farther expanded. He had not attained the power to apply his general principle to the concrete, so as to deduce the latter from the former. It was Socrates who took the first step in comprehending the union of the concrete with the universal. Anaxagoras, then, did not take up a *hostile* position toward such an application. The common belief in Providence *does;* at least it opposes the use of the principle on the large scale, and denies the possibility of discerning the plan of Providence. In isolated cases this plan is supposed to be manifest. Pious persons are encouraged to recognize, in particular circumstances, something more than mere chance; to acknowledge the guiding hand of God; *e.g.,* when help has unexpectedly come to an individual in great perplexity and need. But these instances of providential design are of a limited kind, and concern the accomplishment of nothing more than the desires of the individual in question. But in the history of the world, the *individuals* we have to do with are *peoples;* totalities that are states. We cannot, therefore, be satisfied with what we may call this "peddling" view of providence, to which the belief alluded to limits itself. Equally unsatisfactory is the merely abstract, undefined belief in a providence, when that belief is not brought to bear upon the details of the process which it conducts. On the contrary our earnest endeavor must be directed to the recognition of the ways of Providence, the means it uses, and the historical phenomena in which it manifests itself; and we must show their connection with the general principle above mentioned. But in noticing the recognition of the plan of Divine Providence generally, I have implicitly touched upon a prominent question of the day; *viz.,* that of the possibility of knowing God: or rather, since public opinion has ceased to allow it to be a matter of *question,* the *doctrine* that it is impossible to know God. In direct contravention of what is commanded in Holy Scripture as the highest duty—that we should not merely love, but *know* God—the prevalent dogma involves the denial of what is there said; *viz.,* that it is the spirit (*der Geist*) that leads into truth, knows all things, penetrates even into the deep things of the Godhead. While the Divine Being is thus placed beyond our knowledge, and outside the limit of all human things, we have the convenient licence of wandering as far as we list, in the direction of our own fancies. We are freed from the obligation to refer our knowledge to the divine and true. On the other hand, the vanity and egotism which characterize it find, in this false position, ample justification; and the pious modesty which puts far from it the knowledge of God can well estimate how much furtherance thereby accrues to its own wayward and vain strivings. I have been unwilling to leave out of sight the connection between our thesis—that reason governs and has governed the world—and the question of the possibility of a knowledge of God, chiefly that I might not lose the opportunity of mentioning the imputation against philosophy of being shy of noticing religious truths, or of having occasion to be so; in which is insinuated the suspicion that it has anything but a clear conscience in the presence of these truths. So far from this being the case, the fact is that in recent times philosophy has been obliged to defend the domain of religion against the attacks of several theological systems. In the Christian religion God has revealed Himself, that is, He has given us to understand what He is; so that He is no longer a concealed or secret existence. And this possibility of knowing Him, thus afforded us, renders such knowledge a duty. God wishes no narrow-hearted souls or empty heads for His children; but those whose spirit is of itself indeed, poor, but rich in the knowledge of Him; and who regard this knowledge of God as the only valuable possession. That development of the thinking spirit, which has resulted from the revelation of the Divine Being as its original basis, must ultimately advance to the *intellectual* comprehension of what was presented in the first instance, to *feeling* and *imagination.* The time must eventually come for understanding that rich product of active reason, which the history of the world offers to us. It was for awhile the fashion to profess admiration for the wisdom of God, as displayed in animals, plants, and isolated occurrences. But, if it be allowed that providence manifests itself in such objects and forms of existence, why not also in universal history? This is deemed too great a matter to be thus regarded. But divine wisdom, *i.e.,* reason, is one and the same in the great as in the little; and we must not imagine God to be too weak to exercise His wisdom on the grand scale. Our intellectual striving aims at realizing the conviction that what was *intended* by eternal wisdom, is actually *accomplished* in the domain of existent, active spirit, as well as in that of mere nature. Our mode of treating the subject is, in this aspect, a *theodicæa*—a justification of the ways of God—which Leibnitz attempted metaphysically, in his method, *i.e.*, in indefinite abstract categories—so that the ill that is found in the world may be comprehended, and the thinking spirit reconciled with the fact of the existence of evil. Indeed, nowhere is such a harmonizing view more pressingly demanded than in universal history; and it can be attained only by recognizing the *positive* existence, in which that negative element is a subordinate and vanquished nullity. On the one hand, the ultimate design of the world must be perceived; and, on the other hand, the fact that this design has been actually realized in it, and that evil has not been able permanently to assert a competing position, but this superintending νοῦς, or in "providence." "Reason," whose sovereignty over the world has been maintained, is as indefinite a term as "providence," supposing the term to be used by those who are unable to characterize it distinctly—to show wherein it consists, so as to enable us to decide whether a thing is rational or irrational. An adequate definition of reason is the first desideratum; and whatever boast may be made of strict adherence to it in explaining phenomena. Without such a definition we get no farther than mere words. With these observations we may proceed to the second point of view that has to be considered in this introduction.

II. The inquiry into the *essential destiny* of reason, as far as it is considered in reference to the world, is identical with the question, *what is the ultimate design of the world?* And the expression implies that that design is destined to be realized. Two points of consideration suggest themselves; first, the *import* of this design—its abstract definition; and secondly, its *realization*.

It must be observed at the outset, that the phenomenon we investigate—universal history —belongs to the realm of *spirit*. The term *"world"* includes both physical and psychical nature. Physical nature also plays its part in the world's history, and attention will have to be paid to the fundamental natural relations thus involved. But spirit, and the course of its development, is our substantial object. Our task does not require us to contemplate nature as a rational system in itself, though in its own proper domain it proves itself such, but simply in its relation to *spirit*. On the stage on which we are

observing it—universal history—spirit displays itself in its most concrete reality. Notwithstanding this (or rather for the very purpose of comprehending the *general* principles which this, its form of *concrete reality*, embodies) we must premise some abstract characteristics of the *nature of spirit*. Such an explanation, however, cannot be given here under any other form than that of bare assertion. The present is not the occasion for unfolding the idea of spirit speculatively; for whatever has a place in an introduction, must, as already observed, be taken as simply historical; something assumed as having been explained and proved elsewhere; or whose demonstration awaits the sequel of the science of history itself.

We have therefore to mention here:

(1) The abstract characteristics of the nature of spirit.

(2) What means spirit uses in order to realize its idea.

(3) Lastly, we must consider the shape which the perfect embodiment of spirit assumes —the state.

(1) The nature of spirit may be understood by a glance at its direct opposite—*matter*. As the essence of matter is gravity, so, on the other hand, we may affirm that the substance, the essence of spirit is freedom. All will readily assent to the doctrine that spirit, among other properties, is also endowed with freedom; but philosophy teaches that all the qualities of spirit exist only through freedom; that all are but means for attaining freedom; that all seek and produce this and this alone. It is a result of speculative philosophy, that freedom is the sole truth of spirit. Matter possesses gravity in virtue of its tendency toward a central point. It is essentially composite; consisting of parts that *exclude* each other. It seeks its unity; and therefore exhibits itself as self-destructive, as verging toward its opposite. If it could attain this, it would be matter no longer, it would have perished. It strives after the realization of its idea; for in unity it exists *ideally*. Spirit, on the contrary, may be defined as that which has its centre in itself. It has not a unity outside itself, but has already found it; it exists *in* and *with itself*. Matter has its essence out of itself; spirit is *self-contained existence*. Now this is freedom, exactly. For if I am dependent, my being is referred to something else which I am not; I cannot exist independently of something external. I am free, on the contrary, when my existence depends upon myself. This self-contained existence of spirit is none other than self-consciousness, con-

sciousness of one's own being. Two things must be distinguished in consciousness; first, the fact *that I know;* secondly, *what I know.* In *self* consciousness these are merged in one; for spirit *knows itself.* It involves an appreciation of its own nature, as also an energy enabling it to realize itself; to make itself *actually* that which it is *potentially.* According to this abstract definition it may be said of universal history, that it is the exhibition of spirit in the process of working out the knowledge of that which it is potentially. And as the germ bears in itself the whole nature of the tree, and the taste and form of its fruits, so do the first traces of spirit virtually contain the whole of that history. The Orientals have not attained the knowledge that spirit—man *as such*—is free; and because they do not know this, they are not free. They only know that *one is free.* But on this very account, the freedom of that *one* is only caprice; ferocity—brutal recklessness of passion, or a mildness and tameness of the desires, which is itself only an accident of nature—mere caprice like the former. That *one* is therefore only a despot; not a *free man.* The consciousness of freedom first arose among the Greeks, and therefore they were free; but they, and the Romans likewise, knew only that *some* are free, not man as such. Even Plato and Aristotle did not know this. The Greeks, therefore, had slaves; and their whole life and the maintenance of their splendid liberty, was implicated with the institution of slavery: a fact moreover, which made that liberty on the one hand only an accidental, transient and limited growth; on the other hand, constituted it a rigorous thraldom of our common nature, of the human. The German nations, under the influence of Christianity, were the first to attain the consciousness that man, as man, is free: that it is the *freedom* of spirit which constitutes its essence. This consciousness arose first in religion, the inmost region of spirit; but to introduce the principle into the various relations of the actual world, involves a more extensive problem than its simple implantation; a problem whose solution and application require a severe and lengthened process of culture. In proof of this, we may note that slavery did not cease immediately on the reception of Christianity. Still less did liberty predominate in states; or governments and constitutions adopt a rational organization, or recognize freedom as their basis. That application of the principle to political relations, the thorough moulding and interpenetration of the constitution of society by it, is a process identical with history itself. I have

already directed attention to the distinction here involved, between a principle as such, and its *application; i.e.,* its introduction and carrying out in the actual phenomena of spirit and life. This is a point of fundamental importance in our science, and one which must be constantly respected as essential. And in the same way as this distinction has attracted attention in view of the *Christian* principle of self-consciousness—freedom; it also shows itself as an essential one, in view of the principle of freedom *generally.* The history of the world is none other than the progress of the consciousness of freedom; a progress whose development according to the necessity of its nature it is our business to investigate.

The general statement given above, of the various grades in the consciousness of freedom—and which we applied in the first instance to the fact that the Eastern nations knew only that *one* is free; the Greek and Roman world only that *some* are free; while *we* know that all men absolutely (man *as man*) are free—supplies us with the natural division of universal history, and suggests the mode of its discussion. This is remarked, however, only incidentally and anticipatively; some other ideas must be first explained.

The destiny of the spiritual world, and—since this is the *substantial world,* while the physical remains subordinate to it, or, in the language of speculation, has no truth *as against* the spiritual—*the final cause of the world at large,* we allege to be the *consciousness* of its own freedom on the part of spirit, and *ipso facto,* the *reality* of that freedom. But that this term "freedom," without further qualification, is an indefinite, and incalculable ambiguous term; and that while that which it represents is the *ne plus ultra* of attainment, it is liable to an infinity of misunderstandings, confusions and errors, and to become the occasion for all imaginable excesses—has never been more clearly known and felt than in modern times. Yet, for the present, we must content ourselves with the term itself without further definition. Attention was also directed to the importance of the infinite difference between a principle in the abstract, and its realization in the concrete. In the process before us, the essential nature of freedom—which involves in it absolute necessity—is to be displayed as coming to a consciousness of itself (for it is in its very nature, self-consciousness) and thereby realizing its existence. Itself is its own object of attainment, and the sole aim of spirit. This result it is, at which the process of the world's history has been continually aiming; and to which the sacrifices that have ever and anon been laid on the vast altar of the earth, through the long lapse of ages, have been offered. This is the only aim that sees itself realized and fulfilled; the only pole of repose amid the ceaseless change of events and conditions, and the sole efficient principle that pervades them. This final aim is God's purpose with the world; but God is the absolutely perfect Being, and can, therefore, will nothing other than Himself—His own Will. The nature of His Will—that is, His Nature itself—is what we here call the idea of freedom; translating the language of religion into that of thought. The question, then, which we may next put, is: What means does this principle of freedom use for its realization? This is the second point we have to consider.

(2) The question of the *means* by which freedom develops itself to a world, conducts us to the phenomenon of history itself. Although freedom is, primarily, an undeveloped idea, the means it uses are external and phenomenal; presenting themselves in history to our sensuous vision. The first glance at history convinces us that the actions of men proceed from their needs, their passions, their characters and talents; and impresses us with the belief that such needs, passions and interests are the sole springs of action—the efficient agents in this scene of activity. Among these may, perhaps, be found aims of a liberal or universal kind—benevolence it may be, or noble patriotism; but such virtues and general views are but insignificant as compared with the world and its doings. We may perhaps see the ideal of reason actualized in those who adopt such aims, and within the sphere of their influence; but they bear only a trifling proportion to the mass of the human race; and the extent of that influence is limited accordingly. Passions, private aims, and the satisfaction of selfish desires, are on the other hand, most effective springs of action. Their power lies in the fact that they respect none of the limitations which justice and morality would impose on them; and that these natural impulses have a more direct influence over man than the artificial and tedious discipline that tends to order and self-restraint, law and morality. When we look at this display of passions, and the consequences of their violence; the unreason which is associated not only with them, but even (rather we might say *especially*) with *good* designs and righteous aims; when we see the evil, the vice, the ruin that has befallen the most flourishing kingdoms which the mind of man ever created; we can scarce avoid being filled

with sorrow at this universal taint of corruption: and, since this decay is not the work of mere nature, but of the human will—a moral embitterment—a revolt of the good spirit (if it have a place within us) may well be the result of our reflections. Without rhetorical exaggeration, a simply truthful combination of the miseries that have overwhelmed the noblest of nations and polities, and the finest exemplars of private virtue—forms a picture of most fearful aspect, and excites emotions of the profoundest and most hopeless sadness, counterbalanced by no consolatory result. We endure in beholding it a mental torture, allowing no defence or escape but the consideration that what has happened could not be otherwise; that it is a fatality which no intervention could alter. And at last we draw back from the intolerable disgust with which these sorrowful reflections threaten us, into the more agreeable environment of our individual life—the present formed by our private aims and interests. In short, we retreat into the selfishness that stands on the quiet shore, and thence enjoys in safety the distant spectacle of "wrecks confusedly hurled." But even regarding history as the slaughter-bench at which the happiness of peoples, the wisdom of states, and the virtue of individuals have been victimized—the question involuntarily arises—to what principle, to what final aim these enormous sacrifices have been offered. From this point the investigation usually proceeds to that which we have made the general commencement of our inquiry. Starting from this, we pointed out those phenomena which made up a picture so suggestive of gloomy emotions and thoughtful reflections —as *the very field* that we, for our part, regard as exhibiting only the means for realizing what we assert to be the essential destiny—the absolute aim, or, which comes to the same thing, the true *result* of the world's history. We have all along purposely eschewed "moral reflections" as a method of rising from the scene of historical specialties to the general principles which they embody. Besides, it is not the interest of such sentimentalities really to rise above those depressing emotions; and to solve the enigmas of providence which the considerations that occasioned them present. It is essential to their character to find a gloomy satisfaction in the empty and fruitless sublimities of that negative result. We return them to the point of view which we have adopted; observing that the successive steps (*Momente*) of the analysis to which it will lead us, will also evolve the conditions requisite for answering the inquiries suggested by the panorama of sin and suffering that history unfolds.

The *first* remark we have to make, and which, though already presented more than once, cannot be too often repeated when the occasion seems to call for it—is that what we call *principle, aim, destiny,* or the nature and idea of spirit, is something merely general and abstract. Principle—plan of existence—law—is a hidden, undeveloped essence, which *as such,* however true in itself, is not completely real. Aims, principles, etc. have a place in our thoughts, in our subjective design only; but not yet in the sphere of reality. That which exists for itself only, is a possibility, a potentiality; but has not yet emerged into existence. A *second* element must be introduced in order to produce actuality—*viz.,* actuation, realization; and whose motive power is the will—the activity of man in the widest sense. It is only by this activity that that idea as well as abstract characteristics generally are realized, actualized; for of themselves they are powerless. The motive power that puts them in operation, and gives them determinate existence, is the need, instinct, inclination, and passion of man. That some conception of mine should be developed into act and existence is my earnest desire: I wish to assert my personality in connection with it: I wish to be satisfied by its execution. If I am to exert myself for any object, it must in some way or other be *my* object. In the accomplishment of such or such designs I must at the same time find *my* satisfaction; although the purpose for which I exert myself includes a complication of results, many of which have no interest for me. This is the absolute right of personal existence—to find *itself* satisfied in its activity and labor. If men are to interest themselves for anything, they must (so to speak) have part of their existence involved in it; find their individuality gratified by its attainment. Here a mistake must be avoided. We intend blame, and justly impute it as a fault, when we say of an individual, that he is "interested" (in taking part in such or such transactions), that is, seeks only his private advantage. In reprehending this we find fault with him for furthering his personal aims without any regard to a more comprehensive design; of which he takes advantage to promote his own interest, or which he even sacrifices with this view. But he who is active in *promoting an object,* is not simply "interested," but interested in that object itself. Language faithfully expresses this distinction. Nothing therefore happens, nothing is accomplished, unless the individuals concerned, seek their own satisfaction in the issue. They are particular units of society; *i.e.,* they have special needs, instincts, and interests generally, peculiar to themselves. Among these needs are not only such as we usually call necessities, the stimuli of individual desire and volition, but also those connected with individual views and convictions; or, to use a term expressing less decision, leanings of opinion; supposing the impulses of reflection, understanding, and reason, to have been awakened. In these cases people demand, if they are to exert themselves in any direction, that the object should commend itself to them; that in point of opinion, whether as to its goodness, justice, advantage, profit, they should be able to "enter into it." This is a consideration of especial importance in our age, when people are less than formerly influenced by reliance on others, and by authority; when, on the contrary, they devote their activities to a cause on the ground of their own understanding, their independent conviction and opinion.

We assert then that nothing has been accomplished without interest on the part of the actors; and—if interest be called passion, inasmuch as the whole individuality, to the neglect of all other actual or possible interests and claims, is devoted to an object with every fibre of volition, concentrating all its desires and powers upon it—we may affirm absolutely that *nothing great in the world* has been accomplished without *passion.* Two elements, therefore, enter into the object of our investigation; the first the idea, the second the complex of human passions; the one the warp, the other the woof of the vast arras-web of universal history. The concrete mean and union of the two is liberty, under the conditions of morality in a state. We have spoken of the idea of freedom as the nature of spirit, and the absolute goal of history. Passion is regarded as a thing of sinister aspect, as more or less immoral. Man is required to have no passions. Passion, it is true, is not quite the suitable word for what I wish to express. I mean here nothing more than the human activity as resulting from private interests—special, or if you will, self-seeking designs—with this qualification, that the whole energy of will and character is devoted to their attainment; that other interests (which would in themselves constitute attractive aims) or rather all things else, are sacrificed to them. The object in question is so bound up with the man's will, that it entirely and alone determines the "hue of resolution," and is inseparable from it. It has become the very essence of his volition. For a person is a specific existence; not man in general (a term to which no real existence corresponds) but a particular human being. The term "character" likewise expresses this idiosyncrasy of will and intelligence. But *character* comprehends all peculiarities whatever; the way in which a person conducts himself in private relations, etc., and is not limited to his idiosyncrasy in its practical and active phase. I shall, therefore, use the term "passions"; understanding thereby the particular bent of character, as far as the peculiarities of volition are not limited to private interest, but supply the impelling and actuating force for accomplishing deeds shared in by the community at large. Passion is in the first instance the *subjective,* and therefore the *formal* side of energy, will, and activity—leaving the object or aim still undetermined. And there is a similar relation of formality to reality in merely individual conviction, individual views, individual conscience. It is always a question of essential importance, what is the purport of my conviction, what the object of my passion, in deciding whether the one or the other is of a true and substantial nature. Conversely, if it is so, it will inevitably attain actual existence—be realized.

From this comment on the second essential element in the historical embodiment of an aim, we infer, glancing at the institution of the state in passing, that a state is then well constituted and internally powerful, when the private interest of its citizens is one with the common interest of the state; when the one finds its gratification and realization in the other—a proposition in itself very important. But in a state many institutions must be adopted, much political machinery invented, accompanied by appropriate political arrangements—necessitating long struggles of the understanding before what is really appropriate can be discovered—involving, moreover, contentions with private interest and passions, and a tedious discipline of these latter, in order to bring about the desired harmony. The epoch when a state attains this harmonious condition marks the period of its bloom, its virtue, its vigour, and its prosperity. But the history of mankind does not begin with a *conscious* aim of any kind, as it is the case with the particular circles into which men form themselves of set purpose. The mere social instinct implies a conscious purpose of security for life and property; and when society has been constituted, this purpose becomes more comprehensive. The history of the world begins with its general aim, the realization of the idea of spirit, only in an *implicit*

form, that is, as nature; a hidden, most profoundly hidden, unconscious instinct; and the whole process of history (as already observed) is directed to rendering this unconscious impulse a conscious one. Thus appearing in the form of merely natural existence, natural will—that which has been called the subjective side—physical craving, instinct, passion, private interest, as also opinion and subjective conception—spontaneously present themselves at the very commencement. This vast congeries of volitions, interests and activities, constitute the instruments and means of the world-spirit for attaining its object; bringing it to consciousness, and realizing it. And this aim is none other than finding itself, coming to itself, and contemplating itself in concrete actuality. But that those manifestations of vitality on the part of individuals and peoples, in which they seek and satisfy their own purposes, are, at the same time, the means and instruments of a higher and broader purpose of which they know nothing—which they realize unconsciously—might be made a matter of question; rather has been questioned, and in every variety of form negatived, decried and contemned as mere dreaming and "philosophy." But on this point I announced my view at the very outset, and asserted our hypothesis—which, however, will appear in the sequel, in the form of a legitimate inference—and our belief that reason governs the world, and has consequently governed its history. In relation to this independently universal and substantial existence—all else is subordinate, subservient to it, and the means for its development. The union of universal abstract existence generally with the individual—the subjective—that this alone is truth, belongs to the department of speculation, and is treated in this general form in logic. But in the process of the world's history itself, as still incomplete, the abstract final aim of history is not yet made the distinct object of desire and interest. While these limited sentiments are still unconscious of the purpose they are fulfilling, the universal principle is implicit in them, and is realizing itself through them. The question also assumes the form of the union of *freedom* and *necessity;* the latent abstract process of spirit being regarded as *necessity,* while that which exhibits itself in the conscious will of men, as their interest, belongs to the domain of *freedom.* As the metaphysical connection (*i.e.,* the connection in the idea) of these forms of thought belongs to logic, it would be out of place to analyse it here. The chief and cardinal points only shall be mentioned.

Philosophy shows that the idea advances to an infinite antithesis; that, *viz.*, between the idea in its free, universal form, in which it exists for itself, and the contrasted form of abstract introversion, reflection on itself, which is formal existence-for-self, personality, formal freedom, such as belongs to spirit only. The universal idea exists thus as the substantial totality of things on the one side, and as the abstract essence of free volition on the other side. This reflection of the mind on itself is individual self-consciousness—the polar opposite of the idea in its general form, and therefore existing in absolute limitation. This polar opposite is consequently limitation, particularization, for the universal absolute being; it is the side of its *definite existence;* the sphere of its formal reality, the sphere of the reverence paid to God. To comprehend the absolute connection of this antithesis is the profound task of metaphysics. This limitation originates all forms of particularity of whatever kind. The formal volition wills itself; desires to make its own personality valid in all that it purposes and does: even the pious individual wishes to be saved and happy. This pole of the antithesis, existing for itself, is—in contrast with the Absolute Universal Being—a special separate existence, taking cognizance of specialty only, and willing that alone. In short it plays its part in the region of mere phenomena. This is the sphere of particular purposes, in effecting which individuals exert themselves on behalf of their individuality, give it full play and objective realization. This is also the sphere of happiness and its opposite. He is happy who finds his condition suited to his special character, will, and fancy, and so enjoys himself in that condition. The history of the world is not the theatre of happiness. Periods of happiness are blank pages in it, for they are periods of harmony, periods when the antithesis is in abeyance. Reflection on self—the freedom above described—is abstractly defined as the formal element of the activity of the absolute idea. The realizing *activity* of which we have spoken is the middle term of the syllogism, one of whose extremes is the universal essence, the *idea,* which reposes in the penetralia of spirit; and the other, the complex of external things—objective matter. That activity is the medium by which the universal latent principle is translated into the domain of objectivity.

I will endeavor to make what has been said more vivid and clear by examples.

The building of a house is, in the first instance, a subjective aim and design. On the other hand, we have, as means, the several substances required for the work—iron, wood, stones. The elements are made use of in working up this material: fire to melt the iron, wind to blow the fire, water to set wheels in motion, in order to cut the wood, etc. The result is that the wind, which has helped to build the house, is shut out by the house; so also are the violence of rains and floods, and the destructive powers of fire, so far as the house is made fireproof. The stones and beams obey the law of gravity, press downward, and so high walls are carried up. Thus the elements are made use of in accordance with their nature, and yet to co-operate for a product, by which their operation is limited. Thus the passions of men are gratified; they develop themselves and their aims in accordance with their natural tendencies, and build up the edifice of human society; thus fortifying a position for right and order *against themselves.*

The connection of events above indicated involves also the fact that in history an additional result is commonly produced by human actions beyond that which they aim at and obtain, that which they immediately recognize and desire. They gratify their own interest; but something further is thereby accomplished, latent in the actions in question, though not present to their consciousness, and not included in their design. An analogous example is offered in the case of a man who, from a feeling of revenge—perhaps not an unjust one, but produced by injury on the other's part—burns that other man's house. A connection is immediately established between the deed itself and a train of circumstances not directly included in it, taken abstractedly. In itself it consisted in merely presenting a small flame to a small portion of a beam. Events not involved in that simple act follow of themselves. The part of the beam which was set fire to is connected with its remote portions; the beam itself is united with the woodwork of the house generally, and this with other houses; so that a wide conflagration ensues, which destroys the goods and chattels of many other persons besides his against whom the act of revenge was first directed; perhaps even costs not a few men their lives. This lay neither in the deed abstractedly, nor in the design of the man who committed it. But the action has a further general bearing. In the design of the doer it was only revenge executed against an individual in the destruction of his property, but it is moreover a crime, and that involves punishment also. This may not have been present to the mind of the perpetrator, still less in his intention; but his deed itself, the general principles it calls into play, its substantial content entails it. By this example I wish only to impress on you the consideration that, in a simple act, something further may be implicated than lies in the intention and consciousness of the agent. The example before us involves, however, this additional consideration, that the substance of the act, consequently we may say the act itself, recoils upon the perpetrator—reacts upon him with destructive tendency. This union of the two extremes— the embodiment of a general idea in the form of direct reality, and the elevation of a speciality into connection with universal truth—is brought to pass, at first sight, under the conditions of an utter diversity of nature between the two, and an indifference of the one extreme towards the other. The aims which the agents set before them are limited and special; but it must be remarked that the agents themselves are intelligent thinking beings. The purport of their desires is interwoven with *general, essential* considerations of justice, good, duty, etc.; for mere desire, volition in its rough and savage forms, falls not within the scene and sphere of universal history. Those general considerations, which form at the same time a norm for directing aims and actions, have a determinate purport; for such an abstraction as "good for its own sake" has no place in living reality. If men are to act, they must not only intend the good, but must have decided for themselves whether this or that particular thing is a good. What special course of action, however, is good or not, is determined, as regards the ordinary contingencies of private life, by the laws and customs of a state; and here no great difficulty is presented. Each individual has his position; he knows on the whole what a just, honorable course of conduct is. As to ordinary, private relations, the assertion that it is difficult to choose the right and good—the regarding it as the mark of an exalted morality to find difficulties and raise scruples on that score—may be set down to an evil or perverse will which seeks to evade duties not in themselves of a perplexing nature; or at any rate, to an idly reflective habit of mind—where a feeble will affords no sufficient exercise to the faculties —leaving them therefore to find occupation within themselves, and to expend themselves on moral self-adulation.

It is quite otherwise with the comprehensive relations that history has to do with. In this sphere are presented those momentous collisions between existing, acknowledged duties, laws, and rights, and those contingencies which are adverse to this fixed system; which assail and even destroy its foundations and existence; whose tenor may nevertheless seem good—on the large scale advantageous—yes, even indispensable and necessary. These contingencies realize themselves in history: they involve a general principle of a different order from that on which depends the *permanence* of a people or a state. This principle is an essential phase in the development of the *creating* idea, of truth striving and urging towards itself. Historical men— *world-historical individuals*—are those in whose aims such a general principle lies.

Cæsar, in danger of losing a position, not perhaps at that time of superiority yet at least of equality with the others who were at the head of the state, and of succumbing to those who were just on the point of becoming his enemies, belongs essentially to this category. These enemies, who were at the same time pursuing *their* personal aims, had the form of the constitution, and the power conferred by an appearance of justice, on their side. Cæsar was contending for the maintenance of his position, honor, and safety; and, since the power of his opponents included the sovereignty over the provinces of the Roman Empire, his victory secured for him the conquest of that entire empire; and he thus became, though leaving the form of the constitution, the autocrat of the state. That which secured for him the execution of a design, which in the first instance was of negative import, the autocracy of Rome, was, however, at the same time an independently necessary feature in the history of Rome and of the world. It was not, then, his private gain merely, but an unconscious impulse that occasioned the accomplishment of that for which the time was ripe. Such are all great historical men—whose own particular aims involve those large issues which are the will of the world-spirit. They may be called heroes, inasmuch as they have derived their purposes and their vocation, not from the calm, regular course of things, sanctioned by the existing order; but from a concealed fount—one which has not attained to phenomenal, present existence—from that inner spirit, still hidden beneath the surface, which, impinging on the outer world as on a shell, bursts it in pieces, because it is another kernel than that which belonged to the shell in question. They are men, therefore, who appear to draw the impulse of their life from themselves; and whose deeds have produced a condition of things and a complex of historical relations which appear to be only *their* interest, and *their* work.

Such individuals had no consciousness of the general idea they were unfolding, while prosecuting those aims of theirs; on the contrary, they were practical, political men. But at the same time they were thinking men, who had an insight into the requirements of the time—*what was ripe for development.* This was the very truth for their age, for their world; the species next in order, so to speak, and which was already formed in the womb of time. It was theirs to know this nascent principle; the necessary, directly sequent step in progress, which their world was to take; to make this their aim, and to expend their energy in promoting it. World-historical men, the heroes of an epoch, must, therefore, be recognized as its clear-sighted ones; *their* deeds, *their* words are the best of that time. Great men have formed purposes to satisfy themselves, not others. Whatever prudent designs and counsels they might have learned from others would be the more limited and inconsistent features in their career; for it was they who best understood affairs; from whom *others* learned, and approved, or at least acquiesced in their policy. For that spirit which had taken this fresh step in history is the inmost soul of all individuals; but in a state of unconsciousness which the great men in question aroused. Their fellows, therefore, follow these soul-leaders; for they feel the irresistible power of their own inner spirit thus embodied. If we go on to cast a look at the fate of these world-historical persons, whose vocation it was to be the agents of the world-spirit, we shall find it to have been no happy one. They attained no calm enjoyment; their whole life was labor and trouble; their whole nature was nought else but their master-passion. When their object is attained they fall off like empty hulls from the kernel. They die early, like Alexander; they are murdered, like Cæsar; transported to St. Helena, like Napoleon. This fearful consolation—that historical men have not enjoyed what is called happiness, and of which only private life (and this may be passed under very various external circumstances) is capable—this consolation those may draw from history, who stand in need of it; and it is craved by envy—vexed at what is great and transcendent—striving, therefore, to depreciate it, and to find some flaw in it. Thus in modern times it has been demonstrated *ad nauseam* that princes are generally unhappy on their thrones; in consideration of which the possession of a throne is tolerated, and men acquiesce in the fact that not themselves but the personages in question are its occupants. The free man, we may observe, is not envious, but gladly recognizes what is great and exalted, and rejoices that it exists.

It is in the light of those common elements which constitute the interest and therefore the passions of individuals, that these historical men are to be regarded. They are *great* men, because they willed and accomplished something great; not a mere fancy, a mere intention, but that which met the case and fell in with the needs of the age. This mode of considering them also excludes the so-called "psychological" view, which, serving the purpose of envy most effectually, contrives so to refer all actions to the heart —to bring them under such a subjective aspect —as that their authors appear to have done everything under the impulse of some passion, mean or grand—some *morbid craving*—and on account of these passions and cravings to have been not moral men. Alexander of Macedon partly subdued Greece, and then Asia; therefore he was possessed by a *morbid craving* for conquest. He is alleged to have acted from a craving for fame, for conquest; and the proof that these were the impelling motives is that he did that which resulted in fame. What pedagogue has not demonstrated of Alexander the Great, of Julius Cæsar, that they were instigated by such passions, and were consequently immoral men? Whence the conclusion immediately follows that he, the pedagogue, is a better man than they, because he has not such passions; a proof of which lies in the fact that he does not conquer Asia— vanquish Darius and Porus—but while he enjoys life himself, lets others enjoy it too. These psychologists are particularly fond of contemplating those peculiarities of great historical figures which appertain to them as private persons. Man must eat and drink; he sustains relations to friends and acquaintances; he has passing impulses and ebullitions of temper. "No man is a hero to his valet-de-chambre," is a well-known proverb; I have added—and Goethe repeated it ten years later—"but not because the former is no hero, but because the latter is a valet." He takes off the hero's boots, assists him to bed, knows that he prefers champagne, etc. Historical personages waited upon in historical literature by such psychological valets come poorly off; they are brought down by these their attendants to a level with, or rather a few degrees below the level of, the morality of such exquisite discerners of spirits. The Thersites of Homer who abuses the kings is a standing figure for all times. Blows, that is, beating with a solid cudgel, he does not get in every age, as in the Homeric one; but his envy, his egotism, is the thorn which he has to carry in his flesh; and the undying worm that gnaws him is the tormenting consideration that his excellent views and vituperations remain absolutely without result in the world. But our satisfaction at the fate of thersitism also may have its sinister side.

A world-historical individual is not so unwise as to indulge a variety of wishes to divide his regards. He is devoted to the one aim, regardless of all else. It is even possible that such men may treat other great, even sacred interests, inconsiderately; conduct which is indeed obnoxious to moral reprehension. But so mighty a form must trample down many an innocent flower, crush to pieces many an object in its path.

The special interest of passion is thus inseparable from the active development of a general principle: for it is from the special and determinate and from its negation, that the universal results. Particularity contends with its like, and some loss is involved in the issue. *It* is not the general idea that is implicated in opposition and combat, and that is exposed to danger. It remains in the background, untouched and uninjured. This may be called the *cunning of reason* —that it sets the passions to work for itself, while that which develops its existence through such impulsion pays the penalty, and suffers loss. For it is *phenomenal* being that is so treated, and of this, part is of no value, part is positive and real. The particular is for the most part of too trifling value as compared with the general: individuals are sacrificed and abandoned. The idea pays the penalty of determinate existence and of corruptibility, not from itself, but from the passions of individuals.

But though we might tolerate the idea that individuals, their desires and the gratification of them, are thus sacrificed, and their happiness given up to the empire of chance, to which it belongs; and that as a general rule, individuals come under the category of means to an ulterior end—there is one aspect of human individuality which we should hesitate to regard in that subordinate light, even in relation to the highest; since it is absolutely no subordinate element, but exists in those individuals as inherently eternal and divine. I mean *morality, ethics, religion.* Even when speaking of the realization of the great ideal aim by means of individuals, the *subjective* element in them—their interest and that of their cravings and impulses, their views and judgments, though exhibited as the merely formal side of their existence—was spoken of as having an infinite right to be consulted. The first idea that presents itself in speaking of

means is that of something external to the object and having no share in the object itself. But merely natural things—even the commonest lifeless objects—used as means, must be of such a kind as adapts them to their purpose; they must possess something in common with it. Human beings least of all, sustain the bare external relation of mere means to the great ideal aim. Not only do they in the very act of realizing it, make it the occasion of satisfying personal desires, whose purport is diverse from that aim— but they share in that ideal aim itself; and are for that very reason objects of their own existence; not *formally* merely, as the world of living beings generally is—whose individual life is essentially subordinate to that of man, and is properly used *up* as an instrument. Men, on the contrary, are objects of existence to themselves, as regards the intrinsic import of the aim in question. To this order belongs that in them which we would exclude from the category of mere means—morality, ethics, religion. That is to say, man is an object of existence in himself only in virtue of the divine that is in him—that which was designated at the outset as *reason;* which, in view of its activity and power of self-determination, was called *freedom*. And we affirm, without entering at present on the proof of the assertion, that religion, morality, etc. have their foundation and source in that principle, and so are essentially elevated above all alien necessity and chance. And here we must remark that individuals, to the extent of their freedom, are responsible for the depravation and enfeeblement of morals and religion. This is the seal of the absolute and sublime destiny of man—that he knows what is good and what is evil; that his destiny *is* his very ability to will either good or evil—in one word, that he is the subject of moral imputation, imputation not only of evil, but of good; and not only concerning this or that particular matter, and all that happens *ab extra*, but *also* the good and evil attaching to his individual freedom. The brute alone is simply innocent. It would, however, demand an extensive explanation, as extensive as the analysis of moral freedom itself, to preclude or obviate all the misunderstandings which the statement that what is called innocence imports the entire unconsciousness of evil—is wont to occasion.

In contemplating the fate which virtue, morality, even piety experience in history, we must not fall into the litany of lamentations, that the good and pious often, or for the most part, fare ill in the world, while the evil-disposed and wicked prosper. The term *prosperity* is used in a variety of meanings—riches, outward honour, and the like. But in speaking of something which in and for itself constitutes an aim of existence, that so-called well or ill-faring of these or those isolated individuals cannot be regarded as an essential element in the rational order of the universe. With more justice than happiness—or a fortunate environment for individuals—it is demanded of the grand aim of the world's existence, that it should foster, nay involve the execution and ratification of good, moral, righteous purposes. What makes men morally discontented (a discontent, by the by, on which they somewhat pride themselves) is that they do not find the present adapted to the realization of aims which they hold to be right and just (more especially in modern times, ideals of political constitutions); they contrast unfavorably things as they *are,* with their idea of things as they *ought* to be. In this case it is not private interest nor passion that desires gratification, but reason, justice, liberty; and equipped with this title, the demand in question assumes a lofty bearing, and readily adopts a position not merely of discontent, but of open revolt against the actual condition of the world. To estimate such a feeling and such views aright, the demands insisted upon, and the very dogmatic opinions asserted, must be examined. At no time so much as in our own, have such general principles and notions been advanced, or with greater assurance. If in days gone by, history seems to present itself as a struggle of passions; in our time, though displays of passion are not wanting, it exhibits partly a predominance of the struggle of notions assuming the authority of principles; partly that of passions and interests essentially subjective, but under the mask of such higher sanctions. The pretensions thus contended for as legitimate in the name of that which has been stated as the ultimate aim of reason, pass accordingly, for absolute aims—to the same extent as religion, morals, ethics. Nothing, as before remarked, is now more common than the complaint that the *ideals* which imagination sets up are not realized —that these glorious dreams are destroyed by cold actuality. These ideals, which in the voyage of life founder on the rocks of hard reality, may be in the first instance only subjective, and belong to the idiosyncrasy of the individual, imagining himself the highest and wisest. Such do not properly belong to this category. For the fancies which the individual in his isolation indulges, cannot be the model for universal reality; just as *universal* law is not designed for the units of the mass. These as such may, in fact,

find their interests decidedly thrust into the background. But by the term "ideal" we also understand the ideal of reason, of the good, of the true. Poets, as, *e.g.,* Schiller, have painted such ideals touchingly and with strong emotion, and with the deeply melancholy conviction that they could not be realized. In affirming, on the contrary, that the universal reason *does* realize itself, we have indeed nothing to do with the individual empirically regarded. That admits of degrees of better and worse, since here chance and speciality have received authority from the idea to exercise their monstrous power. Much, therefore, in particular aspects of the grand phenomenon might be found fault with. This subjective fault-finding—which, however, only keeps in view the individual and its deficiency, without taking notice of reason pervading the whole—is easy; and inasmuch as it asserts an excellent intention with regard to the good of the whole, and seems to result from a kindly heart, it feels authorized to give itself airs and assume great consequence. It is easier to discover a deficiency in individuals, in states, and in Providence, than to see their real import and value. For in this merely negative fault-finding a proud position is taken, one which overlooks the object, without having entered into it, without having comprehended its positive aspect. Age generally makes men more tolerant; youth is always discontented. The tolerance of age is the result of the ripeness of a judgment which, not merely as the result of indifference, is satisfied even with what is inferior; but, more deeply taught by the grave experience of life, has been led to perceive the substantial, solid worth of the object in question. The insight then to which —in contradistinction from those ideals—philosophy is to lead us, is, that the real world is as it ought to be, that the truly good, the universal divine reason, is not a mere abstraction, but a vital principle capable of realizing itself. This *good,* this *reason,* in its most concrete form, is God. God governs the world; the actual working of His government, the carrying out of His plan, is the history of the world. This plan philosophy strives to comprehend; for only that which has been developed as the result of it possesses *bona fide* reality. That which does not accord with it is negative, worthless existence. Before the pure light of this divine idea, which is no mere ideal, the phantom of a world whose events are an incoherent concourse of fortuitous circumstances utterly vanishes. Philosophy wishes to discover the substantial purport, the real side of the divine idea, and to justify the so much despised reality of things; for reason is the comprehension of the divine work. But as to what concerns the perversion, corruption, and ruin of religious, ethical, and moral purposes, and states of society generally, it must be affirmed that in their *essence* these are infinite and eternal; but that the forms they assume may be of a limited order, and consequently belong to the domain of mere nature, and be subject to the sway of chance. They are therefore perishable, and exposed to decay and corruption. Religion and morality, in the same way as inherently universal essences, have the peculiarity of being present in the individual soul, in the full extent of their idea, and therefore truly and really; although, they may not manifest themselves in it *in extenso*, and are not applied to fully developed relations. The religion, the morality of a limited sphere of life—that of a shepherd or a peasant, *e.g.*—in its intensive concentration and limitation to a few perfectly simple relations of life, has infinite worth; the same worth as the religion and morality of extensive knowledge, and of an existence rich in the compass of its relations and actions. This inner focus—this simple region of the claims of subjective freedom, the home of volition, resolution, and action, the abstract sphere of conscience—that which comprises the responsibility and moral value of the individual, remains untouched; and is quite shut out from the noisy din of the world's history—including not merely external and temporal changes, but also those entailed by the absolute necessity inseparable from the realization of the idea of freedom itself. But as a general truth this must be regarded as settled: that whatever in the world possesses claims as noble and glorious has nevertheless a higher existence above it. The claim of the world-spirit rises above all special claims.

These observations may suffice in reference to the means which the world-spirit uses for realizing its idea. Stated simply and abstractly, this mediation involves the activity of personal existences in whom reason is present as their absolute, substantial being; but a basis, in the first instance, still obscure and unknown to them. But the subject becomes more complicated and difficult when we regard individuals not merely in their aspect of activity, but, more concretely, in conjunction with a particular manifestation of that activity in their religion and morality—forms of existence which are intimately connected with reason, and share in its absolute claims. Here the relation of mere means to an end disappears, and the chief bearings of this seeming difficulty in reference to the absolute aim of spirit have been briefly considered.

(3) The third point to be analysed is, therefore—what is the object to be realized by these means; *i.e.*, what is the form it assumes in the realm of reality. We have spoken of *means;* but in the carrying out of a subjective, limited aim, we have also to take into consideration the element of a *material,* either already present or which has to be procured. Thus the question would arise: What is the material in which the ideal of reason is wrought out? The primary answer would be—personality itself—human desires—subjectivity generally. In human knowledge and volition, as its material element, reason attains positive existence. We have considered subjective volition where it has an object which is the truth and essence of a reality, *viz.,* where it constitutes a great world-historical passion. As a subjective will, occupied with limited passions, it is dependent, and can gratify its desires only within the limits of this dependence. But the subjective will has also a substantial life—a reality—in which it moves in the region of *essential* being, and has the essential itself as the object of its existence. This essential being is the union of the *subjective* with the *rational* will: it is the moral whole, the *state,* which is that form of reality in which the individual has and enjoys his freedom; but on the condition of his recognizing, believing in, and willing that which is common to the whole. And this must not be understood as if the subjective will of the social unit attained its gratification and enjoyment through that common will; as if this were a means provided for its benefit; as if the individual, in his relations to other individuals, thus limited his freedom, in order that this universal limitation—the mutual constraint of all—might secure a small space of liberty for each. Rather, we affirm, are law, morality, government, and they alone, the positive reality and completion of freedom. Freedom of a low and limited order is mere caprice; which finds its exercise in the sphere of particular and limited desires.

Subjective volition—passion—is that which sets men in activity, that which effects "practical" realization. The idea is the inner spring of action; the state is the actually existing, realized moral life. For it is the unity of the universal, essential will, with that of the individual; and this is "morality." The individual living in this unity has a moral life; possesses a value that consists in this substantiality alone. Sophocles in his *Antigone,* says, "The divine commands are not of yesterday, nor of to-day; no, they have an infinite existence, and no one could say whence they came." The laws of morality are not accidental, but are the essentially rational. It is the very object of the state that what is essential in the practical activity of men, and in their dispositions, should be duly recognized; that it should have a manifest existence, and maintain its position. It is the absolute interest of reason that this moral whole should exist; and herein lies the justification and merit of heroes who have founded states—however rude these may have been. In the history of the world, only those peoples can come under our notice which form a state. For it must be understood that this latter is the realization of freedom, *i.e.*, of the absolute final aim, and that it exists for its own sake. It must further be understood that all the worth which the human being possesses, all spiritual reality, he possesses only through the state. For his spiritual reality consists in this, that his own essence—reason—is objectively present to him, that it possesses objective immediate existence for him. Thus only is he fully conscious; thus only is he a partaker of morality, of a just and moral social and political life. For truth is the unity of the universal and subjective will; and the universal is to be found in the state, in its laws, its universal and rational arrangements. The state is the divine idea as it exists on earth. We have in it, therefore, the object of history in a more definite shape than before; that in which freedom obtains objectivity, and lives in the enjoyment of this objectivity. For law is the objectivity of spirit; volition in its true form. Only that will which obeys law is free; for it obeys itself—it is independent and so free. When the state or our country constitutes a community of existence; when the subjective will of man submits to laws—the contradiction between liberty and necessity vanishes. The rational has necessary existence, as being the reality and substance of things, and we are free in recognizing it as law, and following it as the substance of our own being. The objective and the subjective will are then reconciled, and present one identical homogeneous whole. For the morality of the state is not of that ethical reflective kind, in which one's own conviction bears sway; this latter is rather the peculiarity of the modern time, while the true antique morality is based on the principle of abiding by one's duty. An Athenian citizen did what was required of him, as it were from instinct: but if I reflect on the object of my activity, I must have the consciousness that my will has been called into exercise. But morality

is duty—substantial right—a *"second* nature," as it has been justly called; for the *first* nature of man is his primary merely animal existence.

The development *in extenso* of the idea of the state belongs to the philosophy of jurisprudence; but it must be observed that in the theories of our time various errors are current respecting it, which pass for established truths, and have become fixed prejudices. We will mention only a few of them, giving prominence to such as have a reference to the object of our history.

The error which first meets us is the direct contradictory of our principle that the state presents the realization of freedom; the opinion, *viz.*, that man is free by *nature*, but that in *society,* in the state, to which nevertheless he is irresistibly impelled, he must limit this natural freedom. That man is free by nature is quite correct in one sense; *viz.*, that he is so according to the idea of humanity; but we imply thereby that he is such only in virtue of his destiny— that he has an undeveloped power to become such; for the "nature" of an object is exactly synonymous with its "idea." But the view in question imports more than this. When man is spoken of as "free by nature," the mode of his existence as well as his destiny is implied. His merely natural and primary condition is intended. In this sense a "state of nature" is assumed in which mankind at large are in the possession of their natural rights with the unconstrained exercise and enjoyment of their freedom. This assumption is not indeed raised to the dignity of the historical fact; it would indeed be difficult, were the attempt seriously made, to point out any such condition as actually existing, or as having ever occurred. Examples of a savage state of life can be pointed out, but they are marked by brutal passions and deeds of violence; while, however rude and simple their conditions, they involve social arrangements which (to use the common phrase) *restrain* freedom. That assumption is one of those nebulous images which theory produces; an idea which it cannot avoid originating, but which it fathers upon real existence, without sufficient historical justification.

What we find such a state of nature to be in actual experience answers exactly to the idea of a *merely* natural condition. Freedom as the *ideal* of that which is original and natural, does not exist *as original and natural*. Rather must it be first sought out and won; and that by an incalculable medial discipline of the intellectual and moral powers. The state of nature is, therefore, predominantly that of injustice and violence, of untamed natural impulses, of inhuman deeds and feelings. Limitation is certainly produced by society and the state, but it is a limitation of the mere brute emotions and rude instincts; as also, in a more advanced stage of culture, of the premeditated self-will of caprice and passion. This kind of constraint is part of the instrumentality by which only, the consciousness of freedom and the desire for its attainment, in its true—that is, rational and ideal form—can be obtained. To the ideal of freedom, law and morality are indispensably requisite; and they are in and for themselves, universal existences, objects and aims; which are discovered only by the activity of thought, separating itself from the merely sensuous, and developing itself, in opposition thereto; and which must on the other hand, be introduced into and incorporated with the originally sensuous will, and that contrarily to its natural inclination. The perpetually recurring misapprehension of freedom consists in regarding that term only in its *formal,* subjective sense, abstracted from its essential objects and aims; thus a constraint put upon impulse, desire, passion—pertaining to the particular individual as such—a limitation of caprice and self-will is regarded as a fettering of freedom. We should on the contrary look upon such limitation as the indispensable proviso of emancipation. Society and the state are the very conditions in which freedom is realized.

We must notice a second view, contravening the principle of the development of moral relations into a legal form. The *patriarchal* condition is regarded—either in reference to the entire race of man, or to some branches of it—as exclusively that condition of things in which the legal element is combined with a due recognition of the moral and emotional parts of our nature; and in which justice as united with these, truly and really influences the intercourse of the social units. The basis of the patriarchal condition is the family relation; which develops the *primary* form of conscious morality, succeeded by that of the state as its *second* phase. The patriarchal condition is one of transition, in which the family has already advanced to the position of a race or people; where the union, therefore, has already ceased to be simply a bond of love and confidence, and has become one of plighted service. We must first examine the ethical principle of the family. The family may be reckoned as virtually a single person; since its members have either mutually surrendered their individual personality (and con-

sequently their legal position towards each other, with the rest of their particular interests and desires), as in the case of the parents; or have not yet attained such an independent personality—(the children, who are primarily in that merely natural condition already mentioned). They live, therefore, in a unity of feeling, love, confidence, and faith in each other. And in a relation of natural love, the one individual has the consciousness of himself in the consciousness of the other; he lives out of self; and in this mutual self-renunciation each regains the life that had been virtually transferred to the other; gains, in fact, that other's existence and his own, as involved with that other. The farther interests connected with the necessities and external concerns of life, as well as the development that has to take place within their circle, *i.e.,* of the children, constitute a common object for the members of the family. The spirit of the family —the Penates—form one substantial being, as much as the spirit of a people in the state; and morality in both cases consists in a feeling, a consciousness, and a will, not limited to individual personality and interest, but embracing the common interests of the members generally. But this unity is in the case of the family essentially one of *feeling;* not advancing beyond the limits of the merely *natural.* The piety of the family relation should be respected in the highest degree by the state; by its means the state obtains as its members individuals who are already moral (for as mere *persons* they are not) and who in uniting to form a state bring with them that sound basis of a political edifice—the capacity of feeling one with a whole. But the expansion of the family to a patriarchal unity carries us beyond the ties of blood-relationship —the simply natural elements of that basis; and outside of these limits the members of the community must enter upon the position of independent personality. A review of the patriarchal condition, *in extenso,* would lead us to give special attention to the theocratical constitution. The head of the patriarchal clan is also its priest. If the family in its general relations, is not yet separated from civic society and the state, the separation of religion from it has also not yet taken place; and so much the less since the piety of the hearth is itself a profoundly subjective state of feeling.

We have considered two aspects of freedom, the objective and the subjective; if, therefore, freedom is asserted to consist in the individuals of a state all agreeing in its arrangements, it is evident that only the subjective aspect is regarded. The natural inference from this principle is that no law can be valid without the approval of all. This difficulty is attempted to be obviated by the decision that the minority must yield to the majority; the majority therefore bear the sway. But long ago J. J. Rousseau remarked that in that case there would be no longer freedom, for the will of the *minority* would cease to be respected. At the Polish Diet each single member had to give his consent before any political step could be taken; and this kind of freedom it was that ruined the state. Besides, it is a dangerous and false prejudice that the people *alone* have reason and insight, and know what justice is; for each popular faction may represent itself as the people, and the question as to what constitutes the state is one of advanced science and not of popular decision.

If the principle of regard for the individual will is recognized as the only basis of political liberty, *viz.*, that nothing should be done by or for the state to which all the members of the body politic have not given their sanction, we have, properly speaking, no *constitution*. The only arrangement that would be necessary, would be, first, a centre having no *will* of its own, but which should take into consideration what appeared to be the necessities of the state; and, secondly, a contrivance for calling the members of the state together, for taking the votes, and for performing the arithmetical operations of reckoning and comparing the number of votes for the different propositions, and thereby deciding upon them. The state is an *abstraction*, having even its generic existence in its citizens; but it is an actuality, and its simply generic existence must embody itself in individual will and activity. The want of government and political administration in general is felt; this necessitates the selection and separation from the rest of those who have to take the helm in political affairs, to decide concerning them, and to give orders to other citizens, with a view to the execution of their plans. If, *e.g.*, even the people in a democracy resolve on a war, a general must head the army. It is only by a constitution that the *abstraction*—the state—attains life and reality; but this involves the distinction between those who command and those who obey. Yet obedience seems inconsistent with liberty, and those who command appear to do the very opposite of that which the fundamental idea of the state, *viz.*, that of freedom, requires. It is, however, urged that—though the distinction between commanding and obeying is absolutely necessary, because affairs could not go on

without it—and indeed this seems only a compulsory limitation, external to and even contravening freedom in the abstract—the constitution should be at least so framed that the citizens may obey as little as possible, and the smallest modicum of free volition be left to the commands of the superiors; that the substance of that for which subordination is necessary, even in its most important bearings, should be decided and resolved on by the people—by the will of many or of all the citizens; though it is supposed to be thereby provided that the state should be possessed of vigor and strength as a reality—an individual unity.

The primary consideration is, then, the distinction between the governing and the governed, and the political constitutions in the abstract have been rightly divided into monarchy, aristocracy, and democracy; which gives occasion, however, to the remark that monarchy itself must be further divided into despotism and monarchy proper; that in all the divisions to which the leading idea gives rise, only the generic character is to be made prominent—it being not intended thereby that the particular category under review should be exhausted as a form, order, or kind in its *concrete* development. But especially it must be observed that the above-mentioned divisions admit of a multitude of particular modifications—not only such as lie within the limits of those classes themselves, but also such as are mixtures of several of these essentially distinct classes, and which are consequently misshapen, unstable, and inconsistent forms. In such a collision, the concerning question is: what is the *best constitution;* that is, by what arrangement, organization, or mechanism of the power of the state its object can be most surely attained. This object may indeed be variously understood; for instance, as the calm enjoyment of life on the part of the citizens, or as universal happiness. Such aims have suggested the so-called ideals of constitutions, and, as a particular branch of the subject, ideals of the education of princes (Fenelon), or of the governing body—the aristocracy at large (Plato); for the chief point they treat of is the condition of those subjects who stand at the head of affairs; and in these ideals the concrete details of political organization are not at all considered. The inquiry into the best constitution is frequently treated as if not only the theory were an affair of subjective independent conviction, but as if the introduction of a constitution recognized as the best—or as superior to others—could be the result of a resolve adopted in this theoretical manner; as if the form of a consitution were a matter of free choice, determined by nothing else but reflection. Of this artless fashion was that deliberation—not indeed of the Persian *people*, but of the Persian *grandees*, who had conspired to overthrow the pseudo-Smerdis and the Magi, after their undertaking had succeeded, and when there was no scion of the royal family living—as to what constitution they should introduce into Persia; and Herodotus gives an equally naïve account of this deliberation.

In the present day, the constitution of a country and people is not represented as so entirely dependent on free and deliberate choice. The fundamental but abstractly (and therefore imperfectly) entertained conception of freedom, has resulted in the republic being very generally regarded—in *theory*—as the only just and true political constitution. Many even, who occupy elevated official positions under monarchical constitutions, so far from being opposed to this idea, are actually its supporters; only they see that such a constitution, though the best, cannot be realized under all circumstances; and that, while men are what they are, we must be satisfied with less freedom; the monarchical constitution—under the given circumstances, and the present moral condition of the people—being even regarded as the most advantageous. In this view also, the necessity of a particular constitution is made to depend on the condition of the people in such a way as if the latter were non-essential and accidental. This representation is founded on the distinction which the reflective understanding makes between an idea and the corresponding reality; holding to an abstract and consequently untrue idea; not grasping it in its completeness, or—which is virtually, though not in point of form, the same—not taking a concrete view of a people and a state. We shall have to show, further on, that the constitution adopted by a people makes one substance—one spirit—with its religion, its art and philosophy, or, at least, with its conceptions and thoughts—its culture generally; not to expatiate upon the additional influences, *ab extra*, of climate, of neighbors, of its place in the world. A state is an individual totality, of which you cannot select any particular side, although a supremely important one, such as its political constitution, and deliberate and decide respecting it in that isolated form. Not only is that constitution most intimately connected with and dependent on those other spiritual forces; but the form of the entire moral and intellectual individuality, comprising all the forces it embodies, is only a step in the development of the grand whole—with its place preappointed in the process; a fact which gives the highest sanction to the constitution in question, and establishes its absolute necessity. The origin of a state involves imperious lordship on the one hand, instinctive submission on the other. But even obedience—lordly power, and the fear inspired by a ruler—in itself implies some degree of voluntary connection. Even in barbarous states this is the case; it is not the isolated will of individuals that prevails; individual pretensions are relinquished, and the general will is the essential bond of political union. This unity of the general and the particular is the *idea* itself, manifesting itself as a *state*, and which subsequently undergoes further development within itself. The abstract yet necessitated process in the development of truly independent states is as follows: they begin with regal power, whether of patriarchal or military origin. In the next phase, particularity and individuality assert themselves in the form of aristocracy and democracy. Lastly, we have the subjection of these separate interests to a single power; but which can be absolutely none other than one outside of which those spheres have an independent position, *viz.*, the monarchical. Two phases of royalty, therefore, must be distinguished—a primary and a secondary one. This process is necessitated, so that the form of government assigned to a particular stage of development *must* present itself: it is therefore no matter of choice, but is that form which is adapted to the spirit of the people.

In a constitution the main feature of interest is the self-development of the *rational*, that is, the *political* condition of a people; the setting free of the successive elements of the idea: so that the several powers in the state manifest themselves as separate, attain their appropriate and special perfection, and yet in this independent condition, work together for one object, and are held together by it—*i.e.*, form an organic whole. The state is thus the embodiment of rational freedom, realizing and recognizing itself in an objective form. For its objectivity consists in this—that its successive stages are not merely ideal, but are present in an appropriate reality; and that in their separate and several working, they are absolutely merged in that agency by which the totality—the soul, the individuate unity—is produced, and of which it is the result.

The state is the idea of spirit in the external manifestation of human will and its freedom. It is to the state, therefore, that change in the aspect of history indissolubly attaches itself; and the successive phases of the idea manifest themselves in it as distinct political *principles*. The constitutions under which world-historical peoples have reached their culmination, are peculiar to them; and therefore do not present a generally applicable political basis. Were it otherwise, the differences of similar constitutions would consist only in a peculiar method of expanding and developing that generic basis; whereas they really originate in diversity of principle. From the comparison therefore of the political institutions of the ancient world-historical peoples, it so happens that, for the most recent principle of a constitution—for the principle of our own times—nothing (so to speak) can be learned. In science and art it is quite otherwise; *e.g.*, the ancient philosophy is so decidedly the basis of the modern, that it is inevitably contained in the latter, and constitutes its basis. In this case the relation is that of a continuous development of the same structure, whose foundation-stone, walls, and roof have remained what they were. In art, the Greek itself, in its original form, furnishes us the best models. But in regard to political constitution, it is quite otherwise: here the ancient and the modern have not their essential principle in common. Abstract definitions and dogmas respecting just government—importing that intelligence and virtue ought to bear sway —are, indeed, common to both. But nothing is so absurd as to look to Greeks, Romans, or Orientals, for models for the political arrangements of our time. From the East may be derived beautiful pictures of a patriarchal condition, of paternal government, and of devotion to it on the part of peoples; from Greeks and Romans, descriptions of popular liberty. Among the latter we find the idea of a free constitution admitting all the citizens to a share in deliberations and resolves respecting the affairs and laws of the commonwealth. In our times, too, this is its general acceptation; only with this modification, that—since our states are so large, and there are so many of "the many," the latter, direct action being impossible, should by the indirect method of elective substitution express their concurrence with resolves affecting the common weal; that is, that for legislative purposes generally, the people should be represented by deputies. The so-called representative constitution is that form of government with which we connect the idea of a free constitution; and this notion has become a rooted prejudice. On this theory people and government are separated. But there is a perversity in this antithesis; an ill-intentioned ruse designed to insinuate that the people are the totality of the state. Besides, the basis of this view is the principle of isolated individuality—the absolute validity of the subjective will—a dogma which we have already investigated. The great point is that freedom in its ideal conception has not subjective will and caprice for its principle, but the recognition of the universal will; and that the process by which freedom is realized is the free development of its successive stages. The subjective will is a merely formal determination—a *carte blanche*—not including what it is that is willed. Only the *rational* will is that universal principle which independently determines and unfolds its own being, and develops its successive elemental phases as organic members. Of this Gothic-cathedral architecture the ancients knew nothing.

At an earlier stage of the discussion, we established the two elemental considerations: first, the *idea* of freedom as the absolute and final aim; secondly, the *means* for realizing it, *i.e.*, the subjective side of knowledge and will, with its life, movement, and activity. We then recognized the state as the moral whole and the reality of freedom, and consequently as the objective unity of these two elements. For although we make this distinction into two aspects for our consideration, it must be remarked that they are intimately connected; and that their connection is involved in the idea of each when examined separately. We have, on the one hand, recognized the idea in the definite form of freedom conscious of and willing itself—having itself alone as its object: involving at the same time, the pure and simple idea of reason, and likewise, that which we have called subject— self-consciousness—spirit actually existing in the world. If, on the other hand, we consider subjectivity, we find that subjective knowledge and will is thought. But by the very act of thoughtful cognition and volition, I will the universal object—the substance of absolute reason. We observe, therefore, an essential union between the objective side—the idea—and the subjective side—the personality that conceives and wills it. The *objective* existence of this union is the state, which is therefore the basis and centre of the other concrete elements of the life of a people—of art, of law, of morals, of religion, of science. All the activity of spirit has only this object—the becoming conscious of this union, *i.e.*, of its own freedom. Among the forms of this conscious union *religion* occupies the highest position. In it, spirit—rising above the limitations of temporal and secular existence—becomes conscious of the absolute spirit, and in this consciousness of the self-existent Being, renounces its individual interest; it lays this aside in devotion—a state of mind in which it refuses to occupy itself any longer with the limited and particular. By sacrifice man expresses his renunciation of his property, his will, his individual feelings. The religious concentration of the soul appears in the form of feeling; it nevertheless passes also into reflection; a form of worship (*cultus*) is a result of reflection. The second form of the union of the objective and subjective in the human spirit is *art*. This advances farther into the realm of the actual and sensuous than religion. In its noblest walk it is occupied with representing, not indeed, the spirit of God, but certainly the form of God; and in its secondary aims, that which is divine and spiritual generally. Its office is to render visible the divine; presenting it to the imaginative and intuitive faculty. But the true is the object not only of conception and feeling, as in religion—and of intuition, as in art—but also of the thinking faculty; and this gives us the third form of the union in question—*philosophy*. This is consequently the highest, freest, and wisest phase. Of course we are not intending to investigate these three phases here; they have only suggested themselves in virtue of their occupying the same general ground as the object here considered—the *state*.

The general principle which manifests itself and becomes an object of consciousness in the state, the form under which all that the state includes is brought, is the whole of that cycle of phenomena which constitutes the *culture* of a nation. But the definite *substance* that receives the form of universality, and exists in that concrete reality which is the state—is the spirit of the people itself. The actual state is animated by this spirit, in all its particular affairs—its wars, institutions, etc. But man must also attain a conscious realization of this his spirit and essential nature, and of his original identity with it. For we said that morality is the identity of the *subjective* or *personal* with the *universal* will. Now the mind must give itself an express consciousness of this; and the focus of this knowledge is *religion*. Art and science are only various aspects and forms of the same substantial being. In considering religion, the chief point of inquiry is whether it recognizes the true—the idea—only in its separate, abstract form, or in its true unity; in *separation*—God

being represented in an abstract form as the Highest Being, Lord of heaven and earth, living in a remote region far from human actualities—or in its *unity*—God, as unity of the universal and individual; the individual itself assuming the aspect of positive and real existence in the idea of the incarnation. Religion is the sphere in which a nation gives itself the definition of that which it regards as the true. A definition contains everything that belongs to the essence of an object; reducing its nature to its simple characteristic predicate, as a mirror for every predicate—the generic soul pervading all its details. The conception of God, therefore, constitutes the general basis of a people's character.

In this aspect, religion stands in the closest connection with the political principle. Freedom can exist only where individuality is recognized as having its positive and real existence in the Divine Being. The connection may be further explained thus:—secular existence, as merely temporal—occupied with particular interests—is consequently only relative and unauthorized; and receives its validity only in so far as the universal soul that pervades it—its principle—receives absolute validity; which it cannot have unless it is recognized as the definite manifestation, the phenomenal existence of the Divine Essence. On this account it is that the state rests on religion. We hear this often repeated in our times, though for the most part nothing further is meant than that individual subjects as God-fearing men would be more disposed and ready to perform their duty; since obedience to king and law so naturally follows in the train of reverence for God. This reverence, indeed, since it exalts the general over the special, may even turn upon the latter, become fanatical, and work with incendiary and destructive violence against the state, its institutions, and arrangements. Religious feeling, therefore, it is thought, should be sober, kept in a certain degree of coolness, that it may not storm against and bear down that which should be defended and preserved by it. The possibility of such a catastrophe is at least latent in it.

While, however, the correct sentiment is adopted, that the state is based on religion, the position thus assigned to religion supposes the state already to exist; and that subsequently, in order to maintain it, religion must be brought into it—in buckets and bushels as it were—and impressed upon people's hearts. It is quite true that men must be trained to religion, but not as to something whose existence has yet to begin. For in affirming that the state is based on religion—that it has its roots in it—we virtually assert that the former has proceeded from the latter; and that this derivation is going on now and will always continue; *i.e.*, the principles of the state must be regarded as valid in and for themselves, which can only be in so far as they are recognized as determinate manifestations of the Divine Nature. The form of religion, therefore, decides that of the state and its constitution. The latter actually originated in the particular religion adopted by the nation; so that, in fact, the Athenian or the Roman state was possible only in connection with the specific form of heathenism existing among the respective peoples; just as a Catholic state has a spirit and constitution different from that of a Protestant one.

If that outcry—that urging and striving for the implantation of religion in the community—were an utterance of anguish and a call for help, as it often seems to be, expressing the danger of religion having vanished, or being about to vanish entirely from the state—that would be fearful indeed—worse, in fact, than this outcry supposes; for it implies the belief in a resource against the evil, *viz.*, the implantation and inculcation of religion; whereas religion is by no means a thing to be so produced; its *self-production* (and there can be no other) lies much deeper.

Another and opposite folly which we meet with in our time is that of pretending to invent and carry out political constitutions independently of religion. The Catholic confession, although sharing the Christian name with the Protestant, does not concede to the state an inherent justice and morality—a concession which in the Protestant principle is fundamental. This tearing away of the political morality of the constitution from its natural connection, is necessary to the genius of that religion, inasmuch as it does not recognize justice and morality as independent and substantial. But thus excluded from intrinsic worth—torn away from their last refuge, the sanctuary of conscience, the calm retreat where religion has its abode—the principles and institutions of political legislation are destitute of a real centre, to the same degree as they are compelled to remain abstract and indefinite.

Summing up what has been said of the state, we find that we have been led to call its vital principle, as actuating the individuals who compose it, morality. The state, its laws, its arrangements, constitute the rights of its members; its natural features, its mountains, air, and waters, are *their* country, their fatherland, their outward material property; the history of this state, *their* deeds; what their ancestors have produced, belongs to them and lives in their memory. All is their possession, just as they are possessed by it; for it constitutes their existence, their being.

Their imagination is occupied with the ideas thus presented, while the adoption of these laws, and of a fatherland so conditioned is the expression of their will. It is this matured totality which thus constitutes *one* being, the spirit of *one* people. To it the individual members belong; each unit is the son of his nation, and at the same time, in as far as the state to which he belongs is undergoing development, the son of his age. None remains behind it, still less advances beyond it. This spiritual being (the spirit of his time) is his; he is a representative of it; it is that in which he originated, and in which he lives. Among the Athenians the word *Athens* had a double import; suggesting primarily, a complex of political institutions, but no less, in the second place, that goddess who represented the spirit of the people and its unity.

This spirit of a people is a *determinate* and particular spirit, and is, as just stated, further modified by the degree of its historical development. This spirit, then, constitutes the basis and substance of those other forms of a nation's consciousness, which have been noticed. For spirit in its self-consciousness must become an object of contemplation to itself, and objectivity involves, in the first instance, the rise of differences which make up a total of distinct spheres of objective spirit; in the same way as the soul exists only as the complex of its faculties, which in their form of concentration in a simple unity produce that soul. It is thus *one individuality* which, presented in its essence as God, is honoured and enjoyed in *religion;* which is exhibited as an object of sensuous contemplation in *art;* and is apprehended as an intellectual conception in *philosophy*. In virtue of the original identity of their essence, purport, and object, these various forms are inseparably united with the spirit of the state. Only in connection with this particular religion, can this particular political constitution exist; just as in such or such a state, such or such a philosophy or order of art.

The remark next in order is that each particular national genius is to be treated as only one individual in the process of universal history. For that history is the exhibition of the divine, absolute development of spirit in its highest forms—that gradation by which it attains its truth and consciousness of itself. The forms which these grades of progress assume are the characteristic "national spirits" of history; the peculiar tenor of their moral life, of their government, their art, religion, and science. To realize these grades is the boundless impulse of the world-spirit—the goal of its irresistible urging; for this division into organic members, and the full development of each, is its idea. Universal history is exclusively occupied with showing how spirit comes to a recognition and adoption of the truth: the dawn of knowledge appears; it begins to discover salient principles, and at last it arrives at full consciousness.

Having, therefore, learned the abstract characteristics of the nature of spirit, the means which it uses to realize its idea, and the shape assumed by it in its complete realization in phenomenal existence—namely, the state—nothing further remains for this introductory section to contemplate but

III. *The course of the world's history.* The mutations which history presents have been long characterized in the general, as an advance to something better, more perfect. The changes that take place in nature—how infinitely manifold soever they may be—exhibit only a perpetually self-repeating cycle; in nature there happens "nothing new under the sun," and the multiform play of its phenomena so far induces a feeling of *ennui;* only in those changes which take place in the region of spirit does anything new arise. This peculiarity in the world of mind has indicated in the case of man an altogether different destiny from that of merely natural objects—in which we find always one and the same stable character, to which all change reverts—namely, a *real* capacity for change, and that for the better, an impulse of *perfectibility.* This principle, which reduces change itself under a law, has met with an unfavorable reception from religions—such as the Catholic—and from states claiming as their just right a stereotyped, or at least a stable position. If the mutability of worldly things in general—political constitutions, for instance—is conceded, either religion (as the religion of *truth*) is absolutely excepted, or the difficulty escaped by ascribing changes, revolutions, and abrogations of immaculate theories and institutions, to accidents or imprudence—but principally to the levity and evil passions of man. The principle of perfectibility indeed is almost as indefinite a term as mutability in general; it is without scope or goal, and has no standard by which to estimate the chang-

es in question: the improved, more perfect, state of things towards which it professedly tends is altogether undetermined.

The principle of *development* involves also the existence of a latent germ of being—a capacity or potentiality striving to realize itself. This formal conception finds actual existence in spirit; which has the history of the world for its theatre, its possession, and the sphere of its realization. It is not of such a nature as to be tossed to and fro amid the superficial play of accidents, but is rather the absolute arbiter of things; entirely unmoved by contingencies, which, indeed, it applies and manages for its own purposes. Development, however, is also a property of organized natural objects. Their existence presents itself, not as an exclusively dependent one, subjected to external changes, but as one which expands itself in virtue of an internal unchangeable principle; a simple essence —whose existence, *i.e.,* as a germ, is primarily simple—but which subsequently develops a variety of parts, that become involved with other objects, and consequently live through a continuous process of changes—a process, nevertheless, that results in the very contrary of change, and is even transformed into a *vis conservatrix* of the organic principle, and the form embodying it. Thus the organized *individuum* produces itself; it expands itself *actually* to what it was always *potentially.* So spirit is only that which it attains by its own efforts; it makes itself *actually* what it always was *potentially.* That development (of *natural organisms*) takes place in a direct, unopposed, unhindered manner. Between the idea and its realization, the essential constitution of the original germ and the conformity to it of the existence derived from it, no disturbing influence can intrude. But in relation to spirit it is quite otherwise. The realization of *its* idea is mediated by consciousness and will; these very faculties are, in the first instance, sunk in their primary *merely* natural life; the first object and goal of their striving is the realization of their merely natural destiny— but which, since it is spirit that animates it, is possessed of vast attractions and displays great power and richness. Thus spirit is at war with itself; it has to overcome itself as its most formidable obstacle. That development which in the sphere of nature is a peaceful growth, is in that of spirit, a severe, a mighty conflict with itself. What spirit really strives for is the realization of its ideal being; but in doing so, it hides that goal from its own vision, and is proud and well satisfied in this alienation from it.

Its expansion, therefore, does not present the harmless tranquillity of mere growth, as does that of organic life, but a stern reluctant working against itself. It exhibits, moreover, not the mere formal conception of development, but the attainment of a definite result. The goal of attainment we determined at the outset: it is spirit in its *completeness,* in its essential nature, *i.e.,* freedom. This is the fundamental object, and therefore also the leading principle of the development—that whereby it receives meaning and importance (as in the Roman history, Rome is the object—consequently that which directs our consideration of the facts related); as, conversely, the phenomena of the process have resulted from this principle alone, and only as referred to it, possess a sense of value. There are many considerable periods in history in which this development seems to have been intermitted; in which, we might rather say, the whole enormous gain of previous culture appears to have been entirely lost; after which, unhappily, a new commencement has been necessary, made in the hope of recovering—by the assistance of some remains saved from the wreck of a former civilization, and by dint of a renewed incalculable expenditure of strength and time—one of the regions which had been an ancient possession of that civilization. We behold also *continued* processes of growth; structures and systems of culture in particular spheres, rich in kind, and well developed in every direction. The merely formal and indeterminate view of development in general can neither assign to one form of expansion superiority over the other, nor render comprehensible the object of that decay of older periods of growth; but must regard such occurrences—or, to speak more particularly, the retrocessions they exhibit—as external contingencies; and can only judge of particular modes of development from indeterminate points of view; which—since the development, as such, is all in all—are relative and not absolute goals of attainment.

Universal history exhibits the *gradation* in the development of that principle whose substantial *purport* is the consciousness of freedom. The analysis of the successive grades, in their abstract form, belongs to logic; in their concrete aspect to the philosophy of spirit. Here it is sufficient to state that the first step in the process presents that immersion of spirit in nature which has been already referred to; the second shows it as advancing to the consciousness of its freedom. But this initial separation from nature is imperfect and partial, since it is derived immediately from the merely natural state, is consequently related to it, and is still encumbered with it as an essentially connected element. The third step is the elevation of the soul from this still limited and special form of freedom to its pure universal form; that state in which the spiritual essence attains the consciousness and feeling of itself. These grades are the ground-principles of the general process; but how each of them on the other hand involves within *itself* a process of formation, constituting the links in a dialectic of transition, to particularize this must be reserved for the sequel.

Here we have only to indicate that spirit begins with a germ of infinite possibility, but *only* possibility—containing its substantial existence in an undeveloped form, as the object and goal which it reaches only in its resultant—full reality. In actual existence progress appears as an advancing from the imperfect to the more perfect; but the former must not be understood abstractly as *only* the imperfect, but as something which involves the very opposite of itself—the so-called perfect—as a *germ* or impulse. So—reflectively, at least—*possibility* points to something destined to become actual; the Aristotelian δύναμις is also *potentia,* power and might. Thus the imperfect, as involving its opposite, is a contradiction, which certainly exists, but which is continually annulled and solved; the instinctive movement, the inherent impulse in the life of the soul, to break through the rind of mere nature, sensuousness, and that which is alien to it, and to attain to the light of consciousness, *i.e.,* to itself.

We have already made the remark how the commencement of the history of spirit must be conceived so as to be in harmony with its idea—in its bearing on the representations that have been made of a primitive *"natural* condition," in which freedom and justice are supposed to exist, or to have existed. This was, however, nothing more than an assumption of historical existence, conceived in the twilight of theorizing reflection. A pretension of quite another order—not a mere inference of reasoning, but making the claim of historical fact, and that supernaturally confirmed—is put forth in connection with a different view that is now widely promulgated by a certain class of speculatists. This view takes up the idea of the primitive paradisiacal condition of man, which had been previously expanded by the theologians, after their fashion—involving, *e.g.,* the supposition that God spoke with Adam in Hebrew—but remodelled to suit other requirements. The high authority appealed to in the first instance is the Biblical narrative. But this depicts the primitive condition, partly only in the few well-known traits, but partly either as in man generically—human nature at large—or, so far as Adam is to be taken as an individual, and consequently one person—as existing and completed in *this one*, or *only in one* human pair. The Biblical account by no means justifies us in imagining a *people*, and a historical condition of such people, existing in that primitive form; still less does it warrant us in attributing to them the possession of a perfectly developed knowledge of God and nature. "Nature," so the fiction runs, "like a clear mirror of God's creation, had originally lain revealed and transparent to the unclouded eye of man." [1] Divine truth is imagined to have been equally manifest. It is even hinted, though left in some degree of obscurity, that in this primary condition men were in possession of an indefinitely extended and already expanded body of religious truths immediately revealed by God. This theory affirms that all religions had their historical commencement in this primitive knowledge, and that they polluted and obscured the original truth by the monstrous creations of error and depravity; though in all the mythologies invented by error, traces of that origin and of those primitive true dogmas are supposed to be present and cognizable. An important interest, therefore, accrues to the investigation of the history of ancient peoples, that, *viz.*, of the endeavor to trace their annals up to the point where such fragments of the primary revelation are to be met with in greater purity than lower down.[2]

[1] Fr. von Schlegel, *Philosophy of History*, p. 91, Bohn's Standard Library.

[2] We have to thank this interest for many valuable discoveries in Oriental literature, and for a renewed study of treasures previously known in the department of ancient Asiatic culture, mythology, religions, and history. In Catholic countries, where a refined literary taste prevails, governments have yielded to the requirements of speculative inquiry, and have felt the necessity of allying themselves with learning and philosophy. Eloquently and impressively has the Abbé Lamennais reckoned it among the criteria of the true religion that it must be the universal—that is, catholic—and the oldest in date; and the congregation has labored zealously and diligently in France towards rendering such assertions no longer mere pulpit tirades and authoritative dicta, such as were deemed sufficient formerly. The religion of Buddha—a god-man—which has prevailed to such an enormous extent, has especially attracted attention. The Indian Timûrtis, as also the Chinese abstraction of the trinity, has furnished clearer evidence in point of subject matter. The savants, M. Abel Remusat and M. Saint Martin, on the one hand, have undertaken the most meritorious investigations in the Chinese literature, with a view to make this also a base of operations for researches in the Mongolian and, if such were possible, the Tibetan; on the other hand, Baron von Eckstein, in his way (*i.e.*, adopting from Germany superficial physi-

We owe to the interest which has occasioned these investigations very much that is valuable but this investigation bears direct testimony against itself, for it would seem to be awaiting the issue of an historical demonstration of that which is presupposed by it as historically established. That advanced condition of the knowledge of God, and of other scientific, *e.g.*, astronomical knowledge (such as has been falsely attributed to the Hindus); and the assertion that such a condition occurred at the very beginning of history—or that the religions of various nations were traditionally derived from it, and have developed themselves in degeneracy and depravation (as is represented in the rudely-conceived so-called "emanation system"); all these are suppositions which neither have, nor —if we may contrast with their arbitrary subjective origin, the true conception of history—can attain historical confirmation.

The only consistent and worthy method which philosophical investigation can adopt is to take up history where rationality begins to manifest itself in the actual conduct of the world's affairs (not where it is merely an undeveloped potentiality)—where a condition of things is present in which it realizes itself in consciousness, will, and action. The inorganic existence of spirit—that of abstract freedom—unconscious *torpidity* in respect to good and evil (and consequently to laws), or, if we please to term it so, "blessed ignorance," is itself not a subject of history. *Natural*, and at the same time *religious* morality, is the piety of the *family*. In this social relation, morality consists in the members behaving towards each other *not as individuals*—possessing an independent will; not as persons. The family, therefore, is excluded from that process of development in which history takes its rise. But when this self-involved spiritual unity steps beyond this circle of feeling and natural love, and first attains the consciousness of personality, we have that dark, dull centre of indifference, in which neither nature nor spirit is open and transparent; and for which nature and spirit can become open and transparent

cal conceptions and mannerisms, in the style of Fr. von Schlegel, though with more geniality than the latter) in his periodical, *Le Catholique*—has furthered the cause of that primitive Catholicism generally, and in particular has gained for the savants of the congregation the support of the government; so that it has even set on foot expeditions to the East, in order to discover there treasures still concealed; (from which further disclosures have been anticipated, respecting profound theological questions, particularly on the higher antiquity and sources of Buddhism), and with a view to promote the interests of Catholicism by this circuitous but scientifically interesting method.

only by means of a further process—a very lengthened culture of that will, at length become self-conscious. Consciousness alone is clearness; and is that alone for which God (or any other existence) can be revealed. In its true form, in absolute universality, nothing can be manifested except to consciousness made percipient of it. Freedom is nothing but the recognition and adoption of such universal substantial objects as right and law, and the production of a reality that is accordant with them—the state. Nations may have passed a long life before arriving at this their destination, and during this period, they may have attained considerable culture in some directions. This ante-historical period, consistently with what has been said, lies out of our plan; whether a real history followed it, or the peoples in question never attained a political constitution. It is a great discovery in history, as of a new world, which has been made within rather more than the last twenty years, respecting the Sanskrit and the connection of the European languages with it. In particular, the connection of the German and Indian peoples has been demonstrated, with as much certainty as such subjects allow of. Even at the present time we know of peoples which scarcely form a society, much less a state, but that have been long known as existing; while with regard to others, which in their advanced condition excite our especial interest, tradition reaches beyond the record of the founding of the state, and they experienced many changes prior to that epoch. In the connection just referred to, between the languages of nations so widely separated, we have a result before us, which proves the diffusion of those nations from Asia as a centre, and the so dissimilar development of what had been originally related, as an incontestable fact; not as an inference deduced by that favorite method of combining, and reasoning from, circumstances grave and trivial, which has already enriched and will continue to enrich history with so many fictions given out as facts. But that apparently so extensive range of events lies beyond the pale of history; in fact preceded it.

In our language the term *history* unites the objective with the subjective side, and denotes quite as much the *historia rerum gestarum,* as the *res gestæ* themselves; on the other hand it comprehends not less what has *happened,* than the *narration* of what has happened. This union of the two meanings we must regard as of a higher order than mere outward accident; we must suppose historical narrations to have appeared contemporaneously with historical deeds and events. It is an internal vital principle common to both that produces them synchronously. Family memorials, patriarchal traditions, have an interest confined to the family and the clan. The uniform course of events which such a condition implies is no subject of serious remembrance; though distinct transactions or turns of fortune, may rouse Mnemosyne to form conceptions of them—in the same way as love and the religious emotions provoke imagination to give shape to a previously formless impulse. But it is the state which first presents subject-matter that is not only *adapted* to the prose of history, but involves the production of such history in the very progress of its own being. Instead of merely subjective mandates on the part of government—sufficing for the needs of the moment—a community that is acquiring a stable existence, and exalting itself into a state, requires formal commands and laws—comprehensive and universally binding prescriptions; and thus produces a record as well as an interest concerned with intelligent, definite, and, in their results, lasting transactions and occurrences; on which Mnemosyne, for the behoof of the perennial object of the formation and constitution of the state, is impelled to confer perpetuity. Profound sentiments generally, such as that of love, as also religious intuition and its conceptions, are in themselves complete—constantly present and satisfying; but that outward existence of a political constitution which is enshrined in its rational laws and customs is an *imperfect* present; and cannot be thoroughly understood without a knowledge of the past.

The periods, whether we suppose them to be centuries or millennia, that were passed by nations before history was written among them—and which may have been filled with revolutions, nomadic wanderings, and the strangest mutations—are on that very account destitute of *objective* history, because they present no *subjective* history, no annals. We need not suppose that the records of such periods have accidentally perished; rather, because they were not possible, do we find them wanting. Only in a state cognizant of laws, can distinct transactions take place, accompanied by such a clear consciousness of them as supplies the ability and suggests the necessity of an enduring record. It strikes everyone, in beginning to form an acquaintance with the treasures of Indian literature, that a land so rich in intellectual products, and those of the profoundest order of thought, has no history; and in this respect contrasts most strongly with China—an empire possessing one so remarkable, one going back to the most ancient times. India has not only ancient books relating to religion, and splendid poetical productions, but also ancient codes; the existence of which latter kind of literature has been mentioned as a condition necessary to the origination of history —and yet history itself is not found. But in that country the impulse of organization, in beginning to develop social distinctions, was immediately petrified in the merely natural classification according to *castes;* so that although the laws concern themselves with civil rights, they make even these dependent on natural distinctions; and are especially occupied with determining the relations (wrongs rather than rights) of those classes towards each other, *i.e.,* the privileges of the higher over the lower. Consequently, the element of morality is banished from the pomp of Indian life and from its political institutions. Where that iron bondage of distinctions derived from nature prevails, the connection of society is nothing but wild arbitrariness, transient activity, or rather the play of violent emotion without any goal of advancement or development. Therefore no intelligent reminiscence, no object for Mnemosyne presents itself; and imagination—confused though profound—expatiates in a region, which, to be capable of history, must have had an aim within the domain of reality, and, at the same time, of substantial freedom.

Since such are the conditions indispensable to a history, it has happened that the growth of families to clans, of clans to peoples, and their local diffusion consequent upon this numerical increase—a series of facts which itself suggests so many instances of social complication, war, revolution, and ruin, a process which is so rich in interest, and so comprehensive in extent, has occurred without giving rise to history; moreover, that the extension and organic growth of the empire of articulate sounds has itself remained voiceless and dumb—a stealthy, unnoticed advance. It is a fact revealed by philological monuments that languages, during a rude condition of the nations that have spoken them, have been very highly developed; that the human understanding occupied this theoretical region with great ingenuity and completeness. For grammar, in its extended and consistent form, is the work of thought, which makes its categories distinctly visible therein. It is, moreover, a fact that, with advancing social and political civilization, this systematic completeness of intelligence suffers attrition, and language thereupon becomes poorer and ruder: a singular phenomenon—that the progress towards a more highly intellectual condition, while expanding and cultivating rationality, should disregard that intelligent amplitude and expressiveness—should find it an obstruction and contrive to do without it. Speech is the act of theoretic intelligence in a special sense; it is its *external* manifestation. Exercises of memory and imagination without language are direct manifestations. But this act of theoretic intelligence itself, as also its subsequent development, and the more concrete class of facts connected with it—*viz.,* the spreading of peoples over the earth, their separation from each other, their comminglings and wanderings—remain involved in the obscurity of a voiceless past. They are not acts of will becoming self-conscious—of freedom, mirroring itself in a phenomenal form, and creating for itself a proper reality. Not partaking of this element of substantial, veritable existence, those nations, notwithstanding the development of language among them, never advanced to the possession of a *history.* The rapid growth of language, and the progress and dispersion of nations, assume importance and interest for concrete reason only when they have come in contact with states, or begin to form political constitutions themselves.

After these remarks, relating to the form of the *commencement* of the world's history, and to that ante-historical period which must be excluded from it, we have to state the direction of its course: though here only formerly. The further definition of the subject in the concrete, comes under the head of arrangement.

Universal history, as already demonstrated, shows the development of the consciousness of freedom on the part of spirit, and of the consequent realization of that freedom. This development implies a gradation—a series of increasingly adequate expressions or manifestations of freedom, which result from its idea. The logical, and, as still more prominent, the *dialectical* nature of the idea in general, *viz.,* that it is self-determined—that it assumes successive forms which it successively transcends; and by this very process of transcending its earlier stages, gains an affirmative, and, in fact, a richer and more concrete shape; this necessity of its nature, and the necessary series of pure abstract forms which the idea successively assumes, is exhibited in the department of *logic.* Here we need adopt only one of its results, *viz.,* that every step in the process, as differing from any other, has its determinate peculiar principle. In history this principle is idiosyncrasy of spirit—peculiar national genius. It is within the limitations of this idio-syncrasy that the spirit of the nation, concretely manifested, expresses every aspect of its consciousness and will—the whole cycle of its realization. Its religion, its polity, its ethics, its legislation, and even its science, art, and mechanical skill, all bear its stamp. These special peculiarities find their key in that common peculiarity—the particular principle that characterizes a people; as, on the other hand, in the facts which history presents in detail, that common characteristic principle may be detected. That such or such a specific quality constitutes the peculiar genius of a people, is the element of our inquiry which must be derived from experience, and historically proved. To accomplish this, pre-supposes not only a disciplined faculty of abstraction, but an intimate acquaintance with the idea. The investigator must be familiar *a priori* (if we like to call it so) with the whole circle of conceptions to which the principles in question belong—just as Kepler (to name the most illustrious example in this mode of philosophizing) must have been familiar *a priori* with ellipses, with cubes and squares, and with ideas of their relations, before he could discover, from the empirical data, those immortal "laws" of his, which are none other than forms of thought pertaining to those classes of conceptions. He who is unfamiliar with the science that embraces these abstract elementary conceptions is as little capable, though he may have gazed on the firmament and the motions of the celestial bodies for a lifetime, of *understanding* those laws, as of *discovering* them. From this want of acquaintance with the ideas that relate to the development of freedom proceed a part of those objections which are brought against the philosophical consideration of a science usually regarded as one of mere experience; the so-called *a priori* method, and the attempt to insinuate ideas into the empirical data of history, being the chief points in the indictment. Where this deficiency exists, such conceptions appear alien—not lying within the object of investigation. To minds whose training has been narrow and merely subjective, which have not an acquaintance and familiarity with ideas, they are something strange —not embraced in the notion and conception of the subject which their limited intellect forms. Hence the statement that philosophy does not understand such sciences. It must, indeed, allow that it has not that kind of understanding which is the prevailing one in the domain of those sciences, that it does not proceed according to the categories of such understanding, but ac-cording to the categories of *reason*—though at the same time recognizing that understanding, and its true value and position. It must be observed that in this very process of scientific *understanding*, it is of importance that the essential should be distinguished and brought into relief in contrast with the so-called non-essential. But in order to render this possible, we must know what *is essential;* and that is—in view of the history of the world in general—the consciousness of freedom, and the phases which this consciousness assumes in developing itself. The bearing of historical facts on this category is their bearing on the truly essential. Of the difficulties stated, and the opposition exhibited to comprehensive conceptions in science, part must be referred to the inability to grasp and understand ideas. If in natural history some monstrous hybrid growth is alleged as an objection to the recognition of clear and indubitable classes or species, a sufficient reply is furnished by a sentiment often vaguely urged, that "the exception confirms the rule"; *i.e.,* that is the part of a well-defined rule, to show the conditions in which it applies, or the deficiency or hybridism of cases that are abnormal. Mere nature is too weak to keep its genera and species pure, when conflicting with alien elementary influences. If, *e.g.,* on considering the human organization in its concrete aspect, we assert that brain, heart, and so forth are essential to its organic life, some miserable abortion may be adduced, which has on the whole the human form, or parts of it—which has been conceived in a human body and has breathed after birth therefrom—in which nevertheless no brain and no heart is found. If such an instance is quoted against the general conception of a human being—the objector persisting in using the name, coupled with a superficial idea respecting it—it can be proved that a real, concrete human being is a truly different object, that such a being must have a brain in its head, and a heart in its breast.

A similar process of reasoning is adopted, in reference to the correct assertion that genius, talent, moral virtues, and sentiments, and piety, may be found in every zone, under all political constitutions and conditions; in confirmation of which examples are forthcoming in abundance. If in this assertion, the accompanying distinctions are intended to be repudiated as unimportant or non-essential, reflection evidently limits itself to abstract categories and ignores the specialities of the object in question, which certainly fall under no principle recognized by such categories. That intellectual position which adopts such merely formal points of view, presents a vast field for ingenious questions, erudite views, and striking comparisons; for profound seeming reflections and declamations, which may be rendered so much the more brilliant in proportion as the subject they refer to is indefinite, and are susceptible of new and varied forms in inverse proportion to the importance of the results that can be gained from them, and the certainty and rationality of their issues. Under such an aspect the well-known Indian epopees may be compared with the Homeric; perhaps, since it is the vastness of the imagination by which poetical genius proves itself, preferred to them; as, on account of the similarity of single strokes of imagination in the attributes of the divinities, it has been contended that Greek mythological forms may be recognized in those of India. Similarly the Chinese philosophy, as adopting the One as its basis, has been alleged to be the same as at a later period appeared as Eleatic philosophy and as the Spinozistic system; while in virtue of its expressing itself also in abstract numbers and lines, Pythagorean and Christian principles have been supposed to be detected in it. Instances of bravery and indomitable courage, traits of magnanimity, of self-denial, and self-sacrifice, which are found among the most savage and the most pusillanimous nations, are regarded as sufficient to support the view that in these nations as much of social virtue and morality may be found as in the most civilized Christian states, or even more. And on this ground a doubt has been suggested whether in the progress of history and of general culture mankind have become better; whether their morality has been increased—morality being regarded in a subjective aspect and view, as founded on what the agent holds to be right and wrong, good and evil; not on a principle which is considered to be in and for itself right and good, or a crime and evil, or on a particular religion believed to be the true one.

We may fairly decline on this occasion the task of tracing the formalism and error of such a view, and establishing the true principles of morality, or rather of social virtue in opposition to false morality. For the history of the world occupies a higher ground than that on which morality has properly its position; which is personal character, the conscience of individuals, their particular will and mode of action; *these* have a value, imputation, reward or punishment proper to themselves. What the absolute aim of spirit requires and accomplishes, what providence does, transcends the obligations, and the

liability to imputation and the ascription of good or bad motives, which attach to individuality in virtue of its social relations. They who on moral grounds, and consequently with noble intention, have resisted that which the advance of the spiritual idea makes necessary, stand higher in moral worth than those whose crimes have been turned into the means—under the direction of a superior principle—of realizing the purposes of that principle. But in such revolutions both parties generally stand within the limits of the same circle of transient and corruptible existence. Consequently it is only a formal rectitude, deserted by the living Spirit and by God, which those who stand upon ancient right and order maintain. The deeds of great men, who are the individuals of the world's history, thus appear not only justified in view of that intrinsic result of which they were not conscious, but also from the point of view occupied by the secular moralist. But looked at from this point, moral claims that are irrelevant, must not be brought into collision with world-historical deeds and their accomplishment. The litany of private virtues—modesty, humility, philanthropy, and forbearance—must not be raised against them. The history of the world might, on principle, entirely ignore the circle within which morality and the so much talked of distinction between the moral and the politic lies—not only in abstaining from judgments, for the principles involved, and the necessary reference of the deeds in question to those principles, are a sufficient judgment of them—but in leaving individuals quite out of view and unmentioned. What it has to record is the activity of the spirit of peoples, so that the individual forms which that spirit has assumed in the sphere of outward reality, might be left to the delineation of special histories.

The same kind of formalism avails itself in its peculiar manner of the indefiniteness attaching to genius, poetry, and even philosophy; thinks equally that it finds these everywhere. We have here products of reflective thought; and it is familiarity with those general conceptions which single out and name real distinctions without fathoming the true depth of the matter, that we call culture. It is something merely formal, inasmuch as it aims at nothing more than the analysis of the subject, whatever it be, into its constituent parts, and the comprehension of these in their logical definitions and forms. It is not the free universality of conception necessary for making an abstract principle the object of consciousness. Such a consciousness of thought itself, and of its forms isolated from a particular object, is philosophy. This has, indeed, the condition of its existence in culture; that condition being the taking up of the object of thought, and at the same time clothing it with the form of universality, in such a way that the material content and the form given by the intellect are held in an inseparable state; inseparable to such a degree that the object in question—which, by the analysis of one conception into a multitude of conceptions, is enlarged to an incalculable treasure of thought—is regarded as a merely empirical datum in whose formation thought has had no share.

But it is quite as much an act of thought, of the understanding in particular, to embrace in one simple conception object which of itself comprehends a concrete and large significance (as earth, man, Alexander or Cæsar) and to designate it by one word, as to *resolve* such a conception, duly to isolate in idea the conceptions which it contains, and to give them particular names. And in reference to the view which gave occasion to what has just been said, thus much will be clear—that as reflection produces what we include under the general terms genius, talent, art, science—formal culture on every grade of intellectual development, not only can, but must grow, and attain a mature bloom, while the grade in question is developing itself to a state, and on this basis of civilization is advancing to intelligent reflection and to general forms of thought—as in laws, so in regard to all else. In the very association of men in a state lies the necessity of formal culture—consequently of the rise of the sciences and of a cultivated poetry and art generally. The arts designated *plastic* require besides, even in their technical aspect, the civilized association of men. The poetic art—which has less need of external requirements and means, and which has the element of immediate existence, the voice, as its material—steps forth with great boldness and with matured expression, even under the conditions presented by a people not yet united in a political combination; since, as remarked above, language attains on its own particular ground a high intellectual development, prior to the commencement of civilization.

Philosophy also must make its appearance where political life exists; since that in virtue of which any series of phenomena is reduced within the sphere of culture, as above stated, is the form strictly proper to thought; and thus for philosophy, which is nothing other than the consciousness of this form itself—the thinking of thinking—the material of which its edifice is to be constructed, is already prepared by *general* culture. If in the development of the state itself, periods are necessitated which impel the soul of nobler natures to seek refuge from the present in ideal regions—in order to find in them that harmony with itself which it can no longer enjoy in the discordant real world, where the reflective intelligence attacks all that is holy and deep, which had been spontaneously inwrought into the religion, laws and manners of nations, and brings them down and attenuates them to abstract godless generalities—thought will be compelled to become thinking reason, with the view of effecting, in its own element, the restoration of its principles from the ruin to which they had been brought.

We find then, it is true, among all world-historical peoples, poetry, plastic art, science, even philosophy; but not only is there a diversity in style and bearing generally, but still more remarkably in subject-matter; and this is a diversity of the most important kind, affecting the rationality of that subject-matter. It is useless for a pretentious æsthetic criticism to demand that our good pleasure should not be made the rule for the matter—the substantial part of their contents—and to maintain that it is the beautiful form as such, the grandeur of the fancy, and so forth, which fine art aims at, and which must be considered and enjoyed by a liberal taste and cultivated mind. A healthy intellect does not tolerate such abstractions, and cannot assimilate productions of the kind above referred to. Granted that the Indian epopees might be placed on a level with the Homeric, on account of a number of those qualities of form—grandeur of invention and imaginative power, liveliness of images and emotions, and beauty of diction; yet the infinite difference of matter remains; consequently one of substantial importance and involving the interest of reason, which is immediately concerned with the consciousness of the idea of freedom, and its expression in individuals. There is not only a classical *form*, but a classical order of *subject-matter*; and in a work of art form and subject-matter are so closely united that the former can only be classical to the extent to which the latter is so. With a fantastical, indeterminate material —and *rule* is the essence of *reason*—the form becomes measureless and formless, or mean and contracted. In the same way, in that comparison of the various systems of philosophy of which we have already spoken, the only point of importance is overlooked, namely, the character of that unity which is found alike in the Chinese, the Eleatic, and the Spinozistic philosophy—the distinction between the recognition of that unity as abstract and as concrete—concrete to the extent of being a unity in and by itself—a unity synonymous with spirit. But that co-ordination proves that it recognizes only such an abstract unity; so that while it gives judgment respecting philosophy, it is ignorant of that very point which constitutes the interest of philosophy.

But there are also spheres which, amid all the variety that is presented in the substantial content of a particular form of culture, remain the same. The difference above-mentioned in art, science, philosophy, concerns the thinking reason and freedom, which is the self-consciousness of the former, and which has the same one root with thought. As it is not the brute, but only the man that thinks, he only, and only because he is a thinking being, has freedom. *His* consciousness imports this, that the individual comprehends itself as a *person,* that is, recognizes itself in its single existence as possessing universality, as capable of abstraction from, and of surrendering all speciality; and, therefore, as inherently infinite. Consequently those spheres of intelligence which lie beyond the limits of this consciousness are a common ground among those substantial distinctions. Even morality, which is so intimately connected with the consciousness of freedom, can be very pure while that consciousness is still wanting; as far, that is to say, as it expresses duties and rights only as *objective* commands; or even as far as it remains satisfied with the merely formal elevation of the soul—the surrender of the sensual, and of all sensual motives—in a purely negative, self-denying fashion. The *Chinese* morality, since Europeans have become acquainted with it and with the writings of Confucius, has obtained the greatest praise and proportionate attention from those who are familiar with the Christian morality. There is a similar acknowledgment of the sublimity with which the *Indian* religion and poetry (a statement that must, however, be limited to the higher kind), but especially the Indian philosophy, expatiate upon and demand the removal and sacrifice of sensuality. Yet both these nations are, it must be confessed, *entirely* wanting in the essential consciousness of the idea of freedom. To the Chinese their moral laws are just like natural laws, external, positive commands, claims established by force, compulsory duties or rules of courtesy towards each other. Freedom, through which alone the essential determinations of reason become moral sentiments, is wanting. Morality is a political affair, and its

laws are administered by officers of government and legal tribunals. Their treatises upon it (which are not law books, but are certainly addressed to the subjective will and individual disposition) read, as do the moral writings of the Stoics, like a string of commands stated as necessary for realizing the goal of happiness; so that it seems to be left free to men, on their part, to adopt such commands, to observe them or not; while the conception of an abstract subject, "a wise man" forms the culminating point among the Chinese, as also among the Stoic moralists. Also in the Indian doctrine of the renunciation of the sensuality of desires and earthly interests, positive moral freedom is not the object and end, but the annihilation of consciousness—spiritual and even physical privation of life.

It is the concrete spirit of a people which we have distinctly to recognize, and since it is spirit it can only be comprehended spiritually, that is, by thought. It is this alone which takes the lead in all the deeds and tendencies of that people, and which is occupied in realizing itself, in satisfying its ideal and becoming self-conscious, for its great business is self-production. But for spirit, the highest attainment is self-knowledge; an advance not only to the *intuition,* but to the *thought*—the clear conception of itself. This it must and is also destined to accomplish; but the accomplishment is at the same time its dissolution, and the rise of another spirit, another world-historical people, another epoch of universal history. This transition and connection lead us to the connection of the whole, the idea of the world's history as such, which we have now to consider more closely, and of which we have to give a representation.

History in general is therefore the development of spirit in *time,* as nature is the development of the idea in *space.*

If then we cast a glance over the world's history generally, we see a vast picture of changes and transactions; of infinitely manifold forms of peoples, states, individuals, in unresting succession. Everything that can enter into and interest the soul of man, all our sensibility to *goodness, beauty, and greatness,* is called into play. On every hand aims are adopted and pursued, which we recognize, whose accomplishment we desire—we hope and fear for them. In all these occurrences and changes we behold human action and suffering predominant; everywhere something akin to ourselves, and therefore everywhere something that excites our interest for or against. Sometimes it attracts us by beauty, freedom, and rich variety, sometimes by energy such as enables even vice to make itself interesting. Sometimes we see the more comprehensive mass of some general interest advancing with comparative slowness, and subsequently sacrificed to an infinite complication of trifling circumstances, and so dissipated into atoms. Then, again, with a vast expenditure of power a trivial result is produced; while from what appears unimportant a tremendous issue proceeds. On every hand there is the motliest throng of events drawing us within the circle of its interest, and when one combination vanishes another immediately appears in its place.

The general thought—the category which first presents itself in this restless mutation of individuals and peoples, existing for a time and then vanishing—is that of *change* at large. The sight of the ruins of some ancient sovereignty directly leads us to contemplate this thought of change in its negative aspect. What traveller among the ruins of Carthage, of Palmyra, Persepolis, or Rome, has not been stimulated to reflections on the transiency of kingdoms and men, and to sadness at the thought of a vigorous and rich life now departed—a sadness which does not expend itself on personal losses and the uncertainty of one's own undertakings, but is a disinterested sorrow at the decay of a splendid and highly cultured national life! But the next consideration which allies itself with that of change is that change, while it imports dissolution, involves at the same time the rise of a *new life*—that while death is the issue of life, life is also the issue of death. This is a grand conception; one which the Oriental thinkers attained, and which is perhaps the highest in their metaphysics. In the idea of *metempsychosis* we find it evolved in its relation to individual existence; but a myth more generally known is that of the *phœnix* as a type of the life of *nature;* eternally preparing for itself its funeral pile, and consuming itself upon it; but so that from its ashes is produced the new, renovated, fresh life. But this image is only Asiatic; Oriental not Occidental. Spirit, consuming the envelope of its existence, does not merely pass into another envelope, nor rise rejuvenescent from the ashes of its previous form; it comes forth exalted, glorified, a purer spirit. It certainly makes war upon itself, consumes its own existence; but in this very destruction it works up that existence into a new form, and each successive phase becomes in its turn a material, working on which it exalts itself to a new grade.

If we consider spirit in this aspect—regarding its changes not merely as rejuvenescent transitions, *i.e.*, returns to the same form, but rather as manipulations of itself, by which it multiplies the material for future endeavors—we see it exerting itself in a variety of modes and directions; developing its powers and gratifying its desires in a variety which is inexhaustible; because every one of its creations, in which it has already found gratification, meets it anew as material, and is a new stimulus to plastic activity. The abstract conception of mere change gives place to the thought of spirit manifesting, developing, and perfecting its powers in every direction which its manifold nature can follow. What powers it inherently possesses we learn from the variety of products and formations which it originates. In this pleasurable activity, it has to do only with itself. As involved with the conditions of mere nature, internal and external, it will indeed meet in these not only opposition and hindrance, but will often see its endeavors thereby fail; often sink under the complications in which it is entangled either by nature or by itself. But in such case it perishes in fulfilling its own destiny and proper function, and even thus exhibits the spectacle of self-demonstration as spiritual activity.

The very essence of spirit is activity; it realizes its potentiality, makes itself its own deed, its own work, and thus it becomes an object to itself; contemplates itself as an objective existence. Thus is it with the spirit of a people: it is a spirit having strictly defined characteristics, which erects itself into an objective world, that exists and persists in a particular religious form of worship, customs, constitution, and political laws, in the whole complex of its institutions, in the events and transactions that make up its history. That is its work—that is what this particular nation *is*. Nations are what their deeds are. Every Englishman will say: We are the men who navigate the ocean, and have the commerce of the world; to whom the East Indies belong and their riches; who have a parliament, juries, etc. The relation of the individual to that spirit is that he appropriates to himself this substantial existence; that it becomes his character and capability, enabling him to have a definite place in the world—to be *something*. For he finds the being of the people to which he belongs an already established, firm world, objectively present to him, with which he has to incorporate himself. In this its work, therefore—its world —the spirit of the people enjoys its existence and finds its satisfaction. A nation is moral, virtuous, vigorous, while it is engaged in realizing its grand objects, and defends its work against external violence during the process of giving to its purposes an objective existence. The contradiction between its potential, subjective being—its inner aim and life—and its *actual* being is removed; it has attained full reality, has itself objectively present to it. But this having been attained, the activity displayed by the spirit of the people in question is no longer needed; it has its desire. The nation can still accomplish much in war and peace at home and abroad; but the living substantial soul itself may be said to have ceased its activity. The essential, supreme interest has consequently vanished from its life, for interest is present only where there is opposition. The nation lives the same kind of life as the individual when passing from maturity to old age, in the enjoyment of itself, in the satisfaction of being exactly what it desired and was able to attain. Although its imagination might have transcended that limit, it nevertheless abandoned any such aspirations as objects of *actual endeavor,* if the real world was less than favorable to their attainment, and restricted its aim by the conditions thus imposed. This mere *customary life* (the watch wound up and going on of itself) is that which brings on natural death. Custom is activity without opposition, for which there remains only a formal duration; in which the fulness and zest that originally characterized the aim of life are out of the question—a merely external sensuous existence which has ceased to throw itself enthusiastically into its object. Thus perish individuals, thus perish peoples by a natural death; and though the latter may continue in being, it is an existence without intellect or vitality; having no need of its institutions, because the need for them is satisfied—a political nullity and tedium. In order that a truly universal interest may arise, the spirit of a people must advance to the adoption of some new purpose; but whence can this new purpose originate? It would be a higher, more comprehensive conception of itself, a transcending of its principle, but this very act would involve a principle of a new order, a new national spirit.

Such a new principle does in fact enter into the spirit of a people that has arrived at full development and self-realization; it dies not a simply natural death, for it is not a mere single individual, but a spiritual, generic life; in its case natural death appears to imply destruction through its own agency. The reason of this difference from the single natural individual, is that the spirit of a people exists as a *genus,* and consequently carries within it its own negation,

in the very generality which characterizes it. A people can only die a violent death when it has become naturally dead in itself, as, *e.g.,* the German imperial cities, the German imperial constitution.

It is not of the nature of the all-pervading spirit to die this merely natural death; it does not simply sink into the senile life of mere custom, but, as being a national spirit belonging to universal history, attains to the consciousness of what its work is; it attains to a conception of itself. In fact it is world-historical only in so far as a *universal principle* has lain in its fundamental element, in its grand aim: only so far is the work which such a spirit produces, a moral, political organization. If it be mere desires that impel nations to activity, such deeds pass over without leaving a trace; or their traces are only ruin and destruction. Thus, it was first Chronos —Time—that ruled; the Golden Age, without moral products; and what was produced—the offspring of that Chronos—was devoured by it. It was Jupiter, from whose head Minerva sprang, and to whose circle of divinities belong Apollo and the Muses, that first put a constraint upon Time, and set a bound to its principle of decadence. He is the political god, who produced a moral work—the state.

In the very element of an achievement the quality of generality, of thought, is contained; without thought it has no objectivity; that is its basis. The highest point in the development of a people is this—to have gained a conception of its life and condition, to have reduced its laws, its ideas of justice and morality to a science; for in this unity lies the most intimate unity that spirit can attain to in and with itself. In its work it is employed in rendering itself an object of its own contemplation; but it cannot develop itself objectively in its essential nature, except in *thinking* itself.

At this point, then, spirit is acquainted with its principles—the general character of its acts. But at the same time, in virtue of its very generality, this work of thought is different in point of form from the actual achievements of the national genius, and from the vital agency by which those achievements have been performed. We have then before us a *real* and an *ideal* existence of the spirit of the nation. If we wish to gain the general idea and conception of what the Greeks were, we find it in Sophocles and Aristophanes, in Thucydides and Plato. In these individuals the Greek spirit conceived and thought itself. This is the profounder kind of satisfaction which the spirit of a people attains; but it is "ideal," and distinct from its "real" activity.

At such a time, therefore, we are sure to see a people finding satisfaction in the *idea* of virtue; putting *talk* about virtue partly side by side with actual virtue, but partly in the place of it. On the other hand pure, universal thought, since its nature is universality, is apt to bring the special and spontaneous—belief, trust, customary morality—to reflect upon itself, and its primitive simplicity; to show up the limitation with which it is fettered, partly suggesting reasons for renouncing duties, partly itself *demanding reasons,* and the connection of such requirements with universal thought; and not finding that connection, seeking to impeach the authority of duty generally, as destitute of a sound foundation.

At the same time the isolation of individuals from each other and from the whole makes its appearance; their aggressive selfishness and vanity; their seeking personal advantage and consulting this at the expense of the state at large. That inward principle in transcending its outward manifestations is subjective also in *form*— *viz.,* selfishness and corruption in the unbound passions and egotistic interests of men.

Zeus, therefore, who is represented as having put a limit to the devouring agency of Time, and stayed this transiency by having established something inherently and independently durable —Zeus and his race are themselves swallowed up, and that by the very power that produced them—the principle of thought, perception, reasoning, insight derived from rational grounds, and the requirement of such grounds.

Time is the negative element in the sensuous world. Thought is the same negativity, but it is the deepest, the infinite form of it, in which therefore all existence generally is dissolved; first *finite* existence, *determinate,* limited form: but existence *generally,* in its objective character, is limited; it appears therefore as a mere datum—something immediate, authority—and is either intrinsically finite and limited, or presents itself as a limit for the thinking subject, and its infinite reflection on itself.

But first we must observe how the life which proceeds from death is itself, on the other hand, only individual life; so that, regarding the species as the real and substantial in this vicissitude, the perishing of the individual is a regress of the species into individuality. The perpetuation of the race is, therefore, none other than the monotonous repetition of the same kind of existence. Further, we must remark how perception —the comprehension of being by thought—is the source and birthplace of a new, and in fact higher form, in a principle which while it preserves, dignifies its material. For thought is that *universal,* that *species* which is immortal, which preserves identity with itself. The particular form of spirit not merely passes away in the world by natural causes in time, but is annulled in the automatic self-mirroring activity of consciousness. Because this annulling is an activity of thought, it is at the same time conservative and elevating in its operation. While then, on the one side, spirit annuls the reality, the permanence of that which it *is,* it gains on the other side, the essence, the thought, the universal element of that which *it only was.* Its principle is no longer that immediate import and aim which it was previously, but the *essence* of that import and aim.

The result of this process is then that spirit, in rendering itself objective and making this its being an object of thought, on the one hand destroys the determinate form of its being, on the other hand gains a comprehension of the universal element which it involves, and thereby gives a new form to its inherent principle. In virtue of this, the substantial character of the national spirit has been altered; that is, its principle has risen into another, and in fact a higher principle.

It is of the highest importance in apprehending and comprehending history to have and to understand the thought involved in this transition. The individual traverses as a unity various grades of development, and remains the same individual; in like manner also does a people, till the spirit which it embodies reaches the grade of universality. In this point lies the fundamental, the ideal necessity of transition. This is the soul, the essential consideration, of the philosophical comprehension of history.

Spirit is essentially the result of its own activity: its activity is the transcending of immediate, simple, unreflected existence, the negation of that existence, and the returning into itself. We may compare it with the seed; for with this the plant begins, yet it is also the result of the plant's entire life. But the weak side of life is exhibited in the fact that the commencement and the result are disjoined from each other. Thus also is it in the life of individuals and peoples. The life of a people ripens a certain fruit; its activity aims at the complete manifestation of the principle which it embodies. But this fruit does not fall back into the bosom of the people that produced and matured it; on the contrary, it becomes a poison-draught to it. That poison-draught it cannot let alone, for it has an insatiable thirst for it: the taste of the draught is its annihilation, though at the same time the rise of a new principle.

We have already discussed the final aim of this progression. The principles of the successive phases of spirit that animate the nations, in a necessitated gradation, are themselves only steps in the development of the one universal spirit, which through them elevates and completes itself to a self-comprehending *totality*.

While we are thus concerned exclusively with the idea of spirit, and in the history of the world regard everything as only its manifestation, we have, in traversing the past, however extensive its periods, only to do with what is *present;* for philosophy, as occupying itself with the true, has to do with the *eternally present*. Nothing in the past is lost for it, for the idea is ever present; spirit is immortal; with it there is no past, no future, but an essential *now*. This necessarily implies that the present form of spirit comprehends within it all earlier steps. These have indeed unfolded themselves in succession independently; but what spirit it is it has always been essentially; distinctions are only the development of this essential nature. The life of the ever present spirit is a circle of progressive embodiments, which looked at in one aspect still exist beside each other, and only as looked at from another point of view appear as past. The grades which spirit seems to have left behind it, it still possesses in the depths of its present.

GEOGRAPHICAL BASIS OF HISTORY

Contrasted with the universality of the moral whole and with the unity of that individuality which is its active principle, the *natural* connection that helps to produce the spirit of a people, appears an extrinsic element; but inasmuch as we must regard it as the ground on which that spirit plays its part, it is an *essential* and *necessary* basis. We began with the assertion that, in the history of the world, the idea of spirit appears in its actual embodiment as a series of external forms, each one of which declares itself as an actually existing people. This existence falls under the category of time as well as space, in the way of natural existence; and the special principle, which every world-historical people embodies, has this principle at the same time as a *natural* characteristic. Spirit, clothing itself in this form of nature, suffers its particular phases to assume separate existence; for mutual exclusion is the mode of existence proper to mere nature. These natural distinctions must be first of all regarded as special possibilities, from which the spirit of the people in question germinates, and among them is the geographical basis. It is not our concern to become acquainted with the land occupied by nations as an external locale, but with the natural type of the locality, as intimately connected with the type and character of the people which is the offspring of such a soil. This character is nothing more nor less than the mode and form in which nations make their appearance in history, and take place and position in it. Nature should not be rated too high nor too low: the mild Ionic sky certainly contributed much to the charm of the Homeric poems, yet this alone can produce no Homers. Nor in fact does it continue to produce them; under Turkish government no bards have arisen. We must first take notice of those natural conditions which have to be excluded once for all from the drama of the world's history. In the Frigid and in the Torrid Zone the locality of world-historical peoples cannot be found. For awakening consciousness takes its rise surrounded by natural influences alone, and every development of it is the reflection of spirit back upon itself in opposition to the immediate, unreflected character of mere nature. Nature is therefore one element in this antithetic abstracting process; nature is the first standpoint from which man can gain freedom within himself, and this liberation must not be rendered difficult by natural obstructions. Nature, as contrasted with spirit, is a quantitative mass, whose power must not be so great as to make its single force omnipotent. In the extreme zones man cannot come to free movement; cold and heat are here too powerful to allow spirit to build up a world for *itself*. Aristotle said long ago, "When pressing needs are satisfied, man turns to the general and more elevated." But in the extreme zones such pressure may be said never to cease, never to be warded off; men are constantly impelled to direct attention to nature, to the glowing rays of the sun, and the icy frost. The true theatre of history is therefore the Temperate Zone; or, rather, its northern half, because the earth there presents itself in a continental form, and has a broad breast, as the Greeks say. In the south, on the contrary, it divides itself, and runs out into many points. The same peculiarity shows itself in natural products. The north has many kinds of animals and plants with common characteristics; in the south, where the land divides itself into points, natural forms also present individual features contrasted with each other.

The world is divided into *Old* and *New;* the

name of *New* having originated in the fact that America and Australia have only lately become known to us. But these parts of the world are not only relatively new, but intrinsically so in respect of their entire physical and psychical constitution. Their geological antiquity we have nothing to do with. I will not deny the New World the honour of having emerged from the sea at the world's formation contemporaneously with the old: yet the archipelago between South America and Asia shows a physical immaturity. The greater part of the islands are so constituted that they are, as it were, only a superficial deposit of earth over rocks, which shoot up from the fathomless deep, and bear the character of novel origination. New Holland[1] shows a not less immature geographical character; for in penetrating from the settlements of the English farther into the country, we discover immense streams, which have not yet developed themselves to such a degree as to dig a channel for themselves, but lose themselves in marshes. Of America and its grade of civilization, especially in Mexico and Peru, we have information, but it imports nothing more than that this culture was an entirely national one, which must expire as soon as spirit approached it. America has always shown itself physically and psychically powerless, and still shows itself so. For the aborigines, after the landing of the Europeans in America, gradually vanished at the breath of European activity. In the United States of North America all the citizens are of European descent, with whom the old inhabitants could not amalgamate, but were driven back. The aborigines have certainly adopted some arts and usages from the Europeans, among others that of brandy-drinking, which has operated with deadly effect. In the south the natives were treated with much greater violence, and employed in hard labours to which their strength was by no means competent. A mild and passionless disposition, want of spirit, and a crouching submissiveness towards a Creole, and still more towards a European, are the chief characteristics of the native Americans; and it will be long before the Europeans succeed in producing any independence of feeling in them. The inferiority of these individuals in all respects, even in regard to size, is very manifest; only the quite southern races in Patagonia are more vigorous natures, but still abiding in their natural condition of rudeness and barbarism. When the Jesuits and the Catholic clergy proposed to accustom the Indians to European culture and manners (they have, as is

[1] A former name for Australia.—Ed.

well known, founded a state in Paraguay and convents in Mexico and California), they commenced a close intimacy with them, and prescribed for them the duties of the day, which, slothful though their disposition was, they complied with under the authority of the friars. These prescripts (at midnight a bell had to remind them even of their matrimonial duties) were first, and very wisely, directed to the creation of wants—the springs of human activity generally. The weakness of the American physique was a chief reason for bringing the Negroes to America, to employ their labour in the work that had to be done in the New World; for the Negroes are far more susceptible of European culture than the Indians, and an English traveller has adduced instances of Negroes having become competent clergymen, medical men, etc. (a Negro first discovered the use of the Peruvian bark), while only a single native was known to him whose intellect was sufficiently developed to enable him to study, but who had died soon after beginning, through excessive brandy-drinking. The weakness of the human physique of America has been aggravated by a deficiency in the mere tools and appliances of progress—the want of *horses* and *iron*, the chief instruments by which they were subdued.

The original nation having vanished or nearly so, the effective population comes for the most part from Europe; and what takes place in America is but an emanation from Europe. Europe has sent its surplus population to America in much the same way as from the old imperial cities, where trade-guilds were dominant and trade was stereotyped, many persons escaped to other towns which were not under such a yoke, and where the burden of imposts was not so heavy. Thus arose, by the side of Hamburg, Altona—by Frankfort, Offenbach—by Nürnburg, Fürth—and Carouge by Geneva. The relation between North America and Europe is similar. Many Englishmen have settled there, where burdens and imposts do not exist, and where the combination of European appliances and European ingenuity has availed to realize some produce from the extensive and still virgin soil. Indeed the emigration in question offers many advantages. The emigrants have got rid of much that might be obstructive to their interests at home, while they take with them the advantages of European independence of spirit, and acquired skill; while for those who are willing to work vigorously, but who have not found in Europe opportunities for doing so, a sphere of action is certainly presented in America.

America, as is well known, is divided into two parts, connected indeed by an isthmus, but which has not been the means of establishing intercourse between them. Rather, these two divisions are most decidedly distinct from each other. North America shows us on approaching it, along its eastern shore a wide border of level coast, behind which is stretched a chain of mountains—the Blue Mountains or Appalachians; further north the Alleghanies. Streams issuing from them water the country towards the coast, which affords advantages of the most desirable kind to the United States, whose origin belongs to this region. Behind that mountain chain the St. Lawrence River flows (in connection with huge lakes), from south to north, and on this river lie the northern colonies of Canada. Farther west we meet the basin of the vast Mississippi, and the basins of the Missouri and Ohio, which it receives, and then debouches into the Gulf of Mexico. On the western side of this region we have in like manner a long mountain chain, running through Mexico and the Isthmus of Panama, and, under the names of the Andes or Cordillera, cutting off an edge of coast along the whole west side of South America. The border formed by this is narrower and offers fewer advantages than that of North America. There lie Peru and Chile. On the east side flow eastward the monstrous streams of the Orinoco and Amazons; they form great valleys, not adapted however for cultivation, since they are only wide desert steppes. Towards the south flows the Rio de la Plata, whose tributaries have their origin partly in the Cordilleras, partly in the northern chain of mountains which separates the basin of the Amazon from its own. To the district of the Rio de la Plata belong Brazil, and the Spanish Republics. Colombia is the northern coast-land of South America, at the west of which, flowing along the Andes, the Magdalena debouches into the Caribbean Sea.

With the exception of Brazil, republics have come to occupy South as well as North America. In comparing South America (reckoning Mexico as part of it) with North America, we observe an astonishing contrast.

In North America we witness a prosperous state of things; an increase of industry and population, civil order and firm freedom; the whole federation constitutes but a single state, and has its political centres. In South America, on the contrary, the republics depend only on military force; their whole history is a continued revolution; federated states become disunited; others previously separated become united; and all these changes originate in military revolutions. The more special differences between the two parts of America show us two opposite directions, the one in political respects, the other in regard to religion. South America, where the Spaniards settled and asserted supremacy, is Catholic; North America, although a land of sects of every name, is yet fundamentally, Protestant. A wider distinction is presented in the fact, that South America was conquered, but North America colonized. The Spaniards took possession of South America to govern it, and to become rich through occupying political offices, and by exactions. Depending on a very distant mother country, their desires found a larger scope, and by force, address and confidence they gained a great predominance over the Indians. The North American states were, on the other hand, entirely *colonized,* by Europeans. Since in England, Puritans, Episcopalians, and Catholics were engaged in perpetual conflict, and now one party, now the other, had the upper hand, many emigrated to seek religious freedom on a foreign shore. These were industrious Europeans, who betook themselves to agriculture, tobacco, and cotton planting, etc. Soon the whole attention of the inhabitants was given to labour, and the basis of their existence as a united body lay in the necessities that bind man to man, the desire of repose, the establishment of civil rights, security and freedom, and a community arising from the aggregation of individuals as atomic constituents; so that the state was merely something external for the protection of property. From the Protestant religion sprang the principle of the mutual confidence of individuals—trust in the honourable dispositions of other men; for in the Protestant Church the entire life, its activity generally, is the field for what it deems religious works. Among Catholics, on the contrary, the basis of such a confidence cannot exist; for in secular matters only force and voluntary subservience are the principles of action; and the forms which are called constitutions are in this case only a resort of necessity, and are no protection against mistrust.

If we compare North America further with Europe, we shall find in the former the permanent example of a republican constitution. A subjective unity presents itself; for there is a president at the head of the state, who, for the sake of security against any monarchical ambition, is chosen only for four years. Universal protection for property, and a something approaching entire immunity from public burdens, are facts which are constantly held up to commendation. We have in these facts the fundamental character of the community—the endeavor of the individual after acquisition, commercial profit, and gain; the preponderance of *private* interest, devoting itself to that of the community only for its own advantage. We find, certainly, legal relations, a formal code of laws; but respect for law exists apart from genuine probity, and the American merchants commonly lie under the imputation of dishonest dealings under legal protection. If, on the one side, the Protestant Church develops the essential principle of confidence, as already stated, it thereby involves on the other hand the recognition of the validity of the element of feeling to such a degree as gives encouragement to unseemly varieties of caprice. Those who adopt this standpoint maintain that, as everyone may have his peculiar way of viewing things *generally,* so he may have also a *religion* peculiar to himself. Thence the splitting up into so many sects, which reach the very acme of absurdity; many of which have a form of worship consisting in convulsive movements, and sometimes in the most sensuous extravagances. This complete freedom of worship is developed to such a degree that the various congregations choose ministers and dismiss them according to their absolute pleasure; for the church is no independent existence—having a substantial spiritual being, and correspondingly permanent external arrangement—but the affairs of religion are regulated by the good pleasure for the time being of the members of the community. In North America the most unbounded license of imagination in religious matters prevails, and that religious unity is wanting which has been maintained in European States, where deviations are limited to a few confessions. As to the political condition of North America, the general object of the existence of this state is not yet fixed and determined, and the necessity for a firm combination does not yet exist; for a real state and a real government arise only after a distinction of classes has arisen, when wealth and poverty become extreme, and when such a condition of things presents itself that a large portion of the people can no longer satisfy its necessities in the way in which it has been accustomed so to do. But America is hitherto exempt from this pressure, for it has the outlet of colonization constantly and widely open, and multitudes are continually streaming into the plains of the Mississippi. By this means the chief source of discontent is removed, and the continuation of the existing civil condition is guaranteed. A comparison of the United States of North America with European lands is therefore impossible; for in Europe, such a natural outlet for population, notwithstanding all the emigrations that take place, does not exist. Had the woods of Germany been in existence, the French Revolution would not have occurred. North America will be comparable with Europe only after the immeasurable space which that country presents to its inhabitants shall have been occupied, and the members of the political body shall have begun to be pressed back on each other. North America is still in the condition of having land to begin to cultivate. Only when, as in Europe, the direct increase of agriculturists is checked, will the inhabitants, instead of pressing outwards to occupy the fields, press inwards upon each other—pursuing town occupations, and trading with their fellow-citizens; and so form a compact system of civil society, and require an organized state. The North American federation have no neighbouring state (towards which they occupy a relation similar to that of European states to each other) one which they regard with mistrust, and against which they must keep up a standing army. Canada and Mexico are not objects of fear, and England has had fifty years' experience, that *free* America is more profitable to her than it was in a state of *dependence.* The militia of the North American Republic proved themselves quite as brave in the War of Independence, as the Dutch under Philip II; but generally, where independence is not at stake, less power is displayed, and in the year 1814 the militia held out but indifferently against the English.

America is therefore the land of the future, where, in the ages that lie before us, the burden of the world's history shall reveal itself—perhaps in a contest between North and South America. It is a land of desire for all those who are weary of the historical lumber-room of old Europe. Napoleon is reported to have said: *"Cette vieille Europe m'ennuie."* It is for America to abandon the ground on which hitherto the history of the world has developed itself. What *has* taken place in the New World up to the present time is only an echo of the Old World—the expression of a foreign life; and as a land of the future, it has no interest for us here, for, as regards *history,* our concern must be with that which has been and that which is. In regard to *philosophy,* on the other hand, we have to do with that which (strictly speaking) is neither past nor future, but with that which *is,* which has an eternal existence—with reason; and this is quite sufficient to occupy us.

Dismissing, then, the New World, and the dreams to which it may give rise, we pass over to the Old World—the scene of the world's history; and must first direct attention to the natural elements and conditions of existence which it presents. America is divided into two parts, which are indeed connected by an isthmus, but which forms only an external, material bond of union. The Old World, on the contrary, which lies opposite to America, and is separated from it by the Atlantic Ocean, has its continuity interrupted by a deep inlet—the Mediterranean Sea. The three continents that compose it have an essential relation to each other, and constitute a totality. Their peculiar feature is that they lie round this sea, and therefore have an easy means of communication; for rivers and seas are not to be regarded as disjoining, but as uniting. England and Brittany, Norway and Denmark, Sweden and Livonia, have been united. For the three quarters of the globe the Mediterranean Sea is similarly the uniting element, and the centre of world history. Greece lies here, the focus of light in history. Then in Syria we have Jerusalem, the centre of Judaism and of Christianity; southeast of it lie Mecca and Medina, the cradle of the Mussulman faith; towards the west Delphi and Athens; farther west still, Rome: on the Mediterranean Sea we have also Alexandria and Carthage. The Mediterranean is thus the heart of the Old World, for it is that which conditioned and vitalized it. Without it the history of the world could not be conceived: it would be like ancient Rome or Athens without the forum, where all the life of the city came together. The extensive tract of eastern Asia is severed from the process of general historical development, and has no share in it; so also northern Europe, which took part in the world's history only at a later date, and had no part in it while the Old World lasted; for this was exclusively limited to the countries lying round the Mediterranean Sea. Julius Cæsar's crossing the Alps, the conquest of Gaul and the relation into which the Germans thereby entered with the Roman Empire, makes consequently an epoch in history; for in virtue of this it begins to extend its boundaries beyond the Alps. Eastern Asia and that trans-Alpine country are the extremes of this agitated focus of human life around the Mediterranean, the beginning and end of history, its rise and decline.

The more special geographical distinctions must now be established, and they are to be regarded as essential, rational distinctions, in contrast with the variety of merely accidental circumstances. Of these characteristic differences there are three:—

(1) The arid elevated land with its extensive steppes and plains.

(2) The valley plains—the land of transition permeated and watered by great streams.

(3) The coast region in immediate connection with the sea.

These three geographical elements are the essential ones, and we shall see each quarter of the globe triply divided accordingly. The first is the substantial, unvarying, metallic, elevated region, intractably shut up within itself, but perhaps adapted to send forth impulses over the rest of the world; the second forms centres of civilization, and is the yet undeveloped independence; the third offers the means of connecting the world together, and of maintaining the connection.

(1) *The elevated land.* We see such a description of country in middle Asia inhabited by Mongolians (using the word in a general sense): from the Caspian Sea these steppes stretch in a northerly direction towards the Black Sea. As similar tracts may be cited the deserts of Arabia and of Barbary in Africa; in South America the country round the Orinoco, and in Paraguay. The peculiarity of the inhabitants of this elevated region, which is watered sometimes only by rain, or by the overflowing of a river (as are the plains of the Orinoco)—is the patriarchal life, the division into single families. The region which these families occupy is unfruitful or productive only temporarily: the inhabitants have their property not in the land, from which they derive only a trifling profit, but in the animals that wander with them. For a long time these find pasture in the plains, and when they are depastured, the tribe moves to other parts of the country. They are careless and provide nothing for the winter, on which account therefore, half of the herd is frequently cut off. Among these inhabitants of the upland there exist no legal relations, and consequently there are exhibited among them the extremes of hospitality and rapine; the last more especially when they are surrounded by civilized nations, as the Arabians, who are assisted in their depredations by their horses and camels. The Mongolians feed on mare's milk, and thus the horse supplies them at the same time with appliances for nourishment and for war. Although this is the form of their patriarchal life, it often happens that they cohere together in great masses and, by an impulse

of one kind or another, are excited to external movement. Though previously of peaceful disposition, they then rush as a devastating inundation over civilized lands, and the revolution which ensues has no other result than destruction and desolation. Such an agitation was excited among those tribes under Genghis Khan and Tamerlane: they destroyed all before them; then vanished again, as does an overwhelming forest-torrent—possessing no inherent principle of vitality. From the uplands they rush down into the dells: there dwell peaceful mountaineers—herdsmen who also occupy themselves with agriculture, as do the Swiss. Asia has also such a people: they are however on the whole a less important element.

(2) *The valley plains.* These are plains, permeated by rivers, and which owe the whole of their fertility to the streams by which they are formed. Such a valley-plain is China; India, traversed by the Indus and the Ganges; Babylonia, where the Euphrates and the Tigris flow; Egypt, watered by the Nile. In these regions extensive kingdoms arise, and the foundation of great states begins. For agriculture, which prevails here as the primary principle of subsistence for individuals, is assisted by the regularity of seasons, which require corresponding agricultural operations; property in land commences, and the consequent legal relations; that is to say, the basis and foundation of the state, which becomes possible only in connection with such relations.

(3) *The coast land.* A river divides districts of country from each other, but still more does the sea; and we are accustomed to regard water as the separating element. Especially in recent times has it been insisted upon that states must necessarily have been separated by natural features. Yet on the contrary, it may be asserted as a fundamental principle that nothing *unites* so much as water, for countries are nothing else than districts occupied by streams. Silesia, for instance, is the valley of the Oder; Bohemia and Saxony are the valley of the Elbe; Egypt is the valley of the Nile. With the sea this is not less the case, as has been already pointed out. Only mountains separate. Thus the Pyrenees decidedly separate Spain from France. The Europeans have been in constant connection with America and the East Indies ever since they were discovered; but they have scarcely penetrated into the interior of Africa and Asia, because intercourse by land is much more difficult than by water. Only through the fact of being a sea has the Mediterranean become a focus of national

life. Let us now look at the character of the nations that are conditioned by this third element.

The sea gives us the idea of the indefinite, the unlimited, and infinite; and in *feeling his own infinite* in that infinite, man is stimulated and emboldened to stretch beyond the limited: the sea invites man to conquest, and to piratical plunder, but also to honest gain and to commerce. The land, the mere valley-plain attaches him to the soil; it involves him in an infinite multitude of dependencies, but the sea carries him out beyond these limited circles of thought and action. Those who navigate the sea, have indeed gain for their object, but the means are in this respect paradoxical, inasmuch as they hazard both property and life to attain it. The means therefore are the very opposite to that which they aim at. This is what exalts their gain and occupation above itself, and makes it something brave and noble. Courage is necessarily introduced into trade, daring is joined with wisdom. For the daring which encounters the sea must at the same time embrace wariness —cunning—since it has to do with the treacherous, the most unreliable and deceitful element. This boundless plain is absolutely yielding, withstanding no pressure, not even a breath of wind. It looks boundlessly innocent, submissive, friendly, and insinuating; and it is exactly this submissiveness which changes the sea into the most dangerous and violent element. To this deceitfulness and violence man opposes merely a simple piece of wood; confides entirely in his courage and presence of mind; and thus passes from a firm ground to an unstable support, taking his artificial ground with him. The ship—that swan of the sea, which cuts the watery plain in agile and arching movements or describes circles upon it—is a machine whose invention does the greatest honour to the boldness of man as well as to his understanding. This stretching out of the sea beyond the limitations of the land, is wanting to the splendid political edifices of Asiatic states, although they themselves border on the sea—as for example, China. For them the sea is only the limit, the ceasing of the land; they have no positive relation to it. The activity to which the sea invites, is a quite peculiar one: thence arises the fact that the coastlands almost always separate themselves from the states of the interior although they are connected with these by a river. Thus Holland has severed itself from Germany, Portugal from Spain.

In accordance with these data we may now consider the three portions of the globe with which history is concerned, and here the three characteristic principles manifest themselves in a more or less striking manner: Africa has for its leading classical feature the upland, Asia the contrast of river regions with the upland, Europe the mingling of these several elements.

Africa must be divided into three parts: one is that which lies south of the desert of Sahara—Africa proper—the upland almost entirely unknown to us, with narrow coast-tracts along the sea; the second is that to the north of the desert, European Africa (if we may so call it), a coast-land; the third is the river region of the Nile, the only valley-land of Africa, and which is in connection with Asia.

Africa proper, as far as history goes back, has remained, for all purposes of connection with the rest of the world, shut up; it is the gold-land compressed within itself—the land of childhood, which lying beyond the day of self-conscious history, is enveloped in the dark mantle of night. Its isolated character originates, not merely in its tropical nature, but essentially in its geographical condition. The triangle which it forms (if we take the west coast—which in the Gulf of Guinea makes a strongly indented angle—for one side, and in the same way the east coast to Cape Gardafu for another), is on two sides so constituted for the most part, as to have a very narrow coast tract, habitable only in a few isolated spots. Next to this towards the interior, follows to almost the same extent, a girdle of marsh land with the most luxuriant vegetation, the especial home of ravenous beasts, snakes of all kinds—a border tract whose atmosphere is poisonous to Europeans. This border constitutes the base of a cincture of high mountains, which are only at distant intervals traversed by streams, and where they are so, in such a way as to form no means of union with the interior; for the interruption occurs but seldom below the upper part of the mountain ranges, and only in individual narrow channels, where are frequently found innavigable waterfalls and torrents crossing each other in wild confusion. During the three or three and a half centuries that the Europeans have known this border land and have taken places in it into their possession, they have only here and there (and that but for a short time) passed these mountains, and have nowhere settled down beyond them. The land surrounded by these mountains is an unknown upland, from which on the other hand the Negroes have seldom made their way through. In the sixteenth century occurred, at many very distant points, outbreaks of terrible hordes which rushed down upon the more peaceful inhabitants of the declivities. Whether any internal movement had taken place, or if so, of what character, we do not know. What we do know of these hordes is the contrast between their conduct in their wars and forays themselves—which exhibited the most reckless inhumanity and disgusting barbarism—and the fact that afterwards, when their rage was spent, in the calm time of peace, they showed themselves mild and well disposed towards the Europeans, when they became acquainted with them. This holds good of the Fullahs and of the Mandingo tribes, who inhabit the mountain terraces of the Senegal and Gambia. The second portion of Africa is the river district of the Nile—Egypt; which was adapted to become a mighty centre of independent civilization, and therefore is as isolated and singular in Africa as Africa itself appears in relation to the other parts of the world. The northern part of Africa, which may be specially called that of the *coast territory* (for Egypt has been frequently driven back on itself, by the Mediterranean), lies on the Mediterranean and the Atlantic; a magnificent territory, on which Carthage once lay—the site of the modern Morocco, Algiers, Tunis, and Tripoli. This part was to be, *must* be attached to Europe: the French have lately made a successful effort in this direction: like the Near East, it looks Europe-wards. Here in their turn have Carthaginians, Romans, and Byzantines, Mussulmans, Arabians, had their abode, and the interests of Europe have always striven to get a footing in it.

The peculiarly African character is difficult to comprehend, for the very reason that in reference to it, we must quite give up the principle which naturally accompanies all *our* ideas—the category of universality. In Negro life the characteristic point is the fact that consciousness has not yet attained to the realization of any substantial objective existence—as for example, God, or law—in which the interest of man's volition is involved and in which he realizes his own being. This distinction between himself as an individual and the universality of his essential being, the African in the uniform, undeveloped oneness of his existence has not yet attained; so that the knowledge of an absolute being, an other and a higher than his individual self, is entirely wanting. The Negro, as already observed, exhibits the natural man in his completely wild and untamed state. We must lay aside all thought of reverence and morality, all that we call feeling, if we would rightly comprehend him; there is nothing harmonious with humanity to be found in this type of character. The copious and circumstantial accounts of missionaries completely confirm this, and Mohammedanism appears to be the only thing which in any way brings the Negroes within the range of culture. The Mohammedans too understand better than the Europeans how to penetrate into the interior of the country. The grade of culture which the Negroes occupy may be more nearly appreciated by considering the aspect which *religion* presents among them. That which forms the basis of religious conceptions is the consciousness on the part of man of a higher power —even though this is conceived only as a *vis naturæ*—in relation to which he feels himself a weaker, humbler being. Religion begins with the consciousness that there is something higher than man. But even Herodotus called the Negroes sorcerers: now in *sorcery* we have not the idea of a God, of a moral faith; it exhibits man as the highest power, regarding him as alone occupying a position of command over the power of nature. We have here therefore nothing to do with a spiritual adoration of God, nor with an empire of right. God thunders, but is not on that account recognized as God. For the soul of man, God must be more than a thunderer, whereas among the Negroes this is not the case. Although they are necessarily conscious of dependence upon nature—for they need the beneficial influence of storm, rain, cessation of the rainy period, and so on—yet this does not conduct them to the consciousness of a higher power: it is they who command the elements, and this they call "magic." The kings have a class of ministers through whom they command elemental changes, and every place possesses such magicians, who perform special ceremonies, with all sorts of gesticulations, dances, uproar, and shouting, and in the midst of this confusion commence their incantations. The second element in their religion, consists in their giving an outward form to this supernatural power—projecting their hidden might into the world of phenomena by means of images. What they conceive of as the power in question, is therefore nothing really objective, having a substantial being and different from themselves, but the first thing that comes in their way. This, taken quite indiscriminately, they exalt to the dignity of a "genius"; it may be an animal, a tree, a stone, or a wooden figure. This is their *fetich*—a word to which the Portuguese first gave currency, and which is derived from *feitizo,* magic. Here, in the fetich, a kind of objective independence as contrasted with the arbitrary

fancy of the individual seems to manifest itself; but as the objectivity is nothing other than the fancy of the individual projecting itself into space, the human individuality remains master of the image it has adopted. If any mischance occurs which the fetich has not averted, if rain is suspended, if there is a failure in the crops, they bind and beat or destroy the fetich and so get rid of it, making another immediately, and thus holding it in their own power. Such a fetich has no independence as an object of religious worship; still less has it æsthetic independence as a work of art; it is merely a creation that expresses the arbitrary choice of its maker, and which always remains in his hands. In short there is no relation of dependence in this religion. There is however one feature that points to something beyond; the *worship of the dead,* in which their deceased forefathers and ancestors are regarded by them as a power influencing the living. Their idea in the matter is that these ancestors exercise vengeance and inflict upon man various injuries, exactly in the sense in which this was supposed of witches in the middle ages. Yet the power of the dead is not held superior to that of the living, for the Negroes command the dead and lay spells upon them. Thus the power in question remains substantially always in bondage to the living subject. Death itself is looked upon by the Negroes as no universal natural law; even this, they think, proceeds from evil-disposed magicians. In this doctrine is certainly involved the elevation of man over Nature; to such a degree that the chance volition of man is superior to the merely natural —that he looks upon this as an instrument to which he does not pay the compliment of treating it in a way conditioned by itself, but which he commands.

But from the fact that man is regarded as the highest, it follows that he has no respect for himself; for only with the consciousness of a higher being does he reach a point of view which inspires him with real reverence. For if arbitrary choice is the absolute, the only substantial objectivity that is realized, the mind cannot in such be conscious of any universality. The Negroes indulge, therefore, that perfect *contempt* for humanity, which in its bearing on justice and morality is the fundamental characteristic of the race. They have moreover no knowledge of the immortality of the soul, although spectres are supposed to appear. The undervaluing of humanity among them reaches an incredible degree of intensity. Tyranny is regarded as no wrong, and cannibalism is looked upon as quite customary and proper. Among us instinct deters from it, if we can speak of instinct at all as appertaining to man. But with the Negro this is not the case, and the devouring of human flesh is altogether consonant with the general principles of the African race; to the sensual Negro, human flesh is but an object of sense—mere flesh. At the death of a king hundreds are killed and eaten; prisoners are butchered and their flesh sold in the markets; the victor is accustomed to eat the heart of his slain foe. When magical rites are performed, it frequently happens that the sorcerer kills the first that comes in his way and divides his body among the bystanders. Another characteristic fact in reference to the Negroes is slavery. Negroes are enslaved by Europeans and sold to America. Bad as this may be, their lot in their own land is even worse, since there a slavery quite as absolute exists; for it is the essential principle of slavery, that man has not yet attained a consciousness of his freedom and consequently sinks down to a mere thing—an object of no value. Among the Negroes moral sentiments are quite weak, or more strictly speaking, non-existent. Parents sell their children, and conversely children their parents, as either has the opportunity. Through the pervading influence of slavery all those bonds of moral regard which we cherish towards each other disappear, and it does not occur to the Negro mind to expect from others what we are enabled to claim. The polygamy of the Negroes has frequently for its object the having many children, to be sold, every one of them, into slavery; and very often naïve complaints on this score are heard, as for instance in the case of a Negro in London, who lamented that he was now quite a poor man because he had already sold all his relations. In the contempt of humanity displayed by the Negroes, it is not so much a despising of death as a want of regard for life that forms the characteristic feature. To this want of regard for life must be ascribed the great courage, supported by enormous bodily strength, exhibited by the Negroes, who allow themselves to be shot down by thousands in war with Europeans. Life has a value only when it has something valuable as its object.

Turning our attention in the next place to the category of *political constitution,* we shall see that the entire nature of this race is such as to preclude the existence of any such arrangement. The standpoint of humanity at this grade is mere sensuous volition with energy of will; since universal spiritual laws (for example, that of the morality of the family) cannot be recog-

nized here. Universality exists only as arbitrary subjective choice. The political bond can therefore not possess such a character as that free laws should unite the community. There is absolutely no bond, no restraint upon that arbitrary volition. Nothing but external force can hold the state together for a moment. A ruler stands at the head, for sensuous barbarism can only be restrained by despotic power. But since the subjects are of equally violent temper with their master, they keep him on the other hand within limits. Under the chief there are many other chiefs with whom the former, whom we will call the king, takes counsel, and whose consent he must seek to gain, if he wishes to undertake a war or impose a tax. In this relation he can exercise more or less authority, and by fraud or force can on occasion put this or that chieftain out of the way. Besides this the kings have other specified prerogatives. Among the Ashanti the king inherits all the property left by his subjects at their death. In other places all unmarried women belong to the king, and whoever wishes a wife, must buy her from him. If the Negroes are discontented with their king they depose and kill him. In Dahomey, when they are thus displeased, the custom is to send parrots' eggs to the king, as a sign of dissatisfaction with his government. Sometimes also a deputation is sent, which intimates to him, that the burden of government must have been very troublesome to him, and that he had better rest a little. The king then thanks his subjects, goes into his apartments, and has himself strangled by the women. Tradition alleges that in former times a state composed of women made itself famous by its conquests: it was a state at whose head was a woman. She is said to have pounded her own son in a mortar, to have besmeared herself with the blood, and to have had the blood of pounded children constantly at hand. She is said to have driven away or put to death all the males, and commanded the death of all male children. These furies destroyed everything in the neighborhood, and were driven to constant plunderings, because they did not cultivate the land. Captives in war were taken as husbands: pregnant women had to betake themselves outside the encampment; and if they had born a son, put him out of the way. This infamous state, the report goes on to say, subsequently disappeared. Accompanying the king we constantly find in Negro states, the executioner, whose office is regarded as of the highest consideration, and by whose hands the king, though he makes use of him for putting suspected persons to death, may himself suffer death, if the grandees desire it. Fanaticism, which, notwithstanding the yielding disposition of the Negro in other respects, can be excited, surpasses, when roused, all belief. An English traveller states that when a war is determined on in Ashanti, solemn ceremonies precede it: among other things the bones of the king's mother are laved with human blood. As a prelude to the war, the king ordains an onslaught upon his own metropolis, as if to excite the due degree of frenzy. The king sent word to the English Hutchinson: "Christian, take care, and watch well over your family. The messenger of death has drawn his sword and will strike the neck of many Ashanti; when the drum sounds it is the death signal for multitudes. Come to the King, if you can, and fear nothing for yourself." The drum beat, and a terrible carnage was begun; all who came in the way of the frenzied Negroes in the streets were stabbed. On such occasions the king has all whom he suspects killed, and the deed then assumes the character of a sacred act. Every idea thrown into the mind of the Negro is caught up and realized with the whole energy of his will; but this realization involves a wholesale destruction. These people continue long at rest, but suddenly their passions ferment, and then they are quite beside themselves. The destruction which is the consequence of their excitement, is caused by the fact that it is no positive idea, no thought which produces these commotions; a physical rather than a spiritual enthusiasm. In Dahomey, when the king dies, the bonds of society are loosed; in his palace begins indiscriminate havoc and disorganization. All the wives of the king (in Dahomey their number is exactly 3333) are massacred, and through the whole town plunder and carnage run riot. The wives of the king regard this their death as a necessity; they go richly attired to meet it. The authorities have to hasten to proclaim the new governor, simply to put a stop to massacre.

From these various traits it is manifest that want of self-control distinguishes the character of the Negroes. This condition is capable of no development or culture, and as we see them at this day, such have they always been. The only essential connection that has existed and continued between the Negroes and the Europeans is that of slavery. In this the Negroes see nothing unbecoming them, and the English who have done most for abolishing the slave-trade and slavery, are treated by the Negroes themselves as enemies. For it is a point of first importance with the kings to sell their captured enemies, or

even their own subjects; and viewed in the light of such facts, we may conclude *slavery* to have been the occasion of the increase of human feeling among the Negroes. The doctrine which we deduce from this condition of slavery among the Negroes, and which constitutes the only side of the question that has an interest for our inquiry, is that which we deduce from the Idea: *viz.,* that the "natural condition" itself is one of absolute and thorough injustice, contravention of the right and just. Every intermediate grade between this and the realization of a rational state retains, as might be expected, elements and aspects of injustice; therefore we find slavery even in the Greek and Roman states, as we do serfdom down to the latest times. But thus existing in a state, slavery is itself a phase of advance from the merely isolated sensual existence, a phase of education, a mode of becoming participant in a higher morality and the culture connected with it. Slavery is in and for itself *injustice,* for the essence of humanity is *freedom;* but for this man must be matured. The gradual abolition of slavery is therefore wiser and more equitable than its sudden removal.

At this point we leave Africa, not to mention it again. For it is no historical part of the world; it has no movement or development to exhibit. Historical movements in it—that is, in its northern part—belong to the Asiatic or European world. Carthage displayed there an important transitory phase of civilization; but, as a Phœnician colony, it belongs to Asia. Egypt will be considered in reference to the passage of the human mind from its eastern to its western phase, but it does not belong to the African spirit. What we properly understand by Africa, is the unhistorical, undeveloped spirit, still involved in the conditions of mere nature, and which had to be presented here only as on the threshold of the world's history.

Having eliminated this introductory element, we find ourselves for the first time on the real theatre of history. It now only remains for us to give a prefatory sketch of the geographical basis of the Asiastic and European world. Asia is, characteristically, the *Orient* quarter of the globe—the region of origination. It is indeed a western world for America; but as Europe presents on the whole, the centre and end of the old world, and is absolutely the *West*—so Asia is absolutely the *East.*

In Asia arose the light of spirit, and therefore the history of the world.

We must now consider the various localities

of Asia. Its physical constitution presents direct antitheses, and the essential relation of these antitheses. Its various geographical principles are formations in themselves developed and perfected.

First, the northern slope, Siberia, must be eliminated. This slope, from the Altai chain, with its fine streams, that pour their waters into the northern ocean, does not at all concern us here; because the northern zone, as already stated, lies out of the pale of history. But the remainder includes three very interesting localities. The first is, as in Africa, a massive upland, with a mountain girdle which contains the highest summits in the world. This upland is bounded on the south and southeast, by the Mus-Tag or Imaus, parallel to which, farther south, runs the Himalaya chain. Towards the east, a mountain chain running from south to north, parts off the basin of the Amur. On the north lie the Altai and Songarian mountains; in connection with the latter, in the northwest the Musart and in the west the Belur Tag, which by the Hindu Kush chain are again united with the Mus-Tag.

This high mountain-girdle is broken through by streams, which are dammed up and form great valley plains. These, more or less inundated, present centres of excessive luxuriance and fertility, and are distinguished from the European river districts in their not forming, as those do, proper valleys with valleys branching out from them, but river-plains. Of this kind are the Chinese valley plain, formed by the Hwang Ho and Yangtze Kiang (the Yellow and Blue Streams), next that of India, formed by the Ganges; less important is the Indus, which in the north, gives character to the Punjab, and in the south flows through plains of sand. Farther on, the lands of the Tigris and Euphrates, which rise in Armenia and hold their course along the Persian mountains. The Caspian Sea has similar river valleys; in the east those formed by the Oxus and Jaxartes (Gihon and Sihon) which pour their waters into the Sea of Aral; on the west those of the Cyrus and Araxes (Kur and Aras). The upland and the plains must be distinguished from each other; the third element is their intermixture, which occurs in the Near East. To this belongs Arabia, the land of the desert, the upland of plains, the empire of fanaticism. To this belong Syria and Asia Minor, connected with the sea, and having constant intercourse with Europe.

In regard to Asia the remark above offered respecting geographical differences is especially true; viz., that the rearing of cattle is the business of the upland, agriculture and industrial pursuits that of the valley-plains, while commerce and navigation form the third and last item. Patriarchal independence is strictly bound up with the first condition of society; property and the relation of lord and serf with the second; civil freedom with the third. In the upland, where the various kinds of cattle breeding, the rearing of horses, camels, and sheep (not so much of oxen) deserve attention, we must also distinguish the calm *habitual* life of nomad tribes from the wild and restless character they display in their conquests. These people, without developing themselves in a really historical form, are swayed by a powerful impulse leading them to change their aspect as nations; and although *they* have not attained an historical character, the beginning of history may be traced to them. It must however be allowed that the peoples of the plains are more interesting. In agriculture itself is involved, *ipso facto,* the cessation of a roving life. It demands foresight and solicitude for the future: reflection on a general idea is thus awakened; and herein lies the principle of property and productive industry. China, India, Babylonia, have risen to the position of cultivated lands of this kind. But as the peoples that have occupied these lands have been shut up within themselves, and have not appropriated that element of civilization which the sea supplies (or at any rate only at the commencement of their civilization), and as their navigation of it, to whatever extent it may have taken place, remained without influence on their culture—a relation to the rest of history could only exist in their case, through their being sought out, and their character investigated by others. The mountain-girdle of the upland, the upland itself, and the river-plains, characterize Asia physically and spiritually: but they themselves are not concretely, really, historical elements. The opposition between the extremes is simply recognized, not harmonized; a firm settlement in the fertile plains is for the mobile, restless, roving, condition of the mountain and upland races, nothing more than a constant object of endeavour. Physical features distinct in the sphere of nature, assume an essential historical relation. The Near East has both elements in one, and has, consequently, a relation to Europe; for what is most remarkable in it, this land has not kept for itself, but sent over to Europe. It presents the origination of all religious and political principles, but Europe has been the scene of their development.

Europe, to which we now come, has not the physical varieties which we noticed in Asia and Africa. The European character involves the disappearance of the contrast exhibited by earlier varieties, or at least a modification of it; so that we have the milder qualities of a transition state. We have in Europe no uplands immediately contrasted with plains. The three sections of Europe require therefore a different basis of classification.

The first part is southern Europe, looking towards the Mediterranean. North of the Pyrenees, mountain chains run through France, connected with the Alps that separate and cut off Italy from France and Germany. Greece also belongs to this part of Europe. Greece and Italy long presented the theatre of the world's history; and while the middle and north of Europe were uncultivated, the world-spirit found its home here.

The second portion is the heart of Europe, which Cæsar opened when conquering Gaul. This achievement was one of manhood on the part of the Roman general, and more productive than that youthful one of Alexander, who undertook to exalt the East to a participation in Greek life; and whose work, though in its purport the noblest and fairest for the imagination, soon vanished, as a mere ideal, in the sequel. In this centre of Europe, France, Germany, and England are the principal countries.

Lastly, the third part consists of the northeastern states of Europe—Poland, Russia, and the Slavonic kingdoms. They come only late into the series of historical states, and form and perpetuate the connection with Asia. In contrast with the physical peculiarities of the earlier divisions, these are, as already noticed, not present in a remarkable degree, but counterbalance each other.

CLASSIFICATION OF HISTORIC DATA

In the geographical survey, the course of the world's history has been marked out in its general features. The sun—the light—rises in the east. Light is a simply self-involved existence; but though possessing thus in itself universality, it exists at the same time as an individuality in the sun. Imagination has often pictured to itself the emotions of a blind man suddenly becoming possessed of sight, beholding the bright glimmering of the dawn, the growing light, and the flaming glory of the ascending sun. The boundless forgetfulness of his individuality in this pure splendor, is his first feeling—utter astonishment. But when the sun is risen, this astonishment is diminished; objects around are perceived, and from them the individual proceeds to the contemplation of his own inner being, and thereby the advance is made to the perception of the relation between the two. Then inactive contemplation is quitted for activity; by the close of day man has erected a building constructed from his own inner sun; and when in the evening he contemplates this, he esteems it more highly than the original external sun. For now he stands in a *conscious relation* to his spirit, and therefore a *free* relation. If we hold this image fast in mind, we shall find it symbolizing the course of history, the great day's work of spirit.

The history of the world travels from east to west, for Europe is absolutely the end of history, Asia the beginning. The history of the world has an east κατ' ἐξοχήν; (the term east in itself is entirely relative), for although the earth forms a sphere, history performs no circle round it, but has on the contrary a determinate east, *viz.*, Asia. Here rises the outward physical sun, and in the west it sinks down: here consentaneously rises the sun of self-consciousness, which diffuses a nobler brilliance. The history of the world is the discipline of the uncontrolled natural will, bringing it into obedience to a universal principle and conferring subjective freedom. The East knew and to the present day knows only that *one* is free; the Greek and Roman world, that *some* are free; the German world knows that *all* are free. The first political form therefore which we observe in history, is despotism, the second *democracy* and *aristocracy*, the third *monarchy*.

To understand this division we must remark that as the state is the universal spiritual life, to which individuals by birth sustain a relation of confidence and habit, and in which they have their existence and reality—the first question is, whether their actual life is an unreflecting use and habit combining them in this unity, or whether its constituent individuals are reflective and personal beings having a properly subjective and independent existence. In view of this, *substantial* freedom must be distinguished from *subjective* freedom. Substantial freedom is the abstract undeveloped reason implicit in volition, proceeding to develop itself in the state. But in this phase of reason there is still wanting personal insight and will, that is, subjective freedom, which is realized only in the individual, and which constitutes the reflection of the individual in his own conscience. Where there is merely substantial freedom, commands and laws are regarded as something fixed and abstract, to which the subject holds himself in absolute servitude. These laws need not concur with the desire of the individual, and the subjects are consequently like children, who obey their parents without will or insight of their own. But as subjective freedom arises, and man descends from the contemplation of external reality into his own soul, the contrast suggested by reflection arises, involving the negation of reality. The drawing back from the actual world forms *ipso facto* an antithesis, of which one side is the absolute being—the divine—the other the human subject as an individual. In that immediate, unreflected consciousness which characterizes the East, these two are not yet distinguished. The substantial world is distinct from the individual, but the antithesis has not yet created a schism between spirit.

The first phase, that with which we have to begin, is the East. Unreflected consciousness—substantial, objective, spiritual existence—forms the basis; to which the subjective will first sustains a relation in the form of faith, confidence, obedience. In the political life of the East we find a realized rational freedom, developing itself without advancing to *subjective* freedom. It is the childhood of history. Substantial forms constitute the gorgeous edifices of Oriental empires in which we find all rational ordinances and arrangements, but in such a way, that individuals remain as mere accidents. These revolve round a centre, round the sovereign, who, as patriarch, not as despot in the sense of the Roman imperial constitution, stands at the head. For he has to enforce the moral and substantial: he has to uphold those essential ordinances which are already established; so that what among us belongs entirely to subjective freedom, here proceeds from the entire and general body of the state. The glory of Oriental conception is the one individual as that substantial being to which all belongs, so that no other individual has a separate existence, or mirrors himself in his subjective freedom. All the riches of imagination and nature are appropriated to that dominant existence in which subjective freedom is essentially merged; the latter looks for its dignity *not* in itself, but in that absolute object. All the elements of a complete state—even subjectivity—may be found there, but not yet harmonized with the grand substantial being. For outside the one power—before which nothing can maintain an independent existence—there is only revolting caprice, which, beyond the limits of the central power, roves at will without purpose or result. Accordingly we find the wild hordes breaking out from the upland, falling upon the countries in question, and laying them waste, or settling down in them, and giving up their wild life; but in all cases resultlessly lost in the central substance. This phase of substantiality, since it has not taken up its antithesis into itself and overcome it, directly divides itself into two elements. On the one side, we see duration, stability—empires belonging to mere space, as it were, unhistorical history; as for example, in China, the state based on the family relation; a paternal government, which holds together the constitution by its provident care, its admonitions, retributive or rather disciplinary inflictions; a prosaic empire, because the antithesis of form, *viz.*, infinity, ideality, has not yet asserted itself. On the other side, the form of time stands contrasted with this spatial stability. The states in question, without undergoing any change in themselves, or in the principle of their existence, are constantly changing their position towards each other. They are in ceaseless conflict, which brings on rapid destruction. The opposing principle of individuality enters into these conflicting relations; but it is itself as yet only unconscious, merely natural universality—light, which is not yet the light of the personal soul. This history, too (*i.e.*, of the struggles before-mentioned) is, for the most part, really *unhistorical,* for it is only the repetition of the same majestic ruin. The new element, which in the shape of bravery, prowess, magnanimity, occupies the place of the previous despotic pomp, goes through the same circle of decline and subsidence. This subsidence is therefore not really such, for through all this restless change no advance is made. History passes at this point, and only outwardly, *i.e.*, without connection with the previous phase, to Central Asia. Continuing the comparison with the ages of the individual man, this would be the boyhood of history, no longer manifesting the repose and trustingness of the child, but boisterous and turbulent. The Greek world may then be compared with the period of adolescence, for here we have individualities forming themselves. This is the *second* main principle in human history. Morality is, as in Asia, a principle; but it is morality impressed on individuality, and consequently denoting the free volition of individuals. Here, then, is the union of the moral with the subjective will, or the kingdom of *beautiful freedom,* for the idea is united with a plastic form. It is not yet regarded abstractedly, but immediately bound up with the real, as in a beautiful work of art; the sensuous bears the stamp and expression of the spiritual. This kingdom is consequently true harmony; the world of the most charming, but perishable or quickly passing bloom: it is the natural, unreflecting observance of what is *becoming*—not yet true *morality*. The individual will of the subject adopts unreflectingly the conduct and habit prescribed by justice and the laws. The individual is therefore in unconscious unity with the idea—the social weal. That which in the East is divided into two extremes—the substantial as such, and the individuality absorbed in it—meets here. But these distinct principles are only *immediately* in unity, and consequently involve the highest degree of contradiction; for this æsthetic morality has not yet passed through the struggle of subjective freedom, in its second birth, its *palingenesis;* it is not yet purified to the standard of the free subjectivity that is the essence of true morality.

The third phase is the realm of abstract universality (in which the social aim absorbs all individual aims): it is the Roman State, the severe labors of the *manhood* of history. For true manhood acts neither in accordance with the caprice of a despot, nor in obedience to a graceful caprice of its own; but works for a general aim, one in which the individual perishes and realizes his own private object only in that general aim. The state begins to have an abstract existence, and to develop itself for a definite object, in accomplishing which its members have indeed a share, but not a complete and concrete one. Free *individuals* are sacrificed to the severe demands of the *national* objects, to which they must surrender themselves in this service of abstract generalization. The Roman State is not a repetition of such a state of individuals as the Athenian polis was. The geniality and joy of soul that existed there have given place to harsh and rigorous toil. The interest of history is detached from individuals, but these gain for themselves abstract, formal universality. The universal subjugates the individuals; they have to merge their own interests in it; but in return the abstraction which they themselves embody —that is to say, their personality—is recognized: in their individual capacity they become persons with definite rights as such. In the same sense as individuals may be said to be incorporated in the abstract idea of person, *national individualities* (those of the Roman provinces) have also to experience this fate; in this form of universality their concrete forms are crushed, and incorporated with it as a homogeneous and indifferent mass. Rome becomes a pantheon of all deities, and of all spiritual existence, but these divinities and this spirit do not retain their proper vitality. The development of the state in question proceeds in two directions. On the one hand, as based on reflection—abstract universality—it has the express outspoken antithesis in itself: it therefore essentially involves in itself the struggle which that antithesis supposes; with the necessary issue, that individual caprice, the purely contingent and thoroughly worldly power of *one despot,* gets the better of that abstract universal principle. At the very outset we have the antithesis between the aim of the state as the abstract universal principle on the one hand, and the abstract personality of the individual on the other hand. But when subsequently, in the historical development, individuality gains the ascendant, and the breaking up of the community into its component atoms can only be restrained by external compulsion, then the subjective might of *individual despotism* comes forward to play its part, as if summoned to fulfil this task. For the mere abstract compliance with law implies on the part of the subject of law the supposition that he has not attained to self-

organization and self-control; and this principle of obedience, instead of being hearty and voluntary, has for its motive and ruling power only the arbitrary and contingent disposition of the individual; so that the latter is led to seek consolation for the loss of his freedom in exercising and developing his private right. This is the purely *worldly* harmonization of the antithesis. But in the next place, the pain inflicted by despotism begins to be felt, and spirit driven back into its utmost depths, leaves the godless world, seeks for a harmony in itself, and begins now an inner life—a complete concrete subjectivity, which possesses at the same time a substantiality that is not grounded in mere external existence. Within the soul therefore arises the *spiritual* pacification of the struggle, in the fact that the individual personality, instead of following its own capricious choice, is purified and elevated into universality; a subjectivity that of its own free will adopts principles tending to the good of all—reaches, in fact, a divine personality. To that worldly empire, this spiritual one wears a predominant aspect of opposition, as the empire of a subjectivity that has attained to the knowledge of itself—itself in its essential nature—the empire of spirit in its full sense.

The *German* world appears at this point of development—the fourth phase of world history. This would answer in the comparison with the periods of human life to its *old age.* The old age of *nature* is weakness; but that of *spirit* is its perfect maturity and *strength,* in which it returns to unity with itself, but in its fully developed character as *spirit.* This fourth phase begins with the reconciliation presented in Christianity; but only in the germ, without national or political development. We must therefore regard it as commencing rather with the enormous contrast between the spiritual, religious principle, and the barbarian real world. For spirit as the consciousness of an inner world is, at the commencement, itself still in an abstract form. All that is *secular* is consequently given over to rudeness and capricious violence. The *Mohammedan* principle, the enlightenment of the Oriental world, is the first to contravene this barbarism and caprice. We find it developing itself later and more rapidly than Christianity; for the latter needed eight centuries to grow up into a political form. But that principle of the German world which we are now discussing, attained concrete reality only in the history of the German nations. The contrast of the spiritual principle animating the *ecclesiastical* state, with the rough and wild barbarism of the *secular* state, is here likewise present. The secular *ought* to be in harmony with the spiritual principle, but we find nothing more than the *recognition* of that obligation. The secular power forsaken by the spirit, must in the first instance vanish in presence of the ecclesiastical; but while this latter degrades itself to mere secularity, it loses its influence with the loss of its proper character and vocation. From this corruption of the ecclesiastical element—that is, of the church—results the higher form of rational thought. Spirit once more driven back upon itself, produces its work in an intellectual shape, and becomes capable of realizing the ideal of reason from the secular principle alone. Thus it happens, that in virtue of elements of universality, which have the principle of spirit as their basis, the empire of thought is established actually and concretely. The antithesis of church and state vanishes. The spiritual becomes reconnected with the secular, and develops this latter as an independently organic existence. The state no longer occupies a position of real inferiority to the church, and is no longer subordinate to it. The latter asserts no prerogative, and the spiritual is no longer an element foreign to the state. Freedom has found the means of realizing its ideal—its true existence. This is the ultimate result which the process of history is intended to accomplish, and we have to traverse in detail the long track which has been thus cursorily traced out. Yet length of time is something entirely relative, and the element of spirit is eternity. Duration, properly speaking, cannot be said to belong to it.

FIRST PART

THE ORIENTAL WORLD

We have to begin with the oriental world, but not before the period in which we discover states in it. The diffusion of language and the formation of races lie beyond the limits of history. History is prose, and myths fall short of history. The consciousness of external definite existence only arises in connection with the power to form abstract distinctions and assign abstract predicates; and in proportion as a capacity for expressing laws is acquired, in the same proportion does the ability manifest itself, to comprehend objects in an unpoetical form. While the ante-historical is that which precedes political life, it also lies beyond self-cognizant life; though surmises and suppositions may be entertained respecting that period, these do not amount to facts. The Oriental world has as its inherent and distinctive principle the substantial, in morality. We have the first example of a subjugation of the mere arbitrary will, which is merged in this substantiality. Moral distinctions and requirements are expressed as laws, but so that the subjective will is governed by these laws as by an external force. Nothing subjective in the shape of disposition, conscience, formal freedom, is recognized. Justice is administered only on the basis of external morality, and government exists only as the prerogative of compulsion. Our civil law contains indeed some purely compulsory ordinances. I can be compelled to give up another man's property, or to keep an agreement which I have made; but the moral is not placed by *us* in the mere compulsion, but in the disposition of the subjects, their sympathy with the requirements of law. Morality is in the East likewise a subject of positive legislation, and although the moral prescriptions (the *substance* of their ethics) may be perfect, what should be internal subjective sentiment is made a matter of external arrangement. There is no want of a will to command moral actions, but of a will to perform them because commanded from *within*. Since spirit has not yet attained subjectivity, it wears the appearance of spirituality still involved in the conditions of nature. Since the external and the internal, law and moral sense, are not yet distinguished—still form an undivided unity—so also do religion and the state. The constitution generally is a theocracy, and the kingdom of God is to the same extent also a secular kingdom as the secular kingdom is also divine. What we call God has not yet in the East been realized in consciousness, for our idea of God involves an elevation of the soul to the supersensual. While *we* obey, because what we are required to do is confirmed by an *internal* sanction, there the law is regarded as inherently and absolutely valid without a sense of the want of this subjective confirmation. In the law men recognize not their own will, but one entirely foreign.

Of the several parts of Asia we have already eliminated as unhistorical, upper Asia (so far and so long as its nomad population do not appear on the scene of history), and Siberia. The rest of the Asiatic world is divided into four districts: first, the river-plains, formed by the Yellow and Blue Streams, and the upland of farther Asia—China and the Mongols. Secondly, the valley of the Ganges and that of the Indus. The third theatre of history comprises the river-plains of the Oxus and Jaxartes, the upland of Persia, and the other valley-plains of the Euphrates and Tigris, to which the Near East attaches itself. Fourthly, the river-plain of the Nile.

With *China* and the *Mongols,* the realm of theocratic despotism, history begins. Both have the patriarchal constitution for their principle—so modified in China, as to admit the development of an organized system of secular polity; while among the Mongols it limits itself to the simple form of a spiritual, religious sovereignty. In China the monarch is chief as patriarch. The laws of the state are partly civil ordinances, partly moral requirements; so that the internal law, the knowledge on the part of the individual of the nature of his volition, as his own inmost self —even this is the subject of external statutory enactment. The sphere of subjectivity does not then attain to maturity here, since moral laws are treated as legislative enactments, and law on its part has an ethical aspect. All that we call subjectivity is concentrated in the supreme head of the state, who, in all his legislation has an eye to the health, wealth, and benefit of the whole. Contrasted with this secular empire is the spiritual sovereignty of the Mongols, at the head of which stands the Lama, who is honored as God. In this spiritual empire no secular political life can be developed.

In the second phase—the *Indian* realm—we see the unity of political organization, a perfect civil machinery, such as exists in China, in the first instance, broken up. The several powers of society appear as dissevered and free in relation to each other. The different castes are indeed, fixed; but in view of the religious doctrine that establish them, they wear the aspect of *natural* distinctions. Individuals are thereby still further stripped of proper personality, although it might appear as if they derived gain from the development of the distinctions in question. For though we find the organization of the state no longer, as in China, determined and arranged by the one all-absorbing personality, the distinctions that exist are attributed to nature and so become differences of caste. The unity in which these divisions must finally meet, is a religious one; and thus arises theocratic aristocracy and its despotism. Here begins, therefore, the distinction between the spiritual consciousness and secular conditions; but as the *separation* implied in the above mentioned distinctions is the cardinal consideration, so also we find in the religion the principle of the isolation of the constituent elements of the idea; a principle which posits the harshest antithesis—the conception of the purely abstract unity of God, and of the purely sensual powers of nature. The connection of the two is only a constant change, a restless hurrying from one extreme to the other, a wild chaos of fruitless variation, which must appear as madness to a duly regulated, intelligent consciousness.

The third important form, presenting a contrast to the immovable unity of China and to the wild and turbulent unrest of India, is the *Persian* realm. China is quite peculiarly oriental; India we might compare with Greece; Persia on the other hand with Rome. In Persia namely, the theocratic power appears as a *monarchy*. Now monarchy is that kind of constitution which does indeed unite the members of the body politic in the head of the government as in a point; but regards that head neither as the absolute director nor the arbitrary ruler, but as a power whose will

is regulated by the same principle of law as the obedience of the subject. We have thus a general principle, a law, lying at the basis of the whole, but which, still regarded as a dictum of mere nature, is clogged by an antithesis. The representation, therefore, which spirit makes of itself is, at this grade of progress, of a purely natural kind—light. This universal principle is as much a regulative one for the monarch as for each of his subjects, and the Persian spirit is accordingly clear, illuminated—the idea of a people living in pure morality, as in a sacred community. But this has on the one hand as a merely natural ecclesia, the above antithesis still unreconciled; and its sanctity displays the characteristics of a compulsory, external one. On the other hand this antithesis is exhibited in Persia in its being the empire of hostile peoples, and the union of the most widely differing nations. The Persian unity is not that abstract one of the Chinese Empire; it is adapted to rule over many and various nationalities, which it unites under the mild power of universality as a beneficial sun shining over all—waking them into life and cherishing their growth. This universal principle, occupying the position of a root only, allows the several members a free growth for unrestrained expansion and ramification. In the organization of these several peoples, the various principles and forms of life have full play and continue to exist together. We find in this multitude of nations, roving nomads; then we see in Babylonia and Syria commerce and industrial pursuits in full vigour, the wildest sensuality, the most uncontrolled turbulence. The coasts mediate a connection with foreign lands. In the midst of this confusion the spiritual God of the Jews arrests our attention—like Brahma, existing only for thought, yet jealous and excluding from his being and abolishing all distinct speciality of manifestations, such as are freely allowed in other religions. This Persian Empire, then—since it can tolerate these several principles, exhibits the antithesis in a lively active form, and is not shut up within itself, abstract and calm, as are China and India—makes a real transition in the history of the world.

If Persia forms the *external* transition to Greek life, the internal, *mental* transition is mediated by *Egypt*. Here the antitheses in their abstract form are broken through; a breaking through which effects their nullification. This undeveloped reconciliation exhibits the struggle of the most contradictory principles, which are not yet capable of harmonizing themselves, but, setting up the birth of this harmony as the problem to be solved, make themselves a riddle for themselves and for others, the solution of which is only to be found in the *Greek* world.

If we compare these kingdoms in the light of their various fates, we find the empire of the two Chinese rivers the only durable kingdom in the world. Conquests cannot affect such an empire. The world of the Ganges and the Indus has also been preserved. A state of things so destitute of thought is likewise imperishable, but it is in its very nature destined to be mixed with other races—to be conquered and subjugated. While these two realms have remained to the present day, of the empires of the Tigris and Euphrates on the contrary nothing remains, except, at most, a heap of bricks; for the Persian Kingdom, as that of transition, is by nature perishable, and the kingdoms of the Caspian Sea are given up to the ancient struggle of Iran and Turan. The empire of the solitary Nile is only present *beneath* the ground, in its speechless dead, ever and anon stolen away to all quarters of the globe, and in their majestic habitations; for what remains above ground is nothing else but such splendid tombs.

Section I
CHINA

With the empire of China history has to begin, for it is the oldest, as far as history gives us any information; and its *principle* has such substantiality, that for the empire in question it is at once the oldest and the newest. Early do we see China advancing to the condition in which it is found at this day; for as the contrast between objective existence and subjective freedom of movement in it, is still wanting, every change is excluded, and the fixedness of a character which recurs perpetually, takes the place of what we should call the truly historical. China and India lie, as it were, still outside the world's history, as the mere presupposition of elements whose combination must be waited for to constitute their vital progress. The unity of substantiality and subjective freedom so entirely excludes the distinction and contrast of the two elements, that by this very fact, substance cannot arrive at reflection or itself—at subjectivity. The substantial in its moral aspect, rules therefore, not as the moral disposition of the *subject,* but as the despotism of the *sovereign.*

No people has a so strictly continuous series of writers of history as the Chinese. Other Asiatic peoples also have ancient traditions, but no history. The Vedas of the Indians are not such. The traditions of the Arabs are very old, but are not attached to a political constitution and its development. But such a constitution exists in China, and that in a distinct and prominent form. The Chinese traditions ascend to three thousand years before Christ; and the *Shu-King,* their canonical document, beginning with the government of Yao, places this 2357 years before Christ. It may here be incidentally remarked, that the other Asiatic kingdoms also reach a high antiquity. According to the calculation of an English writer, the Egyptian history, *e.g.*, reaches to 2207 years before Christ, the Assyrian to 2221, the Indian to 2204. Thus the traditions respecting the principal kingdoms of the East reach to about 2300 years before the birth of Christ. Comparing this with the history of the Old Testament, a space of 2400 years, according to the common acceptation, intervened between the Deluge and the Christian era. But Johannes von Müller has adduced weighty objections to this number. He places the Deluge in the year 3473 before Christ—thus about a thousand years earlier—supporting his view by the Septuagint. I remark this only to obviate a difficulty that may appear to arise when we meet with dates of a higher age than 2400 years before Christ, and yet find nothing about the Flood.

The Chinese have certain ancient canonical documents, from which their history, constitution, and religion can be gathered. The Vedas and the Mosaic records are similar books; as also the Homeric poems. Among the Chinese these books are called *Kings,* and constitute the foundation of all their studies. The *Shu-King* contains their history, treats of the government of the ancient kings, and gives the statutes enacted by this or that monarch. The *Y-King* consists of figures, which have been regarded as the bases of the Chinese written character, and this book is also considered the groundwork of the Chinese meditation. For it begins with the abstractions of unity and duality, and then treats of the concrete existences pertaining to these abstract forms of thought. Lastly, the *Shi-King* is the book of the oldest poems in a great variety of styles. The high officers of the kingdom were anciently commissioned to bring with them to the annual festival all the poems composed in their province within the year. The emperor in full court was the judge of these poems, and those recognized as good received public approbation. Besides these three books of archives which are specially honoured and studied, there are besides two others, less important, *viz.*, the *Li-Ki* (or *Li-King*) which records the customs and ceremonial observances pertaining to the imperial dignity, and that of the state function-aries (with an appendix, *Yo-King*, treating of music); and the *Tshun-tsin*, the chronicle of the kingdom Lu, where Confucius appeared. These books are the groundwork of the history, the manners and the laws of China.

This empire early attracted the attention of Europeans, although only vague stories about it had reached them. It was always marvelled at as a country which, self-originated, appeared to have no connection with the outer world.

In the thirteenth century a Venetian (Marco Polo) explored it for the first time, but his re-ports were deemed fabulous. In later times, ev-erything that he had said respecting its extent and greatness was entirely confirmed. By the lowest calculation, China has 150,000,000 inhab-itants; another makes the number 200,000,000, and the highest raises it even to 300,000,000. From the far north it stretches towards the south to India; on the east it is bounded by the vast Pacific, and on the west it extends towards Persia and the Caspian. China proper is overpopulated. On both rivers, the Hwang Ho and the Yangtze Kiang, dwell many millions of human beings, liv-ing on rafts adapted to all the requirements of their mode of life. The population and the thor-oughly organized state-arrangements, descend-ing even to the minutest details, have astonished Europeans; and a matter of especial astonish-ment is the accuracy with which their historical works are executed. For in China the historians are some of the highest functionaries. Two min-isters constantly in attendance on the emperor, are commissioned to keep a journal of every-thing the emperor does, commands, and says, and their notes are then worked up and made use of by the historians. We cannot go further into the minutiæ of their annals, which, as they themselves exhibit no development, would only hinder us in ours. Their history ascends to very ancient times, in which Fohi is named as the dif-fuser of culture, he having been the original civilizer of China. He is said to have lived in the twenty-ninth century before Christ—before the time, therefore, at which the *Shu-King* begins; but the mythical and prehistorical is treated by Chinese historians as perfectly historical. The first region of Chinese history is the north-western corner—China proper—towards that point where the Hwang Ho descends from the mountains; for only at a later period did the Chinese empire extend itself towards the south, to the Yangtze Kiang. The narrative begins with the period in which men lived in a wild state, *i.e.*, in the woods, when they fed on the fruits of the

earth, and clothed themselves with the skins of wild beasts. There was no recognition of definite laws among them. To Fohi (who must be duly distinguished from Fo, the founder of a new re-ligion), is ascribed the instruction of men in building themselves huts and making dwellings. He is said to have directed their attention to the change and return of seasons, to barter and trade; to have established marriage; to have taught that reason came from heaven, and to have giv-en instructions for rearing silkworms, building bridges, and making use of beasts of burden. The Chinese historians are very diffuse on the sub-ject of these various origins. The progress of the history is the extension of the culture thus orig-inated, to the south, and the beginning of a state and a government. The great empire which had thus gradually been formed, was soon broken up into many provinces, which carried on long wars with each other, and were then re-united into a whole. The dynasties in China have often been changed, and the one now dominant is generally marked as the twenty-second. In connection with the rise and fall of these dynasties arose the dif-ferent capital cities that are found in this em-pire. For a long time Nanking was the capital; now it is Peking; at an earlier period other cities. China has been compelled to wage many wars with the Tartars, who penetrated far into the country. The long wall built by Shih Huang Ti, and which has always been regarded as a most astounding achievement, was raised as a barrier against the inroads of the northern nomads. This prince divided the whole empire into thirty-six provinces, and made himself especially remark-able by his attacks on the old literature, es-pecially on the historical books and historical studies generally. He did this with the design of strengthening his own dynasty, by destroying the remembrance of the earlier one. After the historical books had been collected and burned, many hundreds of the *literati* fled to the moun-tains, in order to save what remained. Every one that fell into the emperor's hands experienced the same fate as the books. This book-burning is a very important circumstance, for in spite of it the strictly canonical books were saved, as is generally the case. The first connection of China with the West occurred about 64 A.D. At that epoch a Chinese emperor despatched am-bassadors (it is said) to visit the wise sages of the West. Twenty years later a Chinese general is reported to have penetrated as far as Judea. At the beginning of the eighth century after Christ, the first Christians are reputed to have gone to China, of which visit later visitors assert that they found traces and monuments. A Tartar kingdom, *Lyau-Tong,* existing in the north of China, is said to have been reduced and taken possession of by the Chinese with the help of the western Tartars, about 1100 A.D. This, nevertheless, gave these very Tartars an opportunity of securing a footing in China. Similarly they admitted the Manchus with whom they engaged in war in the sixteenth and seventeenth centuries, which resulted in the present dynasty's obtaining possession of the throne. Yet this new dynasty has not effected further change in the country, any more than did the earlier conquest of the Mongols in the year 1281. The Manchus that live in China have to conform to Chinese laws, and study Chinese sciences.

We pass now from these few dates in Chinese history to the contemplation of the *spirit* of the constitution, which has always remained the same. We can deduce it from the general principle, which is, the immediate unity of the substantial spirit and the individual; but this is equivalent to the spirit of the family, which is here extended over the most populous of countries. The element of subjectivity—that is to say, the reflection upon itself of the individual will in antithesis to the substantial (as the power in which it is absorbed) or the recognition of this power as *one with its own essential being,* in which it knows itself *free*—is not found on this grade of development. The universal will displays its activity immediately through that of the individual: the latter has no self-cognizance at all in antithesis to substantial, positive being, which it does not yet regard as a power standing over against it—as, *e.g.,* in Judaism, the "Jealous God" is known as the negation of the individual. In China the universal will immediately commands what the individual is to do, and the latter complies and obeys with proportionate renunciation of reflection and personal independence. If he does not obey, if he thus virtually separates himself from the substance of his being, inasmuch as this separation is not mediated by a retreat within a personality of his own, the punishment he undergoes does not affect his subjective and internal, but simply his outward existence. The element of subjectivity is therefore as much wanting to this political totality as the latter is on its side altogether destitute of a foundation in the moral disposition of the subject. For the substance is simply an individual—the emperor—whose law constitutes all the disposition. Nevertheless, this ignoring of inclination does not imply caprice, which would itself indicate inclination—that is, sub-

jectivity and mobility. Here we have the one being of the state supremely dominant—the substance, which, still hard and inflexible, resembles nothing but itself, includes no other element.

This relation, then, expressed more definitely and more conformably with its conception, is that of the *family.* On this form of moral union alone rests the Chinese state, and it is objective family piety that characterizes it. The Chinese regard themselves as belonging to their family, and at the same time as children of the state. In the family itself they are not personalities, for the consolidated unity in which they exist as members of it is consanguinity and natural obligation. In the state they have as little independent personality; for there the patriarchal relation is predominant, and the government is based on the paternal management of the emperor, who keeps all departments of the state in order. Five duties are stated in the *Shu-King* as involving grave and unchangeable fundamental relations. 1. The mutual one of the emperor and people. 2. Of the fathers and children. 3. Of an elder and younger brother. 4. Of husband and wife. 5. Of friend and friend. It may be here incidentally remarked, that the number five is regarded as fundamental among the Chinese, and presents itself as often as the number three among us. They have five elements of nature—air, water, earth, metal, and wood. They recognize *four* quarters of heaven and a centre. Holy places, where altars are erected, consist of four elevations, and one in the centre.

The duties of the family are absolutely binding, and established and regulated by law. The son may not accost the father, when he comes into the room; he must seem to contract himself to nothing at the side of the door, and may not leave the room without his father's permission. When the father dies, the son must mourn for three years—abstaining from meat and wine. The business in which he was engaged, even that of the state, must be suspended, for he is obliged to quit it. Even the emperor, who has just commenced his government, does not devote himself to his duties during this time. No marriage may be contracted in the family within the period of mourning. Only the having reached his fiftieth year exempts the bereaved from the excessive strictness of the regulations, which are then relaxed that he may not be reduced in person by them. The sixtieth year relaxes them still further, and the seventieth limits mourning to the color of the dress. A mother is honored equally with a father. When Lord Macartney saw the emperor, the latter was sixty-eight years old (sixty years is among the Chinese a fundamental round number, as one hundred is among us), notwithstanding which he visited his mother every morning on foot, to demonstrate his respect for her. The New Year's congratulations are offered even to the mother of the emperor; and the emperor himself cannot receive the homage of the grandees of the court until he has paid his to his mother. The latter is the first and constant counsellor of her son, and all announcements concerning his family are made in her name. The merits of a son are ascribed not to him, but to his father. When on one occasion the prime minister asked the emperor to confer titles of honour on his father, the emperor issued an edict in which it was said: "Famine was desolating the empire: Thy father gave rice to the starving. What beneficence! The empire was on the edge of ruin: Thy father defended it at the hazard of his life. What fidelity! The government of the kingdom was intrusted to thy father: he made excellent laws, maintained peace and concord with the neighboring princes, and asserted the rights of my crown. What wisdom! The title therefore which I award to him is: beneficent, faithful and wise." The son had done all that is here ascribed to the father. In this way ancestors, a fashion the reverse of ours, obtain titles of honour through their posterity. But in return, every father of a family is responsible for the transgressions of his descendants; duties ascend, but none can be properly said to descend.

It is a great object with the Chinese, to have children who may give them the due honours of burial, pay respect to their memory after death, and decorate their grave. Although a Chinese may have many wives, one only is the mistress of the house, and the children of the subordinate wives have to honor her absolutely as a mother. If a Chinese husband has no children by any of his wives, he may proceed to adoption with a view to this posthumous honour. For it is an indispensable requirement that the grave of parents be annually visited. Here lamentations are annually renewed, and many, to give full vent to their grief, remain there sometimes one or two months. The body of a deceased father is often kept three or four months in the house, and during this time no one may sit down on a chair or sleep in a bed. Every family in China has a hall of ancestors where all the members annually assemble; there are placed representations of those who have filled exalted posts, while the names of those men and women who have been of less importance in the family are inscribed on tablets; the whole family then partake of a meal together, and the poor members are entertained by the more wealthy. It is said that a mandarin who had become a Christian, having ceased to honor his ancestors in this way, exposed himself to great persecutions on the part of his relatives. The same minuteness of regulation which prevails in the relation between father and children, characterizes also that between the elder brother and the younger ones. The former has, though in a less degree than parents, claims to reverence.

This family basis is also the basis of the constitution, if we can speak of such. For although the emperor has the right of a monarch, standing at the summit of a political edifice, he exercises it paternally. He is the patriarch, and everything in the state that can make any claim to reverence is attached to him. For the emperor is chief both in religious affairs and in science—a subject which will be treated of in detail further on. This paternal care on the part of the emperor, and the spirit of his subjects—who like children do not advance beyond the ethical principle of the family circle, and can gain for themselves no independent and civil freedom—makes the whole an empire, administration, and social code, which is at the same time moral and thoroughly prosaic; that is, a product of the understanding without free reason and imagination.

The emperor claims the deepest reverence. In virtue of his position he is obliged personally to manage the government, and must himself be acquainted with and direct the legislative business of the Empire, although the tribunals give their assistance. Notwithstanding this, there is little room for the exercise of his individual will; for the whole government is conducted on the basis of certain ancient maxims of the empire, while his constant oversight is not the less necessary. The imperial princes are therefore educated on the strictest plan. Their physical frames are hardened by discipline, and the sciences are their occupation from their earliest years. Their education is conducted under the emperor's superintendence, and they are early taught that the emperor is the head of the state and therefore must appear as the first and best in everything. An examination of the princes takes place every year, and a circumstantial report of the affair is published through the whole empire, which feels the deepest interest in these matters. China has therefore succeeded in getting the greatest and best governors, to whom the expression "Solomonian wisdom" might be applied; and the present Manchu dynasty has especially distinguished itself by abilities of mind and body. All the ideals of princes and of princely education which have been so numerous and varied since the appearance of Fenelon's *Télémaque* are realized here. In Europe there can be no Solomons. But here are the place and the necessity for such government; since the rectitude, the prosperity, the security of all, depend on the one impulse given to the first link in the entire chain of this hierarchy. The deportment of the emperor is represented to us as in the highest degree simple, natural, noble and intelligent. Free from a proud taciturnity or repelling *hauteur* in speech or manners, he lives in the consciousness of his own dignity and in the exercise of imperial duties to whose observance he has been disciplined from his earliest youth. Besides the imperial dignity there is properly no elevated rank, no nobility among the Chinese; only the princes of the imperial house, and the sons of the ministers enjoy any precedence of the kind, and they rather by their position than by their birth. Otherwise all are equal, and only those have a share in the administration of affairs who have ability for it. Official stations are therefore occupied by men of the greatest intellect and education. The Chinese state has consequently been often set up as an ideal which may serve even us for a model.

The next thing to be considered is the *administration* of the empire. We cannot speak, in reference to China, of a *constitution;* for this would imply that individuals and corporations have independent rights—partly in respect of their particular interests, partly in respect of the entire state. This element must be wanting here, and we can only speak of an administration of the empire. In China, we have the reality of absolute equality, and all the differences that exist are possible only in connection with that administration, and in virtue of the worth which a person may acquire, enabling him to fill a high post in the government. Since equality prevails in China, but without any freedom, despotism is necessarily the mode of government. Among us, men are equal only before the law, and in the respect paid to the property of each; but they have also many interests and peculiar privileges, which must be guaranteed, if we are to have what we call freedom. But in the Chinese Empire these special interests enjoy no consideration on their own account, and the government proceeds from the emperor alone, who sets it in movement as a hierarchy of officials or mandarins. Of these, there are two kinds—learned and military mandarins—the latter corresponding to our officers. The learned mandarins constitute the higher

rank, for, in China, civilians take precedence of the military. Government officials are educated at the schools; elementary schools are instituted for obtaining elementary knowledge. Institutions for higher cultivation, such as our universities, may, perhaps, be said not to exist. Those who wish to attain high official posts must undergo several examinations—usually three in number. To the third and last examination, at which the emperor himself is present, only those can be admitted who have passed the first and second with credit; and the reward for having succeeded in this is the immediate introduction into the highest council of the empire. The sciences, an acquaintance with which is especially required, are the history of the empire, jurisprudence, and the science of customs and usages, and of the organization and administration of government. Besides this, the mandarins are said to have a talent for poetry of the most refined order. We have the means of judging of this, particularly from the romance, *Ju-kiao-li,* or, *The Two Cousins,* translated by Abel Remusat: in this, a youth is introduced who having finished his studies, is endeavoring to attain high dignities. The officers of the army, also, must have some mental acquirements; they too are examined; but civil functionaries enjoy, as stated above, far greater respect. At the great festivals the emperor appears with a retinue of two thousand doctors, *i.e.,* mandarins in civil offices, and the same number of military mandarins. (In the whole Chinese state, there are about 15,000 civil, and 20,000 military mandarins.) The mandarins who have not yet obtained an office, nevertheless belong to the court, and are obliged to appear at the great festivals in the spring and autumn, when the emperor himself guides the plough. These functionaries are divided into eight classes. The first are those that attend the emperor, then follow the viceroys, and so on. The emperor governs by means of administrative bodies, for the most part composed of mandarins. The council of the empire is the highest body of the kind: it consists of the most learned and talented men. From these are chosen the presidents of the other colleges. The greatest publicity prevails in the business of government. The subordinate officials report to the council of the empire, and the latter lay the matter before the emperor, whose decision is made known in the court journal. The emperor often accuses himself of faults; and should his princes have been unsuccessful in their examination, he blames them severely. In every ministry, and in various parts of the empire, there is a censor (*Ko-tao*), who has to give the emperor an account of everything. These censors enjoy a permanent office, and are very much feared. They exercise a strict surveillance over everything that concerns the government, and the public and private conduct of the mandarins, and make their report immediately to the emperor. They have also the right of remonstrating with and blaming *him*. Chinese history gives many examples of the noble-mindedness and courage of these Ko-taos. For example: A censor had remonstrated with a tyrannical sovereign, but had been severely repulsed. Nevertheless, he was not turned away from his purpose, but betook himself once more to the Emperor to renew his remonstrances. Foreseeing his death, he had the coffin brought in with him, in which he was to be buried. It is related of the censors, that, cruelly lacerated by the torturers and unable to utter a sound, they have even written their animadversions with their own blood in the sand. These censors themselves form yet another tribunal which has the oversight of the whole empire. The mandarins are responsible also for performing duties arising from unforeseen exigencies in the state. If famine, disease, conspiracy, religious disturbances occur, they have to report the facts; not, however, to wait for further orders from government, but immediately to act as the case requires. The whole of the administration is thus covered by a network of officials. Functionaries are appointed to superintend the roads, the rivers, and the coasts. Everything is arranged with the greatest minuteness. In particular, great attention is paid to the rivers; in the *Shu-King* are to be found many edicts of the emperor, designed to secure the land from inundations. The gates of every town are guarded by a watch, and the streets are barred all night. Government officers are always answerable to the higher council. Every mandarin is also bound to make known the faults he has committed, every five years; and the trustworthiness of his statement is attested by a board of control—the censorship. In the case of any grave crime not confessed, the mandarins and their families are punished most severely. From all this it is clear that the emperor is the centre, around which everything turns; consequently the well-being of the country and people depends on him. The whole hierarchy of the administration works more or less according to a settled routine, which in a peaceful condition of things becomes a convenient habit. Uniform and regular, like the course of nature, it goes its own way, at one time as at another time; but the emperor is required to be the moving, ever wakeful, spontaneously active soul. If then the personal character of the emperor is not of the order described—namely, thoroughly *moral*, laborious, and, while maintaining dignity, full of energy—everything is relaxed, and the government is paralyzed from head to foot, and given over to carelessness and caprice. For there is no other legal power or institution extant, but this superintendence and oversight of the emperor. It is not their own conscience, their own honour, which keeps the offices of government up to their duty, but an external mandate and the severe sanctions by which it is supported. In the instance of the revolution that occurred in the middle of the seventeenth century, the last emperor of the dynasty was very amiable and honourable; but through the mildness of his character, the reins of government were relaxed, and disturbances naturally ensued. The rebels called the Manchus into the country. The emperor killed himself to avoid falling into the hands of his enemies, and with his blood wrote on the border of his daughter's robe a few words, in which he complained bitterly of the injustice of his subjects. A mandarin, who was with him, buried him, and then killed himself on his grave. The empress and her attendants followed the example. The last prince of the imperial house, who was besieged in a distant province, fell into the hands of the enemy and was put to death. All the other attendant mandarins died a voluntary death.

Passing from the administration to the *jurisprudence* of China, we find the subjects regarded as in a state of nonage, in virtue of the principle of patriarchal government. No independent classes or orders, as in India, have interests of their own to defend. All is directed and superintended from above. All legal relations are definitely settled by rules; free sentiment, the moral standpoint generally, is thereby thoroughly obliterated. It is formally determined by the laws in what way the members of the family should be disposed towards each other, and the transgression of these laws entails in some cases severe punishment. The second point to be noticed here, is the legal externality of the family relations, which becomes almost slavery. Every one has the power of selling himself and his children; every Chinese buys his wife. Only the chief wife is a free woman. The concubines are slaves, and, like the children and every other chattel, may be seized upon in case of confiscation.

A third point is that punishments are generally corporal chastisements. Among us, this would be an insult to honour; not so in China, where the feeling of honour has not yet developed itself. A dose of cudgelling is the most easily forgotten; yet it is the severest punishment for a man of honour, who desires not to be esteemed physically assailable, but who is vulnerable in directions implying a more refined sensibility. But the Chinese do not recognize a subjectivity in honour; they are the subjects rather of corrective than retributive punishment, as are children among us; for *corrective* punishment aims at improvement, that which is *retributive* implies veritable imputation of guilt. In the *corrective,* the deterring principle is only the fear of punishment, not any consciousness of wrong; for here we cannot presume upon any reflection upon the nature of the action itself. Among the Chinese all crimes, those committed against the laws of the family relation, as well as against the State, are punished externally. Sons who fail in paying due honour to their father or mother, younger brothers who are not sufficiently respectful to elder ones, are bastinadoed. If a son complains of injustice done to him by his father, or a younger brother by an elder, he receives a hundred blows with a bamboo, and is banished for three years, *if he is in the right;* if not, he is strangled. If a son should raise his hand against his father, he is condemned to have his flesh torn from his body with red-hot pincers. The relation between husband and wife is, like all other family relations, very highly esteemed, and unfaithfulness—which, however, on account of the seclusion in which the women are kept, can very seldom present itself—meets with severe animadversion. Similar penalties await the exhibition on the part of a Chinese of greater affection to one of his inferior wives than to the matron who heads his establishment, should the latter complain of such disparagement. In China, every mandarin is authorized to inflict blows with the bamboo; even the highest and most illustrious—ministers, viceroys, and even the favorites of the emperor himself—are punished in this fashion. The friendship of the Emperor is not withdrawn on account of such chastisement, and they themselves appear not sensibly touched by it. When, on one occasion, the last English embassy to China was conducted home from the palace by the princes and their retinue, the master of the ceremonies, in order to make room, without any ceremony cleared the way among the princes and nobles with a whip.

As regards responsibility, the distinction between *malice prepense* and blameless or accidental commission of an act is not regarded; for accident among the Chinese is as much charged with blame, as intention. Death is the penalty of accidental homicide. This ignoring of the distinction between accident and intention occasions most of the disputes between the English and the Chinese; for should the former be attacked by the latter—should a ship of war, believing itself attacked, defend itself, and a Chinese be killed as the consequence—the Chinese are accustomed to require that the Englishman who fired the fatal shot should lose his life. Everyone who is in any way connected with the transgressor, shares, especially in the case of crimes against the emperor, the ruin of the actual offender: all his near kinsmen are tortured to death. The printers of an objectionable book and those who read it, are similarly exposed to the vengeance of the law. The direction which this state of things gives to private revenge is singular. It may be said of the Chinese that they are extremely sensitive to injuries and of a vindictive nature. To satisfy his revenge the offended person does not venture to kill his opponent, because the whole family of the assassin would be put to death; he therefore inflicts an injury on himself, to ruin his adversary. In many towns it has been deemed necessary to contract the openings of wells, to put a stop to suicides by drowning. For when anyone has committed suicide, the laws ordain that the strictest investigation shall be made into the cause. All the enemies of the suicide are arrested and put to the torture, and if the person who has committed the insult which led to the act, can be discovered, he and his whole family are executed. In case of insult therefore, a Chinese prefers killing himself rather than his opponent; since in either case he must die, but in the former contingency will have the due honours of burial, and may cherish the hope that his family will acquire the property of his adversary. Such is the fearful state of things in regard to responsibility and non-responsibility; all subjective freedom and moral concernment with an action are ignored. In the Mosaic Laws, where the distinction between *dolus, culpa,* and *casus,* is also not yet clearly recognized, there is nevertheless an asylum opened for the innocent homicide, to which he may betake himself.

There is in China no distinction in the penal code between higher and lower classes. A field-marshal of the empire, who had very much distinguished himself, was traduced on some account, to the emperor; and the punishment for the alleged crime, was that he should be a spy upon those who did not fulfil their duty in clearing away the snow from the streets.

Among the legal relations of the Chinese we have also to notice changes in the rights of possession and the introduction of slavery, which is connected there with it. The soil of China, in which the chief possessions of the Chinese consist, was regarded only at a late epoch as essentially the property of the state. At that time the ninth of all moneys from estates was allotted by law to the emperor. At a still later epoch serfdom was established, and its enactment has been ascribed to the Emperor Shih Huang Ti, who in the year 213 B.C., built the Great Wall; who had all the writings that recorded the ancient rights of the Chinese, burned; and who brought many independent principalities of China under his dominion. His wars caused the conquered lands to become private property, and the dwellers on these lands, serfs. In China, however, the distinction between slavery and freedom is necessarily not great, since all are equal before the emperor—that is, all are alike degraded. As no honour exists, and no one has an individual right in respect of others, the consciousness of debasement predominates, and this easily passes into that of utter abandonment. With this abandonment is connected the great immorality of the Chinese. They are notorious for deceiving wherever they can. Friend deceives friend, and no one resents the attempt at deception on the part of another, if the deceit has not succeeded in its object, or comes to the knowledge of the person sought to be defrauded. Their frauds are most astutely and craftily performed, so that Europeans have to be painfully cautious in dealing with them. Their consciousness of moral abandonment shows itself also in the fact that the religion of Fo is so widely diffused; a religion which regards as the highest and absolute—as God—*pure nothing;* which sets up contempt for individuality, for personal existence, as the highest perfection.

We come, then, to the consideration of the *religious* side of the Chinese polity. In the patriarchal condition the religious exaltation of man has merely a human reference—simple morality and right-doing. The absolute itself, is regarded partly as the abstract, simple rule of this right-doing—eternal rectitude; partly as the *power* which is its sanction. Except in these simple aspects, all the relations of the natural world, the postulates of subjectivity, of heart and soul, are entirely ignored. The Chinese in their patriarchal despotism need no such connection or mediation with the highest Being; for education, the laws of morality and courtesy, and the commands and government of the emperor embody all such connection and mediation as far as they feel the need of it. The emperor, as he is the supreme head of the state, is also the chief of its religion. Consequently, religion is in China essentially state-religion. The distinction between it and Lamaism must be observed, since *the latter* is not developed to a state, but contains religion as a free, spiritual, disinterested consciousness. That *Chinese* religion, therefore, cannot be what *we* call religion. For to us religion means the retirement of the spirit within itself, in contemplating its essential nature, its inmost being. In these spheres, then, man is withdrawn from his relation to the state, and betaking himself to this retirement, is able to release himself from the power of secular government. But in China religion has not risen to this grade, for true faith is possible only where individuals can seclude themselves, can exist for themselves independently of any external compulsory power. In China the individual has no such life, does not enjoy this independence: in any direction he is therefore dependent; in religion as well as in other things; that is, dependent on objects of nature, of which the most exalted is the material heaven. On this depend harvest, the seasons of the year, the abundance and sterility of crops. The emperor, as crown of all, the embodiment of power, alone approaches heaven; individuals, as such, enjoy no such privilege. He it is, who presents the offerings at the four feasts; gives thanks, at the head of his court, for the harvest and invokes blessings on the sowing of the seed. This "heaven" might be taken in the sense of our term "God," as the Lord of nature (we say, for example, "Heaven protect us!"); but such a relation is beyond the scope of Chinese thought, for here the one isolated self-consciousness is substantial being, the emperor himself, the supreme power. Heaven has therefore no higher meaning than nature. The Jesuits indeed, yielded to Chinese notions so far as to call the Christian God, "Heaven"—"*Tien*"; but they were on that account accused to the Pope by other Christian orders. The Pope consequently sent a cardinal to China, who died there. A bishop who was subsequently despatched, enacted that instead of "Heaven," the term "Lord of Heaven" should be adopted. The relation to *Tien* is supposed to be such, that the good conduct of individuals and of the emperor brings blessing; their transgressions on the other hand cause want and evil of all kinds. The Chinese religion involves that primitive element of magical influence over nature, inasmuch as human conduct absolutely determines the course of events. If the emperor behaves well, prosperity cannot but ensue; Heaven must ordain prosperity. A second side of this religion is, that as the general aspect of the relation to Heaven is bound up with the person of the emperor, he has also its more special bearings in his hands; *viz.*, the particular well-being of individuals and provinces. These have each an appropriate *genius* (*Chen*), which is subject to the emperor, who pays adoration only to the general power of heaven, while the several spirits of the natural world follow his laws. He is thus made the proper legislator for heaven as well as for earth. To these genii, each of which enjoys a worship peculiar to itself, certain sculptured forms are assigned. These are disgusting idols, which have not yet attained the dignity of art, because nothing spiritual is represented in them. They are therefore only terrific, frightful and negative; they keep watch—as among the Greeks do the river-gods, the nymphs, and dryads—over single elements and natural objects. Each of the five elements has its genius, distinguished by a particular colour. The sovereignty of the dynasty that occupies the throne of China also depends on a genius, and this one has a yellow colour. Not less does every province and town, every mountain and river possess an appropriate genius. All these spirits are subordinate to the emperor, and in the annual directory of the Empire are registered the functionaries and genii to whom such or such a brook, river, etc., has been intrusted. If a mischance occurs in any part, the genius is deposed as a mandarin would be. The genii have innumerable temples (in Peking nearly 10,000) to which a multitude of priests and convents are attached. These "bonzes" live unmarried, and in all cases of distress are applied to by the Chinese for counsel. In other respects, however, neither they nor the temples are much venerated. Lord Macartney's embassy was even quartered in a temple—such buildings being used as inns. The emperor has sometimes thought fit to secularize many thousands of these convents; to compel the bonzes to return to civil life; and to impose taxes on the estates appertaining to the foundations. The bonzes are soothsayers and exorcists: for the Chinese are given up to boundless superstitions. This arises from the want of subjective independence, and presupposes the very opposite of freedom of spirit. In every undertaking, *e.g.*, if the site of a house, or of a grave, etc., is to be determined, the advice of the soothsayers is asked. In the *Y-King* certain lines are given, which supply fundamental forms and categories —on account of which this book is called the *Book of Fates*. A certain meaning is ascribed to the combination of such lines, and prophetic announcements are deduced from this groundwork. Or a number of little sticks are thrown into the air, and the fate in question is prognosticated from the way in which they fall. What we regard as chance, as natural connection, the Chinese seek to deduce or attain by magical arts; and in this particular also, their want of spiritual religion is manifested.

With this deficiency of genuine subjectivity is connected moreover, the form which Chinese *science* assumes. In mentioning Chinese sciences we encounter a considerable clamour about their perfection and antiquity. Approaching the subject more closely, we see that the sciences enjoy very great respect, and that they are even publicly extolled and promoted by the government. The emperor himself stands at the apex of literature. A college exists whose special business it is to edit the decrees of the emperor, with a view to their being composed in the best style; and this redaction assumes the character of an important affair of state. The mandarins in their notifications have to study the same perfection of style, for the form is expected to correspond with the excellence of the matter. One of the highest governmental boards is the academy of sciences. The emperor himself examines its members; they live in the palace, and perform the functions of secretaries, historians of the empire, natural philosophers, and geographers. Should a new law be proposed, the academy must report upon it. By way of introduction to such report it must give the history of existing enactments; or if the law in question affects foreign countries, a description of them is required. The emperor himself writes the prefaces to the works thus composed. Among recent emperors, *K'ien-Lung* especially distinguished himself by his scientific acquirements. He himself wrote much, but became far more remarkable by publishing the principal works that China has produced. At the head of the commission appointed to correct the press, was a prince of the empire; and after the work had passed through the hands of all, it came once more back to the emperor, who severely punished every error that had been committed.

Though in one aspect the sciences appear thus pre-eminently honoured and fostered, there are wanting to them on the other side that free ground of subjectivity, and that properly scientific interest, which make them a truly theoretical occupation of the mind. A free, ideal, spiritual kingdom has here no place. What may be called scientific is of a merely empirical nature, and is made absolutely subservient to the useful on behalf of the state—its requirements and those of individuals. The nature of their written language is at the outset a great hindrance to the development of the sciences. Rather, conversely, because a true scientific interest does not exist, the Chinese have acquired no better instrument for representing and imparting thought. They have, as is well known, beside a spoken language, a *written language;* which does not express, as ours does, individual sounds—does not present the spoken words to the eye, but represents the ideas themselves by signs. This appears at first sight a great advantage, and has gained the suffrages of many great men—among others, of Leibnitz. In reality, it is anything but such. For if we consider in the first place, the effect of such a mode of writing on the spoken language, we shall find this among the Chinese very imperfect, on account of that separation. For our spoken language is matured to distinctness chiefly through the necessity of finding signs for each single sound, which latter, by reading, we learn to express distinctly. The Chinese, to whom such a means of orthoepic development is wanting, do not mature the modifications of sounds in their language to distinct articulations capable of being represented by letters and syllables. Their spoken language consists of an inconsiderable number of monosyllabic words, which are used with more than one signification. The sole methods of denoting distinctions of meaning are the connection, the accent, and the pronunciation—quicker or slower, softer or louder. The ears of the Chinese have become very sensible to such distinctions. Thus I find that the word *po* has eleven different meanings according to the tone, denoting: glass, to boil, to winnow wheat, to cleave asunder, to water, to prepare, an old woman, a slave, a liberal man, a wise person, a little.

As to their written language, I will specify only the obstacles which it presents to the advance of the sciences. Our written language is very simple for a learner, as we analyze our spoken language into about twenty-five articulations, by which analysis, speech is rendered definite, the multitude of possible sounds is limited, and obscure intermediate sounds are banished: we have to learn only these signs and their combinations. Instead of twenty-five signs of this sort, the Chinese have many thousands to learn. The number necessary for use is reckoned at 9,353, or even 10,516, if we add those recently introduced; and the number of characters generally, for ideas and their combinations as they are presented in books, amounts to from 80,000 to 90,000. As to the sciences themselves, *history* among the Chinese comprehends the bare and definite facts, without any opinion or reasoning upon them. In the same way their *jurisprudence* gives only fixed laws, and their *ethics* only determinate duties, without raising the question of a subjective foundation for them. The Chinese have, however, in addition to other sciences, a *philosophy,* whose elementary principles are of great antiquity, since the *Y-King,* the *Book of Fates,* treats of origination and destruction. In this book are found the purely abstract ideas of unity and duality; the philosophy of the Chinese appears therefore to proceed from the same fundamental ideas as that of Pythagoras.[1] The fundamental principle recognized is *reason—tao;* that essence lying at the basis of the whole, which effects everything. To become acquainted with its forms is regarded among the Chinese also as the highest science; yet this has no connection with the educational pursuits which more nearly concern the state. The works of Lao-tsu, and especially his work *Tao-te-ching,* are celebrated. Confucius visited this philosopher in the sixth century before Christ, to testify his reverence for him. Although every Chinaman is at liberty to study these philosophical works, a particular sect, calling itself *Tao-tse,* "Honorers of Reason," makes this study its special business. Those who compose it are isolated from civil life; and there is much that is enthusiastic and mystic intermingled with their views. They believe, for instance, that he who is acquainted with reason, possesses an instrument of universal power, which may be regarded as all-powerful, and which communicates a supernatural might; so that the possessor is enabled by it to exalt himself to heaven, and is not subject to death (much the same as the universal elixir of life once talked of among us). With the works of Confucius we have become more intimately acquainted. To him, China owes the publication of the *Kings,* and many original works on morality besides, which form the basis of the customs and conduct of the Chinese. In the principal work of Confucius, which has been translated into English, are found correct moral apophthegms; but there is a circumlocution, a reflex character, and circuitousness in the thought, which prevents it from rising above mediocrity. As to the other sciences, they are not regarded as such, but rather as branches of knowledge for the behoof

[1] *Vide* Hegel's *Vorlesungen über die Geschichte der Philosophie,* vol. i. p. 138, etc.

of practical ends. The Chinese are far behind in mathematics, physics, and astronomy, notwithstanding their quondam reputation in regard to them. They knew many things at a time when Europeans had not discovered them, but they have not understood how to apply their knowledge: as, *e.g.*, the magnet, and the art of printing. But they have made no advance in the application of these discoveries. In the latter, for instance, they continue to engrave the letters in wooden blocks and then print them off: they know nothing of movable types. Gunpowder, too, they pretended to have invented before the Europeans; but the Jesuits were obliged to found their first cannon. As to mathematics, they understand well enough how to reckon, but the higher aspect of the science is unknown. The Chinese also have long passed as great astronomers. Laplace has investigated their acquisitions in this department, and discovered that they possess some ancient accounts and notices of lunar and solar eclipses; but these certainly do not constitute a *science*. The notices in question are, moreover, so indefinite, that they cannot properly be put in the category of knowledge. In the *Shu-King*, *e.g.*, we have two eclipses of the sun mentioned in the space of 1,500 years. The best evidence of the state of astronomy among the Chinese, is the fact that for many hundred years the Chinese calendars have been made by Europeans. In earlier times, when Chinese astronomers continued to compose the calendar, false announcements of lunar and solar eclipses often occurred, entailing the execution of the authors. The telescopes which the Chinese have received as presents from the Europeans, are set up for ornament; but they have not an idea how to make further use of them. Medicine, too, is studied by the Chinese, but only empirically; and the grossest superstition is connected with its practice. The Chinese have as a general characteristic, a remarkable skill in imitation, which is exercised not merely in daily life, but also in art. They have not yet succeeded in representing the beautiful, as beautiful; for in their painting, perspective and shadow are wanting. And although a Chinese painter copies European pictures (as the Chinese do everything else), *correctly;* although he observes accurately how many scales a carp has; how many indentations there are in the leaves of a tree; what is the form of various trees, and how the branches bend;—the exalted, the ideal and beautiful is not the domain of his art and skill. The Chinese are, on the other hand, too proud to learn anything from Europeans, although they must often recognize their superiority. A merchant in Canton had a European ship built, but at the command of the governor it was immediately destroyed. The Europeans are treated as beggars, because they are compelled to leave their home, and seek for support elsewhere than in their own country. Besides, the Europeans, just because of their intelligence, have not yet been able to imitate the superficial and perfectly natural cleverness of the Chinese. Their preparation of varnishes, their working of metals, and especially their art of casting them extremely thin, their porcelain manufacture and many other things, have not yet been completely mastered by Europeans.

This is the character of the Chinese people in its various aspects. Its distinguishing feature is, that everything which belongs to spirit—unconstrained morality, in practice and theory, heart, inward religion, science and art properly so-called—is alien to it. The emperor always speaks with majesty and paternal kindness and tenderness to the people; who, however, cherish the meanest opinion of themselves, and believe that they are born only to drag the car of imperial power. The burden which presses them to the ground, seems to them to be their inevitable destiny; and it appears nothing terrible to them to sell themselves as slaves, and to eat the bitter bread of slavery. Suicide, the result of revenge, and the exposure of children, as a common, even daily occurrence, show the little respect in which they hold themselves individually, and humanity in general. And though there is no distinction conferred by birth, and everyone can attain the highest dignity, this very equality testifies to no triumphant assertion of the worth of the inner man, but a servile consciousness—one which has not yet matured itself so far as to recognize distinctions.

Section II

INDIA

India, like China, is a phenomenon antique as well as modern; one which has remained stationary and fixed, and has received a most perfect home-sprung development. It has always been the land of imaginative aspiration, and appears to us still as a fairy region, an enchanted world. In contrast with the Chinese state, which presents only the most prosaic understanding, India is the region of phantasy and sensibility. The point of advance in principle which it exhibits to us may be generally stated as follows: in China the patriarchal principle rules a people in a condition of nonage, the part of whose moral resolution is occupied by the regulating law, and the moral oversight of the emperor. Now it is the interest of spirit that *external* conditions should become *internal* ones; that the natural and the spiritual world should be recognized in the subjective aspect belonging to intelligence; by which process the unity of subjectivity and being generally—or the idealism of existence—is established. This idealism, then, is found in India, but only as an idealism of imagination, without distinct conceptions;—one which does indeed free existence from beginning and matter, but changes everything into the merely imaginative; for although the latter appears interwoven with definite conceptions and thought presents itself as an occasional concomitant, this happens only through accidental combination. Since, however, it is the abstract and absolute thought itself that enters into these dreams as their material, we may say that absolute being is presented here as in the ecstatic state of a dreaming condition. For we have not the dreaming of an actual individual, possessing distinct personality, and simply unfettering the latter from limitation, but we have the dreaming of the unlimited absolute spirit.

There is a beauty of a peculiar kind in women, in which their countenance presents a transparency of skin, a light and lovely roseate hue, which is unlike the complexion of mere health and vital vigor—a more refined bloom, breathed, as it were, by the soul within—and in which the features, the light of the eye, the position of the mouth, appear soft, yielding, and relaxed. This almost unearthly beauty is perceived in women in those days which immediately succeed childbirth; when freedom from the burden of pregnancy and the pains of travail is added to the joy of soul that welcomes the gift of a beloved infant. A similar tone of beauty is seen also in women during the magical somnambulic sleep, connecting them with a world of superterrestrial beauty. A great artist (Schoreel) has moreover given this tone to the dying Mary, whose spirit is already rising to the regions of the blessed, but once more, as it were, lights up her dying countenance for a farewell kiss. Such a beauty we find also in its loveliest form in the Indian world; a beauty of enervation in which all that is rough, rigid, and contradictory is dissolved, and we have only the soul in a state of emotion; a soul, however, in which the death of free self-reliant spirit is perceptible. For should we approach the charm of this flower-life, a charm rich in imagination and genius, in which its whole

environment and all its relations are permeated by the rose-breath of the soul, and the world is transformed into a garden of love—should we look at it more closely, and examine it in the light of human dignity and freedom—the more attractive the first sight of it had been, so much the more unworthy shall we ultimately find it in every respect.

The character of spirit in a state of dream, as the generic principle of the Hindu nature, must be further defined. In a dream, the individual ceases to be conscious of self *as such,* in contradistinction from objective existences. When awake, I exist for myself, and the rest of creation is an external, fixed objectivity, as I myself am for it. As external, the rest of existence expands itself to a rationally connected whole; a system of relations, in which my individual being is itself a member—an individual being united with that totality. This is the sphere of *Understanding.* In the state of dreaming, on the contrary, this separation is suspended. Spirit has ceased to exist for itself in contrast with alien existence, and thus the separation of the external and individual dissolves before its universality—its *essence.* The dreaming Indian is therefore all that we call finite and individual; and, at the same time, as infinitely universal and unlimited, a something intrinsically divine. The Indian view of things is a universal pantheism, a pantheism, however, of imagination, not of thought. One substance pervades the whole of things, and all individualizations are directly vitalized and animated into particular powers. The sensuous matter and content are in each case simply and in the rough taken up, and carried over into the sphere of the universal and immeasurable. It is not liberated by the free power of spirit into a beautiful form, and idealized in the spirit, so that the sensuous might be a merely subservient and compliant expression of the spiritual; but is expanded into the immeasurable and undefined, and the divine is thereby made bizarre, confused, and ridiculous These dreams are not mere fables, a play of the imagination, in which the soul only revelled in fantastic gambols: it is lost in them; hurried to and fro by these reveries, as by something that exists really and seriously for it. It is delivered over to these limited objects as to its lords and gods. Everything, therefore: sun, moon, stars, the Ganges, the Indus, beasts, flowers, everything is a god to it. And while, in this deification, the finite loses its consistency and substantiality, intelligent conception of it is impossible. Conversely the divine, regarded as essentially changeable and unfixed, is also by the base form which it assumes, defiled and made absurd. In this universal deification of all finite existence, and consequent degradation of the divine, the idea of theanthropy, the incarnation of God, is not a particularly important conception. The parrot, the cow, the ape, etc., are likewise incarnations of God, yet are not therefore elevated above their nature. The divine is not individualized to a subject, to concrete spirit, but degraded to vulgarity and senselessness. This gives us a general idea of the Indian view of the universe. *Things* are as much stripped of rationality, of finite consistent stability of cause and effect, as *man* is of the steadfastness of free individuality, of personality, and freedom.

Externally, India sustains manifold relations to the history of the world. In recent times the discovery has been made, that the Sanskrit lies at the foundation of all those further developments which form the languages of Europe; *e.g.,* the Greek, Latin, German. India, moreover, was the centre of emigration for all the western world; but this external historical relation is to be regarded rather as a merely physical diffusion of peoples from this point. Although in India the elements of further developments might be discovered, and although we could find traces of their being transmitted to the west, this transmission has been nevertheless so abstract that that which among later peoples attracts our interest is not anything derived from India, but rather something concrete, which they themselves have formed, and in regard to which they have done their best to forget Indian elements of culture. The spread of Indian culture is prehistorical, for history is limited to that which makes an essential epoch in the development of spirit. On the whole, the diffusion of Indian culture is only a dumb, deedless expansion; that is, it presents no political action. The people of India have achieved no foreign conquests, but have been on every occasion vanquished themselves. And as in this silent way, northern India has been a centre of emigration, productive of merely physical diffusion, India as a *land of desire* forms an essential element in general history. From the most ancient times downwards, all nations have directed their wishes and longings to gaining access to the treasures of this land of marvels, the most costly which the earth presents; treasures of nature—pearls, diamonds, perfumes, rose-essences, elephants, lions, etc.—as also treasures of wisdom. The way by which these treasures have passed to the west, has at all times been a matter of world-historical

importance, bound up with the fate of nations. Those wishes have been realized; this land of desire has been attained; there is scarcely any great nation of the east, nor of the modern European west, that has not gained for itself a smaller or larger portion of it. In the old world, Alexander the Great was the first to penetrate by land to India, but even he only just touched it. The Europeans of the modern world have been able to enter into direct connection with this land of marvels only circuitously from the other side; and by way of the sea, which, as has been said, is the general uniter of countries. The English, or rather the East India Company, are the lords of the land; for it is the necessary fate of Asiatic empires to be subjected to Europeans; and China will, some day or other, be obliged to submit to this fate. The number of inhabitants is near 200,000,000, of whom from 100,000,000 to 112,000,000 are directly subject to the English. The princes who are not immediately subject to them have English agents at their courts, and English troops in their pay. Since the country of the Mahrattas was conquered by the English, no part of India has asserted its independence of their sway. They have already gained a footing in the Burman Empire, and passed the Brahmaputra, which bounds India on the east.

India proper is the country which the English divide into two large sections: the Deccan—the great peninsula which has the Bay of Bengal on the east, and the Indian Sea on the west—and Hindostan, formed by the valley of the Ganges, and extending in the direction of Persia. To the northeast, Hindostan is bordered by the Himalaya, which has been ascertained by Europeans to be the highest mountain range in the world, for its summits are about 26,000 feet above the level of the sea. On the other side of the mountains the level again declines; the dominion of the Chinese extends to that point, and when the English wished to go to Lhasa to the Dalai Lama, they were prevented by the Chinese. Towards the west of India flows the Indus, in which the five rivers are united, which are called the *Pentjâb* (Punjab), into which Alexander the Great penetrated. The dominion of the English does not extend to the Indus; the sect of the Sikhs inhabits that district, whose constitution is thoroughly democratic, and who have broken off from the Indian as well as from the Mohammedan religion, and occupy an intermediate ground—acknowledging only one supreme Being. They are a powerful nation, and have reduced to subjection Kabul and Kashmir. Besides these there dwell along the Indus genuine Indian tribes of the warrior-caste. Between the Indus and its twin-brother, the Ganges, are great plains. The Ganges, on the other hand, forms large kingdoms around it, in which the sciences have been so highly developed, that the countries around the Ganges enjoy a still greater reputation than those around the Indus. The Kingdom of Bengal is especially flourishing. The Nerbudda forms the boundary between the Deccan and Hindostan. The peninsula of the Deccan presents a far greater variety than Hindostan, and its rivers possess almost as great a sanctity as the Indus and the Ganges—which latter has become a general name for all the rivers in India, as the River κατ' ἐξοχήν. We call the inhabitants of the great country which we have now to consider *Indians,* from the river *Indus,* (the English call them *Hindus*). They themselves have never given a name to the whole, for it has never become one empire, and yet we consider it as such.

With regard to the *political* life of the Indians, we must first consider the advance it presents in contrast with China. In China there prevailed an equality among all the individuals composing the empire; consequently all government was absorbed in its centre, the emperor, so that individual members could not attain to independence and subjective freedom. The next degree in advance of this unity is difference, maintaining its independence against the all-subduing power of unity. An organic life requires in the first place one soul, and in the second place, a divergence into differences, which become organic members, and in their several offices develop themselves to a complete system; in such a way, however, that their activity reconstitutes that one soul. This freedom of separation is wanting in China. The deficiency is that diversities cannot attain to independent existence. In this respect, the essential advance is made in India, *viz.:* that independent members ramify from the unity of despotic power. Yet the distinctions which these imply are referred to nature. Instead of stimulating the activity of a soul as their centre of union, and spontaneously realizing that soul—as is the case in organic life, they petrify and become rigid, and by their stereotyped character condemn the Indian people to the most degrading spiritual serfdom. The distinctions in question are the *castes.* In every rational state there are distinctions which must manifest themselves. Individuals must arrive at subjective freedom, and in doing so, give an objective form to these diversities. But Indian culture has not attained to a recognition of free-

dom and inward morality; the distinctions which prevail are only those of occupations, and civil conditions. In a free state also, such diversities give rise to particular classes, so combined, however, that their members can maintain their individuality. In India we have only a division in masses—a division, however, that influences the whole political life and the religious consciousness. The distinctions of class, like that unity in China, remain consequently on the same original grade of *substantiality, i.e.,* they are not the result of the free subjectivity of individuals. Examining the idea of a state and its various functions, we recognize the first essential function as that whose scope is the absolutely universal; of which man becomes conscious first in religion, then in science. God, the divine is the absolutely universal. The highest class therefore will be the one by which the divine is presented and brought to bear on the community —the class of *Brahmans.* The second element or class, will represent subjective power and valour. Such power must assert itself, in order that the whole may stand its ground, and retain its integrity against other such totalities or states. This class is that of the warriors and governors—the *Kshattriyas;* although Brahmans often become governors. The third order of occupation recognized is that which is concerned with the specialities of life, the satisfying of its necessities, and comprehends agriculture, crafts and trade; the class of the *Vaisyas.* Lastly, the fourth element is the class of service, the mere instrument for the comfort of others, whose business it is to work for others for wages affording a scanty subsistence—the caste of *Sudras.* This servile class, properly speaking, constitutes no special organic class in the state, because its members only serve individuals: their occupations are therefore dispersed among them and are consequently attached to that of the previously mentioned castes. Against the existence of "classes" generally, an objection has been brought, especially in modern times, drawn from the consideration of the state in its "aspect" of abstract equity. But equality in civil life is something absolutely impossible; for individual distinctions of sex and age will always assert themselves; and even if an equal share in the government is accorded to all citizens, women and children are immediately passed by, and remain excluded. The distinction between poverty and riches, the influence of skill and talent, can be as little ignored —utterly refuting those abstract assertions. But while this principle leads us to put up with variety of occupations, and distinction of the classes to which they are intrusted, we are met here in India by the peculiar circumstance that the individual belongs to such a class essentially by *birth,* and is bound to it for life. All the concrete vitality that makes its appearance sinks back into death. A chain binds down the life that was just upon the point of breaking forth. The promise of freedom which these distinctions hold out is therewith completely nullified. What birth has separated mere arbitrary choice has no right to join together again: therefore, the castes preserving distinctness from their very origin, are presumed not to be mixed or united by marriage. Yet even Arrian (*Indica* 11) reckoned seven castes, and in later times more than thirty have been made out; which, notwithstanding all obstacles, have arisen from the union of the various classes. Polygamy necessarily tends to this. A Brahman, *e.g.,* is allowed three wives from the three other castes, provided he has first taken one from his own. The offspring of such mixtures originally belonged to no caste, but one of the kings invented a method of classifying these casteless persons, which involved also the commencement of arts and manufactures. The children in question were assigned to particular employments; one section became weavers, another wrought in iron, and thus different classes arose from these different occupations. The highest of these mixed castes consists of those who are born from the marriage of a Brahman with a wife of the warrior caste; the lowest is that of the *Chandālas,* who have to remove corpses, to execute criminals, and to perform impure offices generally. The members of this caste are excommunicated and detested; and are obliged to live separate and far from association with others. The Chandālas are obliged to move out of the way for their superiors, and a Brahman may knock down any that neglect to do so. If a Chandāla drinks out of a pond it is defiled, and requires to be consecrated afresh.

We must next consider the relative position of these castes. Their origin is referred to a myth, which tells us that the Brahman caste proceeded from Brahma's mouth; the warrior caste from his arms; the industrial classes from his loins; the servile caste from his foot. Many historians have set up the hypothesis that the Brahmans originally formed a separate sacerdotal nation, and this fable is especially countenanced by the Brahmans themselves. A people consisting of priests alone is, assuredly, the greatest absurdity, for we know *a priori,* that a distinction of classes can exist only within a

people; in every nation the various occupations of life must present themselves, for they belong to the objectivity of spirit. *One* class necessarily supposes another, and the rise of castes generally, is only a result of the united life of a nation. A nation of priests cannot exist without agriculturists and soldiers. Classes cannot be brought together from without; they are developed only from within. They come forth from the interior of national life, and not conversely. But that these distinctions are here attributed to nature, is a necessary result of the Idea which the East embodies. For while the individual ought properly to be empowered to choose his occupation, in the East, on the contrary, internal subjectivity is not yet recognized as independent; and if distinction obtrude themselves, their recognition is accompanied by the belief that the individual does not choose his particular position for himself, but receives it from nature. In China the people are dependent, without distinction of classes, on the laws and moral decision of the emperor; consequently on a human will. Plato, in his *Republic,* assigns the arrangement in different classes with a view to various occupations, to the choice of the governing body. Here, therefore, a moral, a spiritual power is the arbiter. In India, nature is this governing power. But this natural destiny need not have led to that degree of degradation which we observe here, if the distinctions had been limited to occupation with what is earthly—to forms of objective spirit. In the feudalism of mediæval times, individuals were also confined to a certain station in life; but for all there was a higher being, superior to the most exalted earthly dignity, and admission to holy orders was open to all. This is the grand distinction, that here religion holds the same position towards *all;* that, although the son of a mechanic becomes a mechanic, the son of a peasant a peasant, and free choice is often limited by many restrictive circumstances, the *religious element* stands in the same relation to all, and all are invested with an absolute value by religion. In India the direct contrary is the case. Another distinction between the classes of society as they exist in the Christian world and those in Hindostan is the moral dignity which exists among us in every class, constituting that which man must possess in and through himself. In this respect the higher classes are equal to the lower; and while religion is the higher sphere in which all sun themselves, equality before the law, rights of person and of property, are gained for every class. But by the fact that in India, as already observed, differences extend not only to the objectivity of spirit, but also to its absolute subjectivity, and thus exhaust all its relations—neither morality, nor justice, nor religiosity is to be found.

Every caste has its especial duties and rights. Duties and rights, therefore, are not recognized as pertaining to mankind generally, but as those of a particular caste. While we say, "Bravery is a virtue," the Hindus say, on the contrary, "Bravery is the virtue of the *Kshattriyas*." Humanity generally, human duty and human feeling do not manifest themselves; we find only duties assigned to the several castes. Everything is petrified into these distinctions, and over this petrification a capricious destiny holds sway. Morality and human dignity are unknown; evil passions have their full swing; the spirit wanders into the dream-world, and the highest state is annihilation.

To gain a more accurate idea of what the *Brahmans* are, and in what the Brahmanical dignity consists, we must investigate the Hindu religion and the conceptions it involves, to which we shall have to return further on; for the respective rights of castes have their basis in a religious relation. *Brahmă* (neuter) is the Supreme in religion, but there are besides chief divinities *Brahmâ* (masc.) *Vishnu* or *Krishna,* incarnate in infinitely diverse forms, and *Siva*. These form a connected trinity. Brahmâ is the highest; but Vishnu or Krishna, Siva, the sun moreover, the air, etc., are also Brahm, *i.e.,* substantial unity. To Brahm itself no sacrifices are offered; it is not honoured; but prayers are presented to all other idols. Brahm itself is the substantial unity of all. The highest religious position of man, therefore is, being exalted to Brahm. If a Brahman is asked what Brahm is, he answers: When I fall back within myself, and close all external senses, and say *ôm* to myself, that is Brahm. Abstract unity with God is realized in this abstraction from humanity. An abstraction of this kind may in some cases leave everything else unchanged, as does devotional feeling, momentarily excited. But among the Hindus it holds a negative position towards all that is concrete; and the highest state is supposed to be this exaltation, by which the Hindu raises himself to deity. The Brahmans, in virtue of their birth, are already in possession of the divine. The distinction of castes involves, therefore, a distinction between present deities and mere limited mortals. The other castes may likewise become partakers in a *regeneration;* but they must subject themselves to immense

self-denial, torture, and penance. Contempt of life, and of living humanity, is the chief feature in this ascesis. A large number of the non-Brahmanical population strive to attain *regeneration*. They are called Yogis. An Englishman who, on a journey to Tibet to visit the Dalai Lama, met such a yogi, gives the following account: The yogi was already on the second grade in his ascent to Brahmanical dignity. He had passed the first grade by remaining for twelve years on his legs, without ever sitting or lying down. At first he had bound himself fast to a tree with a rope, until he had accustomed himself to sleep standing. The second grade required him to keep his hands clasped together over his head for twelve years in succession. Already his nails had almost grown into his hands. The third grade is not always passed through in the same way; generally the yogi has to spend a day between *five fires,* that is, between four fires occupying the four quarters of heaven, and the sun. He must then swing backwards and forwards over the fire, a ceremony occupying three hours and three-quarters. Englishmen present at an act of this kind, say that in half an hour the blood streamed forth from every part of the devotee's body; he was taken down and presently died. If this trial is also surmounted, the aspirant is finally buried alive, that is put into the ground in an upright position and quite covered over with soil; after three hours and three-quarters he is drawn out, and if he lives, he is supposed to have at last attained the spiritual power of a Brahman.

Thus only by such negation of his existence does anyone attain Brahmanical power. In its highest degree this negation consists in a sort of hazy consciousness of having attained perfect mental immobility—the annihilation of all emotion and all volition; a condition which is regarded as the highest among the Buddhists also. However pusillanimous and effeminate the Hindus may be in other respects, it is evident how little they hesitate to sacrifice themselves to the highest—to annihilation. Another instance of the same is the fact of wives burning themselves after the death of their husbands. Should a woman contravene this traditional usage, she would be severed from society, and perish in solitude. An Englishman states that he also saw a woman burn herself because she had lost her child. He did all that he could to divert her away from her purpose; at last he applied to her husband who was standing by, but he showed himself perfectly indifferent, as *he had more wives at home*. Sometimes twenty women are seen throwing themselves at once into the Ganges, and on the Himalaya range an English traveller found three women seeking the source of the Ganges, in order to put an end to their life in this holy river. At a religious festival in the celebrated temple of Juggernaut in Orissa, on the Bay of Bengal, where millions of Hindus assemble, the image of the god Vishnu is drawn in procession on a car: about five hundred men set it in motion, and many fling themselves down before its wheels to be crushed to pieces. The whole seashore is already strewed with the bodies of persons who have thus immolated themselves. Infanticide is also very common in India. Mothers throw their children into the Ganges, or let them pine away under the rays of the sun. The morality which is involved in respect for human life, is not found among the Hindus. There are besides those already mentioned, infinite modifications of the same principle of conduct, all pointing to annihilation. This, e.g., is the leading principle of the gymnosophists, as the Greeks called them. Naked fakirs wander about without any occupation, like the mendicant friars of the Catholic Church; live on the alms of others, and make it their aim to reach the highest degree of abstraction—the perfect deadening of consciousness; a point from which the transition to physical death is no great step.

This elevation which others can only attain by toilsome labour is, as already stated, the birthright of the Brahmans. The Hindu of another caste, must, therefore, reverence the Brahman as a divinity; fall down before him, and say to him: "Thou art God." And this elevation cannot have anything to do with moral conduct, but, inasmuch as all internal morality is absent, is rather dependent on a farrago of observances relating to the merest externalities and trivialities of existence. Human life, it is said, ought to be a perpetual worship of God. It is evident how hollow such general aphorisms are, when we consider the concrete forms which they may assume. They require another, a further qualification, if they are to have a meaning. The Brahmans are a present deity, but their spirituality has not yet been reflected inwards in contrast with nature; and thus that which is purely indifferent is treated as of absolute importance. The employment of the Brahmans consists principally in the reading of the Vedas: they only have a right to read them. Were a Sudra to read the Vedas, or to hear them read, he would be severely punished, and burning oil must be poured into his ears. The external observances binding on the Brahmans are prodigiously numerous, and the laws of Manu treat of them as the most essential part of duty. The Brahman must rest on one particular foot in rising, then wash in a river; his hair and nails must be cut in neat curves, his whole body purified, his garments white; in his hand must be a staff of a specified kind; in his ears a golden earring. If the Brahman meets a man of an inferior caste, he must turn back and purify himself. He has also to read in the Vedas, in various ways: each word separately, or doubling them alternately, or backwards. He may not look to the sun when rising or setting, or when overcast by clouds or reflected in the water. He is forbidden to step over a rope to which a calf is fastened, or to go out when it rains. He may not look at his wife when she eats, sneezes, gapes, or is quietly seated. At the mid-day meal he may only have one garment on, in bathing never be quite naked. How minute these directions are, may be especially judged of from the observances binding on the Brahmans in regard to satisfying the calls of nature. This is forbidden to them in a great thoroughfare, on ashes, on ploughed land, on a hill, a nest of white ants, on wood destined for fuel, in a ditch, walking or standing, on the bank of a river, etc. At such a time they may not look at the sun, at water, or at animals. By day they should keep their face generally directed to the north, but by night to the south; only in the shade are they allowed to turn to which quarter they like. It is forbidden to everyone who desires a long life, to step on potsherds, cotton seeds, ashes, or sheaves of corn, or his urine. In the episode Nala, in the poem of *Mahabharata,* we have a story of a virgin who in her 21st year, the age in which the maidens themselves have a right to choose a husband, makes a selection from among her wooers. There are five of them; but the maiden remarks that four of them do not stand firmly on their feet, and thence infers correctly that they are gods. She therefore chooses the fifth, who is a veritable man. But besides the four despised divinities there are two malevolent ones, whom her choice had not favored, and who on that account wish for revenge. They therefore keep a strict watch on the husband of their beloved in every step and act of life, with the design of inflicting injury upon him if he commits a misdemeanour. The persecuted husband does nothing that can be brought against him, until at last he is so incautious as to step on his urine. The genius has now an advantage over him; he afflicts him with a passion for gambling, and so plunges him into the abyss.

While, on the one hand, the Brahmans are subject to these strict limitations and rules, on the other hand their life is sacred; it cannot answer for crimes of any kind; and their property is equally secure from being attacked. The severest penalty which the ruler can inflict upon them amounts to nothing more than banishment. The English wished to introduce trial by jury into India, the jury to consist half of Europeans, half of Hindus, and submitted to the natives, whose wishes on the subject were consulted, the powers with which the panel would be intrusted. The Hindus were for making a number of exceptions and limitations. They said, among other things, that they could not consent that a Brahman should be condemned to death; not to mention other objections, *e.g.*, that looking at and examining a corpse was out of the question. Although in the case of a warrior the rate of interest may be as high as three per cent, in that of a Vaisya four per cent, a Brahman is never required to pay more than two per cent. The Brahman possesses such a power, that heaven's lightning would strike the king who ventured to lay hands on him or his property. For the meanest Brahman is so far exalted above the king, that he would be polluted by conversing with him, and would be dishonored by his daughters choosing a prince in marriage. In Manu's code it is said: "If anyone presumes to teach a Brahman his duty, the king must order that hot oil be poured into the ears and mouth of such an instructor. If one who is only once-born, loads one who is twice-born with reproaches, a red hot iron bar ten inches long shall be thrust into his mouth." On the other hand a Sudra is condemned to have a red hot iron thrust into him from behind if he rests himself in the chair of a Brahman, and to have his foot or his hand hewed off if he pushes against a Brahman with hands or feet. It is even permitted to give false testimony, and to lie before a court of justice, if a Brahman can be thereby freed from condemnation.

As the Brahmans enjoy advantages over the other castes, the latter in their turn have privileges according to precedence, over their inferiors. If a Sudra is defiled by contact with a Pariah, he has the right to knock him down on the spot. Humanity on the part of a higher caste towards an inferior one is entirely forbidden, and a Brahman would never think of assisting a member of another caste, even when in danger. The other castes deem it a great honour when a Brahman takes their daughters as his wives—a thing however, which is permitted him, as already stated, only when he has already taken one from his own caste. Thence arises the freedom the Brahmans enjoy in getting wives. At the great religious festivals they go among the people and choose those that please them best; but they also repudiate them at pleasure.

If a Brahman or a member of any other caste transgresses the above cited laws and precepts, he is himself excluded from his caste, and in order to be received back again, he must have a hook bored through the hips, and be swung repeatedly backwards and forwards in the air. There are also other forms of restoration. A rajah who thought himself injured by an English governor, sent two Brahmans to England to detail his grievances. But the Hindus are forbidden to cross the sea, and these envoys on their return were declared excommunicated from their caste, and in order to be restored to it, they had to be born again from a golden cow. The imposition was so far lightened, that only those parts of the cow out of which they had to creep were obliged to be golden; the rest might consist of wood. These various usages and religious observances to which every caste is subject, have occasioned great perplexity to the English, especially in enlisting soldiers. At first these were taken from the Sudra caste, which is not bound to observe so many ceremonies; but nothing could be done with them, they therefore betook themselves to the Kshattriya class. These however have an immense number of regulations to observe: they may not eat meat, touch a dead body, drink out of a pool in which cattle or Europeans have drunk, not eat what others have cooked, etc. Each Hindu assumes one definite occupation, and that only, so that one must have an infinity of servants; a lieutenant has *thirty*, a major *sixty*. Thus every caste has its own duties; the lower the caste, the less it has to observe; and as each individual has his position assigned by birth, beyond this fixed arrangement everything is governed by caprice and force. In the code of Manu punishments increase in proportion to the inferiority of castes, and there is a distinction in other respects. If a man of a higher caste brings an accusation against an inferior without proof, the former is not punished; if the converse occurs, the punishment is very severe. Cases of theft are exceptional; in this case the higher the caste the heavier is the penalty.

In respect to property the Brahmans have a great advantage, for they pay no taxes. The prince receives half the income from the lands of others; the remainder has to suffice for the cost of cultivation and the support of the laborers. It is an extremely important question, whether the cultivated land in India is recognized as belonging to the cultivator, or belongs to a so-called manorial proprietor. The English themselves have had great difficulty in establishing a clear understanding about it. For when they conquered Bengal, it was of great importance to them, to determine the mode in which taxes were to be raised on property, and they had to ascertain whether these should be imposed on the tenant cultivators or the lord of the soil. They imposed the tribute on the latter; but the result was that the proprietors acted in the most arbitrary manner: drove away the tenant cultivators, and declaring that such or such an amount of land was not under cultivation, gained an abatement of tribute. They then took back the expelled cultivators as daylabourers, at a low rate of wages, and had the land cultivated on their own behalf. The whole income belonging to every village is, as already stated, divided into two parts, of which one belongs to the rajah, the other to the cultivators; but proportionate shares are also received by the provost of the place, the judge, the watersurveyor, the Brahman who superintends religious worship, the astrologer (who is also a Brahman, and announces the days of good and ill omen), the smith, the carpenter, the potter, the washerman, the barber, the physician, the dancing girls, the musician, the poet. This arrangement is fixed and immutable, and subject to no one's will. *All political* revolutions, therefore, are matters of indifference to the common Hindu, for his lot is unchanged.

The view given of the relation of castes leads directly to the subject of religion. For the claims of caste are, as already remarked, not merely secular, but essentially religious, and the Brahmans in their exalted dignity are the very gods bodily present. In the laws of Manu it is said: "Let the king, even in extreme necessity, beware of exciting the Brahmans against him; for they can destroy him with their power—they who create fire, sun, moon, etc." They are servants neither of God nor of his people, but are God himself to the other castes—a position of things which constitutes the perverted character of the Hindu mind. The dreaming unity of spirit and nature, which involves a monstrous bewilderment in regard to all phenomena and relations, we have already recognized as the principle of the Hindu spirit. The Hindu mythology is therefore only a wild extravagance of fancy, in which nothing has a settled form; which takes us abruptly from the meanest to the highest, from the most sublime to the most disgusting and trivial. Thus it is also difficult to discover what the Hindus understand by Brahm. We are apt to take our conception of Supreme Divinity —the One—the Creator of heaven and earth— and apply it to the Indian Brahm. Brahma is distinct from Brahm—the former constituting one personality in contrasted relation to Vishnu and Siva. Many therefore call the supreme existence who is over the first mentioned deity, *Parabrahma*. The English have taken a good deal of trouble to find out what Brahm properly is. Wilford has asserted that Hindu conceptions recognize two heavens: the first, the earthly paradise, the second, heaven in a spiritual sense. To attain them, two different modes of worship are supposed to be required. The one involves external ceremonies, idol-worship; the other requires that the Supreme Being should be honoured in spirit. Sacrifices, purifications, pilgrimages are not needed in the latter. This authority states moreover that there are few Hindus ready to pursue the second way, because they cannot understand in what the pleasure of the second heaven consists, and that if one asks a Hindu whether he worships idols, every one says "Yes!" but to the question, "Do you worship the Supreme Being?" every one answers "No." If the further question is put, "What is the meaning of that practice of yours, that silent meditation which some of your learned men speak of?" they respond, "When I pray to the honour of one of the gods, I sit down, the foot of either leg on the thigh of the other, look towards heaven, and calmly elevate my thoughts with my hands folded in silence; then I say, I am Brahm the Supreme Being. We are not conscious to ourselves of being Brahm, by reason of Maya (the delusion occasioned by the outward world). It is forbidden to pray to him, and to offer sacrifices to him in his own nature; for this would be to adore ourselves. In every case therefore, it is only emanations of Brahm that we address." Translating these ideas then into our own process of thought, we should call Brahm the pure unity of thought in itself—God in the incomplexity of his existence. No temples are consecrated to him, and he receives no worship. Similarly, in the Catholic religion, the Churches are not dedicated to God, but to the saints. Other Englishmen, who have devoted themselves to investigating the conception of Brahm, have thought Brahm to be an unmeaning epithet, applied to all gods: so that Vishnu says, "I am Brahm"; and the sun, the air, the seas are called Brahm. Brahm would on this supposition be substance in its simplicity, which by its very nature expands itself into the limitless variety of phenomenal diversities. For this abstraction, this pure unity, is that which lies at the foundation of all—the root of all definite existence. In the intellection of this unity, all objectivity falls away; for the purely abstract is intellection itself in its greatest vacuity. To attain this death of life during life itself, to constitute this abstraction, requires the disappearance of all moral activity and volition, and of all intellection too, as in the religion of Fo; and this is the object of the penances already spoken of.

The complement to the abstraction Brahm must then be looked for in the concrete complex of things; for the principle of the Hindu religion is the manifestation of diversity. These then, fall outside that abstract unity of thought, and as that which deviates from it, constitute the variety found in the world of sense, the variety of intellectual conceptions in an unreflected sensuous form. In this way the concrete complex of material things is isolated from spirit, and, presented in wild distraction, except as re-absorbed in the pure ideality of Brahm. The other deities are therefore things of sense: mountains, streams, beasts, the sun, the moon, the Ganges. The next stage is the concentration of this wild variety into substantial distinctions, and the comprehension of them as a series of divine persons. Vishnu, Siva, Mahadeva are thus distinguished from Brahma. In the embodiment Vishnu, are presented those incarnations in which God has appeared as man, and which are always historical personages, who effected important changes and new epochs. The power of procreation is likewise a substantial embodiment; and in the excavations, grottos and pagodas of the Hindus, the lingam is always found as symbolizing the male, and the lotus the female *vis procreandi.*

With this duality, abstract unity on the one side and the abstract isolation of the world of sense on the other side, exactly corresponds the double form of *worship,* in the relation of the human subjectivity to God. The one side of this duality of worship, consists in the abstraction of pure self-elevation—the abrogation of real self-consciousness; a negativity which is consequently manifested, on the one hand, in the attainment of torpid unconsciousness—on the other hand, in suicide and the extinction of all that is worth calling life, by self-inflicted tortures. The other side of worship consists in a wild tumult of excess; when all sense of individuality has vanished from consciousness by immersion in the merely natural, with which individuality thus makes itself identical—destroying its consciousness of distinction from nature. In all the pagodas, therefore, prostitutes and dancing girls are kept, whom the Brahmans instruct most carefully in dancing, in beautiful postures and attractive gestures, and who have to comply with the wishes of all comers at a fixed price. Theological doctrine, relation of religion to morality, is here altogether out of the question. On the one hand love, heaven, in short, everything spiritual, is conceived by the fancy of the Hindu; but on the other hand, his conceptions have an actual sensuous embodiment, and he immerses himself by a voluptuous intoxication in the merely natural. Objects of religious worship are thus either disgusting forms produced by art, or those presented by nature. Every bird, every monkey is a present god, an absolutely universal existence. The Hindu is incapable of holding fast an object in his mind by means of rational predicates assigned to it, for this requires reflection. While a universal essence is wrongly transmuted into sensuous objectivity, the latter is also driven from its definite character into universality—a process whereby it loses its footing and is expanded to indefiniteness.

If we proceed to ask how far their religion exhibits the *morality* of the Hindus, the answer must be that the former is as distinct from the latter, as Brahm from the concrete existence of which he is the essence. To *us,* religion is the knowledge of that Being who is emphatically *our* Being, and therefore the substance of our knowledge and volition; the proper office of which latter is to be the mirror of this fundamental substance. But that requires this Being to be *in se* a personality, pursuing divine aims, such as can become the purport of human action. Such an idea of a relation of the Being of God as constituting the universal basis or substance of human action—such a morality cannot be found among the Hindus; for they have not the spiritual as the import of their consciousness. On the one hand, their virtue consists in the abstraction from all activity—the condition they call "Brahm." On the other hand, every action with them is a prescribed external usage; not free activity, the result of inward personality. Thus the moral condition of the Hindus (as already observed) shows itself most abandoned. In this all Englishmen agree. Our judgment of the morality of the Hindus is apt to be warped by representations of their mildness, tenderness, beautiful, and sentimental fancy. But we must reflect that in nations utterly corrupt there are sides of character which may be called tender and noble. We have Chinese poems in which the tenderest relations of love are depicted; in which delineations of deep emotion, humility, modesty, propriety are to be found; and which may be compared with the best that European literature contains. The same characteristics meet us in many Hindu poems; but rectitude, morality, freedom of soul, consciousness of individual right are quite another thing. The annihilating of spiritual and physical existence has nothing concrete in it; and absorption in the abstractly universal has no connection with the real. Deceit and cunning are the fundamental characteristics of the Hindu. Cheating, stealing, robbing, murdering are with him habitual. Humbly crouching and abject before a victor and lord, he is recklessly barbarous to the vanquished and subject. Characteristic of the Hindu's humanity is the fact that he kills no brute animal, founds and supports rich hospitals for brutes, especially for old cows and monkeys—but that through the whole land, no single institution can be found for human beings who are diseased or infirm from age. The Hindus will not tread upon ants, but they are perfectly indifferent when poor wanderers pine away with hunger. The Brahmans are especially immoral. According to English reports, they do nothing but eat and sleep. In what is not forbidden them by the rules of their order they follow natural impulses entirely. When they take any part in public life they show themselves avaricious, deceitful, voluptuous. With those whom they have reason to fear, they are humble enough; for which they avenge themselves on their dependents. "I do not know an honest man among them," says an English authority. Children have no respect for their parents: sons maltreat their mothers.

It would lead us too far to give a detailed notice of Hindu *art* and *science*. But we may make the general remark, that a more accurate acquaintance with its real value has not a little diminished the widely bruited fame of Indian wisdom. According to the Hindu principle of pure self-renouncing ideality, and that variety which goes to the opposite extreme of sensuousness, it is evident that nothing but abstract thought and imagination can be developed. Thus, *e.g.*, their grammar has advanced to a high degree of consistent regularity; but when substantial matter in sciences and works of art is in question, it is useless to look for it here. When the English had become masters of the country, the work of restoring to light the records of Indian culture was

commenced, and William Jones first disinterred the poems of the Golden Age. The English exhibited plays at Calcutta: this led to a representation of dramas on the part of the Brahmans, *e.g.*, the *Sakuntala* of Kalidasa, etc. In the enthusiasm of discovery the Hindu culture was very highly rated; and as, when new beauties are discovered, the old ones are commonly looked down upon with contempt, Hindu poetry and philosophy were extolled as far superior to the Greek. For our purpose the most important documents are the ancient and canonical books of the Hindus, especially the *Vedas*. They comprise many divisions, of which the fourth is of more recent origin. They consist partly of religious prayers, partly of precepts to be observed. Some manuscripts of these Vedas have come to Europe, though in a complete form they are exceedingly rare. The writing is on palm leaves, scratched in with a needle. The Vedas are very difficult to understand, since they date from the most remote antiquity, and the language is a much older Sanskrit. Colebrooke has indeed translated a part, but this itself is perhaps taken from a commentary, of which there are very many.[1] Two great epic poems, *Ramayana* and *Mahabharata*, have also reached Europe. Three quarto volumes of the former have been printed, the second volume is extremely rare. Besides these works, the Puranas must be particularly noticed. The *Puranas* contain the history of a god or of a temple. They are entirely fanciful. Another Hindu classical book is the *Code of Manu*. This Hindu lawgiver has been compared with the Cretan Minos, a name which also occurs among the Egyptians; and certainly this extensive occurrence of the same name is noteworthy and cannot be ascribed to chance. Manu's code of morals (published at Calcutta with an English translation by Sir W. Jones) forms the basis of Hindu legislation. It begins with a theogony, which is not only entirely different from the mythological conceptions of other peoples (as might be expected), but also deviates essentially from the Hindu traditions themselves. For in these also there are only some leading features that pervade the whole. In other respects everything is abandoned to chance, caprice, and fancy; the result of which is that the most multiform traditions, shapes, and names, appear in never ending procession. The time when Manu's

[1] Only recently has Professor Rosen, residing in London, gone thoroughly into the matter and given a specimen of the text with a translation, *Rig-Vedæ Specimen*, ed. Fr. Rosen. Lond. 1830. [More recently, since Rosen's death, the whole *Rig-Veda*, London, 1839, has been published from MSS. left by him.]

code was composed, is also entirely unknown and undetermined. The traditions reach beyond twenty-three centuries before the birth of Christ: a dynasty of the Children of the Sun is mentioned, on which followed one of the Children of the Moon. This much, however, is certain, that the code in question is of high antiquity; and an acquaintance with it is of the greatest importance to the English, as their knowledge of Hindu law is derived from it.

After pointing out the Hindu principle in the distinctions of caste, in religion and literature, we must also mention the mode and form of their *political* existence—the polity of the Hindu *state*. A state is a realization of spirit, such that in it the self-conscious being of spirit, the freedom of the will, is realized as law. Such an institution then, necessarily presupposes the consciousness of free will. In the Chinese state the moral will of the emperor is the law: but so that subjective, inward freedom is thereby repressed, and the law of freedom governs individuals only as from without. In India the primary aspect of subjectivity—*viz.*, that of the imagination—presents a union of the natural and spiritual, in which nature on the one hand, does not present itself as a world embodying reason, nor the spiritual, on the other hand, as consciousness in contrast with nature. Here the antithesis in the principle is wanting. Freedom both as *abstract* will and as *subjective* freedom is absent. The proper basis of the state, the principle of freedom is altogether absent: there cannot therefore be any state in the true sense of the term. This is the first point to be observed: if China may be regarded as nothing else but a state, Hindu political existence presents us with a people, but *no state*. Secondly, while we found a moral despotism in *China,* whatever may be called a relic of political life in *India,* is a despotism *without a principle,* without any rule of morality and religion: for morality and religion (as far as the latter has a reference to human action) have as their indispensable condition and basis the freedom of the will. In India, therefore, the most arbitrary, wicked, degrading despotism has its full swing. China, Persia, Turkey, in fact Asia generally, is the scene of despotism, and, in a bad sense, of tyranny; but it is regarded as contrary to the due order of things, and is disapproved by religion and the moral consciousness of individuals. In those countries, tyranny rouses men to resentment; they detest it and groan under it as a burden. To them it is an accident and an irregularity, not a necessity: it *ought* not to

exist. But in India it is normal: for here there is no sense of personal independence with which a state of despotism could be compared, and which would raise revolt in the soul; nothing approaching even a resentful protest against it is left, except the corporeal smart, and the pain of being deprived of absolute necessaries and of pleasure.

In the case of such a people, therefore, that which we call in its double sense, *history,* is not to be looked for; and here the distinction between China and India is most clearly and strongly manifest. The Chinese possess a most minute history of their country, and it has been already remarked what arrangements are made in China for having everything accurately noted down in their annals. The contrary is the case in India. Though the recent discoveries of the treasures of Indian literature have shown us what a reputation the Hindus have acquired in geometry, astronomy, and algebra—that they have made great advances in philosophy, and that among them grammar has been so far cultivated that no language can be regarded as more fully developed than the Sanskrit—we find the department of *history* altogether neglected, or rather non-existent. For history requires understanding—the power of looking at an object in an independent objective light, and comprehending it in its rational connection with other objects. Those peoples therefore are alone capable of history, and of prose generally, who have arrived at that period of development (and can make that their starting point), at which individuals comprehend their own existence as independent, *i.e.*, possess self-consciousness.

The Chinese are to be rated at what they have made of themselves, looking at them in the entirety of their state. While they have thus attained an existence independent of nature, they can also regard objects as distinct from themselves, as they are actually presented, in a definite form and in their real connection. The Hindus on the contrary are by birth given over to an unyielding destiny, while at the same time their spirit is exalted to ideality; so that their minds exhibit the contradictory processes of a dissolution of fixed rational and definite conceptions in their ideality, and on the other side, a degradation of this ideality to a multiformity of sensuous objects. This makes them incapable of writing history. All that happens is dissipated in their minds into confused dreams. What we call historical truth and veracity—intelligent, thoughtful comprehension of events, and fidelity in representing them—nothing of this sort can be looked for among the Hindus. We may explain this deficiency partly from that excitement and debility of the nerves, which prevent them from retaining an object in their minds, and firmly comprehending it, for in their mode of apprehension a sensitive and imaginative temperament changes it into a feverish dream; partly from the fact, that veracity is the direct contrary to their nature. They even lie knowingly and designedly where misapprehension is out of the question. As the Hindu spirit is a state of dreaming and mental transiency, a self-oblivious dissolution, objects also dissolve for it into unreal images and indefinitude. This feature is absolutely characteristic; and this alone would furnish us with a clear idea of the spirit of the Hindus, from which all that has been said might be deduced.

But history is always of great importance for a people; since by means of that it becomes conscious of the path of development taken by its own spirit, which expresses itself in laws, manners, customs, and deeds. Laws, comprising morals and judicial institutions, are by nature the permanent element in a people's existence. But history presents a people with their own image in a condition which thereby becomes objective to them. Without history their existence in time is blindly self-involved—the recurring play of arbitrary volition in manifold forms. History fixes and imparts consistency to this fortuitous current, gives it the form of universality, and, by so doing, posits a directive and restrictive rule for it. It is an essential instrument in developing and determining the constitution—that is, a rational political condition; for it is the empirical method of producing the universal, inasmuch as it sets up a permanent object for the conceptive powers. It is because the Hindus have no history in the form of annals (*historia*) that they have no history in the form of transactions (*res gestæ*); that is, no growth expanding into a veritable political condition.

Periods of time are mentioned in the Hindu writings, and large numbers which have often an astronomical meaning, but which have still oftener a quite arbitrary origin. Thus it is related of certain kings that they had reigned 70,000 years, or more. Brahma, the first figure in the cosmogony, and self-produced, is said to have lived 20,000 years, etc. Innumerable names of kings are cited—among them the incarnations of Vishnu. It would be ridiculous to regard passages of this kind as anything historical. In their poems kings are often talked of: these may have been historical personages, but they completely vanish in fable; *e.g.*, they retire from the world, and then appear again, after they have passed ten thousand years in solitude. The numbers in question, therefore, have not the value and rational meaning which we attach to them.

Consequently the oldest and most reliable sources of Indian history are the notices of Greek authors, after Alexander the Great had opened the way to India. From them we learn that their institutions were the same at that early period as they are now: Santaracottus (Chandragupta) is marked out as a distinguished ruler in the northern part of India, to which the Bactrian kingdom extended. The Mohammedan historians supply another source of information; for the Mohammedans began their invasions as early as the tenth century. A Turkish slave was the ancestor of the Ghiznian race. His son Mahmoud made an inroad into Hindostan and conquered almost the whole country. He fixed his royal residence west of Kabul, and at his court lived the poet Firdousi. The Ghiznian dynasty was soon entirely exterminated by the sweeping attacks of the Afghans and Moguls. In later times nearly the whole of India has been subjected to the Europeans. What therefore is known of Indian history, has for the most part been communicated through foreign channels: the native literature gives only indistinct data. Europeans assure us of the impossibility of wading through the morasses of Indian statements. More definite information may be obtained from inscriptions and documents, especially from the deeds of gifts of land to pagodas and divinities; but this kind of evidence supplies names only. Another source of information is the astronomical literature, which is of high antiquity. Colebrooke thoroughly studied these writings; though it is very difficult to procure manuscripts, since the Brahmans keep them very close; they are moreover disfigured by the grossest interpolations. It is found that the statements with regard to constellations are often contradictory, and that the Brahmans interpolate these ancient works with events belonging to their own time. The Hindus do indeed possess lists and enumerations of their kings, but these also are of the most capricious character; for we often find twenty kings more in one list than in another; and should these lists even be correct, they could not constitute a history. The Brahmans have no conscience in respect to truth. Captain Wilford had procured manuscripts from all quarters with great trouble and expense; he assembled a considerable number of Brahmans, and commissioned them to make extracts from these works, and to institute inquiries respecting certain remarkable events—about Adam and Eve, the Deluge, etc. The Brahmans, to please their employer, produced statements of the kind required; but there was nothing of the sort in the manuscripts. Wilford wrote many treatises on the subject, till at last he detected the deception, and saw that he had labored in vain. The Hindus have, it is true, a fixed era: they reckon from *Vicramâditya,* at whose splendid court lived Kalidasa, the author of the *Sakuntala.* The most illustrious poets flourished about the same time. "There were nine pearls at the court of Vicramâditya," say the Brahmans: but we cannot discover the date of this brilliant epoch. From various statements, the year 1491 B.C. has been contended for; others adopt the year 50 B.C., and this is the commonly received opinion. Bentley's researches at length placed Vicramâditya in the twelfth century B.C. But still more recently it has been discovered that there were five, or even eight or nine kings of that name in India; so that on this point also we are thrown back into utter uncertainty.

When the Europeans became acquainted with India, they found a multitude of petty kingdoms, at whose head were Mohammedan and Indian princes. There was an order of things very nearly approaching feudal organization; and the kingdoms in question were divided into districts, having as governors Mohammedans, or people of the warrior caste of Hindus. The business of these governors consisted in collecting taxes and carrying on wars; and they thus formed a kind of aristocracy, the prince's council of state. But only as far as their princes are feared and excite fear, have they any power; and no obedience is rendered to them but by force. As long as the prince does not want money, he has troops; and neighboring princes, if they are inferior to him in force, are often obliged to pay taxes, but which are yielded only on compulsion. The whole state of things, therefore, is not that of repose, but of continual struggle; while moreover nothing is developed or furthered. It is the struggle of an energetic will on the part of this or that prince against a feebler one; the history of reigning dynasties, but not of peoples; a series of perpetually varying intrigues and revolts—not indeed of subjects against their rulers, but of a prince's son, for instance, against his father; of brothers, uncles and nephews in contest with each other; and of functionaries against their master. It

might be believed that, though the Europeans found such a state of things, this was the result of the dissolution of earlier superior organizations. It might, for instance, be supposed that the period of the Mogul supremacy was one of prosperity and splendour, and of a political condition in which India was not distracted religiously and politically by foreign conquerors. But the historical traces and lineaments that accidentally present themselves in poetical descriptions and legends, bearing upon the period in question, always point to the same divided condition—the result of war and of the instability of political relations; while contrary representations may be easily recognized as a dream, a mere fancy. This state of things is the natural result of that conception of Hindu life which has been exhibited, and the conditions which it necessitates. The wars of the sects of the Brahmans and Buddhists, of the devotees of Vishnu and of Siva, also contributed their quota to this confusion. There is indeed, a common character pervading the whole of India; but its several states present at the same time the greatest variety; so that in one Indian state we meet with the greatest effeminacy—in another, on the contrary, we find prodigious vigour and savage barbarity.

If then, in conclusion, we once more take a general view of the comparative condition of India and China, we shall see that China was characterized by a thoroughly unimaginative understanding; a prosaic life amid firm and definite reality: while in the Indian world there is, so to speak, no object that can be regarded as real, and firmly defined; none that was not at its first apprehension perverted by the imagination to the very opposite of what it presents to an intelligent consciousness. In China it is the moral which constitutes the substance of the laws, and which is embodied in external strictly determinate relations; while over all hovers the patriarchal providence of the emperor, who like a father, cares impartially for the interest of his subjects. Among the Hindus, on the contrary, instead of this unity, diversity is the fundamental characteristic. Religion, war, handicraft, trade, yes, even the most trivial occupations are parcelled out with rigid separation—constituting as they do the import of the one will which they involve, and whose various requirements they exhaust. With this is bound up a monstrous, irrational imagination, which attaches the moral value and character of men to an infinity of outward actions as empty in point of intellect as of feeling; sets aside all respect for the welfare of man, and even makes a duty of the cruelest and severest contravention of it. Those distinctions being rigidly maintained, nothing remains for the one universal will of the state but pure caprice, against whose omnipotence only the fixed caste-distinctions avail for protection. The Chinese in their prosaic rationality, reverence as the highest, only the abstract supreme lord; and they exhibit a contemptibly superstitious respect for the fixed and definite. Among the Hindus there is no such superstition so far as it presents an antithesis to understanding; rather their whole life and ideas are one unbroken superstition, because among them all is revery and consequent enslavement. Annihilation—the abandonment of all reason, morality and subjectivity—can only come to a positive feeling and consciousness of itself, by extravagating in a boundlessly wild imagination; in which, like a desolate spirit, it finds no rest, no settled composure, though it can content itself in no other way; as a man who is quite reduced in body and spirit finds his existence altogether stupid and intolerable, and is driven to the creation of a dream-world and a delirious bliss in opium.

Section II (Continued)
INDIA, Buddhism[1]

It is time to quit the Dream-State characterizing the Hindu spirit revelling in the most extravagant maze through all natural and spiritual forms; comprising at the same time the coarsest sensuality and anticipations of the profoundest thought, and on that very account, as far as free and rational reality is concerned, sunk in the most self-abandoned, helpless slavery; a slavery, in which the abstract forms into which concrete human life is divided, have become stereotyped, and human rights and culture have been made absolutely dependent upon these distinctions. In contrast with this inebriate dream-life, which in the sphere of reality is bound fast in chains, we have the *unconstrained* dream-life; which, on the one hand, is ruder than the former—as not having advanced so far as to make this distinction of modes of life—but for the same reason, has not sunk into the slavery which this entails. It keeps itself more free, more independently firm in itself: its world of ideas is

consequently compressed into simpler conceptions.

The spirit of the phase just indicated, is involved in the same fundamental principle as that assigned to Hindu conceptions: but it is more concentrated in itself; its religion is simpler, and the accompanying political condition more calm and settled. This phase comprehends peoples and countries of the most varied complexion. We regard it as embracing Ceylon, Farther India with the Burman Empire, Siam, Anam—north of that Tibet, and further on the Chinese upland with its various populations of Mongols and Tartars. We shall not examine the special individualities of these peoples, but merely characterize their religion, which constitutes the most interesting side of their existence. The religion of these peoples is *Buddhism*, which is the most widely extended religion on our globe. In China, Buddha is reverenced as *Fo;* in Ceylon as *Gautama;* in Tibet and among the Mongols this religion has assumed the phase of Lamaism. In China—where the religion of Fo early received a great extension, and introduced a monastic life—it occupies the position of an integrant element of the Chinese principle. As the substantial form of spirit which characterizes China, develops itself only to a unity of *secular* national life, which degrades individuals to a position of constant dependence, religion also remains in a state of dependence. The element of freedom is wanting to it; for its object is the principle of nature in general—heaven, universal matter. But the truth of this alienated form of spirit is *ideal* unity; the elevation above the limitation of nature and of existence at large;—the return of consciousness into the soul. This element, which is contained in Buddhism, has made its way in China, to that extent to which the Chinese have become aware of the unspirituality of their condition, and the limitation that hampers their consciousness. In this religion—which may be generally described as the religion of self-involvement[2]—the elevation of that unspiritual condition to subjectivity, takes place in two ways; one of which is of a negative, the other of an affirmative kind.

The *negative* form of this elevation is the concentration of spirit to the infinite, and must first present itself under theological conditions. It is contained in the fundamental dogma that nothingness is the principle of all things—that all proceeded from and returns to nothingness. The various forms found in the world are only

[1] As in Hegel's original plan and in the first lecture the transition from Indian Brahminism to Buddhism occupies the place assigned it here, and as this position of the chapter on Buddhism agrees better with recent investigations, its detachment from the place which it previously occupied and mention here will appear sufficiently justified.—ED.

[2] Compare Hegel's *Vorlesungen über die Philosophie der Religion,* 2d Edition, Pt. I. p. 384.

modifications of procession. If an analysis of these various forms were attempted, they would lose their quality; for in themselves all things are one and the same inseparable essence, and this essence is nothingness. The connection of this with the metempsychosis can be thus explained: all is but a change of form. The inherent infinity of spirit, infinite concrete self-dependence, is entirely separate from this universe of phenomena. Abstract nothingness is properly that which lies beyond finite existence—what we may call the Supreme Being. This real principle of the universe is, it is said, in eternal repose, and in itself unchangeable. Its essence consists in the absence of activity and volition. For nothingness is abstract unity with itself. To obtain happiness, therefore, man must seek to assimilate himself to this principle by continual victories over himself; and for the sake of this, do nothing, wish nothing, desire nothing. In this condition of happiness, therefore, vice or virtue is out of the question; for the true blessedness is union with nothingness. The more man frees himself from all speciality of existence, the nearer does he approach perfection; and in the annihilation of all activity, in pure passivity, he attains complete resemblance to Fo. The abstract unity in question is not a mere futurity— a spiritual sphere existing beyond our own; it has to do with the present; it is truth for man, and ought to be realized in him. In Ceylon and the Burman Empire—where this Buddhistic faith has its roots—there prevails an idea, that man can attain by meditation, to exemption from sickness, old age and death.

But while this is the *negative* form of the elevation of spirit from immersion in the objective to a subjective realization of itself, this religion also advances to the consciousness of an *affirmative* form. Spirit is the absolute. Yet in comprehending spirit it is a point of essential importance in what determinate form spirit is conceived. When we speak of spirit as universal, we know that for us it exists only in an inward conception; but to attain this point of view, to appreciate spirit in the pure subjectivity of thought and conception, is the result of a longer process of culture. At that point in history at which we have now arrived, the form of spirit is not advanced beyond immediateness. God is conceived in an immediate, unreflected form; not in the form of thought—objectively. But this immediate form is that of humanity. The sun, the stars do not come up to the idea of spirit; but man seems to realize it; and he, as *Buddha, Gautama, Fo*—in the form of a depart-

ed teacher, and in the living form of the Grand Lama—receives divine worship. The abstract understanding generally objects to this idea of a god-man; alleging as a defect that the form here assigned to spirit is an immediate one— that in fact it is none other than man in the concrete. Here the character of a whole people is bound up with the theological view just indicated. The *Mongols*—a race extending through the whole of central Asia as far as Siberia, where they are subject to the Russians—worship the Lama; and with this form of worship a simple political condition, a patriarchal life is closely united; for they are properly a nomad people, and only occasionally are commotions excited among them, when they seem to be beside themselves, and eruptions and inundations of vast hordes are occasioned. Of the lamas there are three: the best known is the Dalai Lama, who has his seat at Lhasa in the kingdom of Tibet. A second is the Tashi Lama, who under the title of Pan-chen-rin-po-che resides at Tashi Lhunpo; there is also a third in southern Siberia. The first two lamas preside over two distinct sects, of which the priests of one wear yellow caps, those of the other, red. The wearers of the yellow caps—at whose head is the Dalai Lama, and among whose adherents is the Emperor of China —have introduced celibacy among the priests, while the red sect allow their marriage. The English have become considerably acquainted with the Tashi Lama and have given us descriptions of him.

The general form which the spirit of the Lamaistic development of Buddhism assumes, is that of a living human being; while in the original Buddhism it is a deceased person. The two hold in common the relationship to a man. The idea of a man being worshipped as God, especially a living man, has in it something paradoxical and revolting; but the following considerations must be examined before we pronounce judgment respecting it. The conception of spirit involves its being regarded as inherently, intrinsically, universal. This condition must be particularly observed, and it must be discovered how in the systems adopted by various peoples this universality is kept in view. It is not the individuality of the subject that is revered, but that which is universal in him; and which among the Tibetans, Hindus, and Asiatics generally, is regarded as the essence pervading all things. This substantial unity of spirit is realized in the lama, who is nothing but the form in which spirit manifests itself; and who does not hold this spiritual essence as his peculiar property, but is regarded as partaking in it only in order to exhibit it to others, that they may attain a conception of spirituality and be led to piety and blessedness. The lama's personality as such, his particular individuality, is therefore subordinate to that substantial essence which it embodies. The second point which constitutes an essential feature in the conception of the lama is the disconnection from nature. The imperial dignity of China involved a supremacy over the powers of nature; while here spiritual power is directly separated from the *vis naturæ*. The idea never crosses the minds of the lama-worshippers to desire of the lama to show himself lord of nature—to exercise magical and miraculous power; for from the being they call God, they look only for spiritual activity and the bestowal of spiritual benefits. Buddha has moreover the express names, "Saviour of Souls," "Sea of Virtue," "the Great Teacher." Those who have become acquainted with the Tashi Lama depict him as a most excellent person, of the calmest temper and most devoted to meditation. Thus also do the lama-worshippers regard him. They see in him a man constantly occupied with religion, and who when he directs his attention to what is human, does so only to impart consolation and encouragement by his blessing, and by the exercise of mercy and the bestowal of forgiveness. These lamas lead a thoroughly isolated life and have a feminine rather than masculine training. Early torn from the arms of his parents the lama is generally a well-formed and beautiful child. He is brought up amid perfect quiet and solitude, in a kind of prison: he is well catered for, and remains without exercise or childish play, so that it is not surprising that a feminine susceptible tendency prevails in his character. The Grand Lamas have under them inferior lamas as presidents of the great fraternities. In Tibet every father who has four sons is obliged to dedicate one to a conventual life. The Mongols, who are especially devoted to Lamaism, this modification of Buddhism, have great respect for all that possesses life. They live chiefly on vegetables, and revolt from killing any animal, even a louse. This worship of the lamas has supplanted Shamanism, that is, the religion of sorcery. The Shamans, priests of this religion, intoxicate themselves with strong drinks and dancing, and while in this state perform their incantations, fall exhausted on the ground, and utter words which pass for oracular. Since Buddhism and Lamaism have taken the place of the Shaman religion, the life of the Mongols has been simple, prescrip-

tive, and patriarchal. Where they take any part in history, we find them occasioning impulses that have only been the groundwork of historical development. There is therefore little to be said about the political administration of the lamas. A vizier has charge of the secular dominion and reports everything to the lama: the government is simple and lenient; and the veneration which the Mongols pay to the lama expresses itself chiefly in their asking counsel of him in political affairs.

Section III

PERSIA

Asia separates itself into two parts, the Near and the Far East; which are essentially different from each other. While the Chinese and Hindus—the two great nations of the Far East, already considered—belong to the strictly Asiatic, namely the Mongolian race, and consequently possess a quite peculiar character, discrepant from ours; the nations of the Near East belong to the Caucasian, *i.e.*, the European stock. They are related to the West, while the Far Eastern peoples are perfectly isolated. The European who goes from Persia to India, observes, therefore, a prodigious contrast. Whereas in the former country he finds himself still somewhat at home, and meets with European dispositions, human virtues and human passions —as soon as he crosses the Indus (*i.e.*, in the *latter* region), he encounters the most repellent characteristics, pervading every single feature of society.

With the Persian Empire we first enter on continuous history. The Persians are the first historical people; Persia was the first empire that passed away. While China and India remained stationary, and perpetuate a natural vegetative existence even to the present time, this land has been subject to those developments and revolutions, which alone manifest a historical condition. The Chinese and the Indian Empires assert a place in the historical series only on their own account and for us. But here in Persia first arises that light which shines itself, and illuminates what is around; for Zoroaster's "light" belongs to the world of consciousness—to spirit as a relation to something distinct from itself. We see in the Persian world a pure exalted unity, as the essence which leaves the special existences that inhere in it, free; as the light, which only manifests what bodies are in themselves; a unity which governs individuals only to excite them to become powerful for themselves—to develop and assert their individuality. Light makes no distinctions: the sun shines on the righteous and the unrighteous, on high and low, and confers on all the same benefit and prosperity. Light is vitalizing only in so far as it is brought to bear on something distinct from itself, operating upon and developing that. It holds a position of antithesis to darkness, and this antithetical relation opens out to us the principle of activity and life. The principle of development begins with the history of Persia. This therefore constitutes strictly the beginning of world-history; for the grand interest of spirit in history, is to attain an unlimited immanence of subjectivity—by an absolute antithesis to attain complete harmony.

Thus the transition which we have to make, is only in the sphere of the Idea, not in the external historical connection. The principle of this transition is that the universal essence, which we recognized in Brahm, now becomes perceptible to consciousness—becomes an object and acquires a positive import for man. Brahm is not worshipped by the Hindus: he is nothing more than a condition of the individual, a religious feeling, a non-objective existence; a relation, which for concrete vitality is that of annihilation. But in becoming objective, this universal essence acquires a positive nature: man becomes free, and thus occupies a position face to face as it were with the highest being, the latter being made objective for him. This form of universality we see exhibited in Persia, involving a separation of man from the universal essence; while at the same time the individual recognizes himself as identical with that essence. In the Chinese and Indian principle, this distinction was not made. We found only a unit of the spiritual and the natural. But spirit still involved in nature has to solve the problem of freeing itself from the latter. Rights and duties in India are intimately connected with special classes, and are therefore only peculiarities attaching to man by the arrangement of nature. In China this unity presents itself under the conditions of *paternal* government. Man is not free there; he possesses no moral element, since he is identical with the external command. In the Persian principle, unity first elevates itself to the distinction from the merely natural; we have the negation of that unreflecting relation which allowed no exercise of mind to intervene between the mandate and its adoption by the will. In the Persian principle this unity is manifested as light, which in this case is not simply light as such, the most universal physical element, but at the same time also *spiritual* purity—the good. Speciality, the involvement with *limited* nature, is consequently abolished. Light, in a physical and spiritual sense, imports, therefore, elevation—freedom from the merely natural. Man sustains a relation to light, to the abstract good, as to something objective, which is acknowledged, reverenced, and evoked to activity by his will. If we look back once more, and we cannot do so too frequently, on the phases which we have traversed in arriving at this point, we perceive in China the totality of a moral whole, but excluding subjectivity;—this totality divided into members, but without independence in its various portions. We found only an external arrangement of this political unity. In India, on the contrary, distinctions made themselves prominent; but the *principle* of separation was unspiritual. We found incipient subjectivity, but hampered with the condition, that the separation in question is insurmountable; and that spirit remains involved in the limitations of nature, and is therefore a self-contradiction. Above this purity of castes is that purity of light which we observe in Persia; that abstract good, to which all are equally able to approach, and in which all equally may be hallowed. The unity recognized therefore, now first becomes a principle, not an external bond of soulless order. The fact that everyone has a share in that principle, secures to him personal dignity.

First as to *geographical position,* we see China and India, exhibiting as it were the dull half-conscious brooding of spirit, in fruitful plains—distinct from which is the lofty girdle of mountains with the wandering hordes that occupy them. The inhabitants of the heights, in their conquest, did not change the spirit of the plains, but imbibed it themselves. But in Persia the two principles, retaining their diversity, became united, and the mountain peoples with their principle became the predominant element. The two chief divisions which we have to mention are: the Persian upland itself, and the valley plains, which are reduced under the dominion of the inhabitants of the uplands. That elevated territory is bounded on the east by the Soliman mountains, which are continued in a northerly direction by the Hindu Kush and Belur Tag. The latter separate the anterior region—Bactriana and Sogdiana, occupying the plains of the Oxus—from the Chinese Upland, which extends as far as Kashgar. That plain of the Oxus itself lies to the north of the Persian upland, which declines on the south towards the Persian Gulf. This is the geographical position of Iran. On its western declivity lies Persia (Farsistan); higher to the north, Kurdistan—beyond this Armenia. Thence extend in a southwesterly direction the river districts of the Tigris and the Euphrates. The elements of the Persian Empire are the Zend race—the old Parsees; next the Assyrian, Median and Babylonian Empire in the region mentioned; but the Persian Empire also includes Asia Minor, Egypt, and Syria, with its line of coast; and thus combines the upland, the valley plains and the coast region.

Chapter 1. *The Zend People*

The Zend people derived their name from the language in which the *Zend Books* are written, *i.e.*, the canonical books on which the religion of the ancient Parsees is founded. Of this religion of the Parsees or Fire-worshippers, there are still traces extant. There is a colony of them in Bombay; and on the Caspian Sea there are some scattered families that have retained this form of worship. Their national existence was put an end to by the Mohammedans. The great *Zardusht*, called Zoroaster by the Greeks, wrote his religious books in the Zend language. Until nearly the last third of the eighteenth century, this language and all the writings composed in it, were entirely unknown to Europeans; when at length the celebrated Frenchman, Anquetil-Duperron, disclosed to us these rich treasures. Filled with an enthusiasm for the Oriental world, which his poverty did not allow him to gratify, he enlisted in a French corps that was about to sail for India. He thus reached Bombay, where he met with the Parsees, and entered on the study of their religious ideas. With indescribable difficulty he succeeded in obtaining their religious books; making his way into their literature, and thus opening an entirely new and wide field of research, but which, owing to his imperfect acquaintance with the language, still awaits thorough investigation.

Where the Zend people, mentioned in the religious books of Zoroaster, lived, is difficult to determine. In Media and Persia the religion of Zoroaster prevailed, and Xenophon relates that Cyrus adopted it: but none of these countries was the proper habitat of the Zend people. Zoroaster himself calls it the pure Aryan: we find a similar name in Herodotus, for he says that the Medes were formerly called Arii—a name with which the designation Iran is connected. South of the Oxus runs a mountain chain in the ancient Bactriana—with which the elevated plains commence, that were inhabited by the Medes, the Parthians, and the Hyrcanians. In the district watered by the Oxus at the commencement of its course, Bactra, probably the modern Balkh, is said to have been situated; from which Kabul and Kashmir are distant only about eight days' journey. Here in Bactriana appears to have been the seat of the Zend people. In the time of Cyrus we find the pure and original faith, and the ancient political and social relations such as they are described in the Zend books, no longer perfect. Thus much appears certain, that the Zend language, which is connected with the Sanskrit, was the language of the Persians, Medes, and Bactrians. The laws and institutions of the people bear an evident stamp of great simplicity. Four classes are mentioned: priests, warriors, agriculturists, and craftsmen. Trade only is not noticed; from which it would appear that the people still remained in an isolated condition. Governors of districts, towns, and roads, are mentioned; so that all points to the social phase of society—the political not being yet developed; and nothing indicates a connection with other states. It is essential to note, that we find here no castes, but only classes, and that there are no restrictions on marriage between these different classes; though the Zend writings announce civil laws and penalties, together with religious enactments.

The chief point, that which especially concerns us here, is the *doctrine* of Zoroaster. In contrast with the wretched hebetude of spirit which we find among the Hindus, a pure ether—an exhalation of spirit—meets us in the Persian conception. In it, spirit emerges from that substantial unity of nature, that substantial destitution of import, in which a separation has not yet taken place—in which spirit has not yet an independent existence in contraposition to its object. This people, namely, attained to the consciousness, that absolute truth must have the form of universality—of unity. This universal, eternal, infinite essence is not recognized at first, as conditioned in any way; it is unlimited identity. This is properly (and we have already frequently repeated it) also the character of Brahm. But this Universal Being became objective, and their spirit became the consciousness of this its essence; while on the contrary among the Hindus this objectivity is only the *natural* one of the Brahmans, and is recognized as pure universality only in the destruction of consciousness. Among the Persians this negative assertion has become a positive one; and man has a relation to Universal Being of such a kind that he remains positive in sustaining it. This One, Universal Being, is indeed not yet recognized as the free unity of thought; not yet "worshipped in spirit and in truth"; but is still clothed with a form—that of light. But light is not a lama, a Brahman, a mountain, a brute, this or that particular existence, but sensuous universality itself; simple manifestation. The Persian religion is therefore no idol-worship; it does not adore individual natural objects, but the universal itself. Light admits, moreover, the signification of the spiritual; it is the form of the good and true, the substantiality of knowledge and volition as well as of all natural things. Light puts man in a position to be able to exercise choice; and he can only choose when he has emerged from that which had absorbed him. But light directly involves an opposite, namely, darkness; just as evil is the antithesis of good. As man could not appreciate good, if evil were not; and as he can be really good only when he has become acquainted with the contrary, so the light does not exist without darkness. Among the Persians, *Ormazd* and *Ahriman* present the antithesis in question. Ormazd is the lord of the kingdom of light—of good; Ahriman that of darkness—of evil. But there is a still higher being from whom both proceeded —a Universal Being not affected by this antithesis, called *Zrvana Akarana*—the Unlimited All. The All, *i.e.*, is something abstract; it does not exist for itself, and Ormazd and Ahriman have arisen from it. This dualism is commonly brought as a reproach against oriental thought; and, as far as the contradiction is regarded as absolute, that is certainly an irreligious understanding which remains satisfied with it. But the very nature of spirit demands antithesis; the principle of dualism belongs therefore to the idea of spirit, which, in its concrete form, essentially involves distinction. Among the Persians, purity and impurity have both become subjects of consciousness; and spirit, in order to comprehend itself, must of necessity place the special and negative existence in contrast with the universal and positive. Only by overcoming this antithesis is spirit twice-born—regenerated. The deficiency in the Persian principle is only that the unity of the antithesis is not completely recognized; for in that indefinite conception of the Uncreated All, whence Ormazd and Ahriman proceeded, the unity is only the absolutely *primal* existence, and does not reduce the contradictory elements to harmony in itself. Ormazd creates of his own free will; but also according to the decree of Zrvana Akarana (the representation wavers); and the harmonizing of the contradiction is only to be found in the contest which Ormazd carries on with Ahriman, and in

which he will at last conquer. Ormazd is the lord of light, and he creates all that is beautiful and noble in the world, which is a kingdom of the sun. He is the excellent, the good, the positive in all natural and spiritual existence. Light is the *body of Ormazd;* thence the worship of fire, because Ormazd is present in all light; but he is not the sun or moon itself. In these the Persians venerate only the light, which is Ormazd. Zoroaster asks Ormazd who he is? He answers: "My name is the ground and centre of all existence; highest wisdom and science; destroyer of the ills of the world, and maintainer of the universe; fulness of blessedness; pure will," etc. That which comes from Ormazd is living, independent, and lasting. Language testifies to his power; prayers are his productions. Darkness is on the contrary the body of Ahriman; but a perpetual fire banishes him from the temples. The chief end of every man's existence is to keep himself pure, and to spread this purity around him. The precepts that have this in view are very diffuse; the moral requirements are however characterized by mildness. It is said: if a man loads you with revilings, and insults, but subsequently humbles himself, call him your friend. We read in the *Vendidad,* that sacrifices consist chiefly of the flesh of clean animals, flowers and fruits, milk and perfumes. It is said there, "As man was created pure and worthy of heaven, he becomes pure again through the law of the servants of Ormazd, which is purity itself; if he purifies himself by sanctity of thought, word, and deed. What is 'pure thought'? That which ascends to the beginning of things. What is 'pure word'? The word of Ormazd, (the word is thus personified and imports the living spirit of the whole revelation of Ormazd). What is 'pure deed'? The humble adoration of the heavenly hosts, created at the beginning of things." It is implied in this that man should be virtuous: his own will, his subjective freedom is presupposed. Ormazd is not limited to particular forms of existence. Sun, moon, and five other stars, which seem to indicate the planets, those illuminating and illuminated bodies, are the primary symbols of Ormazd; the *Amshaspands,* his first sons. Among these, Mithra is also named: but we are at a loss to fix upon the star which this name denotes, as we are also in reference to the others. The *Mithra* is placed in the Zend books among the other stars; yet in the penal code moral transgressions are called "Mithrasins," *e.g.,* breach of promise, entailing 300 lashes; to which in the case of theft, 300 years of punishment in hell are to be added.

Mithra appears here as the presiding genius of man's inward higher life. Later on, great importance is assigned to Mithra as the mediator between Ormazd and men. Even Herodotus mentions the adoration of Mithra. In Rome, at a later date, it became very prevalent as a secret worship; and we find traces of it even far into the Middle Ages. Besides those noticed there are other protecting genii, which rank under the Amshaspands, their superiors; and are the governors and preservers of the world. The council of the seven great men whom the Persian monarch had about him was likewise instituted in imitation of the court of Ormazd. The *fravashi* —a kind of spirit-world—are distinguished from the creatures of the mundane sphere. The *fravashi* are not spirits according to our idea, for they exist in every natural object, whether fire, water, or earth. Their existence is coeval with the origin of things; they are in all places, in highroads, towns, etc., and are prepared to give help to supplicants. Their abode is in Garo-demana, the dwelling of the "blessed," above the solid vault of heaven. As son of Ormazd we find the name Dshemshid: apparently the same as he whom the Greeks call Achæmenes, whose descendants are called Pishdadians—a race to which Cyrus was reported to belong. Even at a later period the Persians seem to have had the designation Achæmenians among the Romans. (Horace, *Odes* III. i. 44). Dshemshid, it is said, pierced the earth with a golden dagger; which means nothing more than that he introduced agriculture. He is said then to have traversed the various countries, originated springs and rivers, and thereby fertilized certain tracts of land, and made the valleys teem with living beings, etc. In the *Zendavesta*, the name Gustasp is also frequently mentioned, which many recent investigators have been inclined to connect with Darius Hystaspes; an idea however that cannot be entertained for a moment, for this Gustasp doubtless belongs to the ancient Zend race—to a period therefore antecedent to Cyrus. Mention is made in the Zend books of the Turanians also, *i.e.*, the nomad tribes of the north; though nothing historical can be thence deduced.

The *ritual observances* of the religion of Ormazd import that men should conduct themselves in harmony with the kingdom of light. The great general commandment is therefore, as already said, spiritual and corporeal purity, consisting in many prayers to Ormazd. It was made specially obligatory upon the Persians, to maintain living existences, to plant trees, to dig wells, to fertilize deserts; in order that life, the posi-

tive, the pure might be furthered, and the dominion of Ormazd be universally extended. External purity is contravened by touching a dead animal, and there are many directions for being purified from such pollution. Herodotus relates of Cyrus, that when he went against Babylon, and the river Gyndes engulfed one of the horses of the chariot of the sun, he was occupied for a year in punishing it, by diverting its stream into small canals, to deprive it of its power. Thus Xerxes, when the sea broke in pieces his bridges, had chains laid upon it as the wicked and pernicious being —Ahriman.

Chapter 2. *The Assyrians, Babylonians, Medes, and Persians*

As the Zend race was the higher spiritual element of the Persian Empire, so in Assyria and Babylonia we have the element of external wealth, luxury, and commerce. Traditions respecting them ascend to the remotest periods of history; but in themselves they are obscure, and partly contradictory; and this contradiction is the less easy to be cleared up, as they have no canonical books or indigenous works. The Greek historian Ctesias is said to have had direct access to the archives of the Persian kings; yet we have only a few fragments remaining. Herodotus gives us much information; the accounts in the Bible are also valuable and remarkable in the highest degree, for the Hebrews were immediately connected with the Babylonians. In regard to the Persians, special mention must be made of the epic, *Shahnama,* by Firdousi—a heroic poem in 60,000 strophes, from which Görres has given a copious extract. Firdousi lived at the beginning of the eleventh century A.D. at the court of Mahmoud the Great, at Ghazni, east of Kabul and Kandahar. The celebrated epic just mentioned has the old heroic traditions of Iran (that is of West Persia proper) for its subject; but it has not the value of a historical authority, since its contents are poetical and its author a Mohammedan. The contest of Iran and Turan is described in this heroic poem. Iran is Persia proper —the mountain land on the south of the Oxus; Turan denotes the plains of the Oxus and those lying between it and the ancient Jaxartes. A hero, Rustan, plays the principal part in the poem; but its narrations are either altogether fabulous, or quite distorted. Mention is made of Alexander, and he is called Ishkander or Skander of Roum. Roum means the Turkish Empire (even now one of its provinces is called Roumelia), but it denotes also the *Roman;* and in the poem Alexander's empire has equally the appellation Roum. Confusions of this kind are quite of a piece with the Mohammedan views. It is related in the poem, that the King of Iran made war on Philip, and that this latter was beaten. The King then demanded Philip's daughter as a wife; but after he had lived a long time with her, he sent her away because her breath was disagreeable. On returning to her father, she gave birth to a son, Skander, who hastened to Iran to take possession of the throne after the death of his father. Add to the above that in the whole of the poem no personage or narrative occurs that can be connected with Cyrus, and we have sufficient data for estimating its historical value. It has a value for us, however, so far as Firdousi therein exhibits the spirit of his time, and the character and interest of modern Persian views.

As regards *Assyria,* we must observe, that it is a rather indeterminate designation. Assyria proper is a part of Mesopotamia, to the north of Babylon. As chief towns of this empire are mentioned, Atur or Assur on the Tigris, and of later origin Nineveh, said to have been founded and built by Ninus, the founder of the Assyrian Empire. In those times one city constituted the whole empire—Nineveh for example: so also Ecbatana in Media, which is said to have had seven walls, between whose inclosures agriculture was carried on; and within whose innermost wall was the palace of the ruler. Thus too, Nineveh, according to Diodorus, was 480 stadia (about 12 German miles—[55 English]) in circumference. On the walls, which were 100 feet high, were fifteen hundred towers, within which a vast mass of people resided. Babylon included an equally immense population. These cities arose in consequence of a twofold necessity; on the one hand, that of giving up the nomad life and pursuing agriculture, handicrafts, and trade in a fixed abode; and, on the other hand, of gaining protection against the roving mountain peoples, and the predatory Arabs. Older traditions indicate that this entire valley district was traversed by nomads, and that this mode of life gave way before that of the cities. Thus Abraham wandered forth with his family from Mesopotamia westwards, into mountainous Palestine. Even at this day the country round Baghdad is thus infested by roving nomads. Nineveh is said to have been built 2050 years before Christ; consequently the founding of the Assyrian Kingdom is of no later date. Ninus reduced under his sway also Babylonia, Media, and Bactriana; the conquest of which latter country is particularly extolled as having displayed the greatest energy;

for Ctesias reckons the number of troops that accompanied Ninus, at 1,700,000 infantry and a proportionate number of cavalry. Bactra was besieged for a very considerable time, and its conquest is ascribed to Semiramis; who with a valiant host is said to have ascended the steep acclivity of a mountain. The personality of Semiramis wavers between mythological and historical representations. To her is ascribed the building of the Tower of Babel, respecting which we have in the Bible one of the oldest of traditions.

Babylon lay to the south, on the Euphrates, in a plain of great fertility and well adapted for agriculture. On the Euphrates and the Tigris there was considerable navigation. Vessels came partly from Armenia, partly from the south, to Babylon, and conveyed thither an immense amount of material wealth. The land round Babylon was intersected by innumerable canals; more for purposes of agriculture, to irrigate the soil and to obviate inundations, than for navigation. The magnificent buildings of Semiramis in Babylon itself are celebrated; though how much of the city is to be ascribed to the more ancient period, is undetermined and uncertain. It is said that Babylon formed a square, bisected by the Euphrates. On one side of the stream was the temple of Bel, on the other the great palaces of the monarchs. The city is reputed to have had a hundred brazen (*i.e.,* copper) gates, its walls being a hundred feet high, and thick in proportion, defended by two hundred and fifty towers. The thoroughfares in the city which led towards the river were closed every night by brazen doors. Ker Porter, an Englishman, about twelve years ago (his whole tour occupied from 1817 to 1820), traversed the countries where ancient Babylon lay: on an elevation he thought he could discover remains still existing of the old Tower of Babel; and supposed that he had found traces of the numerous roads that wound around the tower, and in whose loftiest story the image of Bel was set up. There are besides many hills with remains of ancient structures. The bricks correspond with the description in the Biblical record of the building of the tower. A vast plain is covered by an innumerable multitude of such bricks, although for many thousand years the practice of removing them has been continued; and the entire town of Hilla, which lies in the vicinity of the ancient Babylon, has been built with them. Herodotus relates some remarkable facts in the customs of the Babylonians, which appear to show that they were people living peaceably and neighbourly with each other. When anyone in Babylon fell ill, he was brought to some open place, that every passerby might have the opportunity of giving him his advice. Marriageable daughters were disposed of by auction, and the high price offered for a belle was allotted as a dowry for her plainer neighbor. Such an arrangement was not deemed inconsistent with the obligation under which every woman lay of prostituting herself once in her life in the temple of Mylitta. It is difficult to discover what connection this had with their religious ideas. This excepted, according to Herodotus's account, immorality invaded Babylon only at a later period, when the people became poorer. The fact that the fairer portion of the sex furnished dowries for their less attractive sisters, seems to confirm his testimony so far as it shows a provident care for all; while that bringing of the sick into the public places indicates a certain neighbourly feeling.

We must here mention the *Medes* also. They were, like the Persians, a mountain-people, whose habitations were south and southwest of the Caspian Sea and stretched as far as Armenia. Among these Medes, the Magi are also noticed as one of the six tribes that formed the Median people, whose chief characteristics were fierceness, barbarism, and warlike courage. The capital, Ecbatana, was built by Deioces, not earlier. He is said to have united under his kingly rule the tribes of the Medes, after they had made themselves free a second time from Assyrian supremacy, and to have induced them to build and to fortify for him a palace befitting his dignity. As to the religion of the Medes, the Greeks call all the oriental priests *Magi* which is therefore a perfectly indefinite name. But all the data point to the fact that among the Magi we may look for a comparatively close connection with the Zend religion; but that, although the Magi preserved and extended it, it experienced great modifications in transmission to the various peoples who adopted it. Xenophon says, that Cyrus was the first that sacrificed to God according to the fashion of the Magi. The Medes therefore acted as a medium for propagating the Zend religion.

The Assyrian-Babylonian Empire, which held so many peoples in subjection, is said to have existed for one thousand or fifteen hundred years. The last ruler was Sardanapalus—a great voluptuary, according to the descriptions we have of him. Arbaces, the Satrap of Media, excited the other satraps against him; and in combination with them, led the troops which assembled every year at Nineveh to pay the tribute, against Sardanapalus. The latter, although he had gained many victories, was at last compelled to yield before overwhelming force, and to shut himself up in Nineveh; and, when he could not longer offer resistance, to burn himself there with all his treasure. According to some chronologists, this took place 888 years B.C.; according to others, at the end of the seventh century. After this catastrophe the empire was entirely broken up: it was divided into an Assyrian, a Median, and a Babylonian Empire, to which also belonged the Chaldeans—a mountain people from the north which had united with the Babylonians. These several empires had in their turn various fortunes; though here we meet with a confusion in the accounts which has never been cleared up. Within this period of their existence begins their connection with the Jews and Egyptians. The Jewish people succumbed to superior force; the Jews were carried captive to Babylon, and from them we have accurate information respecting the condition of this empire. According to Daniel's statements there existed in Babylon a carefully appointed organization for government business. He speaks of Magians— from whom the expounders of sacred writings, the soothsayers, astrologers, Wise Men, and Chaldeans who interpreted dreams, are distinguished. The Prophets generally say much of the great commerce of Babylon; but they also draw a terrible picture of the prevailing depravity of manners.

The real culmination of the Persian Empire is to be looked for in connection with the *Persian* people properly so called, which, embracing in its rule all the Near East, came into contact with the Greeks. The Persians are found in extremely close and early connection with the Medes; and the transmission of the sovereignty to the Persians makes no essential difference; for Cyrus was himself a relation of the Median king, and the names of Persia and Media melt into one. At the head of the Persians and Medes, Cyrus made war upon Lydia and its king, Crœsus. Herodotus relates that there had been wars before that time between Lydia and Media, but which had been settled by the intervention of the king of Babylon. We recognize here a system of states, consisting of Lydia, Media, and Babylon. The latter had become predominant and had extended its dominion to the Mediterranean Sea. Lydia stretched eastward as far as the Halys; and the border of the western coast of Asia Minor, the fair Greek colonies, were subject to it; a high degree of culture was thus already present in the Lydian Empire. Art and poetry were blooming there as cultivated by the Greeks. These colonies also were subjected to Persia. Wise men, such as Bias, and still earlier, Thales, advised them to unite themselves in a firm league, or to quit their cities and possessions, and to seek out for themselves other habitations; (Bias meant Sardinia). But such a union could not be realized among cities which were animated by the bitterest jealousy of each other, and who lived in continual quarrel: while in the intoxication of affluence they were not capable of forming the heroic resolve to leave their homes for the sake of freedom. Only when they were on the very point of being subjugated by the Persians, did some cities give up certain for prospective possessions, in their aspiration after the highest good—liberty. Herodotus says of the war against the Lydians, that it made the Persians who were previously poor and barbarous, acquainted for the first time with the luxuries of life and civilization. After the Lydian conquest Cyrus subjugated Babylon. With it he came into possession of Syria and Palestine; freed the Jews from captivity, and allowed them to rebuild their temple. Lastly, he led an expedition against the Massagetæ; engaged with them in the steppes between the Oxus and the Jaxartes, but sustained a defeat, and died the death of a warrior and conqueror. The death of heroes who have formed an epoch in the history of the world, is stamped with the character of their mission. Cyrus thus died in his mission, which was the union of the Near East into one sovereignty without an ulterior object.

Chapter 3. *The Persian Empire and its Constituent Parts*

The Persian Empire is an empire in the *modern* sense—like that which existed in Germany, and the great imperial realm under the sway of Napoleon; for we find it consisting of a number of states, which are indeed dependent, but which have retained their own individuality, their manners, and laws. The general enactments, binding upon all, did not infringe upon their political and social idiosyncrasies, but even protected and maintained them; so that each of the nations that constitute the whole, had its own form of constitution. As light illuminates everything, imparting to each object a peculiar vitality, so the Persian Empire extends over a multitude of nations, and leaves to each one its particular character. Some have even kings of their own; each one its distinct language, arms, way of life, and customs. All this diversity coexists harmoniously under the impartial dominion of light. The Persian Empire comprehends all the three geographical elements, which we classified as distinct. First, the uplands of Persia and Media; next, the valley-plains of the Euphrates and Tigris, whose inhabitants are found united in a developed form of civilization, with Egypt—the valley-plain of the Nile —where agriculture, industrial arts, and sciences flourished; and lastly a third element, *viz.*, the nations who encounter the perils of the sea— the Syrians, the Phœnicians, the inhabitants of the Greek colonies and Greek maritime states in Asia Minor. Persia thus united in itself the three natural principles, while China and India remained foreign to the sea. We find here neither that consolidated totality which China presents, nor that Hindu life, in which an anarchy of caprice is prevalent everywhere. In Persia, the government, though joining all in a central unity, is but a combination of peoples—leaving each of them free. Thereby a stop is put to that barbarism and ferocity with which the nations had been wont to carry on their destructive feuds, and which the Book of Kings and the Book of Samuel sufficiently attest. The lamentations of the Prophets and their imprecations upon the state of things before the conquest, show the misery, wickedness and disorder that prevailed among them, and the happiness which Cyrus diffused over the region of the Near East. It was not given to the Asiatics to unite self-dependence, freedom, and substantial vigour of mind, with culture, *i.e.*, and interest for diverse pursuits and an acquaintance with the conveniences of life. Military valour among them is consistent only with barbarity of manners. It is not the calm courage of order; and when their mind opens to a sympathy with various interests, it immediately passes into effeminacy; allows its energies to sink, and makes men the slaves of an enervated sensuality.

Persia

The Persians—a free mountain and nomad people—though ruling over richer, more civilized, and fertile lands, retained, on the whole, the fundamental characteristics of their ancient mode of life. They stood with one foot on their ancestral territory, with the other on their foreign conquests. In his ancestral land the king was a friend among friends, and as if surrounded by equals. Outside of it, he was the lord to whom all were subject, and bound to acknowledge their dependence by the payment of tribute. Faithful to the Zend religion, the Persians give themselves to the pursuit of piety and the pure worship of Ormazd. The tombs of the kings were in Persia proper; and there the king sometimes visited his countrymen, with whom he lived in relations of the greatest simplicity. He brought with him presents for them, while all other nations were obliged to make presents to him. At the court of the monarch there was a division of Persian cavalry which constituted the *élite* of the whole army, ate at a common table, and were subject to a most perfect discipline in every respect. They made themselves illustrious by their bravery, and even the Greeks awarded a tribute of respect to their valour in the Median wars. When the entire Persian host, to which this division belonged, was to engage in an expedition, a summons was first issued to all the Asiatic populations. When the warriors were assembled, the expedition was undertaken with that character of restlessness, that nomadic disposition which formed the idiosyncrasy of the Persians. Thus they invaded Egypt, Scythia, Thrace, and at last Greece; where their vast power was destined to be shattered. A march of this kind looked almost like an emigration: their families accompanied them. Each people exhibited its national features and warlike accoutrements, and poured forth *en masse*. Each had its own order of march and mode of warfare. Herodotus sketches for us a brilliant picture of this variety of aspect as it presented itself in the vast march of nations under Xerxes (two millions of human beings are said to have accompanied him). Yet, as these peoples were so unequally disciplined, so diverse in strength and bravery, it is easy to understand how the small but well-trained armies of the Greeks, animated by the same spirit, and under matchless leadership, could withstand those innumerable but disorderly hosts of the Persians. The provinces had to provide for the support of the Persian cavalry, which were quartered in the centre of the kingdom. Babylon had to contribute the third part of the supplies in question, and consequently appears to have been by far the richest district. As regards other branches of revenue, each people was obliged to supply the choicest of the peculiar produce which the district afforded. Thus Arabia gave frankincense, Syria purple, etc.

The education of the princes—but especially that of the heir to the throne—was conducted with extreme care. Till their seventh year the sons of the king remained among the women, and did not come into the royal presence. From their seventh year forward they were instructed in hunting, riding, shooting with the bow, and

also in speaking the truth. There is one statement to the effect that the prince received instruction in the Magian lore of Zoroaster. Four of the noblest Persians conducted the prince's education. The magnates of the land, at large, constituted a kind of diet. Among them Magi were also found. They are depicted as free men, animated by a noble fidelity and patriotism. Of such character seem the seven nobles—the counterpart of the Amshaspands who stand around Ormazd—when after the unmasking of the false Smerdis, who on the death of King Cambyses gave himself out as his brother, they assembled to deliberate on the most desirable form of government. Quite free from passion, and without exhibiting any ambition, they agreed that monarchy was the only form of government adapted to the Persian Empire. The sun, and the horse which first saluted them with a neigh, decided the succession in favor of Darius. The magnitude of the Persian dominion occasioned the government of the provinces by viceroys—satraps; and these often acted very arbitrarily to the provinces subjected to their rule, and displayed hatred and envy towards each other; a source of much evil. These satraps were only superior presidents of the provinces, and generally left the subject kings of the countries in possession of regal privileges. All the land and all the water belonged to the great king of the Persians. "Land and water," were the demands of Darius Hystaspes and Xerxes from the Greeks. But the king was only the abstract sovereign: the enjoyment of the country remained to the nations themselves; whose obligations were comprised in the maintenance of the court and the satraps, and the contribution of the choicest part of their property. Uniform taxes first make their appearance under the government of Darius Hystaspes. On the occasion of a royal progress the districts of the empire visited had to give presents to the king; and from the amount of these gifts we may infer the wealth of the unexhausted provinces. Thus the dominion of the Persians was by no means oppressive, either in secular or religious respects. The Persians, according to Herodotus, had no idols—in fact ridiculed anthropomorphic representations of the gods; but they tolerated every religion, although there may be found expressions of wrath against idolatry. Greek temples were destroyed, and the images of the gods broken in pieces.

Syria and Semitic Western Asia

One element—the coast territory—which also belonged to the Persian Empire, is especially represented by Syria. It was peculiarly important to the Persian Empire; for when continental Persia set out on one of its great expeditions, it was accompanied by Phœnician as well as by Greek navies. The Phœnician coast is but a very narrow border, often only two leagues broad, which has the high mountains of Lebanon on the east. On the seacoast lay a series of noble and rich cities, as Tyre, Sidon, Byblus, Berytus, carrying on great trade and commerce; which last, however, was too isolated and confined to that particular country, to allow it to affect the whole Persian state. Their commerce lay chiefly in the direction of the Mediterranean sea, and it reached thence far into the west. Through its intercourse with so many nations, Syria soon attained a high degree of culture. There the most beautiful fabrications in metals and precious stones were prepared, and there the most important discoveries, e.g., of glass and of purple, were made. Written language there received its first development, for in their intercourse with various nations, the need of it was soon felt. (So, to quote another example, Lord Macartney observes that in Canton itself, the Chinese had felt and expressed the need of a more pliable written language.) The Phœnicians discovered and first navigated the Atlantic Ocean. They had settlements in Cyprus and Crete. In the remote island of Thasos, they worked gold mines. In the south and southwest of Spain they opened silver mines. In Africa they founded the colonies of Utica and Carthage. From Gades they sailed far down the African coast, and according to some, even circumnavigated Africa. From Britain they brought tin, and from the Baltic, Prussian amber. This opens to us an entirely new principle. Inactivity ceases, as also mere rude valour; in their place appears the activity of industry, and that considerate courage which, while it dares the perils of the deep, rationally bethinks itself of the means of safety. Here everything depends on man's activity, his courage, his intelligence; while the objects aimed at are also pursued in the interest of man. Human will and activity here occupy the foreground, not nature and its bounty. Babylonia had its determinate share of territory, and human subsistence was there dependent on the course of the sun and the process of nature generally. But the sailor relies upon himself amid the fluctuations of the waves, and eye and heart must be always open. In like manner the principle of industry involves the very opposite of what is received from nature; for natural objects are worked up for use and ornament. In industry

man is an object to himself, and treats nature as something subject to him, on which he impresses the seal of his activity. Intelligence is the valour needed here, and ingenuity is better than mere natural courage. At this point we see the nations freed from the fear of nature and its slavish bondage.

If we compare their *religious* ideas with the above, we shall see in *Babylon,* in the *Syrian* tribes, and in *Phrygia,* first a rude, vulgar, sensual idolatry—a description of which, in its principal features, is given in the Prophets. Nothing indeed more specific than idolatry is mentioned; and this is an indefinite term. The Chinese, the Hindus, the Greeks, practise idolatry; the Catholics, too, adore the images of saints; but in the sphere of thought with which we are at present occupied, it is the powers of nature and of production generally that constitute the object of veneration; and the worship is luxury and pleasure. The Prophets give the most terrible pictures of this, though their repulsive character must be partly laid to the account of the hatred of Jews against neighbouring peoples. Such representations are particularly ample in the Book of Wisdom. Not only was there a worship of natural objects, but also of the universal power of nature—Astarte, Cybele, Diana of Ephesus. The worship paid was a sensuous intoxication, excess, and revelry: sensuality and cruelty are its two characteristic traits. "When they keep their holy days they act as if mad," ["they are mad when they be merry"— English Version], says the Book of Wisdom (14. 28). With a merely sensuous life, this being a form of consciousness which does not attain to general conceptions, cruelty is connected; because nature itself is the highest, so that man has no value, or only the most trifling. Moreover, the genius of such a polytheism involves the destruction of its consciousness on the part of spirit in striving to identify itself with nature, and the annihilation of the spiritual generally. Thus we see children sacrificed, priests of Cybele subjecting themselves to mutilation, men making themselves eunuchs, women prostituting themselves in the temple. As a feature of the court of Babylon it deserves to be remarked that, when Daniel was brought up there, it was not required of him to take part in the religious observances; and moreover that food ceremonially pure was allowed him; that he was in requisition especially for interpreting the dreams of the king, because he had "the spirit of the holy gods." The king proposes to elevate himself above sensuous life by dreams, as indica-tions from a superior power. It is thus generally evident, that the bond of religion was lax, and that here no unity is to be found. For we observe also adorations offered to images of *kings;* the power of nature and the *king* as a spiritual power, are the highest; so that in this form of idolatry there is manifested a perfect contrast to the Persian purity.

We find on the other hand something quite different among the *Phœnicians,* that bold seafaring people. Herodotus tells us that at Tyre, Hercules was worshipped. If the divinity in question is not absolutely identical with the Greek demigod, there must be understood by that name one whose attributes nearly agree with his. This worship is particularly indicative of the character of the people; for it is Hercules of whom the Greeks say, that he raised himself to Olympus by dint of human courage and daring. The idea of the sun perhaps originated that of Hercules as engaged in his twelve labors; but this basis does not give us the chief feature of the myth, which is, that Hercules is that scion of the gods who, by his virtue and exertion, made himself a god by human spirit and valour; and who, instead of passing his life in idleness, spends it in hardship and toil. A *second* religious element is the worship of *Adonis,* which takes place in the towns of the coast (it was celebrated in Egypt also by the Ptolemies); and respecting which we find a notable passage in the Book of Wisdom (14. 13, etc.), where it is said: "The idols were not from the beginning—but were invented through the vain ambition of men, because the latter are short-lived. For a father afflicted with untimely mourning, when he had made an image of his child (Adonis) early taken away, honored him as a god, who was a dead man, and delivered to those that were under him ceremonies and sacrifices" (E. V. nearly). The feast of Adonis was very similar to the worship of Osiris, the commemoration of his death, a funeral festival, at which the women broke out into the most extravagant lamentations over the departed god. In India lamentation is suppressed in the heroism of insensibility; uncomplaining, the women there plunge into the river, and the men, ingenious in inventing penances, impose upon themselves the direst tortures; for they give themselves up to the loss of vitality, in order to destroy consciousness in empty abstract contemplation. Here, on the contrary, human pain becomes an element of worship; in pain man realizes his subjectivity: it is expected of him—he may here indulge self-consciousness and the feeling of actual existence.

Life here regains its value. A universality of pain is established: for death becomes immanent in the Divine, and the deity dies. Among the Persians we saw light and darkness struggling with each other, but here both principles are united in one—the absolute. The negative is here, too, the merely natural; but as the death of a *god,* it is not a limitation attaching to an individual object, but is pure negativity itself. And this point is important, because the generic conception that has to be formed of deity is spirit; which involves its being concrete, and having in it the element of negativity. The qualities of wisdom and power are also concrete qualities, but only as predicates; so that God remains abstract substantial unity, in which differences themselves vanish, and do not become *organic* elements (*Momente*) of this unity. But here the negative itself is a *phase* of deity —the natural—death; the worship appropriate to which is grief. It is in the celebration of the death of Adonis, and of his resurrection, that the concrete is made conscious. Adonis is a youth, who is torn from his parents by a too early death. In China, in the worship of ancestors, these latter enjoy divine honour. But parents in their decease only pay the debt of nature. When a *youth* is snatched away by death, the occurrence is regarded as contrary to the proper order of things; and while affliction at the death of parents is no *just* affliction, in the case of youth death is a paradox. And this is the deeper element in the conception that in the divinity, negativity—antithesis—is manifested; and that the worship rendered to him involves both elements—the pain felt for the divinity snatched away, and the joy occasioned by his being found again.

Judæa

The next people belonging to the Persian Empire, in that wide circle of nationalities which it comprises, is the *Jewish.* We find here, too, a canonical book—the *Old Testament;* in which the views of this people, whose principle is the exact opposite of the one just described, are exhibited. While among the Phœnician people the spiritual was still limited by nature, in the case of the Jews we find it entirely purified; the pure product of thought. Self-conception appears in the field of consciousness, and the spiritual develops itself in sharp contrast to nature and to union with it. It is true that we observed at an earlier stage the pure conception "Brahm"; but only as the universal being of nature; and with this limitation, that Brahm is not himself an object of consciousness. Among the Persians we saw this abstract being become an object for consciousness, but it was that of sensuous intuition—as light. But the idea of light has at this stage advanced to that of "Jehovah"—the *purely One*. This forms the point of separation between the East and the West; spirit descends into the depths of its own being, and recognizes the abstract fundamental principle as the spiritual. Nature, which in the East is the primary and fundamental existence, is now depressed to the condition of a mere creature; and spirit now occupies the first place. God is known as the creator of all men, as he is of all nature, and as absolute causality generally. But this great principle, as further conditioned, is *exclusive* unity. This religion must necessarily possess the element of exclusiveness, which consists essentially in this—that only the one people which adopts it, recognizes the one God, and is acknowledged by Him. The God of the Jewish people is the God only of Abraham and of his seed: national individuality and a special local worship are involved in such a conception of deity. Before him all other gods are false: moreover the distinction between "true" and "false" is quite abstract; for as regards the false gods, not a ray of the divine is supposed to shine into them. But every form of spiritual force, and *a fortiori* every religion is of such a nature, that whatever be its peculiar character, an affirmative element is necessarily contained in it. However erroneous a religion may be, it possesses truth, although in a mutilated phase. In every religion there is a divine presence, a divine relation; and a philosophy of history has to seek out the spiritual element even in the most imperfect forms. But it does not follow that because it is a religion, it is therefore *good*. We must not fall into the lax conception that the content is of no importance but only the form. This latitudinarian tolerance the Jewish religion does not admit, being absolutely exclusive.

The spiritual speaks itself here absolutely free of the sensuous, and nature is reduced to something merely external and undivine. This is the true and proper estimate of nature at this stage; for only at a more advanced phase can the idea attain a reconciliation in this its alien form. Its first utterances will be in opposition to nature; for spirit, which had been hitherto dishonoured, now first attains its due dignity, while nature resumes its proper position. Nature is conceived as having the ground of its existence in another—as something posited, created; and this idea, that God is the lord and creator of na-

ture, leads men to regard God as the exalted One, while the whole of nature is only his robe of glory, and is expended in his service. In contrast with this kind of exaltation, that which the Hindu religion presents is only that of indefinitude. In virtue of the prevailing spirituality the sensuous and immoral are no longer privileged, but disparaged as ungodliness. Only the One—Spirit—the nonsensuous is the truth; Thought exists free for itself, and true morality and righteousness can now make their appearance; for God is honoured by righteousness, and rightdoing is "walking in the way of the Lord." With this is conjoined happiness, life and temporal prosperity as its reward; for it is said: "that thou mayest live long in the land." Here too also we have the possibility of a *historical* view; for the understanding has become prosaic; putting the limited and circumscribed in its proper place, and comprehending it as the form proper to finite existence: Men are regarded as individuals, not as incarnations of God; sun as sun, mountains as mountains—not as possessing spirit and will.

We observe among this people a severe religious ceremonial, expressing a relation to pure thought. The individual as concrete does not become free, because the absolute itself is not comprehended as *concrete* spirit; since spirit still appears posited as non-spiritual—destitute of its proper characteristics. It is true that subjective feeling is manifest—the pure heart, repentance, devotion; but the particular concrete individuality has not become objective to itself in the absolute. It therefore remains closely bound to the observance of ceremonies and of the law, the basis of which latter is pure freedom in its abstract form. The Jews possess that which makes them what they are, through the *One:* consequently the individual has no freedom for itself. Spinoza regards the code of Moses as having been given by God to the Jews for a punishment—a rod of correction. The individual never comes to the consciousness of independence; on that account we do not find among the Jews any belief in the immortality of the soul; for individuality does not exist in and for itself. But though in Judaism the *individual* is not respected, the *family* has inherent value; for the worship of Jehovah is attached to the family, and it is consequently viewed as a substantial existence. But the state is an institution not consonant with the Judaistic principle, and it is alien to the legislation of Moses. In the idea of the Jews, Jehovah is the God of Abraham, of Isaac, and Jacob; who commanded them to depart out of Egypt, and gave them the land of Canaan. The accounts of the patriarchs attract our interest. We see in this history the transition from the patriarchal nomad condition to agriculture. On the whole the Jewish history exhibits grand features of character; but it is disfigured by an exclusive bearing (sanctioned in its religion), towards the genius of other nations (the destruction of the inhabitants of Canaan being even commanded), by want of culture generally, and by the superstition arising from the idea of the high value of their peculiar nationality. Miracles, too, form a disturbing feature in this history—*as history;* for as far as concrete consciousness is not free, concrete perception is also not free; nature is undeified, but not yet understood.

The family became a great nation; through the conquest of Canaan, it took a whole country into possession; and erected a temple for the entire people, in Jerusalem. But properly speaking no *political* union existed. In case of national danger heroes arose, who placed themselves at the head of the armies; though the nation during this period was for the most part in subjection. Later on, kings were chosen, and it was they who first rendered the Jews independent. David even made conquests. Originally the legislation is adapted to a family only; yet in the books of Moses the wish for a king is anticipated. The priests are to choose him: he is not to be a foreigner, not to have horsemen in large numbers, and he is to have few wives. After a short period of glory the kingdom suffered internal disruption and was divided. As there was only one tribe of Levites and one temple, *i.e.*, in Jerusalem, idolatry was immediately introduced. The one God could not be honored in different temples, and there could not be two kingdoms attached to one religion. However spiritual may be the conception of God as objective, the subjective side, the honour rendered to him, is still very limited and unspiritual in character. The two kingdoms, equally infelicitous in foreign and domestic warfare, were at last subjected to the Assyrians and Babylonians; through Cyrus the Israelites obtained permission to return home and live according to their own laws.

Egypt

The Persian Empire is one that has passed away, and we have nothing but melancholy relics of its glory. Its fairest and richest towns—such as Babylon, Susa, Persepolis—are razed to the ground; and only a few ruins mark their ancient site. Even in the more modern great cities of Persia, Ispahan and Shiraz, half of them has become a ruin; and they have not, as is the case with ancient Rome, developed a new life, but have lost their place almost entirely in the remembrance of the surrounding nations. Besides the other lands already enumerated as belonging to the Persian Empire, *Egypt* claims notice, characteristically the land of ruins; a land which from hoar antiquity has been regarded with wonder, and which in recent times also has attracted the greatest interest. Its ruins, the final result of immense labour, surpass in the gigantic and monstrous, all that antiquity has left us.

In Egypt we see united the elements which in the Persian monarchy appeared singly. We found among the Persians the adoration of light, regarded as the essence of universal nature. This principle then develops itself in phases which hold a position of indifference towards each other. The one is the immersion in the sensuous —among the Babylonians and Syrians; the other is the spiritual phase, which is twofold: first as the incipient consciousness of the concrete spirit in the worship of Adonis, and then as pure and abstract thought among the Jews. In the former the concrete is deficient in unity; in the latter the concrete is altogether wanting. The next problem is then, to harmonize these contradictory elements; and this problem presents itself in Egypt. Of the representations which Egyptian antiquity presents us with, one figure must be especially noticed, *viz., the Sphinx,* in itself a riddle, an ambiguous form, half brute, half human. The Sphinx may be regarded as a symbol of the Egyptian spirit. The human head looking out from the brute body, exhibits spirit as it begins to emerge from the merely natural —to tear itself loose therefrom and already to look more freely around it; without, however, entirely freeing itself from the fetters nature had imposed. The innumerable edifices of the Egyptians are half below the ground, and half rise above it into the air. The whole land is divided into a kingdom of life and a kingdom of death. The colossal statue of *Memnon* resounds at the first glance of the young morning sun; though it is not yet the free light of spirit with which it vibrates. Written language is still a hieroglyphic; and its basis is only the sensuous image, not the letter itself.

Thus the memorials of Egypt themselves give us a multitude of forms and images that express its character; we recognize a spirit in them which feels itself compressed; which utters itself, but only in a sensuous mode.

Egypt was always the land of marvels, and

has remained so to the present day. It is from the Greeks especially that we get information respecting it, and chiefly from Herodotus. This intelligent historiographer himself visited the country of which he wished to give an account, and at its chief towns made acquaintance with the Egyptian priests. Of all that he saw and heard, he gives an accurate record; but the deeper symbolism of the Egyptian mythology he has refrained from unfolding. This he regards as something sacred, and respecting which he cannot so freely speak as of merely external objects. Besides him Diodorus Siculus is an authority of great importance; and, among the Jewish historians, Josephus.

In their architecture and hieroglyphics, the thoughts and conceptions of the Egyptians are expressed. A national work in the department of language is wanting: and that not only to us, but to the Egyptians themselves; they could not have any, because they had not advanced to an understanding of themselves. Nor was there any Egyptian history, until at last Ptolemy Philadelphus, he who had the sacred books of the Jews translated into Greek, prompted the high-priest Manetho to write an Egyptian history. Of this we have only extracts, list of kings, which however have occasioned the greatest perplexities and contradictory views. To become acquainted with Egypt, we must for the most part have recourse to the notices of the ancients, and the immense monuments that are left us. We find a number of granite walls on which hieroglyphics are graved, and the ancients have given us explanations of some of them, but which are quite insufficient. In recent times attention has especially been recalled to them, and after many efforts something at least of the hieroglyphic writing has been deciphered. The celebrated Englishman, Thomas Young, first suggested a method of discovery, and called attention to the fact, that there are small surfaces separated from the other hieroglyphics, and in which a Greek translation is perceptible. By comparison Young made out three names—Berenice, Cleopatra, and Ptolemy, and this was the first step is deciphering them. It was found at a later date, that a great part of the hieroglyphics are phonetic, that is, express sounds. Thus the figure of an eye denotes first the eye itself, but secondly the first letter of the Egyptian word that means "eye," (as in Hebrew the figure of a house, ב, denotes the letter *b*, with which the word ברה, house, begins). The celebrated Champollion (the younger), first called attention to the fact that the phonetic hieroglyphs

are intermingled with those which mark conceptions; and thus classified the hieroglyphs and established settled principles for deciphering them.

The *history* of Egypt, as we have it, is full of the greatest contradictions. The mythical is blended with the historical, and the statements are as diverse as can be imagined. European literati have eagerly investigated the lists given by Manetho and have relied upon them, and several names of kings have been confirmed by the recent discoveries. Herodotus says that according to the statements of the priests, gods had formerly reigned over Egypt, and that from the first human king down to the King Sethos 341 generations, or 11,340 years, had passed away; but that the first human ruler was Menes (the resemblance of the name to the Greek Minos and the Hindu Manu is striking). With the exception of the Thebaid, its most southern part, Egypt was said by them to have formed a lake; the delta presents reliable evidence of having been produced by the silt of the Nile. As the Dutch have gained their territory from the sea, and have found means to sustain themselves upon it; so the Egyptians first acquired their country, and maintained its fertility by canals and lakes. An important feature in the history of Egypt is its descent from Upper to Lower Egypt, from the south to the north. With this is connected the consideration that Egypt probably received its culture from Ethiopia; principally from the island Meroe, which, according to recent hypotheses, was occupied by a sacerdotal people. Thebes in Upper Egypt was the most ancient residence of the Egyptian kings. Even in Herodotus's time it was in a state of dilapidation. The ruins of this city present the most enormous specimens of Egyptian architecture that we are acquainted with. Considering their antiquity they are remarkably well preserved: which is partly owing to the perpetually cloudless sky. The centre of the kingdom was then transferred to Memphis, not far from the modern Cairo; and lastly to Sais, in the delta itself. The structures that occur in the locality of this city are of very late date and imperfectly preserved. Herodotus tells us that Memphis was referred to so remote a founder as Menes. Among the later kings must be especially noticed Sesostris, who, according to Champollion, is Ramses the Great. To him in particular are referred a number of monuments and pictures in which are depicted his triumphal processions, and the captives taken in battle. Herodotus speaks of his conquests in Syria, extending even to Colchis; and illustrates his statement by the great similarity between the manners of the Colchians and those of the Egyptians; these two nations and the Ethiopians were the only ones that had always practised circumcision. Herodotus says, moreover, that Sesostris had vast canals dug through the whole of Egypt, which served to convey the water of the Nile to every part. It may be generally remarked that the more provident the government in Egypt was, so much the more regard did it pay to the maintenance of the canals, while under negligent governments the desert got the upper hand; for Egypt was engaged in a constant struggle with the fierceness of the heat and with the water of the Nile. It appears from Herodotus, that the country had become impassable for cavalry in consequence of the canals; while, on the contrary, we see from the books of Moses, how celebrated Egypt once was in this respect. Moses says that if the Jews desired a king, he must not marry too many wives, nor send for horses from Egypt.

Next to Sesostris the Kings Cheops and Chephren deserve special mention. They are said to have built enormous pyramids and closed the temples of the priests. A son of Cheops, Mycerinus, is said to have reopened them; after him the Ethiopians invaded the country, and their king, Sabaco, made himself sovereign of Egypt. But Anysis, the successor of Mycerinus, fled into the marshes—to the mouth of the Nile; only after the departure of the Ethiopians did he make his appearance again. He was succeeded by Setho, who had been a priest of Phtha (supposed to be the same as Hephæstus): under his government, Sennacherib, King of the Assyrians, invaded the country. Setho had always treated the warrior-caste with great disrespect, and even robbed them of their lands; and when he invoked their assistance, they refused it. He was obliged therefore to issue a general summons to the Egyptians, and assembled a host composed of hucksters, artisans, and market people. In the Bible we are told that the enemies fled, and that it was the angels who routed them; but Herodotus relates that fieldmice came in the night and knawed the quivers and bows of the enemy, so that the latter, deprived of their weapons, were compelled to flee. After the death of Setho, the Egyptians (Herodotus tells us), regarded themselves as free, and chose themselves twelve kings, who formed a federal union—as a symbol of which they built the Labyrinth, consisting of an immense number of rooms and halls above and below

ground. In the year 650 B.C. one of these kings, Psammetichus, with the help of the Ionians and Carians (to whom he promised land in Lower Egypt), expelled the eleven other kings. Till that time Egypt had remained secluded from the rest of the world; and at sea it had established no connection with other nations. Psammetichus commenced such a connection, and thereby led the way to the ruin of Egypt. From this point the history becomes clearer, because it is based on Greek accounts. Psammetichus was followed by Necho, who began to dig a canal, which was to unite the Nile with the Red Sea, but which was not completed until the reign of Darius Nothus. The plan of uniting the Mediterranean Sea with the Arabian Gulf, and the wide ocean, is not so advantageous as might be supposed; since in the Red Sea, which on other accounts is very difficult to navigate, there prevails for about nine months in the year a constant north wind, so that it is only during three months that the passage from south to north is feasible. Necho was followed by Psammis, and the latter by Apries, who led an army against Sidon, and engaged with the Tyrians by sea: against Cyrene also he sent an army, which was almost annihilated by the Cyrenians. The Egyptians rebelled against him, accusing him of wishing to lead them to destruction; but this revolt was probably caused by the favor shown by him to the Carians and Ionians. Amasis placed himself at the head of the rebels, conquered the king, and possessed himself of the throne. By Herodotus he is depicted as a humorous monarch, who, however, did not always maintain the dignity of the throne. From a very humble station he had raised himself to royalty by ability, astuteness, and intelligence, and he exhibited in all other relations the same keen understanding. In the morning he held his court of judicature, and listened to the complaints of the people; but in the afternoon, feasted and surrendered himself to pleasure. To his friends, who blamed him on this account, and told him that he ought to give the whole day to business, he made answer: "If the bow is constantly on the stretch, it becomes useless or breaks." As the Egyptians thought less of him on account of his mean descent, he had a golden basin, used for washing the feet, made into the image of a god in high honour among the Egyptians; this he meant as a symbol of his own elevation. Herodotus relates, moreover, that he indulged in excesses as a private man, dissipated the whole of his property, and then betook himself to stealing. This contrast of a vulgar soul and a keen intellect is characteristic in an Egyptian king.

Amasis drew down upon him the ill-will of King Cambyses. Cyrus desired an oculist from the Egyptians; for at that time the Egyptian oculists were very famous, their skill having been called out by the numerous eye-diseases prevalent in Egypt. This oculist, to revenge himself for having been sent out of the country, advised Cambyses to ask for the daughter of Amasis in marriage; knowing well that Amasis would either be rendered unhappy by giving her to him, or on the other hand, incur the wrath of Cambyses by refusing. Amasis would not give his daughter to Cambyses, because the latter desired her as an inferior wife (for his lawful spouse must be a Persian); but sent him, under the name of his own daughter, that of Apries, who afterwards discovered her real name to Cambyses. The latter was so incensed at the deception, that he led an expedition against Egypt, conquered that country, and united it with the Persian Empire.

As to the Egyptian *spirit*, it deserves mention here, that the Elians in Herodotus's narrative call the Egyptians the wisest of mankind. It also surprises us to find among them, in the vicinity of African stupidity, reflective intelligence, a thoroughly rational organization characterizing all institutions, and most astonishing works of art. The Egyptians were, like the Hindus, divided into castes, and the children always continued the trade and business of their parents. On this account, also, the mechanical and technical in the arts was so much developed here; while the hereditary transmission of occupations did not produce the same disadvantageous results in the character of the Egyptians as in India. Herodotus mentions the seven following castes: the priests, the warriors, the neatherds, the swineherds, the merchants (or trading population generally), the interpreters—who seem only at a later date to have constituted a separate class—and, lastly, the seafaring class. Agriculturists are not named here, probably because agriculture was the occupation of several castes, as, *e.g.*, the warriors, to whom a portion of the land was given. Diodorus and Strabo give a different account of these caste-divisions. Only priests, warriors, herdsmen, agriculturists, and artificers are mentioned, to which latter, perhaps, tradesmen also belong. Herodotus says of the priests, that they in particular received arable land, and had it cultivated for rent; for the land generally was in the possession of the priests, warriors, and kings.

Joseph was a minister of the king, according to Holy Scripture, and contrived to make him master of all landed property. But the several occupations did not remain so stereotyped as among the Hindus; for we find the Israelites, who were originally herdsmen, employed also as manual labourers: and there was a king, as stated above, who formed an army of manual labourers alone. The castes are not rigidly fixed, but struggle with and come into contact with one another: we often find cases of their being broken up and in a state of rebellion. The warrior-caste, at one time discontented on account of their not being released from their abodes in the direction of Nubia, and desperate at not being able to make use of their lands, betake themselves to Meroe, and foreign mercenaries are introduced into the country.

Of the *mode of life* among the Egyptians, Herodotus supplies a very detailed account, giving prominence to everything which appears to him to deviate from Greek manners. Thus the Egyptians had physicians specially devoted to particular diseases; the women were engaged in outdoor occupations, while the men remained at home to weave. In one part of Egypt polygamy prevailed; in another, monogamy; the women had but one garment, the men two; they wash and bathe much, and undergo purification every month. All this points to a condition of settled peace. As to arrangements of police, the law required that every Egyptian should present himself, at a time appointed, before the superintendent under whom he lived, and state from what resources he obtained his livelihood. If he could not refer to any, he was punished with death. This law, however, was of no earlier date than Amasis. The greatest care, moreover, was observed in the division of the arable land, as also in planning canals and dikes; under Shabako, the Ethiopian king, says Herodotus, many cities were elevated by dikes.

The business of *courts of justice* was administered with very great care. They consisted of thirty judges nominated by the district, and who chose their own president. Pleadings were conducted in writing, and proceeded as far as the "rejoinder." Diodorus thinks this plan very effectual, in obviating the perverting influence of forensic oratory, and of the sympathy of the judges. The latter pronounced sentence silently, and in a hieroglyphical manner. Herodotus says, that they had a symbol of truth on their breasts, and turned it towards that side in whose favor the cause was decided, or adorned the victorious party with it. The king himself had to take part in judicial business every day. Theft, we are told, was forbidden; but the law commanded that thieves should inform against themselves. If they did so, they were not punished, but, on the contrary, were allowed to keep a fourth part of what they had stolen. This perhaps was designed to excite and keep in exercise that cunning for which the Egyptians were so celebrated.

The *intelligence* displayed in their legislative economy, appears characteristic of the Egyptians. This intelligence, which manifests itself in the practical, we also recognize in the productions of art and science. The Egyptians are reported to have divided the year into twelve months, and each month into thirty days. At the end of the year they intercalated five additional days, and Herodotus says that their arrangement was better than that of the Greeks. The intelligence of the Egyptians especially strikes us in the department of mechanics. Their vast edifices—such as no other nation has to exhibit, and which excel all others in solidity and size— sufficiently prove their artistic skill; to whose cultivation they could largely devote themselves, because the inferior castes did not trouble themselves with political matters. Diodorus Siculus says, that Egypt was the only country in which the citizens did not trouble themselves about the state, but gave their whole attention to their private business. Greeks and Romans must have been especially astonished at such a state of things.

On account of its judicious economy, Egypt was regarded by the ancients as the pattern of a morally regulated condition of things—as an ideal such as Pythagoras realized in a limited select society, and Plato sketched on a larger scale. But in such ideals no account is taken of passion. A plan of society that is to be adopted and acted upon, as an absolutely complete one —in which everything has been considered, and especially the education and habituation to it, necessary to its becoming a second nature—is altogether opposed to the nature of spirit, which makes contemporary life the object on which it acts; itself being the infinite impulse of activity to alter its forms. This impulse also expressed itself in Egypt in a peculiar way. It would appear at first as if a condition of things so regular, so determinate in every particular, contained nothing that had a peculiarity entirely its own. The introduction of a religious element would seem to be an affair of no critical moment, provided the higher necessities of men were satisfied; we should in fact rather expect that it would be introduced in a peaceful way and in ac-

cordance with the moral arrangement of things already mentioned. But in contemplating the *religion* of the Egyptians, we are surprised by the strangest and most wonderful phenomena, and perceive that this calm order of things, bound fast by legislative enactment, is not like that of the Chinese, but that we have here to do with a spirit entirely different—one full of stirring and urgent impulses. We have here the African element, in combination with Oriental massiveness, transplanted to the Mediterranean Sea, that grand *locale* of the display of nationalities; but in such a manner, that here there is no connection with foreign nations—this mode of stimulating intellect appearing superfluous; for we have here a prodigious urgent striving within the nationality itself, and which within its own circle shoots out into an objective realization of itself in the most monstrous productions. It is that African imprisonment of ideas combined with the infinite impulse of the spirit to realize itself objectively, which we find here. But spirit has still, as it were, an iron band around its forehead; so that it cannot attain to the free consciousness of its existence, but produces this only as the problem, the enigma of its being.

The fundamental conception of that which the Egyptians regard as the essence of being, rests on the determinate character of the natural world, in which they live; and more particularly on the determinate physical circle which the Nile and the sun mark out. These two are strictly connected—the position of the sun and that of the Nile; and to the Egyptian this is all in all. The Nile is that which essentially determines the boundaries of the country; beyond the Nilevalley begins the desert; on the north, Egypt is shut in by the sea, and on the south by torrid heat. The first Arab leader that conquered Egypt, writes to the Caliph Omar: "Egypt is first a vast sea of dust; then a sea of fresh water; lastly, it is a great sea of flowers. It never rains there; towards the end of July dew falls, and then the Nile begins to overflow its banks, and Egypt resembles a sea of islands." (Herodotus compares Egypt, during this period, with the islands in the Ægean.) The Nile leaves behind it prodigious multitudes of living creatures: then appear moving and creeping things innumerable; soon after, man begins to sow the ground, and the harvest is very abundant. Thus the existence of the Egyptian does not depend on the brightness of the sun, or the quantity of rain. For him, on the contrary, there exist only those perfectly simple conditions, which form the basis of his mode of life and its occupations.

There is a definite physical cycle, which the Nile pursues, and which is connected with the course of the sun; the latter advances, reaches its culmination, and then retrogrades. So also does the Nile.

This basis of the life of the Egyptians determines moreover the particular tenor of their religious views. A controversy has long been waged respecting the sense of meaning of the Egyptian religion. As early as the reign of Tiberius, the Stoic Chæremon, who had been in Egypt, explains it in a purely materialistic sense. The new Platonists take a directly opposite view, regarding all as symbols of a spiritual meaning, and thus making this religion a pure idealism. Each of these representations is one-sided. Natural and spiritual powers are regarded as most intimately united—(the free spiritual import, however, has *not* been developed at this stage of thought)—but in such a way, that the extremes of the antithesis were united in the harshest contrast. We have spoken of the Nile, of the sun, and of the vegetation depending upon them. This limited view of nature gives the principle of the religion, and its subject-matter is primarily a history. The Nile and the sun constitute the divinities, conceived under human forms; and the course of nature and the mythological history is the same. In the winter solstice the power of the sun has reached its minimum, and must be born anew. Thus also Osiris appears as born; but he is killed by Typhon, his brother and enemy, the burning wind of the desert. Isis, the earth, from whom the aid of the sun and of the Nile has been withdrawn, yearns after him: she gathers the scattered bones of Osiris, and raises her lamentation for him, and all Egypt bewails with her the death of Osiris, in a song which Herodotus calls *Maneros*. Maneros he reports to have been the only son of the first king of the Egyptians, and to have died prematurely; this song being also the Linus-Song of the Greeks, and the only song which the Egyptians have. Here again pain is regarded as something divine, and the same honour is assigned to it here as among the Phœnicians. Hermes then embalms Osiris; and his grave is shown in various places. Osiris is now judge of the dead, and lord of the kingdom of the shades. These are the leading ideas. Osiris, the sun, the Nile; this triplicity of being is united in one knot. The sun is the symbol, in which Osiris and the history of that god are recognized, and the Nile is likewise such a symbol. The concrete Egyptian imagination also ascribes to Osiris and Isis the introduction of agriculture, the invention of the plough, the hoe, etc.; for Osiris gives not only the useful itself—the fertility of the earth—but, moreover, the means of making use of it. He also gives men laws, a civil order and a religious ritual; he thus places in men's hands the means of labour, and secures its result. Osiris is also the symbol of the seed which is placed in the earth, and then springs up—as also of the course of life. Thus we find this heterogeneous duality, the phenomena of nature and the spiritual, woven together into *one* knot.

The parallelism of the course of human life with the Nile, the sun, and Osiris, is not to be regarded as a mere allegory—as if the principle of birth, of increase in strength, of the culmination of vigour and fertility, of decline and weakness, exhibited itself in these different phenomena, in an equal or similar way; but in this variety imagination conceived only *one subject,* one vitality. This unity is, however, quite abstract: the heterogeneous element shows itself therein as pressing and urging, and in a confusion which sharply contrasts with Greek perspicuity. Osiris represents the Nile and the sun: sun and Nile are, on the other hand, symbols of human life—each one is signification and symbol at the same time; the symbol is changed into signification, and this latter becomes symbol of that symbol, which itself then becomes signification. None of these phases of existence is a type without being at the same time a signification; each is both; the one is explained by the other. Thus there arises one pregnant conception, composed of many conceptions, in which each fundamental nodus retains its individuality, so that they are not resolved into a general idea. The general idea—the thought itself, which forms the bond of analogy—does not present itself to the consciousness purely and freely as such, but remains concealed as an internal connection. We have a consolidated individuality, combining various phenomenal aspects; and which on the one hand is fanciful, on account of the combination of apparently disparate material, but on the other hand internally and essentially connected, because these various appearances are a particular prosaic matter of fact.

Besides this fundamental conception, we observe several special divinities, of whom Herodotus reckons three classes. Of the first he mentions eight gods; of the second twelve; of the third an indefinite number, who occupy the position towards the unity of Osiris of specific manifestations. In the first class, fire and its use appears as Phtha, also as Knef, who is besides represented as the Good Genius; but the Nile itself is held to be that Genius, and thus abstractions are changed into concrete conceptions. Ammon is regarded as a great divinity, with whom is associated the determination of the equinox: it is he, moreover, who gives oracles. But Osiris is similarly represented as the founder of oracular manifestations. So the procreative power, banished by Osiris, is represented as a particular divinity. But Osiris is himself this procreative power. Isis is the earth, the moon, the receptive fertility of nature. As an important element in the conception Osiris, *Anubis* (*Thoth*)—the Egyptian Hermes—must be specially noticed. In human activity and invention, and in the economy of legislation, the spiritual, as such, is embodied; and becomes in this form, which is itself determinate and limited, an object of consciousness. Here we have the spiritual, not as one infinite, independent sovereignty over nature, but as a particular existence, side by side with the powers of nature—characterized also by intrinsic particularity. And thus the Egyptians had also specific divinities, conceived as spiritual activities and forces; but partly *intrinsically* limited—partly contemplated under natural symbols.

The Egyptian Hermes is celebrated as exhibiting the spiritual side of their theism. According to Iamblichus, the Egyptian priests immemorially prefixed to all their inventions the name Hermes: Eratosthenes, therefore, called his book, which treated of the entire science of Egypt, *Hermes.* Anubis is called the friend and companion of Osiris. To him is ascribed the invention of writing, and of science generally —of grammar, astronomy, mensuration, music, and medicine. It was he who first divided the day into twelve hours: he was moreover the first lawgiver, the first instructor in religious observances and objects, and in gymnastics and orchestics; and it was he who discovered the olive. But, notwithstanding all these spiritual attributes, this divinity is something quite other than the god of thought. Only particular human arts and inventions are associated with him. Not only so; but he entirely falls back into involvement in existence, and is degraded under physical symbols. He is represented with a dog's head, as an imbruted god; and besides this mask, a particular natural object is bound up with the conception of this divinity; for he is at the same time Sirius, the dog-star. He is thus as limited in respect of what he embodies, as sensuous in the positive existence ascribed to him. It may be incidentally remarked, that as ideas and nature are not distinguished from each other, in

the same way the arts and appliances of human life are not developed and arranged so as to form a rational circle of aims and means. Thus medicine, deliberation respecting corporeal disease, as also the whole range of deliberation and resolve with regard to undertakings in life, was subjected to the most multifarious superstition in the way of reliance on oracles and magic arts. Astronomy was also essentially astrology, and medicine an affair of magic, but more particularly of astrology. All astrological and sympathetic superstition may be traced to Egypt.

Egyptian *worship* is chiefly zoolatry. We have observed the union here presented between the spiritual and the natural: the more advanced and elevated side of this conception is the fact that the Egyptians, while they observed the spiritual as manifested in the Nile, the sun, and the sowing of seed, took the same view of the life of animals. To us zoolatry is repulsive. We may reconcile ourselves to the adoration of the material heaven, but the worship of brutes is alien to us; for the abstract natural element seems to us more generic, and therefore more worthy of veneration. Yet it is certain that the nations who worshipped the sun and the stars by no means occupy a higher grade than those who adore brutes, but contrariwise; for in the brute world the Egyptians contemplate a hidden and incomprehensible principle. We also, when we contemplate the life and action of brutes, are astonished at their instinct, the adaptation of their movements to the object intended, their restlessness, excitability, and liveliness; for they are exceedingly quick and discerning in pursuing the ends of their existence, while they are at the same time silent and shut up within themselves. We cannot make out what it is that "possesses" these creatures, and cannot rely on them. A black tom-cat, with its glowing eyes and its now gliding, now quick and darting movement, has been deemed the presence of a malignant being—a mysterious reserved spectre: the dog, the canary-bird, on the contrary, appear friendly and sympathizing. The lower animals are the truly incomprehensible. A *man* cannot by imagination or conception enter into the nature of a *dog,* whatever resemblance he himself might have to it; it remains something altogether alien to him. It is in two departments that the so-called incomprehensible meets us—in living nature and in spirit. But in very deed it is only in nature that we have to encounter the incomprehensible; for the being manifest to itself is the essence, spirit: spirit understands and comprehends spirit. The obtuse self-consciousness of the Egyptians, therefore, to which the thought of human freedom is not yet revealed, worships the soul as still shut up within and dulled by the physical organization, and sympathizes with brute life. We find a veneration of mere vitality among other nations also: sometimes expressly, as among the Hindus and all the Mongolians; sometimes in mere traces, as among the Jews: "Thou shalt not eat the blood of animals, for in it is the life of the animal." The Greeks and Romans also regarded birds as specially intelligent, believing that what in the human spirit was not revealed, the incomprehensible and higher, was to be found in them. But among the Egyptians this worship of beasts was carried to excess under the forms of a most stupid and non-human superstition. The worship of brutes was among them a matter of particular and detailed arrangement: each district had a brute deity of its own—a cat, an ibis, a crocodile, etc. Great establishments were provided for them; beautiful *mates* were assigned them; and, like human beings, they were embalmed after death. The bulls were buried, but with their horns protruding above their graves; the bulls embodying *Apis* had splendid monuments, and some of the pyramids must be looked upon as such. In one of those that have been opened, there was found in the most central apartment a beautiful alabaster coffin; and on closer examination it was found that the bones inclosed were those of the ox. This reverence for brutes was often carried to the most absurd excess of severity. If a man killed one designedly, he was punished with death; but even the undesigned killing of some animals might entail death. It is related, that once when a Roman in Alexandria killed a cat, an insurrection ensued, in which the Egyptians murdered the aggressor. They would let human beings perish by famine, rather than allow the sacred animals to be killed, or the provision made for them trenched upon. Still more than mere vitality, the universal *vis vitæ* of productive nature was venerated in a phallus-worship; which the Greeks also adopted into the rites paid by them to Dionysus. With this worship the greatest excesses were connected.

The brute form is, on the other hand, turned into a symbol: it is also partly degraded to a mere hieroglyphical sign. I refer here to the innumerable figures on the Egyptian monuments, of sparrow-hawks or falcons, dung-beetles, scarabæi, etc. It is not known what ideas such figures symbolized, and we can scarcely think that a satisfactory view of this very obscure subject is attainable. The dung-beetle is said to be the symbol of generation, of the sun and its course; the Ibis, that of the Nile's overflowing; birds of the hawk tribe, of prophecy, of the year, of pity. The strangeness of these combinations results from the circumstance that we have not, as in our idea of poetical invention, a general conception embodied in an image; but, conversely, we begin with a concept in the sphere of sense, and imagination conducts us into the same sphere again. But we observe the conception liberating itself from the direct animal form, and the continued contemplation of it; and that which was only surmised and aimed at in that form, advancing to comprehensibility and conceivableness. The hidden meaning, the spiritual, emerges as a human face from the brute. The multiform sphinxes, with lions' bodies and virgins' heads —or as male sphinxes ($\dot{\alpha}\nu\delta\rho\acute{o}\sigma\phi\iota\gamma\gamma\epsilon\varsigma$) with beards—are evidence supporting the view, that the meaning of the spiritual is the problem which the Egyptians proposed to themselves; as the enigma generally is not the utterance of something unknown, but is the challenge to discover it—implying a wish to be revealed. But conversely, the human form is also disfigured by a brute face, with the view of giving it a specific and definite expression. The refined art of Greece is able to attain a specific expression through the spiritual character given to an image in the form of beauty, and does not need to deform the human face in order to be understood. The Egyptians appended an explanation to the human forms, even of the gods, by means of heads and masks of brutes; Anubis, *e.g.*, has a dog's head, Isis, a lion's head with bull's horns, etc. The priests, also, in performing their functions, are masked as falcons, jackals, bulls, etc.; in the same way the surgeon, who has taken out the bowels of the dead (represented as fleeing, for he has laid sacrilegious hands on an object once hallowed by life); so also the embalmers and the scribes. The sparrow-hawk, with a human head and outspread wings, denotes the soul flying through material space, in order to animate a new body. The Egyptian imagination also created new forms—combinations of different animals: serpents with bulls' and rams' heads, bodies of lions with rams' heads, etc.

We thus see Egypt intellectually confined by a narrow, involved, close view of nature, but breaking through this; impelling it to self-contradiction, and proposing to itself the problem which that contradiction implies. The principle does not remain satisfied with its primary conditions, but points to that other meaning and spirit which lies concealed beneath the surface.

In the view just given, we saw the Egyptian spirit working itself free from natural forms. This urging, powerful spirit, however, was not able to rest in the subjective conception of that view of things which we have now been considering, but was impelled to present it to external consciousness and outward vision by means of art. For the religion of the Eternal One—the formless—art is not only unsatisfying, but, since its *object* essentially and exclusively occupies the thought, something sinful. But spirit, occupied with the contemplation of particular natural forms—being at the same time a striving and plastic Spirit—changes the direct, natural view, *e.g.*, of the Nile, the sun, etc., to images, in which spirit has a share. It is, as we have seen, symbolizing spirit; and as such, it endeavors to master these symbolizations, and to present them clearly before the mind. The more enigmatical and obscure it is to itself, so much the more does it feel the impulse to labour to deliver itself from its imprisonment, and to gain a clear objective view of itself.

It is the distinguishing feature of the Egyptian spirit, that it stands before us as this mighty taskmaster. It is not splendour, amusement, pleasure, or the like that it seeks. The force which urges it is the impulse of self-comprehension; and it has no other material or ground to work on, in order to teach itself what it is, to realize itself for itself, than this working out its thoughts in stone; and what it engraves on the stone are its enigmas—these hieroglyphs. They are of two kinds: hieroglyphs *proper,* designed rather to express language, and having reference to subjective conception; and a class of hieroglyphs of a different kind, *viz.,* those enormous masses of architecture and sculpture, with which Egypt is covered. While among other nations history consists of a series of events—as, *e.g.,* that of the Romans, who century after century, lived only with a view to conquest, and accomplished the subjugation of the world—the Egyptians raised an empire equally mighty—of achievements in works of art, whose ruins prove their indestructibility, and which are greater and more worthy of astonishment than all other works of ancient or modern time.

Of these works I will mention no others than those devoted to the dead, and which especially attract our attention. These are, the enormous excavations in the hills along the Nile at Thebes, whose passages and chambers are entirely filled with mummies—subterranean abodes as large as the largest mining works of our time: next, the great field of the dead in the plain of Sais, with its walls and vaults: thirdly, those wonders of the world, the Pyramids, whose destination, though stated long ago by Herodotus and Diodorus, has been only recently expressly confirmed—to the effect, *viz.,* that these prodigious crystals, with their geometrical regularity, contain dead bodies: and lastly, that most astonishing work, the tombs of the kings, of which one has been opened by Belzoni in modern times.

It is of essential moment to observe, what importance this realm of the dead had for the Egyptian: we may thence gather what idea he had of man. For in the dead, man conceives of man as stripped of all adventitious wrappages—as reduced to his essential nature. But that which a people regards as man in his essential characteristics, that it is itself—such is its character.

In the first place, we must here cite the remarkable fact which Herodotus tells us, *viz.,* that the Egyptians were the first to express the thought that the soul of man is *immortal.* But this proposition that the soul is immortal, is intended to mean that it is something other than nature—that Spirit is inherently independent. The *ne plus ultra* of blessedness among the Hindus, was the passing over into abstract unity, into nothingness. On the other hand, subjectivity, when free, is inherently infinite: the kingdom of free spirit is therefore the kingdom of the invisible—such as Hades was conceived by the Greeks. This presents itself to men first as the empire of death, to the Egyptians as the *realm of the dead.*

The idea that spirit is immortal, involves this—that the human individual inherently possesses infinite value. The merely Natural appears limited, absolutely dependent upon something other than itself, and has its existence in that other; but immortality involves the inherent infinitude of spirit. This idea is first found among the Egyptians. But it must be added, that the soul was known to the Egyptians previously only as an atom, that is, as something concrete and particular. For with that view is immediately connected the notion of metempsychosis, the idea that the soul of man may also become the tenant of the body of a brute. Aristotle too speaks of this idea, and despatches it in few words. Every subject, he says, has its particular organs, for its peculiar mode of action: so the smith, the carpenter, each for his own craft. In like manner the human soul has its peculiar organs, and the body of a brute cannot be its domicile. Pythagoras adopted the doctrine of metempsychosis; but it could not find much support among the Greeks, who held rather to the concrete. The Hindus have also an indistinct conception of this doctrine, inasmuch as with them the final attainment is absorption in the universal substance. But with the Egyptians the soul—the spirit—is, at any rate, an affirmative being, although only abstractedly affirmative. The period occupied by the soul's migrations was fixed at three thousand years; they affirmed, however, that a soul which had remained faithful to Osiris, was not subject to such a degradation—for such they deem it.

It is well known that the Egyptians embalmed their dead; and thus imparted such a degree of permanence that they have been preserved even to the present day, and may continue as they are for many centuries to come. This indeed seems inconsistent with their idea of immortality; for if the soul has an independent existence, the permanence of the body seems a matter of indifference. But on the other hand it may be said, that if the soul is recognized as a permanent existence, honour should be shown to the body, as its former abode. The Parsees lay the bodies of the dead in exposed places to be devoured by birds; but among them the soul is regarded as passing forth into universal existence. Where the soul is supposed to enjoy continued existence, the body must also be considered to have some kind of connection with this continuance. Among us, indeed, the doctrine of the immortality of the soul assumes the higher form: spirit is in and for itself eternal: its destiny is eternal blessedness. The Egyptians made their dead into mummies; and did not occupy themselves further with them; no honour was paid them beyond this. Herodotus relates of the Egyptians, that when any person died, the women went about loudly lamenting; but the idea of immortality is not regarded in the light of a consolation, among us.

From what was said above, respecting the works for the dead, it is evident that the Egyptians, and especially their kings, made it the business of their life to build their sepulchre, and to give their bodies a permanent abode. It is remarkable that what had been needed for the business of life, was buried with the dead. Thus the craftsman had his tools: designs on the coffin show the occupation to which the deceased had devoted himself; so that we are able to become acquainted with him in all the *minutiæ* of his condition and employment. Many mummies have been found with a roll of papyrus under their arm, and this was formerly regarded as a remarkable treasure. But these rolls contain only various representations of the pursuits of life, together with writings in the demotic character. They have been deciphered, and the discovery has been made, that they are all deeds of purchase, relating to pieces of ground and the like; in which everything is most minutely recorded, even the duties that had to be paid to the royal chancery on the occasion. What, therefore, a person bought during his life, is made to accompany him, in the shape of a legal document, in death. In this monumental way we are made acquainted with the private life of the Egyptians, as with that of the Romans through the ruins of Pompeii and Herculaneum.

After the death of an Egyptian, judgment was passed upon him. One of the principal representations on the sarcophagi is this judicial process in the realm of the dead. Osiris, with Isis behind him appears, holding a balance, while before him stands the soul of the deceased. But judgment was passed on the dead by the living themselves; and that not merely in the case of private persons, but even of kings. The tomb of a certain king has been discovered—very large, and elaborate in its architecture—in whose hieroglyphs the name of the principal person is obliterated, while in the bas-reliefs and pictorial designs the chief figure is erased. This has been explained to import that the honour of being thus immortalized was refused this king by the sentence of the court of the dead.

If death thus haunted the minds of the Egyptians during life, it might be supposed that their disposition was melancholy. But the thought of death by no means occasioned depression. At banquets they had representations of the dead (as Herodotus relates), with the admonition: "Eat and drink—such a one wilt thou become, when thou art dead." Death was thus to them rather a call to enjoy life. Osiris himself dies, and goes down into the realm of death, according to the above-mentioned Egyptian myth. In many places in Egypt, the sacred grave of Osiris was exhibited. But he was also represented as president of the kingdom of the invisible sphere, and as judge of the dead in it; later on, Serapis exercised this function in his place. Of Anubis-Hermes the myth says, that he embalmed the body of Osiris: this Anubis sustained also the office of leader of the souls of the dead; and in the pictorial representations he stands, with a writing tablet in his hand, by the side of Osiris. The reception of the dead into the kingdom of Osiris had also a profounder import, *viz.*, that the individual was united with Osiris. On the lids of the sarcophagi, therefore, the defunct is represented as having himself become Osiris; and in deciphering the hieroglyphs, the idea has been suggested that the kings are called gods. The human and the divine are thus exhibited as united.

If, in conclusion, we combine what has been said here of the peculiarities of the Egyptian spirit in all its aspects, its pervading principle is found to be, that the two elements of reality —spirit sunk in nature, and the impulse to liberate it—are here held together inharmoniously as contending elements. We behold the antithesis of nature and spirit—not the primary immediate unity, nor the concrete unity, where nature is posited only as a basis for the manifestation of spirit; in contrast with the first and second of these unities, the Egyptian unity, combining contradictory elements, occupies a middle place. The two sides of this unity are held in abstract independence of each other, and their veritable union presented only as a problem. We have, therefore, on the *one* side, prodigious confusion and limitation to the particular; barbarous sensuality with African hardness, zoolatry, and sensual enjoyment. It is stated that, in a public market-place, sodomy was committed by a woman with a goat. Juvenal relates that human flesh was eaten and human blood drunk out of revenge. The *other* side is the struggle of spirit for liberation; fancy displayed in the forms created by art, together with the abstract understanding shown in the mechanical labors connected with their production. The same intelligence—the power of altering the form of individual existences, and that steadfast thoughtfulness which can rise above mere phenomena —shows itself in their police and the mechanism of the state, in agricultural economy, etc.; and the contrast to this is the severity with which their customs bind them, and the superstition to which humanity among them is inexorably subject. With a clear understanding of the present, is connected the highest degree of impulsiveness, daring, and turbulence. These features are combined in the stories which Herodotus relates to us of the Egyptians. They much resemble the tales of the *Thousand and One Nights;* and although these have Baghdad as the locality of their narration, their origin is no more limited to this luxurious court, than to the Arabian people, but must be partly traced to Egypt—as Von Hammer also thinks. The Arabian world is quite other than the fanciful and enchanted region there described; it has much more simple passions and interests. Love, martial daring, the horse, the sword, are the darling subjects of the poetry peculiar to the Arabians.

Transition to the Greek World

The Egyptian spirit has shown itself to us as in all respects shut up within the limits of particular conceptions, and, as it were, imbruted in them; but likewise stirring itself within these limits; passing restlessly from one particular form into another. This spirit never rises to the universal and higher, for it seems to be blind to that; nor does it ever withdraw into itself: yet it symbolizes freely and boldly with particular existence, and has already mastered it. All that is now required is to posit that particular existence —which contains the germ of ideality—*as ideal*, and to comprehend universality itself, which is already potentially liberated from the particulars involving it. It is the free, joyful spirit of Greece that accomplishes this, and makes this its starting-point. An Egyptian priest is reported to have said that the Greeks remain eternally children. We may say, on the contrary, that the Egyptians are vigorous *boys*, eager for self-comprehension, who require nothing but clear understanding of themselves in an ideal form, in order to become *young men*. In the Oriental spirit there remains as a basis the massive substantiality of spirit immersed in nature. To the Egyptian spirit it has become impossible, though it is still involved in infinite embarrassment, to remain contented with *that*. The rugged African nature disintegrated that primitive unity, and lighted upon the problem whose solution is free spirit.

That the spirit of the Egyptians presented itself to their consciousness in the form of a *problem,* is evident from the celebrated inscription in the sanctuary of the goddess Neith at Sais: *"I am that which is, that which was, and that which will be; no one has lifted my veil."* This inscription indicates the principle of the Egyptian spirit; though the opinion has often been entertained, that its purport applies to all times. Proclus supplies the addition: *"The fruit which I have produced is Helios."* That which is clear to itself is, therefore, the result of, and the solution of, the problem in question. This lucidity is spirit—the son of Neith the concealed night-loving divinity. In the Egyptian Neith, truth is still a problem. The Greek Apollo is its solution; his utterance is: *"Man, know thyself."* In this dictum is not intended a self-recognition that regards the specialities of one's own weaknesses and defects: it is not the individual that is admonished to become acquainted with his idiosyncrasy, but humanity *in general* is summoned to self-knowledge. This mandate was given for the Greeks, and in the Greek spirit humanity exhibits itself in its clear and developed condition. Wonderfully, then, must the Greek legend surprise us, which relates, that the Sphinx—the great Egyptian symbol—appeared in Thebes, uttering the words: "What is that which in the morning goes on four legs, at midday on two, and in the evening on three?" Œdipus, giving the solution, *man,* precipitated the Sphinx from the rock. The solution and liberation of that Oriental spirit, which in Egypt had advanced so far as to propose the problem, is certainly this: that the inner being of nature is thought, which has its existence only in the human consciousness. But that time-honoured antique solution given by Œdipus, who thus shows himself possessed of knowledge, is connected with a dire ignorance of the character of his own actions. The rise of spiritual illumination in the old royal house is disparaged by connection with abominations, the result of ignorance; and that primeval royalty must, in order to attain true knowledge and moral clearness, first be brought into shapely form, and be harmonized with the spirit of the beautiful, by civil laws and political freedom.

The *inward* or ideal transition, from Egypt to Greece is as just exhibited. But Egypt became a province of the great Persian Kingdom, and the *historical* transition takes place when the Persian world comes in contact with the Greek. Here, for the first time, an historical transition meets us, *viz.,* in the fall of an empire. China and India, as already mentioned, have remained —Persia has not. The transition to Greece is, indeed, internal; but here it shows itself also externally, as a transmission of sovereignty—an occurrence which from this time forward is ever and anon repeated. For the Greeks surrender the sceptre of dominion and of civilization to the Romans, and the Romans are subdued by the Germans. If we examine this fact of transition more closely, the question suggests itself—for example, in this first case of the kind, *viz.,* Persia—why it sank, while China and India remain. In the first place we must here banish from our minds the prejudice in favour of duration, as if it had any advantage as compared with transience: the imperishable mountains are not superior to the quickly dismantled rose exhaling its life in fragrance. In Persia begins the principle of free spirit as contrasted with imprisonment in nature; mere natural existence, therefore, loses its bloom, and fades away. The principle of separation from nature is found in the Persian Empire, which, therefore, occupies a higher grade than those worlds immersed in the natural. The necessity of advance has been thereby proclaimed. Spirit has disclosed its existence, and must complete its development. It is only when dead that the Chinese is held in reverence. The Hindu kills himself, becomes absorbed in Brahm, undergoes a living death in the condition of perfect unconsciousness, or is a present god in virtue of his birth. Here we have no change; no advance is admissible, for progress is only possible through the recognition of the independence of spirit. With the "light" of the Persians begins a spiritual view of things, and here spirit bids adieu to nature. It is here, then, that we first find (as occasion called us to notice above) that the objective world remains free— that the nations are not enslaved, but are left in possession of their wealth, their political constitution, and their religion. And, indeed, this is the side on which Persia itself shows weakness as compared with Greece. For we see that the Persians could erect no empire possessing complete organization; that they could not "inform" the conquered lands with their principle, and were unable to make them into a harmonious whole, but were obliged to be content with an aggregate of the most diverse individualities. Among these nations the Persians secured no inward recognition of the legitimacy of their rule; they could not establish their legal principles of enactments, and in organizing their dominion, they only considered themselves, not the whole extent of their empire. Thus, as Persia did not constitute, politically, *one* spirit, it appeared weak in contrast with Greece. It was not the effeminacy of the Persians (although, perhaps, Babylon infused an enervating element) that ruined them, but the unwieldy, unorganized character of their host, as matched against Greek organization; *i.e.,* the superior principle overcame the inferior. The abstract principle of the Persians displayed its defectiveness as an unorganized, incompacted union of disparate contradictories; in which the Persian doctrine of light stood side by side with Syrian voluptuousness and luxury, with the activity and courage of the sea-braving Phœnicians, the abstraction of pure thought in the Jewish Religion, and the mental unrest of Egypt; an aggregate of elements, which awaited their idealization, and could receive it only in *free individuality.* The Greeks must be looked upon as the people in whom these elements interpenetrated each other: spirit became introspective, triumphed over particularity, and thereby emancipated itself.

SECOND PART

THE GREEK WORLD

Among the Greeks we feel ourselves immediately at home, for we are in the region of spirit; and though the origin of the nation, as also its philological peculiarities, may be traced farther —even to India—the proper emergence, the true palingenesis of spirit must be looked for in Greece first. At an earlier stage I compared the Greek world with the period of adolescence; not, indeed, in *that* sense, that youth bears within it a serious, anticipative destiny, and consequently by the very conditions of its culture urges towards an ulterior aim—presenting thus an inherently incomplete and immature form, and being then most defective when it would deem itself perfect—but in *that* sense, that youth does not yet present the activity of work, does not yet exert itself for a definite intelligent aim, but rather exhibits a concrete freshness of the soul's life. It appears in the sensuous, actual world, as incarnate spirit and spiritualized sense —in a unity which owed its origin to spirit. Greece presents to us the cheerful aspect of youthful freshness, of spiritual vitality. It is here first that advancing spirit makes *itself* the content of its volition and its knowledge; but in such a way that state, family, law, religion, are at the same time objects aimed at by individuality, while the latter *is* individuality only in virtue of those aims. The man, on the other hand, devotes his life to labor for an objective aim; which he pursues consistently, even at the cost of his individuality.

The highest form that floated before Greek imagination was Achilles, the son of the poet, the Homeric youth of the Trojan War. Homer is the element in which the Greek world lives, as man does in the air. The Greek life is a truly youthful achievement. Achilles, the ideal youth, of *poetry*, commenced it: Alexander the Great, the ideal youth of *reality*, concluded it. Both appear in contest with Asia. Achilles, as the principal figure in the national expedition of the Greeks against Troy, does not stand at its head, but is subject to the chief of chiefs; he cannot be made the leader without becoming a fantastic untenable conception. On the contrary, the second youth, Alexander, the freest and finest individuality that the real world has ever produced, advances to the head of this youthful life that has now perfected itself, and accomplishes the revenge against Asia.

We have, then, to distinguish three periods in Greek history: the first, that of the growth of real individuality; the second, that of its independence and prosperity in external conquest (through contact with the previous world-historical people); and the third, the period of its decline and fall, in its encounter with the succeeding organ of world-history. The period from its origin to its internal completeness (that which enables a people to make head against its predecessor) includes its primary culture. If the nation has a basis—such as the Greek world has in the Oriental—a foreign culture enters as an element into its primary condition, and it has a double culture, one original, the other of foreign suggestion. The uniting of these two elements constitutes its training; and the first period ends with the combination of its forces to produce its real and proper vigour, which then turns against the very element that had been its basis. The second period is that of victory and prosperity. But while the nation directs its energies outwards, it becomes unfaithful to its principles at home, and internal dissension follows upon the ceasing of the external excitement. In art and science, too, this shows itself in the separation of the ideal from the real. Here is the point of decline. The third period is that of ruin, through contact with the nation that embodies a higher spirit. The same process, it may be stated once for all, will meet us in the life of every world-historical people.

Section I

THE ELEMENTS OF THE GREEK SPIRIT

Greece is the substantial, which is at the same time *individual*. The universal, as such, is overcome; the submersion in nature no longer exists, and consentaneously the unwieldy character of *geographical* relations has also vanished. The country now under consideration is a section of territory spreading itself in various forms through the sea—a multitude of islands, and a continent which itself exhibits insular features. The Peloponnesus is connected with the continent only by a narrow isthmus: the whole of Greece is indented by bays in numberless shapes. The partition into small divisions of territory is the universal characteristic, while at the same time, the relationship and connection between them is facilitated by the sea. We find here mountains, plains, valleys, and streams of limited extent: no great river, no absolute valley-plain presents itself; but the ground is diversified by mountains and rivers in such a way as to allow no prominence to a single massive feature. We see no such display of physical grandeur as is exhibited in the East, no stream such as the Ganges, the Indus, etc., on whose plains a race delivered over to monotony is stimulated to no change, because its horizon always exhibits one unvarying form. On the contrary, that divided and multiform character everywhere prevails which perfectly corresponds with the varied life of Greek races and the versatility of the Greek spirit.

This is the *elementary character* of the spirit of the Greeks, implying the origination of their culture from independent individualities; a condition in which individuals take their own ground, and are not, from the very beginning, patriarchally united by a bond of *nature*, but realize a union through some other medium—through law and custom having the sanction of spirit. For beyond all other nations that of Greece attained its form by *growth*. At the origin of their national unity, separation as a generic feature—inherent *distinctness* of character—is the chief point that has to be considered. The first phase in the subjugation of this, constitutes the primary period of Greek culture; and only through such distinctness of character, and such a subjugation of it, was the beautiful free Greek spirit produced. Of this principle we must have a clear conception. It is a superficial and absurd idea that such a beautiful and truly free life can be produced by a process so incomplex as the development of a race keeping within the limits of blood-relationship and friendship. Even the plant, which supplies the nearest analogy to such a calm, homogeneous unfolding, lives and grows only by means of the antithetic activities of light, air, and water. The only real antithesis

that spirit can have, is itself spiritual: *viz.*, its inherent heterogeneity, through which alone it acquires the power of realizing itself as spirit. The history of Greece exhibits at its commencement this interchange and mixture of partly homesprung, partly quite foreign stocks; and it was Attica itself, whose people was destined to attain the acme of Hellenic bloom, that was the asylum of the most various stocks and families. Every world-historical people, except the Asiatic kingdoms, which stands detached from the grand historical *catena,* has been formed in this way. Thus the Greeks, like the Romans, developed themselves from a *colluvies*—a conflux of the most various nations. Of the multitude of tribes which we meet in Greece, we cannot say which was the original Greek people, and which immigrated from foreign lands and distant parts of the globe; for the period of which we speak belongs entirely to the unhistorical and obscure. The *Pelasgi* were at that time a principal race in Greece. The most various attempts have been made by the learned to harmonize the confused and contradictory account which we have respecting them, a hazy and obscure period being a special object and stimulus to erudition. Remarkable as the earliest centres of incipient culture are Thrace, the native land of Orpheus, and Thessaly; countries which at a later date retreated more or less into the background. From Phthiotis, the country of Achilles, proceeds the common name *Hellenes*—a name which, as Thucydides remarks, presents itself as little in Homer in this comprehensive sense, as the term *Barbarians*, from whom the Greeks were not yet clearly distinguished. It must be left to special history to trace the several tribes, and their transformations. In general we may assume, that the tribes and individuals were prone to leave their country when too great a population occupied it, and that consequently these tribes were in a migratory condition, and practised mutual depredation. "Even now," says the discerning Thucydides, "the Ozolian Locrians, the Ætolians, and Acarnanians retain their ancient mode of life; the custom of carrying weapons, too, has maintained itself among them as a relic of their ancient predatory habits." Respecting the Athenians, he says that they were the first who laid aside arms in time of peace. In such a state of things agriculture was not pursued; the inhabitants had not only to defend themselves against freebooters, but also to contend with wild beasts (even in Herodotus's time many lions infested the banks of the Nestus and Achelous); at a later time tame cattle became especially an object of plunder, and even after agriculture had become more general, men were still entrapped and sold for slaves. In depicting this original condition of Greece, Thucydides goes still further into detail.

Greece, then, was in this state of turbulence, insecurity, and rapine, and its tribes were continually migrating.

The other element in which the national life of the Hellenes was versed, was the *sea*. The physique of their country led them to this amphibious existence, and allowed them to skim freely over the waves, as they spread themselves freely over the land—not roving about like the nomad populations, nor torpidly vegetating like those of the river districts. Piracy, not trade, was the chief object of maritime occupations; and, as we gather from Homer, it was not yet reckoned discreditable. The suppression of piracy is ascribed to Minos, and Crete is renowned as the land where security was first enjoyed; for there the state of things which we meet with again in Sparta was early realized, *viz.*, the establishment in power of one party, and the subjugation of the other, which was compelled to obey and work for the former.

We have just spoken of heterogeneity as an element of the Greek spirit, and it is well known that the rudiments of Greek civilization are connected with the advent of foreigners. This origin of their moral life the Greeks have preserved, with grateful recollection, in a form of recognition which we may call mythological. In their mythology we have a definite record of the introduction of agriculture by Triptolemus, who was instructed by Ceres, and of the institution of marriage, etc. Prometheus, whose origin is referred to the distant Caucasus, is celebrated as having first taught men the production and the use of fire. The introduction of iron was likewise of great importance to the Greeks; and while Homer speaks only of bronze, Æschylus calls iron "Scythian." The introduction of the olive, of the art of spinning and weaving, and the creation of the horse by Poseidon, belong to the same category.

More historical than these rudiments of culture is the alleged arrival of *foreigners;* tradition tells us how the various states were founded by such foreigners. Thus, Athens owes its origin to Cecrops, an Egyptian, whose history, however, is involved in obscurity. The race of Deucalion, the son of Prometheus, is brought into connection with the various Greek tribes. Pelops of Phrygia, the son of Tantalus, is also mentioned; next, Danaus, from Egypt: from him

descend Acrisius, Danæ, and Perseus. Pelops is said to have brought great wealth with him to the Peloponnesus, and to have acquired great respect and power there. Danaus settled in Argos. Especially important is the arrival of Cadmus, of Phœnician origin, with whom phonetic writing is said to have been introduced into Greece; Herodotus refers it to Phœnicia, and ancient inscriptions then extant are cited to support the assertion. Cadmus, according to the legend, founded Thebes.

We thus observe a colonization by civilized peoples, who were in advance of the Greeks in point of culture: though we cannot compare this colonization with that of the English in North America, for the latter have not been blended with the aborigines, but have dispossessed them; whereas in the case of the settlers in Greece the adventitious and autochthonic elements were mixed together. The date assigned to the arrival of these colonists is very remote—the fourteenth and fifteenth century before Christ. Cadmus is said to have founded Thebes about 1490 B.C., a date with which the Exodus of Moses from Egypt (1500 B.C.) nearly coincides. Amphictyon is also mentioned among the founders of Greek institutions; he is said to have established at Thermopylæ a union between many small tribes of Hellas proper and Thessaly—a combination with which the great Amphictyonic league is said to have originated.

These foreigners, then, are reputed to have established fixed *centres* in Greece by the erection of fortresses and the founding of royal houses. In Argolis, the walls of which the ancient fortresses consisted, were called Cyclopian; some of them have been discovered even in recent times, since, on account of their solidity, they are indestructible.

These walls consist partly of irregular blocks, whose interstices are filled up with small stones —partly of masses of stones carefully fitted into each other. Such walls are those of Tiryns and Mycenæ. Even now the gate with the lions, at Mycenæ, can be recognized by the description of Pausanias. It is stated of Prœtus, who ruled in Argos, that he brought with him from Lycia the Cyclopes who built these walls. It is, however, supposed that they were erected by the ancient Pelasgi. To the fortresses protected by such walls the princes of the heroic times generally attached their dwellings. Especially remarkable are the treasure-houses built by them, such as the Treasure-house of Minyas at Orchomenus, and that of Atreus at Mycenæ. These fortresses, then, were the nuclei of small states;

they gave a greater security to agriculture; they protected commercial intercourse against robbery. They were, however, as Thucydides informs us, not placed in the immediate vicinity of the sea, on account of piracy; maritime towns being of later date. Thus with those royal abodes originated the firm establishment of society. The relation of princes to subjects, and to each other, we learn best from Homer. It did not depend on a state of things established by law, but on superiority in riches, possessions, martial accoutrements, personal bravery, pre-eminence in insight and wisdom, and lastly, on descent and ancestry; for the princes, as heroes, were regarded as of a higher race. Their subjects obeyed them, not as distinguished from them by conditions of caste, nor as in a state of serfdom, nor in the patriarchal relation—according to which the chief is only the head of the tribe or family to which all belong—nor yet as the result of the express necessity for a constitutional government; but only from the need, universally felt, of being held together, and of obeying a ruler accustomed to command—without envy and ill-will towards him. The prince has just so much personal authority as he possesses the ability to acquire and to assert; but as this superiority is only the individually heroic, resting on personal merit, it does not continue long. Thus in Homer we see the suitors of Penelope taking possession of the property of the absent Ulysses, without showing the slightest respect to his son. Achilles, in his inquiries about his father, when Ulysses descends to Hades, indicates the supposition that, as he is old, he will be no longer honoured. Manners are still very simple: princes prepare their own repasts; and Ulysses labours at the construction of his own house. In Homer's *Iliad,* we find a king of kings, a generalissimo in the great national undertaking, but the other magnates environ him as a freely deliberating council; the prince is honoured, but he is obliged to arrange everything to the satisfaction of the others; he indulges in violent conduct towards Achilles, but, in revenge, the latter withdraws from the struggle. Equally lax is the relation of the several chiefs to the people at large, among whom there are always individuals who claim attention and respect. The various peoples do not fight as mercenaries of the prince in his battles, nor as a stupid serf-like herd driven to the contest, nor yet in their own interest; but as the companions of their honored chieftain, as witnesses of his exploits, and his defenders in peril. A perfect resemblance to these relations is also presented in the Greek Pantheon. Zeus is the father of the gods, but each one of them has his own will; Zeus respects them, and they him: he may sometimes scold and threaten them, and they then allow his will to prevail or retreat grumbling; but they do not permit matters to come to an extremity, and Zeus so arranges matters on the whole—by making this concession to one, that to another—as to produce satisfaction. In the terrestrial, as well as in the Olympian world, there is, therefore, only a lax bond of unity maintained; royalty has not yet become monarchy, for it is only in a more extensive society that the need of the latter is felt.

While this state of things prevailed, and social relations were such as have been described, that striking and great event took place—the union of the whole of Greece in a national undertaking, *viz.,* the *Trojan War;* with which began that more extensive connection with Asia which had very important results for the Greeks. (The expedition of Jason to Colchis, also mentioned by the poets, and which bears an earlier date, was, as compared with the war of Troy, a very limited and isolated undertaking.) The occasion of that united expedition is said to have been the violation of the laws of hospitality by the son of an Asiatic prince, in carrying off the wife of his host. Agamemnon assembles the princes of Greece through the power and influence which he possesses. Thucydides ascribes his authority to his hereditary sovereignty, combined with naval power (*Iliad,* ii. 108), in which he was far superior to the rest. It appears, however, that the combination was effected without external compulsion, and that the whole armament was convened simply on the strength of individual consent. The Hellenes were then brought to act unitedly, to an extent of which there is no subsequent example. The result of their exertions was the conquest and destruction of Troy, though they had no design of making it a permanent possession. No external result, therefore, in the way of settlement ensued, any more than an enduring political union, as the effect of the uniting of the nation in the accomplishment of this single achievement. But the poet supplied an imperishable portraiture of their youth and of their national spirit, to the imagination of the Greek people; and the picture of this beautiful human heroism hovered as a directing ideal before their whole development and culture. So likewise, in the *middle ages,* we see the whole of Christendom united to attain one object—the conquest of the Holy Sepulchre; but, in spite of all the victories achieved, with just as little permanent result.

The Crusades are the Trojan War of newly awakened Christendom, waged against the simple, homogeneous clearness of Mohammedanism.

The royal houses perished, partly as the consequence of particular atrocities, partly through gradual extinction. There was no strictly moral bond connecting them with the tribes which they governed. The same relative position is occupied by the people and the royal houses in the Greek tragedy also. The people is the chorus—passive, deedless: the heroes perform the deeds, and incur the consequent responsibility. There is nothing in common between them; the people have no directing power, but only appeal to the gods. Such heroic personalities as those of the princes in question are so remarkably suited for subjects of dramatic art on this very account that they form their resolutions independently, and individually, and are not guided by universal laws binding on every citizen; their conduct and their ruin are individual. The people appears separated from the royal houses, and these are regarded as an alien body, a higher race, fighting out the battles and undergoing the penalties of their fate, for themselves alone. Royalty having performed that which it had to perform, thereby rendered itself superfluous. The several dynasties are the agents of their own destruction, or perish not as the result of animosity, or of struggles on the side of the people: rather the families of the sovereigns are left in calm enjoyment of their power—a proof that the democratic government which followed is not regarded as something absolutely diverse. How sharply do the annals of other times contrast with this!

This fall of the royal houses occurs after the Trojan War, and many changes now present themselves. The Peloponnesus was conquered by the Heraclidæ, who introduced a calmer state of things, which was not again interrupted by the incessant migrations of races. The history now becomes more obscure; and though the several occurrences of the Trojan War are very circumstantially described to us, we are uncertain respecting the important transactions of the time immediately following, for a space of many centuries. No united undertaking distinguishes them, unless we regard as such that of which Thucydides speaks, viz., the war between the Chalcidians and Eretrians in Eubœa, in which many nations took part. The towns vegetate in isolation, or at most distinguish themselves by war with their neighbors. Yet, they enjoy prosperity in this isolated condition, by means of trade; a kind of progress to which their being rent by many party-struggles offers no opposition. In the same way, we observe in the middle ages the towns of Italy—which, both internally and externally, were engaged in continual struggle—attaining so high a degree of prosperity. The flourishing state of the Greek towns at that time is proved, according to Thucydides, also by the colonies sent out in every direction. Thus, Athens colonized Ionia and several islands; and colonies from the Peloponnesus settled in Italy and Sicily. Colonies, on the other hand, became relatively mother states; e.g., Miletus, which founded many cities on the Propontis and the Black Sea. This sending out of colonies, especially during the period between the Trojan War and Cyrus, presents us with a remarkable phenomenon. It can be thus explained. In the several towns the people had the governmental power in their hands, since they gave the final decision in political affairs. In consequence of the long repose enjoyed by them, the population and the development of the community advanced rapidly; and the immediate result was the amassing of great riches, contemporaneously with which fact great want and poverty make their appearance. Industry, in our sense, did not exist; and the lands were soon occupied. Nevertheless a part of the poorer classes would not submit to the degradations of poverty, for everyone felt himself a free citizen. The only expedient, therefore, that remained, was colonization. In another country, those who suffered distress in their own might seek a free soil and gain a living as free citizens by its cultivation. Colonization thus became a means of maintaining some degree of equality among the citizens; but this means is only a palliative, and the original inequality, founded on the difference of property, immediately reappears. The old passions were rekindled with fresh violence, and riches were soon made use of for securing power: thus "tyrants" gained ascendancy in the cities of Greece. Thucydides says, "When Greece increased in riches, tyrants arose in the cities, and the Greeks devoted themselves more zealously to the sea." At the time of Cyrus, the history of Greece acquires its peculiar interest; we see the various states now displaying their particular character. This is the date, too, of the formation of the distinct Greek spirit. Religion and political institutions are developed with it, and it is these important phases of national life which must now occupy our attention.

In tracing up the rudiments of *Greek culture*, we first recall attention to the fact, that the physical condition of the country does not exhibit such a characteristic unity, such a uniform mass, as to exercise a powerful influence over the inhabitants. On the contrary, it is diversified, and produces no decided impression. Nor have we here the unwieldy unity of a family or national combination; but, in the presence of scenery and displays of elemental power broken up into fragmentary forms, men's attention is more largely directed to themselves, and to the extension of their immature capabilities. Thus we see the Greeks, divided and separated from each other, thrown back upon their inner spirit and personal energy, yet at the same time most variously excited and cautiously circumspect. We behold them quite undetermined and irresolute in the presence of nature, dependent on its contingencies, and listening anxiously to each signal from the external world; but, on the other hand, intelligently taking cognizance of and appropriating that outward existence, and showing boldness and independent vigour in contending with it. These are the simple elements of their culture and religion. In tracing up their mythological conceptions, we find natural objects forming the basis—not *en masse,* however; only in dissevered forms. The Diana of Ephesus (that is, nature as the universal mother), the Cybele and Astarte of Syria—such comprehensive conceptions remained Asiatic, and were not transmitted to Greece. For the Greeks only *watch* the objects of nature, and form *surmises* respecting them; inquiring, in the depth of their souls, for the hidden meaning. According to Aristotle's dictum, that philosophy proceeds from wonder, the Greek view of nature also proceeds from wonder of this kind. Not that in their experience, spirit meets something extraordinary, which it compares with the common order of things; for the intelligent view of a regular course of nature, and the reference of phenomena to that standard, do not yet present themselves; but the Greek spirit was excited to wonder at the *natural* in nature. It does not maintain the position of stupid indifference to it as something existing, and there an end of it; but regards it as something in the first instance foreign, in which, however, it has a presentiment of confidence, and the belief that it bears something within it which is friendly to the human spirit, and to which it may be permitted to sustain a positive relation. This *wonder,* and this *presentiment,* are here the fundamental categories; though the Hellenes did not content themselves with these moods of feelings but projected the hidden meaning, which was the

subject of the surmise, into a distinct conception as an object of consciousness. The natural holds its place in their minds only after undergoing some transformation by spirit—not immediately. Man regards nature only as an excitement to his faculties, and only the spiritual which he has evolved from it can have any influence over him. Nor is this commencement of the spiritual apprehension of nature to be regarded as an explanation suggested by *us;* it meets us in a multitude of conceptions formed by the Greeks themselves. The position of curious surmise, of attentive eagerness to catch the meaning of nature, is indicated to us in the comprehensive idea of *Pan.* To the Greeks, Pan did not represent the *objective* whole, but that indefinite neutral ground which involves the element of the *subjective;* he embodies that thrill which pervades us in the silence of the forests; he was, therefore, especially worshipped in sylvan Arcadia: (a "panic terror" is the common expression for a groundless fright). Pan, this thrill-exciting being, is also represented as playing on the flute; we have not the bare internal presentiment, for Pan makes himself audible on the seven-reeded pipe. In what has been stated we have, on the one hand, the indefinite, which, however, holds communication with man; on the other hand, the fact that such communication is only a subjective imagining, an explanation furnished by the percipient himself. On the same principle the Greeks listened to the murmuring of the fountains, and asked what might be thereby signified; but the signification which they were led to attach to it was not the objective meaning of the fountain, but the subjective—that of the subject itself, which further exalts the Naiad to a Muse. The naiads, or fountains, are the external, objective origin of the Muses. Yet the immortal songs of the Muses are not that which is heard in the murmuring of the fountains; they are the productions of the thoughtfully listening spirit, *creative* while *observant.* The interpretation and explanation of nature and its transformations, the indication of their sense and import, is the act of the subjective spirit; and to this the Greeks attached the name μαντεία. The general idea which this embodies, is the form in which man realizes his relationship to nature. Μαντεία has reference both to the matter of the exposition and to the expounder who divines the weighty import in question. Plato speaks of it in reference to dreams, and to that delirium into which men fall during sickness; an interpreter, μάντις, is wanted to explain these dreams and this delirium. That nature answered the questions which the Greek put to her, is in this converse sense true, that he obtained an answer to the questions of nature from his own spirit. The insight of the seer becomes thereby purely poetical; spirit supplies the signification which the natural image expresses. Everywhere the Greeks desired a clear presentation and interpretation of the natural. Homer tells us, in the last book of the *Odyssey,* that while the Greeks were overwhelmed with sorrow for Achilles, a violent agitation came over the sea: the Greeks were on the point of dispersing in terror, when the experienced Nestor arose and interpreted the phenomenon to them. Thetis, he said, was coming, with her nymphs, to lament for the death of her son. When a pestilence broke out in the camp of the Greeks, the priest, Calchas, explained that Apollo was incensed at their not having restored the daughter of his priest Chryses when a ransom had been offered. The oracle was originally interpreted exactly in this way. The oldest oracle was at Dodona, (in the district of the modern Janina). Herodotus says that the first priestesses of the temple there, were from Egypt; yet this temple is stated to be an ancient Greek one. The rustling of the leaves of the sacred oaks was the form of prognostication there. Bowls of metal were also suspended in the grove. But the sounds of the bowls dashing against each other were quite indefinite, and had no objective sense; the sense, the signification, was imparted to the sounds only by the human beings who heard them. Thus also the Delphic priestesses, in a senseless, distracted state, in the intoxication of enthusiasm ($\mu\alpha\nu\iota\alpha$), uttered unintelligible sounds; and it was the $\mu\alpha\nu\tau\iota\varsigma$ who gave to these utterances a definite meaning. In the cave of Trophonius the noise of subterranean waters was heard, and apparitions were seen: but these indefinite phenomena acquired a meaning only through the interpreting, comprehending spirit. It must also be observed, that these excitements of spirit are in the first instance external, natural impulses. Succeeding them are internal changes taking place in the human being himself—such as dreams, or the delirium of the Delphic priestess—which require to be made intelligible by the $\mu\alpha\nu\tau\iota\varsigma$. At the commencement of the *Iliad,* Achilles is excited against Agamemnon, and is on the point of drawing his sword; but on a sudden he checks the movement of his arm, and recollects himself in his wrath, reflecting on his relation to Agamemnon. The poet explains this by saying that it was Pallas-Athene (wisdom or consideration)

that restrained him. When Ulysses among the Phæacians, has thrown his discus farther than the rest, and one of the Phæacians shows a friendly disposition towards him, the poet recognizes in him Pallas-Athene. Such an explanation denotes the perception of the inner meaning, the sense, the underlying truth; and the poets were in this way the teachers of the Greeks —especially Homer. $M\alpha\nu\tau\epsilon\iota\alpha$ in fact is poesy, not a capricious indulgence of fancy, but an imagination which introduces the spiritual into the natural—in short, a richly intelligent perception. The Greek spirit, on the whole, therefore, is free from superstition, since it changes the *sensuous* into the *sensible*—the intellectual, so that decisions are derived from spirit; although superstition comes in again from another quarter, as will be observed when impulsions from another source than the spiritual, are allowed to tell upon opinion and action.

But the stimuli that operated on the spirit of the Greeks are not to be limited to these objective and subjective excitements. The traditional element derived from foreign countries, the culture, the divinities and ritual observances transmitted to them *ab extra* must also be included. It has been long a much vexed question whether the arts and the religion of the Greeks were developed independently or through foreign suggestion. Under the conduct of a one-sided understanding the controversy is interminable; for it is no less a fact of history that the Greeks derived conceptions from India, Syria, and Egypt, than that the Greek conceptions are peculiar to themselves, and those others alien. Herodotus (II. 53) asserts, with equal decision, that *"Homer and Hesiod invented a theogony for the Greeks,* and assigned to the gods their appropriate epithets" (a most weighty sentence, which has been the subject of deep investigation, especially by Creuzer), and in another place, that Greece took the names of its divinities from Egypt, and that the Greeks made inquiry at Dodona, whether they ought to adopt these names or not. This appears self-contradictory: it is, however, quite consistent; for the fact is that the Greeks evolved the spiritual from the materials which they had received. The natural, as *explained* by man—*i.e.,* its internal essential element—is, as a universal principle, the beginning of the divine. Just as in art the Greeks may have acquired a mastery of technical matters from others, from the Egyptians especially, so in their religion the commencement might have been from without; but by their independent spirit they transformed the one as well as the other.

Traces of such foreign rudiments may be generally discovered, (Créuzer, in his *Symbolik*, dwells especially on this point). The amours of Zeus appear indeed as something isolated, extraneous, adventitious, but it may be shown that foreign theogonic representations form their basis. Hercules is, among the Hellenes, that spiritual humanity which by native energy attains Olympus through the twelve far-famed labours: but the foreign idea that lies at the basis is the sun, completing its revolution through the twelve signs of the zodiac. The mysteries were only such ancient rudiments, and certainly contained no greater wisdom than already existed in the consciousness of the Greeks. All Athenians were initiated in the mysteries—Socrates excepted, who refused initiation, because he knew well that science and art are not the product of mysteries, and that wisdom never lies among arcana. True science has its place much rather in the open field of consciousness.

In summing up the constituents of the *Greek spirit,* we find its fundamental characteristic to be that the freedom of spirit is conditioned by and has an essential relation to some stimulus supplied by nature. Greek freedom of thought is excited by an alien existence; but it is free because it transforms and virtually reproduces the stimulus by its own operation. This phase of spirit is the medium between the loss of individuality on the part of man (such as we observe in the Asiatic principle, in which the spiritual and divine exists only under a natural form), and infinite subjectivity as pure certainty of itself—the position that the ego is the ground of all that can lay claim to substantial existence. The Greek spirit as the medium between these two, begins with nature, but transforms it into a mere objective form of its (spirit's) own existence; spirituality is therefore not yet absolutely free; not yet absolutely *self*-produced— is not self-stimulation. Setting out from surmise and wonder, the Greek spirit advances to definite conceptions of the hidden meanings of nature. In the subject itself too, the same harmony is produced. In man, the side of his subjective existence which he owes to nature is the heart, the disposition, passion, and variety of temperament: this side is then developed in a spiritual direction to free individuality; so that the character is not placed in a relation to universally valid moral authorities, assuming the form of duties, but the moral appears as a nature peculiar to the individual—an exertion of will, the result of disposition and individual constitution.

This stamps the Greek character as that of *individuality conditioned by beauty,* which is produced by spirit, transforming the merely natural into an expression of its own being. The activity of spirit does not yet possess in itself the material and organ of expression, but needs the excitement of nature and the matter which nature supplies: it is not free, self-determining spirituality, but mere naturalness formed to spirituality—spiritual individuality. The Greek spirit is the plastic artist, forming the stone into a work of art. In this formative process the stone does not remain mere stone—the form being only superinduced from without; but it is made an expression of the spiritual, even contrary to its nature, and thus *trans*formed. Conversely, the artist *needs* for his spiritual conceptions, stone, colours, sensuous forms to express his idea. Without such an element he can no more be conscious of the idea himself, than give it an objective form for the contemplation of others; since it cannot in thought alone become an object to him. The Egyptian spirit also was a similar labourer in matter, but the natural had not yet been subjected to the spiritual. No advance was made beyond a struggle and contest with it; the natural still took an independent position and formed one side of the image, as in the body of the Sphinx. In Greek beauty the sensuous is only a sign, an expression, an envelope, in which spirit manifests itself.

It must be added, that while the Greek spirit is a transforming artist of this kind, it knows itself free in its productions; for it is their creator, and they are what is called the "work of man." They are, however, not merely this, but eternal truth—the energizing of spirit in its innate essence, and quite as really not created as created by man. He has a respect and veneration for these conceptions and images—this Olympian Zeus, this Pallas of the Acropolis—and in the same way for the laws, political and ethical, that guide his actions. But he, the human being, is the womb that conceived them, he the breast that suckled them, he the spiritual to which their grandeur and purity are owing. Thus he feels himself calm in contemplating them, and not only free in himself, but possessing the consciousness of his freedom; thus the honour of the human is swallowed up in the worship of the divine. Men honour the divine in and for itself, but at the same time as their deed, their production, their phenomenal existence; thus the divine receives its honour through the respect paid to the human, and the human in virtue of the honour paid to the divine.

Such are the qualities of that *beautiful individuality*, which constitutes the centre of the Greek character. We must now consider the several radiations which this idea throws out in realizing itself. All issue in works of art, and we may arrange under three heads: the *subjective* work of art, that is, the culture of the man himself; the *objective* work of art, *i.e.*, the shaping of the world of divinities; lastly, the *political* work of art, the form of the Constitution, and the relations of the individuals who compose it.

Section II

PHASES OF INDIVIDUALITY ÆSTHETICALLY CONDITIONED

Chapter 1. *The Subjective Work of Art*

Man with his necessities sustains a practical relation to external nature, and in making it satisfy his desires, and thus using it up, has recourse to a system of *means*. For natural objects are powerful and offer resistance in various ways. In order to subdue them, man introduces other natural agents; thus turns nature against itself, and invents *instruments* for this purpose. These human inventions belong to spirit, and such an instrument is to be respected more than a mere natural object. We see, too, that the Greeks are accustomed to set an especial value upon them, for in Homer, man's delight in them appears in a very striking way. In the notice of Agamemnon's sceptre, its origin is given in detail: mention is made of doors which turn on hinges, and of accoutrements and furniture, in a way that expresses satisfaction. The honour of human invention in subjugating nature is ascribed to the gods.

But, on the other hand, man uses nature for *ornament*, which is intended only as a token of wealth and of that which man has made of himself. We find ornament, in this interest, already very much developed among the Homeric Greeks. It is true that both barbarians and civilized nations ornament themselves; but barbarians content themselves with mere ornament; they intend their persons to please by an *external* addition. But ornament by its very nature is destined only to beautify something other than itself, *viz.*, the human body, which is man's immediate environment, and which, in common with nature at large, he has to transform. The spiritual interest of primary importance is, therefore, the development of the body to a perfect organ for the will—an adaptation which may, on the one hand, itself be the means for ulterior objects, and, on the other hand, appear as an object *per se*. Among the Greeks, then, we find this boundless impulse of individuals to *display themselves*, and to find their enjoyment in so doing. Sensuous enjoyment does not become the basis of their condition when a state of repose has been obtained, any more than the dependence and stupor of superstition which enjoyment entails. They are too powerfully excited, too much bent upon developing their individuality, absolutely to adore nature, as it manifests itself in its aspects of power and beneficence. That peaceful condition which ensued when a predatory life had been relinquished, and liberal nature had afforded security and leisure, turned their energies in the direction of self-assertion— the effort to dignify themselves. But while, on the one side, they have too much independent personality to be subjugated by superstition, that sentiment has not gone to the extent of making them *vain;* on the contrary, essential conditions must be first satisfied, before this can become a matter of vanity with them. The exhilarating sense of personality, in contrast with sensuous subjection to nature, and the need, not of mere pleasure, but of the display of individual powers, in order thereby to gain special distinction and consequent enjoyment, constitute therefore the chief characteristic and principal occupation of the Greeks. Free as the bird singing in the sky, the individual only expresses what lies in his untrammelled human nature to have his importance recognized. This is the *subjective* beginning of Greek art, in which the human being elaborates his physical being, in free, beautiful movement and agile vigour, to a work of art. The Greeks first trained their own persons to beautiful configurations before they attempted the expression of such in marble and in paintings. The innocuous contests of *games,* in which every one exhibits his powers, is of very ancient date. Homer gives a noble description of the games conducted by Achilles, in honour of Patroclus; but in all his poems there is no notice of statues of the gods, though he mentions the sanctuary at Dodona, and the treasure-house of Apollo at Delphi. The games in Homer consist in wrestling and boxing, running, horse and chariot races, throwing the discus or javelin, and archery. With these exercises are united dance and song, to express and form part of the enjoyment of social exhilaration, and which arts likewise blossomed into beauty. On the shield of Achilles, Hephæstus represents, among other things, how beautiful youths and maidens move as quickly "with well-taught feet," as the potter turns his wheel. The multitude stand round enjoying the spectacle; the divine singer accompanies the song with the harp, and two chief dancers perform their evolutions in the centre of the circle.

These games and æsthetic displays, with the pleasures and honours that accompanied them, were at the outset only private, originating in particular occasions; but in the sequel they became an affair of the nation, and were fixed for certain times at appointed places. Besides the Olympic games in the sacred district of Elis, there were also held the Isthmian, the Pythian, and Nemean, at other places.

If we look at the inner nature of these sports, we shall first observe how sport itself is opposed to serious business, to dependence and need. This wrestling, running, contending was no serious affair; bespoke no obligation of defence, no necessity of combat. Serious occupation is labour that has reference to some want. I or nature must succumb; if the one is to continue, the other must fall. In contrast with this kind of seriousness, however, sport presents the higher seriousness; for in it nature is wrought into spirit, and although in these contests the subject has not advanced to the highest grade of serious thought, yet in this exercise of his physical powers, man shows his freedom, viz., that he has transformed his body to an organ of spirit.

Man has immediately in one of his organs, the voice, an element which admits and requires a more extensive purport than the mere sensuous present. We have seen how song is united with the dance, and ministers to it: but, subsequently song makes itself independent, and requires musical instruments to accompany it; it then ceases to be unmeaning, like the modulations of a bird, which may indeed express emotion, but which have no objective import; but it requires an import created by imagination and spirit, and which is then further formed into an objective work of art.

Chapter 2. The Objective Work of Art

If the subject of song as thus developed among the Greeks is made a question, we should say that its essential and absolute purport is religious. We have examined the idea embodied in the Greek spirit; and religion is nothing else than this idea made objective as the essence of being. According to that idea, we shall observe also that the divine involves the vis naturæ only as an element suffering a process of transforma-tion to spiritual power. Of this natural element, as its origin, nothing more remains than the accord of analogy involved in the representation they formed of spiritual power; for the Greeks worshipped God as spiritual. We cannot, therefore, regard the Greek divinity as similar to the Indian—some power of nature for which the human shape supplies only an outward form. The essence is the spiritual itself, and the natural is only the point of departure. But on the other hand, it must be observed, that the divinity of the Greeks is not yet the absolute, free spirit, but spirit in a particular mode, fettered by the limitations of humanity—still dependent as a determinate individuality on external conditions. Individualities, objectively beautiful, are the gods of the Greeks. The divine spirit is here so conditioned as to be not yet regarded as abstract spirit, but has a specialized existence—continues to manifest itself in sense; but so that the sensuous is not its substance, but is only an element of its manifestation. This must be our leading idea in the consideration of the Greek mythology, and we must have our attention fixed upon it so much the more firmly, as—partly through the influence of erudition, which has whelmed essential principles beneath an infinite amount of details, and partly through that destructive analysis which is the work of the abstract understanding—this mythology, together with the more ancient periods of Greek history, has become a region of the greatest intellectual confusion.

In the idea of the Greek spirit we found the two elements, nature and spirit, in such a relation to each other, that nature forms merely the point of departure. This degradation of nature is in the Greek mythology the turning point of the whole—expressed as the war of the gods, the overthrow of the Titans by the race of Zeus. The transition from the Oriental to the Occidental spirit is therein represented, for the Titans are the merely physical, natural existences, from whose grasp sovereignty is wrested. It is true that they continue to be venerated, but not as governing powers; for they are relegated to the verge of the world. The Titans are powers of Nature, Uranus, Gæa, Oceanus, Selene, Helios, etc. Chronos expresses the dominion of abstract time, which devours its children. The unlimited power of reproduction is restrained, and Zeus appears as the head of the new divinities, who embody a spiritual import, and are themselves spirit.[1] It is not possible to express this transition more

[1] See Hegel's Vorles, über die Philos. der Religion, II. p. 102, sqq. (2d edition).

distinctly and naïvely than in this myth; the new dynasty of divinities proclaim their peculiar nature to be of a spiritual order.

The second point is, that the new divinities retain natural elements, and consequently in themselves a determinate relation to the powers of nature, as was previously shown. Zeus has his lightnings and clouds, and Hera is the creatress of the *natural*, the producer of crescent vitality. Zeus is also the political god, the protector of morals and of hospitality. Oceanus, as such, is only the element of nature which his name denotes. Poseidon has still the wildness of that element in his character; but he is also an ethical personage; to him is ascribed the building of walls and the production of the Horse. Helios is the sun as a natural element. This light, according to the analogy of spirit, has been transformed to self-consciousness, and Apollo has proceeded from Helios. The name Λύκειος points to the connection with light; Apollo was a herdsman in the employ of Admetus, but oxen not subjected to the yoke were sacred to Helios: his rays, represented as arrows, kill the python. The idea of light as the natural power constituting the basis of the representation, cannot be dissociated from this divinity; especially as the other predicates attached to it are easily united with it, and the explanations of Müller and others, who deny that basis, are much more arbitary and far-fetched. For Apollo is the prophesying and discerning god—light, that makes everything clear. He is, moreover, the healer and strengthener; as also the destroyer, for he kills men. He is the propitiating and purifying god, *e.g.*, in contravention of the Eumenides, the ancient subterrene divinities, who exact hard, stern justice. He himself is pure; he has no wife, but only a sister, and is not involved in various disgusting adventures, like Zeus; moreover, he is the discerner and declarer, the singer and leader of the dances, as the sun leads the harmonious dance of stars. In like manner, the naiads became the Muses. The mother of the gods, Cybele, continuing to be worshipped at Ephesus as Artemis, is scarcely to be recognized as the Artemis of the Greeks, the chaste huntress and destroyer of wild beasts. Should it be said that this change of the natural into the spiritual is owing to our allegorizing, or that of the later Greeks, we may reply, that this transformation of the natural to the spiritual is the Greek spirit itself. The epigrams of the Greeks exhibit such advances from the sensuous to the spiritual. But the abstract understanding cannot comprehend this blending of the natural with the spiritual.

It must be further observed, that the Greek gods are to be regarded as individualities—not abstractions, like "knowledge," "unity," "time," "heaven," "necessity." Such abstractions do not form the substance of these divinities; they are no allegories, no abstract beings, to which various attributes are attached, like the Horatian *"necessitas clavis trabalibus."* As little are the divinities symbols, for a symbol is only a sign, an adumbration of something else. The Greek gods express of themselves what they are. The eternal repose and clear intelligence that dignifies the head of Apollo, is not a symbol, but the expression in which spirit manifests itself, and shows itself present. The gods are personalities, concrete individualities: an allegorical being has no qualities, but is itself one quality and no more. The gods are, moreover, special characters, since in each of them one peculiarity predominates as the characteristic one; but it would be vain to try to bring this circle of characters into a system. Zeus, perhaps, may be regarded as ruling the other gods, but not with substantial power; so that they are left free to their own idiosyncrasy. Since the whole range of spiritual and moral qualities was appropriated by the gods, the unity, which stood above them all, necessarily remained abstract; it was therefore formless and unmeaning fact—necessity, whose oppressive character arises from the absence of the spiritual in it; whereas the gods hold a friendly relation to men, for they are spiritual natures. That higher thought, the knowledge of unity as God—the One Spirit—lay beyond that grade of thought which the Greeks had attained.

With regard to the *adventitious* and special that attaches to the Greek gods, the question arises, where the external origin of this adventitious element is to be looked for. It arises partly from local characteristics, the scattered condition of the Greeks at the commencement of their national life, fixing as this did on certain points, and consequently introducing local representations. The local divinities stand alone, and occupy a much greater extent than they do afterwards, when they enter into the circle of the divinities, and are reduced to a limited position; they are conditioned by the particular consciousness and circumstances of the countries in which they appear. There are a multitude of Herculeses and Zeuses, that have their local history like the Indian gods, who also at different places possess temples to which a peculiar legend attaches. A similar relation occurs in the case of the Catholic saints and their legends; though here, not the several localities, but the one *Mater Dei* supplies the point of departure, being afterwards localized in the most diversified modes. The Greeks relate the liveliest and most attractive stories of their gods, to which no limit can be assigned, since rich fancies were always gushing forth anew in the living spirit of the Greeks. A second source from which adventitious specialities in the conception of the gods arose is that worship of nature, whose representations retain a place in the Greek myths, as certainly as they appear there also in a regenerated and transfigured condition.

The preservation of the original myths, brings us to the famous chapter of the *"mysteries,"* already mentioned. These mysteries of the Greeks present something which, as unknown, has attracted the curiosity of all times, under the supposition of profound wisdom. It must first be remarked that their antique and primary character, in virtue of its very antiquity, shows their destitution of excellence—their inferiority; that the more refined truths are not expressed in these mysteries, and that the view which many have entertained is incorrect, *viz.,* that the unity of God, in opposition to polytheism, was taught in them. The mysteries were rather antique rituals; and it is as unhistorical as it is foolish to assume that profound philosophical truths are to be found there; since, on the contrary, only natural ideas—ruder conceptions of the metamorphoses occurring everywhere in nature, and of the vital principle that pervades it—were the subjects of those mysteries. If we put together all the historical data pertinent to the question, the result we shall inevitably arrive at will be that the mysteries did not constitute a system of doctrines, but were sensuous ceremonies and exhibitions, consisting of symbols of the universal operations of nature, as, *e.g.,* the relation of the earth to celestial phenomena. The chief basis of the representations of Ceres and Proserpine, Bacchus and his train, was the universal principle of nature; and the accompanying details were obscure stories and representations, mainly bearing on the universal vital force and its metamorphoses. An analogous process to that of nature, spirit has also to undergo; for it must be twice-born, *i.e.,* abnegate itself; and thus the representations given in the mysteries called attention, though only feebly, to the nature of spirit. In the Greeks they produced an emotion of shuddering awe; for an instinctive dread comes over men, when a signification is perceived in a form, which as a sensuous phenomenon does not express that signification, and

which therefore both repels and attracts— awakes surmises by the import that reverberates through the whole, but at the same time a thrill of dread at the repellent form. Æschylus was accused of having profaned the mysteries in his tragedies. The indefinite representations and symbols of the mysteries, in which the profound import is only surmised, are an element alien to the clear pure forms, and threaten them with destruction; on which account the gods of art remain separated from the gods of the mysteries, and the two spheres must be strictly dissociated.

Most of their gods the Greeks received from foreign lands, as Herodotus states expressly with regard to Egypt, but these exotic myths were transformed and spiritualized by the Greeks; and that part of the foreign theogonies which accompanied them, was, in the mouth of the Hellenes, worked up into a legendary narrative which often redounded to the disadvantage of the divinities. Thus also the brutes which continued to rank as gods among the Egyptians were degraded to external signs, accompanying the spiritual god. While they have each an individual character, the Greek gods are also represented as human, and this anthropomorphism is charged as a defect. On the contrary (we may immediately rejoin), man as the spiritual constitutes the element of truth in the Greek gods, which rendered them superior to all elemental deities, and all mere abstractions of the One and Highest Being. On the other side it is alleged as an advantage of the Greek gods that they are represented as men—that being regarded as not the case with the Christian God. Schiller says:

> *While the gods remained more human,*
> *The men were more divine.*

But the Greek gods must not be regarded as more human than the Christian God. Christ is much more a *man:* he lives, dies, suffers death on the cross, which is infinitely more human than the humanity of the Greek idea of the beautiful. But in referring to this common element of the Greek and the Christian religions, it must be said of both that, if a manifestation of God is to be supposed at all, his natural form must be that of spirit, which for sensuous conception is essentially the human; for no other form can lay claim to spirituality. God appears indeed in the sun, in the mountains, in the trees, in everything that has life; but a natural appearance of this kind is not the form proper to spirit: here God is cognizable only in the mind of the percipient. If God himself is to be manifested in a corresponding expression, that can only be the human form: for from this the spiritual beams forth. But if it were asked: Does God *necessarily* manifest himself? The question must be answered in the affirmative; for there is no essential existence that does not manifest itself. The real defect of the Greek religion, as compared with the Christian, is, therefore, that in the former the *manifestation* constitutes the highest mode in which the divine being is conceived to exist—the sum and substance of divinity; while in the Christian religion the manifestation is regarded only as a *temporary phase* of the divine. Here the *manifested* God dies, and elevates himself to glory; only after death is Christ represented as sitting at the right hand of God. The Greek god, on the contrary, exists for his worshippers perennially *in the manifestation*—only in marble, in metal or wood, or as figured by the imagination.

But why did God not appear to the Greeks in the flesh? Because man was not duly estimated, did not obtain honour and dignity, till he had more fully elaborated and developed himself in the attainment of the freedom implicit in the æsthetic manifestation in question; the form and shaping of the divinity therefore continued to be the product of individual views. One element in spirit is that it produces itself—*makes* itself what it is: and the other is that it is originally free—that freedom is its *nature* and its idea. But the Greeks, since they had not attained an intellectual conception of themselves, did not yet realize spirit in its universality, had not the idea of man and the essential unity of the divine and human nature according to the Christian view. Only the self-reliant, truly subjective spirit can bear to dispense with the phenomenal side, and can venture to assign the divine nature to spirit alone. It then no longer needs to inweave the natural into its idea of the spiritual, in order to hold fast its conception of the divine, and to have its unity with the divine, externally visible; but while free thought *thinks* the phenomenal, it is content to leave it as it is; for it also *thinks* that union of the finite and the infinite, and recognizes it not as a mere accidental union, but as the absolute—the eternal idea itself. Since subjectivity was not comprehended in all its depth by the Greek spirit, the true reconciliation was not attained in it, and the human spirit did not yet assert its true position. This defect showed itself in the fact of fate as pure subjectivity appearing superior to the gods; it also shows itself in the fact, that men derive their resolves not yet from themselves, but from their oracles. Neither human nor divine subjectivity,

recognized as infinite, has as yet, absolutely decisive authority.

Chapter 3. *The Political Work of Art*

The state unites the two phases just considered, *viz.*, the subjective and the objective work of art. In the state, spirit is not a mere object, like the deities, nor, on the other hand, is it merely subjectively developed to a beautiful physique. It is here a living, universal spirit, but which is at the same time the self-conscious spirit of the individuals composing the community.

The *democratical* constitution alone was adapted to the spirit and political condition in question. In the East we recognized despotism, developed in magnificent proportions, as a form of government strictly appropriate to the dawn-land of history. Not less adapted is the democratical form in Greece, to the part assigned to it in the same great drama. In Greece, *viz.*, we have the freedom of the individual, but it has not yet advanced to such a degree of abstraction, that the subjective unit is conscious of direct dependence on the substantial principle—the state as such. In this grade of freedom, the individual will is unfettered in the entire range of its vitality, and embodies that substantial principle, according to its particular idiosyncrasy. In Rome, on the other hand, we shall observe a harsh sovereignty dominating over the individual members of the state; as also in the German Empire, a monarchy, in which the individual is connected with and has *devoirs* to perform not only in regard to the monarch, but to the whole monarchical organization.

The democratical state is not patriarchal, does not rest on a still unreflecting, undeveloped confidence, but implies laws, with the consciousness of their being founded on an equitable and moral basis, and the recognition of these laws as positive. At the time of the kings, no political life had as yet made its appearance in Hellas; there are, therefore, only slight traces of legislation. But in the interval from the Trojan War till near the time of Cyrus, its necessity was felt. The first lawgivers are known under the name of The Seven Sages—a title which at that time did not imply any such character as that of the sophists—teachers of wisdom, designedly proclaiming the right and true—but merely thinking men, whose thinking stopped short of science, properly so called. They were *practical* politicians; the good counsels which two of them—Thales of Miletus and Bias of Priene—gave to the Ionian cities, have been already mentioned. Thus Solon was commissioned by the Athenians to give them laws, as those then in operation no longer sufficed. Solon gave the Athenians a constitution by which all obtained equal rights, yet not so as to render the democracy a quite abstract one. The main point in democracy is moral disposition. *Virtue* is the basis of democracy, remarks Montesquieu; and this sentiment is as important as it is true in reference to the idea of democracy commonly entertained. The substance of justice, the common weal, the general interest, is the main consideration; but it is so only as custom, in the form of objective will, so that morality properly so called—subjective conviction and intention—has not yet manifested itself. Law exists, and is in point of substance, the law of freedom—rational and valid *because it is law, i.e.,* without ulterior sanction. As in beauty the natural element—its sensuous coefficient—remains, so also in this customary morality, laws assume the form of a necessity of nature. The Greeks occupy the middle ground of *beauty* and have not yet attained the higher standpoint of truth. While custom and wont is the form in which the right is willed and done, that form is a stable one, and has not yet admitted into it the foe of immediacy—reflection and subjectivity of will. The interests of the community may, therefore, continue to be intrusted to the will and resolve of the citizens, and this must be the basis of the Greek constitution; for no principle has as yet manifested itself, which can contravene such choice conditioned by custom, and hinder its realizing itself in action. The democratic constitution is here the only possible one: the citizens are still unconscious of particular interests, and therefore of a corrupting element: the objective will is in their case not disintegrated. Athene the goddess is Athens itself—*i.e.,* the real and concrete spirit of the citizens. The divinity ceases to inspire their life and conduct, only when the Will has retreated within itself—into the *adytum* of cognition and conscience—and has posited the infinite schism between the subjective and the objective. The above is the true position of the democratic polity; its justification and absolute necessity rest on this still immanent objective morality. For the modern conceptions of democracy this justification cannot be pleaded. These provide that the interests of the community, the affairs of state, shall be discussed and decided by the people; that the individual members of the community shall deliberate, urge their respective opinions, and give their votes; and this on the ground that the interests of the state and its concerns are the interests of such individual members.

All this is very well; but the essential condition and distinction in regard to various phases of democracy is: *What is the character of* these individual members? They are absolutely authorized to assume their position, only in as far as their will is still *objective Will*—not one that wishes this or that, not mere "good" will. For good will is something particular—rests on the morality of individuals, on their conviction and subjective feeling. That very subjective freedom which constitutes the principle and determines the peculiar form of freedom in *our* world, which forms the absolute basis of our political and religious life, could not manifest itself in Greece otherwise than as a *destructive* element. Subjectivity was a grade not greatly in advance of that occupied by the Greek spirit; that phase must of necessity soon be attained: but it plunged the Greek world into ruin, for the polity which that world embodied was not calculated for this side of humanity, did not recognize this phase; since it had not made its appearance when that polity began to exist. Of the Greeks in the first and genuine form of their freedom, we may assert, that they had no conscience; the habit of living for their country without further reflection, was the principle dominant among them. The consideration of the state in the abstract, which to our understanding is the essential point, was alien to them. Their grand object was their country in its living and real aspect —*this actual* Athens, this Sparta, these temples, these altars, this form of social life, this union of fellow-citizens, these manners and customs. To the Greek his country was a necessary of life, without which existence was impossible. It was the Sophists—the "Teachers of Wisdom"—who first introduced subjective reflection, and the new doctrine that each man should act according to his own conviction. When reflection once comes into play, the inquiry is started whether the principles of law cannot be improved. Instead of holding by the existing state of things, *internal* conviction is relied upon; and thus begins a subjective independent freedom, in which the individual finds himself in a position to bring everything to the test of his own conscience, even in defiance of the existing constitution. Each one has his "principles," and that view which accords with his private judgment he regards as *practically* the best, and as claiming practical realization. This decay even Thucydides notices, when he speaks of every one's thinking that things are going on badly when he has not a hand in the management.

To this state of things, in which every one presumes to have a judgment of his own, confidence in great men is antagonistic. When, in earlier times, the Athenians commission Solon to legislate for them, or when Lycurgus appears at Sparta as lawgiver and regulator of the state, it is evidently not supposed that the people in general think that they know best what is politically right. At a later time also, it was distinguished personages of plastic genius in whom the people placed their confidence: Cleisthenes, *e.g.*, who made the constitution still more democratic than it had been—Miltiades, Themistocles, Aristides, and Cimon, who in the Median wars stand at the head of Athenian affairs—and Pericles, in whom Athenian glory centres as in its focus. But as soon as any of these great men had performed what was needed, envy intruded, *i.e.*, the recoil of the sentiment of equality against conspicuous talent, and he was either imprisoned or exiled. Finally, the sycophants arose among the people, aspersing all individual greatness, and reviling those who took the lead in public affairs.

But there are three other points in the condition of the Greek republics that must be particularly observed.

1. With democracy in that form in which alone it existed in Greece, *oracles* are intimately connected. To an independent resolve, a consolidated subjectivity of the will (in which the latter is determined by preponderating reasons) is absolutely indispensable; but the Greeks had not this element of strength and vigour in their volition. When a colony was to be founded, when it was proposed to adopt the worship of foreign deities, or when a general was about to give battle to the enemy, the oracles were consulted. Before the battle of Platæa, Pausanias took care that an augury should be taken from the animals offered in sacrifice, and was informed by the soothsayer Tisamenus that the sacrifices were favorable to the Greeks provided they remained on the hither side of the Asopus, but the contrary, if they crossed the stream and began the battle. Pausanias, therefore, awaited the attack. In their private affairs, too, the Greeks came to a determination not so much from subjective conviction as from some extraneous suggestion. With the advance of democracy we observe the oracles no longer consulted on the most important matters, but the particular views of popular orators influencing and deciding the policy of the state. As at this time Socrates relied upon his "Dæmon," so the popular leaders and the people relied on their individual convictions in forming their decisions. But contemporaneously with this were introduced corruption, disorder, and an unintermitted process of change in the constitution.

2. Another circumstance that demands special attention here, is the element of slavery. This was a necessary condition of an æsthetic democracy, where it was the right and duty of every citizen to deliver or to listen to orations respecting the management of the state in the place of public assembly, to take part in the exercise of the gymnasia, and to join in the celebration of festivals. It was a necessary condition of such occupations, that the citizens should be freed from handicraft occupations; consequently, that what among us is performed by free citizens, the work of daily life, should be done by slaves. Slavery does not cease until the will has been infinitely self-reflected, until right is conceived as appertaining to every freeman, and the term freeman is regarded as a synonym for man in his generic nature as endowed with reason. But here we still occupy the standpoint of morality as mere wont and custom, and therefore known only as a peculiarity attaching to a certain kind of existence.

3. It must also be remarked, thirdly, that such democratic constitutions are possible only in small states, states which do not much exceed the compass of cities. The whole polis of the Athenians is united in the one city of Athens. Tradition tells that Theseus united the scattered Demes into an integral totality. In the time of Pericles, at the beginning of the Peloponnesian War, when the Spartans were marching upon Attica, its entire population took refuge in the city. Only in such cities can the interests of all be similar; in large empires, on the contrary, diverse and conflicting interests are sure to present themselves. The living together in one city, the fact that the inhabitants see each other daily, render a common culture and a *living* democratic polity possible. In democracy, the main point is that the character of the citizen be plastic, all "of a piece." He must be present at the critical stages of public business; he must take part in decisive crises with his entire personality, not with his vote merely; he must mingle in the heat of action—the passion and interest of the whole man being absorbed in the affair, and the warmth with which a resolve was made being equally ardent during its execution. That unity of opinion to which the whole community must be brought must be produced in the individual members of the state by *oratorical suasion*. If this were attempted by *writing*, in an abstract,

lifeless way, no general fervour would be excited among the social units; and the greater the number, the less weight would each individual vote have. In a large empire a general inquiry might be made, votes might be gathered in the several communities, and the results reckoned up—as was done by the French Convention. But a political existence of this kind is destitute of life, and the world is *ipso facto* broken into fragments and dissipated into a mere paper-world. In the French Revolution, therefore, the republican constitution never actually became a democracy: tyranny, despotism, raised its voice under the mask of freedom and equality.

We come now to the second period of Greek History. The first period saw the Greek spirit attain its æsthetic development and reach maturity—realize its *essential being*. The second shows it manifesting itself, exhibits it in its full glory as producing a work for the world, asserting its principle in the struggle with an antagonistic force, and triumphantly maintaining it against that attack.

The Wars with the Persians

The period of contact with the preceding world-historical people, is generally to be regarded as the *second* in the history of any nation. The world-historical contact of the Greeks was with the Persians; in that, Greece exhibited itself in its most glorious aspect. The occasion of the Median wars was the revolt of the Ionian cities against the Persians, in which the Athenians and Eretrians assisted them. That which, in particular, induced the Athenians to take their part, was the circumstance that the son of Pisistratus, after his attempts to regain sovereignty in Athens had failed in Greece, had betaken himself to the king of the Persians. The Father of history has given us a brilliant description of these Median wars, and for the object we are now pursuing we need not dwell long upon them. At the beginning of the Median wars, Lacedæmon was in possession of the hegemony, partly as the result of having subjugated and enslaved the free nation of the Messenians, partly because it had assisted many Greek states to expel their tyrants. Provoked by the part the Greeks had taken in assisting the Ionians against him, the Persian King sent heralds to the Greek cities to require them to give water and earth, *i.e.*, to acknowledge his supremacy. The Persian envoys were contemptuously sent back, and the Lacedæmonians went so far as to throw them into a well—a deed, however, of which they afterwards so deeply repented, as to send two

Lacedæmonians to Susa in expiation. The Persian King then despatched an army to invade Greece. With its vastly superior force the Athenians and Platæans, without aid from their compatriots, contended at Marathon under Miltiades, and gained the victory. Afterwards, Xerxes came down upon Greece with his enormous masses of nations (Herodotus gives a detailed description of this expedition); and with the terrible array of land-forces was associated the not less formidable fleet. Thrace, Macedon, and Thessaly were soon subjugated; but the entrance into Greece proper, the Pass of Thermopylæ, was defended by three hundred Spartans and seven hundred Thespians, whose fate is well known. Athens, voluntarily deserted by its inhabitants, was ravaged; the images of the gods which it contained were "an abomination" to the Persians, who worshipped the amorphous, the unformed. In spite of the disunion of the Greeks, the Persian fleet was beaten at Salamis; and this glorious battle-day presents the three greatest tragedians of Greece in remarkable chronological association: for Æschylus was one of the combatants, and helped to gain the victory, Sophocles danced at the festival that celebrated it, and on the same day Euripides was born. The host that remained in Greece, under the command of Mardonius, was beaten at Platæa by Pausanias, and the Persian power was consequently broken at various points.

Thus was Greece freed from the pressure which threatened to overwhelm it. Greater battles, unquestionably, have been fought; but these live immortal not in the historical records of nations only, but also of science and of art, of the noble and the moral generally. For these are world-historical victories; they were the salvation of culture and spiritual vigour, and they rendered the Asiatic principle powerless. How often, on other occasions, have not men sacrificed everything for one grand object! How often have not warriors fallen for duty and country! But here we are called to admire not only valour, genius and spirit, but the purport of the contest, the effect, the result, which are unique in their kind. In all other battles a particular interest is predominant; but the immortal fame of the Greeks is none other than their due, in consideration of the noble cause for which deliverance was achieved. In the history of the world it is not the formal valour that has been displayed, not the so-called merit of the combatants, but the importance of the cause itself, that must decide the fame of the achievement. In the case before us, the interest of the world's history hung trembling in the balance. Oriental despotism, a world united under one lord and sovereign, on the one side, and separate states, insignificant in extent and resources, but animated by free individuality, on the other side, stood front to front in array of battle. Never in history has the superiority of spiritual power over material bulk, and that of no contemptible amount, been made so gloriously manifest. This war, and the subsequent development of the states which took the lead in it, is the most brilliant period of Greece. Everything which the Greek principle involved, then reached its perfect bloom and came into the light of day.

The Athenians continued their wars of conquest for a considerable time, and thereby attained a high degree of prosperity; while the Lacedæmonians, who had no naval power, remained quiet. The antagonism of Athens and Sparta now commences—a favorite theme for historical treatment. It may be asserted that it is an idle inquiry, which of these two states justly claims the superiority, and that the endeavour should rather be, to exhibit each as in its own department a necessary and worthy phase of the Greek spirit. On Sparta's behalf, e.g., many categories may be referred to in which she displays excellence; strictness in point of morals, subjection to discipline, etc., may be advantageously cited. But the leading principle that characterizes this state is political virtue, which Athens and Sparta have, indeed, in common, but which in the one state developed itself to a work of art, viz., free individuality—in the other retained its substantial form. Before we speak of the Peloponnesian War, in which the jealousy of Sparta and Athens broke out into a flame, we must exhibit more specifically the fundamental character of the two states, their distinctions in a political and moral respect.

Athens

We have already become acquainted with Athens as an asylum for the inhabitants of the other districts of Greece, in which a very mixed population was congregated. The various branches of human industry, agriculture, handicraft, and trade (especially by sea), were united in Athens, but gave occasion to much dissension. An antagonism had early arisen between ancient and wealthy families and such as were poorer. Three parties, whose distinction had been grounded on their local position and the mode of life which that position suggested, were then fully recognized. These were, the Pediæans— inhabitants of the plain, the rich and aristocratic; the Diacrians—mountaineers, cultivators of the vine and olive, and herdsmen, who were the most numerous class; and between the two, the Paralians, inhabitants of the coast, the moderate party. The polity of the state was wavering between aristocracy and democracy. Solon effected, by his division into four property-classes, a medium between these opposites. All these together formed the popular assembly for deliberation and decision on public affairs; but the offices of government were reserved for the three superior classes. It is remarkable that even while Solon was still living and actually present, and in spite of his opposition, Pisistratus acquired supremacy. The constitution had, as it were, not yet entered into the blood and life of the community; it had not yet become the habit of moral and civil existence. But it is still more remarkable that Pisistratus introduced no legislative changes, and that he presented himself before the Areopagus to answer an accusation brought against him. The rule of Pisistratus and of his sons appears to have been needed for repressing the power of great families and factions—for accustoming them to order and peace, and the citizens generally, on the other hand, to the Solonian legislation. This being accomplished, that rule was necessarily regarded as superfluous, and the principles of a free code enter into conflict with the power of the Pisistratidæ. The Pisistratidæ were expelled, Hipparchus killed, and Hippias banished. Then factions were revived; the Alcmæonidæ, who took the lead in the insurrection, favored democracy; on the other hand, the Spartans aided the adverse party of Isagoras, which followed the aristocratic direction. The Alcmæonidæ, with Cleisthenes at their head, kept the upper hand. This leader made the constitution still more democratic than it had been; the φυλαί, of which hitherto there had been only four, were increased to ten, and this had the effect of diminishing the influence of the clans. Lastly, Pericles rendered the constitution yet more democratic by diminishing the essential dignity of the Areopagus, and bringing causes that had hitherto belonged to it, before the demos and the tribunals. Pericles was a statesman of plastic antique character: when he devoted himself to public life, he renounced private life, withdrew from all feasts and banquets, and pursued without intermission his aim of being useful to the state—a course of conduct by which he attained such an exalted position, that Aristophanes calls him the Zeus of Athens. We cannot but admire him in the highest degree: he stood at the head of a light-minded but highly refined and cultivated people; the only means by which he could obtain influence and authority over them, was his personal character and the impression he produced of his being a thoroughly noble man, exclusively intent upon the weal of the state, and of superiority to his fellow-citizens in native genius and acquired knowledge. In force of individual character no statesman can be compared with him.

As a general principle, the democratic constitution affords the widest scope for the development of great political characters; for it excels all others in virtue of the fact that it not only *allows of* the display of their powers on the part of individuals, but *summons* them to use those powers for the general weal. At the same time, no member of the community can obtain influence unless he has the power of satisfying the intellect and judgment, as well as the passions and volatility, of a cultivated people.

In Athens a vital freedom existed, and a vital equality of manners and mental culture; and if inequality of property could not be avoided, it nevertheless did not reach an extreme. Together with this equality, and within the compass of this freedom, all diversities of character and talent, and all variety of idiosyncrasy could assert themselves in the most unrestrained manner, and find the most abundant stimulus to development in its environment; for the predominant elements of Athenian existence were the independence of the social units and a culture animated by the spirit of beauty. It was Pericles who originated the production of those eternal monuments of sculpture, whose scanty remains astonish posterity; it was before this people that the dramas of Æschylus and Sophocles were performed, and later on those of Euripides—which, however, do not exhibit the same plastic moral character, and in which the principle of corruption is more manifest. To this people were addressed the orations of Pericles: from it sprung a band of men whose genius has become classical for all centuries; for to this number belong, besides those already named, Thucydides, Socrates, Plato, and Aristophanes—the last of whom preserved entire the political seriousness of his people at the time when it was being corrupted; and who, imbued with this seriousness, wrote and dramatized with a view to his country's weal. We recognize in the Athenians great industry, susceptibility to excitement, and development of individuality within the sphere of spirit conditioned by the morality of custom. The blame with which we find them visited in Xenophon and Plato, attaches rather to that later period

when misfortune and the corruption of the democracy had already supervened. But if we would have the verdict of the ancients on the political life of Athens, we must turn, not to Xenophon, nor even to Plato, but to those who had a thorough acquaintance with the state in its full vigour, who managed its affairs and have been esteemed its greatest leaders, *i.e.,* to its statesmen. Among these, Pericles is the Zeus of the human Pantheon of Athens. Thucydides puts into his mouth the most profound description of Athenian life, on the occasion of the funeral obsequies of the warriors who fell in the second year of the Peloponnesian War. He proposes to show for what a city and in support of what interests they had died; and this leads the speaker directly to the essential elements of the Athenian community. He goes on to paint the character of Athens, and what he says is most profoundly thoughtful, as well as most just and true. "We love the beautiful," he says, "but without ostentation or extravagance; we philosophize without being seduced thereby into effeminacy and inactivity (for when men give themselves up to thought, they get further and further from the practical—from activity for the public, for the common weal). We are bold and daring; but this courageous energy in action does not prevent us from giving ourselves an account of what we undertake (we have a clear consciousness respecting it); among other nations, on the contrary, martial daring has its basis in deficiency of culture: we know best how to distinguish between the agreeable and the irksome; notwithstanding which, we do not shrink from perils." Thus Athens exhibited the spectacle of a state whose existence was essentially directed to realizing the beautiful, which had a thoroughly cultivated consciousness respecting the serious side of public affairs and the interests of man's spirit and life, and united with that consciousness, hardly courage and practical ability.

Sparta

Here we witness on the other hand rigid abstract virtue—a life devoted to the state, but in which the activity and freedom of individuality are put in the background. The polity of Sparta is based on institutions which do full justice to the interest of the state, but whose object is a lifeless equality—not free movement. The very first steps in Spartan history are very different from the early stages of Athenian development. The Spartans were Dorians—the Athenians, Ionians; and this national distinction has an influence on their constitution also. In reference to the mode in which the Spartan state originated, we observe that the Dorians invaded the Peloponnesus with the Heracleidæ, subdued the indigenous tribes, and condemned them to slavery; for the Helots were doubtless aborigines. The fate that had befallen the Helots, was suffered at a later epoch by the Messenians; for inhuman severity of this order was innate in Spartan character. While the Athenians had a family life, and slaves among them were inmates of the house, the relation of the Spartans to the subjugated race was one of even greater harshness than that of the Turks to the Greeks; a state of warfare was constantly kept up in Lacedæmon. In entering upon office, the Ephors made an unreserved declaration of war against the Helots, and the latter were habitually given up to the younger Spartans to be practised upon in their martial exercises. The Helots were on some occasions set free, and fought against the enemy; moreover, they displayed extraordinary valour in the ranks of the Spartans; but on their return they were butchered in the most cowardly and insidious way. As in a slave-ship the crew are constantly armed, and the greatest care is taken to prevent an insurrection, so the Spartans exercised a constant vigilance over the Helots, and were always in a condition of war, as against enemies.

Property in land was divided, even according to the constitution of Lycurgus (as Plutarch relates) into equal parts, of which 9,000 only belonged to the Spartans—*i.e.*, the inhabitants of the city—and 30,000 to the Lacedæmonians or Periæci. At the same time it was appointed, in order to maintain this equality, that the portions of ground should not be sold. But how little such an institution avails to effect its object, is proved by the fact, that in the sequel Lacedæmon owed its ruin chiefly to the inequality of possessions. As daughters were capable of inheriting, many estates had come by marriage into the possession of a few families, and at last all the landed property was in the hands of a limited number; as if to show how foolish it is to attempt a forced equality—an attempt which, while ineffective in realizing its professed object, is also destructive of a most essential point of liberty, the free disposition of property. Another remarkable feature in the legislation of Lycurgus, is his forbidding all money except that made of iron, an enactment which necessitated the abolition of all foreign business and traffic. The Spartans moreover had no naval force—a force indispensable to the support and furtherance of commerce; and on occasions when such a force was required, they had to apply to the Persians for it.

It was with an especial view to promote similarity of manners, and a more intimate acquaintance of the citizens with each other, that the Spartans had meals in common—a community, however, which disparaged family life; for eating and drinking is a private affair, and consequently belongs to domestic retirement. It was so regarded among the Athenians; with them association was not material but spiritual, and even their banquets, as we see from Xenophon and Plato, had an intellectual tone. Among the Spartans, on the other hand, the costs of the common meal were met by the contributions of the several members, and he who was too poor to offer such a contribution was consequently excluded.

As to the political constitution of Sparta, its basis may be called democratic, but with considerable modifications which rendered it almost an aristocracy and oligarchy. At the head of the state were two kings, at whose side was a senate (γερουσία), chosen from the best men of the state, and which also performed the functions of a court of justice—deciding rather in accordance with moral and legal customs, than with written laws.[1] The γερουσία was also the highest state-council—the Council of the Kings, regulating the most important affairs. Lastly, one of the highest magistracies was that of the *ephors*, respecting whose election we have no definite information; Aristotle says that the mode of choice was exceedingly childish. We learn from Aristotle that even persons without nobility or property could attain this dignity. The ephors had full authority to convoke popular assemblies, to put resolutions to the vote, and to propose laws, almost in the same way as the *tribuni plebis* in Rome. Their power became tyrannical, like that which Robespierre and his party exercised for a time in France.

While the Lacedæmonians directed their entire attention to the state, intellectual culture—art and science—was not domiciled among them. The Spartans appeared to the rest of the Greeks, stiff, coarse, awkward beings, who could not transact business involving any degree of intricacy, or at least performed it very clumsily. Thucydides makes the Athenians say to the

[1] Otfried Müller, in his *History of the Dorians*, gives too dignified an aspect to this fact; he says that justice was, as it were, imprinted on their minds. But such an imprinting is always something indefinite; laws must be *written*, that it may be distinctly known what is forbidden and what is allowed.

Spartans: "You have laws and customs which have nothing in common with others; and besides this, you proceed, when you go into other countries, neither in accordance with these, nor with the traditionary usages of Hellas." In their intercourse at home, they were, on the whole, honourable; but as regarded their conduct towards other nations, they themselves plainly declared that they held their own good pleasure for the commendable, and what was advantageous for the right. It is well known that in Sparta (as was also the case in Egypt) the taking away of the necessaries of life, under certain conditions, was permitted; only the thief must not allow himself to be discovered. Thus the two states, Athens and Sparta, stand in contrast with each other. The morality of the latter is rigidly directed to the maintenance of the state; in the former we find a similar ethical relation, but with a cultivated consciousness, and boundless activity in the production of the beautiful—subsequently, of the true also.

This Greek morality, though extremely beautiful, attractive and interesting in its manifestation, is not the highest point of view for spiritual self-consciousness. It wants the form of infinity, the reflection of thought within itself, the emancipation from the natural element—(the sensuous that lurks in the character of beauty and divinity)—and from that immediacy, which attaches to their ethics. Self-comprehension on the part of thought is wanting—illimitable self-consciousness—demanding, that what is regarded by me as right and morality should have its confirmation in myself, from the testimony of my own spirit; that the beautiful (the idea as manifested in sensuous contemplation or conception) may also become the true—an inner, supersensuous world. The standpoint occupied by the æsthetic spiritual unity which we have just described, could not long be the resting-place of spirit; and the element in which further advance and corruption originated, was that of subjectivity—inward morality, individual reflection, and an inner life generally. The perfect bloom of Greek life lasted only about sixty years—from the Median wars, B.C. 492, to the Peloponnesian War, B.C. 431. The principle of subjective morality which was inevitably introduced, became the germ of corruption, which, however, showed itself in a different form in Athens from that which it assumed in Sparta: in Athens, as levity in public conduct, in Sparta, as private depravation of morals. In their fall, the Athenians showed themselves not only amiable, but great and noble—to such a degree that we cannot but lament it; among the Spartans, on the contrary, the principle of subjectivity develops itself in vulgar greed and issues in vulgar ruin.

The Peloponnesian War

The principle of corruption displayed itself first in the external political development, in the contest of the states of Greece with each other, and the struggle of factions within the cities themselves. The Greek morality had made Hellas unfit to form one common state; for the dissociation of small states from each other, and the concentration in cities, where the interest and the spiritual culture pervading the whole, could be identical, was the necessary condition of that grade of freedom which the Greeks occupied. It was only a momentary combination that occurred in the Trojan War, and even in the Median wars a union could not be accomplished. Although the tendency towards such a union is discoverable, the bond was but weak, its permanence was always endangered by jealousy, and the contest for the hegemony set the states at variance with each other. A general outbreak of hostilities in the Peloponnesian War was the consummation. Before it, and even at its commencement, Pericles was at the head of the Athenian nation—that people most jealous of its liberty; it was only his elevated personality and great genius that enabled him to maintain his position. After the wars with the Medes, Athens enjoyed the hegemony; a number of allies—partly islands, partly towns—were obliged to contribute to the supplies required for continuing the war against the Persians; and instead of the contribution being made in the form of fleets or troops, the subsidy was paid in money. Thereby an immense power was concentrated in Athens; a part of the money was expended in great architectural works, in the enjoyment of which, since they were products of spirit, the allies had some share. But that Pericles did not devote the whole of the money to works of art, but also made provision for the demos in other ways, was evident after his death, from the quantity of stores amassed in several magazines, but especially in the naval arsenal. Xenophon says: "Who does not stand in need of Athens? Is she not indispensable to all lands that are rich in corn and herds, in oil and wine—to all who wish to traffic either in money or in mind—to craftsmen, sophists, philosophers, poets, and all who desire what is worth seeing or hearing in sacred and public matters?"

In the Peloponnesian War, the struggle was

essentially between Athens and Sparta. Thucydides has left us the history of the greater part of it, and his immortal work is the absolute gain which humanity has derived from that contest. Athens allowed herself to be hurried into the extravagant projects of Alcibiades; and when these had already much weakened her, she was compelled to succumb to the Spartans, who were guilty of the treachery of applying for aid to Persia, and who obtained from the king supplies of money and a naval force. They were also guilty of a still more extensive treason, in abolishing democracy in Athens and in the cities of Greece generally, and in giving a preponderance to factions that desired oligarchy, but were not strong enough to maintain themselves without foreign assistance. Lastly, in the peace of Antalcidas, Sparta put the finishing stroke to her treachery, by giving over the Greek cities in Asia Minor to Persian dominion.

Lacedæmon had therefore, both by the oligarchies which it had set up in various countries, and by the garrisons which it maintained in some cities—as, *e.g.*, Thebes—obtained a great preponderance in Greece. But the Greek states were far more incensed at Spartan oppression than they had previously been at Athenian supremacy. With Thebes at their head, they cast off the yoke, and the Thebans became for a moment the most distinguished people in Hellas. But it was to two distinguished men among its citizens that Thebes owed its entire power—Pelopidas and Epaminondas; as for the most part in that state we find the subjective preponderant. In accordance with this principle, lyrical poetry, that which is the expression of subjectivity, especially flourished there; a kind of subjective amenity of nature shows itself also in the so-called Sacred Legion which formed the kernel of the Theban host, and was regarded as consisting of persons connected by amatory bonds; while the influence of subjectivity among them was especially proved by the fact, that after the death of Epaminondas, Thebes fell back into its former position. Weakened and distracted, Greece could no longer find safety in itself, and needed an authoritative prop. In the towns there were incessant contests; the citizens were divided into factions, as in the Italian cities of the middle ages. The victory of one party entailed the banishment of the other; the latter then usually applied to the enemies of their native city, to obtain their aid in subjugating it by force of arms. The various states could no longer co-exist peaceably: they prepared ruin for each other, as well as for themselves.

We have, then, now to investigate the *corruption* of the Greek world in its profounder import, and may denote the principle of that corruption as *subjectivity obtaining emancipation for itself*. We see subjectivity obtruding itself in various ways. Thought—the subjectively universal—menaces the beautiful religion of Greece, while the passions of individuals and their caprice menace its political constitution. In short, subjectivity, comprehending and manifesting itself, threatens the existing state of things in every department—characterized as that state of things is by immediacy. Thought, therefore, appears here as the principle of decay—decay, *viz.*, of substantial morality; for it introduces an antithesis, and asserts essentially rational principles. In the oriental states, in which there is no such antithesis, moral freedom cannot be realized, since the highest principle is abstraction. But when thought recognizes its positive character, as in Greece, it establishes principles; and these bear to the real world the relation of essence to form. For the concrete vitality found among the Greeks is customary morality—a life for religion, for the state, without further reflection, and without analysis leading to abstract definitions, which must lead away from the concrete embodiment of them, and occupy an antithetical position to that embodiment. Law is part of the existing state of things, with spirit *implicit* in it. But as soon as thought arises, it investigates the various political constitutions: as the result of its investigation it forms for itself an idea of an improved state of society, and demands that this ideal should take the place of things as they are.

In the principle of Greek freedom, inasmuch as it is freedom, is involved the self-emancipation of thought. We observed the dawn of thought in the circle of men mentioned above under their well-known appellation of the Seven Sages. It was they who first uttered general propositions; though at that time wisdom consisted rather in a concrete insight. Parallel with the advance in the development of religious art and with political growth, we find a progressive strengthening of thought, its enemy and destroyer; and at the time of the Peloponnesian War science was already developed. With the Sophists began the process of reflection on the existing state of things, and of ratiocination. That very diligence and activity which we observed among the Greeks in their practical life, and in the achievement of works of art, showed itself also in the turns and windings which these ideas took; so that, as material things are changed, worked up and used for other than their original purposes, similarly the essential being of spirit—what is thought and known—is variously handled; it is made an object about which the mind can employ itself, and this occupation becomes an interest in and for itself. The movement of thought—that which goes on within its sphere—a process which had formerly no interest, acquires attractiveness on its own account. The cultivated Sophists, who were not erudite or scientific men, but masters of subtle turns of thought, excited the admiration of the Greeks. For all questions they had an answer; for all interests of a political or religious order they had general points of view; and in the ultimate development of their art, they claimed the ability to prove everything, to discover a justifiable side in every position. In a democracy it is a matter of the first importance to be able to speak in popular assemblies, to urge one's opinions on public matters. Now this demands the power of duly presenting before them that point of view which we desire them to regard as essential. For such a purpose, intellectual culture is needed, and this discipline the Greeks acquired under their Sophists. This mental culture then became the means, in the hands of those who possessed it, of enforcing their views and interests on the demos: the expert Sophist knew how to turn the subject of discussion this way or that way at pleasure, and thus the doors were thrown wide open to all human passions. A leading principle of the Sophists was, that "Man is the measure of all things"; but in this, as in all their apophthegms, lurks an ambiguity, since the term "man" may denote spirit in its depth and truth, or in the aspect of mere caprice and private interest. The Sophists meant man simply as subjective, and intended in this dictum of theirs, that mere liking was the principle of right, and that advantage to the individual was the ground of final appeal. This sophistic principle appears again and again, though under different forms, in various periods of history; thus even in our own times subjective opinion of what is right—mere feeling— is made the ultimate ground of decision.

In beauty, as the Greek principle, there was a concrete unity of spirit, united with reality, with country and family, etc. In this unity no fixed point of view had as yet been adopted within the spirit itself, and thought, as far as it transcended this unity, was still swayed by mere liking. But Anaxagoras himself had taught, that thought itself was the absolute essence of the world. And it was in *Socrates,* that at the be-

ginning of the Peloponnesian War, the principle of subjectivity—of the absolute inherent independence of thought—attained free expression. He taught that man has to discover and recognize in himself what is the right and good, and that this right and good is in its nature universal. Socrates is celebrated as a teacher of morality, but we should rather call him the *inventor of morality*. The Greeks had a *customary* morality; but Socrates undertook to teach them what moral virtues, duties, etc. were. The moral man is not he who merely wills and does that which is right, not the merely innocent man, but he who has the consciousness of what he is doing.

Socrates, in assigning to insight, to conviction, the determination of men's actions, posited the individual as capable of a final moral decision, in contraposition to country and to customary morality, and thus made himself an oracle, in the Greek sense. He said that he had a δαιμόνιον within him, which counselled him what to do, and revealed to him what was advantageous to his friends. The rise of the inner world of subjectivity was the rupture with the existing reality. Though Socrates himself continued to perform his duties as a citizen, it was not the actual state and its religion, but the world of thought that was his true home. Now the question of the existence and nature of the gods came to be discussed. The disciple of Socrates, Plato, banished from his ideal state Homer and Hesiod, the originators of that mode of conceiving of religious objects which prevailed among the Greeks; for he desiderated a higher conception of what was to be reverenced as divine—one more in harmony with thought. Many citizens now seceded from practical and political life, to live in the ideal world. The principle of Socrates manifests a revolutionary aspect towards the Athenian state; for the peculiarity of this state was that customary morality was the form in which its existence was moulded, *viz.*, an inseparable connection of thought with actual life. When Socrates wishes to induce his friends to reflection, the discourse has always a negative tone; he brings them to the consciousness that they do not know what the right is. But when on account of the giving utterance to that principle which was advancing to recognition, Socrates is condemned to death, the sentence bears, on the one hand, the aspect of unimpeachable rectitude —inasmuch as the Athenian people condemns its deadliest foe—but, on the other hand, that of a deeply tragical character, inasmuch as the Athenians had to make the discovery that what they reprobated in Socrates had already struck firm root among themselves, and that they must be pronounced guilty or innocent with him. With this feeling they condemned the accusers of Socrates, and declared him guiltless. In Athens that higher principle which proved the ruin of the Athenian state advanced in its development without intermission. Spirit had acquired the propensity to gain satisfaction for itself—to reflect. Even in decay the spirit of Athens appears majestic, because it manifests itself as the free, the liberal, exhibiting its successive phases in their pure idiosyncrasy, in that form in which they really exist. Amiable and cheerful even in the midst of tragedy is the light-heartedness and nonchalance with which the Athenians accompany their morality to its grave. We recognize the higher interest of the new culture in the fact that the people made themselves merry over their own follies, and found great entertainment in the comedies of Aristophanes, which have the severest satire for their contents, while they bear the stamp of the most unbridled mirth.

In Sparta the same corruption is introduced, since the social unit seeks to assert his individuality against the moral life of the community: but there we have merely the isolated side of particular subjectivity—corruption in its undisguised form, blank immorality, vulgar selfishness and venality. All these passions manifest themselves in Sparta, especially in the persons of its generals, who, for the most part living at a distance from their country, obtain an opportunity of securing advantages at the expense of their own state as well as of those to whose assistance they are sent.

The Macedonian Empire

After the fall of Athens, Sparta took upon herself the hegemony; but misused it, as already mentioned, so selfishly, that she was universally hated. Thebes could not long sustain the part of humiliating Sparta, and was at last exhausted in the war with the Phocians. The Spartans and the Phocians—the former because they had surprised the citadel of Thebes, the latter because they had tilled a piece of land belonging to the Delphic Apollo—had been sentenced to pay considerable sums of money. Both states however refused payment; for the Amphictyonic Council had not much more authority than the old German Diet, which the German princes obeyed only so far as suited their inclination. The Phocians were then to be punished by the Thebans; but by an egregious piece

of violence, by desecrating and plundering the temple at Delphi, the former attained momentary superiority. This deed completes the ruin of Greece; the sanctuary was desecrated, the god so to speak, killed; the last support of unity was thereby annihilated; reverence for that which in Greece had been as it were always the final arbiter—its monarchical principle—was displaced, insulted, and trodden under foot.

The next step in advance is then that quite simple one, that the place of the dethroned oracle should be taken by another deciding will —a *real* authoritative *royalty*. The foreign Macedonian king—Philip—undertook to avenge the violation of the oracle, and forthwith took its place, by making himself lord of Greece. Philip reduced under his dominion the Hellenic states, and convinced them that it was all over with their independence, and that they could no longer maintain their own footing. The charge of littleness, harshness, violence, and political treachery—all those hateful characteristics with which Philip has so often been reproached—did not extend to the young Alexander, when he placed himself at the head of the Greeks. He had no need to incur such reproaches; he had not to form a military force, for he found one already in existence. As he had only to mount Bucephalus, and take the rein in hand, to make him obsequious to his will, just so he found that Macedonian phalanx prepared for his purpose; that rigid well-trained iron mass, the power of which had been demonstrated under Philip, who copied it from Epaminondas.

Alexander had been educated by the deepest and also the most comprehensive thinker of antiquity—Aristotle; and the education was worthy of the man who had undertaken it. Alexander was initiated into the profoundest metaphysics: therefore his nature was thoroughly refined and liberated from the customary bonds of mere opinion, crudities and idle fancies. Aristotle left this grand nature as untrammelled as it was before his instructions commenced; but impressed upon it a deep perception of what the true is, and formed the spirit which nature had so richly endowed, to a plastic being, rolling freely like an orb through its circumambient ether.

Thus accomplished, Alexander placed himself at the head of the Hellenes, in order to lead Greece over into Asia. A youth of twenty, he commanded a thoroughly experienced army, whose generals were all veterans, well versed in the art of war. It was Alexander's aim to avenge Greece for all that Asia had inflicted upon it for so many years, and to fight out at last the ancient feud and contest between the east and the west. While in this struggle he retaliated upon the Oriental world what Greece had suffered from it, he also made a return for the rudiments of culture which had been derived thence, by spreading the maturity and culmination of that culture over the east; and, as it were, changed the stamp of subjugated Asia and assimilated it to a Hellenic land. The grandeur and the interest of this work were proportioned to his genius, to his peculiar youthful individuality, the like of which in so beautiful a form we have not seen a second time at the head of such an undertaking. For not only were the genius of a commander, the greatest spirit, and consummate bravery united in him, but all these qualities were dignified by the beauty of his character as a man and an individual. Though his generals are devoted to him, they had been the long tried servants of his father; and this made his position difficult: for his greatness and youth is a humiliation to them, as inclined to regard themselves and the achievements of the past, as a complete work; so that while their envy, as in Clitus' case, arose to blind rage, Alexander also was excited to great violence.

Alexander's expedition to Asia was at the same time a journey of discovery; for it was he who first opened the Oriental world to the Europeans, and penetrated into countries—as, *e.g.*, Bactria, Sogdiana, northern India—which have since been hardly visited by Europeans. The arrangement of the march, and not less the military genius displayed in the disposition of battles, and in tactics generally, will always remain an object of admiration. He was great as a commander in battles, wise in conducting marches and marshalling troops, and the bravest soldier in the thick of the fight. Even the death of Alexander, which occurred at Babylon in the three and thirtieth year of his age, gives us a beautiful spectacle of his greatness, and shows in what relation he stood to his army: for he takes leave of it with the perfect consciousness of his dignity.

Alexander had the good fortune to die at the proper time; *i.e.*, it may be called good fortune, but it is rather a necessity. That he may stand before the eyes of posterity as a youth, an early death must hurry him away. Achilles, as remarked above, *begins* the Greek world, and his antitype Alexander *concludes* it: and these youths not only supply a picture of the fairest kind in their own persons, but at the same time afford a complete and perfect type of Hellenic

existence. Alexander finished his work and completed his ideal; and thus bequeathed to the world one of the noblest and most brilliant of visions, which our poor reflections only serve to obscure. For the great world-historical form of Alexander, the modern standard applied by recent historical "philistines," that of virtue or morality, will by no means suffice. And if it be alleged in depreciation of his merit, that he had no successor, and left behind no dynasty, we may remark that the Greek kingdoms that arose in Asia after him, are his dynasty. For two years he was engaged in a campaign in Bactria, which brought him into contact with the Massagetæ and Scythians; and there arose the Græco-Bactrian kingdom which lasted for two centuries. Thence the Greeks came into connection with India, and even with China. The Greek dominion spread itself over northern India, and Sandracottus (Chandragupta) is mentioned as the first who emancipated himself from it. The same name presents itself indeed among the Hindus, but for reasons already stated, we can place very little dependence upon such mention. Other Greek kingdoms arose in Asia Minor, in Armenia, in Syria, and Babylonia. But Egypt especially, among the kingdoms of the successors of Alexander, became a great centre of science and art; for a great number of its architectural works belong to the time of the Ptolemies, as has been made out from the deciphered inscriptions. Alexandria became the chief centre of commerce, the point of union for eastern manners and tradition with western civilization. Besides these, the Macedonian kingdom, that of Thrace, stretching beyond the Danube, that of Illyria, and that of Epirus, flourished under the sway of Greek princes.

Alexander was also extraordinarily attached to the sciences, and he is celebrated as next to Pericles the most liberal patron of the arts. Meier says in his *History of Art,* that his intelligent love of art would have secured him an immortality of fame not less than his conquests.

Section III

THE FALL OF THE GREEK SPIRIT

This third period in the history of the Hellenic world, which embraces the protracted development of the evil destiny of Greece, interests us less. Those who had been Alexander's generals, now assuming an independent appearance on the stage of history as kings, carried on long wars with each other, and experienced, almost all of them, the most romantic revolutions of fortune. Especially remarkable and prominent in this respect is the life of Demetrius Poliorcetes.

In Greece the states had preserved their existence: brought to a consciousness of their weakness by Philip and Alexander, they contrived to enjoy an apparent vitality, and boasted of an unreal independence. That self-consciousness which independence confers, they could not have; and diplomatic statesmen took the lead in the several states, orators who were not at the same time generals, as was the case formerly, *e.g.*, in the person of Pericles. The countries of Greece now assume various relations to the different monarchs, who continued to contend for the sovereignty of the Greek states—partly also for their favour, especially for that of Athens: for Athens still presented an imposing figure—if not as a power, yet certainly as the centre of the higher arts and sciences, especially of philosophy and rhetoric. Besides it kept itself more free from the gross excess, coarseness and passions which prevailed in the other states, and made them contemptible; and the Syrian and Egyptian kings deemed it an honour to make Athens large presents of corn and other useful supplies. To some extent too the kings of the period reckoned it their greatest glory to render and to keep the Greek cities and states independent. The *emancipation of Greece* had as it were, become the general watchword; and it passed for a high title of fame to be called the *deliverer* of Greece. If we examine the hidden political bearing of this word, we shall find that it denotes the prevention of any indigenous Greek state from obtaining decided superiority, and keeping all in a state of weakness by separation and disorganization.

The special peculiarity by which each Greek state was distinguished from the others consisted in a difference similar to that of their glorious divinities, each one of whom has his particular character and peculiar being, yet so that this peculiarity does not derogate from the divinity common to all. When therefore, this divinity has become weak and has vanished from the states, nothing but the bare particularity remains; the repulsive speciality which obstinately and waywardly asserts itself, and which on that very account assumes a position of absolute dependence and of conflict with others. Yet the feeling of weakness and misery led to combinations here and there. The *Ætolians* and their allies as a predatory people, set up injustice, violence, fraud, and insolence to others, as

their charter of rights. Sparta was governed by infamous tyrants and odious passions, and in this condition was dependent on the Macedonian kings. The Bœotian subjective character had, after the extinction of Theban glory, sunk down into indolence and the vulgar desire of coarse sensual enjoyment. The *Achæan* league distinguished itself by the aim of its union (the expulsion of tyrants), by rectitude and the sentiment of community. But this too was obliged to take refuge in the most complicated policy. What we see here on the whole is a *diplomatic* condition, an infinite involvement with the most manifold foreign interests, a subtle intertexture and play of parties, whose threads are continually being combined anew.

In the internal condition of the states, which, enervated by selfishness and debauchery, were broken up into factions—each of which on the other hand directs its attention to foreign lands, and with treachery to its native country begs for the favours of the kings—the point of interest is no longer the fate of these states, but the great *individuals*, who arise amid the general corruption, and honourably devote themselves to their country. They appear as great tragic characters, who with their genius, and the most intense exertion, are yet unable to extirpate the evils in question; and perish in the struggle, without having had the satisfaction of restoring to their fatherland, repose, order and freedom, nay, even without having secured a reputation with posterity free from all stain. Livy says in his prefatory remarks: "In our times we can neither endure our faults nor the means of correcting them." And this is quite as applicable to these last of the Greeks, who began an undertaking which was as honourable and noble, as it was sure of being frustrated. Agis and Cleomenes, Aratus and Philopœmen, thus sunk under the struggle for the good of their nation. Plutarch sketches for us a highly characteristic picture of these times, in giving us a representation of the importance of individuals during their continuance.

The third period of the history of the Greeks brings us to their contact with that people which was to play the next part on the theatre of the world's history; and the chief excuse for this contact was, as pretexts had previously been, the liberation of Greece. After Perseus the last Macedonian king, in the year 168 B.C. had been conquered by the Romans and brought in triumph to Rome, the Achæan league was attacked and broken up, and at last in the year 146 B.C. Corinth was destroyed. Looking at Greece as Polybius describes it, we see how a noble nature, such as his, has nothing left for it but to despair at the state of affairs and to retreat into philosophy; or if it attempts to act, can only die in the struggle. In deadly contraposition to the multiform variety of passion which Greece presents —that distracted condition which whelms good and evil in one common ruin—stands a blind fate, an iron power ready to show up that degraded condition in all its weakness, and to dash it to pieces in miserable ruin; for cure, amendment, and consolation are impossible. And this crushing destiny is the *Roman power*.

THIRD PART

THE ROMAN WORLD

Napoleon, in a conversation which he once had with Goethe on the nature of tragedy, expressed the opinion that its modern phase differed from the ancient, through our no longer recognizing a destiny to which men are absolutely subject, and that policy occupies the place of the ancient fate. This therefore he thought must be used as the modern form of destiny in tragedy, the irresistible power of circumstances to which individuality must bend. Such a power is the *Roman world,* chosen for the very purpose of casting the moral units into bonds, as also of collecting all deities and all spirits into the pantheon of universal dominion, in order to make out of them an abstract universality of power. The distinction between the Roman and the Persian principle is exactly this—that the former stifles all vitality, while the latter allowed of its existence in the fullest measure. Through its being the aim of the state that the social units in their moral life should be sacrificed to it, the world is sunk in melancholy: its heart is broken, and it is all over with the natural side of spirit, which has sunk into a feeling of unhappiness. Yet only from this feeling could arise the supersensuous, the free spirit in Christianity.

In the Greek principle we have seen spiritual existence in its exhilaration, its cheerfulness and enjoyment: spirit had not yet drawn back into abstraction; it was still involved with the natural element, the idiosyncrasy of individuals; on which account the virtues of individuals themselves became moral works of art. Abstract universal personality had not yet appeared, for spirit must first develop itself to that form of abstract universality which exercised the severe discipline over humanity now under consideration. Here, in Rome, then, we find that free universality, that abstract freedom, which on the one hand sets an abstract state, a political constitution and power, over *concrete* individuality; on the other side creates a personality in opposition to that universality, the inherent freedom of the *abstract* ego, which must be distin-

guished from individual idiosyncrasy. For personality constitutes the fundamental condition of legal right: it appears chiefly in the category of property, but it is indifferent to the concrete characteristics of the living spirit with which individuality is concerned. These two elements, which constitute Rome—political universality on the one hand, and the abstract freedom of the individual on the other—appear, in the first instance, in the form of subjectivity. This subjectivity, this retreating into one's self which we observed as the corruption of the Greek spirit, becomes here the ground on which a new side of the world's history arises. In considering the Roman world, we have not to do with a concretely spiritual life, rich in itself; but the world-historical element in it is the *abstractum* of universality, and the object which is pursued with soulless and heartless severity, is mere *dominion,* in order to enforce that *abstractum.*

In Greece, *democracy* was the fundamental condition of political life, as in the east, *despotism;* here we have *aristocracy* of a rigid order, in a state of opposition to the people. In Greece also the democracy was rent asunder, but only in the way of factions; in Rome it is principles that keep the entire community in a divided state—they occupy a hostile position towards, and struggle with, each other: first the aristocracy with the kings, then the plebs with the aristocracy, till democracy gets the upper hand; then first arise factions in which originated that later aristocracy of commanding individuals which subjugated the world. It is this dualism that, properly speaking, marks Rome's inmost being.

Erudition has regarded the Roman history from various points of view, and has adopted very different and opposing opinions: this is especially the case with the more ancient part of the history, which has been taken up by three different classes of *literati*—historians, philologists, and jurists. The historians hold to the grand features, and show respect for the history as such; so that we may after all see our way best under their guidance, since they allow the validity of the records in the case of leading events. It is otherwise with the philologists, by whom generally received traditions are less regarded, and who devote more attention to small details which can be combined in various ways. These combinations gain a footing first as historical hypotheses, but soon after as established facts. To the same degree as the philologists in their department, have the jurists in that of Roman law, instituted the minutest examination and involved their inferences with hypothesis. The result is that the most ancient part of Roman history has been declared to be nothing but fable; so that this department of inquiry is brought entirely within the province of learned criticism, which always finds the most to do where the least is to be got for the labour. While, on the one side, the poetry and the myths of the Greeks are said to contain profound historical truths, and are thus transmuted into history, the Romans, on the contrary, have myths and poetical views affiliated upon them; and epopees are affirmed to be at the basis of what has been hitherto taken for prosaic and historical.

With these preliminary remarks we proceed to describe the *locality*.

The Roman world has its centre in Italy; which is extremely similar to Greece, and, like it, forms a peninsula, only not so deeply indented. Within this country, the city of Rome itself formed the centre of the centre. Napoleon in his memoirs takes up the question, which city—if Italy were independent and formed a totality—would be best adapted for its capital. Rome, Venice, and Milan may put forward claims to the honour; but it is immediately evident that none of these cities would supply a centre. Northern Italy constitutes a basin of the river Po, and is quite distinct from the body of the peninsula; Venice is connected only with higher Italy, not with the south; Rome, on the other hand, would, perhaps, be naturally a centre for middle and lower Italy, but only artificially and violently for those lands which were subjected to it in higher Italy. The Roman state rests geographically, as well as historically, on the element of force.

The locality of Italy, then, presents no natural unity—as the valley of the Nile; the unity was similar to that which Macedonia by its sovereignty gave to Greece; though Italy wanted that permeation by one spirit, which Greece possessed through equality of culture; for it was inhabited by very various races. Niebuhr has pref-

aced his Roman history by a profoundly erudite treatise on the peoples of Italy; but from which no connection between them and the Roman history is visible. In fact, Niebuhr's *History* can only be regarded as a *criticism* of Roman history, for it consists of a series of treatises which by no means possess the unity of history.

We observed subjective inwardness as the general principle of the Roman world. The course of Roman history, therefore, involves the expansion of undeveloped subjectivity, inward conviction of existence, to the visibility of the real world. The principle of subjective inwardness receives positive application in the first place only from without, through the particular volition of the sovereignty, the government, etc. The development consists in the purification of inwardness to abstract personality, which gives itself reality in the existence of private property; the mutually repellent social units can then be held together only by despotic power. The general course of the Roman world may be defined as this: the transition from the inner sanctum of subjectivity to its direct opposite. The development is here not of the same kind as that in Greece—the unfolding and expanding of its own substance on the part of the principle; but it is the transition to its opposite, which latter does not appear as an element of corruption, but is demanded and posited by the principle itself.

As to the particular sections of the Roman history, the common division is that into the monarchy, the republic, and the empire—as if in these forms different principles made their appearance; but the same principle, that of the Roman spirit, underlies their development. In our division, we must rather keep in view the course of history generally. The annals of every world-historical people were divided above into three periods, and this statement must prove itself true in this case also. *The first period* comprehends the rudiments of Rome, in which the elements which are essentially opposed, still repose in calm unity; until the contrarieties have acquired strength, and the unity of the state becomes a powerful one, through that antithetical condition having been produced and maintained within it. In this vigorous condition the state directs its forces outwards, *i.e.*, in the *second period*, and makes its *début* on the theatre of general history; this is the noblest period of Rome, the Punic Wars and the contact with the antecedent world-historical people. A wider stage is opened, towards the east; the history at the epoch of this contact has been treated by the noble Polybius. The Roman Empire now acquired that world-conquering extension which paved the way for its fall. Internal distraction supervened, while the antithesis was developing itself to self-contradiction and utter incompatibility; it closes with despotism, which marks the *third period*. The Roman power appears here in its pomp and splendour; but it is at the same time profoundly ruptured within itself, and the Christian religion, which begins with the imperial dominion, receives a great extension. The third period comprises the contact of Rome with the north and the German peoples, whose turn is now come to play their part in history.

Section I

ROME TO THE TIME OF THE SECOND PUNIC WAR

Chapter 1. *The Elements of the Roman Spirit*

Before we come to the Roman history, we have to consider the *elements of the Roman spirit* in general, and mention and investigate the origin of Rome with a reference to them. Rome arose *outside recognized countries, viz.*, in an angle where three different districts met—those of the Latins, Sabines, and Etruscans; it was not formed from some ancient stem, connected by natural patriarchal bonds, whose origin might be traced up to remote times (as seems to have been the case with the Persians, who, however, even then ruled a large empire); but Rome was from the very beginning, of artificial and violent, not spontaneous growth. It is related that the descendants of the Trojans, led by Æneas to Italy, founded Rome; for the connection with Asia was a much cherished tradition, and there are in Italy, France, and Germany itself (Xanten) many towns which refer their origin, or their names, to the fugitive Trojans. Livy speaks of the ancient tribes of Rome, the Ramnenses, Titienses, and Luceres. Now if we look upon these as distinct nations, and assert that they were really the elements from which Rome was formed, a view which in recent times has very often striven to obtain currency, we directly subvert the historical tradition. All historians agree that at an early period, shepherds, under the leadership of chieftains, roved about on the hills of Rome; that the first Roman community constituted itself as a predatory state; and that it was with difficulty that the scattered inhabitants of the vicinity were thus united. The details of these circumstances are also given. Those preda-

tory shepherds received every contribution to their community that chose to join them, (Livy calls it a *colluvies*). The rabble of all the three districts between which Rome lay, was collected in the new city. The historians state that this point was very well chosen on a hill close to the river, and particularly adapted to make it an asylum for all delinquents. It is equally historical that in the newly formed state there were no women, and that the neighboring states would enter into no *connubia* with it: both circumstances characterize it as predatory union, with which the other states wished to have no connection. They also refused the invitation to their religious festivals; and only the Sabines—a simple agricultural people, among whom, as Livy says, prevailed a *tristis atque tetrica superstitio* —partly from superstition, partly from fear, presented themselves at them. The seizure of the Sabine women is also a universally received historical fact. This circumstance itself involves a very characteristic feature, *viz.*, that religion is used as a means for furthering the purposes of the infant state. Another method of extension was the conveying to Rome of the inhabitants of neighboring and conquered towns. At a later date there was also a voluntary migration of foreigners to Rome; as in the case of the so celebrated family of the Claudii, bringing their whole *clientela*. The Corinthian Demaratus, belonging to a family of consideration, had settled in Etruria; but as being an exile and a foreigner, he was little respected there, and his son, Lucumo, could no longer endure this degradation. He betook himself to Rome, says Livy, because a *new* people and a *repentin a atque ex virtute nobilitas* were to be found there. Lucumo attained, we are told, such a degree of respect, that he afterwards became king.

It is this peculiarity in the founding of the state which must be regarded as the essential basis of the idiosyncrasy of Rome. For it directly involves the severest discipline, and self-sacrifice to the grand object of the union. A state which had first to form itself, and which is based on force, must be held together by force. It is not a moral, liberal connection, but a compulsory condition of subordination, that results from such an origin. The Roman *virtus* is valour; not, however, the merely personal, but that which is essentially connected with a union of associates; which union is regarded as the supreme interest, and may be combined with lawless violence of all kinds. While the Romans formed a union of this kind, they were not, indeed, like the Lacedæmonians, engaged in an internal contest with a conquered and subjugated people; but there arose a distinction and a struggle between *patricians* and *plebeians*. This distinction was mythically adumbrated in the hostile brothers, Romulus and Remus. Remus was buried on the Aventine mount; this is consecrated to the evil genii, and to it are directed the secessions of the plebs. The question comes, then, how this distinction originated? It has been already said, that Rome was formed by robber-herdsmen, and the concourse of rabble of all sorts. At a later date, the inhabitants of captured and destroyed towns were also conveyed thither. The weaker, the poorer, the later additions of population are naturally underrated by, and in a condition of dependence upon those who originally founded the state, and those who were distinguished by valour, and also by wealth. It is not necessary, therefore, to take refuge in a hypothesis which has recently been a favourite one—that the patricians formed a particular race.

The dependence of the plebeians on the patricians is often represented as a perfectly legal relation—indeed, even a sacred one; since the patricians had the *sacra* in their hands, while the plebs would have been godless, as it were, without them. The plebeians left to the patricians their hypocritical stuff (*ad decipiendam plebem,* Cicero) and cared nothing for their *sacra* and auguries; but in disjoining political rights from these ritual observances, and making good their claim to those rights, they were no more guilty of a presumptuous sacrilege than the Protestants, when they emancipated the political power of the state and asserted the freedom of conscience. The light in which, as previously stated, we must regard the relation of the patricians and plebeians is that those who were poor, and consequently helpless, were compelled to attach themselves to the richer and more respectable, and to seek for their *patrocinium:* in this relation of protection on the part of the more wealthy, the protected are called *clientes.* But we find very soon a fresh distinction between the plebs and the *clientes.* In the contentions between the patricians and the plebeians, the *clientes* held to their *patroni,* though belonging to the plebs as decidedly as any class. That this relation of the *clientes* had not the stamp of right and law is evident from the fact, that with the introduction and knowledge of the laws among all classes, the cliental relation gradually vanished; for as soon as individuals found protection in the law, the temporary necessity for it could not but cease.

In the first predatory period of the state, every citizen was necessarily a soldier, for the state was based on war; this burden was oppressive, since every citizen was obliged to maintain himself in the field. This circumstance, therefore, gave rise to the contracting of enormous debts—the patricians becoming the creditors of the plebeians. With the introduction of laws, this arbitrary relation necessarily ceased; but only gradually, for the patricians were far from being immediately inclined to release the plebs from the cliental relation; they rather strove to render it permanent. The laws of the Twelve Tables still contained much that was undefined; very much was still left to the arbitrary will of the judge, the patricians alone being judges; the antithesis, therefore, between patricians and plebeians, continues till a much later period. Only by degrees do the plebeians scale all the heights of official station, and attain those privileges which formerly belonged to the patricians alone.

In the life of the Greeks, although it did not any more than that of the Romans originate in the patriarchal relation, family love and the family tie appeared at its very commencement, and the peaceful aim of their social existence had for its necessary condition the extirpation of freebooters both by sea and land. The founders of Rome, on the contrary—Romulus and Remus—are, according to the tradition, themselves freebooters—represented as from their earliest days thrust out from the family and as having grown up in a state of isolation from family affection. In like manner, the first Romans are said to have got their wives, not by free courtship and reciprocated inclination, but by force. This commencement of the Roman life in savage rudeness excluding the sensibilities of natural morality, brings with it one characteristic element—harshness in respect to the family relation; a selfish harshness, which constituted the fundamental condition of Roman manners and laws, as we observe them in the sequel. We thus find family relations among the Romans not as a beautiful, free relation of love and feeling; the place of confidence is usurped by the principle of severity, dependence, and subordination. Marriage, in its strict and formal shape, bore quite the aspect of a mere contract; the wife was part of the husband's property (*in manum conventio*), and the marriage ceremony was based on a *coemptio,* in a form such as might have been adopted on the occasion of any other purchase. The husband acquired a power over his wife, such as he had over his daughter; nor less over her property; so that everything which she gained, she gained for her husband. During the good times of the republic, the celebration of marriages included a religious ceremony—*confarreatio*—but which was omitted at a later period. The husband obtained not less power than by the *coemptio,* when he married according to the form called *usus;* that is, when the wife remained in the house of her husband without having been absent a *trinoctium* in a year. If the husband had not married in one of the forms of the *in manum conventio,* the wife remained either in the power of her father, or under the guardianship of her *agnates,* and was free as regarded her husband. The Roman matron, therefore, obtained honour and dignity only through independence of her husband, instead of acquiring her honour through her husband and by marriage. If a husband who had married under the freer condition—that is, when the union was not consecrated by the *confarreatio*—wished to separate from his wife, he dismissed her without further ceremony. The relation of sons was perfectly similar: they were, on the one hand, about as dependent on the paternal power as the wife on the matrimonial; they could not possess property, it made no difference whether they filled a high office in the state or not (though the *peculia castrensia,* and *adventitia* were differently regarded); but on the other hand, when they were emancipated, they had no connection with their father and their family. An evidence of the degree in which the position of children was regarded as analogous to that of slaves, is presented in the *imaginaria servitus (mancipium),* through which emancipated children had to pass. In reference to inheritance, morality would seem to demand that children should share equally. Among the Romans, on the contrary, testamentary caprice manifests itself in its harshest form.

Thus perverted and demoralized, do we here see the fundamental relations of ethics. The immoral active severity of the Romans in this private side of character, necessarily finds its counterpart in the passive severity of their political union. For the severity which the Roman experienced from the state he was compensated by a severity, identical in nature, which he was allowed to indulge towards his family—a servant on the one side, a despot on the other. This constitutes the Roman greatness, whose peculiar characteristic was stern inflexibility in the union of individuals with the state, and with its law and mandate. In order to obtain a nearer view of this spirit, we must not merely keep in view the actions of Roman heroes, confronting the enemy as soldiers or generals, or appearing as ambassadors—since in these cases they belong, with their whole mind and thought, only to the state and its mandate, without hesitation or yielding—but pay particular attention also to the conduct of the plebs in times of revolt against the patricians. How often in insurrection and in anarchical disorder was the plebs brought back into a state of tranquillity by a mere form, and cheated of the fulfilment of its demands, righteous or unrighteous! How often was a dictator, *e.g.,* chosen by the senate, when there was neither war nor danger from an enemy, in order to get the plebeians into the army, and to bind them to strict obedience by the military oath! It took Licinius ten years to carry laws favourable to the plebs; the latter allowed itself to be kept back by the mere formality of the veto on the part of other tribunes, and still more patiently did it wait for the long-delayed execution of these laws. It may be asked: by what were such a disposition and character produced? Produced it cannot be, but it is essentially latent in the origination of the state from that primal robber-community, as also in the idiosyncrasy of the people who composed it, and lastly, in that phase of the world spirit which was just ready for development. The elements of the Roman people were Etruscan, Latin, and Sabine; these must have contained an inborn natural adaptation to produce the Roman spirit. Of the spirit, the character, and the life of the ancient Italian peoples we know very little—thanks to the non-intelligent character of Roman historiography! —and that little, for the most part, from the Greek writers on Roman history. In contrast with that primeval wild poetry and transmutation of the finite which we observe in the east, in contrast with the beautiful, harmonious poetry and well-balanced freedom of spirit among the Greeks, of the general character of the Romans we may say that the *prose* of life makes its appearance—the self-consciousness of finiteness, the abstraction of the understanding and a rigorous principle of personality, which even in the family does not expand itself to natural morality, but remains the unfeeling non-spiritual unit, and recognizes the uniting bond of the several social units only in abstract universality.

This extreme prose of the spirit we find in Etruscan art, which though technically perfect and so far true to nature, has nothing of Greek ideality and beauty: we also observe it in the development of Roman law and in the Roman religion.

To the constrained, non-spiritual, and unfeeling intelligence of the Roman world we owe the origin and the development of *positive law*. For we saw above how in the east relations in their very nature belonging to the sphere of outward or inward morality were made legal mandates; even among the Greeks, morality was at the same time juristic right, and on that very account the constitution was entirely dependent on morals and disposition, and had not yet a fixity of principle within it, to counterbalance the mutability of men's inner life and individual subjectivity. The Romans then completed this important separation, and discovered a principle of right, which is external, *i.e.*, one not dependent on disposition and sentiment. While they have thus bestowed upon us a valuable gift, in point of *form*, we can use and enjoy it without becoming victims to that sterile understanding—without regarding it as the *ne plus ultra* of wisdom and reason. They were its victims, living beneath its sway; but they thereby secured for others freedom of spirit, *viz.*, that inward freedom which has consequently become emancipated from the sphere of the limited and the external. Spirit, soul, disposition, religion have now no longer to fear being involved with that abstract juristical understanding. Art too has its external side; when in art the mechanical side has been brought to perfection, free art can arise and display itself. But those must be pitied who knew of nothing but that mechanical side, and desired nothing further; as also those who, when art has arisen, still regard the mechanical as the highest.

We see the Romans thus bound up in that abstract understanding which pertains to finiteness. This is their highest characteristic, consequently also their highest consciousness, in religion. In fact, constraint was the religion of the Romans; among the Greeks, on the contrary, it was the cheerfulness of free fantasy. We are accustomed to regard Greek and Roman religion as the same, and use the names Jupiter, Minerva, etc. as Roman deities, often without distinguishing them from those of Greeks. This is admissible inasmuch as the Greek divinities were more or less introduced among the Romans; but as the Egyptian religion is by no means to be regarded as identical with the Greek, merely because Herodotus and the Greeks form to themselves an idea of the Egyptian divinities under the names "Latona," "Pallas," etc., so neither must the Roman be confounded with the Greek. We have said that in the Greek religion the thrill of awe suggested by nature was fully developed

to something spiritual—to a free conception, a spiritual form of fancy—that the Greek spirit did not remain in the condition of inward fear, but proceeded to make the relation borne to man by nature a relation of freedom and cheerfulness. The Romans, on the contrary, remained satisfied with a dull, stupid subjectivity; consequently, the external was only an object—something alien, something hidden. The Roman spirit, which thus remained involved in subjectivity, came into a relation of constraint and dependence, to which the origin of the word *religio* (*lig-are*) points. The Roman had always to do with something *secret;* in everything he believed in and sought for something *concealed;* and while in the Greek religion everything is open and clear, present to sense and contemplation—not pertaining to a future world, but something friendly and of this world—among the Romans everything exhibits itself as mysterious, duplicate: they saw in the object first itself, and then that which lies concealed in it: their history is pervaded by this duplicate mode of viewing phenomena. The city of Rome had besides its proper name another secret one, known only to a few. It is believed by some to have been *Valentia*, the Latin translation of *Roma;* others think it was *Amor* (*Roma* read backwards). Romulus, the founder of the state, had also another, a sacred name—*Quirinus*—by which title he was worshipped: the Romans too were also called *Quirites*. (This name is connected with the term *curia:* in tracing its etymology, the name of the Sabine town *Cures* has been had recourse to.)

Among the Romans the religious thrill of awe remained undeveloped; it was shut up to the mere subjective certainty of its own existence. Consciousness has therefore given itself no spiritual objectivity—has not elevated itself to the theoretical contemplation of the eternally divine nature, and to freedom in that contemplation; it has gained no religious substantiality for itself from spirit. The bare subjectivity of conscience is characteristic of the Roman in all that he does and undertakes—in his covenants, political relations, obligations, family relations, etc.; and all these relations receive thereby not merely a legal sanction, but as it were a solemnity analogous to that of an oath. The infinite number of ceremonies at the *comitia*, on assuming offices, etc., are expressions and declarations that concern this firm bond. Everywhere the *sacra* play a very important part. Transactions, naturally the most alien to constraint, became a *sacrum*, and were petrified, as it were, into that.

To this category belongs, *e.g.*, in strict marriages, the *confarreatio,* and the auguries and auspices generally. The knowledge of these *sacra* is utterly uninteresting and wearisome, affording fresh material for learned research as to whether they are of Etruscan, Sabine, or other origin. On their account the Roman people have been regarded as extremely pious, both in positive and negative observances; though it is ridiculous to hear recent writers speak with unction and respect of these *sacra.* The patricians were especially fond of them; they have therefore been elevated in the judgement of some, to the dignity of sacerdotal families, and regarded as the sacred *gentes*—the possessors and conservators of Roman religion: the plebeians then become the godless element. On this head what is pertinent has already been said. The ancient kings were at the same time also *reges sacrorum.* After the royal dignity had been done away with, there still remained a *rex sacrorum;* but he, like all the other priests, was subject to the *pontifex maximus,* who presided over all the *sacra,* and gave them such a rigidity and fixity as enabled the patricians to maintain their religious power so long.

But the essential point in pious feeling is the subject matter with which it occupies itself, though it is often asserted, on the contrary, in modern times, that if pious feelings exist, it is a matter of indifference what object occupies them. It has been already remarked of the Romans that their religious subjectivity did not expand into a free spiritual and moral comprehensiveness of being. It can be said that their piety did not develop itself into religion; for it remained essentially formal, and this formalism took its real side from another quarter. From the very definition given, it follows that it can only be of a finite, unhallowed order, since it arose outside the secret sanctum of religion. The chief characteristic of Roman religion is therefore a hard and dry contemplation of certain voluntary aims, which they regard as existing absolutely in their divinities, and whose accomplishment they desire of them as embodying absolute power. These purposes constitute that for the sake of which they worship the gods, and by which, in a constrained, limited way, they are bound to their deities. The Roman religion is therefore the entirely *prosaic* one of narrow aspirations, expediency, profit. The divinities peculiar to them are entirely prosaic; they are conditions, sensations, or useful arts, to which their dry fancy, having elevated them to independent power, gave objectivity; they are partly abstractions, which could only become frigid allegories—partly conditions of being which appear as bringing advantage or injury, and which were presented as objects of worship in their original bare and limited form. We can but briefly notice a few examples. The Romans worshipped Pax, Tranquillitas, Vacuna (Repose), Angeronia (Sorrow and Grief), as divinities; they consecrated altars to the Plague, to Hunger, to Mildew (Robigo), to Fever, and to the Dea Cloacina. Juno appears among the Romans not merely as Lucina, the obstetric goddess, but also as Juno Ossipagina, the divinity who forms the bones of the child, and as Juno Unxia, who anoints the hinges of the doors at marriages (a matter which was also reckoned among the *sacra*). How little have these prosaic conceptions in common with the beauty of the spiritual powers and deities of the Greeks! On the other hand, Jupiter as Jupiter Capitolinus represents the generic essence of the Roman Empire, which is also personified in the divinities Roma and Fortuna Publica.

It was the Romans especially who introduced the practice of not merely supplicating the gods in time of need, and celebrating *lectisternia,* but of also making solemn promises and vows to them. For help in difficulty they sent even into foreign countries, and imported foreign divinities and rites. The introduction of the gods and most of the Roman temples thus arose from necessity—from a vow of some kind, and an obligatory, not disinterested acknowledgment of favours. The Greeks on the contrary erected and instituted their beautiful temples, and statues, and rites, from love to beauty and divinity for their own sake.

Only one side of the Roman religion exhibits something attractive, and that is the festivals, which bear a relation to country life, and whose observance was transmitted from the earliest times. The idea of the *Saturnian* time is partly their basis, the conception of a state of things antecedent to and beyond the limits of civil society and political combination; but their import is partly taken from nature generally—the sun, the course of the year, the seasons, months, etc., (with astronomical intimations)—partly from the particular aspects of the course of nature, as bearing upon pastoral and agricultural life. There were festivals of sowing and harvesting and of the seasons; the principal was that of the Saturnalia, etc. In this aspect there appears much that is naïve and ingenuous in the tradition. Yet this series of rites, on the whole, presents a very limited and prosaic appearance;

deeper views of the great powers of nature and their generic processes are not deducible from them; for they are entirely directed to external vulgar advantage, and the merriment they occasioned, degenerated into a buffoonery unrelieved by intellect. While among the Greeks their tragic art developed itself from similar rudiments, it is on the other hand remarkable that among the Romans the scurrilous dances and songs connected with the rural festivals, were kept up till the latest periods without any advance from this naïve but rude form to anything really artistic.

It has already been said that the Romans adopted the *Greek* gods (the mythology of the Roman poets is entirely derived from the Greeks); but the worship of these beautiful gods of the imagination appears to have been among them of a very cold and superficial order. Their talk of Jupiter, Juno, Minerva, sounds like a mere theatrical mention of them. The Greeks made their Pantheon the embodiment of a rich intellectual material, and adorned it with bright fancies; it was to them an object calling forth continual invention and exciting thoughtful reflection; and an extensive, nay inexhaustible treasure has thus been created for sentiment, feeling and thought, in their mythology. The spirit of the Romans did not indulge and delight itself in that play of a thoughtful fancy; the Greek mythology appears lifeless and exotic in their hands. Among the Roman poets, especially Virgil, the introduction of the gods is the product of a frigid understanding and of imitation. The gods are used in these poems as machinery, and in a merely superficial way; regarded much in the same way as in our didactic treatises on the belles-lettres, where among other directions we find one relating to the use of such machinery in epics—in order to produce astonishment.

The Romans were as essentially different from the Greeks in respect to their public *games*. In these the Romans were, properly speaking, only spectators. The mimetic and theatrical representation, the dancing, foot-racing, and wrestling, they left to manumitted slaves, gladiators, or criminals condemned to death. Nero's deepest degradation was his appearing on a public stage as a singer, lyrist, and combatant. As the Romans were only spectators, these diversions were something foreign to them; they did not enter into them with their whole souls. With increasing luxury the taste for the baiting of beasts and men became particularly keen. Hundreds of bears, lions, tigers, elephants, crocodiles, and ostriches, were produced, and slaughtered for mere amusement. A body consisting of hundreds, nay thousands of gladiators, when entering the amphitheatre at a certain festival to engage in a sham sea-fight, addressed the emperor with the words: "Those who are devoted to death salute thee," to excite some compassion. In vain! the whole were devoted to mutual slaughter. In place of human sufferings in the depths of the soul and spirit, occasioned by the contradictions of life, and which find their solution in destiny, the Romans instituted a cruel reality of corporeal sufferings: blood in streams, the rattle in the throat which signals death, and the expiring gasp were the scenes that delighted them.

This cold negativity of naked murder exhibits at the same time that murder of all spiritual objective aim which had taken place in the soul. I need only mention in addition, the auguries, auspices, and Sibylline Books, to remind you how fettered the Romans were by superstitions of all kinds, and that they pursued exclusively their own aims in all the observances in question. The entrails of beasts, flashes of lightning, the flight of birds, the Sibylline dicta determined the administration and projects of the state. All this was in the hands of the patricians, who consciously made use of it as a mere outward means of constraint to further their own ends and oppress the people.

The distinct elements of Roman religion are, according to what has been said, subjective religiosity and a ritualism having for its object purely superficial external aims. Secular aims are left entirely free, instead of being limited by religion—in fact they are rather justified by it. The Romans are invariably pious, whatever may be the substantial character of their actions. But as the sacred principle here is nothing but an empty form, it is exactly of such a kind that it can be an instrument in the power of the devotee; it is taken possession of by the individual, who seeks his private objects and interests; whereas the truly divine possesses on the contrary a concrete power in itself. But where there is only a powerless form, the individual—the will, possessing an independent concreteness able to make that form its own, and render it subservient to its views—stands above it. This happened in Rome on the part of the patricians. The possession of sovereignty by the patricians is thereby made firm, sacred, incommunicable, peculiar: the administration of government, and political privileges, receive the character of hallowed private property. There does not exist therefore a substantial national unity, not that beautiful and moral necessity of united life in the polis; but every *gens* is itself firm, stern, having its own *penates* and *sacra;* each has its own political character, which it always preserves: strict, aristocratic severity distinguished the Claudii; benevolence towards the people, the Valerii; nobleness of spirit, the Cornelii. Separation and limitation were extended even to marriage, for the *connubia* of patricians with plebeians were deemed profane. But in that very subjectivity of religion we find also the principle of arbitrariness: and while, on the one hand, we have arbitrary choice invoking religion to bolster up private possession, we have, on the other hand, the revolt of arbitrary choice against religion. For the same order of things can, on the one side, be regarded as privileged by its religious form, and, on the other side, wear the aspect of being merely a matter of choice—of arbitrary volition on the part of man. When the time was come for it to be degraded to the rank of a mere form, it was necessarily known and treated as a form, trodden under foot, represented as formalism.

The inequality which enters into the domain of sacred things forms the transition from religion to the bare reality of political life. The consecrated inequality of will and of private property constitutes the fundamental condition of the change. The Roman principle admits of *aristocracy* alone as the constitution proper to it, but which directly manifests itself only in an antithetical form—internal inequality. Only from necessity and the pressure of adverse circumstances is this contradiction momentarily smoothed over; for it involves a duplicate power, the sternness and malevolent isolation of whose components can only be mastered and bound together by a still greater sternness, into a unity maintained by force.

Chapter 2. *The History of Rome to the Second Punic War*

In the first period, several successive stages display their characteristic varieties. The Roman state here exhibits its first phase of growth, under kings; then it receives a republican constitution, at whose head stand consuls. The struggle between patricians and plebeians begins; and after this has been set at rest by the concession of the plebeian demands, there ensues a state of contentment in the internal affairs of Rome, and it acquires strength to combat victoriously with the nation that preceded it on the stage of general history. As regards the accounts of the first

Roman kings, every datum has met with flat contradiction as the result of criticism; but it is going too far to deny them all credibility. Seven kings in all are mentioned by tradition; and even the "higher criticism" is obliged to recognize the last links in the series as perfectly historical. Romulus is called the founder of this union of freebooters; he organized it into a military state. Although the traditions respecting him appear fabulous, they only contain what is in accordance with the Roman spirit as above described. To the second king, Numa, is ascribed the introduction of the religious ceremonies. This trait is very remarkable from its implying that religion was introduced later than political union, while among other peoples religious traditions make their appearance in the remotest periods and before all civil institutions. The king was at the same time a priest (*rex* is referred by etymologists to ῥέζειν—to sacrifice). As is the case with states generally, the political was at first united with the sacerdotal, and a theocratical state of things prevailed. The king stood here at the head of those who enjoyed privileges in virtue of the *sacra*.

The separation of the distinguished and powerful citizens as senators and patricians took place as early as the first kings. Romulus is said to have appointed 100 *patres*, respecting which however, the higher criticism is sceptical. In religion, arbitrary ceremonies—the *sacra*—became fixed marks of distinction, and peculiarities of the *gentes* and orders. The internal organization of the state was gradually realized. Livy says that as Numa established all divine matters, so Servius Tullius introduced the different classes, and the census, according to which the share of each citizen in the administration of public affairs was determined. The patricians were discontented with this scheme, especially because Servius Tullius abolished a part of the debts owed by the plebeians, and gave public lands to the poorer citizens, which made them possessors of landed property. He divided the people into six classes, of which the first together with the knights formed ninety-eight centuries, the inferior classes proportionately fewer. Thus, as they voted by centuries, the class first in rank had also the greatest weight in the state. It appears that previously the patricians had the power exclusively in their hands, but that after Servius's division they had merely a preponderance; which explains their discontent with his institutions. With Servius the history becomes more distinct; and under him and his predecessor, the elder Tarquinius, traces of prosperity are exhibited. Niebuhr is surprised that according to Dionysius and Livy, the most ancient constitution was democratic, inasmuch as the vote of every citizen had equal weight in the assembly of the people. But Livy only says that Servius abolished the *suffragium viritim*. Now in the *comitia curiata*—the cliental relation, which absorbed the plebs, extending to all—the patricians alone had a vote, and *populus* denoted at that time only the patricians. Dionysius therefore does not contradict himself, when he says that the constitution according to the laws of Romulus was strictly aristocratic.

Almost all the kings were foreigners, a circumstance very characteristic of the origin of Rome. Numa, who succeeded the founder of Rome, was according to the tradition, one of the Sabines—a people which under the reign of Romulus, led by Tatius, is said to have settled on one of the Roman hills. At a later date however the Sabine country appears as a region entirely separated from the Roman state. *Numa* was followed by *Tullus Hostilius,* and the very name of this king points to his foreign origin. *Ancus Martius,* the fourth king, was the grandson of Numa. *Tarquinius Priscus* sprang from a Corinthian family, as we had occasion to observe above. *Servius Tullius* was from Corniculum, a conquered Latin town; *Tarquinius Superbus* was descended from the elder Tarquinius. Under this last king Rome reached a high degree of prosperity: even at so early a period as this, a commercial treaty is said to have been concluded with the Carthaginians; and to be disposed to reject this as mythical would imply forgetfulness of the connection which Rome had, even at that time, with the Etrurians and other bordering peoples whose prosperity depended on trade and maritime pursuits. The Romans were probably even then acquainted with the art of writing, and already possessed that clear-sighted comprehension which was their remarkable characteristic, and which led to that perspicuous historical composition for which they are famous.

In the growth of the inner life of the state, the power of the patricians had been much reduced; and the kings often courted the support of the people, as we see was frequently the case in the mediæval history of Europe, in order to steal a march upon the patricians. We have already observed this in Servius Tullius. The last king, Tarquinius Superbus, consulted the senate but little in state affairs; he also neglected to supply the place of its deceased members, and acted in every respect as if he aimed at its utter dissolution. Then ensued a state of political excitement which only needed an occasion to break out into open revolt. An insult to the honour of a matron—the invasion of that *sanctum sanctorum*—by the son of the king, supplied such an occasion. The kings were banished in the year 244 of the city and 510 of the Christian Era (that is, if the building of Rome is to be dated 753 B.C.), and the royal dignity abolished forever.

The kings were expelled by the patricians, not by the plebeians; if therefore the patricians are to be regarded as possessed of "divine right" as being a sacred race, it is worthy of note that we find them here contravening such legitimation; for the king was their high priest. We observe on this occasion with what dignity the sanctity of marriage was invested in the eyes of the Romans. The principle of subjectivity and piety (*pudor*) was with them the religious and guarded element; and its violation becomes the occasion of the expulsion of the kings, and later on of the decemvirs too. We find monogamy therefore also looked upon by the Romans as an understood thing. It was not introduced by an express law; we have nothing but an incidental testimony in the institutes, where it is said that marriages under certain conditions of relationship are not allowable, because a man may not have two wives. It is not until the reign of Diocletian that we find a law expressly determining that no one belonging to the Roman empire may have two wives, "since according to a pretorian edict also, infamy attaches to such a condition" (*cum etiam in edicto prætoris hujusmodi viri infamia notati sunt*). Monogamy therefore is regarded as naturally valid, and is based on the principle of subjectivity.

Lastly, we must also observe that royalty was not abrogated here as in Greece by suicidal destruction on the part of the royal races, but was exterminated in hate. The king, himself the chief priest, had been guilty of the grossest profanation; the principle of subjectivity revolted against the deed, and the patricians, thereby elevated to a sense of independence, threw off the yoke of royalty. Possessed by the same feeling, the plebs at a later date rose against the patricians, and the Latins and the allies against the Romans; until the equality of the social units was restored through the whole Roman dominion (a multitude of slaves, too, being emancipated), and they were held together by simple despotism.

Livy remarks that Brutus hit upon the right epoch for the expulsion of the kings, for that if it had taken place earlier, the state would have suffered dissolution. What would have happened, he asks, if this homeless crowd had been liberated earlier, when living together had not yet produced a mutual conciliation of dispositions? The constitution now became in *name* republican. If we look at the matter more closely, it is evident (Livy ii. 1) that no other essential change took place than the transference of the power which was previously *permanent* in the king, to *two annual* consuls. These two, equal in power, managed military and judicial as well as administrative business; for prætors, as supreme judges, do not appear till a later date.

At first all authority remained in the hands of the consuls; and at the beginning of the republic, externally and internally, the state was in evil plight. In the Roman history a period occurs as troubled as that in the Greek which followed the extinction of the dynasties. The Romans had first to sustain a severe conflict with their expelled king, who had sought and found help from the Etrurians. In the war against Porsena, the Romans lost all their conquests and even their independence: they were compelled to lay down their arms and to give hostages; according to an expression of Tacitus (*Histories,* III. 72) it seems as if Porsena had even taken Rome. Soon after the expulsion of the kings we have the contest between the patricians and plebeians; for the abolition of royalty had taken place exclusively to the advantage of the aristocracy, to which the royal power was transferred, while the plebs lost the protection which the kings had afforded it. All magisterial and juridical power, and all property in land, was at this time in the hands of the patricians; while the people, continually dragged out to war, could not employ themselves in peaceful occupations: handicrafts could not flourish, and the only acquisition the plebeians could make was their share in the booty. The patricians had their territory and soil cultivated by slaves, and assigned some of their land to their clients, who on condition of paying taxes and contributions —as tenant cultivators, therefore—had the usufruct of it. This relation, on account of the form in which the dues were paid by the *clientes,* was very similar to vassalage: they were obliged to give contributions towards the marriage of the daughters of the *patronus,* to ransom him or his sons when in captivity, to assist them in obtaining magisterial offices, and to make up the losses sustained in suits at law. The administration of justice was likewise in the hands of the patri-

cians, and that without the limitations of definite and written laws—a desideratum which at a later period the decemvirs were created to supply. All the power of government belonged moreover to the patricians, for they were in possession of all offices—first of the consulship, afterwards of the military tribuneship and censorship (instituted A.U.C. 311)—by which the actual administration of government as likewise the oversight of it, was left to them alone. Lastly, it was the patricians who constituted the senate. The question as to how that body was recruited appears very important. But in this matter no systematic plan was followed. Romulus is said to have founded the senate, consisting then of one hundred members; the succeeding kings increased this number, and Tarquinius Priscus fixed it at three hundred. Junius Brutus restored the senate, which had very much fallen away, *de novo.* In after times it would appear that the censors and sometimes the dictators filled up the vacant places in the senate. In the Second Punic War, A.U.C. 538, a dictator was chosen, who nominated one hundred and seventy-seven new senators: he selected those who had been invested with curule dignities, the plebeian ædiles, tribunes of the people and quæstors, citizens who had gained *spolia opima* or the *corona civica.* Under Cæsar the number of the senators was raised to eight hundred; Augustus reduced it to six hundred. It has been regarded as great negligence on the part of the Roman historians, that they give us so little information respecting the composition and redintegration of the senate. But this point which appears to us to be invested with infinite importance, was not of so much moment to the Romans at large; they did not attach so much weight to formal arrangements, for their principal concern was *how* the government was conducted. How, in fact, can we suppose the constitutional rights of the ancient Romans to have been so well defined, and that at a time which is even regarded as mythical and its traditionary history as epical?

The people were in some such oppressed condition as, *e.g.,* the Irish were a few years ago in the British Isles, while they remained at the same time entirely excluded from the government. Often they revolted and made a secession from the city. Sometimes they also refused military service; yet it always remains a very striking fact that the senate could so long resist superior numbers irritated by oppression and practised in war; for the main struggle lasted for more than a hundred years. In the fact that the people could so long be kept in check is manifested its respect for legal order and the *sacra*. But of necessity the plebeians at last secured their righteous demands, and their debts were often remitted. The severity of the patricians their creditors, the debts due to whom they had to discharge by slave-work, drove the plebs to revolts. At first it demanded and received only what it had already enjoyed under the kings—landed property and protection against the powerful. It received assignments of land, and tribunes of the people—functionaries, that is to say, who had the power to put a veto on every decree of the senate. When this office commenced, the number of tribunes was limited to two: later there were ten of them; which however was rather injurious to the plebs, since all that the senate had to do was to gain over one of the tribunes, in order to thwart the purpose of all the rest by his single opposition. The plebs obtained at the same time the *provocatio ad populum:* that is, in every case of magisterial oppression, the condemned person might appeal to the decision of the people—a privilege of infinite importance to the plebs, and which especially irritated the patricians. At the repeated desire of the people the *decemviri* were nominated, the tribunate of the people being suspended, to supply the desideratum of a determinate legislation; they perverted, as is well known, their unlimited power to tyranny, and were driven from power on an occasion entailing similar disgrace to that which led to the punishment of the kings. The dependence of the *clientela* was in the meantime weakened; after the decemviral epoch, the *clientes* are less and less prominent and are merged in the plebs, which adopts resolutions (*plebiscita*); the senate by itself could only issue *senatus consulta,* and the tribunes, as well as the senate, could now impede the *comitia* and elections. By degrees, the plebeians effected their admissibility to all dignities and offices; but, at first, a plebeian consul, ædile, censor, etc., was not equal to the patrician one, on account of the *sacra* which the latter kept in his hands; and a long time intervened after this concession before a plebeian actually became a consul. It was the *tribunis plebis,* Licinius, who established the whole cycle of these political arrangements in the second half of the fourth century, A.U.C. 387. It was he also who chiefly commenced the agitation for the *lex agraria,* respecting which so much has been written and debated among the learned of the day. The agitators for this law excited during every period very great commo-

tions in Rome. The plebeians were practically excluded from almost all the landed property, and the object of the agrarian laws was to provide lands for them—partly in the neighborhood of Rome, partly in the conquered districts, to which colonies were to be then led out. In the time of the republic we frequently see military leaders assigning lands to the people; but in every case they were accused of striving after royalty, because it was the kings who had exalted the plebs. The agrarian law required that no citizen should possess more than five hundred *jugera:* the patricians were consequently obliged to surrender a large part of their property. Niebuhr, in particular, has undertaken extensive researches respecting the agrarian laws, and has conceived himself to have made great and important discoveries: he says, *viz.,* that an infringement of the sacred right of property was never thought of, but that the state had only assigned a portion of the public lands for the use of the plebs, having always had the right of disposing of them as its own property. I only remark in passing that Hegewisch had made this discovery before Niebuhr, and that Niebuhr derived the particular data on which his assertion rests from Appian and Plutarch; that is from Greek authors, respecting whom he himself allows that we should have recourse to only in an extreme case. How often does Livy, as well as Cicero and others, speak of the agrarian laws, while nothing definite can be inferred from their statements!

This is another proof of the inaccuracy of the Roman historians. The whole affair ends in nothing but a useless question of jurisprudence. The land which the patricians had taken into possession or in which colonies settled, was originally public land; but it also certainly belonged to those in possession, and our information is not at all promoted by the assertion that it always remained public land. This discovery of Niebuhr's turns upon a very immaterial distinction, existing perhaps in his ideas, but not in reality. The Licinian law was indeed carried, but soon transgressed and utterly disregarded. Licinius Stolo himself, who had first "agitated" for the law, was punished because he possessed a larger property in land than was allowed, and the patricians opposed the execution of the law with the greatest obstinacy. We must here call especial attention to the distinction which exists between the Roman, the Greek, and our own circumstances. Our civil society rests on other principles, and in it such measures are not necessary. Spartans and Athenians, who had not arrived at such an abstract idea of the state as was so tenaciously held by the Romans, did not trouble themselves with abstract rights, but simply desired that the citizens should have the means of subsistence; and they required of the state that it should take care that such should be the case.

This is the chief point in the first period of Roman history, that the plebs attained the right of being eligible to the higher political offices, and that, by a share which they too managed to obtain in the land and soil, the means of subsistence were assured to the citizens. By this union of the patriciate and the plebs, Rome first attained true internal consistency; and only after this had been realized could the Roman power develop itself externally. A period of satisfied absorption in the common interest ensues, and the citizens are weary of internal struggles. When after civil discords nations direct their energies outward, they appear in their greatest strength; for the previous excitement continues, and no longer having its object within, seeks for it without. This direction given to the Roman energies was able for a moment to conceal the defect of that union; equilibrium was restored, but without an essential centre of unity and support. The contradiction that existed could not but break out again fearfully at a later period; but previously to this time the greatness of Rome had to display itself in war and the conquest of the world. The power, the wealth, the glory derived from these wars, as also the difficulties to which they led, kept the Romans together as regards the internal affairs of the state. Their courage and discipline secured their victory. As compared with the Greek or Macedonian, the Roman art of war has special peculiarities. The strength of the phalanx lay in its mass and in its massive character. The Roman legions also present a close array, but they had at the same time an articulated organization: they united the two extremes of massiveness on the one hand, and of dispersion into light troops on the other hand: they held firmly together, while at the same time they were capable of ready expansion. Archers and slingers preceded the main body of the Roman army when they attacked the enemy, afterwards leaving the decision to the sword.

It would be a wearisome task to pursue the wars of the Romans in Italy; partly because they are in themselves unimportant, even the often empty rhetoric of the generals in Livy cannot very much increase the interest; partly on account of the unintelligent character of the Roman annalists, in whose pages we see the Romans carrying on war only with "enemies" without learning anything further of their individuality, e.g., the Etruscans, the Samnites, the Ligurians, with whom they carried on wars during many hundred years. It is singular in regard to these transactions that the Romans, who have the justification conceded by world-history on their side, should also claim for themselves the minor justification in respect to manifestoes and treaties on occasion of minor infringements of them, and maintain it as it were after the fashion of advocates. But in political complications of this kind, either party may take offence at the conduct of the other, if it pleases, and deems it expedient to be offended. The Romans had long and severe contests to maintain with the Samnites, the Etruscans, the Gauls, the Marsi, the Umbrians, and the Bruttii, before they could make themselves masters of the whole of Italy. Their dominion was extended thence in a southerly direction; they gained a secure footing in Sicily, where the Carthaginians had long carried on war; then they extended their power towards the west: from Sardinia and Corsica they went to Spain. They thus soon came into frequent contact with the Carthaginians, and were obliged to form a naval power in opposition to them. This transition was easier in ancient times than it would perhaps be now, when long practice and superior knowledge are required for maritime service. The mode of warfare at sea was not very different from that on land.

We have thus reached the end of the first epoch of Roman history, in which the Romans by their retail military transactions had become capitalists in a strength proper to themselves, and with which they were to appear on the theatre of the world. The Roman dominion was, on the whole, not yet very greatly extended: only a few colonies had settled on the other side of the Po, and on the south a considerable power confronted that of Rome. It was the Second Punic War, therefore, that gave the impulse to its terrible collision with the most powerful states of the time; through it the Romans came into contact with Macedonia, Asia, Syria, and subsequently also with Egypt. Italy and Rome remained the centre of their great far-stretching empire, but this centre was, as already remarked, not the less an artificial, forced, and compulsory one. This grand period of the contact of Rome with other states, and of the manifold complications thence arising, has been depicted by the noble Achæan, Polybius, whose fate it was to observe the fall of his country through the disgraceful passions of the Greeks and the baseness and inexorable persistency of the Romans.

Section II

ROME FROM THE SECOND PUNIC WAR TO THE EMPERORS

The second period, according to our division, begins with the Second Punic War, that epoch which decided and stamped a character upon Roman dominion. In the First Punic War, the Romans had shown that they had become a match for the mighty Carthage, which possessed a great part of the coast of Africa and southern Spain, and had gained a firm footing in Sicily and Sardinia. The Second Punic War laid the might of Carthage prostrate in the dust. The proper element of that state was the sea; but it had no original territory, formed no nation, had no national army; its hosts were composed of the troops of subjugated and allied peoples. In spite of this, the great Hannibal with such a host, formed from the most diverse nations, brought Rome near to destruction. Without any support he maintained his position in Italy for sixteen years against Roman patience and perseverance; during which time however the Scipios conquered Spain and entered into alliances with the princes of Africa. Hannibal was at last compelled to hasten to the assistance of his hard-pressed country; he lost the battle of Zama in the year 552 A.U.C. and after six and thirty years revisited his paternal city, to which he was now obliged to offer pacific counsels. The Second Punic War thus eventually established the undisputed power of Rome over Carthage; it occasioned the hostile collision of the Romans with the king of Macedonia, who was conquered five years later. Now Antiochus, the king of Syria, is involved in the *mêlée*. He opposed a huge power to the Romans, was beaten at Thermopylæ and Magnesia, and was compelled to surrender to the Romans Asia Minor as far as the Taurus. After the conquest of Macedonia both that country and Greece were declared free by the Romans—a declaration whose meaning we have already investigated, in treating of the preceding historical nation. It was not till this time that the Third Punic War commenced, for Carthage had once more raised its head and excited the jealousy of the Romans. After long resistance it was taken and laid in ashes. Nor could the Achæan league now long maintain itself in the face of Roman ambition: the Romans were eager for war, destroyed Corinth in the same year as Carthage, and made Greece a province. The fall of Carthage and the subjugation of Greece were the central points from which the Romans gave its vast extent to their sovereignty.

Rome seemed now to have attained perfect security; no external power confronted it: she was the mistress of the Mediterranean—that is, of the *media terra* of all civilization. In this period of victory, its morally great and fortunate personages, especially the Scipios, attract our attention. They were morally fortunate, although the greatest of the Scipios met with an end outwardly unfortunate, because they devoted their energies to their country during a period when it enjoyed a sound and unimpaired condition. But after the feeling of patriotism, the dominant instinct of Rome, had been satisfied, destruction immediately invades the state regarded *en masse;* the grandeur of *individual* character becomes stronger in intensity, and more vigorous in the use of means, on account of contrasting circumstances. We see the internal contradiction of Rome now beginning to manifest itself in another form; and the epoch which concludes the second period is also the second mediation of that contradiction. We observed that contradiction previously in the struggle of the patricians against the plebeians: now it assumes the form of private interest, contravening patriotic sentiment; and respect for the state no longer holds these opposites in the necessary equipoise. Rather, we observe now side by side with wars for conquest, plunder and glory, the fearful spectacle of civil discords in Rome, and intestine wars. There does not follow, as among the Greeks after the Median wars, a period of brilliant splendour in culture, art and science, in which spirit enjoys inwardly and ideally that which it had previously achieved in the world of action. If inward satisfaction was to follow the period of that external prosperity in war, the principle of Roman life must be more concrete. But if there were such a concrete life to evolve as an object of consciousness from the depths of their souls by imagination and thought, what would it have been! Their chief spectacles were triumphs, the treasures gained in war, and captives from all nations, unsparingly subjected to the yoke of abstract sovereignty. The concrete element, which the Romans actually find within themselves, is only this unspiritual unity, and any definite thought or feeling of a non-abstract kind, can lie only in the idiosyncrasy of individuals. The tension of virtue is now relaxed, because the danger is past. At the time of the First Punic War, necessity united the hearts of all for the saving of Rome. In the following wars too, with Macedonia, Syria, and the Gauls in upper Italy, the existence of the entire state was still concerned. But after the danger from Carthage and Macedon was over, the subsequent wars were more and more the mere consequences of victories, and nothing else was needed than to gather in their fruits. The armies were used for particular expeditions, suggested by policy, or for the advantages of individuals—for acquiring wealth, glory, *sovereignty* in the abstract. The relation to other nations was purely that of force. The national individuality of peoples did not, as early as the time of the Romans, excite respect, as is the case in modern times. The various peoples were not yet recognized as legitimated; the various states had not yet acknowledged each other as real essential existences. Equal right to existence entails a union of states, such as exists in modern Europe, or a condition like that of Greece, in which the states had an equal right to existence under the protection of the Delphic god. The Romans do not enter into such a relation to the other nations, for their god is only the *Jupiter Capitolinus;* neither do they respect the *sacra* of the other nations (any more than the plebeians those of the patricians); but as conquerors in the strict sense of the term, they plunder the palladia of the nations. Rome kept standing armies in the conquered provinces, and proconsuls and proprætors were sent into them as viceroys. The equites collected the taxes and tributes, which they farmed under the state. A net of such fiscal farmers (*publicani*) was thus drawn over the whole Roman world. Cato used to say, after every deliberation of the senate: *"Ceterum censeo Carthaginem esse delendam";* and Cato was a thorough Roman. The Roman principle thereby exhibits itself as the cold abstraction of sovereignty and power, as the pure egotism of the will in opposition to others, involving no moral element of determination, but appearing in a concrete form only in the shape of individual interests. Increase in the number of provinces issued in the aggrandizement of individuals within Rome itself, and the corruption thence arising. From Asia, luxury and debauchery were brought to Rome. Riches flowed in after the fashion of spoils in war, and were not the fruit of industry and honest activity; in the same way as the marine had arisen, not from the necessities of commerce, but with a warlike

object. The Roman state, drawing its resources from rapine, came to be rent in sunder by quarrels about dividing the spoil. For the first occasion of the breaking out of contention within it, was the legacy of Attalus, king of Pergamus, who had bequeathed his treasures to the Roman state. Tiberius Gracchus came forward with the proposal to divide it among the Roman citizens; he likewise renewed the Licinian agrarian laws, which had been entirely set aside during the predominance of individuals in the state. His chief object was to procure property for the free citizens, and to people Italy with citizens instead of slaves. This noble Roman, however, was vanquished by the grasping nobles, for the Roman constitution was no longer in a condition to be saved by the constitution itself. Caius Gracchus, the brother of Tiberius, prosecuted the same noble aim as his brother and shared the same fate. Ruin now broke in unchecked, and, as there existed no generally recognized and absolutely essential object to which the country's energy could be devoted, individualities and physical force were in the ascendant. The enormous corruption of Rome displays itself in the war with Jugurtha, who had gained the senate by bribery and so indulged himself in the most atrocious deeds of violence and crime. Rome was pervaded by the excitement of the struggle against the Cimbri and Teutones, who assumed a menacing position towards the state. With great exertions the latter were utterly routed in Provence, near Aix; the others in Lombardy, at the Adige, by Marius the conqueror of Jugurtha. Then the Italian allies, whose demand of Roman citizenship had been refused, raised a revolt; and while the Romans had to sustain a struggle against a vast power in Italy, they received the news that, at the command of Mithridates, 80,000 Romans had been put to death in Asia Minor. Mithridates was King of Pontus, governed Colchis and the lands of the Black Sea as far as the Tauric peninsula, and could summon to his standard in his war with Rome the populations of the Caucasus, of Armenia, Mesopotamia, and a part of Syria, through his son-in-law Tigranes. Sulla, who had already led the Roman hosts in the Social War, conquered him. Athens, which had hitherto been spared, was beleaguered and taken, but "for the sake of their fathers," as Sulla expressed himself, not destroyed. He then returned to Rome, reduced the popular faction, headed by Marius and Cinna, became master of the city, and commenced systematic massacres of Roman citizens of consideration. Forty senators and six hundred knights were sacrificed to his ambition and lust of power.

Mithridates was indeed defeated, but not overcome, and was able to begin the war anew. At the same time, Sertorius, a banished Roman, arose in revolt in Spain, carried on a contest there for eight years, and perished only through treachery. The war against Mithridates was terminated by Pompey; the king of Pontus killed himself when his resources were exhausted. The Servile War in Italy is a contemporaneous event. A great number of gladiators and mountaineers had formed a union under Spartacus, but were vanquished by Crassus. To this confusion was added the universal prevalence of piracy, which Pompey rapidly reduced by a large armament.

We thus see the most terrible and dangerous powers arising against Rome; yet the military force of this state is victorious over all. Great individuals now appear on the stage as during the times of the fall of Greece. The biographies of Plutarch are here also of the deepest interest. It was from the disruption of the state, which had no longer any consistency or firmness in itself, that these colossal individualities arose, instinctively impelled to restore that political unity which was no longer to be found in men's dispositions. It is their misfortune that they cannot maintain a pure morality, for their course of action contravenes things as they are, and is a series of transgressions. Even the noblest—the Gracchi—were not merely the victims of injustice and violence from without, but were themselves involved in the corruption and wrong that universally prevailed. But that which these individuals purpose and accomplish has on its side the higher sanction of the world-spirit and must eventually triumph. The idea of an organization for the vast empire being altogether absent, the senate could not assert the authority of government. The sovereignty was made dependent on the people—that people which was now a mere mob, and was obliged to be supported by corn from the Roman provinces. We should refer to Cicero to see how all affairs of state were decided in riotous fashion, and with arms in hand, by the wealth and power of the grandees on the one side, and by a troop of rabble on the other. The Roman citizens attach themselves to individuals who flatter them, and who then become prominent in factions, in order to make themselves masters of Rome. Thus we see in Pompey and Cæsar the two foci of Rome's splendor coming into hostile opposition: on the one side, Pompey with the senate, and there-

fore apparently the defender of the Republic —on the other, Cæsar with his legions and a superiority of genius. This contest between the two most powerful individualities could not be decided at Rome in the forum. Cæsar made himself master in succession, of Italy, Spain, and Greece, utterly routed his enemy at Pharsalus, forty-eight years before Christ, made himself sure of Asia, and so returned victor to Rome.

In this way the world-wide sovereignty of Rome became the property of a single possessor. This important change must not be regarded as a thing of chance; it was *necessary*— postulated by the circumstances. The democratic constitution could no longer be really maintained in Rome, but only kept up in appearance. Cicero, who had procured himself great respect through his high oratorical talent, and whose learning acquired him considerable influence, always attributes the corrupt state of the republic to individuals and their passions. Plato, whom Cicero professedly followed, had the full consciousness that the Athenian state, as it presented itself to him, could not maintain its existence, and therefore sketched the plan of a perfect constitution accordant with his views. Cicero, on the contrary, does not consider it impossible to preserve the Roman Republic, and only desiderates some temporary assistance for it in its adversity. The nature of the state, and of the Roman state in particular, transcends his comprehension. Cato, too, says of Cæsar: "His virtues be execrated, for they have ruined my country!" But it was not the mere accident of Cæsar's existence that destroyed the republic— it was *necessity*. All the tendencies of the Roman principle were to sovereignty and military force: it contained in it no spiritual centre which it could make the object, occupation, and enjoyment of its spirit. The aim of patriotism, that of preserving the state, ceases when the lust of personal dominion becomes the impelling passion. The citizens were alienated from the state, for they found in it no objective satisfaction; and the interests of individuals did not take the same direction as among the Greeks, who could set against the incipient corruption of the practical world, the noblest works of art in painting, sculpture, and poetry, and especially a highly cultivated philosophy. Their works of art were only what they had collected from every part of Greece, and therefore not productions of their own; their riches were not the fruit of industry, as was the case in Athens, but the result of plunder. Elegance—culture—was foreign to the Romans *per se;* they sought to obtain it from the Greeks, and for this purpose a vast number of Greek slaves were brought to Rome. Delos was the centre of this slave trade, and it is said that sometimes on a single day, ten thousand slaves were purchased there. To the Romans, Greek slaves were their poets, their authors, the superintendents of their manufactories, the instructors of their children.

The republic could not longer exist in Rome. We see, especially from Cicero's writings, how all public affairs were decided by the private authority of the more eminent citizens—by their power, their wealth; and what tumultuary proceedings marked all political transactions. In the republic, therefore, there was no longer any security; *that* could be looked for only in a single will. Cæsar, who may be adduced as a paragon of Roman adaptation of means to ends—who formed his resolves with the most unerring perspicuity, and executed them with the greatest vigor and practical skill, without any superfluous excitement of mind—Cæsar, judged by the great scope of history, did the right; since he furnished a mediating element, and that kind of political bond which men's condition required. Cæsar effected two objects: he calmed the internal strife, and at the same time originated a new one outside the limits of the empire. For the conquest of the world had reached hitherto only to the circle of the Alps, but Cæsar opened a new scene of achievement: he founded the theatre which was on the point of becoming the centre of history. He then achieved universal sovereignty by a struggle which was decided not in Rome itself, but by his conquest of the whole Roman world. His position was indeed hostile to the republic, but, properly speaking, only to its shadow; for all that remained of that republic was entirely powerless. Pompey, and all those who were on the side of the senate, exalted their *dignitas auctoritas,* their individual rule, as the power of the republic; and the mediocrity which needed protection took refuge under this title. Cæsar put an end to the empty formalism of this title, made himself master, and held together the Roman world by force, in opposition to isolated factions. In spite of this, we see the noblest men of Rome supposing Cæsar's rule to be a merely adventitious thing, and the entire position of affairs to be dependent on his individuality. So thought Cicero, so Brutus and Cassius. They believed that if this one individual were out of the way, the republic would be *ipso facto* restored. Possessed by this remarkable hallucination, Brutus, a man of highly noble character, and Cassius, endowed with greater practical

energy than Cicero, assassinated the man whose virtues they appreciated. But it became immediately manifest that only a *single* will could guide the Roman state, and now the Romans were compelled to adopt that opinion; since in all periods of the world a political revolution is sanctioned in men's opinions, when it repeats itself. Thus Napoleon was twice defeated, and the Bourbons twice expelled. By repetition that which at first appeared merely a matter of chance and contingency, becomes a real and ratified existence.

Section III

Chapter 1. *Rome Under the Emperors*

During this period the Romans come into contact with the people destined to succeed them as a world-historical nation; and we have to consider that period in two essential aspects, the *secular* and the *spiritual.* In the secular aspect two leading phases must be specially regarded: first, the position of *the ruler;* and secondly, the conversion of mere individuals into *persons*—the world of legal relations.

The first thing to be remarked respecting the *imperial rule* is that the Roman government was so abstracted from interest, that the great transition to that rule hardly changed anything in the constitution. The popular assemblies alone were unsuited to the new state of things and disappeared. The emperor was *princeps senatus,* censor, consul, tribune: he united all their nominally continuing offices in himself; and the military power, here the most essentially important, was exclusively in his hands. The constitution was an utterly unsubstantial form, from which all vitality, consequently all might and power, had departed; and the only means of maintaining its existence were the legions which the emperor constantly kept in the vicinity of Rome. Public business was indeed brought before the senate, and the emperor appeared simply as one of its members; but the senate was obliged to obey, and whoever ventured to gainsay his will was punished with death, and his property confiscated. Those therefore who had certain death in anticipation, killed themselves, that if they could do nothing more they might at least preserve their property to their family. Tiberius was the most odious to the Romans on account of his power of dissimulation: he knew very well how to make good use of the baseness of the senate, in extirpating those among them whom he feared. The power of the emperor rested, as we have said, on the army, and the

Pretorian bodyguard which surrounded him. But the legions, and especially the Pretorians, soon became conscious of their importance, and arrogated to themselves the disposal of the imperial throne. At first they continued to show some respect for the family of Cæsar Augustus, but subsequently the legions chose their own generals; such, *viz.*, as had gained their good will and favor, partly by courage and intelligence, partly also by bribes, and indulgence in the administration of military discipline.

The emperors conducted themselves in the enjoyment of their power with perfect simplicity, and did not surround themselves with pomp and splendour in Oriental fashion. We find in them traits of simplicity which astonish us. Thus, *e.g.*, Augustus writes a letter to Horace, in which he reproaches him for having failed to address any poem to him, and asks him whether he thinks that that would disgrace him with posterity. Sometimes the senate made an attempt to regain its consequence by nominating the emperor: but their nominees were either unable to maintain their ground, or could do so only by bribing the Pretorians. The choice of the senators and the constitution of the senate was moreover left entirely to the caprice of the emperor. The political institutions were united in the person of the emperor; no moral bond any longer existed; the will of the emperor was supreme, and before him there was absolute equality. The freedmen who surrounded the emperor were often the mightiest in the empire; for caprice recognizes no distinction. In the person of the emperor, isolated subjectivity has gained a perfectly unlimited realization. Spirit has renounced its proper nature, inasmuch as limitation of being and of volition has been constituted an unlimited absolute existence. This arbitrary choice, moreover, has only one limit, the limit of all that is human—*death;* and even death became a theatrical display. Nero, *e.g.*, died a death, which may furnish an example for the noblest hero as for the most resigned of sufferers. Individual subjectivity thus entirely emancipated from control has no inward life, no prospective nor retrospective emotions, no repentance, nor hope, nor fear—not even thought; for all these involve fixed conditions and aims, while here every condition is purely contingent. The springs of action are none other than desire, lust, passion, fancy— in short, caprice absolutely unfettered. It finds so little limitation in the will of others that the relation of will to will may be called that of absolute sovereignty to absolute slavery. In the whole known world, no will is imagined that is not subject to the will of the emperor. But under the sovereignty of that one, everything is in a condition of *order;* for as it actually *is*, it is in due order, and government consists in bringing all into harmony with the sovereign *one*. The concrete element in the character of the emperors is therefore of itself of no interest, because the concrete is not of essential importance. Thus there were emperors of noble character and noble nature, and who highly distinguished themselves by mental and moral culture. Titus, Trajan, the Antonines, are known as such characters, rigorously strict in self-government; yet even these produced no change in the state. The proposition was never made during their time, to give the Roman Empire an organization of free social relationship: they were only a kind of happy chance, which passes over without a trace and leaves the condition of things as it was. For these persons find themselves here in a position in which they cannot be said to act, since no object confronts them in opposition; they have only to will—well or ill—and it *is* so. The praiseworthy emperors, Vespasian and Titus, were succeeded by that coarsest and most loathsome tyrant, Domitian: yet the Roman historian tells us that the Roman world enjoyed tranquillizing repose under him. Those single points of light, therefore, effected no change; the whole empire was subject to the pressure of taxation and plunder; Italy was depopulated; the most fertile lands remained untilled: and this state of things lay as a fate on the Roman world.

The second point which we have particularly to remark, is the position taken by individuals as *persons*. Individuals were perfectly equal (slavery made only a trifling distinction) and without any political right. As early as the termination of the Social War, the inhabitants of the whole of Italy were put on an equal footing with Roman citizens; and under Caracalla all distinction between the subjects of the entire Roman empire was abolished. Private right developed and perfected this equality. The right of property had been previously limited by distinctions of various kinds, which were now abrogated. We observed the Romans proceeding from the principle of abstract subjectivity, which now realizes itself as personality in the recognition of private right. Private right, *viz.*, is this: that the social unit as such enjoys consideration in the state, in the reality which he gives to himself—*viz.*, in property. The living political body, that Roman feeling which animated it as its soul, is now brought back to the isolation of a lifeless private right. As, when the physical body suffers dissolution, each point gains a life of its own, but which is only the miserable life of worms; so the political organism is here dissolved into atoms—*viz.*, private persons. Such a condition is Roman life at this epoch: on the one side, fate and the abstract universality of sovereignty; on the other, the *individual* abstraction. "Person," which involves the recognition of the independent dignity of the social unit, not on the ground of the display of the life which he possesses—in his complete individuality—but as the abstract *individuum*.

It is the pride of the social units to enjoy absolute importance as private persons; for the ego is thus enabled to assert unbounded claims; but the substantial interest thus comprehended —the *meum*—is only of a superficial kind, and the development of private right, which this high principle introduced, involved the decay of political life. The emperor *domineered* only, and could not be said to *rule;* for the equitable and moral medium between the sovereign and the subjects was wanting—the bond of a constitution and organization of the state, in which a gradation of circles of social life, enjoying independent recognition, exists in communities and provinces, which, devoting their energies to the general interest, exert an influence on the general government. There are indeed *curiæ* in the towns, but they are either destitute of weight, or used only as means for oppressing individuals, and for systematic plunder. That, therefore, which was abidingly present to the minds of men was not their country, or such a moral unity as that supplies: the whole state of things urged them to yield themselves to fate, and to strive for a perfect indifference to life— an indifference which they sought either in freedom of thought or in directly sensuous enjoyment. Thus man was either at war with existence, or entirely given up to mere sensuous existence. He either recognized his destiny in the task of acquiring the means of enjoyment through the favor of the emperor, or through violence, testamentary frauds, and cunning; or he sought repose in philosophy, which alone was still able to supply something firm and independent: for the systems of that time— Stoicism, Epicureanism, and Scepticism—although within their common sphere opposed to each other, had the same general purport, *viz.*, rendering the soul absolutely indifferent to everything which the real world had to offer. These philosophies were therefore widely extended among the cultivated: they produced in man a self-reliant immobility as the result of

thought, *i.e.*, of the activity which produces the universal. But the inward reconciliation by means of philosophy was itself only an abstract one—in the pure principle of personality; for thought, which, as perfectly refined, made itself its own object, and thus harmonized itself, was entirely destitute of a real object, and the immobility of Scepticism made aimlessness itself the object of the will. This philosophy knew nothing but the negativity of all that assumed to be real and was the counsel of despair to a world which no longer possessed anything stable. It could not satisfy the living spirit, which longed after a higher reconciliation.

Chapter 2. *Christianity*

It has been remarked that Cæsar inaugurated the modern world on the side of *reality*, while its spiritual and inward existence was unfolded under Augustus. At the beginning of that empire, whose principle we have recognized as finiteness and particular subjectivity exaggerated to infinitude, the salvation of the world had its birth in the same principle of subjectivity— *viz.*, as a *particular person,* in abstract subjectivity, but in such a way that conversely, finiteness is only the *form* of his appearance, while infinity and absolutely independent existence constitute the essence and substantial being which it embodies. The Roman world, as it has been described—in its desperate condition and the pain of abandonment by God—came to an open rupture with reality, and made prominent the general desire for a satisfaction such as can only be attained in "the inner man," the soul, thus preparing the ground for a higher spiritual world. Rome was the fate that crushed down the gods and all genial life in its hard service, while it was the power that purified the human heart from all speciality. Its entire condition is therefore analogous to a place of birth, and its pain is like the travail-throes of another and higher spirit, which manifested itself in connection with the *Christian religion.* This higher spirit involves the reconciliation and emancipation of spirit; while man obtains the consciousness of spirit in its universality and infinity. The absolute object, *truth,* is spirit; and as man himself is spirit, he is present to himself in that object, and thus in his absolute object has found essential being and *his own* essential being. But in order that the objectivity of essential being may be done away with, and spirit be no longer alien to itself, may be *with* itself, the naturalness of spirit—that in virtue of which man is a special, empirical existence—must be removed;

so that the alien element may be destroyed, and the reconciliation of spirit be accomplished.

God is thus recognized as *spirit*, only when known as the triune. This new principle is the axis on which the history of the world turns. This is *the goal* and the *starting point* of history. "When the fulness of the time was come, God sent His Son," is the statement of the Bible. This means nothing else than that *self-consciousness* had reached the phases of development [*momente*], whose resultant constitutes the idea of spirit, and had come to feel the necessity of comprehending those phases absolutely. This must now be more fully explained. We said of the Greeks, that the law for their spirit was: "Man, know thyself." The Greek spirit was a consciousness of spirit, but under a limited form, having the element of nature as an essential ingredient. Spirit may have had the upper hand, but the unity of the superior and the subordinate was itself still natural. Spirit appeared as specialized in the idiosyncrasies of the genius of the several Greek nationalities and of their divinities, and was represented by *art*, in whose sphere the sensuous is elevated only to the middle ground of beautiful form and shape, but not to pure thought. The element of subjectivity that was wanting to the Greeks, we found among the Romans: but as it was merely formal and in itself indefinite, it took its material from passion and caprice;—even the most shameful degradations could be here connected with a divine dread (*vide* the declaration of Hispala respecting the Bacchanalia, Livy xxxix. 13). This element of subjectivity is afterwards further realized as personality of individuals—a realization which is exactly adequate to the principle, and is equally abstract and formal. As such an ego, I am infinite to myself, and my phenomenal existence consists in the property recognized as mine, and the recognition of my personality. This inner existence goes no further; all the applications of the principle merge in this. Individuals are thereby posited as atoms; but they are at the same time subject to the severe rule of the *One*, which as *monas monadum* is a power over private persons. That private right is therefore, *ipso facto*, a nullity, an ignoring of the personality; and the supposed condition of right turns out to be an absolute destitution of it. This contradiction is the misery of the Roman world. Each person is, according to the principle of his personality, entitled only to possession, while the person of persons lays claim to the possession of all these individuals, so that the right assumed by the social unit is at once abrogated and robbed of validity. But the misery of this contradiction is the *discipline of the world. Zucht* (discipline) is derived from *ziehen* (to draw). This "drawing" must be towards something; there must be some fixed unity in the background in whose direction that drawing takes place, and for which the subject of it is being trained, in order that the standard of attainment may be reached. A renunciation, a disaccustoming, is the means of leading to an absolute basis of existence. That contradiction which afflicts the Roman world is the very state of things which constitutes such a discipline, the discipline of that culture which compels personality to display its nothingness. But it is reserved for us of a later period to regard this as a training; to those who are thus trained, it seems a blind destiny, to which they submit in the stupor of suffering. The higher condition, in which the soul itself feels pain and longing—in which man is not only "drawn," but feels that the drawing is into himself—is still absent. What has been reflection on our part must arise in the mind of the subject of this discipline, in the form of a consciousness that in himself he is miserable and null. Outward suffering must, as already said, be merged in a sorrow of the inner man. He must feel himself as the negation of himself; he must see that his misery is the misery of his nature—that he is in himself a divided and discordant being. This state of mind, this self-chastening, this pain occasioned by our individual nothingness—the wretchedness of our self, and the longing to transcend this condition of soul—must be looked for elsewhere than in the properly Roman world. It is this which gives to the *Jewish people* their world historical importance and weight; for from this state of mind arose that higher phase in which spirit came to absolute self-consciousness—passing from that alien form of being which is its discord and pain, and mirroring itself in its own essence. The state of feeling in question we find expressed most purely and beautifully in the Psalms of David, and in the Prophets, the chief burden of whose utterances is the thirst of the soul after God, its profound sorrow for its transgressions, and the desire for righteousness and holiness. Of this spirit we have the mythical representation at the very beginning of the Jewish canonical books, in the account of the Fall. Man, created in the image of God, lost, it is said, his state of absolute contentment, by eating of the tree of the knowledge of good and evil. Sin consists here only in knowledge: this is the sinful element, and by it man is stated to have trifled away his natural happiness. This is a deep truth, that evil lies in consciousness: for the brutes are neither evil nor good; the merely natural man quite as little.[1] Consciousness occasions the separation of the ego, in its boundless freedom as arbitrary choice, from the pure essence of the will—*i.e.*, from the good. Knowledge, as the disannulling of the unity of mere nature, is the Fall, which is no casual conception, but the eternal history of spirit. For the state of innocence, the paradisaical condition, is that of the brute. Paradise is a park, where only brutes, not men, can remain. For the brute is one with God only implicitly. Only man's spirit (that is) has a self-cognizant existence. This existence for self, this consciousness, is at the same time separation from the universal and divine spirit. If I hold to my abstract freedom, in contraposition to the good, I adopt the standpoint of evil. The Fall is therefore the eternal mythus of man—in fact, the very transition by which he becomes man. Persistence in this standpoint is, however, evil, and the feeling of pain at such a condition, and of longing to transcend it, we find in David, when he says: "Lord, create for me a pure heart, a new *steadfast* Spirit." This feeling we observe even in the account of the Fall; though an announcement of reconciliation is not made there, but rather one of continuance in misery. Yet we have in this narrative the *prediction* of reconciliation in the sentence, "The serpent's head shall be bruised"; but still more profoundly expressed where it is stated that when God saw that Adam had eaten of that tree, he said, "Behold Adam is become as one of us, knowing good and evil." God confirms the words of the serpent. Implicitly and explicitly, then, we have the truth that man through spirit—through cognition of the universal and the particular—comprehends God Himself. But it is only God that declares this—not man: the latter remains, on the contrary, in a state of internal discord. The joy of reconciliation is still distant from humanity; the absolute and final repose of his whole being is not yet discovered to man. It exists, in the first instance, only for God. As far as the present is concerned, the feeling of pain at his condition is regarded as a final award. The satisfaction which man enjoys at first, consists in the finite and temporal blessings conferred on the chosen family and the possession of the Land of Canaan. His repose is not found in God. Sacrifices are, it is true, offered to Him in the temple, and atonement made by outward offerings and

inward penitence. But that mundane satisfaction in the chosen family, and its possession of Canaan, was taken from the Jewish people in the chastisement inflicted by the Roman Empire. The Syrian kings did indeed oppress it, but it was left for the Romans to annul its individuality. The Temple of Zion is destroyed; the God-serving nation is scattered to the winds. Here every source of satisfaction is taken away, and the nation is driven back to the standpoint of that primeval mythus—the standpoint of that painful feeling which humanity experiences when thrown upon itself. Opposed to the universal *fatum* of the Roman world, we have here the consciousness of evil and the direction of the mind Godwards. All that remains to be done, is that this fundamental idea should be expanded to an objective universal sense, and be taken as the concrete existence of man—as the completion of his nature. Formerly the Land of Canaan and themselves as the people of God had been regarded by the Jews as that concrete and complete existence. But this basis of satisfaction is now lost, and thence arises the sense of misery and failure of hope in God, with whom that happy reality had been essentially connected. Here, then, misery is not the stupid immersion in a blind fate, but a boundless energy of longing. Stoicism taught only that the negative *is not*—that pain must not be recognized as a veritable existence; but *Jewish* feeling persists in acknowledging reality and desires harmony and reconciliation within its sphere; for that feeling is based on the Oriental unity of nature—*i.e.*, the unity of reality, of subjectivity, with the substance of the one esssential being. Through the loss of mere outward reality spirit is driven back within itself; the side of reality is thus refined to universality, through the reference of it to the one. The Oriental antithesis of light and darkness is transferred to spirit, and the darkness becomes sin. For the abnegation of reality there is no compensation but subjectivity itself—the human will as intrinsically universal; and thereby alone does reconciliation become possible. Sin is the discerning of good and evil as separation; but this discerning likewise heals the ancient hurt, and is the fountain of infinite reconciliation. The discerning in question brings with it the destruction of that which is external and alien in consciousness, and is consequently the return of subjectivity into itself. This, then, adopted into the actual self-consciousness of the world is the *reconciliation of the world*. From that unrest of infinite sorrow, in which the two sides of the an-

[1] I was alive without the law once, etc. Romans, 7. 9.

tithesis stand related to each other, is developed the unity of God with reality (which latter had been posited as negative), *i.e.*, with subjectivity which had been separated from Him. The infinite loss is counterbalanced only by its infinity and thereby becomes infinite gain. The recognition of the identity of the subject and God was introduced into the world when *the fulness of time was come:* the consciousness of this identity is the recognition of God in his true essence. The material of truth is *spirit* itself—inherent vital movement. The nature of God as pure spirit, is manifested to man *in the Christian religion.*

But what is spirit? It is the one immutably homogeneous infinite—pure identity—which in its second phase separates itself from itself and makes this second aspect its own polar opposite, *viz.,* as existence for and in self as contrasted with the universal. But this separation is annulled by the fact that atomistic subjectivity, as simple relation to itself is itself the universal, the identical with self. If spirit be defined as absolute reflection within itself in virtue of its absolute duality—love, on the one hand, as comprehending the emotional, knowledge, on the other hand, as spirit—it is recognized as *triune:* the "Father" and the "Son," and that duality which essentially characterizes it as "Spirit." It must further be observed, that *in* this truth, the relation of man *to* this truth is also posited. For spirit makes itself its own opposite and is the return from this opposite into itself. Comprehended in pure ideality, that antithetic form of spirit is the Son of God; reduced to limited and particular conceptions, it is the world-nature and finite spirit: finite spirit itself therefore is posited as a constituent element in the divine being. Man himself therefore is comprehended in the idea of God, and this comprehension may be thus expressed—that the unity of man with God is posited in the Christian religion. But this unity must not be superficially conceived, as if God were only man, and man, without further condition, were God. Man, on the contrary, is God only in so far as he annuls the merely natural and limited in his spirit and elevates himself to God. That is to say, it is obligatory on him who is a partaker of the truth, and knows that he himself is a constituent of the divine idea, to give up his merely natural being: for the natural is the unspiritual. In this idea of God, then, is to be found also the *reconciliation* that heals the pain and inward suffering of man. For suffering itself is henceforth recognized as an instrument necessary for producing the unity

of man with God. This implicit unity exists in the first place only for the thinking speculative consciousness; but it must also exist for the sensuous, representative consciousness—it must become an object for the world—it must *appear,* and that in the sensuous form appropriate to spirit, which is the human.

Christ has appeared—a man who is God— God who is man; and thereby peace and reconciliation have accrued to the world. Our thoughts naturally revert to the Greek anthropomorphism, of which we affirmed that it did not go far enough. For that natural elation of soul which characterized the Greeks did not rise to the subjective freedom of the ego itself, to the inwardness that belongs to the Christian religion, to the recognition of spirit as a *definite positive being.* The appearance of the Christian God involves further its being *unique* in its kind; it can occur only once, for God is realized as subject, and as manifested subjectivity is exclusively one individual. The lamas are ever and anon chosen anew; because God is known in the East as substance, whose infinity of form is recognized merely in an unlimited multeity of outward and particular manifestations. But subjectivity as infinite relation to self, has its form *in itself,* and as manifested, must be a unity excluding all others. Moreover, the sensuous existence in which spirit is embodied is only a transitional phase. Christ dies; only as dead, is he exalted to heaven and sits at the right hand of God; only thus is he spirit. He himself says: "When I am no longer with you, the Spirit will guide you into all truth." Not till the Feast of Pentecost were the Apostles filled with the Holy Ghost. To the Apostles, Christ as living, was not that which he was to them subsequently as the spirit of the Church, in which he became to them for the first time an object for their truly spiritual consciousness. On the same principle, we do not adopt the right point of view in thinking of Christ only as a historical bygone personality. So regarded, the question is asked: what are we to make of his birth, his father and mother, his early domestic relations, his miracles, etc.?— *i.e.,* what is he *unspiritually* regarded? Considered only in respect of his talents, character and morality, as a teacher and so forth, we place him in the same category with Socrates and others, though his morality may be ranked higher. But excellence of character, morality, etc.—all this is not the *ne plus ultra* in the requirements of spirit—does not enable man to gain the speculative idea of spirit for his conceptive faculty. If Christ is to be looked upon only as an excellent, even impeccable individual, and nothing more, the conception of the speculative idea, of absolute truth is ignored. But this is the desideratum, the point from which we have to start. Make of Christ what you will, exegetically, critically, historically—demonstrate as you please, how the doctrines of the Church were established by councils, attained currency as the result of this or that episcopal interest or passion, or originated in this or that quarter; let all such circumstances have been what they might—the only concerning question is: what is the idea or the truth in and for itself?

Further, the real attestation of the divinity of Christ is the witness of one's own spirit—not miracles; for only spirit recognizes spirit. The miracles may lead the way to such recognition. A miracle implies that the natural course of things is interrupted: but it is very much a question of relation what we call the "natural course"; and the phenomena of the magnet might, under cover of this definition, be reckoned miraculous. Nor does the miracle of the divine mission of Christ prove anything; for Socrates likewise introduced a new self-consciousness on the part of spirit, diverse from the traditional tenor of men's conceptions. The main question is not his divine mission but the revelation made in Christ and the purport of his mission. Christ himself blames the Pharisees for desiring miracles of him, and speaks of false prophets who will perform miracles.

We have next to consider how the Christian view resulted in the formation of the Church. To pursue the rationale of its development from the idea of Christianity would lead us too far, and we have here to indicate only the general phases which the process assumed. The first phase is the founding of the Christian religion, in which its principle is expressed with unrestrained energy, but in the first instance abstractly. This we find in the Gospels, where the infinity of spirit, its elevation into the spiritual world, is the main theme. With transcendent boldness does Christ stand forth among the Jewish people. "Blessed are the pure in heart, for they shall see God," he proclaims in the Sermon on the Mount—a dictum of the noblest simplicity, and pregnant with an elastic energy of rebound against all the adventitious appliances with which the human soul can be burdened. The pure heart is the domain in which God is present to man: he who is imbued with the spirit of this apophthegm is armed against all alien bonds and superstitions. The other utterances are of the same tenor: "Blessed are the peacemak-

ers; for they shall be called the children of God"; and, "Blessed are they which are persecuted for righteousness' sake: for theirs is the kingdom of heaven"; and, "Be ye perfect, even as your Father which is in heaven is perfect." Christ enforces here a completely unmistakable requirement. The infinite exaltation of spirit to absolute purity is placed at the beginning as the foundation of all. The form of the instrumentality by which that result is to be accomplished is not yet given, but the result itself is the subject of an absolute command. As regards the relation of this standpoint of spirit to secular existence, we find that spiritual purity presented as the substantial basis. "Seek ye first the kingdom of God and his righteousness, and all things shall be added unto you"; and, "The sufferings of this present time are not worthy to be compared with that glory."[1] Here Christ says that outward sufferings, as such, are not to be feared or fled from, for they are nothing as compared with that glory. Further on, this doctrine, as the natural consequence of its appearing in an abstract form, assumes a *polemical* direction. "If thy right eye offend thee, pluck it out and cast it from thee: if thy right hand offend thee, cut it off and cast it from thee. It is better that one of thy members should perish, and not that thy whole body should be cast into hell." Whatever might disturb the purity of the soul, should be destroyed. So in reference to property and worldly gain, it is said: "Care not for your life, what ye shall eat and drink, nor for your body, what ye shall put on. Is not the life more than meat, and the body more than raiment? Behold the fowls of the air: for they sow not, neither do they reap, nor gather into barns; yet your heavenly Father feedeth them. Are ye not much better than they?" Labor for subsistence is thus reprobated: "Wilt thou be perfect, go and sell what thou hast, and give it to the poor, so shalt thou have a treasure in heaven, and come, follow me." Were this precept directly complied with, a social revolution must take place; the poor would become the rich. Of such supreme moment, it is implied, is the doctrine of Christ, that all duties and moral bonds are unimportant as compared with it. To a youth who wishes to delay the duties of discipleship till he has buried his father, Christ says: "Let the dead bury their dead—follow thou me." "He that loveth father or mother more than me is not worthy of me." He said: "Who is my mother? and who are my brethren? and stretched his hand out over his

[1] The words in the text occur in Romans, 8. 18, but the import of Matthew, 5. 12, is nearly the same.

disciples and said, "Behold my mother and my brethren! For he that doeth the will of my Father in heaven, the same is my brother, and sister and mother." Yes, it is even said: "*Think not that I am come to send peace on the earth. I am not come to send peace but the sword. For I am come to set a man against his father, and the daughter against her mother, and the mother-in-law against her daughter-in-law.*" Here then is an abstraction from all that belongs to reality, even from moral ties. We may say that nowhere are to be found such revolutionary utterances as in the Gospels; for everything that had been respected, is treated as a matter of indifference—as worthy of no regard.

The next point is the development of this principle; and the whole sequel of history is the history of its development. Its first realization is the formation, by the friends of Christ, of a society—a church. It has been already remarked that only after the death of Christ could the spirit come upon his friends; that only then were they able to conceive the true idea of God, *viz.*, that in Christ man is redeemed and reconciled: for in him the idea of eternal truth is recognized, the essence of man acknowledged to be spirit, and the fact proclaimed that only by stripping himself of his finiteness and surrendering himself to pure self-consciousness, does he attain the truth. Christ—man as man—in whom the unity of God and man has appeared, has in his death, and his history generally, himself presented the eternal history of spirit—a history which every man has to accomplish in himself, in order to exist as spirit, or to become a child of God, a citizen of his kingdom. The followers of Christ, who combine on this principle and live in the spiritual life as their aim, form the *Church*, which is the Kingdom of God. "Where two or three are gathered together in my name," (*i.e.*, "in the character of partakers in my being") says Christ, "there am I in the midst of them." The church is a real present life in the spirit of Christ.

It is important that the Christian religion be not limited to the teachings of Christ himself: it is in the Apostles that the completed and developed truth is first exhibited. This complex of thought unfolded itself in the Christian community. That community, in its first experiences, found itself sustaining a double relation—first, a relation to the Roman world, and secondly, to the truth whose development was its aim. We will pursue these different relations separately.

The Christian community found itself in the Roman world, and in this world the extension of the Christian religion was to take place. That community must therefore keep itself removed from all activity in the state, constitute itself a separate company, and not react against the decrees, views, and transactions of the state. But as it was secluded from the state, and consequently did not hold the emperor for its absolute sovereign, it was the object of persecution and hate. Then was manifested that infinite inward liberty which it enjoyed, in the great steadfastness with which sufferings and sorrows were patiently borne for the sake of the highest truth. It was less the miracles of the Apostles that gave to Christianity its outward extension and inward strength, than the substance, the truth of the doctrine itself. Christ himself says: "Many will say to me at that day: Lord, Lord! have we not prophesied in thy name, have we not cast out devils in thy name, have we not in thy name done many wonderful deeds? Then will I profess unto them: I never knew you, depart from me all ye workers of iniquity."

As regards its other relation, *viz.*, that to the truth, it is especially important to remark that the *dogma*—the theoretical—was already matured within the Roman world, while we find the development of the state from that principle a much later growth. The Fathers of the Church and the councils constituted the dogma; but a chief element in this constitution was supplied by the previous development of *philosophy*. Let us examine more closely how the philosophy of the time stood related to religion. It has already been remarked that the Roman inwardness and subjectivity, which presented itself only abstractly, as soulless personality in the exclusive position assumed by the ego, was refined by the philosophy of stoicism and scepticism to the form of universality. The ground of thought was thereby reached, and God was known in thought as the One Infinite. The universal stands here only as an unimportant predicate—not itself a subject, but requiring a concrete particular application to make it such. But the one and universal, the illimitable conceived by fancy, is essentially Oriental; for measureless conceptions, carrying all limited existence beyond its proper bounds, are indigenous to the east. Presented in the domain of thought itself, the Oriental *One* is the invisible and non-sensuous God of the Israelitish people, but whom they also make an object of conception as a person. This principle became world-historical with Christianity.

In the Roman world, the union of the east and west had taken place in the first instance by means of conquest: it took place now inwardly, psychologically, also—the spirit of the east spreading over the west. The worship of Isis and that of Mithra had been extended through the whole Roman world; spirit, lost in the outward and in limited aims, yearned after an infinite. But the west desired a deeper, purely inward universality—an infinite possessed at the same time of positive qualities. Again, it was in Egypt—in Alexandria, viz., the centre of communication between the east and the west—that the problem of the age was proposed for thought; and the solution now found was spirit. There the two principles came into scientific contact, and were scientifically worked out. It is especially remarkable to observe there learned Jews such as Philo connecting abstract forms of the concrete, which they derived from Plato and Aristotle, with their conception of the infinite, and recognizing God according to the more concrete idea of spirit, under the definition of the Λόγος. So, also, did the profound thinkers of Alexandria comprehend the unity of the Platonic and Aristotelian philosophy; and their speculative thinking attained those abstract ideas which are likewise the fundamental purport of the Christian religion. The application, by way of postulate, to the pagan religion, of ideas recognized as true, was a direction which philosophy had already taken among the heathen. Plato had altogether repudiated the current mythology, and, with his followers, was accused of atheism. The Alexandrians, on the contrary, endeavoured to demonstrate a speculative truth in the Greek conceptions of the gods: and the Emperor Julian the Apostate resumed the attempt, asserting that the pagan ceremonials had a strict connection with rationality. The heathen felt, as it were, obliged to give to their divinities the semblance of something higher than sensuous conceptions; they therefore attempted to spiritualize them. Thus much is also certain, that the Greek religion contains a degree of reason; for the substance of spirit is reason, and its product must be something rational. It makes a difference, however, whether reason is explicitly developed in religion, or merely adumbrated by it, as constituting its hidden basis. And while the Greeks thus spiritualized their sensuous divinities, the Christians also, on their side, sought for a profounder sense in the historical part of their religion. Just as Philo found a deeper import shadowed forth in the Mosaic record and idealized what he considered the bare shell of the narrative, so also did the Christians treat their records—partly

with a polemic view, but still more largely from a free and spontaneous interest in the process. But the instrumentality of philosophy in introducing these dogmas into the Christian religion is no sufficient ground for asserting that they were foreign to Christianity and had nothing to do with it. It is a matter of perfect indifference where a thing originated; the only question is: "Is it true in and for itself?" Many think that by pronouncing the doctrine to be Neo-Platonic, they have *ipso facto* banished it from Christianity. Whether a Christian doctrine stands exactly thus or thus in the Bible, the point to which the exegetical scholars of modern times devote all their attention, is not the only question. The letter kills, the spirit makes alive: this they say themselves, yet pervert the sentiment by taking the *understanding* for the *spirit*. It was the Church that recognized and established the doctrines in question, i.e., the spirit of the Church; and it is itself an article of doctrine: "I believe in a Holy Church";[1] as Christ himself also said: "The Spirit will guide you into all truth." In the Nicene Council (A.D. 325), was ultimately established a fixed confession of faith, to which we still adhere: this confession had not, indeed, a speculative *form,* but the profoundly speculative is most intimately inwoven with the manifestation of Christ himself. Even in John (ἐν ἀρχῇ ἦν ὁ λόγος καὶ ὁ λόγος ἦν πρὸς τὸν Θεὸν, καὶ Θεὸς ἦν ὁ λόγος) we see the commencement of a profounder comprehension. The profoundest thought is connected with the personality of Christ, with the historical and external; and it is the very grandeur of the Christian religion that, with all this profundity, it is easy of comprehension by our consciousness in its outward aspect, while, at the same time, it summons us to penetrate deeper. It is thus adapted to every grade of culture and yet satisfies the highest requirements.

Having spoken of the relation of the Christian community to the Roman world on the one side, and to the truth contained in its doctrines on the other side, we come to the third point, in which both doctrine and the external world are concerned, the *Church.* The Christian community is the kingdom of Christ—its influencing present spirit being Christ: for this kingdom has an actual existence, not a merely future one. This spiritual actuality has, therefore, also a phenomenal existence; and that, not only as contrasted with heathenism, but with secular existence

---

[1] In the Lutheran ritual, "*a* holy Catholic Church" is substituted for "*the* Holy Catholic Church," in the creed.

generally. For the Church, as presenting this outward existence, is not merely a *religion* as opposed to another religion, but is at the same time a particular form of secular existence, occupying a place side by side with other secular existence. The religious existence of the Church is governed by Christ; the secular side of its government is left to the free choice of the members themselves. Into this kingdom of God an organization must be introduced. In the first instance, all the members know themselves filled with the spirit; the whole community perceives the truth and gives expression to it; yet, together with this common participation of spiritual influence, arises the necessity of a presidency of guidance and teaching—a body distinct from the community at large. Those are chosen as presidents who are distinguished for talents, character, fervor of piety, a holy life, learning, and culture generally. The presidents—those who have a superior acquaintance with that substantial life of which all are partakers, and who are instructors in that life, those who establish what is truth, and those who dispense its enjoyment—are distinguished from the community at large, as persons endowed with knowledge and governing power are from the governed. To the intelligent presiding body, the spirit comes in a fully revealed and *explicit* form; in the mass of the community that spirit is only *implicit*. While, therefore, in the presiding body, the spirit exists as self-appreciating and self-cognizant, it becomes an authority in spiritual as well as in secular matters—an authority for the truth and for the relation of each individual to the truth, determining how he should conduct himself so as to act in accordance with the truth. This distinction occasions the rise of an *ecclesiastical kingdom* in the kingdom of God. Such a distinction is inevitable; but the existence of an authoritative government for the spiritual, when closely examined, shows that human subjectivity in its proper form has not yet developed itself. In the heart, indeed, the evil will is surrendered, but the will, as human, is not yet interpenetrated by the deity; the human will is emancipated only abstractly, not in its concrete reality, for the whole sequel of history is occupied with the realization of this concrete freedom. Up to this point, finite freedom has been only annulled, to make way for infinite freedom. The latter has not yet penetrated secular existence with its rays. Subjective freedom has not yet attained validity as such: insight does not yet rest on a basis of its own, but is content to inhere in the spirit of an extrinsic authority.

That *spiritual* kingdom has, therefore, assumed the shape of an *ecclesiastical* one, as the relation of the substantial being and essence of spirit to human freedom. Besides the interior organization already mentioned, we find the Christian community assuming also a definite external position, and becoming the possessor of property of its own. As property belonging to the spiritual world, it is presumed to enjoy special protection; and the immediate inference from this is that the Church has no dues to pay to the state, and that ecclesiastical persons are not amenable to the jurisdiction of the secular courts. This entails the government by the Church itself of ecclesiastical property and ecclesiastical persons. Thus there originates with the Church the contrasted spectacle of a body consisting only of private persons and the power of the emperor on the secular side; on the other side, the perfect democracy of the spiritual community, choosing its own president. Priestly consecration, however, soon changes this democracy into aristocracy; though the further development of the Church does not belong to the period now under consideration, but must be referred to the world of a later date.

It was then through the Christian religion that the absolute idea of God, in its true conception, attained consciousness. Here man, too, finds himself comprehended in his true nature, given in the specific conception of "the Son." Man, finite when regarded *for himself,* is yet at the same time the image of God and a fountain of infinity *in himself.* He is the object of his own existence —has in himself an infinite value, an eternal destiny. Consequently he has his true home in a supersensuous world—an infinite subjectivity, gained only by a rupture with mere natural existence and volition, and by his labour to break their power within him. This is religious self-consciousness. But in order to enter the sphere and display the active vitality of that religious life, humanity must become capable of it. This capability is the δύναμις for that ἐνέργεια. What therefore remains to be considered is those conditions of humanity which are the necessary corollary to the consideration that man is absolute self-consciousness—his spiritual nature being the starting-point and presupposition. These conditions are themselves not yet of a concrete order, but simply the first *abstract principles,* which are won by the instrumentality of the Christian religion for the *secular state.* First, under Christianity slavery is impossible; for man is man, in the abstract essence of his nature, is contemplated in God; each unit of mankind is an object of the grace of God and of the divine purpose: "God will have *all* men to be saved." Utterly excluding all speciality, therefore, man, in and for himself, in his simple quality of man, has infinite value; and this infinite values abolishes, *ipso facto*, all particularity attaching to birth or country. The other, the second principle, regards the subjectivity of man in its bearing on the fortuitous—on chance. Humanity has this sphere of free spirituality in and for itself, and everything else must proceed from it. The place appropriated to the abode and presence of the divine spirit, the sphere in question, is spiritual subjectivity, and is constituted the place to which all contingency is amenable. It follows thence that what we observed among the Greeks, as a form of customary morality, cannot maintain its position in the Christian world. For *that* morality is spontaneous unreflected wont; while the Christian principle is independent subjectivity—the soil on which grows the true. Now an unreflected morality cannot continue to hold its ground against the principle of subjective freedom. Greek freedom was that of hap and "genius"; it was still conditioned by slaves and oracles; but now the principle of absolute freedom in God makes its appearance. Man now no longer sustains the relation of dependence, but of love—in the consciousness that he is a partaker in the divine existence. In regard to particular aims, man now forms his own determinations and recognizes himself as plenipotentiary in regard to all finite existence. All that is special retreats into the background before that spiritual sphere of subjectivity, which takes a secondary position only in presence of the divine spirit. The superstition of oracles and auspices is thereby entirely abrogated: man is recognized as the absolute authority in crises of decision.

It is the two principles just treated of, that now attach to spirit in this its self-contained phase. The inner shrine of man is designed, on the one hand, to train the citizen of the religious life to bring himself into harmony with the spirit of God; on the other hand, this is the *point du départ* for determining secular relations, and its condition is the theme of Christian history. The change which piety effects must not remain concealed in the recesses of the heart, but must become an actual, present world, complying with the conditions prescribed by that absolute spirit. Piety of heart does not, *per se,* involve the submission of the subjective will, in its external relations, to that piety. On the contrary we see all passions increasingly rampant in the sphere of reality, because that sphere is looked down upon with contempt, from the lofty position attained by the world of mind, as one destitute of all claim and value. The problem to be solved is therefore the imbuing of the sphere of unreflected spiritual existence with the *idea* of spirit. A general observation here suggests itself. From time immemorial it has been customary to assume an opposition between reason and religion, as also between *religion and the world;* but on investigation this turns out to be only a *distinction.* Reason in general is the positive existence of spirit, divine as well as human. The distinction between religion and the world is only this: that religion as such, is reason in the soul and heart, that it is a temple in which truth and freedom in God are presented to the conceptive faculty. The state, on the other hand, regulated by the selfsame reason, is a temple of human freedom concerned with the perception and volition of a reality, whose purport may itself be called divine. Thus freedom in the state is preserved and established by religion, since moral rectitude in the state is only the carrying out of that which constitutes the fundamental principle of religion. The process displayed in history is only the manifestation of religion as human reason—the production of the religious principle which dwells in the heart of man, under the form of secular freedom. Thus the discord between the inner life of the heart and the actual world is removed. To realize this is, however, the vocation of another people, or other peoples, *viz.,* the *German.* In ancient Rome itself, Christianity cannot find a ground on which it may become actual and develop an empire.

Chapter 3. *The Byzantine Empire*

With Constantine the Great, the Christian religion ascended the throne of the empire. He was followed by a succession of Christian emperors, interrupted only by Julian—who however, could do but little for the prostrate ancient faith. The Roman Empire embraced the whole civilized earth, from the western ocean to the Tigris—from the interior of Africa, to the Danube (Pannonia, Dacia). Christianity soon spread through the length and breadth of this enormous realm. Rome had long ceased to be the exclusive residence of the emperors. Many of Constantine's predecessors had resided in Milan or other places; and he himself established a second court in the ancient Byzantium, which received the name of Constantinople. From the first its population consisted chiefly of Christians, and Constantine lavished every appliance to render this new abode equal in splendour to the old. The empire still remained in its integrity till Theodosius the Great made permanent a separation that had been only occasional, and divided it between his two sons. The reign of Theodosius displayed the last faint glimmer of that splendour which had glorified the Roman world. Under him the pagan temples were shut, the sacrifices and ceremonies abolished, and paganism itself forbidden: gradually however it entirely vanished of itself. The heathen orators of the time cannot sufficiently express their wonder and astonishment at the monstrous contrast between the days of their forefathers and their own. "Our temples have become tombs. The places which were formerly adorned with the holy statues of the gods are now covered with sacred bones [relics of the martyrs]; men who have suffered a shameful death for their crimes, whose bodies are covered with stripes, and whose heads have been embalmed, are the object of veneration." All that was contemned is exalted; all that was formerly revered, is trodden in the dust. The last of the pagans express this enormous contrast with profound lamentation.

The Roman Empire was divided between the two sons of Theodosius. The elder, Arcadius, received the Eastern Empire: ancient Greece, with Thrace, Asia Minor, Syria, Egypt; the younger, Honorius, the Western: Italy, Africa, Spain, Gaul, Britain. Immediately after the death of Theodosius, confusion entered, and the Roman provinces were overwhelmed by alien peoples. Already, under the Emperor Valens, the Visigoths, pressed by the Huns, had solicited a domicile on the hither side of the Danube. This was granted them, on the condition that they should defend the border provinces of the empire. But maltreatment roused them to revolt. Valens was beaten and fell on the field. The later emperors paid court to the leader of these Goths. Alaric, the bold Gothic chief, turned his arms against Italy. Stilicho, the general and minister of Honorius, stayed his course, A.D. 403, by the battle of Pollentia, as at a later date he also routed Radagaisus, leader of the Alani, Suevi, and others. Alaric now attacked Gaul and Spain and, on the fall of Stilicho, returned to Italy. Rome was stormed and plundered by him A.D. 410. Afterwards Attila advanced on it with the terrible might of the Huns—one of those purely Oriental phenomena, which, like a mere storm-torrent, rise to a furious height and bear down everything in their course, but in a brief space are so completely spent that nothing is seen of them but the traces they have left in the ruins which they have occasioned. Attila pressed into Gaul, where, A.D. 451, a vigorous resistance was offered him by Ætius, near Chalons on the Marne. Victory remained doubtful. Attila subsequently marched upon Italy and died in the year 453. Soon afterwards however Rome was taken and plundered by the Vandals under Genseric. Finally, the dignity of the western emperors became a farce, and their empty title was abolished by Odoacer, king of the Heruli.

The Eastern Empire long survived, and in the west a new Christian population was formed from the invading barbarian hordes. Christianity had at first kept aloof from the state, and the development which it experienced related to doctrine, internal organization, discipline, etc. But now it had become dominant: it was now a political power, a political motive. We now see Christianity under two forms: on the one side, barbarian nations whose culture was yet to begin, who have to acquire the very rudiments of science, law, and polity; on other side, civilized peoples in possession of Greek science and a highly refined oriental culture. Municipal legislation among them was complete—having reached the highest perfection through the labors of the great Roman jurisconsults; so that the *corpus juris* compiled at the instance of the Emperor Justinian still excites the admiration of the world. Here the Christian religion is placed in the midst of a developed civilization, which did not proceed from it. There, on the contrary, the process of culture has its very first step still to take, and that within the sphere of Christianity.

These two empires, therefore, present a most remarkable contrast, in which we have before our eyes a grand example of the necessity of a people's having its culture *developed* in the spirit of the Christian religion. The history of the highly civilized Eastern Empire—where as we might suppose, the spirit of Christianity could be taken up in its truth and purity—exhibits to us a millennial series of uninterrupted crimes, weaknesses, basenesses and want of principle; a most repulsive and consequently a most uninteresting picture. It is evident here how Christianity may be abstract and how, as such it is powerless, on account of its very purity and intrinsic spirituality. It may even be entirely separated from the world, as, *e.g.*, in Monasticism—which originated in Egypt. It is a common notion and saying, in reference to the power of religion, abstractly considered, over the hearts of men, that if Christian love were universal, private and political life would both be perfect, and the state of mankind would be thoroughly righteous and moral. Such representations may be a pious *wish,* but do not possess truth; for religion is something internal, having to do with conscience alone. To it all the passions and desires are opposed, and in order that heart, will, intelligence may become true, they must be *thoroughly educated;* right must become custom—habit; practical activity must be elevated to rational action; the state must have a rational organization, and then at length does the will of individuals become a truly righteous one. Light shining in darkness may perhaps give colour, but not a picture animated by spirit. The Byzantine Empire is a grand example of how the Christian religion may maintain an abstract character among a cultivated people, if the whole organization of the state and of the laws is not reconstructed in harmony with its principle. At Byzantium, Christianity had fallen into the hands of the dregs of the population—the lawless mob. Popular license, on the one side, and courtly baseness, on the other side, take refuge under the sanction of religion and degrade the latter to a disgusting object. In regard to religion, two interests obtained prominence: first, the settlement of doctrine; and secondly, the appointment to ecclesiastical offices. The settlement of doctrine pertained to the councils and Church authorities; but the principle of Christianity is freedom—subjective insight. These matters therefore, were special subjects of contention for the populace; violent civil wars arose, and everywhere might be witnessed scenes of murder, conflagration and pillage, perpetrated in the cause of Christian dogmas. A famous schism, *e.g.,* occurred in reference to the dogma of the Τρισάγιον. The words read: "Holy, Holy, Holy, is the Lord God of Zebaoth." To this, one party, in honor of Christ, added—"who was crucified for us." Another party rejected the addition, and sanguinary struggles ensued. In the contest on the question whether Christ were ὁμοούσιος or ὁμοιούσιος—that is, of *the same* or of *similar* nature with God—the one letter ι cost many thousands their lives. Especially notorious are the contentions about images, in which it often happened, that the emperor declared for the images and the patriarch against, or conversely. Streams of blood flowed as the result. Gregory Nazianzen says somewhere: "This city [Constantinople] is full of handicraftsmen and slaves, who are all profound theologians, and preach in their workshops and in the streets. If you want a man to change a piece of silver, he instructs you in what consists the distinction between the Father and the Son: if you ask the price of a loaf of bread, you receive for answer —that the Son is inferior to the Father; and if you ask, whether the bread is ready, the rejoinder is that the genesis of the Son was from nothing." The idea of spirit contained in this doctrine was thus treated in an utterly unspiritual manner. The appointment to the Patriarchate at Constantinople, Antioch and Alexandria, and the jealousy and ambition of the patriarchs likewise occasioned many intestine struggles. To all these religious contentions was added the interest in the gladiators and their combats, and in the parties of the blue and green colour, which likewise occasioned the bloodiest encounters; a sign of the most fearful degradation, as proving that all feeling for what is serious and elevated is lost, and that the delirium of religious passion is quite consistent with an appetite for gross and barbarous spectacles.

The chief points in the Christian religion were at last, by degrees, established by the councils. The Christians of the Byzantine Empire remained sunk in the dream of superstition—persisting in blind obedience to the patriarchs and the priesthood. Image-worship, to which we alluded above, occasioned the most violent struggles and storms. The brave Emperor Leo the Isaurian, in particular, persecuted images with the greatest obstinacy, and in the year 754, image-worship was declared by a council to be an invention of the devil. Nevertheless, in the year 787 the Empress Irene had it restored under the authority of a Nicene council, and the Empress Theodora definitively established it— proceeding against its enemies with energetic rigour. The iconoclastic patriarch received two hundred blows, the bishops trembled, the monks exulted, and the memory of this orthodox proceeding was celebrated by an annual ecclesiastical festival. The west, on the contrary, repudiated image-worship as late as the year 794, in the council held at Frankfort; and, though retaining the images, blamed most severely the superstition of the Greeks. Not till the later middle ages did image-worship meet with universal adoption as the result of quiet and slow advances.

The Byzantine Empire was thus distracted by passions of all kinds *within,* and pressed by the barbarians—to whom the emperors could offer but feeble resistance—*without.* The realm was in a condition of perpetual insecurity. Its general aspect presents a disgusting picture of imbecility; wretched, nay, insane passions, stifle the growth of all that is noble in thoughts, deeds, and persons. Rebellion on the part of generals, depositions of the emperors by their means or through the intrigues of the courtiers, assassination or poisoning of the emperors by their own wives and sons, women surrendering themselves to lusts and abominations of all kinds—such are the scenes which history here brings before us; till at last, about the middle of the fifteenth century (A.D. 1453), the rotten edifice of the Eastern Empire crumbled in pieces before the might of the vigorous Turks.

FOURTH PART

THE GERMAN WORLD

The German spirit is the spirit of the new world. Its aim is the realization of absolute truth as the unlimited self-determination of freedom—*that* freedom which has its own absolute form itself as its purport.[1] The destiny of the German peoples is to be the bearers of the Christian principle. The principle of spiritual freedom—of reconciliation, was introduced into the still simple, unformed minds of those peoples; and the part assigned them in the service of the world spirit was that of not merely possessing the idea of freedom as the substratum of their religious conceptions, but of producing it in free and spontaneous developments from their subjective self-consciousness.

In entering on the task of dividing the German world into its natural periods, we must remark that we have not, as was the case in treating of the Greeks and Romans, a double external relation—backwards to an earlier world-historical people, and forwards to a later one—to guide us. History shows that the process of development among the peoples now under consideration was an altogether different one. The Greeks and Romans had reached maturity within, ere they directed their energies outwards. The Germans, on the contrary, began with self-diffusion—deluging the world, and overpowering in their course the inwardly rotten, hollow political fabrics of the civilized nations. Only then did their *development* begin, kindled by a foreign culture, a foreign religion, polity and legislation. The process of culture they underwent consisted in taking up foreign elements and reductively amalgamating them with their own national life. Thus their history presents an introversion, the attraction of alien forms of life and the bring-

ing these to bear upon their own. In the Crusades, indeed, and in the discovery of America, the western world directed its energies outwards. But it was not thus brought in contact with a world-historical people that had preceded it; it did not dispossess a principle that had previously governed the world. The relation to an extraneous principle here only *accompanies* the history, does not bring with it essential changes in the nature of those conditions which characterize the peoples in question, but rather wears the aspect of internal evolution.[2]

The relation to other countries and periods is thus entirely different from that sustained by the Greeks and Romans. For the Christian world is the world of completion; the grand principle of being is realized, consequently the end of days is fully come. The idea can discover in Christianity no point in the aspirations of spirit that is not satisfied. For its individual members, the church is, it is true, a preparation for an eternal state as something future; since the units who compose it, in their isolated and several capacity, occupy a position of particularity: but the church has also the spirit of God actually present in it, it forgives the sinner and is a present kingdom of heaven. Thus the Christian world has no absolute existence outside its sphere, but only a relative one which is already implicitly vanquished, and in respect to which its only concern is to make it apparent that this conquest has taken place. Hence it follows that an external reference ceases to be the characteristic element determining the epochs of the modern world. We have therefore to look for another principle of division.

The German world took up the Roman culture and religion in their completed form. There was indeed a German and northern religion, but it had by no means taken deep root in the soul; Tacitus therefore calls the Germans: *"Securi*

[1] That is: The supreme law of the universe is recognized as identical with the dictates of conscience—becomes a "law of liberty." Morality—that authority which has the incontestable right to determine men's actions, which therefore is the only absolutely *free* and unlimited power—is no longer a compulsory enactment, but the free choice of human beings. The good man would make law for himself if he found none made for him.

[2] The influence of the Crusades and of the discovery of America was simply *reflex*. No other phase of humanity was thereby merged in Christendom.

adversus Deos." The Christian religion which they adopted, had received from councils and Fathers of the Church, who possessed the whole culture, and in particular, the philosophy of the Greek and Roman world, a perfected dogmatic system; the Church, too, had a completely developed hierarchy. To the native tongue of the Germans, the Church likewise opposed one perfectly developed—the Latin. In art and philosophy a similar alien influence predominated. What of Alexandrian and of formal Aristotelian philosophy was still preserved in the writings of Boethius, and elsewhere, became the fixed basis of speculative thought in the west for many centuries. The same principle holds in regard to the form of the secular sovereignty. Gothic and other chiefs gave themselves the name of Roman patricians, and at a later date the Roman Empire was restored. Thus the German world appears, superficially, to be only a continuation of the Roman. But there lived in it an entirely *new spirit*, through which the world was to be regenerated, the free spirit, *viz.*, which reposes on itself, the absolute self-determination of subjectivity. To this self-involved subjectivity, the corresponding objectivity stands opposed as absolutely alien. The distinction and antithesis which is evolved from these principles, is that of *church* and *state*. On the one side, the church develops itself, as the embodiment of absolute truth; for it is the consciousness of this truth, and at the same time the agency for rendering the individual harmonious with it. On the other side stands secular consciousness, which, with its aims, occupies the world of limitation—the *state*, based on heart or mutual confidence and subjectivity generally. European history is the exhibition of the growth of each of these principles severally, in church and state; then of an antithesis on the part of both —not only of the one to the other, but appearing within the sphere of each of these bodies themselves (since each of them is itself a totality); lastly, of the harmonizing of the antithesis.

The *three periods* of this world will have to be treated accordingly.

The *first* begins with the appearance of the German nations in the Roman Empire—the incipient development of these peoples, converts to Christianity, and now established in the possession of the west. Their barbarous and simple character prevents this initial period from possessing any great interest. The Christian world then presents itself as "Christendom"—one mass, in which the spiritual and the secular form only different aspects. This epoch extends to Charlemagne.

The *second period* develops the two sides of the antithesis to a logically consequential independence and opposition—the Church for itself as a *theocracy*, and the state for itself as a *feudal monarchy*. Charlemagne had formed an alliance with the Holy See against the Lombards and the factions of the nobles in Rome. A union thus arose between the spiritual and the secular power, and a kingdom of heaven on earth promised to follow in the wake of this conciliation. But just at this time, instead of a spiritual kingdom of heaven, the inwardness of the Christian principle wears the appearance of being altogether directed outwards and leaving its proper sphere. Christian freedom is perverted to its very opposite, both in a religious and secular respect; on the one hand, to the severest bondage, on the other hand, to the most immoral excess—a barbarous intensity of every passion. In this period two aspects of society are to be especially noticed: the first is the formation of states—superior and inferior suzerainties exhibiting a regulated subordination, so that every relation becomes a firmly-fixed private right, excluding a sense of universality. This regulated subordination appears in the *feudal system*. The second aspect presents the antithesis of *Church and state*. This antithesis exists solely because the Church, to whose management the spiritual was committed, itself sinks down into every kind of worldliness—a worldliness which appears only the more detestable, because all passions assume the sanction of religion.

The time of Charles V's reign, *i.e.*, the first half of the sixteenth century, forms the end of the second, and likewise the beginning of the *third period*. Secularity appears now as gaining a consciousness of its intrinsic worth—becomes aware of its having a value of its own in the morality, rectitude, probity and activity of man. The consciousness of independent validity is aroused through the restoration of Christian freedom. The Christian principle has now passed through the terrible discipline of culture, and it first attains truth and reality through the Reformation. This third period of the German world extends from the Reformation to our own times. The principle of free spirit is here made the banner of the world, and from this principle are evolved the universal axioms of reason. Formal thought—the understanding—had been already developed; but thought received its true material first with the Reformation, through the reviviscent concrete consciousness of free spirit.

From that epoch thought began to gain a culture properly its own: principles were derived from it which were to be the norm for the constitution of the state. Political life was now to be consciously regulated by reason. Customary morality, traditional usage lost its validity; the various claims insisted upon, must prove their legitimacy as based on rational principles. Not till this era is the freedom of spirit realized.

We may distinguish these periods as Kingdoms of the Father, the Son, and the Spirit.[1] The Kingdom of the Father is the consolidated, undistinguished mass, presenting a self-repeating cycle, mere change—like that sovereignty of Chronos engulfing his offspring. The Kingdom of the Son is the manifestation of God merely in a *relation* to secular existence—shining upon it as upon an alien object. The Kingdom of the Spirit is the harmonizing of the antithesis.

These epochs may be also compared with the earlier empires. In the German æon, as the realm of totality, we see the distinct *repetition of the earlier epochs*. Charlemagne's time may be compared with the Persian Empire; it is the period of substantial unity—this unity having its foundation in the inner man, the heart, and both in the spiritual and the secular still abiding in its simplicity.

To the Greek world and its merely *ideal* unity, the time preceding Charles V answers; where *real* unity no longer exists, because all phases of particularity have become fixed in privileges and peculiar rights. As in the interior of the realms themselves, the different estates of the realm, with their several claims, are isolated, so do the various states in their foreign aspects occupy a *merely external* relation to each other. A *diplomatic policy* arises, which in the interest of a European balance of power, unites them *with* and *against* each other. It is the time in which the world becomes clear and manifest to itself (discovery of America). So too does consciousness gain clearness *in* the supersensuous world and *respecting* it. Substantial objective religion brings itself to sensuous clearness in the

sensuous element (Christian art in the age of Pope Leo), and also becomes clear to itself in the element of inmost truth. We may compare this time with that of Pericles. The introversion of spirit begins (Socrates—Luther), though Pericles is wanting in this epoch. Charles V possesses enormous possibilities in point of outward appliances, and appears absolute in his power; but the inner spirit of Pericles, and therefore the absolute means of establishing a free sovereignty, are not in him. This is the epoch when spirit becomes clear to itself in separations occurring in the realm of reality; now the distinct elements of the German world manifest their essential nature.

The third epoch may be compared with the Roman world. The unity of a universal principle is here quite as decidedly present, yet not as the unity of abstract universal sovereignty, but as the hegemony of self-cognizant thought. The authority of rational aim is acknowledged, and privileges and particularities melt away before the common object of the state. Peoples will the right in and for itself; regard is not had exclusively to particular conventions between nations, but principles enter into the considerations with which diplomacy is occupied. As little can religion maintain itself apart from thought, but either advances to the comprehension of the idea, or, compelled by thought itself, becomes intensive belief—or lastly, from despair of finding itself at home in thought, flees back from it in pious horror, and becomes superstition.

Section I

THE ELEMENTS OF THE CHRISTIAN GERMAN WORLD

Chapter 1. *The Barbarian Migrations*

Respecting this first period, we have on the whole little to say, for it affords us comparatively slight materials for reflection. We will not follow the Germans back into their forests, nor investigate the origin of their migrations. Those forests of theirs have always passed for the abodes of free peoples, and Tacitus sketched his celebrated picture of Germany with a certain love and longing, contrasting it with the corruption and artificiality of that world to which he himself belonged. But we must not on this account regard such a state of barbarism as an exalted one, or fall into some such error as Rousseau's, who represents the condition of the American savages as one in which man is in possession of true freedom. Certainly there is an

---

[1] The conception of a mystical *regnum Patris, regnum Filii,* and *regnum Spiritus Sancti* is perfectly familiar to metaphysical theologians. The first represents the period in which deity is not yet manifested—remains *self-involved*. The second is that of manifestation in an individual being, standing *apart from* mankind generally—"the Son." The third is that in which this barrier is broken down, and an intimate mystical communion ensues between God in Christ and the regenerated, when God is "all in all." This remark may serve to prevent misconception as to the tone of the remainder of the paragraph. The mention of the Greek myth will appear pertinent in the view of those who admit what seems a very reasonable explanation of it—*viz.*, as an adumbration of the *self-involved* character of the prehistorical period.

immense amount of misfortune and sorrow of which the savage knows nothing; but this is a merely negative advantage, while freedom is essential positive. It is only the blessings conferred by affirmative freedom that are regarded as such in the highest grade of consciousness.

Our first acquaintance with the Germans finds each individual enjoying an independent freedom; and yet there is a certain community of feeling and interest, though not yet matured to a political condition. Next we see them inundating the Roman Empire. It was partly the fertility of its domains, partly the necessity of seeking other habitations, that furnished the inciting cause. In spite of the wars in which they engage with the Romans, individuals, and even entire clans, enter their service as soldiers. Even so early as the battle of Pharsalia we find German cavalry united with the Roman forces of Cæsar. In military service and intercourse with civilized peoples, they became acquainted with their advantages—advantages tending to the enjoyment and convenience of life, but also, and principally, those of mental cultivation. In the later emigrations, many nations—some entirely, others partially—remained behind in their original abodes.

Accordingly, a distinction must be made between the German nations who remained in their ancient habitations and those who spread themselves over the Roman Empire, and mingled with the conquered peoples. Since in their migratory expeditions the Germans attached themselves to their leaders of their own free choice, we find a peculiar duplicate condition of the great Teutonic families (Eastern and Western Goths; Goths in all parts of the world and in their original country; Scandinavians and Normans in Norway, but also appearing as knightly adventurers in the wide world). However different might be the fates of these peoples, they nevertheless had one aim in common —to procure themselves possessions, and to develop themselves in the direction of political organization. This process of growth is equally characteristic of all. In the west, in Spain and Portugal, the Suevi and Vandals are the first settlers, but are subdued and dispossessed by the Visigoths. A great *Visigothic* kingdom was established, to which Spain, Portugal, and a part of southern France belonged. The second kingdom is that of the *Franks*—a name which, from the end of the second century, was given in common to the Istævonian races between the Rhine and the Weser. They established themselves between the Moselle and the Scheldt, and under their leader, Clovis, pressed forward into Gaul as far as the Loire. He afterwards reduced the Franks on the lower Rhine, and the Alemanni on the upper Rhine; his sons subjugated the Thuringians and Burgundians. The third kingdom is that of the *Ostrogoths* in Italy, founded by Theodoric, and highly flourishing beneath his rule. The learned Romans Cassiodorus and Boëthius filled the highest offices of state under Theodoric. But this Ostrogothic kingdom did not last long; it was destroyed by the Byzantines under Belisarius and Narses. In the second half (568) of the sixth century, the *Lombards* invaded Italy and ruled for two centuries, till this kingdom also was subjected to the Frank sceptre by Charlemagne. At a later date, the Normans also established themselves in lower Italy. Our attention is next claimed by the *Burgundians,* who were subjugated by the Franks, and whose kingdom forms a kind of partition wall between France and Germany. The *Angles* and *Saxons* entered Britain and reduced it under their sway. Subsequently, the Normans make their appearance here also.

These countries, previously a part of the Roman empire, thus experienced the fate of subjugation by the barbarians. In the first instance, a great contrast presented itself between the already civilized inhabitants of those countries and the victors; but this contrast terminated in the hybrid character of the new nations that were now formed. The whole mental and moral existence of such states exhibits a divided aspect; in their inmost being we have characteristics that point to an alien origin. This distinction strikes us even on the surface, in their *language,* which is an intermixture of the ancient Roman, already united with the vernacular, and the German. We may class these nations together as *Romanic*—comprehending thereby Italy, Spain, Portugal, and France. Contrasted with these stand three others, more or less *German-speaking* nations, which have maintained a consistent tone of uninterrupted fidelity to native character—Germany itself, Scandinavia, and England. The last was, indeed, incorporated in the Roman Empire, but was affected by Roman culture little more than superficially—like Germany itself—and was again Germanized by Angles and Saxons. *Germany proper* kept itself pure from any admixture; only the southern and western border, on the Danube and the Rhine, had been subjugated by the Romans. The portion between the Rhine and the Elbe remained thoroughly national. This part of Germany was inhabited by several tribes. Besides the Ripuarian Franks and those established by Clovis in the districts of the Maine, four leading tribes—the Alemanni, the Boioarians, the Thuringians, and the Saxons—must be mentioned. The *Scandinavians* retained in their fatherland a similar purity from intermixture; and also made themselves celebrated by their expeditions, under the name of Normans. They extended their chivalric enterprises over almost all parts of Europe. Part of them went to Russia, and there became the founders of the Russian Empire; part settled in northern France and Britain; another established principalities in lower Italy and Sicily. Thus a part of the Scandinavians founded states in foreign lands, another maintained its nationality by the ancestral hearth.

We find, moreover, in the east of Europe, the great *Slavonic* nation, whose settlements extended west of the Elbe to the Danube. The Magyars (Hungarians) settled in between them. In Moldavia, Wallachia, and northern Greece appear the Bulgarians, Servians, and Albanians, likewise of Asiatic origin—left behind as broken barbarian remains in the shocks and countershocks of the advancing hordes. These people did, indeed, found kingdoms and sustain spirited conflicts with the various nations that came across their path. Sometimes, as an advanced guard, an intermediate nationality, they took part in the struggle between Christian Europe and unchristian Asia. The Poles even liberated beleaguered Vienna from the Turks; and the Slavs have to some extent been drawn within the sphere of Occidental reason. Yet this entire body of peoples remains excluded from our consideration, because hitherto it has not appeared as an independent element in the series of phases that reason has assumed in the world. Whether it will do so hereafter, is a question that does not concern us here; for in history we have to do with the past.

The German nation was characterized by the sense of natural totality—an idiosyncrasy which we may call *heart*.[1] "Heart" is that undeveloped, indeterminate totality of spirit, in reference to the will, in which satisfaction of soul is attained in a correspondingly general and indeterminate way. *Character* is a particular form of will and interest asserting itself; but the quality in question has no particular aim—riches, honour, or the like; in fact does not concern itself with any *objective* condition, but with the entire condition of the soul—a general sense of enjoyment. Will in the case of such an idiosyncrasy is exclusively *formal* will[2]—its purely subjective freedom exhibits itself as self-will. To the disposition thus designated, every particular object of attraction seems important, for "heart" surrenders itself entirely to each; but as, on the other hand, it is not interested in the quality of such aim in the abstract, it does not become exclusively absorbed in that aim, so as to pursue it with violent and evil passion—does not go the length of abstract vice. In the idiosyncrasy we term "heart," no such absorption of interest presents itself; it wears, on the whole, the appearance of "well-meaning." *Character* is its direct opposite.

This is the abstract principle innate in the German peoples, and that subjective side which they present to the objective in Christianity. "Heart" has no particular object; in Christianity we have the absolute *object*—all that can engage and occupy human subjectivity. Now it is the desire of satisfaction without further definition or restriction, that is involved in "heart"; and it is exactly that for which we found an appropriate application in the principle of Christianity. The indefinite as substance, in objectivity, is the purely universal—God; while the reception of the individual will to a participation in His favour is the complementary element in the Christian concrete unity. The absolutely universal is that which contains in it all determinations, and in virtue of this is itself indeterminate. Subject is the absolutely determinate; and these two are identical.[3] This was

---

[1] The word *Gemüth* has no exactly corresponding term in English. It is used further on synonymously with *Herz*, and the openness to various emotions and impressions which it implies, may perhaps be approximately rendered by "heart." Yet it is but an awkward substitute.

[2] Formal will or subjective freedom is inclination or mere casual liking, and is opposed to substantial or objective will—also called objective freedom—which denotes the principles that form the basis of society, and that have been spontaneously adopted by particular nations or by mankind generally. The latter as well as the former may lay claim to being a manifestation of human will. For however rigid the restraints which those principles impose on individuals, they are the result of no extraneous compulsion brought to bear on the community at large, and are recognized as rightfully authoritative even by the individuals whose physical comfort or relative affections they most painfully contravene. Unquestioning homage to unreasonable despotism, and the severe rubrics of religious penance, can be traced to no natural necessity or stimulus *ab extra*. The principles in which these originate, may rather be called *the settled and supreme determination* of the community that recognizes them. The term "objective will" seems therefore not unfitly used to describe the psychological phenomena in question. The term *"substantial* will" (as opposed to "formal will"), denoting the same phenomena, needs no defence or explanation. The third term, "objective freedom," used synonymously with the two preceding, is justified on the ground of the unlimited dominion exercised by such principles as those mentioned above. *"Deus solus liber."* (See remarks to this effect on page 169 of the Introduction, and elsewhere.)

[3] Pure self—pure subjectivity or personality—not only excludes all that is manifestly objective, all that is

exhibited above as the material content in Christianity; here we find it subjectively as "heart." Subject must then also gain an objective form, that is, be expanded to an object. It is necessary that for the indefinite susceptibility which we designate "heart," the absolute also should assume the form of an object, in order that man on his part may attain a consciousness of his unity with that object. But this recognition of the absolute requires the purification of man's subjectivity—requires it to become a real, concrete self, a sharer in general interests as a denizen of the world at large, and that it should act in accordance with large and liberal aims, recognize law, and find satisfaction in it. Thus we find here two principles corresponding the one with the other, and recognize the adaptation of the German peoples to be, as we stated above, the bearers of the higher principle of spirit.

We advance then to the consideration of the German principle in its primary phase of existence, *i.e.,* the earliest historical condition of the German nations. Their quality of "heart" is in its first appearance quite abstract, undeveloped and destitute of any particular object; for substantial aims are not involved in "heart" itself. Where this susceptibility stands alone, it appears as a want of character—mere inanity. "Heart" as purely abstract, is dulness; thus we see in the original condition of the Germans a barbarian dulness, mental confusion and vagueness. Of the *religion* of the Germans we know little. The Druids belonged to Gaul and were extirpated by the Romans. There was indeed, a peculiar northern mythology; but how slight a hold the religion of the Germans had upon their hearts has been already remarked, and it is also evident from the fact that the Germans were easily converted to Christianity. The Saxons, it is true, offered considerable resistance to Charlemagne; but this was directed, not so much against the religion he brought with him, as against oppression itself. Their religion had no profundity; and the same may be said of their *ideas* of *law.* Murder was not regarded and punished as a crime: it

evidently not-self, but also abstracts from any peculiar conditions that may temporarily adhere to it, *e.g.,* youth or age, riches or poverty, a present or a future state. Thus though it seems, *prima facie,* a fixed point or atom, it is absolutely unlimited. By loss or degradation of bodily and mental faculties, it is possible to conceive one's self degraded to a position which it would be impossible to distinguish from that which we attribute to the brutes, or by increase and improvement of those faculties, indefinitely elevated in the scale of being, while yet self—personal identity—is retained. On the other hand, absolute being in the Christian concrete view, is an infinite self. The absolutely limited is thus shown to be identical with the absolutely unlimited.

was expiated by a pecuniary fine. This indicates a deficiency in depth of sentiment, that absence of a power of abstraction and discrimination that marks their peculiar temperament, a temperament which leads them to regard it only as an injury to the community when one of its members is killed, and nothing further. The blood-revenge of the Arabs is based on the feeling that the honour of the family is injured. Among the Germans the community had no dominion over the individual, for the element of freedom is the first consideration in their union in a social relationship. The ancient Germans were famed for their love of freedom; the Romans formed a correct idea of them in this particular from the first. Freedom has been the watchword in Germany down to the most recent times, and even the league of princes under Frederick II had its origin in the love of liberty. This element of freedom, in passing over to a social relationship, can establish only popular communities; so that these communities constitute the whole state, and every member of the community, as such, is a free man. Homicide could be expiated by a pecuniary mulct, because the individuality of the free man was regarded as sacred, permanently and inviolably, whatever he might have done. The community or its presiding power, with the assistance of members of the community, delivered judgment in affairs of private right, with a view to the protection of person and property. For affairs affecting the body politic at large, for wars and similar contingencies, the whole community had to be consulted. The second point to be observed is, that social nuclei were formed by free confederation, and by voluntary attachment to military leaders and princes. The connection in this case was that of *fidelity;* for fidelity is the second watchword of the Germans, as freedom was the first. Individuals attach themselves with free choice to an individual, and without external prompting make this relation an inviolable one. This we find neither among the Greeks nor the Romans. The relation of Agamemnon and the princes who accompanied him was not that of feudal suit and service: it was a free association merely for *a particular purpose*—a hegemony. But the German confederations have their being not in a relation to a mere external aim or cause, but in a relation to the spiritual self—the subjective inmost personality. Heart, disposition, the concrete subjectivity in its integrity, which does not attach itself to any abstract bearing of an object, but regards the whole of it as a condition of attachment—making itself dependent on the person *and* the cause—renders this relation a compound of fidelity to a person and obedience to a principle.

The union of the two relations—of individual freedom in the community, and of the bond implied in association—is the main point in the formation of the state. In this, duties and rights are no longer left to arbitrary choice but are determined as fixed relations; involving, moreover, the condition that the state be the soul of the entire body, and remain its sovereign, that from it should be derived particular aims and the authorization both of political acts and political agents, the generic character and interests of the community constituting the permanent basis of the whole. But here we have the peculiarity of the German states, that contrary to the view thus presented, social relations do not assume the character of general definitions and laws, but are entirely split up into *private* rights and *private* obligations. They perhaps exhibit a social or communal mould or stamp, but nothing *universal;* the laws are absolutely particular, and the rights are privileges. Thus the state was a patchwork of private rights, and a rational political life was the tardy issue of wearisome struggles and convulsions.

We have said, that the Germans were predestined to be the bearers of the Christian principle, and to carry out the idea as the absolutely rational aim. In the first instance we have only vague volition, in the background of which lies the true and infinite. The true is present only as an unsolved problem, for their soul is not yet purified. A long process is required to complete this purification so as to realize concrete spirit. Religion comes forward with a challenge to the violence of the passions, and rouses them to madness. The excess of passions is aggravated by evil conscience, and heightened to an insane rage; which perhaps would not have been the case, had that opposition been absent. We behold the terrible spectacle of the most fearful extravagance of passion in all the royal houses of that period. Clovis, the founder of the Frank monarchy, is stained with the blackest crimes. Barbarous harshness and cruelty characterize all the succeeding Merovingians; the same spectacle is repeated in the Thuringian and other royal houses. The Christian principle is certainly the problem implicit in their souls; but these are primarily still crude. The will—potentially true—mistakes itself, and separates itself from the true and proper aim by particular, limited aims. Yet it is in this struggle with itself and contrariety to its bias, that it realizes its

wishes; it contends against the object which it really desires, and thus accomplishes it; for implicitly, *potentially,* it is *reconciled.* The spirit of God lives in the church; it is the inward impelling spirit. But it is in the world that spirit is to be realized—in a material not yet brought into harmony with it. Now this material is the subjective will, which thus has a contradiction in itself. On the religious side, we often observe a change of this kind: a man who has all his life been fighting and hewing his way—who with all vehemence of character and passion, has struggled and revelled in secular occupations—on a sudden repudiates it all, to betake himself to religious seclusion. But in the world, secular business cannot be thus repudiated; it demands accomplishment, and ultimately the discovery is made that spirit finds the goal of its struggle and its harmonization in that very sphere which it made the object of its resistance—it finds that *secular pursuits are a spiritual occupation.*

We thus observe that individuals and peoples regard that which is their misfortune as their greatest happiness and, conversely, struggle against their happiness as their greatest misery. *La vérité, en la repoussant, on l'embrasse.* Europe comes to the truth while, and to the degree in which, she has repulsed it. It is in the agitation thus occasioned that providence especially exercises its sovereignty; realizing its absolute aim—its honour—as the result of unhappiness, sorrow, private aims and the unconscious will of the nations of the earth.

While, therefore, in the West this long process in the world's history—necessary to that purification by which spirit in the concrete is realized—is commencing, the purification requisite for developing *spirit in the abstract* which we observe carried on contemporaneously in the East is more quickly accomplished. The latter does not need a long process, and we see it produced rapidly, even suddenly, in the first half of the seventh century, in Mohammedanism.

Chapter 2. *Mohammedanism*

On the one hand, we see the *European* world forming itself anew—the nations taking firm root there, to produce a world of free reality expanded and developed in every direction. We behold them beginning their work by bringing all social relations under the form of *particularity*—with dull and narrow intelligence splitting that which in its nature is generic and normal, into a multitude of chance contingencies; rendering that which ought to be simple principle and law a tangled web of convention. In short, while the West began to shelter itself in a political edifice of chance, entanglement and particularity, the very opposite direction necessarily made its appearance in the world, to produce the balance of the totality of spiritual manifestation. This took place in the *revolution of the East,* which destroyed all particularity and dependence, and perfectly cleared up and purified the soul and disposition; making the abstract One the absolute object of attention and devotion, and to the same extent, pure subjective consciousness—the knowledge of this One alone—the only aim of reality; making the *unconditioned* the *condition of existence.*

We have already become acquainted with the nature of the Oriental principle, and seen that its highest being is only negative; that with it the positive imports an abandonment to mere nature, the enslavement of spirit to the world of realities. Only among the Jews have we observed the principle of pure unity elevated to a thought; for only among them was adoration paid to the One, as an object of thought. This unity then remained, when the purification of the mind to the conception of abstract spirit had been accomplished; but it was freed from the particularity by which the worship of Jehovah had been hampered. Jehovah was only the God of that one people—the God of Abraham, of Isaac and Jacob: only with the Jews had this God made a covenant; only to this people had he revealed himself. That speciality of relation was done away with in Mohammedanism. In this spiritual universality, in this unlimited and indefinite purity and simplicity of conception, human personality has no other aim than the realization of this universality and simplicity. *Allah* has not the affirmative, limited aim of the Judaic God. The worship of the One is the only final aim of Mohammedanism, and subjectivity has this worship for the sole occupation of its activity, combined with the design to subjugate secular existence to the One. This One has indeed the quality of spirit; yet because subjectivity suffers itself to be absorbed in the object, this One is deprived of every concrete predicate; so that neither does subjectivity become on its part spiritually free, nor on the other hand is the object of its veneration concrete. But Mohammedanism is not the Hindu, not the monastic immersion in the absolute. Subjectivity is here living and unlimited—an energy which enters into secular life with a purely negative purpose, and busies itself and interferes with the world, only in such a way as shall promote the pure adoration of the One. The object of Mo-

hammedan worship is purely intellectual; no image, no representation of Allah is tolerated. Mohammed is a prophet but still man—not elevated above human weaknesses. The leading features of Mohammedanism involve this, that in actual existence nothing can become fixed, but that everything is destined to expand itself in activity and life in the boundless amplitude of the world, so that the worship of the One remains the only bond by which the whole is capable of uniting. In this expansion, this active energy, all limits, all national and caste distinctions vanish; no particular race, political claim of birth or possession is regarded—only *man* as a *believer.* To adore the One, to believe in him, to fast—to remove the sense of speciality and consequent separation from the infinite, arising from corporeal limitation—and to give alms—that is, to get rid of particular private possession—these are the essence of Mohammedan injunctions; but the highest merit is to die for the faith. He who perishes for it in battle is sure of Paradise.

The Mohammedan religion originated among the Arabs. Here spirit exists in its simplest form, and the sense of the formless has its especial abode; for in their deserts nothing can be brought into a firm consistent shape. The flight of Mohammed from Mecca in the year 622 begins the Moslem era. Even during his life, and under his own leadership, but especially by following up his designs after his death under the guidance of his successors, the Arabs achieved their vast conquests. They first came down upon Syria and conquered its capital Damascus in the year 634. They then passed the Euphrates and Tigris and turned their arms against Persia, which soon submitted to them. In the west they conquered Egypt, northern Africa and Spain, and pressed into southern France as far as the Loire, where they were defeated by Charles Martel near Tours, in 732. Thus the dominion of the Arabs extended itself in the west. In the east they reduced successively Persia, as already stated, Samarkand, and the southwestern part of Asia Minor. These conquests, as also the spread of their religion, took place with extraordinary rapidity. Whoever became a convert to Islam gained a perfect equality of rights with all Mussulmans. Those who rejected it, were, during the earliest period, slaughtered. Subsequently, however, the Arabs behaved more leniently to the conquered; so that, if they were unwilling to go over to Islam, they were only required to pay an annual poll-tax. The towns that immediately submitted, were obliged to pay the victor a *tithe* of all their possessions; those which had to be captured, a *fifth*.

Abstraction swayed the minds of the Mohammedans. Their object was to establish an abstract worship, and they struggled for its accomplishment with the greatest enthusiasm. This enthusiasm was *fanaticism,* that is, an enthusiasm for something abstract—for an abstract thought which sustains a negative position towards the established order of things. It is the essence of fanaticism to bear only a desolating destructive relation to the concrete; but that of Mohammedanism was, at the same time, capable of the greatest elevation—an elevation free from all petty interests and united with all the virtues that appertain to magnanimity and valour. *La religion et la terreur* was the principle in this case, as with Robespierre, *la liberté et la terreur*. But real life is nevertheless concrete and introduces particular aims; conquest leads to sovereignty and wealth, to the conferring of prerogatives on a dynastic family, and to a union of individuals. But all this is only contingent and built on sand; it is to-day, and to-morrow is not. With all the passionate interest he shows, the Mohammedan is really indifferent to this social fabric, and rushes on in the ceaseless whirl of fortune. In its spread Mohammedanism founded many kingdoms and dynasties. On this boundless sea there is a continual onward movement; nothing abides firm. Whatever curls up into a form remains all the while transparent, and in that very instant glides away. Those dynasties were destitute of the bond of an organic firmness: the kingdoms, therefore, did nothing but degenerate; the individuals that composed them simply vanished. Where, however, a noble soul makes itself prominent—like a billow in the surging of the sea—it manifests itself in a majesty of freedom, such that nothing more noble, more generous, more valiant, more devoted was ever witnessed. The particular determinate object which the individual embraces is grasped by him entirely—with the whole soul. While Europeans are involved in a multitude of relations, and form, so to speak, "a bundle" of them—in Mohammedanism the individual is *one* passion and *that alone;* he is superlatively cruel, cunning, bold, or generous. Where the sentiment of love exists, there is an equal *abandon*—love the most fervid. The ruler who loves the slave, glorifies the object of his love by laying at his feet all his magnificence, power and honour—forgetting sceptre and throne for him; but, on the other hand, he will sacrifice him just as recklessly. This reckless fervour shows itself also in the glowing

warmth of the Arab and Saracen poetry. That glow is the perfect freedom of fancy from every fetter—an absorption in the life of its object and the sentiment it inspires, so that selfishness and egotism are utterly banished.

Never has enthusiasm, as such, performed greater deeds. Individuals may be enthusiastic for what is noble and exalted in various particular forms. The enthusiasm of a people for its independence has also a definite aim. But abstract and therefore all-comprehensive enthusiasm— restrained by nothing, finding its limits nowhere, and absolutely indifferent to all beside—is that of the Mohammedan East.

Proportioned to the rapidity of the Arab conquests was the speed with which the arts and sciences attained among them their highest bloom. At first we see the conquerors destroying everything connected with art and science. Omar is said to have caused the destruction of the noble Alexandrian library. "These books," said he, "either contain what is in the Koran, or something else: in either case they are superfluous." [1] But soon afterwards the Arabs became zealous in promoting the arts and spreading them everywhere. Their empire reached the summit of its glory under the Caliphs Al-Mansur and Harun al-Rashid. Large cities arose in all parts of the empire, where commerce and manufactures flourished, splendid palaces were built, and schools created. The learned men of the empire assembled at the caliph's court, which not merely shone outwardly with the pomp of the costliest jewels, furniture and palaces, but was resplendent with the glory of poetry and all the sciences. At first the caliphs still maintained entire that simplicity and plainness which characterized the Arabs of the desert (the Caliph Abu-Bekr is particularly famous in this respect), and which acknowledged no distinction of station and culture. The meanest Saracen, the most insignificant old woman approached the caliph as his equals. Unreflecting naïveté does not stand in need of culture; and in virtue of the freedom of his spirit, each one sustains a relation of equality to the ruler.

The great empire of the caliphs did not last long: for on the basis presented by universality nothing is firm. The great Arabian empire fell about the same time as that of the Franks: thrones were demolished by slaves and by fresh invading hordes—the Seljuks and Mongols—and

---

[1] "If these writings of the Greeks agree with the book of God, they are useless and need not be preserved; if they disagree, they are pernicious and ought to be destroyed."—ED.

new kingdoms founded, new dynasties raised to the throne. The Osman race at last succeeded in establishing a firm dominion, by forming for themselves a firm centre in the Janizaries. Fanaticism having cooled down, no moral principle remained in men's souls. In the struggle with the Saracens, European valour had idealized itself to a fair and noble chivalry. Science and knowledge, especially that of philosophy, came from the Arabs into the West. A noble poetry and free imagination were kindled among the Germans by the East—a fact which directed Goethe's attention to the Orient and occasioned the composition of a string of lyric pearls, in his *Westöstlicher Diwan,* which in warmth and felicity of fancy cannot be surpassed. But the East itself, when by degrees enthusiasm had vanished, sank into the grossest vice. The most hideous passions became dominant, and as sensual enjoyment was sanctioned in the first form which Mohammedan doctrine assumed, and was exhibited as a reward of the faithful in Paradise, it took the place of fanaticism. At present, driven back into its Asiatic and African quarters, and tolerated only in one corner of Europe through the jealousy of Christian powers, Islam has long vanished from the stage of history at large, and has retreated into Oriental ease and repose.

Chapter 3. *The Empire of Charlemagne*

The empire of the Franks, as already stated, was founded by Clovis. After his death, it was divided among his sons. Subsequently, after many struggles and the employment of treachery, assassination and violence, it was again united, and once more divided. Internally the power of the kings was very much increased, by their having become princes in *conquered* lands. These were indeed parcelled out among the Frank freemen; but very considerable permanent revenues accrued to the king, together with what had belonged to the emperors, and the spoils of confiscation. These therefore the king bestowed as personal, *i.e.,* not heritable, *beneficia,* on his warriors, who in receiving them entered into a personal obligation to him, became his vassals, and formed his feudal array. The very opulent bishops were united with them in constituting the king's council, which however did not circumscribe the royal authority. At the head of the feudal array was the *major domus.* These *majores domus* soon assumed the entire power and threw the royal authority into the shade, while the kings sank into a torpid condition and became mere puppets. From the

former sprang the dynasty of the Carlovingians. Pepin le Bref, the son of Charles Martel, was in the year 752 raised to the dignity of King of the Franks. Pope Zacharias released the Franks from their oath of allegiance to the still living Childeric III—the last of the Merovingians—who received the tonsure, *i.e.,* became a monk, and was thus deprived of the royal distinction of long hair. The last of the Merovingians were utter weaklings, who contented themselves with the name of royalty, and gave themselves up almost entirely to luxury—a phenomenon that is quite common in the dynasties of the east and is also met with again among the last of the Carlovingians. The *majores domus,* on the contrary, were in the very vigour of ascendant fortunes, and were in such close alliance with the feudal nobility, that it became easy for them ultimately to secure the throne.

The Popes were most severely pressed by the Lombard kings and sought protection from the Franks. Out of gratitude Pepin undertook to defend Stephen II. He led an army twice across the Alps and twice defeated the Lombards. His victories gave splendour to his newly established throne, and entailed a considerable heritage on the Chair of St. Peter. In A.D. 800 the son of Pepin—Charlemagne—was crowned Emperor by the Pope, and hence originated the firm union of the Carlovingians with the Papal See. For the Roman Empire continued to enjoy among the barbarians the prestige of a great power, and was ever regarded by them as the centre from which civil dignities, religion, laws and all branches of knowledge—beginning with written characters themselves—flowed to them. Charles Martel, after he had delivered Europe from Saracen domination, was, himself and his successors, dignified with the title of "Patrician" by the people and senate of Rome; but Charlemagne was crowned Emperor, and that by the Pope himself.

There were now, therefore, *two* empires, and in them the Christian confession was gradually divided into two churches, the *Greek* and the *Roman.* The Roman Emperor was the born defender of the Roman Church, and this position of the Emperor towards the Pope seemed to declare that the Frank sovereignty was only a continuation of the Roman Empire.

The empire of Charlemagne had a very considerable extent. Franconia proper stretched from the Rhine to the Loire. Aquitania, south of the Loire, was in 768—the year of Pepin's death—entirely subjugated. The Frank Empire also included Burgundy, Alemannia (southern

Germany between the Lech, the Maine, and the Rhine), Thuringia, which extended to the Saale, and Bavaria. Charlemagne likewise conquered the Saxons, who dwelt between the Rhine and the Weser, and put an end to the Lombard dominion, so that he became master of upper and central Italy.

This great empire Charlemagne formed into a systematically organized state, and gave the Frank dominion settled institutions adapted to impart to it strength and consistency. This must however not be understood, as if he first introduced the *constitution* of his empire in its whole extent, but as implying that institutions partly already in existence, were developed under his guidance, and attained a more decided and unobstructed efficiency. The king stood at the head of the officers of the empire, and the principle of hereditary monarchy was already recognized. The king was likewise master of the armed force, as also the largest landed proprietor, while the supreme judicial power was equally in his hands. The *military constitution* was based on the "*arrière-ban.*" Every freeman was bound to arm for the defence of the realm, and had to provide for his support in the field for a certain time. This militia (as it would now be called) was under the command of counts and margraves, which latter presided over large districts on the borders of the empire—the "Marches." According to the general partition of the country, it was divided into provinces [or counties] over each of which a count presided. Over these again, under the later Carlovingians, were dukes, whose seats were large cities, such as Cologne, Ratisbon, and the like. Their office gave occasion to the division of the country into duchies: thus there was a Duchy of Alsatia, Lorraine, Frisia, Thuringia, Rhætia. These dukes were appointed by the Emperor. Peoples that had retained their hereditary princes after their subjugation, lost this privilege and received dukes, when they revolted; this was the case with Alemannia, Thuringia, Bavaria, and Saxony. But there was also a kind of standing army for readier use. The vassals of the Emperor, namely, had the enjoyment of estates on the condition of performing military service, whenever commanded. And with a view to maintain these arrangements, commissioners (*missi*) were sent out by the Emperor, to observe and report concerning the affairs of the empire, and to inquire into the state of judicial administration and inspect the royal estates.

Not less remarkable is the management of the *revenues of the state*. There were no direct taxes and few tolls on rivers and roads, of which several were farmed out to the higher officers of the empire. Into the treasury flowed on the one hand judicial fines, on the other hand the pecuniary satisfactions made for not serving in the army at the Emperor's summons. Those who enjoyed *beneficia,* lost them on neglecting this duty. The chief revenue was derived from the crown-lands, of which the Emperor had a great number, on which royal palaces were erected. It had been long the custom for the kings to make progresses through the chief provinces, and to remain for a time in each palatinate; the due preparations for the maintenance of the court having been already made by marshals, chamberlains, etc.

As regards the *administration of justice,* criminal causes and those which concern real property were tried before the communal assemblies under the presidency of a count. Those of less importance were decided by at least seven free men, an elective bench of magistrates, under the presidency of the Centgraves. The supreme jurisdiction belonged to the royal tribunals, over which the king presided in his palace: to these the feudatories, spiritual and temporal, were amenable. The royal commissioners mentioned above gave especial attention in their inquisitorial visits to the judicial administration, heard all complaints, and punished injustice. A spiritual and a temporal envoy had to go their circuit four times a year.

In Charlemagne's time the ecclesiastical body had already acquired great weight. The bishops presided over great cathedral establishments, with which were also connected seminaries and scholastic institutions. For Charlemagne endeavoured to restore science, then almost extinct, by promoting the foundation of schools in towns and villages. Pious souls believed that they were doing a good work and earning salvation by making presents to the Church; in this way the most savage and barbarous monarchs sought to atone for their crimes. Private persons most commonly made their offerings in the form of a bequest of their entire estate to religious houses, stipulating for the enjoyment of the usufruct only for life or for a specified time. But it often happened that, on the death of a bishop or abbot, the temporal magnates and their retainers invaded the possessions of the clergy, and fed and feasted there till all was consumed; for religion had not yet such an authority over men's minds as to be able to bridle the rapacity of the powerful. The clergy were obliged to appoint stewards and bailiffs to manage their estates;

besides this, guardians had charge of all their secular concerns, led their men-at-arms into the field, and gradually obtained from the king territorial jurisdiction, when the ecclesiastics had secured the privilege of being amenable only to their own tribunals, and enjoyed immunity from the authority of the royal officers of justice (the counts). This involved an important step in the change of political relations, inasmuch as the ecclesiastical domains assumed more and more the aspect of independent provinces enjoying a freedom surpassing anything to which those of secular princes had yet made pretensions. Moreover the clergy contrived subsequently to free themselves from the burdens of the state, and opened the churches and monasteries as asylums—that is, inviolable sanctuaries for all offenders. This institution was on the one hand very beneficial as a protection in cases of violence and oppression; but it was perverted on the other hand into a means of impunity for the grossest crimes. In Charlemagne's time, the law could still demand from conventual authorities the surrender of offenders. The bishops were tried by a judicial bench consisting of bishops; as vassals they were properly subject to the royal tribunal. Afterwards the monastic establishments sought to free themselves from episcopal jurisdiction also: and thus they made themselves independent even of the Church. The bishops were chosen by the clergy and the religious communities at large; but as they were also vassals of the sovereign, their feudal dignity had to be conferred by him. The contingency of a contest was avoided by the obligation to choose a person approved of by the king.

The imperial tribunals were held in the palace where the Emperor resided. The sovereign himself presided in them, and the magnates of the imperial court constituted with him the supreme judicial body. The deliberations of the imperial council on the affairs of the empire did not take place at appointed times, but as occasions offered, at military reviews in the spring, at ecclesiastical councils and on court-days. It was especially these court-days, to which the feudal nobles were invited—when the king held his court in a particular province, generally on the Rhine, the centre of the Frank Empire—that gave occasion to the deliberations in question. Custom required the sovereign to assemble twice a year a select body of the higher temporal and ecclesiastical functionaries, but here also the king had decisive power. These conventions are therefore of a different character from the imperial diets of later times, in which the nobles assume a more independent position.

Such was the state of the Frank Empire—that first consolidation of Christianity into a political form proceeding from itself, the Roman Empire having been swallowed up by Christianity. The constitution just described looks excellent; it introduced a firm military organization and provided for the administration of justice within the empire. Yet after Charlemagne's death it proved itself utterly powerless—externally defenceless against the invasions of the Normans, Hungarians, and Arabs, and internally inefficient in resisting lawlessness, spoliation, and oppression of every kind. Thus we see, side by side with an excellent constitution, the most deplorable condition of things, and therefore confusion in all directions. Such political edifices need, for the very reason that they originate suddenly, the additional strengthening afforded by negativity evolved within themselves: they need reactions in every form, such as manifest themselves in the following period.

Section II

THE MIDDLE AGES

While the *first* period of the German world ends brilliantly with a mighty empire, the *second* is commenced by the reaction resulting from the antithesis occasioned by that infinite falsehood which rules the destinies of the *Middle Ages* and constitutes their life and spirit. This reaction is, *first,* that of the particular nationalities against the universal sovereignty of the Frank Empire—manifesting itself in the splitting up of that great empire. The *second reaction* is that of individuals against legal authority and the executive power, against subordination, and the military and judicial arrangements of the constitution. This produced the *isolation* and therefore *defencelessness* of individuals. The universality of the power of the state disappeared through this reaction: individuals sought protection with the powerful, and the latter became oppressors. Thus was gradually introduced a condition of universal dependence, and this protecting relation is then systematized into the feudal system. The *third reaction* is that of the Church, the reaction of the spiritual element against the existing order of things. Secular extravagances of passion were repressed and kept in check by the Church, but the latter was itself secularized in the process, and abandoned its proper position. From that moment begins the introversion of the secular principle. These relations and reactions all go to constitute the history of the Middle Ages, and the culminating point of this period is *the Crusades;* for with them arises a universal instability, but one through which the states of Christendom first attain internal and external independence.

Chapter 1. *The Feudality and the Hierarchy*

The *first reaction* is that of particular nationality against the universal sovereignty of the Franks. It appears indeed, at first sight, as if the Frank Empire was divided by the mere choice of its sovereigns; but another consideration deserves attention, *viz.*, that this division was popular, and was accordingly maintained by the peoples. It was, therefore, not a mere dynastic act— which might appear unwise, since the princes thereby weakened their own power—but a restoration of those distinct nationalities which had been held together by a connecting bond of irresistible might and the genius of a great man. Louis the Pious, son of Charlemagne, divided the empire among his three sons. But subsequently, by a second marriage, another son was born to him—Charles the Bald. As he wished to give him also an inheritance, wars and contentions arose between Louis and his other sons, whose already received portion would have to be diminished by such an arrangement. In the first instance, therefore, a private interest was involved in the contest; but that of the nations which composed the empire made the issue not indifferent to them. The western Franks had already identified themselves with the Gauls, and with them originated a reaction against the German Franks, as also at a later epoch one on the part of Italy against the Germans. By the treaty of Verdun, A.D. 843, a division of the empire among Charlemagne's descendants took place; the whole Frank Empire, some provinces excepted, was for a moment again united under Charles the Gross. It was, however, only for a short time that this weak prince was able to hold the vast empire together; it was broken up into many smaller sovereignties, which developed and maintained an independent position. These were the Kingdom of Italy, which was itself divided, the two Burgundian sovereignties —Upper Burgundy, of which the chief centres were Geneva and the convent of St. Maurice in Valaise, and Lower Burgundy between the Jura, the Mediterranean and the Rhone—Lorraine, between the Rhine and the Meuse, Normandy, and Brittany. France proper was shut in between these sovereignties; and thus limited did Hugh Capet find it when he ascended the throne.

Eastern Franconia, Saxony, Thuringia, Bavaria, Swabia, remained parts of the German Empire. Thus did the unity of the Frank monarchy fall to pieces. The internal arrangements of the Frank Empire also suffered a gradual but total decay; and the first to disappear was the military organization. Soon after Charlemagne we see the Norsemen from various quarters making inroads into England, France, and Germany. In England seven dynasties of Anglo-Saxon kings were originally established, but in the year 827 Egbert united these sovereignties into a single kingdom. In the reign of his successor the Danes made very frequent invasions and pillaged the country. In Alfred the Great's time they met with vigorous resistance, but subsequently the Danish King Canute conquered all England. The inroads of the *Normans* into France were contemporaneous with these events. They sailed up the Seine and the Loire in light boats, plundered the towns, pillaged the convents, and went off with their booty. They beleaguered Paris itself, and the Carlovingian kings were reduced to the base necessity of purchasing a peace. In the same way they devastated the towns lying on the Elbe; and from the Rhine plundered Aix-la-Chapelle and Cologne, and made Lorraine tributary to them. The Diet of Worms, in 882, did indeed issue a general proclamation, summoning all subjects to rise in arms, but they were compelled to put up with a disgraceful composition. These storms came from the north and the west. The eastern side of the empire suffered from the inroads of the *Magyars*. These barbarian peoples traversed the country in wagons, and laid waste the whole of southern Germany. Through Bavaria, Swabia, and Switzerland they penetrated into the interior of France and reached Italy. The *Saracens* pressed forward from the south. Sicily had been long in their hands: they thence obtained a firm footing in Italy, menaced Rome—which diverted their attack by a composition—and were the terror of Piedmont and Provence.

Thus these three peoples invaded the empire from all sides in great masses, and in their desolating marches almost came into contact with each other. France was devastated by the Normans as far as the Jura; the Hungarians reached Switzerland, and the Saracens Valaise. Calling to mind that organization of the *"arrière-ban,"* and considering it in juxtaposition with this miserable state of things, we cannot fail to be struck with the inefficiency of all those far-famed institutions, which at such a juncture ought to have shown themselves most effective. We might be inclined to regard the picture of the noble and rational constitution of the Frank monarchy under Charlemagne—exhibiting itself as strong, comprehensive, and well ordered, internally and externally—as a baseless figment. Yet it actually existed; the entire political system being held together only by the power, the greatness, the regal soul of this one man, not based on the spirit of the people, not having become a vital element in it. It was superficially induced—an *a priori* constitution like that which Napoleon gave to Spain, and which disappeared with the physical power that sustained it. That, on the contrary, which renders a constitution real, is that it exists as objective freedom—the substantial form of volition—as duty and obligation acknowledged by the subjects themselves. But obligation was not yet recognized by the German spirit, which hitherto showed itself only as "heart" and subjective choice; for it there was as yet no subjectivity involving unity, but only a subjectivity conditioned by a careless superficial self-seeking. Thus that constitution was destitute of any firm bond; it had no objective support in subjectivity; for, in fact, no constitution was as yet possible.

This leads us to the *second reaction*—that of individuals against the authority of law. The capacity of appreciating legal order and the common weal is altogether absent, has no vital existence in the peoples themselves. The duties of every free citizen, the authority of the judge to give judicial decisions, that of the count of a province to hold his court, and interest in the laws as such, are no longer regarded as valid now that the strong hand from above ceases to hold the reins of sovereignty. The brilliant administration of Charlemagne had vanished without leaving a trace, and the immediate consequence was the general defencelessness of individuals. The need of protection is sure to be felt in some degree in every well-organized state: each citizen knows his rights and also knows that for the security of possession the social state is absolutely necessary. Barbarians have not yet attained this sense of need, the want of protection from others. They look upon it as a limitation of their freedom if their rights must be guaranteed them by others. Thus, therefore, the impulse towards a firm organization did not exist: men must first be placed in a defenceless condition, before they were sensible of the necessity of the organization of a state. The political edifice had to be reconstructed from the very foundations. The commonwealth as then organized had no vitality or firmness at all either in itself or in the minds of the people; and its weakness manifested itself in the fact that it was unable to give protection to its individual members. As observed above, the idea of duty was not present in the spirit of the Germans; it had to be restored. In the first instance volition could only be arrested in its wayward career in reference to the merely external point of *possession;* and to make it feel the importance of the protection of the state, it had to be violently dislodged from its obtuseness and impelled by necessity to seek union and a social condition. Individuals were therefore obliged to consult for themselves by taking refuge with individuals, and submitted to the authority of certain powerful persons, who constituted a private possession and personal sovereignty out of that authority which formerly belonged to the commonwealth. As *officers of the state,* the counts did not meet with obedience from those committed to their charge, and they were as little desirous of it. Only for *themselves* did they covet it. They assumed to themselves the power of the state, and made the authority with which they had been intrusted as a *beneficium,* a heritable possession. As in earlier times the king or other magnates conferred fiefs on their vassals by way of rewards, now, conversely, the weaker and poorer surrendered their possessions to the strong, for the sake of gaining efficient protection. They committed their estates to a lord, a convent, an abbot, a bishop (*feudum oblatum*), and received them back, encumbered with feudal obligations to these superiors. Instead of freemen they became vassals, feudal dependants, and their possession a *beneficium.* This is the constitution of the feudal system. *"Feudum"* is connected with *"fides";* the fidelity implied in this case is a bond established on unjust principles, a relation that does indeed contemplate a legitimate object, but whose import is not a whit the less injustice; for the fidelity of vassals is not an obligation to the commonwealth, but a private one—*ipso facto* therefore subject to the sway of chance, caprice, and violence. Universal injustice, universal lawlessness is reduced to a system of dependence on and obligation to individuals, so that the mere formal side of the matter, the mere fact of compact constitutes its sole connection with the principle of right.

Since every man had to protect himself, the martial spirit, which in point of external defence seemed to have most ignominiously vanished, was reawakened; for torpidity was roused to action partly by extreme ill-usage, partly by the greed and ambition of individuals. The valour that now manifested itself, was displayed not on behalf of the state, but of private interests. In every district arose castles; fortresses were erected, and that for the defence of private property, and with a view to plunder the tyranny. In the way just mentioned, the political totality was ignored at those points where individual authority was established, among which the seats of bishops and archbishops deserve especial mention. The bishoprics had been freed from the jurisdiction of the judicial tribunals, and from the operations of the executive generally. The bishops had stewards on whom at their request the emperors conferred the jurisdiction which the counts had formerly exercised. Thus there were detached ecclesiastical domains —ecclesiastical districts which belonged to a saint. Similar suzerainties of a secular kind were subsequently constituted. Both occupied the position of the previous provinces or counties. Only in a few towns where communities of freemen were independently strong enough to secure protection and safety, did relics of the ancient free constitution remain. With these exceptions the free communities entirely disappeared, and became subject to the prelates or to the counts and dukes, thenceforth known as seigneurs and princes. The imperial power was extolled in general terms, as something very great and exalted: the Emperor passed for the secular head of entire Christendom: but the more exalted the *ideal* dignity of the emperors, the more limited was it in reality. France derived extraordinary advantage from the fact that it entirely repudiated this baseless assumption, while in Germany the advance of political development was hindered by that pretence of power. The kings and emperors were no longer chiefs of the *state,* but of the *princes,* who were indeed their vassals, but possessed sovereignty and territorial lordships of their own. The whole social condition therefore, being founded on individual sovereignty, it might be supposed that the advance to a state would be possible only through the return of those individual sovereignties to an official relationship. But to accomplish this, a superior power would have been required, such as was not in existence; for the feudal lords themselves determined how far they were still dependent on the general constitution of the state. No authority of law and right is valid any longer; nothing but chance power—the crude caprice of particular as opposed to universally valid right; and this struggles against equality of rights and laws. Inequality of political privileges, the allotment being the work of the purest haphazard, is the predominant feature. It is impossible that a monarchy can arise from such a social condition through the subjugation of the several minor powers under the chief of the state, as such. Reversely, the former were gradually transformed into principalities and became united with the principality of the chief, thus enabling the authority of the king and of the state to assert itself. While, therefore, the bond of political unity was still wanting, the several seigneuries attained their development independently.

In France the dynasty of Charlemagne, like that of Clovis, became extinct through the weakness of the sovereigns who represented it. Their dominion was finally limited to the petty sovereignty of Laon; and the last of the Carlovingians, Duke Charles of Lorraine, who laid claim to the crown after the death of Louis V, was defeated and taken prisoner. The powerful Hugh Capet, Duke of France, was proclaimed king. The title of king, however, gave him no real power; his authority was based on his territorial possessions alone. At a later date, through purchase, marriage, and the dying out of families, the kings became possessed of many feudal domains; and their authority was frequently invoked as a protection against the oppressions of the nobles. The royal authority in France became heritable at an early date, because the fiefs were heritable; though at first the kings took the precaution to have their sons crowned during their lifetime. France was divided into many sovereignties: the Duchy of Guienne, the Earldom of Flanders, the Duchy of Gascony, the Earldom of Toulouse, the Duchy of Burgundy, the Earldom of Vermandois; Lorraine too had belonged to France for some time. Normandy had been ceded to the Normans by the kings of France, in order to secure a temporary repose from their incursions. From Normandy Duke William passed over into England and conquered it in the year 1066. Here he introduced a fully developed feudal constitution—a network which, to a great extent, encompasses England even at the present day. And thus the dukes of Normandy confronted the comparatively feeble kings of France with a power of no inconsiderable pretensions.—Germany was composed of the great duchies of Saxony, Swabia, Bavaria, Carinthia, Lorraine and Burgundy, the margraviate of Thuringia, etc., with several bishoprics and archbishoprics. Each of those duchies again was divided into several fiefs, enjoying more or less independence. The Emperor seems often to have united several duchies under his immediate sovereignty. The Emperor Henry III was, when he ascended the throne, lord of many large dukedoms; but he weakened his own power by enfeoffing them to others. Germany was radically a free nation, and had not, as France had, any dominant family as a central authority; it continued an elective empire. Its princes refused to surrender the privilege of choosing their sovereign for themselves; and at every new election they introduced new restrictive conditions, so that the imperial power was degraded to an empty shadow. In Italy we find the same political condition. The German emperors had pretensions to it: but their authority was valid only so far as they could support it by direct force of arms, and as the Italian cities and nobles deemed their own advantage to be promoted by submission. Italy was, like Germany, divided into many larger and smaller dukedoms, earldoms, bishoprics, and seigneuries. The Pope had very little power, either in the north or in the south; which latter was long divided between the Lombards and the Greeks, until both were overcome by the Normans. Spain maintained a contest with the Saracens, either defensive or victorious, through the whole mediæval period, till the latter finally succumbed to the more matured power of Christian civilization.

Thus all right vanished before individual might; for equality of rights and rational legislation, where the interests of the political totality, of the state, are kept in view, had no existence.

The *third reaction,* noticed above, was that of the element of universality against the real world as split up into particularity. This reaction proceeded from below upwards—from that condition of isolated possession itself; and was then promoted chiefly by the Church. A sense of the *nothingness* of its condition seized on the world as it were universally. In that condition of utter isolation, where only the unsanctioned might of individuals had any validity men could find no repose, and Christendom was, so to speak, agitated by the tremor of an evil conscience. In the eleventh century, the fear of the approaching final judgment and the belief in the speedy dissolution of the world, spread through all Europe. This dismay of soul impelled men to the most irrational proceedings. Some bestowed the whole of their possessions on the Church, and passed their lives in continual penance; the majority dissipated their worldly all in riotous debauchery. The Church alone increased its riches by the hallucinations, through donations and bequests.

About the same time too, terrible famines swept away their victims: human flesh was sold in open market. During this state of things, lawlessness, brutal lust, the most barbarous caprice, deceit and cunning, were the prevailing moral features. Italy, the centre of Christendom, presented the most revolting aspect. Every virtue was alien to the times in question; consequently *virtus* had lost its proper meaning: in common use it denoted only violence and oppression, sometimes even libidinous outrage. This corrupt state of things affected the clergy equally with the laity. Their own advowees had made themselves masters of the ecclesiastical estates intrusted to their keeping, and lived on them quite at their own pleasure, restricting the monks and clergy to a scanty pittance. Monasteries that refused to accept advowees were compelled to do so; the neighbouring lords taking the office upon themselves or giving it to their sons. Only bishops and abbots maintained themselves in possession, being able to protect themselves partly by their own power, partly by means of their retainers; since they were, for the most part, of noble families.

The bishoprics being secular fiefs, their occupants were bound to the performance of imperial and feudal service. The investiture of the bishops belonged to the sovereigns, and it was their interest that these ecclesiastics should be attached to them. Whoever desired a bishopric, therefore, had to make application to the king; and thus a regular trade was carried on in bishoprics and abbacies. Usurers who had lent money to the sovereign received compensation by the bestowal of the dignities in question; the worst of men thus came into possession of spiritual offices. There could be no question that the clergy ought to have been chosen by the religious community, and there were always influential persons who had the right of electing them; but the king compelled them to yield to his orders. Nor did the papal dignity fare any better. Through a long course of years the counts of Tusculum near Rome conferred it on members of their own family, or on persons to whom they had sold it for large sums of money. The state of things became at last so intolerable, that laymen as well as ecclesiastics of energetic character opposed its continuance. The Emperor Henry III put an end to the strife of factions by nominating the Popes himself and supporting them by his authority in defiance of the opposition of the Roman nobility. Pope Nicholas

II decided that the Popes should be chosen by the cardinals; but as the latter partly belonged to dominant families, similar contests of factions continued to accompany their election. Gregory VII (already famous as Cardinal Hildebrand) sought to secure the independence of the Church in this frightful condition of things, by two measures especially. *First,* he enforced the *celibacy of the clergy.* From the earliest times, it must be observed, the opinion had prevailed that it was commendable and desirable for the clergy to remain unmarried. Yet the annalists and chroniclers inform us that this requirement was but indifferently complied with. Nicholas II had indeed pronounced the married clergy to be a new sect; but Gregory VII proceeded to enforce the restriction with extraordinary energy, excommunicating all the married clergy and all laymen who should hear Mass when they officiated. In this way the ecclesiastical body was shut up within itself and excluded from the morality of the state. His *second* measure was directed against *simony, i.e.,* the sale of or arbitrary appointment to bishoprics and to the Papal See itself. Ecclesiastical offices were thenceforth to be filled by the clergy, who were capable of administering them; an arrangement which necessarily brought the ecclesiastical body into violent collision with secular seigneurs.

These were the two grand measures by which Gregory purposed to emancipate the Church from its condition of dependence and exposure to secular violence. But Gregory made still further demands on the secular power. The transference of benefices to a new incumbent was to receive validity simply in virtue of his ordination by his ecclesiastical superior, and the Pope was to have exclusive control over the vast property of the ecclesiastical community. The Church as a divinely constituted power, laid claim to supremacy over secular authority— founding that claim on the abstract principle that the divine is superior to the secular. The Emperor at his coronation, a ceremony which only the Pope could perform, was obliged to promise upon oath that he would always be obedient to the Pope and the Church. Whole countries and states, such as Naples, Portugal, England, and Ireland came into a formal relation of vassalage to the papal chair.

Thus the Church attained an independent position: the bishops convoked synods in the various countries, and in these convocations the clergy found a permanent centre of unity and support. In this way the Church attained the most influential position in secular affairs. It arrogated to itself the award of princely crowns, and assumed the part of mediator between sovereign powers in war and peace. The contingencies which particularly favored such interventions on the part of the Church were the marriages of princes. It frequently happened that princes wished to be divorced from their wives; but for such a step they needed the permission of the Church. The latter did not let slip the opportunity of insisting upon the fulfilment of demands that might have been otherwise urged in vain, and thence advanced till it had obtained universal influence. In the chaotic state of the community generally, the intervention of the authority of the Church was felt as a necessity. By the introduction of the "Truce of God," feuds and private revenge were suspended for at least certain days in the week, or even for entire weeks; and the Church maintained this armistice by the use of all its ghostly appliances of excommunication, interdict, and other threats and penalties. The secular possessions of the Church brought it however into a relation to other secular princes and lords, which was alien to its proper nature; it constituted a formidable secular power in contraposition to them, and thus formed in the first instance a centre of opposition against violence and arbitrary wrong. It withstood especially the attacks upon the ecclesiastical foundations—the secular lordships of the bishops; and on occasion of opposition on the part of vassals to the violence and caprice of princes, the former had the support of the Pope. But in these proceedings the Church brought to bear against opponents only a force and arbitrary resolve of the same kind as their own, and mixed up in secular interest with its interest as an ecclesiastical, *i.e.,* a divinely substantial power. Sovereigns and peoples were by no means incapable of discriminating between the two, or of recognizing the worldly aims that were apt to intrude as motives for ecclesiastical intervention. They therefore stood by the Church as far as they deemed it their interest to do so; otherwise they showed no great dread of excommunication or other ghostly terrors. Italy was the country where the authority of the Popes was least respected; and the worst usage they experienced was from the Romans themselves. Thus what the Popes acquired in point of land and wealth and direct sovereignty, they lost in influence and consideration.

We have then to probe to its depths the *spiritual element* in the Church—the form of its power. The essence of the Christian principle has already been unfolded; it is the principle of mediation. Man realizes his spiritual essence only when he conquers the natural that attaches to him. This conquest is possible only on the supposition that the human and the divine nature are essentially one, and that man, so far as he is spirit, also possesses the essentiality and substantiality that belong to the idea of deity. The condition of the mediation in question is the consciousness of this unity; and the intuition of this unity was given to man in Christ. The object to be attained is therefore, that man should lay hold on this consciousness, and that it should be continually excited in him. This was the design of the *Mass:* in the *Host,* Christ is set forth as actually present; the piece of bread consecrated by the priest is the present God, subjected to human contemplation and ever and anon offered up. One feature of this representation is correct, inasmuch as the sacrifice of Christ is here regarded as an actual and eternal transaction, Christ being not a mere sensuous and single, but a completely universal, *i.e.,* divine *individuum;* but on the other hand it involves the error of isolating the sensuous phase; for the Host is adored even apart from its being partaken of by the faithful, and the presence of Christ is not exclusively limited mental vision and spirit. Justly therefore did the Lutheran Reformation make this dogma an especial ob-, ject of attack. Luther proclaimed the great doctrine that the Host had spiritual value and Christ was received only on the condition of *faith* in him; apart from this, the Host, he affirmed, was a mere external thing, possessed of no greater value than any other thing. But the Catholic falls down before the Host; and thus the merely outward has sanctity ascribed to it. The Holy as a mere thing has the character of externality; thus it is capable of being taken possession of by another to my exclusion: it may come into an alien hand, since the process of appropriating it is not one that takes place in spirit, but is conditioned by its quality as an external object. The highest of human blessings is in the hands of others. Here arises *ipso facto* a separation between those who possess this blessing and those who have to receive it from others—between the *clergy* and the *laity.* The laity as such are alien to the divine. This is the absolute schism in which the Church in the Middle Ages was involved: it arose from the recognition of the holy as something external. The clergy imposed certain conditions, to which the laity must conform if they would be partakers of the holy. The entire development of *doctrine,*

spiritual insight and the knowledge of divine things, belonged exclusively to the Church: it has to ordain, and the laity have simply to believe: obedience is their duty—the obedience of faith, without insight on their part. This position of things rendered faith a matter of external legislation, and resulted in compulsion and the stake.

The generality of men are thus cut off from the Church; and on the same principle they are severed from the holy in every form. For on the same principle as that by which the clergy are the medium between man on the one hand and God and Christ on the other hand, the layman cannot directly apply to the divine being in his prayers, but only through mediators— human beings who conciliate God for him, the dead, the perfect—*Saints.* Thus originated the adoration of the Saints, and with it that conglomerate of fables and falsities with which the Saints and their biographies have been invested. In the East the worship of images had early become popular, and after a lengthened struggle had triumphantly established itself: an image, a picture, though sensuous, still appeals rather to the imagination; but the coarser natures of the West desired something more immediate as the object of their contemplation, and thus arose the worship of relics. The consequence was a formal resurrection of the dead in the mediæval period, every pious Christian wished to be in possession of such sacred earthly remains. Among the Saints the chief object of adoration was the *Virgin Mary.* She is certainly the beautiful concept of pure love—a mother's love; but spirit and thought stand higher than even this; and in the worship of this conception that of God in spirit was lost, and Christ himself was set aside. The element of mediation between God and man was thus apprehended and held as something external. Thus through the perversion of the principle of freedom, absolute slavery became the established law. The other aspects and relations of the spiritual life of Europe during this period flow from this principle. Knowledge, comprehension of religious doctrine, is something of which spirit is judged incapable; it is the exclusive possession of a class, which has to determine the true. For man may not presume to stand in a direct relation to God; so that, as we said before, if he would apply to Him, he needs a mediator—a saint. This view imports the denial of the essential unity of the divine and human; since man, as such, is declared incapable of recognizing the divine and of approaching thereto. And while humanity is thus separated from the supreme good, no change of heart, as such, is insisted upon—for this would suppose that the unity of the divine and the human is to be found in man himself—but the terrors of Hell are exhibited to man in the most terrible colours, to induce him to escape from them, not by moral amendment, but in virtue of something external—the *"means of grace."* These, however, are an *arcanum* to the laity; another—the "confessor," must furnish him with them. The individual has to confess, is bound to expose all the particulars of his life and conduct to the view of the confessor, and then is informed what course he has to pursue to attain spiritual safety. Thus the Church took the place of *conscience:* it put men in leading strings like children, and told them that man could not be freed from the torments which his sins had merited by any amendment of his own moral condition, but by outward actions, *opera operata*—actions which were not the promptings of his own good will, but performed by command of the ministers of the Church; *e.g.,* hearing Mass, doing penance, going through a certain number of prayers, undertaking pilgrimages—actions which are unspiritual, stupefy the soul, and which are not only mere external ceremonies, but are such as can be even vicariously performed. The supererogatory works ascribed to the Saints, could be purchased, and the spiritual advantage which they merited, secured to the purchaser. Thus was produced an utter derangement of all that is recognized as good and moral in the Christian Church: only external requirements are insisted upon, and these can be complied with in a merely external way. A condition the very reverse of freedom is intruded into the principle of freedom itself.

With this perversion is connected the absolute separation of the spiritual from the secular principle generally. There are two divine kingdoms—the intellectual in the heart and cognitive faculty, and the socially ethical whose element and sphere is secular existence. It is science alone that can comprehend the kingdom of God and the socially moral world as one idea, and that recognizes the fact that the course of time has witnessed a process ever tending to the realization of this unity. But piety as such has nothing to do with the secular: it may make its appearance in that sphere on a mission of mercy, but this stops short of a strict socially ethical connection with it—does not come up to the idea of freedom. Religious feeling is extraneous to history, and has no history; for history is rather the empire of spirit recognizing

itself in its *subjective* freedom, as the economy of social morality in the state. In the middle ages that embodying of the divine in actual life was wanting; the antithesis was not harmonized. Social morality was represented as worthless, and that in its *three* most essential particulars.

One phase of social morality is that connected with love—with the emotions called forth in the *marriage relation.* It is not proper to say that celibacy is contrary to nature, but that it is adverse to social morality. Marriage was indeed reckoned by the Church among the sacraments; but notwithstanding the position thus assigned it, it was degraded, inasmuch as celibacy was reckoned as the more holy state. A second point of social morality is presented in *activity*—the workman has to perform for his subsistence. His dignity consists in his depending entirely on his diligence, conduct, and intelligence, for the supply of his wants. In direct contravention of this principle, *pauperism,* laziness, inactivity, was regarded as nobler: and the immoral thus received the stamp of consecration. A *third* point of morality is, that *obedience* be rendered to the moral and rational, as an obedience to laws which I recognize as just; that it be not that blind and unconditional compliance which does not know what it is doing, and whose course of action is a mere groping about without clear consciousness or intelligence. But it was exactly this latter kind of obedience that passed for the most pleasing to God; a doctrine that exalts the obedience of slavery, imposed by the arbitrary will of the Church, above the true obedience of freedom.

In this way the three vows of chastity, poverty, and obedience turned out the very opposite of what they assumed to be, and in them all social morality was degraded. The Church was no longer a *spiritual* power, but an *ecclesiastical* one; and the relation which the secular world sustained to it was unspiritual, automatic, and destitute of independent insight and conviction. As the consequence of this, we see everywhere vice, utter absence of respect for conscience, shamelessness, and a distracted state of things, of which the entire history of the period is the picture in detail.

According to the above, the Church of the Middle Ages exhibits itself as a manifold *self-contradiction.* For subjective spirit, although testifying of the absolute, is at the same time *limited* and definitely existing spirit, as intelligence and will. Its limitation begins in its taking up this distinctive position, and here consentaneously begins its contradictory and self-alienated phase; for that intelligence and will are not imbued with the truth, which appears in relation to them as something *given*. This externality of the absolute object of comprehension affects the consciousness thus: that the absolute object presents itself as a merely sensuous, external thing—common outward existence —and yet claims to be absolute: in the mediæval view of things this absolute demand is made upon spirit. The second form of the contradiction in question has to do with the relation which the Church itself sustains. The true spirit exists in man—is *his* spirit; and the individual gives himself the certainty of this identity with the absolute, in worship—the Church sustaining merely the relation of a teacher and directress of this worship. But here, on the contrary, we have an ecclesiastical body, like the Brahmins in India, in possession of the truth—not indeed by birth, but in virtue of knowledge, teaching and training—yet with the proviso that this alone is not sufficient, an external form, an unspiritual title being judged essential to actual possession. This outward form is ordination, whose nature is such that the consecration imparted inheres essentially like a sensuous quality in the individual, whatever be the character of his soul—be he irreligious, immoral, or absolutely ignorant. The third kind of contradiction is the Church itself, in its acquisition as an outward existence, of possessions and an enormous property—a state of things which, since that church despises or professes to despise riches, is none other than a lie.

And we found the state, during the mediæval period, similarly involved in contradictions. We spoke above of an imperial rule, recognized as standing by the side of the church and constituting its secular arm. But the power thus acknowledged is invalidated by the fact that the imperial dignity in question is an empty title, not regarded by the Emperor himself or by those who wish to make him the instrument of their ambitious views, as conferring solid authority on its possessor; for passion and physical force assume an independent position, and own no subjection to that merely abstract conception. But *secondly,* the bond of union which holds the mediæval state together, and which we call fidelity, is left to the arbitrary choice of men's disposition which recognizes no objective duties. Consequently, this fidelity is the most *unfaithful* thing possible. German honour in the Middle Ages has become a proverb; but examined more closely as history exhibits it we find it a veritable *Punica fides* or *Græca fides;* for the princes and vassals of the Emperor are true and honourable only to their selfish aims, individual advantage and passions, but utterly untrue to the Empire and the Emperor; because in "fidelity" in the abstract, their subjective caprice receives a sanction, and the state is not organized as a moral totality. A *third* contradiction presents itself in the character of individuals, exhibiting, as they do, on the one hand, piety—religious devotion, the most beautiful in outward aspect, and springing from the very depths of sincerity —and, on the other hand, a barbarous deficiency in point of intelligence and will. We find an acquaintance with abstract truth, and yet the most uncultured, the rudest ideas of the secular and the spiritual: a truculent delirium of passion and yet a Christian sanctity which renounces all that is worldly, and devotes itself entirely to holiness. So self-contradictory, so deceptive is this mediæval period; and the polemical zeal with which its excellence is contended for is one of the absurdities of our times. Primitive barbarism, rudeness of manners, and childish fancy are not revolting; they simply excite our pity. But the highest purity of soul defiled by the most horrible barbarity; the truth, of which a knowledge has been acquired, degraded to a mere tool by falsehood and self-seeking; that which is most irrational, coarse and vile, established and strengthened by the religious sentiment—this is the most disgusting and revolting spectacle that was ever witnessed, and which only philosophy can comprehend and so justify. For such an antithesis must arise in man's consciousness of the holy while this consciousness still remains primitive and immediate; and the profounder the truth to which spirit comes into an *implicit* relation, while it has not yet become aware of its own presence in that profound truth, so much the more alien is it to itself in this its unknown form: but only as the result of this alienation does it attain its true harmonization.

We have then contemplated the Church as the *reaction* of the spiritual against the secular life of the time; but this reaction is so conditioned that it only subjects to itself that against which it reacts—does not reform it. While the spiritual, repudiating its proper sphere of action, has been acquiring secular power, a secular sovereignty has also consolidated itself and attained a systematic development—the *feudal system.* As through their isolation, men are reduced to a dependence on their individual power and might, every point in the world on which a human being can maintain his ground becomes an *energetic* one. While the individual still remains destitute of the defence of laws and is protected only by his own exertion, life, activity and excitement everywhere manifest themselves. As men are certain of eternal salvation through the instrumentality of the Church, and to this end are bound to obey it only in its spiritual requirements, their ardour in the pursuit of worldly enjoyment increases, on the other hand, in inverse proportion to their fear of its producing any detriment to their spiritual weal; for the Church bestows *indulgences*, when required, for oppressive, violent, and vicious actions of all kinds.

The period from the eleventh to the thirteenth century witnessed the rise of an impulse which developed itself in various forms. The inhabitants of various districts began to build enormous churches—cathedrals, erected to contain the whole community. Architecture is always the first art, forming the inorganic phase, the domiciliation of the divinity; not till this is accomplished does art attempt to exhibit to the worshippers the divinity himself—the objective. Maritime commerce was carried on with vigour by the cities on the Italian, Spanish, and Flemish coasts, and this stimulated the productive industry of their citizens at home. The sciences began in some degree to revive: the scholastic philosophy was in its glory. Schools for the study of law were founded at Bologna and other places, as also for that of medicine. It is on the rise and growing importance of the towns that all these creations depend as their main condition; a favourite subject of historical treatment in modern times. And the rise of such communities was greatly desiderated. For the towns, like the Church, present themselves as reactions against feudal violence—as the earliest legally and regularly constituted power. Mention has already been made of the fact that the possessors of power compelled others to put themselves under their protection. Such centres of safety were castles, churches, and monasteries, round which were collected those who needed protection. These now became burghers, and entered into a cliental relation to the lords of such castles or to monastic bodies. Thus a firmly established community was formed in many places. Many cities and fortified places still existed in Italy, in the south of France, and in Germany on the Rhine, which dated their existence from the ancient Roman times, and which originally possessed municipal rights, but subsequently lost them under the rule of feudal governors. The citizens, like their rural neighbors, had been reduced to vassalage.

The principle of free possession however began to develop itself from the *protective* relation of feudal protection; *i.e.*, freedom originated in its direct contrary. The feudal lords or great barons enjoyed, properly speaking, no free or absolute possession, any more than their dependents; they had unlimited power over the latter, but at the same time they also were vassals of princes higher and mightier than themselves, and to whom they were under engagements—which, it must be confessed, they did not fulfil except under compulsion. The ancient Germans had known of none other than free possession; but this principle had been perverted into its complete opposite, and now for the first time we behold the few feeble commencements of a reviving sense of freedom. Individuals brought into closer relation by the soil which they cultivated, formed among themselves a kind of union, confederation, or *conjuratio*. They agreed to be and to perform on their own behalf that which they had previously been and performed in the service of their feudal lord alone. Their first united undertaking was the erection of a tower in which a bell was suspended: the ringing of the bell was a signal for a general rendezvous, and the object of the union thus appointed was the formation of a kind of militia. This is followed by the institution of a municipal government, consisting of magistrates, jurors, consuls, and the establishment of a common treasury, the imposition of taxes, tolls, etc. Trenches are dug and walls built for the common defence, and the citizens are forbidden to erect fortresses for themselves individually. In such a community, handicrafts, as distinguished from agriculture, find their proper home. Artisans necessarily soon attained a superior position to that of the tillers of the ground, for the latter were forcibly driven to work; the former displayed activity really their own, and a corresponding diligence and interest in the result of their labours. Formerly artisans had been obliged to get permission from their liege lords to sell their work, and thus earn something for themselves: they were obliged to pay them a certain sum for this privilege of market, besides contributing a portion of their gains to the baronial exchequer. Those who had houses of their own were obliged to pay a considerable quit-rent for them; on all that was imported and exported, the nobility imposed large tolls, and for the security afforded to travellers they exacted safe-conduct money. When at a later date these communities became stronger, all such feudal rights were purchased from the nobles, or the cession of them compulsorily extorted: by degrees the towns secured an independent jurisdiction and likewise freed themselves from all taxes, tolls, and rents. The burden which continued the longest was the obligation the towns were under to make provision for the Emperor and his whole retinue during his stay within their precincts, as also for seigneurs of inferior rank under the same circumstances. The trading class subsequently divided itself into *guilds,* to each of which were attached particular rights and obligations. The factions to which episcopal elections and other contingencies gave rise, very often promoted the attainment by the towns of the rights above-mentioned. As it would not infrequently happen that two rival bishops were elected to the same see, each one sought to draw the citizens into his own interest, by granting them privileges and freeing them from burdens. Subsequently arose many feuds with the clergy, the bishops and abbots. In some towns they mantained their position as lords of the municipality; in others the citizens got the upper hand, and obtained their freedom. Thus, *e.g.,* Cologne threw off the yoke of its bishop; Mayence on the other hand remained subject. By degrees cities grew to be independent republics: first and foremost in Italy, then in the Netherlands, Germany, and France. They soon come to occupy a peculiar position with respect to the *nobility.* The latter united itself with the corporations of the towns, and constituted as, *e.g.,* in Berne, a particular guild. It soon assumed special powers in the corporations of the towns and attained a dominant position; but the citizens resisted the usurpation and secured the government to themselves. The rich citizens (*populus crassus*) now excluded the nobility from power. But in the same way as the party of the nobility was divided into factions—especially those of Ghibellines and Guelfs, of which the former favored the Emperor, the latter the Pope—that of the citizens also was rent in sunder by intestine strife. The victorious faction was accustomed to exclude its vanquished opponents from power. The *patrician* nobility which supplanted the feudal aristocracy, deprived the common people of all share in the conduct of the state, and thus proved itself no less oppressive than the original noblesse. The history of the cities presents us with a continual change of constitutions, according as one party among the citizens or the other, this faction or that, got the upper hand. Originally a select body of citizens chose the magistrates; but as in such elections the victorious faction always had the greatest influence, no other means of securing impartial functionaries was left, but the election of foreigners to the office of judge and *podésta.* It also frequently happened that the cities chose foreign princes as supreme seigneurs, and intrusted them with the *signoria.* But all of these arrangements were only of short continuance; the princes soon misused their sovereignty to promote their own ambitious designs and to gratify their passions, and in a few years were once more deprived of their supremacy.

Thus the history of these cities presents on the one hand, in ind'vidual characters marked by the most terrible or the most admirable features, an astonishingly interesting picture; on the other hand, it repels us by assuming, as it unavoidably does, the aspect of mere chronicles. In contemplating the restless and ever-varying impulses that agitate the very heart of these cities and the continual struggles of factions, we are astonished to see on the other side industry, commerce by land and sea, in the highest degree prosperous. It is the same principle of lively vigour, which, nourished by the internal excitement in question, produces this phenomenon.

We have contemplated the Church, which extended its power over all the sovereignties of the time, and the cities, where a social organization on a basis of right was first resuscitated, as powers reacting against the authority of princes and feudal lords. Against these two rising powers, there followed a reactionary movement of princely authority; the Emperor now enters on a struggle with the Pope and the cities. The Emperor is recognized as the apex of Christian, *i.e.,* secular power, the Pope on the other hand as that of ecclesiastical power, which had now however become as decidedly a secular dominion. In theory, it was not disputed that the Roman Emperor was the head of Christendom—that he possessed the *dominium mundi*—that since all Christian states belonged to the Roman Empire, their princes owed him allegiance in all reasonable and equitable requirements. However satisfied the emperors themselves might be of the validity of this claim, they had too much good sense to attempt seriously to enforce it: but the empty title of Roman Emperor was a sufficient inducement to them to exert themselves to the utmost to acquire and maintain it in Italy. The Othos especially cherished the idea of the continuation of the old Roman Empire, and were ever and anon summoning the German princes to join them in an expedition to Rome with a view to coronation there; an undertaking in which they were often deserted by them and had to undergo the shame of a retreat. Equal disappointment was experienced by those Italians who hoped for deliverance at the hands of the Emperor from the ochlocracy that domineered over the cities, or from the violence of the feudal nobility in the country at large. The Italian princes who had invoked the presence of the Emperor and had promised him aid in asserting his claims drew back and left him in the lurch; and those who had previously expected salvation for their country then broke out into bitter complaints that their beautiful country was devastated by barbarians, their superior civilization trodden under foot, and that right and liberty, deserted by the Emperor, must also perish. Especially touching and deep are the lamentations and reproaches which Dante addresses to the Emperors.

The second complication with Italy was that struggle which contemporaneously with the former was sustained chiefly by the great Swabians, the house of *Hohenstaufen,* and whose object was to bring back the secular power of the Church, which had become independent, to its original dependence on the state. The Papal See was also a secular power and sovereignty, and the Emperor asserted the superior prerogative of choosing the Pope and investing him with his secular sovereignty. It was these rights of the state for which the Emperors contended. But to that secular power which they withstood, they were at the same time subject, in virtue of its spiritual pretensions: thus the contest was an interminable contradiction. Contradictory as the varying phases of the contest, in which reconciliation was ever alternating with renewed hostilities, was also the instrumentality employed in the struggle. For the power with which the Emperors made head against their enemy—the princes, their servants and subjects, were divided in their own minds, inasmuch as they were bound by the strongest ties of allegiance to the Emperor and to his enemy at one and the same time. The chief interest of the princes lay in that very assumption of independence in reference to the state, against which on the part of the Papal See the Emperor was contending; so that they were willing to stand by the Emperor in cases where the empty dignity of the imperial crown was impugned, or on some particular occasions—*e.g.,* in a contest with the cities—but abandoned him when he aimed at seriously asserting his authority against the secular power of the clergy, or against other princes.

As, on the one hand, the German Emperors sought to realize their title in Italy, so, on the other hand, Italy had its political centre in Germany. The interests of the two countries were thus linked together, and neither could gain political consolidation within itself. In the brilliant period of the *Hohenstaufen* dynasty, individuals of commanding character sustained the dignity of the throne; sovereigns like Frederick Barbarossa, in whom the imperial power manifested itself in its greatest majesty, and who by his personal qualities succeeded in attaching the subject princes to his interests. Yet brilliant as the history of the Hohenstaufen dynasty may appear, and stirring as might have been the contest with the Church, the former presents on the whole nothing more than the tragedy of this house itself, and the latter had no important result in the sphere of spirit. The cities were indeed compelled to acknowledge the imperial authority, and their deputies swore to observe the decisions of the Roncalian Diet; but they kept their word no longer than they were compelled to do so. Their sense of obligation depended exclusively on the direct consciousness of a superior power ready to enforce it. It is said that when the Emperor Frederick I asked the deputies of the cities whether they had not sworn to the conditions of peace, they answered: "Yes, but not that we would observe them." The result was that Frederick I at the Peace of Constance (1183) was obliged to concede to them a virtual independence; although he appended the stipulation that in this concession their feudal obligations to the German Empire were understood to be reserved. The contest between the Emperors and the Popes regarding investitures was settled at the close of 1122 by Henry V and Pope Calixtus II on these terms: the Emperor was to invest with the sceptre; the Pope with the ring and crosier; the chapter were to elect the bishops in the presence of the Emperor or of imperial commissioners; then the Emperor was to invest the bishop as a secular feudatory with the *temporalia,* while the ecclesiastical investiture was reserved for the Pope. Thus the protracted contest between the secular and spiritual powers was at length set at rest.

Chapter 2. *The Crusades*

The Church gained the victory in the struggle referred to in the previous chapter; and in this way secured as decided a supremacy in Germany, as she did in the other states of Europe by a calmer process. She made herself mistress of all the relations of life, and of science and art; and she was the permanent repository of spiritual treasures. Yet notwithstanding this full and complete development of ecclesiastical life, we find a deficiency and consequent craving manifesting itself in Christendom, and which drove it out of itself. To understand this want, we must revert to the nature of the Christian religion itself, and particularly to that aspect of it by which it has a footing in the present in the consciousness of its votaries.

The objective doctrines of Christianity had been already so firmly settled by the councils of the Church, that neither the mediæval nor any other philosophy could develop them further, except in the way of exalting them intellectually, so that they might be satisfactory as presenting the *form* of thought. And one essential point in this doctrine was the recognition of the divine nature as not in any sense an *other-world* existence, but as in unity with human nature in the present and actual. But this presence is at the same time exclusively spiritual presence. Christ as a particular human personality has left the world; his *temporal* existence is only a past one —*i.e.*, it exists only in mental conception. And since the divine existence on earth is essentially of a spiritual character, it cannot appear in the form of a Dalai Lama. The Pope, however high his position as Head of Christendom and Vicar of Christ, calls himself only the Servant of Servants. How then did the Church realize Christ as a *definite and present existence?* The principal form of this realization was, as remarked above, the Holy Supper, in the form it presented as the Mass: in this the life, suffering, and death of the actual Christ were verily present, as an eternal and daily repeated sacrifice. Christ appears as a definite and present existence in a sensuous form as the *Host*, consecrated by the priest; so far all is satisfactory: that is to say, it is the Church, the spirit of Christ, that attains in this ordinance direct and full assurance. But the most prominent feature in this sacrament is, that the process by which deity is manifested, is conditioned by the limitations of particularity—that the Host, this *thing*, is set up to be adored as God. The Church then might have been able to content itself with this sensuous presence of deity; but when it is once granted that God exists in external phenomenal presence, this external manifestation immediately becomes infinitely varied; for the need of this presence is infinite. Thus innumerable instances will occur in the experience of the Church, in which Christ has appeared to one and another, in various places; and still more frequently his divine Mother, who as standing nearer to humanity, is a second mediator between the Mediator and man (the miracle-working images of the Virgin are in their way Hosts, since they supply a benign and gracious presence

of God). In all places, therefore, there will occur manifestations of the heavenly, in specially gracious appearances, the stigmata of Christ's Passion, etc.; and the divine will be realized in *miracles* as detached and isolated phenomena. In the period in question the Church presents the aspect of a world of miracle; to the community of devout and pious persons natural existence has utterly lost its stability and certainty: rather, absolute certainty has turned against it, and the divine is not conceived of by Christendom under conditions of universality as the law and nature of spirit, but reveals itself in isolated and detached phenomena, in which the rational form of existence is utterly perverted.

In this complete development of the Church, *we* may find a deficiency: but what can be felt as a want by *it?* What compels *it*, in this state of perfect satisfaction and enjoyment, to wish for something else within the limits of its own principles—without apostatizing from itself? Those miraculous images, places, and times, are only isolated points, momentary appearances— are not an embodiment of deity, not of the highest and absolute kind. The Host, the supreme manifestation, is to be found indeed in innumerable churches; Christ is therein transubstantiated to a present and particular existence: but this itself is of a vague and general character; it is not his actual and very presence as particularized in *space*. That presence has passed away, as regards *time;* but as spatial and as concrete in *space* it has a mundane permanence in this particular spot, this particular village, etc. It is then this mundane existence which Christendom desiderates, which it is resolved on attaining. Pilgrims in crowds had indeed been able to enjoy it; but the approach to the hallowed localities is in the hands of the infidels, and it is a reproach to Christendom that the holy places and the Sepulchre of Christ in particular are not in possession of the Church. In this feeling Christendom was united; consequently the *Crusades* were undertaken, whose object was not the furtherance of any special interests on the part of the several states that engaged in them, but simply and solely the conquest of the Holy Land.

The West once more sallied forth in hostile array against the East. As in the expedition of the Greeks against Troy, so here, the invading hosts were entirely composed of independent feudal lords and knights; though they were not united under a real individuality, as were the Greeks under Agamemnon or Alexander. Christendom, on the contrary, was engaged in an undertaking whose object was the securing of the *definite and present existence*—the real culmination of individuality. This object impelled the West against the East, and this is the essential interest of the Crusades.

The first and immediate commencement of the Crusades was made in the West itself. Many thousands of Jews were massacred, and their property seized; and after this terrible prelude Christendom began its march. The monk, Peter the Hermit of Amiens, led the way with an immense troop of rabble. This host passed in the greatest disorder through Hungary, and robbed and plundered as they went; but their numbers dwindled away, and only a few reached Constantinople. For rational considerations were out of the question; the mass of them believed that God would be their immediate guide and protector. The most striking proof that enthusiasm almost robbed the nations of Europe of their senses is supplied by the fact that at a later time troops of children ran away from their parents and went to Marseilles, there to take ship for the Holy Land. Few reached it; the rest were sold by the merchants to the Saracens as slaves.

At last, with much trouble and immense loss, more regular armies attained the desired object; they beheld themselves in possession of all the holy places of note—Bethlehem, Gethsemane, Golgotha, and even the *Holy Sepulchre*. In the whole expedition, in all the acts of the Christians, appeared that enormous contrast (a feature characteristic of the age)—the transition on the part of the crusading host from the greatest excesses and outrages to the profoundest contrition and humiliation. Still dripping with the blood of the slaughtered inhabitants of Jerusalem, the Christians fell down on their faces at the tomb of the Redeemer, and directed their fervent supplications to him.

Thus did Christendom come into the possession of its highest good. Jerusalem was made a kingdom, and the entire feudal system was introduced there—a constitution which, in presence of the Saracens, was certainly the worst that could be adopted. Another Crusade in the year 1204 resulted in the conquest of Constantinople and the establishment of a Latin Empire there. Christendom, therefore, had appeased its religious craving; it could now veritably walk unobstructed in the footsteps of the Saviour. Whole shiploads of earth were brought from the Holy Land to Europe. Of Christ himself no corporeal relics could be obtained, for he was arisen: the Sacred Handkerchief, the Cross, and lastly the Sepulchre, were the most venerated

memorials. But in the grave is found the real point of retroversion; it is in the grave that all the vanity of the sensuous perishes. At the Holy Sepulchre the vanity of opinion passes away; there all is seriousness. In the negation of that *definite and present embodiment, i.e.,* of the sensuous, it is that the turning-point in question is found, and those words have an application: "Thou wouldst not suffer thy Holy One to see corruption." Christendom was not to find its ultimatum of truth in the grave. At this sepulchre the Christian world received a second time the response given to the disciples when they sought the body of the Lord there: *"Why seek ye the living among the dead? He is not here, but is risen."* You must not look for the principle of your religion in the sensuous, in the grave among the dead, but in the living spirit in yourselves. We have seen how the vast idea of the union of the finite with the infinite was perverted to such a degree as that men looked for a *definite embodiment* of the infinite in a mere isolated outward object. Christendom found the empty Sepulchre, but not the union of the secular and the eternal; and so it lost the Holy Land. It was practically undeceived; and the result which it brought back with it was of a negative kind: *viz.,* that the *definite embodiment* which it was seeking, was to be looked for in *subjective consciousness alone,* and in no external object; that the definite form in question, presenting the union of the secular with the eternal, is spiritual self-cognizant independence of the individual. Thus the world attains the conviction that man must look within himself for that *definite embodiment* of being which is of a divine nature: subjectivity thereby receives absolute authorization, and claims to determine for itself the relation to the divine.[1] This then was the absolute result of the Crusades, and from them we may date the commencement of self-reliance and spontaneous activity. The West bade an eternal farewell to the East at the Holy Sepulchre, and gained a comprehension of its own principle of subjective infinite freedom. Christendom never appeared again on the scene of history as *one* body.

Crusades of another kind, bearing somewhat the character of wars with a view to mere secular conquest, but which involved a religious interest also, were the contests waged by Spain against the Saracens in the peninsula itself. The Christians had been shut up in a corner by the

---

[1] All human actions, projects, institutions, etc., begin to be brought to the bar of "principle"—the sanctum of subjectivity—for absolute decision on their merits, instead of being referred to an extraneous authority.

Arabs; but they gained upon their adversaries in strength, because the Saracens in Spain and Africa were engaged in war in various directions, and were divided among themselves. The Spaniards, united with Frank knights, undertook frequent expeditions against the Saracens; and in this collision of the Christians with the chivalry of the East, with its freedom and perfect independence of soul, the former became also partakers in this freedom. Spain gives us the fairest picture of the knighthood of the Middle Ages, and its hero is the Cid. Several Crusades, the records of which excite our unmixed loathing and detestation, were undertaken against the south of France also. There an æsthetic culture had developed itself: the troubadours had introduced a freedom of manners similar to that which prevailed under the Hohenstaufen Emperors in Germany; but with this difference, that the former had in it something affected, while the latter was of a more genuine kind. But as in upper Italy, so also in the south of France fanatical ideas of purity had been introduced;[1] a Crusade was therefore preached against that country by papal authority. St. Dominic entered it with a vast host of invaders, who, in the most barbarous manner, pillaged and murdered the innocent and the guilty indiscriminately, and utterly laid waste the fair region which they inhabited.

Through the Crusades the Church reached the completion of its authority: it had achieved the perversion of religion and of the divine spirit; it had distorted the principle of Christian freedom to a wrongful and immoral slavery of men's souls; and in so doing, far from abolishing lawless caprice and violence and supplanting them by a virtuous rule of its own, it had even enlisted them in the service of ecclesiastical authority. In the Crusades the Pope stood at the head of the secular power: the Emperor appeared only in a subordinate position, like the other princes, and was obliged to commit both the initiative and the executive to the Pope, as the manifest generalissimo of the expedition. We have already seen the noble house of Hohenstaufen presenting the aspect of chivalrous, dignified and cultivated opponents of the papal power, when spirit had given up the contest. We have seen how they were ultimately obliged to yield to the Church, which, elastic enough to sustain any attack, bore down all opposition and would not move a step towards conciliation. The fall of the Church was

not to be effected by open violence; it was from within, by the power of spirit and by an influence that wrought its way upwards, that ruin threatened it. Respect for the papacy could not but be weakened by the very fact that the lofty aim of the Crusades, the satisfaction expected from the enjoyment of the sensuous presence, was not attained. As little did the Popes succeed in keeping possession of the Holy Land. Zeal for the holy cause was exhausted among the princes of Europe. Grieved to the heart by the defeat of the Christians, the Popes again and again urged them to advance to the rescue; but lamentations and entreaties were vain, and they could effect nothing. Spirit, disappointed with regard to its craving for the highest form of the sensuous presence of deity, fell back upon itself. A rupture, the first of its kind and profound as it was novel, took place. From this time forward we witness religious and intellectual movements in which spirit, transcending the repulsive and irrational existence by which it is surrounded, either finds its sphere of exercise within itself, and draws upon its own resources for satisfaction, or throws its energies into an actual world of general and morally justified aims, which are therefore aims consonant with freedom. The efforts thus originated are now to be described: they were the means by which spirit was to be prepared to comprehend the grand purpose of its freedom in a form of greater purity and moral elevation.

To this class of movements belongs in the first place the establishment of monastic and chivalric orders, designed to carry out those rules of life which the Church had distinctly enjoined upon its members. That renunciation of property, riches, pleasures, and free will, which the Church had designated as the highest of spiritual attainments, was to be a reality—not a mere profession. The existing monastic and other institutions that had adopted this vow of renunciation had been entirely sunk in the corruption of worldliness. But now spirit sought to realize in the sphere of the principle of negativity, purely in itself, what the Church had demanded. The more immediate occasion of this movement was the rise of numerous heresies in the south of France and Italy, whose tendency was in the direction of enthusiasm; and the unbelief which was now gaining ground, but which the Church justly deemed not so dangerous as those heresies. To counteract these evils, new *monastic orders* were founded, the chief of which was that of the Franciscans, or Mendicant Friars, whose founder, St. Francis of Assisi, a

---

[1] The term "Cathari" ($\kappa\alpha\theta\alpha\rho o\iota$), *Purists*, was one of the most general designations of the dissident sects in question. The German word *"Ketzer"* = *heretic* is by some derived from it.

man possessed by an enthusiasm and ecstatic passion that passed all bounds, spent his life in continually striving for the loftiest purity. He gave an impulse of the same kind to his order; the greatest fervour of devotion, the sacrifice of all pleasures in contravention of the prevailing worldliness of the Church, continual penances, the severest poverty (the Franciscans lived on daily alms)—were therefore peculiarly characteristic of it. Contemporaneously with it arose the Dominican order, founded by St. Dominic; its special business was preaching. The mendicant friars were diffused through Christendom to an incredible extent; they were, on the one hand, the standing apostolic army of the Pope, while, on the other hand, they strongly protested against his worldliness. The Franciscans were powerful allies of Louis of Bavaria in his resistance of the papal assumptions, and they are said to have been the authors of the position, that a general council was higher authority than the Pope; but subsequently they too sank down into a torpid and unintelligent condition. In the same way the ecclesiastical *Orders of Knighthood* contemplated the attainment of purity of spirit. We have already called attention to the peculiar chivalric spirit which had been developed in Spain through the struggle with the Saracens: the same spirit was diffused as the result of the Crusades through the whole of Europe. The ferocity and savage valour that characterized the predatory life of the barbarians—pacified and brought to a settled state by possession, and restrained by the presence of equals—was elevated by religion and then kindled to a noble enthusiasm through contemplating the boundless magnanimity of oriental prowess. For Christianity also contains the element of boundless abstraction and freedom; the oriental chivalric spirit found therefore in occidental hearts a response which paved the way for their attaining a nobler virtue than they had previously known. Ecclesiastical orders of knighthood were instituted on a basis resembling that of the monastic fraternities. The same conventual vow of renunciation was imposed on their members—the giving up of all that was worldly. But at the same time they undertook the defence of the pilgrims: their first duty therefore was knightly bravery; ultimately, they were also pledged to the sustenance and care of the poor and the sick. The Orders of Knighthood were divided into three: that of St. John, that of the Temple, and the Teutonic Order. These associations are essentially distinguished from the self-seeking principle of feudalism. Their members sacrificed themselves with almost suicidal bravery for a common interest. Thus these orders transcended the circle of their immediate environment, and formed a network of fraternal coalition over the whole of Europe. But their members sank down to the level of vulgar interests, and the Orders became in the sequel a provisional institute for the nobility generally, rather than anything else. The Order of the Temple was even accused of forming a religion of its own, and of having renounced Christ in the creed which, under the influence of the oriental spirit, it had adopted.

A second impulsion, having a similar origin, was that in the direction of *science*. The development of thought, the abstractly universal, now had its commencement. Those fraternal associations themselves, having a common object, in whose service their members were enlisted, point to the fact that a general principle was beginning to be recognized, and which gradually became conscious of its power. Thought was first directed to theology, which now became philosophy under the name of scholastic divinity. For philosophy and theology have the divine as their common object; and although the theology of the Church was a stereotyped dogma, the impulse now arose to justify this body of doctrine in the view of thought. "When we have arrived at faith," says the celebrated scholastic, Anselm, "it is a piece of negligence to stop short of convincing ourselves, by the aid of thought, of that to which we have given credence." But thus conditioned thought was not free, for its material was already posited *ab extra;* it was to the proof of this material that philosophy devoted its energies. But thought suggested a variety of questions, the complete answer to which was not given directly in the symbols of the Church; and since the Church had not decided respecting them, they were legitimate subjects of controversy. Philosophy was indeed called an *ancilla fidei,* for it was in subjection to that material of the Church's creed, which had been already definitely settled; but yet it was impossible for the opposition between thought and belief not to manifest itself. As Europe presented the spectacle of chivalric contests generally, passages of arms and tournaments, it was now the theatre for intellectual jousting also. It is incredible to what an extent the abstract forms of thought were developed, and what dexterity was acquired in the use of them. This intellectual tourneying for the sake of exhibiting skill, and as a diversion (for it was not the doctrines themselves, but only the forms in which they were couched that made the subject of debate), was chiefly prosecuted and brought to perfection in France. France, in fact, began at that time to be regarded as the centre of Christendom: there the scheme of the first Crusades originated, and French armies carried it out: there the popes took refuge in their struggles with the German emperors and with the Norman princes of Naples and Sicily, and there for a time they made a continuous sojourn. We also observe in the period subsequent to the Crusades, commencements of art—of painting, *viz.*, even during their continuance a peculiar kind of poetry had made its appearance. Spirit, unable to satisfy its cravings, created for itself by imagination fairer forms and in a calmer and freer manner than the actual world could offer.

Chapter 3. *The Transition from Feudalism to Monarchy*

The moral phenomena above mentioned, tending in the direction of a general principle, were partly of a subjective, partly of a speculative order. But we must now give particular attention to the practical political movements of the period. The advance which that period witnessed, presents a negative aspect in so far as it involves the termination of the sway of individual caprice and of the isolation of power. Its affirmative aspect is the rise of a supreme authority whose dominion embraces all—a political power properly so called, whose subjects enjoy an equality of rights, and in which the will of the individual is subordinated to that common interest which underlies the whole. This is the advance from feudalism to *monarchy*. The principle of feudal sovereignty is the *outward* force of individuals—princes, liege lords; it is a force destitute of *intrinsic* right. The subjects of such a constitution are vassals of a superior prince or seigneur, to whom they have stipulated duties to perform: but whether they perform these duties or not depends upon the seigneur's being able to induce them so to do, by force of character or by grant of favours: conversely, the recognition of those feudal claims themselves was extorted by violence in the first instance; and the fulfilment of the corresponding duties could be secured only by the constant exercise of the power which was the sole basis of the claims in question. The monarchical principle also implies a supreme authority, but it is an authority over persons possessing no independent power to support their individual caprice; where we have no longer caprice opposed to caprice; for the supremacy implied in monarchy is essentially a power emanating from a political body, and is pledged to the furtherance of that equitable purpose on which the constitution of a state is based. Feudal sovereignty is a polyarchy: we see nothing but lords and serfs; in monarchy, on the contrary, there is one lord and no serf, for servitude is abrogated by it, and in it right and law are recognized; it is the source of real freedom. Thus in monarchy the caprice of individuals is kept under, and a common gubernatorial interest established. In the suppression of those isolated powers, as also in the resistance made to that suppression, it seems doubtful whether the desire for a lawful and equitable state of things, or the wish to indulge individual caprice, is the impelling motive. Resistance to kingly authority is entitled liberty, and is lauded as legitimate and noble when the idea of arbitrary will is associated with that authority. But by the arbitrary will of an individual exerting itself so as to subjugate a whole body of men, a community is formed; and comparing this state of things with that in which every point is a centre of capricious violence, we find a much smaller number of points exposed to such violence. The great extent of such a sovereignty necessitates general arrangements for the purposes of organization, and those who govern in accordance with those arrangements are at the same time, in virtue of their office itself, obedient to the state: vassals become officers of state, whose duty it is to execute the laws by which the state is regulated. But since this monarchy is developed from feudalism, it bears in the first instance the stamp of the system from which it sprang. Individuals quit their isolated capacity and become members of estates and corporations; the vassals are powerful only by combination as an order; in contraposition to them the cities constitute powers in virtue of their communal existence. Thus the authority of the sovereign inevitably ceases to be mere arbitrary sway. The consent of the estates and corporations is essential to its maintenance; and if the prince wishes to have that consent, he must will what is just and reasonable.

We now see a constitution embracing various orders, while feudal rule knows no such orders. We observe the transition from feudalism to monarchy taking place in three ways:

1. Sometimes the lord paramount gains a mastery over his independent vassals, by subjugating their individual power—thus making himself sole ruler.

2. Sometimes the princes free themselves from the feudal relation altogether, and become the territorial lords of certain states.

3. Lastly, the lord paramount unites the particular lordships that own him as their superior with his own particular suzerainty, in a more peaceful way, and thus becomes master of the whole.

These processes do not indeed present themselves in history in that pure and abstract form in which they are exhibited here: often we find more modes than one appearing contemporaneously; but one or the other always predominates. The cardinal consideration is that the basis and essential condition of such a political formation is to be looked for in the *particular nationalities* in which it had its birth. Europe presents particular nations, constituting a unity in their very nature, and having the absolute tendency to form a state. All did not succeed in attaining this political unity: we have now to consider them severally in relation to the change thus introduced.

First, as regards the Roman Empire, the connection between *Germany* and *Italy* naturally results from the idea of that empire: the secular dominion united with the spiritual was to constitute one whole; but this state of things was rather the object of constant struggle than one actually attained. In Germany and Italy the transition from the feudal condition to monarchy involved the entire abrogation of the former: the vassals became independent monarchs.

Germany had always embraced a great variety of stocks: Swabians, Bavarians, Franks, Thuringians, Saxons, Burgundians: to these must be added the Slavs of Bohemia, Germanized Slavs in Mecklenburg, in Brandenburg, and in a part of Saxony and Austria; so that no such combination as took place in France was possible. Italy presented a similar state of things. The Lombards had established themselves there, while the Greeks still possessed the Exarchate and lower Italy: the Normans too established a kingdom of their own in lower Italy, and the Saracens maintained their ground for a time in Sicily. When the rule of the house of Hohenstaufen was terminated, barbarism got the upper hand throughout Germany; the country being broken up into several sovereignties, in which a forceful despotism prevailed. It was the maxim of the electoral princes to raise only weak princes to the imperial throne; they even sold the imperial dignity to foreigners. Thus the unity of the state was virtually annulled. A number of centres of power were formed, each of which was a predatory state: the legal constitution recognized by feudalism was dissolved, and gave place to undisguised violence and plunder; and powerful princes made themselves lords of the country. After the interregnum, the Count of Hapsburg was elected Emperor, and the House of Hapsburg continued to fill the imperial throne with but little interruption. These emperors were obliged to create a force of their own, as the princes would not grant them an adequate power attached to the empire. But that state of absolute anarchy was at last put an end to by associations having general aims in view. In the cities themselves we see associations of a minor order; but now *confederations of cities* were formed with a common interest in the suppression of predatory violence. Of this kind was the *Hanseatic League* in the north, the *Rhenish League* consisting of cities lying along the Rhine, and the *Swabian League*. The aim of all these confederations was resistance to the feudal lords; and even princes united with the cities, with a view to the subversion of the feudal condition and the restoration of a peaceful state of things throughout the country. What the state of society was under feudal sovereignty is evident from the notorious association formed for executing criminal justice: it was a private tribunal, which, under the name of the *Vehmgericht*, held secret sittings; its chief seat was the northwest of Germany. A peculiar *peasant association* was also formed. In Germany the peasants were bondsmen; many of them took refuge in the towns, or settled down as freemen in the neighborhood of the towns (*Pfahlbürger*); but in Switzerland a peasant fraternity was established. The peasants of Uri, Schwyz, and Unterwalden were under imperial governors; for the Swiss governments were not the property of private possessors, but were official appointments of the empire. These the sovereigns of the Hapsburg line wished to secure to their own house. The peasants, with club and iron-studded mace, returned victorious from a contest with the haughty steel-clad nobles, armed with spear and sword, and practised in the chivalric encounters of the tournament. Another invention also tended to deprive the nobility of the ascendancy which they owed to their accoutrements—that of *gunpowder*. Humanity needed it, and it made its appearance forthwith. It was one of the chief instruments in freeing the world from the dominion of physical force, and placing the various orders of society on a level. With the distinction between the weapons they used, vanished also that between lords and serfs. And before gunpowder fortified places were no longer impregnable, so that strongholds and castles now lose their importance. We may indeed be led to lament the decay or the depreciation of the practical value of personal valour—the bravest, the noblest may be shot down by a cowardly wretch at safe distance in an obscure lurking-place; but, on the other hand, gunpowder has made a rational, considerate bravery—spiritual valour—the essential to martial success. Only through this instrumentality could that superior order of valour be called forth, that valour in which the heat of personal feeling has no share; for the discharge of firearms is directed against a body of men—an abstract enemy, not individual combatants. The warrior goes to meet deadly peril calmly, sacrificing himself for the common weal; and the valour of cultivated nations is characterized by the very fact, that it does not rely on the strong arm alone, but places its confidence essentially in the intelligence, the generalship, the character of its commanders; and, as was the case among the ancients, in a firm combination and unity of spirit on the part of the forces they command.

In *Italy,* as already noticed, we behold the same spectacle as in Germany—the attainment of an independent position by isolated centres of power. In that country, warfare in the hands of the condottieri became a regular business. The towns were obliged to attend to their trading concerns, and therefore employed mercenary troops, whose leaders often became feudal lords; Francis Sforza even made himself Duke of Milan. In Florence, the Medici, a family of merchants, rose to power. On the other hand, the larger cities of Italy reduced under their sway several smaller ones and many feudal chiefs. A papal territory was likewise formed. There, also, a very large number of feudal lords had made themselves independent; by degrees they all became subject to the one sovereignty of the Pope. How thoroughly equitable in the view of social morality such a subjugation was is evident from Machiavelli's celebrated work, *The Prince.* This book has often been thrown aside in disgust, as replete with the maxims of the most revolting tyranny; but nothing worse can be urged against it than that the writer, having the profound consciousness of the necessity for the formation of a state, has here exhibited the principles on which alone states could be founded in the circumstances of the times. The chiefs who asserted an isolated independence, and the power they arrogated, must be entirely subdued; and though we cannot reconcile with our idea of freedom, the means which he proposes as the only efficient ones, and regards as perfectly justifiable—inasmuch as they involve

the most reckless violence, all kinds of deception, assassination, and so forth—we must nevertheless confess that the feudal nobility, whose power was to be subdued, were assailable in no other way, since an indomitable contempt for principle, and an utter depravity of morals, were thoroughly engrained in them.

In *France* we find the converse of that which occurred in Germany and Italy. For many centuries the kings of France possessed only a very small domain, so that many of their vassals were more powerful than themselves: but it was a great advantage to the royal dignity in France, that the principle of hereditary monarchy was firmly established there. The consideration it enjoyed was increased by the circumstance that the corporations and cities had their rights and privileges confirmed by the king, and that the appeals to the supreme feudal tribunal—the Court of Peers, consisting of twelve members enjoying that dignity—became increasingly frequent. The king's influence was extended by his affording that protection which only the throne could give. But that which essentially secured respect for royalty, even among the powerful vassals, was the increasing personal power of the sovereign. In various ways, by inheritance, by marriage, by force of arms, etc., the kings had come into possession of many earldoms and several duchies. The dukes of Normandy had, however, become kings of England; and thus a formidable power confronted France, whose interior lay open to it by way of Normandy. Besides this there were powerful duchies still remaining; nevertheless, the king was not a mere feudal suzerain like the German emperors, but had become a territorial possessor: he had a number of barons and cities under him, who were subject to his immediate jurisdiction; and Louis IX succeeded in rendering appeals to the royal tribunal common throughout his kingdom. The towns attained a position of greater importance in the state. For when the king needed money, and all his usual resources—such as taxes and forced contributions of all kinds—were exhausted, he made application to the towns and entered into separate negotiations with them. It was Philip the Fair who, in the year 1302, first convoked the deputies of the towns as a Third Estate in conjunction with the clergy and the barons. All indeed that they were in the first instance concerned with was the authority of the sovereign as the power that had convoked them, and the raising of taxes as the object of their convocation; but the states nevertheless secured an importance and weight in the kingdom and, as the natural result, an influence on legislation also. A fact which is particularly remarkable is the proclamation issued by the kings of France, giving permission to the bondsmen on the crown lands to purchase their freedom at a moderate price. In the way we have indicated the kings of France very soon attained great power; while the flourishing state of the poetic art in the hands of the troubadours, and the growth of the scholastic theology, whose especial centre was Paris, gave France a culture superior to that of the other European states, and which secured the respect of foreign nations.

England, as we have already had occasion to mention, was subjugated by William the Conqueror, Duke of Normandy. William introduced the feudal system into it, and divided the kingdom into fiefs, which he granted almost exclusively to his Norman followers. He himself retained considerable crown possessions; the vassals were under obligation to perform service in the field, and to aid in administering justice: the king was the guardian of all vassals under age; they could not marry without his consent. Only by degrees did the barons and the towns attain a position of importance. It was especially in the disputes and struggles for the throne that they acquired considerable weight. When the oppressive rule and fiscal exactions of the kings became intolerable, contentions and even war ensued: the barons compelled King John to swear to Magna Charta, the basis of English liberty, *i.e.,* more particularly of the privileges of the nobility. Among the liberties thus secured, that which concerns the administration of justice was the chief: no Englishman was to be deprived of personal freedom, property, or life without the judicial verdict of his peers. Every one, moreover, was to be entitled to the free disposition of his property. Further, the king was to impose no taxes without the consent of the archbishops, bishops, earls, and barons. The towns, also, favoured by the kings in opposition to the barons, soon elevated themselves into a Third Estate and to representation in the Commons' House of Parliament. Yet the king was always very powerful, if he possessed strength of character: his crown estates procured for him due consideration; in later times, however, these were gradually alienated, given away, so that the king was reduced to apply for subsidies to the Parliament.

We shall not pursue the minute and specifically historic details that concern the incorporation of principalities with states, or the dis-

sensions and contests that accompanied such incorporations. We have only to add that the kings, when by weakening the feudal constitution, they had attained a higher degree of power, began to use that power against each other in the undisguised interest of their own dominion. Thus France and England carried on wars with each other for a century. The kings were always endeavouring to make foreign conquests; the towns, which had the largest share of the burdens and expenses of such wars, were opposed to them, and in order to placate them the kings granted them important privileges.

The *Popes* endeavoured to make the disturbed state of society to which each of these changes gave rise an occasion for the intervention of their authority; but the interest of the growth of states was too firmly established to allow them to make their own interest of absolute authority valid against it. Princes and peoples were indifferent to papal clamour urging them to new Crusades. The Emperor Louis set to work to deduce from Aristotle, the Bible, and the Roman Law a refutation of the assumptions of the Papal See; and the electors declared at the diet held at Rense in 1338, and afterwards still more decidedly at the Imperial Diet held at Frankfort, that they would defend the liberties and hereditary rights of the empire, and that to make the choice of a Roman Emperor or king valid, no papal confirmation was needed. So, at an earlier date, 1302, on occasion of a contest between Pope Boniface and Philip the Fair, the Assembly of the States convoked by the latter had offered opposition to the Pope. For states and communities had arrived at the consciousness of independent moral worth. Various causes had united to weaken the papal authority: the Great Schism of the Church, which led men to doubt the Pope's infallibility, gave occasion to the decisions of the Councils of Constance and Basle, which assumed an authority superior to that of the Pope, and therefore deposed and appointed Popes. The numerous attempts directed against the ecclesiastical system confirmed the necessity of a reformation. Arnold of Brescia, Wickliffe, and Huss met with sympathy in contending against the dogma of the papal vicegerency of Christ, and the gross abuses that disgraced the hierarchy. These attempts were, however, only partial in their scope. On the one hand, the time was not yet ripe for a more comprehensive onslaught; on the other hand, the assailants in question did not strike at the heart of the matter, but (especially the two latter) attacked the teaching of the Church chiefly with the weapons of erudition, and consequently failed to excite a deep interest among the people at large.

But the ecclesiastical principle had a more dangerous foe in the incipient formation of political organizations, than in the antagonists above referred to. A common object, an aim intrinsically possessed of perfect moral validity,[1] presented itself to secularity in the formation of states; and to this aim of community the will, the desire, the caprice of the individual submitted themselves. The hardness characteristic of the self-seeking quality of "heart," maintaining its position of isolation, the knotty heart of oak underlying the national temperament of the Germans, was broken down and mellowed by the terrible discipline of the Middle Ages. The two iron rods which were the instruments of this discipline were the Church and serfdom. The Church drove the "heart" to desperation—made spirit pass through the severest bondage, so that the soul was no longer its own; but it did not degrade it to Hindu torpor, for Christianity is an intrinsically spiritual principle and, as such, has a boundless elasticity. In the same way serfdom, which made a man's body not his own but the property of another, dragged humanity through all the barbarism of slavery and unbridled desire, and the latter was destroyed by its own violence. It was not so much *from* slavery as *through* slavery that humanity was emancipated. For barbarism, lust, injustice constitute evil: man, bound fast in its fetters, is unfit for morality and religiousness; and it is from this intemperate and ungovernable state of volition that the discipline in question emancipated him. The Church fought the battle with the violence of rude sensuality in a temper equally wild and terroristic with that of its antagonist: it prostrated the latter by dint of the terrors of hell, and held it in perpetual subjection, in order to break down the spirit of barbarism and to tame it into repose. Theology declares that every man has this struggle to pass through, since he is by nature evil, and only by passing through a state of mental laceration arrives at the certainty of reconciliation. But granting this, it must on the other hand be maintained, that the form of the contest is very much altered when the conditions of its commencement are different, and when that reconciliation has had an actual realization. The path of torturous discipline is in that case dispensed with (it does indeed make

its appearance at a later date, but in a quite different form), for the waking up of consciousness finds man surrounded by the element of a moral state of society. The phase of negation is, indeed, a necessary element in human development, but it has now assumed the tranquil form of education, so that all the terrible characteristics of that inward struggle vanish.

Humanity has now attained the consciousness of a real internal harmonization of spirit, and a good conscience in regard to actuality—to secular existence. The human spirit has come to stand on its own basis. In the self-consciousness to which man has thus advanced, there is no revolt against the divine, but a manifestation of that better subjectivity, which recognizes the divine in its own being; which is imbued with the good and true, and which directs its activities to general and liberal objects bearing the stamp of rationality and beauty.

Art and Science as Putting a Period to the Middle Ages

Humanity beholds its spiritual firmament restored to serenity. With that tranquil settling down of the world into political order, which we have been contemplating, was conjoined an exaltation of spirit to a nobler grade of humanity in a sphere involving more comprehensive and concrete interests than that with which political existence is concerned. The sepulchre, that *caput mortuum* of spirit, and the ultramundane cease to absorb human attention. The principle of a specific and definite embodiment of the infinite, that desideratum which urged the world to the Crusades, now developed itself in a quite different direction, *viz.*, in secular existence asserting an independent ground: spirit made its embodiment an outward one and found a congenial sphere in the secular life thus originated. The Church, however, maintained its former position, and retained the principle in question in its original form. Yet even in this case, that principle ceased to be limited to a bare outward existence [a sacred *thing*, the Host, *e.g.*]: it was transformed and elevated by *art*. Art spiritualizes, animates the mere outward and material object of adoration with a form which expresses soul, sentiment, spirit; so that piety has not a bare sensuous embodiment of the infinite to contemplate, and does not lavish its devotion on a mere *thing*, but on the higher element with which the material object is imbued—that expressive form with which *Spirit* has invested it.

It is one thing for the mind to have before

---

[1] That is, not a personal aim, whose self-seeking character is its condemnation, but a general and liberal, consequently a *moral* aim.

it a mere thing—such as the Host *per se,* a piece of stone or wood, or a wretched daub; quite another thing for it to contemplate a painting, rich in thought and sentiment, or a beautiful work of sculpture, in looking at which, soul holds converse with soul and spirit with spirit. In the former case, spirit is torn from its proper element, bound down to something utterly alien to it—the sensuous, the nonspiritual. In the latter, on the contrary, the sensuous object is a beautiful one, and the spiritual form with which it is endued gives it a soul and contains truth in itself. But on the one hand, this element of truth as thus exhibited is manifested only in a sensuous mode, not in its appropriate form; on the other hand, while religion normally involves independence of that which is essentially a mere outward and material object—a mere thing— that kind of religion which is now under consideration finds no satisfaction in being brought into connection with the beautiful: the coarsest, ugliest, poorest representations will suit its purpose *equally well*—perhaps better. Accordingly real masterpieces, *e.g.,* Raphael's Madonnas, do not enjoy distinguished veneration, or elicit a multitude of offerings: inferior pictures seem, on the contrary, to be especial favourites and to be made the object of the warmest devotion and the most generous liberality. Piety passes by the former for this very reason, that were it to linger in their vicinity it would feel an inward stimulus and attraction; an excitement of a kind which cannot but be felt to be alien, where all that is desiderated is a sense of mental bondage in which self is lost—the stupor of abject dependence. Thus art in its very nature transcended the principle of the Church. But as the former manifests itself only under sensuous limitations, it is at first regarded as a harmless and indifferent matter. The Church, therefore, continued to follow it; but as soon as the free spirit in which art originated advanced to thought and science, a separation ensued.

For art received a further support and experienced an elevating influence as the result of the *study of antiquity;* (the name *humaniora* is very expressive, for in those works of antiquity honour is done to the human and to the development of humanity): through this study the West became acquainted with the true and eternal element in the activity of man. The outward occasion of this revival of science was the fall of the Byzantine Empire. Large numbers of Greeks took refuge in the west and introduced Greek literature there; and they brought with them not only the knowledge of the Greek language but also the treasures to which that knowledge was the key. Very little of Greek literature had been preserved in the convents, and an acquaintance with the language could scarcely be said to exist at all. With the Roman literature it was otherwise; in regard to that, ancient traditions still lingered: Virgil was thought to be a great magician (in Dante he appears as the guide in Hell and Purgatory). Through the influence of the Greeks, then, attention was again directed to the ancient Greek literature; the West had become capable of enjoying and appreciating it; quite other ideals and a different order of virtue from that with which mediæval Europe was familiar were here presented; an altogether novel standard for judging of what was to be honoured, commended, and imitated was set up. The Greeks in their works exhibited quite other moral commands than those with which the West was acquainted; scholastic formalism had to make way for a body of speculative thought of a widely different complexion: Plato became known in the West, and in him a new human world presented itself. These novel ideas met with a principal organ of diffusion in the newly discovered *art of printing,* which, like the use of gunpowder, corresponds with modern character, and supplied the desideratum of the age in which it was invented, by tending to enable men to stand in an ideal connection with each other. So far as the study of the ancients manifested an interest in human deeds and virtues, the Church continued to tolerate it, not observing that in those alien works an altogether alien spirit was advancing to confront it.

As a *third* leading feature demanding our notice in determining the character of the period, might be mentioned that urging of spirit *outwards*—that desire on the part of man to become acquainted with *his* world. The chivalrous spirit of the maritime heroes of Portugal and Spain opened a new way to the East Indies and discovered America. This progressive step also, involved no transgression of the limits of ecclesiastical principles or feeling. The aim of Columbus was by no means a merely secular one: it presented also a distinctly religious aspect; the treasures of those rich Indian lands which awaited his discovery were destined in his intention to be expended in a new Crusade, and the heathen inhabitants of the countries themselves were to be converted to Christianity. The recognition of the spherical figure of the earth led man to perceive that it offered him a definite and limited object, and navigation had been benefited by the new found instrumentality of the magnet, enabling it to be something better than mere coasting: thus technical appliances make their appearance when a need for them is experienced.

These three events—the so-called Revival of Learning, the flourishing of the fine arts, and the discovery of America and of the passage to India by the Cape—may be compared with that *blush of dawn,* which after long storms first betokens the return of a bright and glorious day. This day is the day of universality, which breaks upon the world after the long, eventful, and terrible night of the Middle Ages—a day which is distinguished by science, art, and inventive impulse—that is, by the noblest and highest, and which humanity, rendered free by Christianity and emancipated through the instrumentality of the Church, exhibits as the eternal and veritable substance of its being.

Section III
THE MODERN TIME

We have now arrived at the third period of the German world, and thus enter upon the period of spirit conscious that it is free, inasmuch as it wills the true, the eternal—that which is in and for itself universal.

In this third period also, three divisions present themselves. First, we have to consider the *Reformation* in itself—the all-enlightening *sun,* following on that blush of dawn which we observed at the termination of the mediæval period; next, the unfolding of that state of things which succeeded the Reformation; and lastly, the modern times, dating from the end of the last century.

Chapter 1. *The Reformation*

The reformation resulted from the *corruption of the Church.* That corruption was not an accidental phenomenon; it was not the mere *abuse* of power and dominion. A corrupt state of things is very frequently represented as an "abuse"; it is taken for granted that the foundation was good—the system, the institution itself faultless—but that the passion, the subjective interest, in short, the arbitrary volition of men has made use of that which in itself was good to further its own selfish ends, and that all that is required to be done is to remove these adventitious elements. On this showing the institute in question escapes obloquy, and the evil that disfigures it appears something foreign to it. But when accidental abuse of a good thing really oc-

curs, it is limited to particularity. A great and general corruption affecting a body of such large and comprehensive scope as a church, is quite another thing. The corruption of the Church was a native growth; the principle of that corruption is to be looked for in the fact that the specific and definite embodiment of deity which it recognizes, is sensuous—that the external in a coarse material form, is enshrined in its inmost being. (The refining transformation which art supplied was not sufficient.) The higher spirit, that of the world, has already expelled the spiritual from it; it finds nothing to interest it in the spiritual or in occupation with it; thus it retains that specific and definite embodiment; *i.e.,* we have the sensuous immediate subjectivity, not refined by it to spiritual subjectivity. Henceforth it occupies *a position of inferiority to the world-spirit;* the latter has already transcended it, for it has become capable of recognizing the sensuous as sensuous, the merely outward as merely outward; it has learned to occupy itself with the finite in a finite way, and in this very activity to maintain an independent and confident position as a valid and rightful subjectivity.[1]

The element in question which is innate in the ecclesiastical principle only reveals itself as a corrupting one when the Church has no longer any opposition to contend with—when it has become firmly established. Then its elements are free to display their tendencies without let or hindrance. Thus it is that externality in the Church itself which becomes evil and corruption, and develops itself as a negative principle in its own bosom. The forms which this corruption assumes are coextensive with the relations which the Church itself sustains, into which consequently this vitiating element enters.

The ecclesiastical piety of the period displays the very essence of superstition—the fettering of the mind to a sensuous object, a mere thing—in the most various forms: slavish deference to *authority;* for spirit, having renounced its proper nature in its most essential quality, has lost its freedom, and is held in adamantine bondage to what is alien to itself; a credulity of the most absurd and childish character in regard to *miracles,* for the divine is supposed to manifest

---

[1] The Church, in its devotion to mere ceremonial observances, *supposes* itself to be engaged with the spiritual, while it is really occupied with the sensuous. The world towards the close of the mediæval period, is equally devoted to the sensuous, but labours under no such hallucination as to the character of its activity; and it has ceased to feel compunction at the *merely secular* nature of its aims and actions, such as it might have felt, e.g., in the eleventh century.

itself in a perfectly disconnected and limited way, for purely finite and particular purposes; lastly, lust of power, riotous debauchery, all the forms of barbarous and vulgar corruption, hypocrisy, and deception—all this manifests itself in the Church; for in fact the sensuous in it is not subjugated and trained by the understanding; it has become free, but only in a rough and barbarous way. On the other hand, the *virtue* which the Church presents, since it is negative only in opposition to sensual appetite, is but abstractly negative; it does not know how to exercise a moral restraint in the indulgence of the senses; in actual life nothing is left for it but avoidance, renunciation, inactivity.

These contrasts which the Church exhibits— of barbarous vice and lust, on the one hand, and an elevation of soul that is ready to renounce all worldly things, on the other hand—became still wider in consequence of the energetic position which man is sensible of occupying in his subjective power over outward and material things in the natural world, in which he feels himself free, and so gains for himself an absolute right. The Church whose office it is to save souls from perdition, makes this salvation itself a mere external appliance, and is now degraded so far as to perform this office in a merely external fashion. The *remission of sins*—the highest satisfaction which the soul craves, the certainty of its peace with God, that which concerns man's deepest and inmost nature—is offered to man in the most grossly superficial and trivial fashion, *to be purchased for mere money;* while the object of this sale is to procure means for dissolute excess. One of the objects of this sale was indeed the building of St. Peter's, that magnificent chef-d'œuvre of Christian fabrics erected in the metropolis of religion. But, as that paragon of works of art, the Athene and her temple-citadel at Athens, was built with the money of the allies and issued in the loss of both allies and power; so the completion of this church of St. Peter and Michael Angelo's *Last Judgment* in the Sistine Chapel, were the doomsday and the ruin of this proud spiritual edifice.

The time-honoured and cherished *sincerity of the German people* is destined to effect this revolution out of the honest truth and simplicity of its heart. While the rest of the world are urging their way to India, to America—straining every nerve to gain wealth and to acquire a secular dominion which shall encompass the globe, and on which the sun shall never set—we find a simple *monk* looking for that specific embodi-

ment of deity which Christendom had formerly sought in an earthly sepulchre of stone, rather in the deeper abyss of the absolute ideality of all that is sensuous and external—in the spirit and the heart—the heart, which, wounded unspeakably by the offer of the most trivial and superficial appliances to satisfy the cravings of that which is inmost and deepest, now detects the perversion of the absolute relation of truth in its minutest features, and pursues it to annihilation. Luther's simple doctrine is that the specific embodiment of deity—infinite subjectivity, that is true spirituality, Christ—is in no way present and actual in an outward form, but as essentially spiritual is obtained only in being reconciled to God, *in faith and spiritual enjoyment*. These two words express everything. That which this doctrine desiderates is not the recognition of a sensuous object as God, nor even of something merely conceived, and which is not actual and present, but of a reality that is not sensuous. This abrogation of externality imports the reconstruction of all the doctrines, and the reform of all the superstition into which the Church consistently wandered, and in which its spiritual life was dissipated. This change especially affects the doctrine of works; for works include what may be performed under any mental conditions—not necessarily in faith, in one's own soul, but as mere external observances prescribed by authority. Faith is by no means a bare assurance respecting mere finite things, an assurance which belongs only to limited mind, as, *e.g.*, the belief that such or such a person existed and said this or that; or that the Children of Israel passed dry-shod through the Red Sea, or that the trumpets before the walls of Jericho produced as powerful an impression as our cannons; for although nothing of all this had been related to us, our knowledge of God would not be the less complete. In fact it is not a belief in something that is absent, past, and gone, but the subjective assurance of the eternal, of absolute truth, the truth of God. Concerning this assurance, the Lutheran Church affirms that the Holy Spirit alone produces it—*i.e.*, that it is an assurance which the individual attains, not in virtue of his particular idiosyncrasy, but of his essential being. The Lutheran doctrine therefore involves the entire substance of Catholicism, with the exception of all that results from the element of externality—as far as the Catholic Church insists upon that externality. Luther therefore could not do otherwise than refuse to yield an iota in regard to that doctrine of the Eucharist in which the whole question is concentrated. Nor could he concede to the Reformed Church, that Christ is a mere commemoration, a mere reminiscence: in this respect his view was rather in accordance with that of the Catholic Church, *viz.*, that Christ is an actual presence, though only in faith and in spirit. He maintained that the spirit of Christ really fills the human heart—that Christ therefore is not to be regarded as merely a historical person, but that man sustains *an immediate relation to him in spirit*.

While, then, the individual knows that he is filled with the divine spirit, all the relations that spring from that vitiating element of externality which we examined above are *ipso facto* abrogated: there is no longer a distinction between priests and laymen; we no longer find one class in possession of the substance of the truth, as of all the spiritual and temporal treasures of the Church; but the heart, the emotional part of man's spiritual nature, is recognized as that which can and ought to come into possession of the truth; and this subjectivity is the common property of *all mankind*. Each has to accomplish the work of reconciliation in his own soul. Subjective spirit has to receive the spirit of truth into itself, and give it a dwelling place there. Thus that absolute inwardness of soul which pertains to religion itself and freedom in the Church are both secured. Subjectivity therefore makes the objective purport of Christianity, *i.e.*, the doctrine of the Church, its own. In the Lutheran Church the subjective feeling and the conviction of the individual is regarded as equally necessary with the objective side of truth. Truth with Lutherans is not a finished and completed thing; the subject himself must be imbued with truth, surrendering his particular being in exchange for the substantial truth, and making that truth his own. Thus subjective spirit gains emancipation in the truth, abnegates its particularity, and comes to itself in realizing the truth of its being. Thus Christian freedom is actualized. If subjectivity be placed in feeling only, without that objective side, we have the standpoint of the merely natural will.

In the proclamation of these principles is unfurled the new, the latest standard round which the peoples rally—the banner of *free spirit*, independent, though finding its life in the truth, and enjoying independence only in it. This is the banner under which we serve, and which we bear. Time, since that epoch, has had no other work to do than the formal imbuing of the world with this principle, in bringing the reconciliation implicit into objective and explicit realiza-

tion. Culture is essentially concerned with form; the work of culture is the production of the form of universality, which is none other than thought.[1] Consequently law, property, social morality, government, constitutions, etc., must be conformed to general principles, in order that they may accord with the idea of free will and be rational. Thus only can the spirit of truth manifest itself in subjective will—in the particular shapes which the activity of the will assumes. In virtue of that degree of intensity which subjective free spirit has attained, elevating it to the form of universality, objective spirit attains manifestation. This is the sense in which we must understand the state to be based on religion. States and laws are nothing else than religion manifesting itself in the relations of the actual world.

This is the essence of the Reformation: man is in his very nature destined to be free.

At its commencement, the Reformation concerned itself only with particular aspects of the Catholic Church: Luther wished to act in union with the whole Catholic world and expressed a desire that councils should be convened. His theses found supporters in every country. In answer to the charge brought against Luther and the Protestants, of exaggeration, nay, even of calumnious misrepresentation in their descriptions of the corruption of the Church, we may refer to the statements of Catholics themselves, bearing upon this point, and particularly to those contained in the official documents of ecclesiastical councils. But Luther's onslaught, which was at first limited to particular points, was soon extended to the doctrines of the Church; and leaving individuals, he attacked institutions at large—conventual life, the secular lordships of the bishops, etc. His writings now controverted not merely isolated dicta of the Pope and the councils, but the very principle on which such a mode of deciding points in dispute was based—in fact, *the authority of the Church*. Luther repudiated that authority, and set up in its stead the *Bible* and the testimony of the human spirit. And it is a fact of the weightiest import that the Bible has become the basis of the Christian Church: henceforth each indi-

---

[1] The community of principle which *really* links together individuals of the same class, and in virtue of which they are similarly related to other existences, assumes a *form* in human consciousness; and that form is the thought or idea which summarily comprehends the constituents of generic character. The primary meaning of the word ἰδέα and of the related terms εἶδος and *species*, is "form." Every "universal" in thought has a corresponding generic principle in reality, to which it gives intellectual expression or *form*.

vidual enjoys the right of deriving instruction for himself from it, and of directing his conscience in accordance with it. We see a vast change in the principle by which man's religious life is guided: the whole system of tradition, the whole fabric of the Church becomes problematical, and its authority is subverted. Luther's translation of the Bible has been of incalculable value to the German people. It has supplied them with a people's book, such as no nation in the Catholic world can boast; for though the latter have a vast number of minor productions in the shape of prayer-books, they have no generally recognized and classical book for popular instruction. In spite of this it has been made a question in modern times whether it is judicious to place the Bible in the hands of the people. Yet the few disadvantages thus entailed are far more than counterbalanced by the incalculable benefits thence accruing: narratives, which in their external shape might be repellent to the heart and understanding, can be discriminatingly treated by the religious sense, which, holding fast the substantial truth, easily vanquishes any such difficulties. And even if the books which have pretensions to the character of people's books were not so superficial as they are, they would certainly fail in securing that respect which a book claiming such a title ought to inspire in *individuals*. But to obviate this difficulty is no easy matter, for even should a book adapted to the purpose in every other respect be produced, every country parson would have some fault to find with it, and think to better it. In France the need of such a book has been very much felt; great premiums have been offered with a view to obtaining one, but, from the reason stated, without success. Moreover, the existence of a people's book presupposes as its primary condition an ability to read on the part of the people; an ability which in Catholic countries is not very commonly to be met with.

The denial of the authority of the Church necessarily led to a separation. The Council of Trent stereotyped the principles of Catholicism, and made the restoration of concord impossible. Leibnitz at a later time discussed with Bishop Bossuet the question of the union of the churches; but the Council of Trent remains the insurmountable obstacle. The *churches* became hostile *parties,* for even in respect to secular arrangements a striking difference manifested itself. In the non-Catholic countries the conventual establishments and episcopal foundations were broken up, and the rights of the then proprietors ignored. Educational arrangements were altered; the fast and holy days were abolished. Thus there was also a secular reform—a change affecting the state of things outside the sphere of ecclesiastical relations: in many places a rebellion was raised against the temporal authorities. In Münster the Anabaptists expelled the bishop and established a government of their own; and the peasants rose *en masse* to emancipate themselves from the yoke of serfdom. But the world was not yet ripe for a transformation of its political condition as a consequence of ecclesiastical reformation.

The Catholic Church also was essentially influenced by the Reformation: the reins of discipline were drawn tighter, and the greatest occasions of scandal, the most crying abuses were abated. Much of the intellectual life of the age that lay outside its sphere, but with which it had previously maintained friendly relations, it now repudiated. The Church came to a dead stop—"hitherto and no farther!" It severed itself from advancing science, from philosophy and humanistic literature; and an occasion was soon offered of declaring its enmity to the scientific pursuits of the period. The celebrated Copernicus had discovered that the earth and the planets revolve round the sun, but the Church declared against this addition to human knowledge. Galileo, who had published a statement in the form of a dialogue of the evidence for and against the Copernican discovery (declaring indeed his own conviction of its truth), was obliged to crave pardon for the offence on his knees. The Greek literature was not made the basis of culture; education was intrusted to the Jesuits. Thus does the spirit of the Catholic world in general sink behind the spirit of the age.

Here an important question solicits investigation: why the Reformation was limited to certain nations, and why it did not permeate the whole Catholic world. The Reformation originated in Germany, and struck firm root only in the purely German nations; outside of Germany itself it established itself in Scandinavia and England. But the Romanic and Slavonic nations kept decidedly aloof from it. Even south Germany has only partially adopted the Reformation—a fact which is consistent with the mingling of elements which is the general characteristic of its nationality. In Swabia, Franconia, and the Rhine countries there were many convents and bishoprics, as also many free imperial towns; and the reception or rejection of the Reformation very much depended on the influences which these ecclesiastical and civil bodies respectively exercised; for we have already no-

ticed that the Reformation was a change influencing the political life of the age as well as its
religious and intellectual condition. We must
further observe, that authority has much greater
weight in determining men's opinions than people are inclined to believe. There are certain
fundamental principles which men are in the
habit of receiving on the strength of authority;
and it was mere authority which in the case of
many countries decided for or against the adoption of the Reformation. In Austria, in Bavaria,
in Bohemia, the Reformation had already made
great progress; and though it is commonly said
that when truth has once penetrated men's souls,
it cannot be rooted out again, it was indisputably stifled in the countries in question, by force
of arms, by stratagem or persuasion. The *Slavonic nations* were *agricultural*. This condition
of life brings with it the relation of lord and
serf. In agriculture the agency of nature predominates; human industry and subjective activity are on the whole less brought into play in
this department of labour than elsewhere. The
Slavonians therefore did not attain so quickly
or readily as other nations the fundamental
sense of pure individuality—the consciousness
of universality—that which we designated
above as "political power," and could not share
the benefits of dawning freedom. But the *Romanic nations* also—Italy, Spain, Portugal, and
in part France—were not imbued with the Reformed doctrines. Physical force perhaps did
much to repress them; yet this alone would not
be sufficient to explain the fact, for when the
spirit of a nation craves anything no force can
prevent its attaining the desired object: nor
can it be said that these nations were deficient
in culture; on the contrary, they were in advance of the Germans in this respect. It was
rather owing to the fundamental character of
these nations, that they did not adopt the Reformation. But what is this peculiarity of character which hindered the attainment of spiritual
freedom? We answer: the pure inwardness of
the German nation was the proper soil for the
emancipation of spirit; the Romanic nations, on
the contrary, have maintained in the very depth
of their soul—in their spiritual consciousness—
the principle of *disharmony:* [1] they are a product of the fusion of Roman and German blood,
and still retain the heterogeneity thence resulting. The German cannot deny that the French,

[1] The acknowledgment of an external power authorized to command the entire soul of man was not supplanted in their case by a deference to conscience and
subjective principle (*i. e.,* the union of objective and
subjective freedom) as the supreme authority.

the Italians, the Spaniards, possess more determination of character, that they pursue a
settled aim (even though it have a fixed idea for
its object) with perfectly clear consciousness
and the greatest attention, that they carry out
a plan with great circumspection, and exhibit
the greatest decision in regard to specific objects. The French call the Germans *entiers,* "entire," *i.e.,* stubborn; they are also strangers to
the whimsical originality of the English. The
Englishman attaches his idea of liberty to the
special; he does not trouble himself about the
understanding, but on the contrary feels himself so much the more at liberty, the more his
course of action or his license to act contravenes
the understanding, *i.e.,* runs counter to general
principles. On the other hand, among the Romanic peoples we immediately encounter that
internal schism, that holding fast by an abstract
principle, and, as the counterpart of this, an
absence of the totality of spirit and sentiment
which we call "heart"; there is not that medita-
tive introversion of the soul upon itself; in their
inmost being they may be said to be alienated
from themselves. With them the inner life is a
region whose depth they do not appreciate; for
it is given over "bodily" to particular interests,
and the infinity that belongs to spirit is not to
be looked for there. Their inmost being is not
their own. They leave it as an alien and indifferent matter, and are glad to have its concerns
settled for them by another. That other to which
they leave it is the Church. They have indeed
something to do with it themselves; but since
that which they have to do is not self-originated
and self-prescribed, not their very own, they are
content to leave the affair to be settled in a
superficial way. *"Eh bien,"* said Napoleon, "we
shall go to Mass again, and my good fellows will
say: 'That is the word of command!' " This is
the leading feature in the character of these nations—the separation of the religious from the
secular interest, *i.e.,* from the special interest of
individuality; and the ground of this separation
lies in their inmost soul, which has lost its independent entireness of being, its profoundest
unity. Catholicism does not claim the essential
direction of the secular; religion remains an indifferent matter on the one side, while the other
side of life is dissociated from it, and occupies a
sphere exclusively its own. Cultivated French-
men therefore feel an antipathy to Protestantism because it seems to them something pedantic, dull, minutely captious in its morality; since
it requires that spirit and thought should be
directly engaged in religion: in attending Mass

and other ceremonies, on the contrary, no exertion of thought is required, but an imposing sensuous spectacle is presented to the eye, which does not make such a demand on one's attention as entirely to exclude a little chat, while yet the duties of the occasion are not neglected.

We spoke above of the *relation which the new doctrine sustained to secular life,* and now we have only to exhibit that relation in detail. The development and advance of spirit from the time of the Reformation onwards consist in this, that spirit, having now gained the consciousness of its Freedom, through that process of mediation which takes place between man and God— that is, in the full recognition of the objective process as the existence [the positive and definite manifestation] of the divine essence—now takes it up and follows it out in building up the edifice of secular relations. That harmony which has resulted from the painful struggles of history, involves the recognition of the secular as capable of being an embodiment of truth; whereas it had been formerly regarded as evil only, as incapable of good—the latter being considered essentially ultramundane. It is now perceived that morality and justice in the state are also divine and commanded by God, and that in point of substance there is nothing higher or more sacred. One inference is that *marriage* is no longer deemed less holy than *celibacy.* Luther took a wife to show that he respected marriage, defying the calumnies to which he exposed himself by such a step. It was his duty to do so, as it was also to eat meat on Fridays; to prove that such things are lawful and right, in opposition to the imagined superiority of abstinence. The family introduces man to community—to the relation of interdependence in society; and this union is a moral one: while, on the other hand, the monks, separated from the sphere of social morality, formed as it were the standing army of the Pope, as the janizaries formed the basis of the Turkish power. The marriage of the priests entails the disappearance of the outward distinction between laity and clergy.

Moreover, the repudiation of work no longer earned the reputation of sanctity; it was acknowledged to be more commendable for men to rise from a state of dependence by *activity,* intelligence, and industry, and make themselves independent. It is more consonant with justice that he who has money should spend it even in luxuries, than that he should give it away to idlers and beggars; for he bestows it on an equal number of persons by so doing, and these must

at any rate have worked diligently for it. Industry, crafts, and trades now have their moral validity recognized, and the obstacles to their prosperity which originated with the Church, have vanished. For the Church had pronounced it a sin to lend money on interest: but the necessity of so doing led to the direct violation of her injunctions. The Lombards (a fact which accounts for the use of the term *lombard* in French to denote a loan-office), and particularly the House of Medici, advanced money to princes in every part of Europe. The third point of sanctity in the Catholic Church—blind *obedience,* was likewise denuded of its false pretensions. Obedience to the laws of the state, as the rational element in volition and action, was made the principle of human conduct. In this obedience man is free, for all that is demanded is that the particular should yield to the general. Man himself has a conscience; consequently the subjection required of him is a free allegiance. This involves the possibility of a development of reason and freedom, and of their introduction into human relations; and reason and the divine commands are now synonymous. The rational no longer meets with contradiction on the part of the religious conscience; it is permitted to develop itself in its own sphere without disturbance, without being compelled to resort to force in defending itself against an adverse power. But in the Catholic Church, that adverse element is unconditionally sanctioned. Where the Reformed doctrine prevails, princes may still be bad governors, but they are no longer sanctioned and solicited thereto by the promptings of their religious conscience. In the Catholic Church, on the contrary, it is nothing singular for the conscience to be found in opposition to the laws of the state. Assassinations of sovereigns, conspiracies against the state, and the like, have often been supported and carried into execution by the priests.

This harmony between the state and the church has now attained *immediate* realization.[1] We have, as yet, no reconstruction of the state, of the system of jurisprudence, etc., for thought must first discover the essential principle of right. The laws of freedom had first to be expanded to a system as deduced from an absolute principle of right. Spirit does not assume this complete form immediately after the Reformation; it limits itself at first to direct and simple changes, as, *e.g.,* the doing away with conventual

---

[1] That is, the harmony in question simply exists; its development and results have not yet manifested themselves.

establishments and episcopal jurisdiction, etc. The reconciliation between God and the world was limited in the first instance to an abstract form; it was not yet expanded into a system by which the moral world could be regulated.

In the first instance this reconciliation must take place in the individual soul, must be realized by feeling; the individual must gain the assurance that the spirit dwells in him—that, in the language of the Church, a brokenness of heart has been experienced, and that divine grace has entered into the heart thus broken. By nature man is not what he ought to be; only through a transforming process does he arrive at truth. The general and speculative aspect of the matter is just this—that the human heart is not what it should be. It was then required of the individual that he should know what he is in himself; that is, the teaching of the Church insisted upon man's becoming conscious that he is evil. But the individual is evil only when the natural manifests itself in mere sensual desire— when an unrighteous will presents itself in its untamed, untrained, violent shape; and yet it is required that such a person should know that he is depraved and that the good spirit dwells in him; in fact, he is required to have a direct consciousness of and to "experience" that which was presented to him as a speculative and implicit truth. The reconciliation having, then, assumed this abstract form, men tormented themselves with a view to force upon their souls the consciousness of their sinfulness and to know themselves as evil. The most simple souls, the most innocent natures were accustomed in painful introspection to observe the most secret workings of the heart, with a view to a rigid examination of them. With this duty was conjoined that of an entirely opposite description; it was required that man should attain the consciousness that the good spirit dwells in him— that divine grace has found an entrance into his soul. In fact, the important distinction between the knowledge of abstract truth and the knowledge of what has actual existence was left out of sight. Men became the victims of a tormenting uncertainty as to whether the good spirit has an abode in them, and it was deemed indispensable that the entire process of spiritual transformation should become perceptible to the individual himself. An echo of this self-tormenting process may still be traced in much of the religious poetry of that time; the Psalms of David which exhibit a similar character were then introduced as hymns into the ritual of Protestant Churches. Protestantism took this turn of minute and painful introspection, possessed with the conviction of the importance of the exercise, and was for a long time characterized by a self-tormenting disposition and an aspect of spiritual wretchedness; which, in the present day, has induced many persons to enter the Catholic pale, that they might exchange this inward uncertainty for a formal broad certainty based on the imposing totality of the Church. A more refined order of reflection upon the character of human actions was introduced into the Catholic Church also. The Jesuits analysed the first rudiments of volition (*velleitas*) with as painful minuteness as was displayed in the pious exercises of Protestantism; but they had a science of casuistry which enabled them to discover a good reason for everything, and so get rid of the burden of guilt which this rigid investigation seemed to aggravate.

With this was connected another remarkable phenomenon, common to the Catholic with the Protestant world. The human mind was driven into the inward, the abstract, and the religious element was regarded as utterly alien to the secular. That lively consciousness of his subjective life and of the inward origin of his volition that had been awakened in man, brought with it the belief in *evil*, as a vast power the sphere of whose malign dominion is the secular. This belief presents a parallelism with the view in which the sale of indulgences originated: for as eternal salvation could be secured for money, so by paying the price of one's salvation through a compact made with the Devil, the riches of the world and the unlimited gratification of desires and passions could be secured. Thus arose that famous legend of Faust, who in disgust at the unsatisfactory character of speculative science, is said to have plunged into the world and purchased all its glory at the expense of his salvation.

Faust, if we may trust the poet, had the enjoyment of all that the world could give, in exchange for his soul's weal; but those poor women who were called *witches* were reputed to get nothing more by the bargain than the gratification of a petty revenge by making a neighbour's cow go dry or giving a child the measles. But in awarding punishment it was not the magnitude of the injury in the loss of the milk or the sickness of the child that was considered; it was the abstract power of the Evil One in them that was attacked. The belief in this abstract, special power whose dominion is the world—in the Devil and his devices—occasioned an incalculable number of *trials for witchcraft* both in

Catholic and Protestant countries. It was impossible to prove the guilt of the accused; they were only suspected: it was therefore only a direct knowledge on which this fury against the evil principle professed to be based. It was indeed necessary to have recourse to evidence, but the basis of these judicial processes was simply the belief that certain individuals were possessed by the power of the Evil One. This delusion raged among the nations in the sixteenth century with the fury of a pestilence. The main impulse was suspicion. The principle of suspicion assumes a similarly terrible shape during the sway of the Roman emperors, and under Robespierre's Reign of Terror; when mere disposition, unaccompanied by any overt act or expression, was made an object of punishment. Among the Catholics, it was the Dominicans to whom (as was the Inquisition in all its branches) the trials for witchcraft were intrusted. Father Spee, a noble Jesuit, wrote a treatise against them (he is also the author of a collection of fine poems bearing the title of *Trutznachtigall*), giving a full exposure of the terrible character of criminal justice in proceedings of this kind. Torture, which was only to be applied once, was continued until a confession was extorted. If the accused fainted under the torture it was averred that the Devil was giving them sleep: if convulsions supervened, it was said that the Devil was laughing in them; if they held out steadfastly, the Devil was supposed to give them power. These persecutions spread like an epidemic sickness through Italy, France, Spain, and Germany. The earnest remonstrances of enlightened men, such as Spee and others, already produced a considerable effect. But it was Thomasius, a professor of Halle, who first opposed this prevalent superstition with very decided success. The entire phenomenon is in itself most remarkable when we reflect that we have not long been quit of this frightful barbarity (even as late as the year 1780 a witch was publicly burned at Glarus in Switzerland). Among the Catholics persecution was directed against heretics as well as against witches: we might say indeed that they were placed in one category; the unbelief of the heretics was regarded as none other than the indwelling principle of evil—a possession similar to the other.

Leaving this abstract form of subjectiveness we have now to consider the *secular* side, the constitution of the state and the advance of universality, the recognition of the universal laws of freedom. This is the second and the essential point.

Chapter 2. *Influence of the Reformation on Political Development*

In tracing the course of the political development of the period, we observe in the first place the consolidation of monarchy, and the monarch invested with an authority emanating from the state. The incipient stage in the rise of royal power, and the commencement of that unity which the states of Europe attained, belong to a still earlier period. While these changes were going forward, the entire body of private obligations and rights which had been handed down from the middle age, still retained validity. Infinitely important is this form of private rights, which the organic constituents of the executive power of the state have assumed. At their apex we find a fixed and positive principle—the exclusive right of one family to the possession of the throne, and the hereditary succession of sovereigns further restricted by the law of primogeniture. This gives the state an immovable centre. The fact that Germany was an elective empire prevented its being consolidated into one state; and for the same reason Poland has vanished from the circle of independent states. The state must have a final decisive will: but if an individual is to be the final deciding power, he must be so in a direct and natural way, not as determined by choice and theoretic views, etc. Even among the free Greeks the oracle was the external power which decided their policy on critical occasions; here *birth* is the oracle— something independent of any arbitrary volition. But the circumstance that the highest station in a monarchy is assigned to a family seems to indicate that the sovereignty is the private property of that family. As such, that sovereignty would seem to be divisible; but since the idea of division of power is opposed to the principle of the state, the rights of the monarch and his family required to be more strictly defined. Sovereign possession is not a peculium of the individual ruler, but is consigned to the dynastic family as a trust; and the *estates of the realm* possess security that that trust shall be faithfully discharged, for they have to guard the unity of the body politic. Thus, then, royal possession no longer denotes a kind of private property, private possession of estates, demesnes, jurisdiction, etc., but has become a state-property— a function pertaining to and involved with the state.

Equally important, and connected with that just noticed, is the change of executive powers, functions, duties, and rights, which naturally belong to the state, but which had become private property and private contracts or obligations— into possession conferred by the state. The rights of seigneurs and barons were annulled, and they were obliged to content themselves with official positions in the state. This transformation of the rights of vassals into official functions took place in the several kingdoms in various ways. In *France, e.g.,* the great barons, who were governors of provinces, who could claim such offices as a matter of right, and who, like the Turkish pashas, maintained a body of troops with the revenues thence derived—troops which they might at any moment bring into the field against the king—were reduced to the position of mere landed proprietors or court nobility, and those pashalics became offices held under the government; or the nobility were employed as officers —generals of the army, an army belonging to the *state*. In this aspect the origination of *standing armies* is so important an event; for they supply the monarchy with an independent force and are as necessary for the security of the central authority against the rebellion of the subject individuals as for the defence of the state against foreign enemies. The fiscal system indeed had not as yet assumed a systematic character—the revenue being derived from customs, taxes and tolls in countless variety, besides the subsidies and contributions paid by the estates of the realm; in return for which the right of presenting a statement of grievances was conceded to them, as is now the case in Hungary.

In *Spain* the spirit of chivalry had assumed a very beautiful and noble form. This chivalric spirit, this knightly dignity, degraded to a mere inactive sentiment of honour, has attained notoriety as the Spanish *grandezza*. The grandees were no longer allowed to maintain troops of their own, and were also withdrawn from the command of the armies; destitute of power they had to content themselves as private persons with an empty title. But the means by which the royal power in Spain was consolidated, was the *Inquisition*. This, which was established for the persecution of those who secretly adhered to Judaism, and of Moors and heretics, soon assumed a political character, being directed against the enemies of the state. Thus the Inquisition confirmed the despotic power of the king: it claimed supremacy even over bishops and archbishops, and could cite them before its tribunal. The frequent confiscation of property, one of the most customary penalties, tended to enrich the treasury of the state. Moreover, the Inquisition was a tribunal which took cognizance of mere suspicion; and

while it consequently exercised a fearful authority over the clergy, it had a peculiar support in the national pride. For every Spaniard wished to be considered Christian by descent, and this species of vanity fell in with the views and tendency of the Inquisition. Particular provinces of the Spanish monarchy, as, *e.g.*, Aragon, still retained many peculiar rights and privileges; but the Spanish kings from Philip II downwards proceeded to suppress them altogether.

It would lead us too far to pursue in detail the process of the depression of the aristocracy in the several states of Europe. The main scope of this depressing process was, as already stated, the curtailment of the private rights of the feudal nobility, and the transformation of their seigneurial authority into an official position in connection with the state. This change was in the interest of both the king and the people. The powerful barons seemed to constitute an intermediate body charged with the defence of liberty; but properly speaking, it was only their own privileges which they maintained against the royal power on the one hand, and the citizens on the other hand. The barons of England extorted Magna Charta from the king; but the citizens gained nothing by it, on the contrary they remained in their former condition. Polish liberty too, meant nothing more than the freedom of the barons in contraposition to the king, the nation being reduced to a state of absolute serfdom. When liberty is mentioned, we must always be careful to observe whether it is not really the assertion of private interests which is thereby designated. For although the nobility were deprived of their sovereign power, the people were still oppressed in consequence of their absolute dependence, their serfdom, and subjection to aristocratic jurisdiction; and they were partly declared utterly incapable of possessing property, partly subjected to a condition of bond-service which did not permit of their freely selling the products of their industry. The supreme interest of emancipation from this condition concerned the power of the state as well as the subjects—that emancipation which now gave them as citizens the character of free individuals, and determined that what was to be performed for the commonwealth should be a matter of just allotment, not of mere chance. The aristocracy of possession maintains that possession against both, *viz.*, against the power of the state at large and against individuals. But the aristocracy have a position assigned them, as the support of the throne, as occupied and active on behalf of the state and the common weal, and at the same time as maintaining the freedom of the citizens. This in fact is the prerogative of that class which forms the link between the sovereign and the people—to undertake to discern and to give the first impulse to that which is intrinsically rational and universal; and this recognition of and occupation with the universal must take the place of positive personal right. This subjection to the head of the state of that intermediate power which laid claim to positive authority was now accomplished, but this did not involve the emancipation of the subject class. This took place only at a later date, when the idea of right in and for itself arose in men's minds. Then the sovereigns relying on their respective peoples, vanquished the caste of unrighteousness; but where they united with the barons, or where the latter maintained their freedom against the kings, those positive rights or rather wrongs continued.

We observe also as an essential feature now first presenting itself in the political aspect of the time, a connected *system of states* and a relation of states to each other. They became involved in various wars: the kings having enlarged their political authority, now turn their attention to foreign lands, insisting upon claims of all kinds. The aim and real interest of the wars of the period is invariably conquest.

Italy especially had become such an object of desire, and was a prey to the rapacity of the French, the Spaniards, and at a later date, of the Austrians. In fact, absolute disintegration and dismemberment has always been an essential feature in the national character of the inhabitants of Italy, in ancient as well as in modern times. Their stubborn individuality was exchanged for a union the result of force, under the Roman dominion; but as soon as this bond was broken, the original character reappeared in full strength. In later times, as if finding in them a bond of union otherwise impossible, after having escaped from a selfishness of the most monstrous order and which displayed its perverse nature in crimes of every description, the Italians attained a taste for the *fine arts:* thus their civilization, the mitigation of their selfishness, reached only the grade of beauty, not that of rationality—the higher unity of thought. Consequently, even in poetry and song the Italian nature is different from ours. Improvisation characterizes the genius of the Italians; they pour out their very souls in art and the ecstatic enjoyment of it. Enjoying a *naturel* so imbued with art, the state must be an affair of comparative indifference, a merely cas-

ual matter to the Italians. But we have to observe also that the wars in which *Germany* engaged, were not particularly honourable to it: it allowed Burgundy, Lorraine, Alsace, and other parts of the empire to be wrested from it. From these wars between the various political powers there arose common interests, and the object of that community of interest was the maintenance of severalty—the preservation to the several states of their independence—in fact, the *"balance of power."* The motive to this was of a decidedly "practical" kind, *viz.*, the protection of the several states from conquest. The union of the states of Europe as the means of shielding individual states from the violence of the powerful—the preservation of the balance of power, had now taken the place of that general aim of the elder time, the defence of Christendom, whose centre was the papacy. This new political motive was necessarily accompanied by a diplomatic condition—one in which all the members of the great European system, however distant, felt an interest in that which happened to any one of them. Diplomatic policy had been brought to the greatest refinement in Italy, and was thence transmitted to Europe at large. Several princes in succession seemed to threaten the stability of the balance of power in Europe. When this combination of states was just commencing, Charles V was aiming at universal monarchy; for he was Emperor of Germany and King of Spain to boot: the Netherlands and Italy acknowledged his sway, and the whole wealth of America flowed into his coffers. With this enormous power, which, like the contingencies of fortune in the case of private property, had been accumulated by the most felicitous combinations of political dexterity, among other things by marriage, but which was destitute of an internal and reliable bond, he was nevertheless unable to gain any advantage over France, or even over the German princes; nay he was even compelled to a peace by Maurice of Saxony. His whole life was spent in suppressing disturbances in all parts of his empire and in conducting foreign wars. The balance of power in Europe was similarly threatened by Louis XIV. Through that depression of the grandees of his kingdom which Richelieu and after him Mazarin had accomplished, he had become an absolute sovereign. France, too, had the consciousness of its intellectual superiority in a refinement of culture surpassing anything of which the rest of Europe could boast. The pretensions of Louis were founded not on extent of dominion (as was the case with Charles V) so much as on that culture which distinguished his people, and which at that time made its way everywhere with the language that embodied it, and was the object of universal admiration: they could therefore plead a higher justification than those of the German Emperor. But the very rock on which the vast military resources of Philip II had already foundered, the heroic resistance of the Dutch, proved fatal also to the ambitious schemes of Louis. Charles XII also presented a remarkably menacing aspect; but his ambition had a quixotic tinge and was less sustained by intrinsic vigour. Through all these storms the nations of Europe succeeded in maintaining their individuality and independence.

An external relation in which the states of Europe had an interest in common, was that sustained to *the Turks*—the terrible power which threatened to overwhelm Europe from the east. The Turks of that day had still a sound and vigorous nationality, whose power was based on conquest, and which was therefore engaged in constant warfare, or at least admitted only a temporary suspension of arms. As was the case among the Franks, the conquered territories were divided among their warriors as personal, not heritable possessions; when in later times the principle of hereditary succession was adopted, the national vigour was shattered. The flower of the Osman force, the Janizaries, were the terror of the Europeans. Their ranks were recruited from a body of Christian boys of handsome and vigorous proportions, brought together chiefly by means of annual conscriptions among the Greek subjects of the Porte, strictly educated in the Moslem faith, and exercised in arms from early youth. Without parents, without brothers or sisters, without wives, they were, like the monks, an altogether isolated and terrible corps. The eastern European powers were obliged to make common cause against the Turks—*viz.*, Austria, Hungary, Venice, and Poland. The battle of Lepanto saved Italy, and perhaps all Europe, from a barbarian inundation.

An event of special importance following in the train of the Reformation was the *struggle of the Protestant Church* for political existence. The Protestant Church, even in its original aspect, was too intimately connected with secular interests not to occasion secular complications and political contentions respecting political possession. The subjects of Catholic princes become Protestant have and make claims to ecclesiastical property, change the nature of the tenure, and repudiate or decline the discharge of those ecclesiastical functions to whose due performance the emoluments are attached (*jura stolæ*). Moreover a Catholic government is bound to be the *brachium seculare* of the Church; the Inquisition, *e.g.*, never put a man to death, but simply declared him a heretic, as a kind of jury; he was then punished according to civil laws. Again, innumerable occasions of offence and irritation originated with processions and feasts, the carrying of the Host through the streets, withdrawals from convents, etc. Still more excitement would be felt when an Archbishop of Cologne attempted to make his archiepiscopate a secular princedom for himself and his family. Their confessors made it a matter of conscience with Catholic princes to wrest estates that had been the property of the Church out of the hands of the heretics. In Germany, however, the condition of things was favorable to Protestantism in as far as the several territories which had been imperial fiefs, had become independent principalities. But in countries like Austria, the princes were indifferent to Protestants, or even hostile to them; and in France they were not safe in the exercise of their religion except as protected by fortresses. War was the indispensable preliminary to the security of Protestants; for the question was not one of simple conscience, but involved decisions respecting public and private property which had been taken possession of in contravention of the rights of the Church, and whose restitution it demanded. A condition of absolute mistrust supervened; absolute, because mistrust bound up with the religious conscience was its root. The Protestant princes and towns formed at that time a feeble union, and the defensive operations they conducted were much feebler still. After they had been worsted, Maurice, the Elector of Saxony, by an utterly unexpected and adventurous piece of daring, extorted a peace, itself of doubtful interpretation, and which left the real sources of embitterment altogether untouched. It was necessary to fight out the battle from the very beginning. This took place in the Thirty Years' War, in which first Denmark and then Sweden undertook the cause of freedom. The former was compelled to quit the field, but the latter under Gustavus Adolphus, that hero of the north of glorious memory, played a part which was so much the more brilliant inasmuch as it began to wage war with the vast force of the Catholics, alone—without the help of the Protestant states of the empire. The powers of Europe, with a few exceptions, precipitate themselves on Germany—flowing back towards it as to the fountain from which they had originally issued, and where now the right of inwardness that has come to manifest itself in the sphere of religion, and that of internal independence and severalty is to be fought out. The struggle ends without an ideal result—without having attained the consciousness of a principle as an intellectual concept—in the exhaustion of all parties, in a scene of utter desolation, where all the contending forces have been wrecked; it issues in letting parties simply take their course and maintain their existence on the basis of external power. The issue is in fact exclusively of a *political* nature.

In *England* also, war was indispensable to the establishment of the Protestant Church: the struggle was in this case directed against the sovereigns, who were secretly attached to Catholicism because they found the principle of absolute sway confirmed by its doctrines. The fanaticized people rebelled against the assumption of absolute sovereign power, importing that kings are responsible to God alone (*i.e.*, to the Father Confessor), and in opposition to Catholic externality, unfurled the banner of extreme subjectivity in Puritanism—a principle which, developing itself in the real world, presents an aspect partly of enthusiastic elevation, partly of ridiculous incongruity. The enthusiasts of England, like those of Münster, were for having the state governed directly by the fear of God; the soldiery sharing the same fanatical views prayed while they fought for the cause they had espoused. But a military leader now has the physical force of the country and consequently the government in his hands: for in the state there must be government, and Cromwell knew what governing is. He, therefore, made himself ruler and sent that praying parliament about their business. With his death however his right to authority vanished also, and the old dynasty regained possession of the throne. Catholicism, we may observe, is commended to the support of princes as promoting the security of their government—a position supposed to be particularly manifest if the Inquisition be connected with the government; the former constituting the bulwark of the latter. But such a security is based on a slavish religious obedience, and is limited to those grades of human development in which the political constitution and the whole legal system still rest on the basis of actual positive possession; but if the constitution and laws are to be founded on a veritable eternal right, then security is to be found only in the Protestant religion, in whose principle rational subjective freedom also attains development. The *Dutch* too offered a vigorous opposition to the Catholic principle as bound up with the Spanish sovereignty. Belgium was still attached to the Catholic religion and remained subject to Spain: on the contrary, the northern part of the Netherlands—Holland—stood its ground with heroic valor against its oppressors. The trading class, the guilds, and companies of marksmen formed a militia whose heroic courage was more than a match for the then famous Spanish infantry. Just as the Swiss peasants had resisted the chivalry of Austria, so here the trading cities held out against disciplined troops. During this struggle on the continent itself, the Dutch fitted out fleets and deprived the Spaniards of part of their colonial possessions, from which all their wealth was derived. As independence was secured to Holland in its holding to the Protestant principle, so that of *Poland* was lost through its endeavor to suppress that principle in the case of dissidents.

Through the Peace of Westphalia the Protestant Church had been acknowledged as an independent one, to the great confusion and humiliation of Catholicism. This peace has often passed for the palladium of Germany, as having established its political constitution. But this constitution was in fact a confirmation of the particular rights of the countries into which Germany had been broken up. It involves no thought, no conception of the proper aim of a state. We should consult *Hippolytus a lapide* (a book which, written before the conclusion of the peace, had a great influence on the condition of the empire), if we would become acquainted with the character of that German freedom of which so much is made. In the peace in question the establishment of a complete particularity, the determination of all relations on the principle of private right is the object manifestly contemplated—a *constituted anarchy*, such as the world had never before seen; *i.e.*, the position that an empire is properly a unity, a totality, a state, while yet all relations are determined so exclusively on the principle of private right that the privilege of all the constituent parts of that empire to act for themselves contrarily to the interest of the whole, or to neglect that which its interest demands and which is even required by law—is guaranteed and secured by the most inviolable sanctions. Immediately after this settlement, it was shown what the *German Empire* was as a state in relation to other states: it waged ignominious wars with the Turks, for deliverance from whom Vienna was indebted to Poland. Still more ignominious was its relation to France, which took possession in time of peace of free cities, the bulwarks of Germany, and of flourishing provinces, and retained them undisturbed.

This constitution, which completely terminated the career of Germany as an empire, was chiefly the work of Richelieu, by whose assistance—Romish cardinal though he was—religious freedom in Germany was preserved. Richelieu, with a view to further the interests of the state whose affairs he superintended, adopted the exact opposite of that policy which he promoted in the case of its enemies; for he reduced the latter to political impotence by ratifying the political independence of the several parts of the empire, while at home he destroyed the independence of the Protestant party. His fate has consequently resembled that of many great statesmen, inasmuch as he has been cursed by his countrymen, while his enemies have looked upon the work by which he ruined them as the most sacred goal of their desires—the consummation of their rights and liberties.

The result of the struggle, therefore, was the forcibly achieved and now politically ratified coexistence of religious parties, forming political communities whose relations are determined according to prescriptive principles of civil or of private right.

The Protestant Church increased and so perfected the stability of its political existence by the fact that one of the states which had adopted the principles of the Reformation raised itself to the position of an independent European power. This power was destined to start into a new life with Protestantism: *Prussia, viz.,* which, making its appearance at the end of the seventeenth century, was indebted, if not for origination yet certainly for the consolidation of its strength, to Frederick the Great; and the Seven Years' War was the struggle by which that consolidation was accomplished. Frederick II demonstrated the independent vigour of his power by resisting that of almost all Europe—the union of its leading states. He appeared as the hero of Protestantism, and that not individually merely, like Gustavus Adolphus, but as the ruler of a state. The Seven Years' War was indeed in itself not a war of religion; but it was so in view of its ultimate issues, and in the disposition of the soldiers as well as of the potentates under whose banner they fought. The Pope consecrated the sword of Field Marshal Daun, and the chief object which the allied powers proposed to themselves was the crushing of Prussia as the bulwark of the Protestant Church. But Frederick the Great not only made Prussia one of the great powers of Europe as a Protestant power, but was also a philosophical king—an altogether peculiar and unique phenomenon in modern times. There had been English kings who were subtle theologians, contending for the principle of absolutism: Frederick, on the contrary, took up the Protestant principle in its secular aspect; and though he was by no means favorable to religious controversies and did not side with one party or the other, he had the consciousness of universality, which is the profoundest depth to which spirit can attain, and is thought conscious of its own inherent power.

Chapter 3. *The* Eclaircissement *and Revolution*

Protestantism had introduced the *principle* of subjectivity, importing religious emancipation and inward harmony, but accompanying this with the *belief* in subjectivity as evil, and in a power whose embodiment is "the world." Within the Catholic pale also, the casuistry of the Jesuits brought into vogue interminable investigations, as tedious and wire-drawn as those in which the scholastic theology delighted, respecting the subjective spring of the will and the motives that affect it. This dialectic, which unsettles all particular judgments and opinions, transmuting the evil into good and good into evil, left at last nothing remaining but the mere action of subjectivity itself, the *abstractum* of spirit—*thought*. Thought contemplates everything under the form of universality and is consequently the impulsion towards and production of the universal. In that elder scholastic theology, the real subject-matter of investigation, the doctrine of the church, remained an ultramundane affair; in the Protestant theology also spirit still sustained a relation to the ultramundane; for, on the one side, we have the will of the individual—the spirit of man—I myself, and, on the other, the grace of God, the Holy Ghost; and so in the wicked, the Devil. But in thought, self moves within the limits of its own sphere; that with which it is occupied—its objects are as absolutely present to it; for in thinking I must elevate the object to universality. This is utter and absolute freedom, for the pure ego, like pure light, is with itself alone; thus, that which is diverse from itself, sensuous or spiritual, no longer presents an object of dread, for in contemplating such diversity it is inwardly free and can freely confront it. A practical interest makes use of, consumes the objects offered to it: a theoretical interest calmly contemplates them, assured that in themselves they present no alien element. Consequently, the *ne plus ultra* of inwardness, of subjectiveness, is thought. Man is not free, when he is not thinking; for except when thus engaged he sustains a relation to the world around him as to another, an alien, form of being. This comprehension, the penetration of the ego into and beyond other forms of being with the most profound self-certainty directly involves the harmonization of Being: for it must be observed that the unity of thought with its object is already *implicitly* present, for reason is the substantial basis of consciousness as well as of the external and natural. Thus that which presents itself as the object of thought is no longer an absolutely distinct form of existence, not of an alien and grossly substantial nature.

Thought is the grade to which spirit has now advanced. It involves the harmony of Being in its purest essence, challenging the external world to exhibit the same reason which subject possesses. Spirit perceives that nature—the world —must also be an embodiment of reason, for God created it on principles of reason. An interest in the contemplation and comprehension of the present world became universal. Nature embodies universality, inasmuch as it is nothing other than sorts, genera, power, gravitation, etc., phenomenally presented. Thus *experimental science* became the science of the world; for experimental science involves, on the one hand, the observation of phenomena, on the other hand, also, the discovery of the Law, the essential being, the hidden force that causes those phenomena—thus reducing the data supplied by observation to their simple principles. Intellectual consciousness was first extricated from that sophistry of thought, which unsettles everything, by Descartes. As it was the purely German nations among whom the principle of *spirit* first manifested itself, so it was by the Romanic nations that the *abstract idea* (to which the character assigned them above, *viz.*, that of internal schism, more readily conducted them) was first comprehended. Experimental science therefore very soon made its way among them (in common with the Protestant English), but especially among the Italians. It seemed to men as if God had but just created the moon and stars, plants and animals, as if the laws of the universe were now established for the first time; for only then did they feel a real interest in the universe, when they recognized their own reason in the reason which pervades it. The human eye became *clear,* perception quick, thought active and interpretative. The discovery of the laws of nature enabled men to contend against the monstrous supersti-

tion of the time, as also against all notions of mighty alien powers which magic alone could conquer. The assertion was even ventured on, and that by Catholics not less than by Protestants, that the external, with which the church insisted upon associating superhuman virtue, was external and material, and nothing more— that the Host was simply *dough,* the relics of the saints mere *bones.* The independent authority of subjectivity was maintained against belief founded on authority, and the laws of nature were recognized as the only bond connecting phenomena with phenomena. Thus all miracles were disallowed: for nature is a system of known and recognized laws; man is at home in it, and that only passes for truth in which he finds himself at home; he is free through the acquaintance he has gained with nature. Nor was thought less vigorously directed to the spiritual side of things: right and morality came to be looked upon as having their foundation in the actual present will of man, whereas formerly it was referred only to the command of God enjoined *ab extra,* written in the Old and New Testament, or appearing in the form of particular right in old parchments, as *privilegia,* or in international compacts. What the nations acknowledge as international right was deduced empirically from observation (as in the work of Grotius); then, the source of the existing civil and political law was looked for, after Cicero's fashion, in those instincts of men which nature has planted in their hearts, *e.g.,* the social instinct; next, the principle of security for the person and property of the citizens, and of the advantage of the commonwealth—that which belongs to the class of "reasons of state." On these principles private rights were, on the one hand, despotically contravened, but, on the other hand, such contravention was the instrument of carrying out the general objects of the state in opposition to mere positive or prescriptive claims. Frederick II may be mentioned as the ruler who inaugurated the new epoch in the sphere of practical life—that epoch in which practical *political interest* attains universality, and receives an absolute sanction. Frederick II merits especial notice as having comprehended the general object of the state, and as having been the first sovereign who kept the general interest of the state steadily in view, ceasing to pay any respect to particular interests when they stood in the way of the common weal. His immortal work is a domestic code, the Prussian municipal law. How the head of a household energetically provides and governs with a view to the weal of that household and of his dependents—of this he has given a unique specimen.

These general conceptions, deduced from actual and present consciousness, the laws of nature and the substance of what is right and good, have received the name of *reason*. The recognition of the validity of these laws was designated by the term *éclaircissement (Aufklärung)*. From France it passed over into Germany and created a new world of ideas. The absolute criterion, taking the place of all authority based on religious belief and positive laws of right (especially political right), is the verdict passed by spirit itself on the character of that which is to be believed or obeyed. After a free investigation in open day, Luther had secured to mankind spiritual freedom and the reconciliation in the concrete: he triumphantly established the position that man's eternal destiny must be wrought out *in himself*. But the *import* of that which is to take place in him, what truth is to become vital in him, was taken for granted by Luther as something already given, something revealed by religion. *Now*, the principle was set up that this import must be capable of actual investigation, something of which I can gain an inward conviction, and that to this basis of inward demonstration every dogma must be referred.

This principle of thought makes its appearance in the first instance in a general and abstract form; and is based on the axiom of contradiction and identity. The results of thought are thus posited as finite, and the *éclaircissement* utterly banished and extirpated all that was speculative from things human and divine. Although it is of incalculable importance that the multiform complex of things should be reduced to its simplest conditions and brought into the form of universality, yet this still abstract principle does not satisfy the living spirit, the concrete human soul.

This formally absolute principle brings us to *the last stage in history, our world, our own time*.

Secular life is the positive and definite embodiment of the spiritual kingdom—the kingdom of the *will* manifesting itself in outward existence. Mere impulses are also forms in which the inner life realizes itself; but these are transient and disconnected; they are the ever-changing applications of volition. But that which is just and moral belongs to the essential, independent, intrinsically universal will; and if we would know what right really is, we must abstract from inclination, impulse, and desire as the particular; *i.e.*, we must know what the will is in itself. For benevolent, charitable, so-cial impulses are nothing more than impulses—to which others of a different class are opposed. What the will is in itself can be known only when these specific and contradictory forms of volition have been eliminated. Then will appears as will, in its abstract essence. The will is free only when it does not will anything alien, extrinsic, foreign to itself (for as long as it does so, it is dependent), but wills itself alone—wills the will. This is absolute will—the volition to be free. Will making itself its own object is the basis of all right and obligation—consequently of all statutory determinations of right, categorical imperatives, and enjoined obligations. The freedom of the will *per se*, is the principle and substantial basis of all right—is itself absolute, inherently eternal right, and the supreme right in comparison with other specific rights; nay, is even that by which man becomes man, and is therefore the fundamental principle of spirit. But the next question is: how does will assume a definite form? For in willing itself, it is nothing but an identical reference to itself; but, in point of fact, it wills something specific: there *are*, we know, distinct and special duties and rights. A particular application, a definite form of will, is desiderated; for pure will is its own object, its own application, which, as far as this showing goes, is no object, no application. In fact, in this form it is nothing more than *formal* will. But the metaphysical process by which this abstract will develops itself, so as to attain a definite form of freedom, and how rights and duties are evolved therefrom, this is not the place to discuss. It may however be remarked that the same principle obtained speculative recognition in Germany, in the *Kantian* philosophy. According to it the simple unity of self-consciousness, the ego, constitutes the absolutely independent freedom, and is the fountain of all general conceptions, *i.e.*, all conceptions elaborated by thought—theoretical reason; and likewise of the highest of all practical determinations—practical reason, as free and pure will; and rationality of will is none other than the maintaining one's self in pure freedom—willing this and this alone—right purely for the sake of right, duty purely for the sake of duty. Among the Germans this view assumed no other form than that of tranquil theory; but the French wished to give it practical effect. Two questions, therefore, suggest themselves: Why did this principle of freedom remain merely formal? and why did the French alone, and not the Germans, set about realizing it?

With the formal principle more significant

categories were indeed connected: one of the chief of these (for instance) was society, and that which is advantageous for society: but the aim of society is itself political—that of the State (vid., *Droits de l'homme et du citoyen, 1791*)—the conservation of *natural* rights; but natural right is freedom, and, as further determined, it is *equality* of rights before the law. A direct connection is manifest here, for equality, *parity,* is the result of the comparison of many; the "many" in question being human beings, whose essential characteristic is the same, *viz.,* freedom. That principle remains formal, because it originated with abstract thought—with the understanding, which is primarily the self-consciousness of pure reason, and as direct is abstract. As yet, nothing further is developed from it, for it still maintains an adverse position to religion, *i.e.,* to the concrete absolute substance of the universe.

As respects the second question—why the French immediately passed over from the theoretical to the practical, while the Germans contented themselves with theoretical abstraction, it might be said: the French are hot-headed; but this is a superficial solution: the fact is that the formal principle of philosophy in Germany encounters a concrete real world in which spirit finds inward satisfaction and in which conscience is at rest. For, on the one hand, it was the *Protestant world* itself which advanced so far in thought as to realize the absolute culmination of self-consciousness; on the other hand, Protestantism enjoys, with respect to the moral and legal relations of the real world, a tranquil confidence in the disposition of men—a sentiment, which, constituting one and the same thing with religion, is the fountain of all the equitable arrangements that prevail with regard to private right and the constitution of the state. In Germany the *éclaircissement* was conducted in the interest of theology: in France it immediately took up a position of hostility to the Church. In Germany the entire compass of secular relations had already undergone a change for the better; those pernicious ecclesiastical institutes of celibacy, voluntary pauperism, and laziness, had been already done away with; there was no dead weight of enormous wealth attached to the church, and no constraint put upon morality—a constraint which is the source and occasion of vices; there was not that unspeakably hurtful form of iniquity which arises from the interference of spiritual power with secular law, nor that other of the Divine Right of Kings, *i.e.,* the doctrine that the arbitrary will of princes, in

virtue of their being "the Lord's anointed," is divine and holy: on the contrary, their will is regarded as deserving of respect only so far as in association with reason, it wisely contemplates right, justice, and the weal of the community. The principle of thought, therefore, had been so far conciliated already; moreover, the Protestant world had a conviction that in the harmonization which had previously been evolved the principle which would result in a further development of equity in the political sphere was already present.

Consciousness that has received an abstract culture, and whose sphere is the understanding, can be indifferent to religion, but religion is the general form in which truth exists for *non-abstract* consciousness. And the Protestant religion does not admit of two kinds of consciences, while in the Catholic world the holy stands on the one side and on the other side abstraction opposed to religion, that is, to its superstition and its truth. That formal, individual will is in virtue of the abstract position just mentioned made the basis of political theories; right in society is that which the law wills, and the will in question appears as an isolated *individual* will; thus the state, as an aggregate of many individuals, is not an independently substantial unity, and the truth and essence of right in and for itself—to which the will of its individual members ought to be conformed in order to be true, free will; but the volitional atoms are made the starting point, and each will is represented as absolute.

An *intellectual principle* was thus discovered to serve as a basis for the state—one which does not, like previous principles, belong to the sphere of opinion, such as the social impulse, the desire of security for property, etc., nor owe its origin to the religious sentiment, as does that of the divine appointment of the governing power—but the principle of certainty, which is identity with my self-consciousness, stopping short however of that of truth, which needs to be distinguished from it. This is a vast discovery in regard to the profoundest depths of being and freedom. The consciousness of the spiritual is now the essential basis of the political fabric, and *philosophy* has thereby become dominant. It has been said that the *French Revolution* resulted from philosophy, and it is not without reason that philosophy has been called "Weltweisheit"; for it is not only truth in and for itself, as the pure essence of things, but also truth in its living form as exhibited in the affairs of the world. We should not, therefore, contradict the assertion that the Revolution received its first impulse from philosophy. But this philosophy is, in the first instance, only abstract thought, not the concrete comprehension of absolute truth— intellectual positions between which there is an immeasurable chasm.

The principle of the freedom of the will, therefore, asserted itself against existing right. Before the French Revolution, it must be allowed, the power of the grandees had been diminished by Richelieu, and they had been deprived of privileges; but, like the clergy, they retained all the prerogatives which gave them an advantage over the lower class. The political condition of France at that time presents nothing but a confused mass of privileges altogether contravening thought and reason—an utterly irrational state of things, and one with which the greatest corruption of morals, of spirit was associated—an empire characterized by destitution of right, and which, when its real state begins to be recognized, becomes shameless destitution of right. The fearfully heavy burdens that pressed upon the people, the embarrassment of the government to procure for the court the means of supporting luxury and extravagance, gave the first impulse to discontent. The new spirit began to agitate men's minds: oppression drove men to investigation. It was perceived that the sums extorted from the people were not expended in furthering the objects of the state, but were lavished in the most unreasonable fashion. The entire political system appeared one mass of injustice. The change was necessarily violent, because the work of transformation was not undertaken by the government. And the reason why the government did not undertake it was that the court, the clergy, the nobility, the parliaments themselves, were unwilling to surrender the privileges they possessed, either for the sake of expediency or that of abstract right; moreover, because the government as the concrete centre of the power of the state, could not adopt as its principle abstract individual wills, and reconstruct the state on this basis; lastly, because it was Catholic, and therefore the idea of freedom—reason embodied in laws—did not pass for the final absolute obligation, since the holy and the religious conscience are separated from them. The conception, the idea of right asserted its authority *all at once,* and the old framework of injustice could offer no resistance to its onslaught. A constitution, therefore, was established in harmony with the conception of right, and on this foundation all future legislation was to be based. Never since the sun had stood in the firmament and the planets revolved around him had it been perceived that man's existence centres in his head, *i.e.,* in thought, inspired by which he builds up the world of reality. Anaxagoras had been the first to say that νοῦς governs the world; but not until now had man advanced to the recognition of the principle that thought ought to govern spiritual reality. This was accordingly a glorious mental dawn. All thinking beings shared in the jubilation of this epoch. Emotions of a lofty character stirred men's minds at that time; a spiritual enthusiasm thrilled through the world, as if the reconciliation between the divine and the secular was now first accomplished.

The two following points must now occupy our attention: 1st. The course which the revolution in France took; 2d. How that revolution became world-historical.

1. Freedom presents two aspects: the one concerns its substance and purport—its objectivity —the thing itself; the other relates to the form of freedom, involving the consciousness of his activity on the part of the individual; for freedom demands that the individual recognize himself in such acts, that they should be veritably his, it being his interest that the result in question should be attained. The three elements and powers of the state in actual working must be contemplated according to the above analysis, their examination in detail being referred to the *Lectures on the Philosophy of Right.*

(1) *Laws* of rationality—of intrinsic right— objective or real freedom: to this category belong freedom of property and freedom of person. Those relics of that condition of servitude which the feudal relation had introduced are hereby swept away, and all those fiscal ordinances which were the bequest of the feudal law, its tithes and dues, are abrogated. Real liberty requires, moreover, freedom in regard to trades and professions, the permission to every one to use his abilities without restriction, and the free admission to all offices of state. This is a summary of the elements of real freedom, and which are not based on feeling, for feeling allows of the continuance even of serfdom and slavery, but on the thought and self-consciousness of man recognizing the spiritual character of his existence.

(2) But the agency which gives the laws practical effect is the *government* generally. Government is primarily the formal execution of the laws and the maintenance of their authority: in respect to foreign relations it prosecutes the interest of the state; that is, it assists

the independence of the nation as an individuality against other nations; lastly, it has to provide for the internal weal of the state and all its classes—what is called administration: for it is not enough that the citizen is allowed to pursue a trade or calling, it must also be a source of gain to him; it is not enough that men are permitted to use their powers, they must also find an opportunity of applying them to purpose. Thus the state involves a body of abstract principles and a practical application of them. This application must be the work of a subjective will, a will which resolves and decides. Legislation itself, the invention and positive enactment of these statutory arrangements, is an application of such general principles. The next step, then, consists in determination and execution. Here then the question presents itself: what is the decisive will to be? The ultimate decision is the prerogative of the monarch: but if the state is based on liberty, the many wills of individuals also desire to have a share in political decisions. But the *many* are *all;* and it seems but a poor expedient, rather a monstrous inconsistency, to allow only a few to take part in those decisions, since each wishes that his volition should have a share in determining what is to be law for him. The few assume to be the deputies, but they are often only the *despoilers* of the many. Nor is the sway of the majority over the minority a less palpable inconsistency.

(3) This collision of subjective wills leads therefore to the consideration of a third point, that of *disposition*—an *ex animo* acquiescence in the laws; not the mere customary observance of them, but the cordial recognition of laws and the constitution as in principle fixed and immutable, and of the supreme obligation of individuals to subject their particular wills to them. There may be various opinions and views respecting laws, constitution, and government, but there must be a disposition on the part of the citizens to regard all these opinions as subordinate to the substantial interest of the state, and to insist upon them no further than that interest will allow; moreover, nothing must be considered higher and more sacred than good will towards the state; or, if religion be looked upon as higher and more sacred, it must involve nothing really alien or opposed to the constitution. It is, indeed, regarded as a maxim of the profoundest wisdom entirely to separate the laws and constitution of the state from religion, since bigotry and hypocrisy are to be feared as the results of a state religion. But although the aspects of religion and the state are different, they are radically *one;* and the laws find their highest confirmation in religion.

Here it must be frankly stated that with the Catholic religion no rational constitution is possible; for government and people must reciprocate that final guarantee of disposition, and can have it only in a religion that is not opposed to a rational political constitution.

Plato in his *Republic* makes everything depend upon the government, and makes disposition the principle of the state; on which account he lays the chief stress on education. The modern theory is diametrically opposed to this, referring everything to the individual will. But here we have no guarantee that the will in question has that right disposition which is essential to the stability of the state.

In view then of these leading considerations we have to trace the course of the *French Revolution* and the remodelling of the state in accordance with the idea of right. In the first instance purely abstract philosophical principles were set up: disposition and religion were not taken into account. The first constitutional form of government in France was one which recognized royalty; the monarch was to stand at the head of the state, and on him, in conjunction with his ministers, was to devolve the executive power; the legislative body, on the other hand, was to make the laws. But this constitution involved from the very first an internal contradiction; for the legislature absorbed the whole power of the administration: the budget, affairs of war and peace, and the levying of the armed force were in the hands of the Legislative Chamber. Everything was brought under the head of law. The budget however is in its nature something diverse from law, for it is annually renewed, and the power to which it properly belongs is that of the government. With this, moreover, is connected the indirect nomination of the ministry and officers of state, etc. The government was thus transferred to the Legislative Chamber, as in England to the Parliament. This constitution was also vitiated by the existence of absolute mistrust; the dynasty lay under suspicion, because it had lost the power it formerly enjoyed, and the priests refused the oath. Neither government nor constitution could be maintained on this footing, and the ruin of both was the result. A government of some kind however is always in existence. The question presents itself then, whence did it emanate? Theoretically, it proceeded from the people; really and truly from the National Convention and its Committees. The forces now dominant are the abstract principles—freedom, and, as it exists within the limits of the subjective will—virtue. This virtue has now to conduct the government in opposition to the many, whom their corruption and attachment to old interests, or a liberty that has degenerated into license, and the violence of their passions, render unfaithful to virtue. Virtue is here a simple abstract principle and distinguishes the citizens into two classes only —those who are favorably disposed and those who are not. But disposition can only be recognized and judged of by disposition. *Suspicion* therefore is in the ascendant; but virtue, as soon as it becomes liable to suspicion, is already condemned. Suspicion attained a terrible power and brought to the scaffold the monarch, whose subjective will was in fact the religious conscience of a Catholic. Robespierre set up the principle of virtue as supreme, and it may be said that with this man virtue was an earnest matter. *Virtue* and *terror* are the order of the day; for subjective virtue, whose sway is based on disposition only, brings with it the most fearful tyranny. It exercises its power without legal formalities, and the punishment it inflicts is equally simple—*death*. This tyranny could not last; for all inclinations, all interests, reason itself revolted against this terribly consistent liberty, which in its concentrated intensity exhibited so fanatical a shape. An organized government is introduced, analogous to the one that had been displaced; only that its chief and monarch is now a mutable Directory of Five, who may form a moral, but have not an individual unity; under them also suspicion was in the ascendant, and the government was in the hands of the legislative assemblies; this constitution therefore experienced the same fate as its predecessor, for it had proved to itself the absolute necessity of a governmental *power*. Napoleon restored it as a military power, and followed up this step by establishing himself as an individual will at the head of the state: he knew how to rule, and soon settled the internal affairs of France. The *avocats,* idealogues, and abstract-principle men who ventured to show themselves he sent "to the right about," and the sway of mistrust was exchanged for that of respect and fear. He then, with the vast might of his character, turned his attention to foreign relations, subjected all Europe, and diffused his liberal institutions in every quarter. Greater victories were never gained, expeditions displaying greater genius were never conducted: but never was the powerlessness of victory exhibited in a clearer light than then. The disposition of the peoples, *i.e.,* their religious disposition and that of their nationality, ultimately precipitated this colossus; and in France constitutional monarchy, with the *Charte* as its basis, was restored. But here again the antithesis of disposition and mistrust made its appearance. The French stood in a mendacious position to each other, when they issued addresses full of devotion and love to the monarchy, and loading it with benediction. A fifteen years' farce was played. For although the *Charte* was the standard under which all were enrolled, and though both parties had sworn to it, yet, on the one side, the ruling disposition was a Catholic one, which regarded it as a matter of conscience to destroy the existing institutions. Another breach, therefore, took place, and the government was overturned. At length, after forty years of war and confusion indescribable, a weary heart might fain congratulate itself on seeing a termination and tranquillization of all these disturbances. But although one main point is set at rest, there remains, on the one hand, that rupture which the Catholic principle inevitably occasions; on the other hand, that which has to do with men's subjective will. In regard to the latter, the main feature of incompatibility still presents itself, in the requirement that the ideal general will should also be the *empirically* general—*i.e.,* that the units of the state, in their individual capacity, should rule, or at any rate take part in the government. Not satisfied with the establishment of rational rights, with freedom of person and property, with the existence of a political organization in which are to be found various circles of civil life each having its own functions to perform, and with that influence over the people which is exercised by the intelligent members of the community, and the confidence that is felt in them, "*Liberalism*" sets up in opposition to all this the atomistic principle, that which insists upon the sway of individual wills; maintaining that all government should emanate from their express power and have their express sanction. Asserting this formal side of freedom —this abstraction—the party in question allows no political organization to be firmly established. The particular arrangements of the government are forthwith opposed by the advocates of liberty as the mandates of a particular will, and branded as displays of arbitrary power. The will of the many expels the ministry from power, and those who had formed the opposition fill the vacant places; but the latter having now become the government, meet with hostility from the many, and share the same fate. Thus agitation and unrest are perpetuated. This collision, this nodus, this problem is that with which history is now occupied, and whose solution it has to work out in the future.

2. We have now to consider the French Revolution in its organic connection with the *history of the world;* for in its substantial import that event is world-historical, and that contest of formalism which we discussed in the last paragraph must be properly distinguished from its wider bearings. As regards outward diffusion, its principle gained access to almost all modern states, either through conquest or by express introduction into their political life. Particularly all the Romanic nations, and the Roman Catholic world in special—*France, Italy, Spain*—were subjected to the dominion of Liberalism. But it became bankrupt everywhere; first, the grand firm in France, then its branches in Spain and Italy; twice, in fact, in the states into which it had been introduced. This was the case in Spain, where it was first brought in by the Napoleonic constitution, then by that which the Cortes adopted—in Piedmont, first when it was incorporated with the French Empire, and a second time as the result of internal insurrection; so in Rome and in Naples it was twice set up. Thus Liberalism as an abstraction, emanating from France, traversed the Roman world; but religious slavery held that world in the fetters of political servitude. For it is a false principle that the fetters which bind right and freedom can be broken without the emancipation of conscience —that there can be a revolution without a reformation. These countries, therefore, sank back into their old condition—in Italy with some modifications of the outward political condition. Venice and Genoa, those ancient aristocracies, which could at least boast of legitimacy, vanished as rotten despotisms. Material superiority in power can achieve no enduring results: Napoleon could not coerce Spain into freedom any more than Philip II could force Holland into slavery.

Contrasted with these Romanic nations we observe the other powers of Europe, and especially the Protestant nations. *Austria* and *England* were not drawn within the vortex of internal agitation, and exhibited great, immense proofs of their internal solidity. *Austria* is not a kingdom, but an empire, *i.e.*, an aggregate of many political organizations. The inhabitants of its chief provinces are not German in origin and character, and have remained unaffected by "ideas." Elevated neither by education nor religion, the lower classes in some districts have remained in a condition of serfdom, and the nobility have been kept down, as in Bohemia; in other quarters, while the former have continued the same, the barons have maintained their despotism, as in Hungary. Austria has surrendered that more intimate connection with Germany which was derived from the imperial dignity, and renounced its numerous possessions and rights in Germany and the Netherlands. It now takes its place in Europe as a distinct power, involved with no other. *England,* with great exertions, maintained itself on its old foundations; the English *Constitution* kept its ground amid the general convulsion, though it seemed so much the more liable to be affected by it, as a public Parliament, that habit of assembling in public meeting which was common to all orders of the state, and a free press, offered singular facilities for introducing the French principles of liberty and equality among all classes of the people. Was the English nation too backward in point of culture to apprehend these general principles? Yet in no country has the question of liberty been more frequently a subject of reflection and public discussion. Or was the English constitution so entirely a free constitution, had those principles been already so completely realized in it, that they could no longer excite opposition or even interest? The English nation may be said to have approved of the emancipation of France; but it was proudly reliant on its own constitution and freedom, and instead of imitating the example of the foreigner, it displayed its ancient hostility to its rival, and was soon involved in a popular war with France.

The Constitution of England is a complex of mere *particular rights* and particular privileges: the government is essentially administrative— that is, conservative of the interests of all particular orders and classes; and each particular church, parochial district, county, society, takes care of itself, so that the government, strictly speaking, has nowhere less to do than in England. This is the leading feature of what Englishmen call their liberty, and is the very antithesis of such a centralized administration as exists in France, where down to the least village the maire is named by the Ministry or their agents. Nowhere can people less tolerate free action on the part of others than in France: there the Ministry combines in itself all administrative power, to which, on the other hand, the Chamber of Deputies lays claim. In England, on the contrary, every parish, every subordinate division and association has a part of its own to perform. Thus the common interest is concrete, and particular interests are taken cognizance of and determined in view of that common interest. These arrangements, based on particular interests, render a general system impossible. Consequently, abstract and general principles have no attraction for Englishmen, are addressed in their case to inattentive ears. The particular interests above referred to have positive rights attached to them, which date from the antique times of feudal law, and have been preserved in England more than in any other country. By an inconsistency of the most startling kind, we find them contravening equity most grossly; and of institutions characterized by real freedom there are nowhere fewer than in England. In point of private right and freedom of possession they present an incredible deficiency: sufficient proof of which is afforded in the rights of primogeniture, involving the necessity of purchasing or otherwise providing military or ecclesiastical appointments for the younger sons of the aristocracy.

The *Parliament governs,* although Englishmen are unwilling to allow that such is the case. It is worthy of remark that what has been always regarded as the period of the corruption of a republican people presents itself here; *viz.,* election to seats in Parliament by means of bribery. But this also they call freedom—the power to sell one's vote, and to purchase a seat in Parliament.

But this utterly inconsistent and corrupt state of things has nevertheless one advantage, that it provides for the possibility of a government— that it introduces a majority of men into Parliament who are statesmen, who from their very youth have devoted themselves to political business and have worked and lived in it. And the nation has the correct conviction and perception that there must be a government, and is therefore willing to give its confidence to a body of men who have had experience in governing; for a general sense of particularity involves also a recognition of that form of particularity which is a distinguishing feature of one class of the community—that knowledge, experience, and facility acquired by practice, which the aristocracy who devote themselves to such interests exclusively possess. This is quite opposed to the appreciation of principles and abstract views which everyone can understand at once, and which are besides to be found in all constitutions and charters. It is a question whether the reform in Parliament now on the tapis, consistently carried out, will leave the possibility of a government.

The material existence of England is based on commerce and industry, and the English have undertaken the weighty responsibility of being the missionaries of civilization to the world; for their commercial spirit urges them to traverse every sea and land, to form connections with barbarous peoples, to create wants and stimulate industry, and first and foremost to establish among them the conditions necessary to commerce, *viz.,* the relinquishment of a life of lawless violence, respect for property, and civility to strangers.

Germany was traversed by the victorious French hosts, but German nationality delivered it from this yoke. One of the leading features in the political condition of Germany is that code of rights which was certainly occasioned by French oppression, since this was the especial means of bringing to light the deficiencies of the old system. The fiction of an empire has utterly vanished. It is broken up into sovereign states. Feudal obligations are abolished, for freedom of property and of person have been recognized as fundamental principles. Offices of state are open to every citizen, talent and adaptation being of course the necessary conditions. The government rests with the official world, and the personal decision of the monarch constitutes its apex; for a final decision is, as was remarked above, absolutely necessary. Yet with firmly established laws, and a settled organization of the state, what is left to the sole arbitrament of the monarch is, in point of substance, no great matter. It is certainly a very fortunate circumstance for a nation, when a sovereign of noble character falls to its lot; yet in a great state even this is of small moment, since its strength lies in the reason incorporated in it. Minor states have their existence and tranquillity secured to them more or less by their neighbours: they are therefore, properly speaking, not independent, and have not the fiery trial of war to endure. As has been remarked, a share in the government may be obtained by every one who has a competent knowledge, experience, and a morally regulated will. Those who know ought to govern—οἱ ἄριστοι, not ignorance and the presumptuous conceit of "knowing better." Lastly, as to disposition, we have already remarked that in the Protestant Church the reconciliation of religion with legal right has taken place. In the Protestant world there is no sacred, no religious conscience in a state of separation from, or perhaps, even hostility to, secular right.

This is the point which consciousness has attained, and these are the principal phases of that form in which the principle of freedom has realized itself; for the history of the world is nothing but the development of the idea of freedom. But objective freedom—the laws of *real* freedom—demand the subjugation of the mere contingent will, for this is in its nature formal. If the objective is in itself rational, human insight and conviction must correspond with the reason which it embodies, and then we have the other essential element—subjective freedom—also realized. We have confined ourselves to the consideration of that progress of the idea and have been obliged to forego the pleasure of giving a detailed picture of the prosperity, the periods of glory that have distinguished the career of peoples, the beauty and grandeur of the character of individuals, and the interest attaching to their fate in weal or woe. Philosophy concerns itself only with the glory of the idea mirroring itself in the history of the world. Philosophy escapes from the weary strife of passions that agitate the surface of society into the calm region of contemplation; that which interests it is the recognition of the process of development which the idea has passed through in realizing itself— *i.e.,* the idea of freedom, whose reality is the consciousness of freedom and nothing short of it.

That the history of the world, with all the changing scenes which its annals present, is this process of development and the realization of spirit—this is the true *Theodicæa,* the justification of God in history. Only *this* insight can reconcile spirit with the history of the world—*viz.,* that what has happened, and is happening every day, is not only not "without God," but is essentially His work.

PRINTED IN THE U. S. A.

THE GREAT IDEAS, *Volumes 2 and 3*

••••••••••••••••••••••••••••••••••	FAMILY
ANGEL	FATE
ANIMAL	FORM
ARISTOCRACY	GOD
ART	GOOD AND EVIL
ASTRONOMY	GOVERNMENT
BEAUTY	HABIT
BEING	HAPPINESS
CAUSE	HISTORY
CHANCE	HONOR
CHANGE	HYPOTHESIS
CITIZEN	IDEA
CONSTITUTION	IMMORTALITY
COURAGE	INDUCTION
CUSTOM AND	INFINITY
CONVENTION	JUDGMENT
DEFINITION	JUSTICE
DEMOCRACY	KNOWLEDGE
DESIRE	LABOR
DIALECTIC	LANGUAGE
DUTY	LAW
EDUCATION	LIBERTY
ELEMENT	LIFE AND DEATH
EMOTION	LOGIC
ETERNITY	LOVE
EVOLUTION	MAN
EXPERIENCE	MATHEMATICS